MARCEL PROUST
Selected Letters
1918–1922

MARCEL PROUST

Selected Letters

VOLUME 4
1918–1922

Edited by Philip Kolb

Translated with an Introduction by
Joanna Kilmartin

Foreword by
Alain de Botton

Afterword by
Jocelyne Kolb

HarperCollins*Publishers*

HarperCollins*Publishers*
77–85 Fulham Palace Road,
Hammersmith, London w6 8jb

First published in 2000 by HarperCollins*Publishers* Ltd
Correspondance de Marcel Proust Volumes XVII, XVIII, XIX, XX, XXI,
edited by Philip Kolb, copyright © Librairie Plon 1989, 1990, 1991, 1992, 1993
English Translation copyright © HarperCollins 2000
Introduction copyright © Joanna Kilmartin 2000
Foreword copyright © Alain de Botton 2000
Afterword copyright © Jocelyne Kolb 2000

A catalogue record for this book is available from
the British Library

ISBN 0 00 257032 7

Photoset in PostScript Linotype Janson by
Rowland Phototypesetting Ltd, Bury St Edmunds, Suffolk

Printed and bound in Great Britain by
Caledonian International Book Manufacturing Ltd, Glasgow

All rights reserved. No part of this publication may be
reproduced, stored in a retrieval system, or transmitted,
in any form or by any means, electronic, mechanical,
photocopying, recording or otherwise, without the prior
permission of the publishers.

CONTENTS

ACKNOWLEDGMENTS　xv
FOREWORD BY ALAIN DE BOTTON　xvii
INTRODUCTION　xxiii
TRANSLATOR'S NOTE　1

1　To Walter Berry, 4 January 1918　3
2　To Madame Soutzo, 4 January 1918　5
3　To Jacques-Émile Blanche, before 17 January 1918　6
4　To André Gide, 20 January 1918　9
5　To Jacques-Émile Blanche, 20 January 1918　13
6　To Madame Scheikévitch, 21 January 1918　15
7　To Madame Scheikévitch, 21 January 1918　17
8　From Jacques-Émile Blanche, 23 January 1918　19
9　To Jacques-Émile Blanche, 24 January 1918　20
10　To the Abbé Mugnier, 14 February 1918　22
11　To Lucien Daudet, 19 February 1918　24
12　To Jacques Porel, 19 February 1918　27
13　To Lionel Hauser, 3 April 1918　29
14　To Madame Marthe Bibesco, after 4 April 1918　31
15　To Madame Catusse, before 9 April 1918　33
16　To Charles d'Alton, 9 April 1918　34
17　To Madame Soutzo, 9 April 1918　36
18　To Jacques de Lacretelle, 20 April 1918　39
19　To Lionel Hauser, 29 April 1918　42
20　To Lucien Daudet, 11 May 1918　47
21　To Madame Soutzo, 3 July 1918　48
22　To Madame Hecht, around September 1918　50
23　To Madame de Polignac, September 1918　53

Contents

24	To Jean-Louis Vaudoyer, between 18 and 25 October 1918	56
25	To Lionel Hauser, 23 or 24 October 1918	57
26	To Madame Straus, 12 November 1918	61
27	To Clément de Maugny, after 18 January 1919	63
28	To Walter Berry, 21 January 1919	64
29	To Mademoiselle Louise Baignères, 24 or 25 January 1919	67
30	To Madame Straus, 25 January 1919	71
31	To Madame Soutzo, 1 February 1919	73
32	To Gaston Gallimard, around 22 May 1919	75
33	To Madame de Noailles, 27 May 1919	77
34	To Henri Ghéon, early June 1919	79
35	To Jean Cocteau, before 19 June 1919	82
36	To Jacques Porel, after 15 July 1919	84
37	To Daniel Halévy, 19 July 1919	86
38	To Abel Desjardins, July 1919	88
39	To Jean de Gaigneron, 1 August 1919	89
40	To Daniel Halévy, before 13 August 1919	90
41	To Robert de Montesquiou, late August 1919	92
42	To Paul Morand, after 10 October 1919	93
43	To Emmanuel Berl, 26 October 1919	96
44	To Paul Souday, 10 November 1919	97
45	To Gaston Gallimard, before 3 December 1919	100
46	To Jacques Boulenger, 20 December 1919	103
47	To Rosny *aîné*, before 23 December 1919	105
48	To the Abbé Mugnier, late December 1919	109
49	To Jean de Pierrefeu, 4 January 1920	111
50	To Jacques Boulenger, 10–11 January 1920	113
51	To Fernand Vandérem, 15 January 1920	116
52	To Madame Greffulhe, 19 January 1920	118
53	To Louis Martin-Chauffier, around January 1920	120

54	To Marcel Boulenger, before 24 January 1920	122
55	To Jacques Rivière, 26 January 1920	123
56	To Pierre de Polignac, early February 1920	127
57	To Jean-Louis Vaudoyer, early February 1920	128
58	To Madame Soutzo, 17 or 18 February 1920	130
59	To Robert de Flers, 22 February 1920	132
60	To Madame Straus, after 15 March 1920	133
61	To Lionel Hauser, after 8 April 1920	135
62	To Robert Vallery-Radot, after 10 April 1920	137
63	To Henri de Régnier, 14 April 1920	138
64	To Jacques Rivière, after 20 May 1920	141
65	To Maurice Montabré, around June 1920	142
66	To Jacques Porel, 16 June 1920	144
67	To Jacques Rivière, after 2 July 1920	144
68	To *L'Intransigeant*, end July or early August 1920	146
69	To Paul Morand, end August 1920	147
70	To Madame Sert, 1 September 1920	149
71	To Sydney Schiff, 1 or 2 September 1920	150
72	To Lucien Daudet, 15 or 16 September 1920	153
73	To Madame de Madrazo, after 15 September 1920	155
74	To Robert Proust, after 18 September 1920	156
75	To Madame de Chevigné, October 1920	158
76	To Madame Straus, 18 October 1920	159
77	To Paul Souday, around 6 or 7 November 1920	160
78	To Jacques Rivière, 7 or 8 November 1920	163
79	To Madame Soutzo, around 8 November 1920	164
80	To Henri de Régnier, 28 November 1920	165
81	To Émile Henriot, 2 December 1920	167
82	To Jacques Boulenger, 4 December 1920	169
83	To Harry Swann, 10 or 11 December 1920	172
84	To Antoine Bibesco, 11 December 1920	174

85	To Madame de Noailles, after 12 December 1920	175
86	To Madame Léon Daudet, December 1920	177
87	To Madame de Chevigné, December 1920	179
88	To Madame de Clermont-Tonnerre, 30 December 1920	180
89	To Madame de Clermont-Tonnerre, 1 or 2 January 1921	182
90	To Madame Léon Daudet, early January 1921	183
91	To Gaston Gallimard, 11 January 1921	185
92	To Jacques-Émile Blanche, 16 January 1921	188
93	To Paul Souday, after 15 January 1921	191
94	To Gaston Gallimard, between 14 and 19 January 1921	192
95	To Jacques-Émile Blanche, second half of January 1921	194
96	To Louis Martin-Chauffier, 3 or 4 February 1921	196
97	To Jacques Rivière, 7 February 1921	198
98	To Jacques Boulenger, 5 March 1921	199
99	To Gaston Gallimard, 6 March 1921	201
100	To Lionel Hauser, after 7 March 1921	202
101	To Rosny aîné, after 8 March 1921	204
102	From Robert de Montesquiou, 22 March 1921	205
103	To Gaston Gallimard, 22 or 23 March 1921	206
104	To Robert de Montesquiou, after 22 March 1921	208
105	To François Mauriac, second half of March 1921	209
106	To Lionel Hauser, around 7 April 1921	210
107	To Robert de Montesquiou, 18 or 19 April 1921	211
108	To André Gide, 23 April 1921	213
109	To Jean-Louis Vaudoyer, 1 May 1921	216
110	From André Gide, 3 May 1921	217
111	To Paul Souday, 11 May 1921	219
112	To Robert de Montesquiou, after 17 May 1921	221

113	To Louis de Robert, before 26 May 1921	224
114	To Emile Mâle, 1 June 1921	225
115	To Armand de Guiche, 17 June 1921	226
116	To François Mauriac, around 25 June 1921	230
117	To Jacques Boulenger, end of June 1921	232
118	To Walter Berry, 2 July 1921	235
119	To Sydney Schiff, 16 July 1921	237
120	To Léon Daudet, after 15 July 1921	238
121	To Joseph Gahier, after 18 July 1921	240
122	From Jacques Rivière, 20 August 1921	240
123	To Jacques Boulenger, early September 1921	241
124	To Lionel Hauser, 2 or 3 September 1921	243
125	To Gaston Gallimard, 10 September 1921	243
126	To Henri Duvernois, 10 September 1921	246
127	To Roger Allard, before 13 September 1921	248
128	To Jacques Rivière, 12 or 13 September 1921	249
129	From Jacques Rivière, 11 September 1921	251
130	To Jacques Rivière, 13 or 14 September 1921	252
131	To Gaston Gallimard, 19 September 1921	253
132	To Madame de Chevigné, around September 1921	256
133	To Jacques Boulenger, 14 October 1921	257
134	To André Lang, second half of October 1921	258
135	To Jacques Boulenger, 24 or 25 November 1921	260
136	To Robert Proust, 28 November 1921	262
137	To Jacques Rivière, 29 November 1921	264
138	To Jacques Boulenger, 29 November 1921	266
139	To Gaston Gallimard, 4 or 5 December 1921	269
140	To Gaston Gallimard, 7 or 8 December 1921	271
141	To Walter Berry, 8 December 1921	273
142	To Armand de Guiche, 9 or 10 December 1921	276
143	From Walter Berry, 13 December 1921	277

144	To Madame de Guiche, 18 December 1921	279
145	To Etienne de Beaumont, after 17 December 1921	281
146	To Etienne de Beaumont, 31 December 1921	283
147	To Gustave Tronche, early January 1922	284
148	To Walter Berry, 6 January 1922	285
149	To Louisa de Mornand, 10 January 1922	286
150	To Clément de Maugny, first half of January 1922	287
151	To Gaston Gallimard, 18 January 1922	288
152	To Benjamin Crémieux, 18 or 19 January 1922	291
153	To Clément de Maugny, January 1922	292
154	To Gaston Gallimard, 28 January 1922	293
155	To Paul Morand, 28 January 1922	295
156	From Paul Morand, 29 January 1922	296
157	To Gaston Gallimard, 1 February 1922	297
158	To Gaston Gallimard, 3 February 1922	298
159	To Madame Soutzo, 5 February 1922	299
160	To Madame de Clermont-Tonnerre, 20 February 1922	302
161	To Madame Soutzo, 28 February 1922	303
162	To Camille Vettard, around March 1922	306
163	To Paul Helleu, around March or April 1922	307
164	To Ernst Robert Curtius, 7 or 8 March 1922	307
165	To Rosny *aîné*, 10 March 1922	308
166	To Louis Martin-Chauffier, before 22 March 1922	309
167	To Jacques Boulenger, 22 March 1922	312
168	To Léon Daudet, 22 March 1922	313
169	From Léon Daudet, 23 March 1922	315
170	To Philippe Berthelot, after 22 March 1922	316
171	To Pierre-André May, 26 March 1922	318
172	From André Gide, 5 April 1922	319

173	To Paul Souday, 7 April 1922	320
174	To Sydney Schiff, 7 to 8 April 1922	321
175	To André Gide, 11 April 1922	324
176	To Émile Henriot, 13 April 1922	325
177	To Madame Maurice Pouquet, 19 April 1922	327
178	To Robert de Flers, 29 April 1922	330
179	To François Mauriac, end April or early May 1922	332
180	To Binet-Valmer, 1 May 1922	332
181	To Henri Bergson, early May 1922	334
182	To John Middleton Murry, early May 1922	335
183	From François Mauriac, early May 1922	335
184	To Gaston Gallimard, 3 May 1922	336
185	To Roger Allard, before 8 May 1922	337
186	From Madame Straus, 13 May 1922	339
187	To Paul Souday, around mid-May 1922	341
188	To Jacques Boulenger, around 15 May 1922	344
189	To Francis Jammes, after 15 May 1922	345
190	To Madame de Saint-Marceaux, after 16 May 1922	347
191	To Jacques Benoist-Méchin, 17 May 1922	349
192	To Gaston Gallimard, 17 or 18 May 1922	351
193	To Madame Laure Hayman, 18 May 1922	353
194	To Gabriel de La Rochefoucauld, after 18 May 1922	355
195	To Binet-Valmer, 24 May 1922	356
196	To Walter Berry, after 23 May 1922	357
197	From Edmond Jaloux, 26 May 1922	358
198	From Henri de Régnier, 27 May 1922	359
199	To Edmond Jaloux, 27 May 1922	360
200	To Henri de Régnier, 28 May 1922	361
201	To Sydney Schiff, 30 May 1922	364

202	To Jacques Benoist-Méchin, end of May 1922	365
203	From Jacques Rivière, 8 June 1922	366
204	To Walter Berry, 10 June 1922	367
205	To Madame Hennessy, 13 June 1922	368
206	To André Gide, 13 June 1922	370
207	From André Gide, 14 June 1922	371
208	To Benjamin Crémieux, 15 June 1922	372
209	To Jacques Boulenger, around 15 June 1922	373
210	To Abel Bonnard, 15 June 1922	375
211	To Jacques de Lacretelle, 16 June 1922	377
212	To Paul Morand, 16 June 1922	378
213	To Jean-Louis Vaudoyer, after 17 June 1922	380
214	To Edmond Jaloux, before 23 June 1922	382
215	To Camille Vettard, after 24 June 1922	383
216	To Gaston Gallimard, 25 June 1922	385
217	To Jacques Rivière, after 1 July 1922	387
218	To Edmond Jaloux, after 1 July 1922	388
219	To Sir Philip Sassoon, June or July 1922	391
220	To Madame Soutzo, early July 1922	392
221	To Gaston Gallimard, 2 or 3 July 1922	394
222	To Madame Soutzo, after 2 July 1922	396
223	To André Chaumeix, 4 or 5 July 1922	396
224	To Sydney Schiff, 5 July 1922	398
225	To Percy Wyndham Lewis, 7 July 1922	400
226	To Edmond Jaloux, 15 July 1922	401
227	To Jacques Delgado, 16 July 1922	403
228	To Jean Schlumberger, 16 July 1922	403
229	To Paul Brach, after 16 July 1922	406
230	To Sydney Schiff, 18 July 1922	407
231	To Gaston Gallimard, 20 July 1922	409
232	From Jacques Rivière, 22 July 1922	412
233	To Charles Du Bos, 23 July 1922	415

234	To Paul Brach, 27 July 1922	417
235	To Jacques Porel, 27 July 1922	418
236	To Benjamin Crémieux, 5 or 6 August 1922	419
237	To Paul Brach, 9 August 1922	421
238	From Jules Romains, 16 August 1922	422
239	To Henri Ghéon, after 17 August 1922	424
240	To Camille Vettard, around 20 August 1922	426
241	To Henri Duvernois, after 21 August 1922	428
242	To Daniel Halévy, before 26 August 1922	429
243	To Suzy Proust, 25 or 26 August 1922	430
244	To Charles Maurras, 28 August 1922	431
245	From Jacques Rivière, 3 September 1922	433
246	To Gaston Gallimard, 3 September 1922	435
247	To Armand de Guiche, after 4 September 1922	436
248	To Henri Duvernois, after 6 September 1922	438
249	From Sydney Schiff, 9 September 1922	439
250	To Gaston Gallimard, 14 September 1922	440
251	To Edmond Jaloux, around mid-September 1922	442
252	To Ernst Robert Curtius, 17 or 18 September 1922	443
253	To Jacques Rivière, 20 September 1922	444
254	To Jacques Rivière, 23 September 1922	445
255	To René Gillouin, end September 1922	446
256	To Gaston Gallimard, 3 October 1922	447
257	To Charles Scott-Moncrieff, 9 or 10 October 1922	448
258	From Charles Scott-Moncrieff, 12 October 1922	449
259	To Céleste Albaret, after 10 October 1922	450
260	To Céleste Albaret, after 12 October 1922	450
261	To Céleste Albaret, October 1922	451
262	From Reynaldo Hahn, after 21 October 1922	451
263	To Céleste Albaret, October 1922	453

264	From Jacques Rivière, 23 or 24 October 1922	454
265	To Jacques Rivière, 24 October 1922	454
266	From Jacques Rivière, October 1922	455
267	To Jacques Rivière, 25 October 1922	455
268	To Henri Duvernois, 28 or 29 October 1922	456
269	To Jacques Rivière, 30 October or 1 November 1922	458
270	Céleste Albaret to Jacques Rivière, early November 1922	459
271	Reynaldo Hahn to Jacques Rivière, 18 November 1922	459
	AFTERWORD: PHILIP KOLB AND PROUST by Jocelyne Kolb	461
	INDEX	481

ACKNOWLEDGMENTS

The preparation of this volume was made possible by three grants, for which the publishers, editor and translator are most grateful: from the Translations Program of the National Endowment for the Humanities, Washington, U.S.A., an independent federal agency; from the French Ministry of Culture; and from the Wheatland Foundation, New York.

Special thanks are due to the University of Illinois Research Board for its support throughout this project, to the staff of the University of Illinois Library, and to the resources and expert assistance of the personnel of the Kolb-Proust Archive at the University of Illinois.

FOREWORD

Alain de Botton

Aside from delight at finding such a fascinating and revealing selection of his letters, admirers of Proust may have to overcome one niggling anxiety before embarking on it: an awareness that Proust himself wouldn't have been very happy to hear that we were intending to read his letters.

Few writers have insisted more forcefully that we should concentrate on the work, not the life. In *Contre Sainte-Beuve*, Proust famously took issue with Sainte-Beuve's thesis that the private lives of writers should be studied for the light they can shed on literature. He argued that what artists reveal of themselves through their letters or at dinner parties is a superficial social self, which gives us no key to their greatness, and may indeed distract us from it: 'What one gives to sociability . . . is not the deep self which is only to be found by disregarding other people and the self that knows other people.'

He even suggested in a letter to his English friend Sydney Schiff that all good writers should be disappointing in the flesh: 'True, there are people who are better than their books, but that's because their books aren't *Books*.' Something has gone wrong for a writer, implied Proust, if his letters to his friends and his dinnertime chats are more interesting than his works.

But respect for Proust shouldn't dissuade us from ignoring this argument for at least the time it takes to read Joanna Kilmartin and Philip Kolb's great volume, if only because studying a writer's life in no way precludes us from *also* taking an interest in the work. (We should note in passing that Proust happened to be an avid reader of the biographies and letters of the writers he loved.)

We should also feel less guilty about disregarding Proust's advice because his own letters help to flesh out the very thesis proposed in *Contre Sainte-Beuve*. It is striking how different the Proust we meet in these letters is from the one we know from his novel. We actively feel the divide between the social and the private self which Proust had sketched out for us in his essay 'The Method of Sainte-Beuve'. There are fewer extended reflections here, and surprisingly few psychological analyses; he does not discuss art in depth, nor tell so many jokes. What he often does is to try to seduce whoever he is writing to into giving him what he wants, which is typically affection of some kind.

Proust suffered from unusually strong doubts about his own chances of being liked ('Oh! Making a nuisance of myself, that has always been my nightmare,' he once wrote). He had, one might say, an exaggerated notion of how 'friendly' he needed to be in order to have any friends. At the same time, he craved affection ('My only consolation when I am really sad is to love and to be loved'), and confessed to a range of anxieties familiar to any emotional paranoiac: 'What did they think of us?' 'Were we not tactless?' 'Did they like us?' as well as 'the fear of being forgotten in favour of someone else'. It is these anxieties we often find in his approach to social life.

Proust's overwhelming priority in almost every encounter and letter – at least in his youth – was to ensure that he would be liked, remembered and thought well of. 'Not only did he dizzy his hosts and hostesses with verbal compliments, but he ruined himself on flowers and ingenious gifts,' recalled his friend Jacques-Émile Blanche after his death. His immense psychological insight was often wholly directed towards identifying the appropriate word, smile or flower to win others over. And it worked. He excelled at the art of making friends: he acquired an enormous number, they loved his company, were devoted to him, and wrote a pile of adulatory books after his death – designed as much to display their acquaintance with him as to reveal what he was like – with titles like *My Friend Marcel Proust* (by Marcel Duplay), *My Friendship with Marcel Proust* (by Fernand Gregh) and *Letters to a Friend* (by Marie Nordlinger). The accounts of these friends tell us:

That he was generous:

> I can still see him, wrapped in his fur coat, even in springtime, sitting at a table in Larue's restaurant, and I can still see the gesture of his delicate hand as he tried to make you let him order the most extravagant supper, accepting the head waiter's biased suggestions, offering you champagne, exotic fruits and grapes on their vine-plant which he had noticed on the way in . . . He told you there was no

better way of proving your friendship than by accepting. (GEORGES DE LAURIS)

That he was munificent:

In restaurants, and everywhere where there was a chance, Marcel would give enormous tips. This was the case even in the slightest railway station buffet where he would never return. (GEORGES DE LAURIS)

That he liked to add a 200 per cent service charge:

If a dinner cost him ten francs, he would add twenty francs for the waiter. (FERNAND GREGH)

That he was not merely exorbitant:

The legend of Proust's generosity should not develop to the detriment of that of his goodness. (PAUL MORAND)

That he didn't talk only about himself:

He was the best of listeners. Even in his intimate circle his constant care to be modest and polite prevented him from pushing himself forward and from imposing subjects of conversation. These he found in others' thoughts. Sometimes he spoke about sport and motor-cars and showed a touching desire for information. He took an interest in you, instead of trying to make you interested in himself. (GEORGES DE LAURIS)

That he was curious:

Marcel was passionately interested in his friends. Never have I seen less egoism, or egotism . . . He wanted to distract you. He was happy to see others laughing and he laughed. (GEORGES DE LAURIS)

That he didn't forget what was important:

Never, right up to the end, neither his frenzied work, nor his suffering made him forget his friends – because he certainly never put all his poetry into his books, he put as much into his life. (WALTER BERRY)

That he was modest:

> What modesty! You apologized for everything: for being present, for speaking, for being quiet, for thinking, for expressing your dazzlingly meandering thoughts, even for lavishing your incomparable praise. (ANNA DE NOAILLES)

That he was a great talker:

> One can never say it enough: Proust's conversation was dazzling, bewitching. (MARCEL PLANTEVIGNES)

That one never got bored at his house:

> During dinner, he would carry his plate over to each guest; he would eat soup next to one, the fish, or half a fish besides another, and so on until the end of a meal; one can imagine that by the fruit, he had gone all the way around. It was testimony of kindness, of good will towards everyone, because he would have been distraught that anyone would have wanted to complain; and he thought both to make a gesture of individual politeness and to assure, with his usual perspicacity, that everyone was in an agreeable mood. Indeed, the results were excellent, and one never got bored at his house. (GABRIEL DE LA ROCHEFOUCAULD)

Yet Proust was often disappointed in his friends, and this could spill over into caustic remarks about friendship itself. Despite the dazzling conversation and dinner parties, he wrote in his novel:

That he could just as well have befriended a settee:

> The artist who gives up an hour of work for an hour of conversation with a friend knows that he is sacrificing a reality for something that does not exist (our friends being friends only in the light of an agreeable folly which travels with us through life and to which we readily accommodate ourselves, but which at the bottom of our hearts we know to be no more reasonable than the delusion of the man who talks to the furniture because he believes that it is alive).

That talking is a futile activity:

> Conversation, which is friendship's mode of expression, is a superficial digression which gives us nothing worth acquiring. We may talk for a lifetime without doing more than indefinitely repeat the vacuity of a minute.

That friendship is a shallow effort

> ... directed towards making us sacrifice the only part of ourselves that is real and incommunicable (otherwise than by means of art) to a superficial self.

And that friendship is in the end no more than

> ... a lie which seeks to make us believe that we are not irremediably alone.

It doesn't mean he was callous. It doesn't mean he was a misanthrope. It doesn't mean he never had an urge to see friends (an urge he described as a 'craving to see people which attacks both men and women and inspires a longing to throw himself out of the window in the patient who has been shut away from his family and friends in an isolation clinic'). The dark thoughts on friendship taken from his novel reflect Proust's sense that he could not fully be himself with other people – or rather he couldn't be himself *and* have the affection he needed. The reason was that he was far too perceptive about other people for his own good. None of his friends ever quite seemed to match his incredible demands for loyalty and kindness. When Proust met a palm-reader in 1918, the woman was said to have taken a glance at his hand, looked at his face for a moment, then remarked simply, 'What do you want from me, Monsieur? It should be you reading *my* character.' But this miraculous understanding of others did not lead to cheerful conclusions. 'I feel infinite sadness at seeing how few people are genuinely kind,' he said, and judged in his novel that most people had something rather wrong with them:

> The most perfect person in the world has a certain defect which shocks us or makes us angry. One man is of rare intelligence, sees everything from the loftiest viewpoint, never speaks ill of anyone, but will pocket and forget letters of supreme importance which he himself asked you to let

him post for you, and so makes you miss a vital engagement without offering you any excuse, with a smile, because he prides himself upon never knowing the time. Another is so refined, so gentle, so delicate in his conduct that he never says anything to you about yourself that you would not be glad to hear, but you feel that he suppresses, that he keeps buried in his heart, where they turn sour, other, quite different opinions.

In an essay for a commemorative volume published after Proust's death, his friend Lucien Daudet wrote that he possessed

> an unenviable power of divination, he discovered all the pettiness, often hidden, of the human heart, and it horrified him: the most insignificant lies, the mental reservations, the secrecies, the fake disinterestedness, the kind word which has an ulterior motive, the truth which has been slightly deformed for convenience, in short, all the things which worry us in love, sadden us in friendship and make our dealings with others banal were for Proust a subject of constant surprise, sadness or irony.

It was because Proust was both unusually honest and unusually affectionate that he felt keenly the divide between his private and social selves, so keenly that he came to judge that social life and art were fundamentally rather than occasionally incompatible. This real self would go into the novel, the social self into the letters and the dinner parties.

Until now, English readers have had no possibility of studying closely Proust's social self in the last years of his life. Through this magnificent work of scholarship, we can now add to our knowledge of Proust's novel a knowledge of his day-to-day activities, and hence follow for ourselves the fascinating nuances of the divide between this great novelist's private and social selves.

INTRODUCTION

This is the fourth and final volume of the translation of Marcel Proust's correspondence. It opens a few months before the last campaigns of the First World War and ends with Proust's premature death, at the age of fifty-two, in November 1922. The letters were selected by Philip Kolb from the twenty-one volumes which he compiled, edited and published over nearly half a century. In an afterword to this book, Jocelyne Kolb tells the story of her father's remarkable achievement.

In January 1918, Proust is awaiting proofs of *Within a Budding Grove*, the second book of his vast, cyclical work *In Search of Lost Time*. He is in a state of frustration: the continuity essential to its understanding has been lost. *Swann's Way* had appeared in 1913, published at his expense with Bernard Grasset after having been rejected by four publishers, among them the distinguished firm of La Nouvelle revue française recently founded by André Gide. This first book won him many readers, but preparations for the rest ceased when Grasset's firm closed for the duration of the war. Thus, when Gide confessed his mistake, Proust abandoned Grasset without hesitation. He now had the publishers he had always wanted. But the war years had afforded him the time to rethink the central part of his great work, the scheme of which had been clear in his mind since about 1906 – the last page of *Time Regained*, we learn from these letters, was written before the first page of *Swann's Way* – and his letters to his new editor, Gaston Gallimard, show him rewriting each book on proof. Crucially, he introduces a major new sequence of *Sodom and Gomorrah*. By 1922, his original novel has been expanded by some two thirds.

When Gallimard objects to this unorthodox method of proof-correcting, Proust retorts: 'Since you are good enough to see a certain richness which you like in my books, remind yourself that it is precisely due to the extra nourishment with which I reinfuse them through living.' And as we watch, these additions are transmuted from reality into fiction. But alas for Proust, the more he enriches his work, the greater the delay between books. His grand architectural design is not yet apparent, and to critics who accuse him of writing his memoirs, of ignoring plot and composition, he replies with patient analyses of his method and rigorous structure. Plagued by accusations of snobbery, he settles the question by pointing out that, in his books, 'the calumniated social class, which is always in the wrong, which utters nothing but imbecilities, is the vulgar, tasteless class, is so-called high society'. Written as he undertakes the unending task of recreating his masterpiece, these letters, whether clearing up a misconception or expressing his appreciation to the discerning few, will prove invaluable to our understanding of it.

Proust is as good company in his letters as he was in life: droll, mischievous, mercurial, his self-deprecation and ceremonious manners masking a formidable erudition. He himself kept few letters: the entire surviving correspondence – equal in length to *In Search of Lost Time* – is almost wholly one-sided. In the present selection, he corresponds regularly for the first time with critics and fellow-writers, to whom he writes with unconventional informality. Despite becoming a public figure with the award of the Prix Goncourt to *Within a Budding Grove* in 1919, he abhors the role of a 'man-of-letters'. His literary colleagues respond not only to his books but also to his profoundly original essays for the most famous literary magazine of the day, the *NRF*, edited by the charming, modest Jacques Rivière, perhaps his most discerning reader.

But he still keeps up with lifelong friends made at the Lycée Condorcet in Paris salons and during summer seasons in the villas of fashionable Trouville and Cabourg. Some have been scattered by the war. Except for Guiche, he has lost touch with the quartet of aristocrats (one has been killed in action) who together stood for Saint-Loup, and even with his intimate friend Reynaldo Hahn. Others are distanced by marriage, and his congratulations have an air of reproach. Lionel Hauser, his match in epistolary wit, continued to offer him financial and moral advice which, as ever, he ignores. His dear Madame Straus is ailing, but he has a new confidante in the wealthy, worldly Princesse Soutzo, and a new literary friend in the English man-of-letters Sydney Schiff. He has grown closer to André Gide. And he has discovered an affinity with an urbane, cultivated American, Walter Berry, with whom he shares the desire for a just peace.

At the turn of the century, Proust had espoused the cause of

Dreyfus. Now he espouses the cause of reconciliation with Germany, and for the same reasons: a passionate sense of justice and a detestation of the evils of nationalism. Thus his devotion, much insisted upon in these letters, to the arch anti-Dreyfusard, anti-Semite and enemy of reconciliation, Léon Daudet, requires explanation. As a youth, Proust was never happier than with Alphonse Daudet and his family; Léon, a distinguished critic, was not only his earliest admirer but also the protective elder brother of his past lover, Lucien. Naming Daudet and his collaborator Charles Maurras, Proust's narrator protests in *Within a Budding Grove* that 'what brings men together is not a community of views but a consanguinity of minds'. But it comes as a relief when even Proust, in 1922, finally admits to finding Daudet's rhetoric 'unbearable'.

The end of the war brings a new social realism. Writers emerge from the trenches and the Goncourt judges nearly give the prize to a young soldier, Roland Dorgelès; Proust is seen as belonging to a bygone era. The sense of insecurity this induces, and his apprehension about the reception of *Sodom and Gomorrah*, lead him to embark on a long, almost embarrassing courtship of the critics, especially of Jacques Boulenger, his 'St George of Literature', but he nevertheless pounces on self-serving dishonesty (Henri Ghéon) and disingenuousness (Jean de Pierrefeu, Paul Souday, Frédéric Vandérem).

In fact, Proust embraces the post-war transformation of society with enthusiasm. He tells Cocteau, who brings out his Cubist-inspired *Le Coq et l'Arlequin* in 1919, that his aphorisms about music and painting 'prove that we think alike about Modern Art'. The parties he attends in a last 'fling', with their charades and jazz-inspired dances, have the burlesque quality of Cocteau's *Parade*. He seizes on Summer Time, introduced during the war, as a metaphor for the effects of change. When Einstein receives the Nobel Prize for Physics, Proust is baffled, if flattered, to be compared to him: 'I don't understand a word of his theories [but] apparently our ways of distorting Time are analogous'. He is suspicious of comparisons to Freud; accused, to his disgust, of fashionable self-analysis, he comments: 'I had the misfortune to begin my book with the word "I".' Marie Bonaparte will shortly translate Freud, but Proust won't live to read him (the interesting question, did Freud read Proust? remains unanswered). The psychology of his novel, he tells Rivière, is not mere 'plane psychology' but rather 'psychology in Time'.

In 1919, in *Pastiches et mélanges*, Proust publishes his old articles for the *Figaro*. These include his incomparable parodies, which he shows to the Abbé Mugnier. 'I would like you to become better acquainted with my mind,' he writes to Huysmans's former confessor, 'with my common sense, which Descartes tells us is universal.' He amuses himself by adding a new pastiche of Saint-Simon by way of teasing friends, portraying them as figures of the Régence, and of debunking the pretensions of the Napoleonic aristocracy. *Pastiches et mélanges* also contains his early essays on Sainte-Beuve. Between 1918 and 1921, he pursues his contempt for that critic's literary judgment in four major critical essays for the *NRF*. The first is a preface for a book by Jacques-Émile Blanche, whose complacency provokes a strangely bitter exchange of letters in which the painter, stung by Proust's savage irony, threatens to take back his famous portrait. The essays 'On Flaubert's Style', 'Preface to Morand' and 'Concerning Baudelaire' follow at yearly intervals. The subject of Flaubert becomes central to a disputatious correspondence of labyrinthine complexity which involves the *NRF* and ends up by frustrating his ambition to develop his essays in a book of literary criticism. Once again, Proust has proved himself to be his own worst enemy.

On the subject of style, he returns again and again to his admiration for the classics, in particular for Racine. In a postscript to a letter thanking the writer Martin-Chauffier for his 'infallible accuracy of aim' in a review of *The Guermantes Way*, he talks of the seventeenth century, 'that admirable epoch', and of 'its sense of reality, its underlying vigour, its strongly felt impressions, of which an apparent solemnity should never lessen our awareness'. He discusses their work with few contemporary novelists: François Mauriac, Edmond Jaloux, Henri de Régnier. In a letter to Régnier in 1920, he compares the design of Régnier's novel *La Double Maîtresse* to his own, asking: 'doesn't the "peripeteia" in my book, as in yours, hang upon the sudden recall of a sensation?' The contemporary he most admires is Jean Giraudoux, and he is mortified when, in an article devoted to him, Giraudoux confines himself to details of his private life picked up from Paul Morand's outrageously indiscreet 'Ode to Marcel Proust', published in 1919.

In 1921, his innovatory style receives a generous tribute from Gide, who confesses to 'going for days not daring to pick up a pen [...], convinced that this is the only way to write'. But the majority of critics are baffled by its 'convultions'. When Souday claims to have triumphed over a 132-word sentence in *The Guermantes Way*,

Proust teases him: 'I think you are over-generous when you suggest that it becomes clear on a third reading, speaking for myself, I find it incomprehensible.' And when Souday mocks his grammar, Proust parodies him deliciously, and, Molière-like, delivers a lecture on the foolishness of grammarians. His style in these letters resembles his narrator's, except in one respect: his compliments, and his expressions of gratitude to a critic or of sympathy to a mourner, the one stemming from an over-developed sense of politeness, the other from a cult of grief inherited from his mother, can indeed seem unduly flowery and convoluted (an epistolary convention of the day not confined to the French: see the typical style of Proust's translator Charles Scott-Moncrieff in a letter written in English).

Proustian metaphors and emblems crop up in letter after letter: the significance of the 'telescope' as opposed to the 'microscope', the revelations to be found in a photograph or a person's handwriting, the associations of a name (he seeks help with etymologies, with Brichot's dissertations in the 'little train' in mind) or the qualities of asparagus (we learn the source of the Duc de Guermantes's quip about its rigidity) and so on. Above all, he returns repeatedly to the theme of the time that must elapse before an innovator is recognized as a classic, citing Baudelaire and the banned poems, and the 'scandal' of Manet's *Olympia*.

Certain crucial scenes in *In Search of Lost Time* come about almost by accident. It is moving to discover that the scene of Bergotte's death in *The Captive* was written in a state of ecstasy after visiting the Jeu de Paume with Jean-Louis Vaudoyer in 1921 to see once more 'the most beautiful picture in the world', Vermeer's *View of Delft*. 'I have a shining memory,' he writes to Vaudoyer in 1922, 'of the morning when you tenderly guided my faltering steps towards that Vermeer in which the gables are like precious specimens of Chinese art.' And the charm of a critic's address inspires another famous passage: 'I much regret not having chatted to you about street-traders: for I've just finished a long passage for *Sodom and Gomorrah* on the cries of Paris.'

Proust was not writing for posterity in his letters. The notion that they might be published horrified him. Letter-writing, for him, was a form of private conversation. The only letters published in his lifetime were in answer to questionnaires which, as a celebrity, he received from the press. He is asked for his opinion on topics ranging from his choice of French paintings and, should the necessity arise, of manual labour (writing, naturally!), to Classicism, the 'introspective' novel (an essay which contains a wonderful sentence about his efforts to record his own sleep) and the new lending libraries. Obliged in each case to condense his thoughts, he turns out to be an admirable journalist.

In 1906, convinced of the worth and originality of his scheme, Proust turned his back on society and (except when an 'outing' suited its demands) committed himself to his novel. (Its genesis is explained in a long letter to Rosny.) His routine, dictated by work and asthma, involved turning night into day. The physical complications of his illness, whose psychosomatic nature he evidently understood, prove fatal only because, with characteristic stubbornness, he scorns the advice of doctors, treating it with an array of drugs and nostrums and a dangerously abstemious diet. And he has so long exploited it to protect his seclusion, so often claimed to be on the point of death, that people are sceptical. (Morand's 'Ode' begins: 'I say: / You're looking very well. / You reply, / Dear friend, I nearly died three times today.') He also uses it shamelessly to cajole friends into shouldering the burden of practical worries which threaten his capacity to work, such as the intractable problem, a running theme in this correspondence, of his sequestrated funds held by a German bank. And in 1919, forced to leave the security of his shuttered room at the Boulevard Haussmann (its fug captured by Morand in his 'Ode': 'Céleste, / sweet for all her sternness, dunks me in the dark juices / of your bedroom / that smells of warm cork and the cold grate'), he even enrols them to sell his furniture, down to the cork which had lined its walls.

Even before the Goncourt, *Within a Budding Grove* sells out, and he nags Gallimard about reprints: 'I would appear to be copying my parody of the Goncourts if I told you that the book is on every table in China and Japan'. *The Guermantes Way* and the first part of *Sodom and Gomorrah* appear to universal praise in 1920 and 1921. When the second part expands to the point where it has to be divided into three volumes, he writes to reassure the despairing Gallimard: '*Sodom II* will be the richest book, in terms of psychology and range of feeling, I've yet given you.' Nevertheless, he expects its subject to shock his readers (doubly so after an advertisement for 'a *Sodome II*, a *Sodome III*, a *Sodome IV* and, I'm almost sure, a *Sodome V* and a *Sodome VI* as well') and is bemused when critics, and even 'Guermantes ladies', far from being scandalized, see it as 'a moral tale'.

Surprisingly perhaps, he is always ready to discuss the 'keys' to the characters, places and 'furniture' in his novel, with the proviso that 'there are so many to every door that in reality there are none.' He devotes letters on the subject to Jacques de Lacretelle in 1918 about *Swann's Way* (identifying Gilberte) and in 1919 to Lucien Daudet about the personalities in *The Guermantes Way*. In an entertaining exposition of 'Guermantes wit' to Paul Souday, he explains that his source for Oriane's witticisms was 'not somebody well-born, but Bizet's widow, Madame Straus' (also, we learn, the owner of her red shoes). 'The prototype of Swann,' he states in a comical letter to a stranger called Harry Swann, 'was Charles Haas: Haas the friend of princes, the Israelite of the Jockey Club,' and he expounds on the phonetic values of his choice of names. In 1921, he tries unconvincingly to reassure Robert de Montesquiou that he is not the Baron de Charlus; yet within months is explaining to Gallimard that the prickly Count's death has allowed him to enrich Charlus's character. Two courtesans model for Odette (poor Laure Hayman is castigated for recognizing herself). To Guiche he writes that his mother-in-law Mme Greffulhe is not the Duchesse but the Princesse de Guermantes. And to Mme de Chevigné that, inasmuch as she is the Duchesse de Guermantes, she is 'the subject of essays in every newspaper in England, America and Switzerland, of theses in Sweden and lectures in Holland'. His 'unattainable great lady' of the early novels, Mme de Chevigné has completely misunderstood his intentions, and he confesses to her that, 'festering', he had compared her to an 'old crow' in a letter to Guiche. Her obtuseness about her true role, he tells her truthfully, 'is one of the few great sorrows still capable of afflicting a man at the end of his life who has renounced everything'.

'Silence alone is strength, all the rest is weakness', a line from Alfred de Vigny, is Proust's favourite maxim. But despite his passion for secrecy, he is compulsively indiscreet. In personal relations he demands, but does not always get, openness, and his touchiness about imagined slights leads him to pick a quarrel with anybody who falls short of his standards of friendship. But he is always remorseful. The forgiving Hauser remarks that he was doubtless 'drunk on glory'. To Gallimard and Rivière, both of whom must have found him exasperating as author and friend, he excuses himself with touching tenderness. And he shows a genuine concern for his old sparring partner, Montesquiou, in his pathetic state in old age.

His letters also testify to the reckless streak in his complex nature: he cannot resist a gamble, whether in love or on the Stock Exchange. To Hauser's reproaches of his extravagance in both, he retorts with an accusation of 'Cornelian accountancy' in a letter of extraordinary depth of feeling. He confesses to acts of impulse. He visits a brothel after the departure of his secretary, Henri Rochat, and 'six months of enforced chastity'. He scatters a fortune in tips at the Ritz; and brings back a bottle of port ('Bin 345') which he swallows at a sitting. He gets into a fight in the bar at Le Bœuf sur le Toit, enjoys the company of 'apaches' and jumps at the chance of a duel. It is perhaps not too fanciful to suggest that, in sacrificing himself to his book, he was gambling with death, a constant presence in these letters.

Proust can be ribald, even scatological. To Lucien Daudet and Hauser in 1918, and later to Madame de Clermont-Tonnerre and François Mauriac, he is explicit about the physical nature of his love for the undeserving Rochat. But his violent protests when perspicacious critics detect transpositions of gender in his novel, and his outbursts of schoolboy humour when teasing Walter Berry about his womanizing, suggest a hypocritical desire to be considered part of the conventional masculine world. Gide, who justly reproaches him with hypocrisy for his hostility to 'inverts' in *Sodom and Gomorrah*, is amazed when, at their subsequent meeting, Proust cheerfully confesses his homosexuality. But the 'valleys of brimstone and pitch' gradually become a metaphor in his letters for his physical and mental torments.

As these letters follow the course of the war, the Russian Revolution, the peace and the preoccupations of postwar French society, we have a picture of an enlightened and often prophetic observer. Furthermore, they show us why Proust was such a great comic writer, and provide us with a manifesto of his aims as writer and moralist: objectivity, honesty, common sense. Among the human qualities he most admires, we learn, is stoicism. His own becomes unbearably moving as death approaches. In a letter to Gallimard written shortly before he succumbs to pneumonia, despairing not for himself but for his books, he compares his lonely task, still incomplete, with that of Fabre's burrowing wasp in an echo of Françoise's stratagems for 'establishing the greatness of her house': 'doubled up, like her, and totally bereft, I devote myself to providing them with the future denied to me.'

Joanna Kilmartin

TRANSLATOR'S NOTE

The letters in this volume have been selected from volumes XVII to XXI of *Correspondance de Marcel Proust*, texte établi, présenté et annoté par Philip Kolb (Paris, Librairie Plon, 1989–1993).

I am grateful to Dennis Enright for having translated the verse cited in letters up to the end of 1921. I am also indebted, for their literary and period knowledge, to André Choremi, Madeleine Enright, Dominique de Grunne, Professor Jocelyne Kolb, Dr Robin Marsack, Professor John Weightman, Francis Wyndham and the late Michael Wishart.

For the sake of continuity, I have added twenty-eight letters to Professor Kolb's selection from his complete edition, the majority of them from volume XXI, and have quoted in the footnotes from others that do not appear in his selection. I have translated, or paraphrased, some but far from all of his exhaustive footnotes, and have added others for the benefit of the English reader or, again, for the sake of narrative. Jean-Yves Tadié's biography, *Marcel Proust* (N.R.F./Gallimard, Paris, 1996) was the source for certain additional notes, and, for domestic details, the translation of Céleste Albaret's *Monsieur Proust* (Collins/Harvill Press, 1976; trs. Barbara Bray).

In the footnotes, N.R.F. refers to Proust's publishers, *La Nouvelle revue française*, *NRF* to the literary magazine of the same name. The numerals I, II, III, IV, V, VI refer to *Swann's Way, Within a Budding Grove, The Guermantes Way, Sodom and Gomorrah, The Captive & The Fugitive* and *Time Regained* in the six-volume translation of *À la recherche du temps perdu* entitled *In Search of Lost Time* (Chatto & Windus, 1992; trs. C.K. Scott-Moncrieff and Terence Kilmartin; revised by Dennis Enright). *AS-B* and *CS-B* refer to Proust's non-fiction, selected and translated in *Against Sainte-Beuve and Other Essays* (Penguin, 1994; trs. John Sturrock) and collected in *Contre Sainte-Beuve* (N.R.F./Gallimard, La Bibliothèque de la Pléiade, Paris, 1971). *MP-GG* refers to *Marcel Proust Gaston Gallimard, Correspondance 1912–1922* (N.R.F./Gallimard, Paris, 1989).

There is much talk of money in these letters; for the period, £1 equalled c. 51 FF.

1   To Walter Berry[1]

[Friday 4 January 1918]

My dear friend,

I'm very behindhand in thanking you for your delightful note. But I've been out of my mind with worry these past few days over the health of somebody very dear to me.[2] Yet another reason why, as you say, the year has begun under a cloud. Otherwise, I would have invited you to come and dine at the Ritz. But I was too discouraged to do more than pace up and down in the snow outside my front door. However, all goes well now.

Would that the same could be said of that other cloud, the one you meant, the War! If it can (in so far as a war can 'go well' while piling up the dead and leaving the living in ruins, though people would die just the same if we were beaten, and that would be a thousand times worse), we owe it to our American friends, spurred into action by Walter Berry.

I wonder if you read Daniel Halévy's[3] article on the Americans in last week's *Débats*. If not, I'll try and find it for you. Or else write to Halévy. It portrays the women of the North, who are moved to think that 'they've come so far'.[4] It's a short piece, and doesn't in fact add up to much. But the tone is right, being sober and sincere.

For the twentieth time at least, the war has taken on a new aspect in the eyes of the very people waging it. Lloyd George now says: 'War nowadays is a question of tonnage.'[5] That's your field (among so many). Yet each successive formula seems to me too rigid. Fashions in strategy change,[6] even in wartime, as they do in medicine. I dislike a medicine that puts its trust solely in serums etc.

Our wishes are identical: for a happy outcome to the war. And yet, for me, such an outcome cannot be wholly happy, because then, having done all the good you can for France, you will be off on your travels and I shall never see you again. But you must have left behind, in countless other countries and countless other towns, hearts that remember and miss you, as mine will. Meanwhile, as long as the common suffering confines us to the same Ark, and the Flood has not yet subsided, let us try to ensure that I see you occasionally, you, the pearl of your collection, as you were saying about Mme G.[7] Speaking of whom, I've written out for her, in a copy of *Swann*,[8] my various impressions on seeing her.[9] You must tell me when we meet if there is some way of sending it to her, and if so, how.

Warmest regards,
Marcel Proust

P.S. The night before last, walking through the snow and slipping on the ice, I was accosted by two American soldiers who asked me the way to the Hotel Bedford. I didn't know that it was round the corner from me, on the rue de l'Arcade. They having almost no French and I no English, it was in silence that I set off in search of the Bedford, which was soon found. And, like the women of the North, I was moved, thinking: 'they've come so far'.

1. Walter Van Rensselaer Berry (1859–1927). American international lawyer who had campaigned for US entry into the war. Now President of the US Chamber of Commerce in Paris.

2. Princesse Soutzo: see following letter.

3. See letter 37, n. 1. Proust had long admired Halévy's war commentaries for their objectivity.

4. 'Suddenly, the battalion came to a halt. The young soldiers, a little weary, leant on their upturned rifles, arms folded. Women came out of their houses to gaze at them, thronging the narrow pavements, and one woman near me murmured: "So far, just fancy, they've come so far".' Halévy, *Journal des Débats*, 30 December 1917.

5. Proust quotes a speech reported in *Le Temps*, 16 December.

6. See Saint-Loup's theories on military strategy expounded to his fellow-officers at Doncières: III, 118–30.

7. Mrs John W. Garrett, wife of a senior American diplomat currently *en poste* at The Hague. Allusion to Berry's connoisseurship, not only of art and books, but also of women.

8. Proust habitually refers to all volumes of his novel as *Swann*.

9. See Proust's dedicatory letter to Mrs Garrett in a complimentary copy of *Within a Budding Grove*, April 1919: 'I've written a few lines [...] on the delicious sensation I had one evening when you called goodnight to me from beneath the arcades at the Ritz, and your voice rose, pure as a nightingale's, from the depths of shadowy branches.' Cf. the scene at the restaurant at Rivebelle: II, 455.

2 To Madame Soutzo[1]

[Friday 4 January 1918]

Princesse,

You are Madame de Noailles's *Bittô*[2] in this charming photograph. The pose of the little foot I'm more accustomed to see peeking out from beneath your skirt as you recline fits the rhythm of a dance. As for your arm and neck, they have a rhythmic fall that is yours alone.

While you were ill,[3] I didn't go to 'a single place worth mentioning', as Saint-Simon says[4] (which isn't to say that I went to unmentionable places). I've mostly been trudging through snow and fog. I don't think that can be the reason for my having the first signs of bronchitis, it usually being in bed that I catch cold. But it prolongs my attacks,[5] which now last till eleven o'clock at night.

I'm going to try something drastic, however risky, so as to be able to come and chat to you between nine and ten on Monday or Tuesday (preferably Monday, for you say 'next week', and I'm impatient to see you). Not to tire you, I'll leave on the stroke of ten. I shall join you for dinner, unless the smell of the 'fruits of the earth'[6] is forbidden by Antoinette,[7] whom I certainly hope to see.

Till Monday, Princesse. I gaze meanwhile at the image of the room[8] that has been the scene of all my 'outings' for the past year and of which I so often think when at home.[9] I should perhaps have been 'going about' more, especially at a time when you were unable to receive me, but I was too unhappy, too united with you in your suffering. What a start to the year!

Yours respectfully,
Marcel Proust

---

1. Princesse Soutzo, *née* Hélène Chrissoveloni (1879–1975). Graeco-Romanian by origin, enormously rich, dazzling in looks and personality, she was awaiting a divorce in order to marry Proust's friend Paul Morand.
2. A Spanish dancer in a poem by their mutual friend Anna de Noailles.
3. Mme Soutzo was recovering from an appendectomy in her suite at the Ritz.
4. Allusion to Saint-Simon's remark in his *Mémoires* that the Chevalier de Soissons

'had never in his life known a man worth mentioning'. Proust was embarking on a long pastiche of Saint-Simon.

5. Proust had suffered from severe asthma since childhood. He had adopted a routine, supported by a daily cocktail of drugs, which allowed him to sleep by day and work from his bed by night. Any break in this routine required extra stimulants.

6. Allusion to the title of André Gide's novel *Les Nourritures terrestres*. Proust himself abhorred cooking smells, usually having food sent in and eating little and late.

7. Mme Soutzo's personal maid.

8. The photograph showed Mme Soutzo in her drawing-room at the Ritz.

9. Proust had lived alone in an apartment at 102 Boulevard Haussmann since his widowed mother's death in 1905.

3 *To Jacques-Émile Blanche*[1]

[Shortly before 17 January 1918]

Dear friend,

I don't understand your letter telling me that I'll see that you harbour neither rancour nor resentment. But dear friend, need you really be such, not to hold a grudge against me when, towards you, I am all gratitude and admiring affection? You are the one who no longer wants my preface[2] (which I find only natural), who says that the book is already too long, Émile-Paul[3] being unprepared etc. (And greatly honoured though I am, and highly gratified, I confess that if he really has had to leave out the preface at the last moment, I'm more than happy not to tire myself needlessly in writing it. You tell me that Boylesve[4] readily accepted the same fate. I can't tell you how much I admire Boylesve. Every three months, searching for papers, I come across a twelve-page letter, sealed but never sent, which I wrote him about *Le Meilleur Ami*. Moreover, he has a hundred times my literary 'standing'. Only he isn't ill, and I'm worse than ill. Consequently, were this preface unpublished in the book, it would inconvenience me.)

I quite understand that you should no longer want it, and how, dear friend, could I blame you? But when I was 'all for it', how could you, for your part, blame me for *your* change of mind? Where are the grounds for 'rancour' in that? I sincerely hope I never give you reason to show me your lack of it, for I trust that I should always do as you would wish.

On the other hand, permit me to say, if it's not taking too

daring a liberty, that I think you overdo your lack of rancour with regard to Forain,[5] and it's not without sadness that I learn from your letter of your intention to devote a still more eulogistic essay to him. Let us not rake up the subject of Léon Daudet,[6] to whom I owe a huge debt of gratitude, for whom my close affection has outlasted twenty years of absence and whose book is full of such wonderfully comic portraits.[7] Mine[8] gave me no pleasure, but knowing that he meant to please me, I'm extremely grateful to him; yours[9] I would have found very hurtful had it been a good likeness, but despite what you say, it is nothing of the sort. Which is not to say that I didn't deplore its inclusion. But the two cases are very different. Forain, as you well know and say yourself, is a wicked and malicious man. I quite understand your not paying him back in his own coin for his behaviour by saying that he lacks talent etc. But at least you could say nothing at all, taking your lead from Vigny: 'Silence alone is strength, all the rest is weakness'.[10]

I'm wrong to call it weakness, for I know very well that when in the same situation myself (but not when my friends are), my instinctive, unfeigned reaction is also not to bear a grudge. I remember how my seconds upset me by refusing to let me shake hands with Lorrain after our duel.[11] (Even though they were right.) The worst harm, the only real harm, the wicked do to us is that by making it impossible for us to meet their wickedness with goodness, they make us a little wicked ourselves. But keep telling yourself this: whatever you do out of magnanimity, Forain, being incapable of understanding, and judging you by himself, will assume you do to placate him. It's all very well for a Tolstoy to turn the other cheek. But rightly or wrongly, and I think wrongly, you are seen as the very reverse of kind or charitable. Yet another reason why, after his monstrous behaviour, your enthusiasm will be misinterpreted (what's more, I'm sure that many painters are the unsuspecting victims of his spite). Publish your article after his death. *A body of work* deserves the tribute of admiration. I would have certain scruples about giving you this advice (if I wasn't certain that you would ignore it), for it's sad to deprive the nobler sides of an artist's being of the joys of such admiration. Now Forain, in spite of everything, must possess a nobler side, for his work comes from somewhere, after all. And I believe that Whistler's paradox about wicked geniuses and saintly fools holds true.[12] But these noble parts[13] have no need of plaudits, their true joy lying in Creation. And as for his ignoble side, since it renders him impervious to whatever is disinterested or moving, he will take your panegyric as evidence for the success of his intimidation.

Dear friend, I've talked to you with a frankness that is displeasing, futile, naïve. And yet I sometimes think that had we seen more of one another since Auteil,[14] I could have spared you many imprudent acts of kindness and perhaps other things besides. I say this in all humility, knowing that the only one to have benefited from this intimacy would have been your

Marcel Proust

1. Jacques-Émile Blanche (1861–1942), painter and critic; his portrait of Proust as a young dandy, painted in 1893 (now in the Musée d'Orsay), is the one most often reproduced.

2. Proust had agreed to write the preface to Blanche's *Propos de Peintre: De David à Degas*, a collection of essays on painters and their circle.

3. Blanche's publisher.

4. René Boylesve (1867–1926), Academician, middle-brow novelist, author of *Le Meilleur Ami* (1909).

5. Jean-Louis Forain (1852–1931), painter and caricaturist; a virulent anti-Semite with whom Proust had quarelled bitterly over the Dreyfus Affair.

6. Léon Daudet (1868–1942), essayist, critic and polemicist, eldest son of Alphonse Daudet. Co-founder with Charles Maurras of the anti-Semitic, ultra-Nationalist movement Action Française, Léon Daudet had orchestrated the campaign against Captain Alfred Dreyfus, whose cause Proust had espoused.

7. Allusion to Daudet's *Salons et Journaux* (1917), literary sketches of artists and intellectuals in Parisian society at the turn of the century.

8. 'Around 7.30, there arrived [at the Café Weber] a pale, doe-eyed young man, sucking on or fingering the ends of his dark, drooping moustache and swaddled in layers of wool like a Chinese curio. Having ordered grapes and a glass of water, he announced that he had just risen from bed, had influenza, would return to bed, was unable to stand the din, and then, his suspicious glances becoming teasing, dissolved into enchanting laughter and stayed. Soon, in hesitant bursts, there dropped from his lips remarks of an astonishing originality, observations of a fiendish acuity. His improvised images flew round [. . .] like those of some Mercutio or Puck, following several thoughts at once; quick to excuse himself for his pleasantries, torn by ironic scruples, he was by nature complex, nervous, ingratiating. This was the author of that original, often astonishing book, so full of promise, *Du Côté de chez Swann*: this was Marcel Proust.' Daudet, *op. cit.*, 298–9.

9. 'What bitter fruit could he have swallowed, Jacques-Émile Blanche, what emetic herb, to give him those pinched lips puckered up like an anxious dressmaker's in that pale, round face? I always think of him behind a door, wringing his hands, twisting his legs, whispering gossip too trivial even to shock[. . .].' Daudet, *op. cit.*, 226.

10. 'Seul le silence est grand; tout le reste est faiblesse'. Line from 'La Mort du loup' by Alfred de Vigny.

11. In 1897, Proust called out Jean Lorrain, a scurrilous columnist, for insinuating a sexual relationship between him and Lucien Daudet, Léon's younger brother. A harmless exchange of shots ensued; Proust's seconds were Jean Béraud, a painter, and Gustave 'Sword-thrust' Borda, whose obituary he was to write: see *CS-B*, 549–50.

12. James McNeill Whistler (1834–1903), a painter whom Proust had long admired. The quotation is unidentified.

13. *Les nobles parties*: a euphemism for the sexual organs.

14. Blanche still lived in the family home in Auteuil, the countrified Paris suburb where Proust, too, was brought up.

4   To André Gide[1]

20 January 1918

Dear friend,

Your letter touches me deeply, also saddens me, because of what you see as my indiscretion, above all gives me pleasure, because I gather that you have found happiness. But the source of this happiness[2] must not, I beg you, since you don't trust me absolutely, be revealed to me, not even partially (at present I am completely in the dark). La Bruyère rightly says: 'All trust is dangerous unless absolute; there are few circumstances in which one should not either reveal all or conceal all. One has already given away too much of one's secret to him from whom one feels obliged to conceal some particular.'[3]

I would add that I'm not curious, not even in the best sense of the word. The only situation where I would mind a friend keeping a secret from me is one where I might be of immediate service to him, where his heart or else his self-esteem was involved. Indeed, I must often have told you that however much of a bungler when it comes to myself, always letting the things I desire slip through my fingers, I can be extremely skilful on behalf of others, for I unite two qualities seldom met with in the same human being: a certain perspicacity on the one hand and, on the other, a total lack of amour propre and the complete inability to betray a friend. I thus missed my true vocation, which was to be a go-between[4] or a professional witness at duels. Moreover, it's often the compensation of those who bungle everything for themselves to procure success for others.

As for the indiscretion which you attribute to me – and which is completely contrary to my nature – your misunderstanding probably came about like this: when you were last here I thought of something you had written (in *Isabelle*, I think) about liking Jammes[5] for his way of telling stories.[6] Seized with the spirit of emulation, I told you a few, or tried to. But they concerned people whom I didn't know, or may once have sat beside at a dinner and have never seen since. To repeat their statements, about which there was nothing in the least confidential, is not what I call indiscretion.

Alas, where my friends are concerned, I find their confidential opinions come back to me, they having confided them to somebody whom they thought discreet, who then repeated them to somebody else, and so on. Now, I am the last person to do that. I am capable of being critical to a greater or lesser degree of people who mean nothing to me. But of a friend (and for the past three years I have thought of you as a friend), that, for me, would be unthinkable.

Dear friend, I would be horrified if, to show me that you believed me, you were to take me into your confidence about anything, no matter what. It would only make me miserable. And you, if you're happy, must have the strength to keep your happiness to yourself. The least confidence entails loss. Happiness is not increased by sharing it, despite what Hugo rightly says about maternal love.[7]

In short, I implore you to tell me nothing.

I doubt if I'll be able to see you on your way through Paris. The reason is this: at present, my attacks are seldom over till late at night; for instance, I couldn't receive visitors at the hour when you last saw me. It comes from having exhausted myself over a friend who has had an operation;[8] I had to comply with the visiting hours permitted by her doctor, and, like the swing of a pendulum, my illness took its revenge. I suppose things will gradually improve (I have days – all too rare – of relative respite) and certainly hope so, for I still haven't received my proofs from the N.R.F.[9] and shall have to 'put my back into it' when they eventually arrive. On no account complain to the N.R.F. about this delay (the printer lost an exercise-book;[10] nobody at the N.R.F. knew who had sent it to him etc.). I have already complained, more perhaps than I should have done; I should therefore be very vexed were you to add your reproaches to my grievances. Nor would it do any good, the printer having promised to get a move on.

Dear friend, you would give me great pleasure, and show me

that you anticipate a little from my book, by not reading it until it is in print, or at least until I tell you that the proofs have reached a stage where any changes will be minor ones. At present, you would get a totally false impression. Not only that, even these incomplete proofs are no more than the beginnings of a book. Now, I'm publishing the entire work at once, regardless of all the arguments I shall be given to the contrary,[11] so that I may be judged on the whole.[12] Thus, a hundred pages read on their own, even if definitive (and they're far from being that!) would give a wrong idea of something for which I have sacrificed a very great deal. If it would amuse you to see my work-in-progress – though my book is scarcely worth the trouble! – I ask nothing better than to let you have the proofs once you know the printed book. But afterwards, I beg you, not before. Naturally, should there be a passage here and there that might interest you, I'll gladly send you proofs, once corrected. But in those I await there is nothing that could appeal to you, nor make sense except in the context of the whole.

Forgive my having talked so long about such trifling matters as my health and my book. But if by chance I cannot see you on your 'flying visit', much as I hope to do so, I wanted you to know that it won't be for want of eagerness on my part. And that if, on the other hand, I wait for the right moment to show you my book, it is precisely because your opinion means so much to me. But will it ever appear? The printer[13] has been saying for more than a month that if he doesn't send proofs it's because he has no staff, and in the next breath that it's because he has sent me all there are for the first volume ... The N.R.F., on the other hand, barely aware of this state of affairs, leave it to me to remind him of the existence of an exercise-book amounting to a good third of a book for which I haven't had proofs, before they remember it for themselves! Finally, I send off exercise-book after exercise-book of which I don't possess copies. Will they get lost in transit? I've said, written and telephoned all this to the N.R.F., in the person of Madame Lemarié,[14] so there's no point in repeating it, she has been very helpful and we are in agreement. But there was a moment when I was very tempted to leave the publisher (the N.R.F.) which I prefer to any other, whose esteem is my greatest pride, for another, less exalted,[15] where at least my ideas would have been certain to see the light of print.

In any case, I expect to receive a good many proofs any day now. There is no time to be lost in my present state of health, especially when you consider that my manuscripts are barely decipherable,[16] that the first proofs will continue to arrive bearing no resemblance whatsoever to a text which nobody could read, and of which, once I'm gone, nobody will be able to make sense.

Goodbye, dear friend, I've talked only about myself and yet I think only of you.

Your admirer, your friend,
Marcel Proust

1. André Gide (1869–1951), novelist and critic, leading member of the group which, in 1908, founded the distinguished literary review *La Nouvelle revue française* (universally known as the *NRF*), its publishing house, N.R.F. Éditions and, in 1913, the avant-garde Théâtre du Vieux Colombier. Despite their rejection of *Swann's Way* in 1912, the N.R.F. had been Proust's publishers since 1916.

2. See references to 'Michel' in entries for August 1917 in Gide's *Journals* (Penguin, 1984).

3. 'Toute confiance est dangereuse, si elle n'est pas entière. Il y a peu de conjonctures où il ne faille tout dire ou tout cacher. On a déjà trop dit de son secret à celui à qui on croit devoir une circonstance.' La Bruyère, *Les Caractères ou les moeurs de ce siècle*.

4. A role that Proust had played formerly. In *Swann's Way*, M. de Charlus plays a similar role between Swann and Odette.

5. Francis Jammes (1868–1938), poet, novelist and mystic.

6. Said by Gide in *Isabelle* to be 'the delight of evening gatherings'.

7. Allusion to lines in Victor Hugo's *Feuilles d'automne*: 'A mother's love, the love no-one forgets/ [. . .] / To each his share and to all the whole', an echo of Proust's own strong feelings on the subject of maternal love.

8. Mme Soutzo: see letter 2.

9. Proofs of *Within a Budding Grove* were long overdue. (The N.R.F. were also preparing their own edition of *Swann's Way*.)

10. Proust's texts were transcribed from exercise-books in which he wrote by hand, like those into which Françoise pastes the narrator's long additions, which she calls his 'paperies': VI, 432–4.

11. When *Swann's Way* was published in 1913, Proust was persuaded against his better judgment to split it into two volumes for commercial reasons.

12. In 1913, Proust thought he had finished his great novel, but having embarked on the expansion of sequels to *Swann's Way* when publication was suspended by the war, he was anxious that they should now appear in quick succession for the better understanding of the work as a whole.

13. Imprimerie de la Semeuse. Most printers were still in the armed services.

14. Berthe Lemarié, Gaston Gallimard's deputy at the N.R.F..

15. Allusion to Bernard Grasset, the first publisher of *Swann's Way*.

16. See Proust to Albert Nahmias, his secretary in 1912: 'Do you still want to

emulate Oedipus and decipher the sphinx-like riddles of my handwriting? If so, I can send you some exercise-books which exceed in obscurity anything ever seen.'
Selected Letters, Volume Three, letter 46.

5 To Jacques-Émile Blanche

[Sunday evening 20 January 1918]

Dear friend,
    Without having begun to say what I wanted to say, when I received your missives I was already conscious of the length of an overlong preface. Consequently, this exercise-book (which I put in a separate package simply to avoid confusion) could have gone off to you more than three days ago. But for the last three days I've had such violent attacks of breathlessness that I could no more write you a letter than I could eat, drink or sleep.
    Today, it's over, I'm up, I've been out for my room to be cleaned, and I'm sending two packages round to you; one contains everything you lent me, corrected proofs etc., and the other, the exercise-book with the preface, one or two sentences of which will need re-writing on proof.
    I would gladly have mentioned dear Helleu's 'Reimses'[1] but wasn't sure you had them, well though I remember your friendly encouragement of him (did I ever tell you what a good friend he has been to me since?).[2]
    I dare say you'll reproach me for having quoted from the book rather than from your revised text.[3] The reason is that I had already done so before I had the revised text, and also because my eyes would have had difficulty in deciphering it. But you know your own variants, and you can easily substitute the right quotations for those of mine which you say are now obsolete. Regarding these, I have a small confession to make to you nevertheless. In principle, and as a question of doctrine, it seems to me absurd to give preference to a first version, a sketch etc. Sainte-Beuve always claimed never to find the original fire in later editions etc.[4] That is tantamount to denying the entire organic process whereby an author develops and fructifies. Therefore, for me to state that your second versions are inferior would, I feel, be idiotic. I would look like those people who admire Molière not for *La Misanthrope* but for *L'Étourdi,* Musset not for *Nuits* but for *La Ballade à la lune,* in short,

for everything that Molière and Musset tried to put behind them in favour of higher artistic forms.

That and my stated principle apart, it can happen, accidentally, that a first growth has a sap which too much pruning will inhibit. I wonder if that is not sometimes the case (as far as I can tell) in your *Essais et Portraits*. Assuming the mere *possibility*, wouldn't it be as well for the public to have an alternative version, in my quotations, for the sake of comparison, as when Claudel published three 'states' (which seems to me insane) of the same play? Only the poet can make the choice and the sacrifice, but might it not be to your advantage if the preface-writer adduces documentary evidence? It's for you to say.

At the beginning of the proofs, I wish to expand a little on the Auteuil Voyage through Time[5] (four or five lines), and to add a few words in praise of your approach, about which I haven't said enough. I'm so unused to distinguishing between 'style and substance' in a writer.

Now, as to the preface itself, I suppose you've given serious thought to all the trouble we shall bring upon ourselves, all the outrage (I don't give a damn for myself, but I can see it being skilfully manipulated so as to make you quarrel with me). In any case, you are the sole judge. Throw these pages on the fire if you wish, and I'll applaud your wisdom. I shall be very proud and pleased if you publish them at the forefront of your book, while feeling at the same time, for at least five reasons, that it's hardly wise. I see at least five possible routes, each more dangerous than the last, leading to this rotunda.[6] But I repeat, I gladly accept responsibility for what is mine. (I noted the little post-scriptum on Forain with displeasure. It serves no purpose that I can see.)

Ever yours, in affectionate and grateful admiration,
Marcel Proust

---

1. Paul Helleu (1859–1927), fashionable painter and etcher to whom Elstir is compared: IV, 390. In his preface, Proust was to insert a reference to Helleu's 'exquisite plans and transpositions' for the stained-glass in Reims cathedral: *AS-B*, 248.

2. In 1906, Helleu had presented him with a landscape of Versailles, where Proust had taken refuge in a hotel after his mother's death.

3. Allusion to an earlier book of essays, entitled *Essais et Portraits*, some of which Blanche had revised for inclusion in *Propos de peintre*.

4. 'Have you ever read the *first* edition of *Atala*, the *first* edition of *Le Génie du*

Christianisme? There you find the primitive Chateaubriand, in my opinion, the truest in feeling and style, a Chateaubriand who [...] offers us not only unique beauties, exotic incongruities and an abundance of sap, but an extravagance of vegetation which is almost indescribable.' Sainte-Beuve, *Les Causeries du Lundi*, I, 434 *et seq.*

5. 'The Auteuil of my childhood – of my childhood and his own youth – that Jacques Blanche evokes, I can understand that he should hark delightedly back to it, as to anything which has emigrated from the visible world into the invisible, anything which has been converted into memories [...]. But that Auteuil interests me still more as one small corner of the earth observable at two quite far-apart epochs of its voyage through Time.' Proust, 'Preface', *AS-B*, 245.

6. *rotonde*, both a circular building (such as the Pantheon) and a point where roads meet from various directions.

6   To Madame Scheikévitch[1]

[Monday, 21 January 1918]

Madame,

I write you this illogical and very silly note to say, firstly, that I was *very* hurt by things you have said about me since we last met,[2] and next, that I'll be still more so if I go on being 'vexed' with you because of it. To begin with, I thought it best to say nothing: 'Silence alone is strength; all the rest is weakness'.[3] But then I found this silence too painful to keep up, especially now, when you must have so many worries over Russia.

I didn't wish you a 'Happy New Year' because I was very wounded and 'wrathy', but if you like, we can treat the whole thing as 'a silent bar',[4] alter the calendar, just as one does when crossing from Russia into France, and pretend that today is only the first of January. In the book about which you were so indulgent, and in its successor, of which you alone possess handwritten extracts,[5] my young man counted on New Year's Day to become friends again with Gilberte.[6] I no longer share his illusions,[7] and I know, like you, that traits of character persist.

But all I can think of at the moment is the sorrow that your country must be causing you. I might have been able to get some news of what to expect from that quarter from Pechkoff,[8] but I haven't been back to the Crillon since I last dined there with you, which must be nearly two months ago now.

However, I go to the Ritz from time to time, when I can get up, to see the Princesse Soutzo. But never at the same times as you, alas, my health being so bad at the moment that it's very late before my attacks are over. I would like to think that you are happier than me, although that's not saying much; and I doubt, alas, if there is much comfort for you in Lenin's regime.[9] Have you at least managed to fend off the money worries it has caused you without too much difficulty? You are surrounded by friends who are more competent than I am in financial matters, and I imagine they give you good advice. But they can't expunge your grief at seeing one of your countries so completely divorced from the other. Your Russian roots can only serve to bring us closer together, now that they are a source of sorrow to you. One longs for the people one loves to be happy, and one loves them all the more when they are not. Moreover, you mustn't be offended by what I say about Russia. Present politics aside, which it would take too long to discuss here, you know that I'll always be faithful to the Russia of Tolstoy, Dostoevsky, Borodin – and Madame Scheikévitch. It's purely for reasons of euphony, and also because of failing eyesight, that my enumeration of writers is so short, and of composers so null, that I don't mention a single one of those I most admire.

Your respectful friend,
Marcel Proust

1. Marie Scheikévitch, a young, cultivated, Russian-born divorcée who had been one of Proust's rare confidantes on the progress of his novel.

2. Realizing that Mme Scheikévitch would be penniless following the October Revolution, Proust had offered to share the proceeds of the sale of his family furniture with her (she had refused); her offence, it seems, was to have revealed his secret to Mme Soutzo.

3. See letter 3, n. 10.

4. See *The Guermantes Way*: 'What man does not know that when a woman whom he is going to pay says to him "Don't let's talk about money", the remark must be regarded as what is called in music "a silent bar".' III, 298.

5. In 1915, in a dedicatory letter for her copy of *Swann's Way*, he had copied out passages from *Within a Budding Grove* and summarized for her the future story of Albertine. See *Selected Letters Volume Three*, letter 208. See also *AS-B*, 237–42.

6. See I, 490–96; II, 67–70.

7. In 1913, he had sent her a torn-off galley from his proofs of *Swann's Way*; a passage from the exquisite ending to 'Combray', it included the following sentence: 'the Méséglise and Guermantes ways left me exposed, in later life, to much disillusionment and even to many mistakes.' See I, 222.

8. Maxim Gorki's adopted son, invalided out of the French army and staying at the Hotel Crillon.

9. Soviet decrees of 21 January had included the confiscation of private property and the cancellation of interest payments on Russian bonds.

7   To Madame Scheikévitch

[Shortly after 21 January 1918]

My dear Madame Scheikévitch,

    I must express myself very badly, since I hurt your feelings out of what respect alone prevents my calling the tenderest of motives. I mean that I wrote to you simply to say: 'Can we not make up and be friends'. But can one rightfully say that, if one begins with the sham of concealing a grievance? Yet how was I to believe that this grievance was unfounded, when something I had written to you and you alone had been divulged, to my very considerable moral and material harm (naturally, *to* here means the effect, not the intent!) and my even greater sorrow. But let's make it our New Year's present to one another to say no more about these things and truly forget them. As for talking about them to others, I don't even need to ask you not to do that, you would *devastate* me. One day, in the second volume of *Swann*, you'll see how a true thing is transformed in a novel. You'll recognize it. You won't need to tell me. Meanwhile, let's drop the subject.

    I'm extremely sorry to hear of your financial difficulties, and equally so for my impotence in the matter. I would dearly like to relieve you of your worries. But allow me to tell you that from a practical and immediate standpoint, your plans for work[1] (which I was not slow to encourage) now seem, contrary to what I first thought, ill-advised for the development of your gifts and the future course of your life. I don't want to discourage you with my own example, not pretending to be an author sought after by the 'leading dailies', but even at a time when one thought that Venice was about to fall I couldn't profit from it, if one can say that of the saddest of all possible news, to 'place' an article of mine on Venice.[2]

    It's true that you also have a remarkable talent for drawing: your Abbé Mugniers are masterpieces.[3] But I have a very old friend (in every sense of the word old) whose financial situation has been one of my chief worries over the past two years. You don't know her, and certainly wouldn't be flattered by the comparison from an artistic point of view. But she had outlets among dealers who knew her etc., and even so, believe me, all came to naught. No, since chance has surrounded you with so many [...] and [...][4] among your intimate friends (and it's also chance that leads me to pick on their names), would it not be simplest for them to advance you the interest on coupons which Russia will certainly be bound to honour sooner or later? It would be nothing to people like that, and such a relief to you, not to have to give it another thought.

However, there is something of a literary nature which might be possible without your having to write a single line. Since you are on such close terms with *Le Temps*,[5] tell them that you are willing to write a daily article, purely for money, preferably of the 'man-bites-dog' kind. The supposed writer will be you, but to spare you the sickening tedium, the one who will write it, from the first line to the last, with a pleasure you cannot imagine, will be me. And it goes without saying that we won't share the fees but that all will be for you, the whole point being to earn you money without your having to lift a finger. While I'm writing the articles, you'll be receiving your guests, or dreaming in front of your flowers, and I will be so happy to think that I'm working for you. And every evening, Céleste[6] will bring you my copy. I may appear to be contradicting what I said earlier, but it's only from *quantity*, from a daily article, that one can achieve a respectable income. How does this appeal to you, dear collaborator?

Awaiting your call to arms, I conserve my strength by not prolonging a letter in which I no longer remember if I have sufficiently assured you of my tender and respectful affection.

Marcel Proust

1. Mme Scheikévitch had consulted Proust about writing a novel.

2. Allusion to Italy's defeat at Caporetto in October 1917, when it was feared that Venice would be abandoned to the Austrians. Proust had offered the *Figaro* an early version of the chapter on Venice near the end of *The Fugitive*.

3. i.e. sketches of the Abbé Mugnier: see following letter.

4. The names suppressed are those of well-known bankers.

5. Allusion to Mme Scheikévitch's lover, Adrien Hébrard, editor of *Le Temps*.

6. Céleste Albaret, *née* Gineste (1891–1984). Céleste had become Proust's housekeeper in 1914, later marrying his regular taxi-driver, Odilon Albaret. Among Proust's friends, she was famous for her imposing presence and native wit. There is an affectionate portrayal of her forthright character, and the 'strange genius' of her speech, in *Sodom and Gomorrah*: IV, 282–6.

8 From Jacques-Émile Blanche

19, rue du Docteur-Blanche, XVIe
[23 January 1918]

Dear Marcel,

I scarcely expected the bombshell which descended upon me yesterday evening. For anything to do with the book, send for M. Émile-Paul, or go and see him, he will tell you how things stand. In fact, I was in the process of collating the pieces from which I had intended to make *one* book[1] and which, totalling some 900 pages, were retrieved from the printer nine months ago. I never dreamt of depriving myself of your preface, and whatever the mysterious Xs and Ys report to you about my supposed remarks[2] (which you throw back in my face), they are better informed than I am.

The emphasis which you have placed from the start, and continue to place, on my understanding the courage and risks involved in associating your name with mine should have made me think twice.

Not to name your informants, as is your wont, is worse than appointing them. Kindly take the first opportunity to tell them *never to set foot in my house again.*

I cannot have dealings by telephone, still less by letter, with someone who hides behind others. When I saw you again after so many years that evening at the Théâtre Astruc,[3] you immediately started talking about what the Xs and Ys had said to you about me. I more or less challenged you to give me what journalists call your 'sources'. You said you would think about it. Nothing came of it. I should have persisted. This time, I leave it to you to choose between your anonymous informants and me.

My first impulse was to return your manuscript and take back the portrait I painted of you some twenty-five years ago, as Degas did to me.[4] But having slept on it, I decided never again to act in the heat of the moment. In one of the remarkable letters you wrote me, you say, à propos of Forain and Léon Daudet, that one must learn how not to forget; this is a unique opportunity to put that lesson into practice. Never have I felt so mortally offended.

Very sorrowfully yours,
J-É. Blanche

Kindly make the contents of this letter known to those whom it may concern.

1. See letter 3, n. 2. Blanche now intended to make two books out of his essays.
2. Proust had written reproaching Blanche for having gossiped about his preface.
3. The occasion was the Paris première of Mussorgsky's *Boris Godunov* in 1913. The Théâtre Astruc (now the Théâtre des Champs-Élysées), was named for Diaghilev's associate, the impresario Gabriel Astruc.
4. See letter 3, n. 1. The portrait was to hang in Proust's bedroom until his death. Apparently Degas had reclaimed his portrait by Blanche when, contrary to his strict instructions, Blanche had allowed it to be reproduced in an art magazine.

9 To Jacques-Émile Blanche

[Tuesday 24 January 1918]

Dear friend,

Yours was hardly a pleasant letter to receive. I no longer recognized you. Your parting shot: 'This is my opportunity to learn how not to forget', applied to the letter of unmitigated affection I had written you, filled me with something akin to horror. What's more, you quote this advice as coming from me and you cite Léon Daudet and Forain. I made no attempt whatsoever to influence you regarding your attitude to Léon Daudet, making it clear that he is a friend to whom I owe a great deal and a writer whom I admire, and I'm only sorry that our friends should so seldom be our friends' friends. As for Forain, I merely advocated silence, that you might emulate mine after his outrageous conduct towards me.

My behaviour towards you has been nothing if not friendly, for which, furthermore, I deserve no credit, having the greatest affection for you. Or rather, I had, till I came to the last words of your letter, words which I swear I never expected to hear from you. But I shall forget them. As you say, it's almost twenty-five years since you did my portrait, and my having loved you for so long without wavering must have brewed some sympathetic ferments in my soul, some beneficial bacteria capable of destroying in a few hours the harmful ones created by two phrases of hate insinuated into your personality, not belonging there. I refuse to believe that it was you writing at that moment. So as never to be tempted to re-read them, I shall excise those three lines from your letter and burn them.

As for myself, I can only think that not merely have my thoughts, my feelings, been misunderstood, but my handwriting has been misread, since you believe that I was talking about the risks I run and the courage I show in writing this preface. I said *exactly the opposite*! What I said was: 'If you're worried lest my name, my preface, might make trouble for you, don't think that you'll hurt my feelings by not publishing it.' That, I believe, was an act of true affection, whereby I pocketed all literary pride, whereby I was thinking only of my friendship for you and of what was in your best interests. To think that my reward, far from being, like Forain's, a surfeit of bouquets, should be your notion of taking back the portrait you did of me at Auteuil!

Dear friend, such things leave me baffled, wondering if one of us is not mad.

I shall ignore what you said to me about printers and Émile-Paul, for I don't understand a word of it, and furthermore it would not make the least difference if I did. Your suggestion that I pay them a visit shows what a peculiar notion you have of my health and that you don't read my letters properly, for I've told you that not once in the past two years have my attacks ended early enough for me to be able to get out to consult an oculist.[1]

Goodbye, dear friend, do as you wish and what you wish.[2] I'm too saddened by your letter to continue with mine, and too united by the tenderest of memories to the old Blanche to be capable, without pain to myself, of exchanging any but the most tender words with the new. Assuring you once more of my friendship, my admiration, my gratitude,

Marcel Proust

1. In fact, Céleste relates that she was sent out to the optician for a selection of spectacles. See Céleste Albaret, *Monsieur Proust*, 271–2.

2. Blanche's *Propos de peintre: De David à Degas*, containing Proust's preface, was to be published in March 1919. It is dedicated 'To Marcel Proust, in memory of the Auteuil of his childhood and my youth, and in homage to the author of *Du Côté de chez Swann*'.

10 To the Abbé Mugnier[1]

[Thursday evening, 14 February 1918]

Monsieur l'Abbé,

You know the art of doing good, you practise it in the subtlest of ways and even upon the stoniest hearts. I had, so to speak, promised myself so much unhappiness from this dinner[2] that I had had the folly to refuse it. For unhappiness alone has something to teach us, and can put us back on the hard, straight path of truth. But the Princesse, knowing that I would find the temptation irresistible and thus paying me a delicate compliment on my taste, said to me: 'No, do come, I've invited the Abbé for you.' The Abbé was hardly there for me, alas, but to have seen his smile, to have received his kindly handshake at dinner, was already pleasure enough. And today's pneumatique[3] (as I suppose we must call it) makes up for the evening's disappointment.

I thank you from the bottom of my heart. You speak of the Chartraine[4] cathedral and the Perche hawthorns.[5] Occasionally, in poor Calmette's day, I would write the leading article in the *Figaro*.[6] The readers felt cheated and the management complained that it wasn't newsworthy. I've found one or two of these pieces, having looked them out for you. I couldn't find the Church, but the hawthorns[7] were there, very faded, keeping their imperishable scent for me alone. For a long time, whenever I was to dine in your company, I would stuff them into the pocket of my pelisse.[8] Mme de Béarn, Mme Rehbinder[9] and the rest would arrive. But no Abbé. And, like the character in Labiche,[10] I would take my hawthorns away again. It was my maid who forgot to slip them into my pelisse the other night. I also found some of the pastiches about which Lemaître[11] was so kind. I couldn't find the least bad, though the weakest may still make you smile. But I can only 'lend' them to you. I don't possess copies, and back-numbers of the *Figaro* for those dates no longer exist. And I intend bringing them out in a volume of essays,[12] once the six volumes of my *Swann* are published.

If I wish to submit these few pieces to you, it's because, while having the wisdom to content myself with listening when in your company, I would nevertheless like you to become better acquainted with my mind (I use it without self-satisfaction, I assure you, but with common sense, which Descartes tells us is universal).[13] Yet how could I send you *Swann*, so discouraging in its length, so shocking in its licentiousness, above all, so harrowing? *Les Plaisirs et les jours*[14] is redeemed by France's preface, but these are pages written at school, when I was fifteen years old, as is only too obvious. My prefaces and annotations to Ruskin[15] are of no interest to anybody except to an admirer of Ruskin, and even he would be somewhat disillusioned. It would be less pretentious to show you some pastiches. So many people spend their lives doing them involuntarily that I may be excused if I have put a few together for my own amusement, as well as for the sensual pleasure of holding down the pedal to prolong the music of those to whom one could listen for ever.[16] Now I could show you my pink and white hawthorns in a different guise, by tearing the faded bouquet from the forbidden book.[17] Let my vacillations, Monsieur l'Abbé, be a homage to my admiring and grateful respect.

Marcel Proust

1. Arthur Mugnier (1853–1944), confessor to the leading writers of his day. Although a mere parish priest admired for his goodness, he was much sought after in society for his wit. His *Journals* contain many references to Proust.

2. A dinner given the night before at the Ritz by Mme Soutzo.

3. An express letter transmitted by means of compressed air through a tube. Commonly known as a 'pneu'.

4. An epithet for Chartres. See the description of Combray church: I, 72–3.

5. Allusion to the countryside around Illiers, the village near Chartres where Proust spent childhood summers and which stands for Combray in *Swann's Way*.

6. Proust wrote for the *Figaro* between 1906 and 1912. Its long-serving editor Gaston Calmette (1858–1914) was shot dead in his office by Mme Joseph Caillaux, wife of the Germanophile finance minister against whom he had campaigned.

7. 'Épines blanches, épines roses' ('White hawthorns, pink hawthorns'): I, 164–8.

8. Winter or summer, Proust was never without this fur-trimmed overcoat, even keeping it on at table and in the theatre.

9. Comtesse René de Béarn, Comtesse Wladimir Rehbinder.

10. Allusion to Eugène Labiche's comedy *La Clé*: a maid is repeatedly told to take the soup away because 'the master isn't home yet'.

11. Jules Lemaître (1853–1914). Proust himself called his pastiches 'literary criticism in action'. Parodies of Balzac, Faguet, Flaubert, the Goncourts, Michelet and Renan, they were immediately acknowledged as masterpieces of comic writing.

12. The pastiches, together with Proust's pre-war essays, articles and prefaces,

were to be published in 1919 under the title *Pastiches et mélanges*, and re-published in 1971 in *Contre Sainte-Beuve*. Except for the pastiches, which remain untranslated, a large selection is translated in *Against Sainte-Beuve and Other Essays*. See translator's note, p. 1.

13. Allusion to Descartes's *Discours de la méthode* (1637): 'Nothing in the world is more fairly distributed than common sense, for each believing himself to be well-endowed with it, even those hardest to please in all other respects never desire more than they already possess.'

14. Proust's first book. Published in a de-luxe edition by Calmann-Lévy in 1886, with a preface by Anatole France and illustrations by the society painter Madeleine Lemaire, it consisted of a miscellany from *Le Banquet*, a short-lived magazine edited by Proust and his schoolfellows at the Lycée Condorcet. The book was re-published in 1971, together with Proust's unfinished novel *Jean Santeuil* (Bibliothèque de la Pléiade.) Translated as *Pleasures and Regrets* (Peter Owen, 1986; trs. Louise Varèse).

15. Proust's translations of Ruskin's *The Bible of Amiens* and *Sesame and Lilies* appeared in 1904 and 1905; his prefaces, of which the most notable is the essay 'Days of Reading', are translated in *AS-B*.

16. Proust was to use the same image in his critical essay 'On Flaubert's Style', to be published in 1920. See *AS-B* 269.

17. Presumably from galleys of *Within a Budding Grove*.

11 To Lucien Daudet[1]

[Tuesday evening 19 February 1918]

My dearest,

I come home feeling very sad after the most unbelievable day to find both your book[2] and your letter. First, dearest Lucien, I neither understand nor believe that you can like my book[3] (especially since you're only at the beginning) unless it's out of a kindness that can call upon the very greatest intelligence. I believe you may like some of the succeeding volumes and, once you are further on, a few pages of this one. But the beginning, as far as I remember (not having a copy to refer to), is very poor, except perhaps for an attempt on the very first page to mark an interval and an evolution.[4] Possibly also a page where I receive a letter from Gilberte, and even before that, where I write a letter to Swann.[5] But I don't suppose that this can mean much to you.

I feared your judgment, but I swear I would never have sent you my book had I first known yours. It gives me such an exalted view of you (and I've only read a few pages, you'll see why in a minute) that I'm horrified to think that I've shown you my work. What is my poor style, painful even to me, compared to your luminous music? What are these tales, which may have a flicker of life, beside sentences which contain all the beauty of nature, all the laws of the mind? Your dedication to your grandmother[6] alone is an unforgettable piece of writing, while I'm incapable of such skill, such flexibility, such tenderness, such musicality, such breadth. Or rather, you are unaware of it, and perhaps we (I less so) are worthier for a detachment which allows us to discern in ourselves the nature of others, something that will never be discerned by self-centred, self-satisfied writers. You hover over the world with power and grace, and the last dinosaur comes naturally to your pen.[7]

My dearest Lucien, I said that I had read only a few pages of your astonishing book because of an incredible day coming on top of a great many sleepless days and nights. To understand my inability to read or write, you should know that the person with whom I've been living for the past *six months*,[8] to whom you've shown such touching kindness, left on holiday today, and that, after much hesitation, I decided not to accompany him (other than to the station). The fatigue of all that would have been exhausting enough in itself, and yet, in recompense, there was the extraordinarily joyful sensation of solitude suddenly regained, such that I couldn't refrain from singing at the top of my voice on the station platform. But within an hour of being alone, as a result of the stimulants I had taken, and above all the almost total chastity to which I've been condemned for so long, I fell from grace. While there was nothing wrong with that in itself, nervous tension, added to fatigue, plunged me into a state of despair and hebetude bordering on madness. Had I not been incapable of the slightest movement, I think I would have followed by the next train. As it was, with no fewer than *seventeen* important letters waiting to be answered on my bedside table, notably one to which replying or not replying meant losing or not losing 24,000 francs, always a gigantic sum to me and almost tragically so at the moment, I found the effort beyond me, preferring to lose the money.

But to read your wonderfully generous praises and, after that, the first pages of your book, suddenly raised my morale to such heights that I found just enough strength to write to you, but for nothing else. I'm not saying that the person who has just left has nothing to do with it, but, the agitation brought about by his departure and, as I told you, my ignominious evening, created in me a sort of transient sorrow, an absurd remorse, almost a factitious passion. Thus, the goodness you have shown him makes it easier for me to write to you than to anybody else. And then your letter, and your book, lifted me into a sphere where fatigue seems non-existent.

Kindly don't mention his departure (nothing to do with a quarrel!) (not my wish but his request). I'll inform each of my visitors in turn (as I told him I would), but I'll gain twenty-four hours in one case, forty-eight in another, perhaps more for all concerned (by all concerned, I mean my few confidants) if you say nothing. And that means a very great deal to me.

Thank you again for all your kindness, for the attention you have paid to things of which nobody could be a better judge.[9] Alas, I rather fear that this exquisite sympathy with naïve ignorance[10] may also be the sentiment, applied in this instance to a culture which cannot plead naïvety, that has dictated praises which leave me embarrassed and yet, this evening, for all my gratitude, I cannot say very happy.

With fondest love, my dearest,
Marcel

1. Lucien Daudet (1878–1946), writer and painter, Alphonse Daudet's handsome younger son; in 1896, he and Proust had had an intense, short-lived affair that had grown into long-lasting friendship.

2. Daudet had sent him the typescript of his novel *La Dimension nouvelle*.

3. Proust had sent Daudet proofs of *Within a Budding Grove*.

4. Allusion to the original chapter-heading of *Within a Budding Grove*, Part One: 'Change of course whereby characters take a new direction', referring to a 'new' Cottard (now a professor) and a 'new' Swann.

5. II, 83–4; II, 73–4.

6. Mme Jules Allard, Daudet's maternal grandmother, who died in 1909.

7. 'Come to me, still heavy with dreams, not to say the nightmare of waking, let me heal your shattered hopes. Why seek to understand? The reality of your senses is enough. Submit: the first man could survive, despite sharing the earth with the last dinosaur.' Daudet, *op. cit.*, 11.

8. Henri Rochat, a Swiss-born waiter from the Ritz whom Proust had taken on as his secretary. All references to Rochat were excised from this letter by Daudet, and have been transcribed and translated from the autograph, prior to the sale of 200 letters from Proust to Daudet at Christie's, London, in November 1996.

9. Daudet's had been the most perceptive review of *Swann's Way* to appear in 1913.

10. In his novel, Daudet gives the following speech to a soldier: 'There are women who wear necklaces and bracelets, who smell good and go dancing. There are men who sleep with them and earn a packet. They're too stupid to give us a thought. The other sort, those who think of us, are too poor to suffer alone, and our poverty keeps them company.' Daudet, *op. cit.*, 99.

12 To Jacques Porel[1]

Tuesday [evening, 19 February 1918]

Dear friend,
    Thanks to my having reached an advanced age, as you so kindly reminded me the other day, I now receive a good many letters announcing engagements. But I'm certain that, of them all, yours must be the prettiest. I'm not saying that it would merit inclusion in a collection of 'model discourses', such books being fatuous and unworthy of this gem. But if they were well done, and contained only the most exquisite things, then the place of honour, between two choice Sévignés, would surely go to this 'letter from a young man announcing his forthcoming marriage'.
    And yet, no, for you're not 'a' young man, you're Porel the Flighty. And I'm not sorry that Céleste had the effrontery to say so, and I to repeat it, when it has given you the opportunity, in conversation, in correspondence, of defending yourself so gracefully. It's a delightful thing to be flighty as long as one knows when to fold one's wings. Everything you say about your fiancée is charming. I envy you, I envy her, and in the joyless solitude of my cork-lined room,[2] I find consolation in your happiness.
    By a coincidence which is nothing if not prosaic, within an hour of your finishing your letter to me and keeping your appointment with the President of the Argentine Chamber of Commerce, I had finished reading it and was keeping mine with the President of the American Chamber of Commerce, who is nothing if not charming. What a pair of commercial travellers we are!
    Dear friend, I believe that you'll not only make a delectable husband, you'll be an exemplary married man. For it's only in the graceful sense that I think of you as flighty. But this youthful volatility is, I fancy, powered and driven by a very great moral seriousness.
    As for meeting your fiancée, that, my dear chap, seems to me

as difficult as it is tempting. We can't possibly dine together. Nobody eats as messily as I do, according to you. It might put an end to your hopes of marriage.

Kindly give my respects to your Mother and Sister[3] (you probably don't realize that I know them – personally, that is, for as you can imagine, Madame Réjane's art filled my inner life. I had never known sorrows like those of Germinie Lacerteux,[4] and I feel them still, often being stirred for hours on end by the memory of that heart-breaking voice. I just wanted to say that I knew them personally, though not at all well). Your Mother once called me a Boche.[5] With such proof of intimacy, I believe I may ask you to tell her that I share her joy.

Your devoted
Marcel Proust

If a 'settled' man is not to be obnoxious, he should first have been flighty, like Porel. For then he settles down not out of inertia, but because he has at last found the best.

The three lines of this P.S. are not crossed out but underlined, the better for you to ponder them.

1. Jacques Porel, born 1883, the acknowledged son of the famous actress Réjane, *née* Gabrielle Réju (1859–1920). Proust borrowed aspects of her life and acting for his tragedienne, Berma.

2. In 1910, to insulate himself from the pollen, dust and noise of the street, Proust had had his bedroom walls lined with cork.

3. Madame Philip Duncan Wilson, *née* Germaine Porel.

4. Eponymous heroine of Edmond de Goncourt's novel of working-class life. Proust was aged nineteen when he saw Réjane play the role in a dramatized version. He was to call it 'the play at which "my childhood" sobbed the most, as he [Edmond de Goncourt] would have put it. How much that was due to Réjane, I don't know, but I emerged so red-eyed that impressionable members of the audience came up to me thinking I had been beaten.' 'The Goncourts', *AS-B*, 311.

5. Proust detested such jingoism: cf VI, 69. On this occasion, in 1914, he was probably deploring the ban on playing works by German composers.

13 To Lionel Hauser[1]

[Wednesday 3 April 1918]

My dear Lionel,

Your letter fills me with consternation. For one thing, I see that my postal service really is impossibly bad if you haven't received the letter in which I answered your objections to the epithet 'Leonardesque'.[2] As I told you, I meant by that to suggest a multiplicity of gifts (Hugo had *Les Quatre vents de l'esprit* and Mme de Noailles *Le Coeur innombrable*[3]). I had no desire, in the wake of those aesthetes who attribute to Duccio what we have always believed to be by Giotto etc.,[4] to deny Leonardo authorship of *St John the Baptist*. But I admit to finding this crisis in my communications, worrying though it is (less so than the terrible illness which seems to be threatening me),[5] not nearly as upsetting as what you tell me about your mobilization.[6] Unless you are to remain in Paris, I fear it means a painful separation for Madame Hauser, and, for you, a change in your way of life that may not suit you. I am extremely upset by this news.

Yet very few things upset me (naturally, I don't mean public events and private griefs; I'm surrounded by only too many heartrending examples of those). I've lost all respect in the eyes of my fellow tenants, because instead of going down below for the Gothas, I go outside during air-raids,[7] while Céleste, having descended from her empyrean into the underworld, coughs and catches her death of cold in the cellars: 'De profundis clamavi'.[8]

I've long noticed (à propos of the shelling of St Gervais[9]) that the Israelites[10] have a particular fondness for the names and rites of the Catholic Church. Names escape me for the moment, but for instance, the Halphens live at 'The Monastery', Mme Henri de Rothschild inhabits the Abbey of Vaux-de-Cernay, Mme Singer Neufmoustiers also something like a Monastery, Mme Porgès another Abbey, somebody else a Commandery, etc., etc.[11] Similarly, at the wedding of Mme Jules Porgès's daughter, I remember that there were so many crucifixes, missals etc. that a very bad-mannered friend who had come with me asked the mistress of the house whether, still being rather new to it all, she had not mixed up the Sacraments and confused marriage with First Communion. Which brings us back to St Gervais, where the victims include a General Francfort (who is, I believe, a cousin of my landlady-aunt[12]) and several Mendelssohns, a name more usually associated with the 'Songs without Words' from Berlin. And *tutti quanti*. In the circumstances, the Chief Rabbi's visit seemed to me to lack the purely ecumenical character which the press found so moving, and the Pope can hardly have read the casualty list, if he finds the disaster all the more deplorable for the 'particularly fervent Catholics' involved. Unless, of course, the 'Good Friday Spell' had touched them with its instant grace.[13] But Catholics or Jews, I'm not any the less appalled by this hecatomb.

Regarding what you say about my Mexican Tramways,[14] since I stupidly failed to take your good advice and invest the money from the sale of my armchairs,[15] it might be as well to compensate by selling the Mexicans. I enclose instructions to sell just in case, which you can either send to the London Bank[16] or tear up, as you please.

I trust that M. Léon Neuburger[17] has been persuaded to leave Paris and abandon the green pastures of the boulevard Émile Augier for the time being. 'To plant is one thing, but to go down to the cellars at that age'.[18] Should you see him, kindly give him my respectful regards. Respectful is not an epithet I can use in your case, your being of call-up age. But I remain your ever-grateful friend.

Marcel Proust

I have good news of my brother,[19] who is in Italy, and of his wife,[20] who is also there as a nurse.

1. Lionel Hauser (1868–1958), head of Warburg's Bank, Paris. He and Proust being related through their mothers, he had agreed to act as Proust's stockbroker and man of business – though not without reservations, for he was well aware of Proust's love of gambling on the Stock Exchange.

2. A compliment on Hauser's epistolary and financial skills.

3. Title of Victor Hugo's last book of collected poems, and of Anna de Noailles's first book of collected poems.

4. Proust apparently alludes to the attribution of the so-called Rucellai *Madonna* in S. Maria Novella, Florence, and to the Louvre's *St John the Baptist*.

5. Proust, who had symptoms of facial paralysis and aphasia, feared a brain tumour.

6. Hauser had been notified that he was due for call-up, which would mean resigning his business activities.

7. Paris was now being subjected to air-raids by the new German night-bomber. See *Time Regained*, where the narrator walks the streets in an air-raid: VI, 137–9.

8. 'Out of the depths have I cried to thee, O Lord'. Psalm CXXX.

9. Fashionable Catholic church which had received a direct hit during Good Friday Vespers from the German long-range gun, 'Big Bertha'. Many of the casualties were leading Jews.

10. A term for old-established Jewish families.

11. See M. de Charlus's mockery of the Blochs for renting La Commanderie: IV, 584–5.

12. Proust's maternal aunt, Mme Georges Weil: see letter 22, n. 9.

13. Allusion to the Faith Motif from the Good Friday music in Wagner's *Parsifal*.

14. Speculative shares which Proust had bought without Hauser's knowledge.

15. See letter 6, n. 2.

16. Paris branch of the London & County Westminster Bank.

17. Hauser's uncle, Léon Neuburger, a retired banker.

18. Proust paraphrases a line from La Fontaine's 'The Old Man and the Three Youths': 'An octogenarian was planting. / To build is one thing; but to plant at that age!' *Fables*, Book XI, 8.

19. Professor Robert Proust (1878–1931), eminent surgeon who had been mentioned in despatches for operating under fire. French divisions had been sent to the Western Front to stiffen Italian resistance to the Austrians.

20. *Née* Marthe Dubois-Amiot (1878–1953).

14 To Madame Marthe Bibesco[1]

[Shortly after 4 April 1918]

Princesse,

My feelings for you resemble, in this one respect at least, that of which Musset speaks, saying: 'When so many other knots bind you to grief'.[2] Naturally, my grief on receiving Antoine's[3] letter cannot be two-fold, like the grief (uncured,[4] incurable, I hope) that I felt at Emmanuel's death.[5] For then I suffered not only from knowing Antoine to be unhappy, but also from having to accept the idea that I would never again see the person who was one of my dearest companions on the face of this earth. This second half of my suffering I cannot feel, or only indistinctly, since I never knew Mademoiselle Lahovary. But perhaps that in itself makes my other sorrow, the one linked to you, even more cruel. For I'm well aware that my not having known the person whom you have lost estranges us at a time when, as always happens, you must be feeling closer to an old servant whom she had known, a gardener to whom she had spoken, a dressmaker who had made her a frock, than to me. From now on, anybody or anything not in some way connected with her will necessarily be alien to you. And yet, perhaps I am not entirely a stranger, so intent are my dim, relentless thoughts on conjuring up the person whom you will never see again. If I may say so, a shared and too recent pain has so united us in Emmanuel's memory that you unconsciously lead me towards a person whom I would have dearly liked to know. She will always elude me, but I shall think of her constantly.

The shock of this tragedy has affected me in exactly the same way as that of Emmanuel's so recent death, and to such an extent that there are moments when I think it never happened, that my suffering has doubled, as one sees double, that I am re-living the same sorrow twice over. But of what help can my thoughts be to you, Princesse; I am neither the gardener nor the old servant, and even such promises as I could make you from personal experience – not that you will be cured, which would horrify you, but that one of these days the unbearable pain will turn into the blessed memory of a person who will never again leave you – are the kind of promises in which, at a certain stage of unhappiness, one cannot believe. I can only remain devastated by your grief and lay at your feet my sorrow and respect.

Marcel Proust

1. Princesse Bibesco, *née* Marthe Lahovary (1887–1973), member of two families of Romanian statesmen.

2. 'Quand par tant d'autres nœuds tu tiens à la douleur'. Alfred de Musset, 'Don Paez II', *Premières Pensées*.

3. Prince Antoine Bibesco (1878–1951), her cousin by marriage. His letter to Proust had announced the suicide of her younger sister, Marguerite Lahovary.

4. Proust coins the word *inguérie* to chime with *inguérissable*, meaning incurable.

5. Prince Emmanuel Bibesco (1877–1917), Antoine's brother. Proust had last seen him in the throes of a distressing illness before he, too, committed suicide. As young men, Proust and the Bibesco brothers had travelled together in France and the Netherlands, visiting the churches and art galleries which were to play so important a part in his novel.

15 To Madame Catusse[1]

[Shortly before 9 April 1918]

Dear Madame,

I'm deeply touched by your note. I do indeed follow these fearful events with an anxious heart, and do not say, with Gautier:

> 'Like Goethe at Weimar on his divan
> Cut off from the rest of the world
> ... I paid no heed to the hurricane
> That battered on my fastened windows.
> But fashioned my *Enamels and Cameos*.'[2]

I'm far from sharing such detachment, believe me. I must confess that Gothas and guns hold no fear for me personally. It's not a question of bravado, I'm often afraid of lesser things. It's simply a fact. But to be the only one not to go down to the cellars puts me in an awkward situation in the house, for I'm thought, quite wrongly, to despise those who do. Unfortunately, my indifference is not shared by Céleste, who spends her time there. And I'm afraid that she may end up by leaving me, but as there is only one floor above us, ours being the lowest house in the street, I don't like to dissuade her; I would never forgive myself if she came to harm because of me. I shall stay on here in any case. I would have loved to take La Tour,[3] as you so kindly suggest. And I would have been the quietest of tenants. But I'm afraid that the greenery at this time of year would bring on my asthma; above all, I'm not sure if my military status is permanent.[4] Two important reasons for staying in Paris. Cabourg[5] is nearer than Nice but seems to me as dangerous as Paris for Céleste. So I think the best thing is: either she stays here with me or, if she's frightened, she can go home, and I'll find somebody else. Besides, I would be afraid of not finding milk[6] in Nice. Beaumont[7] had to come back from Cannes for that very reason.

I'm too tired to thank you properly for your kindness, but I was touched to the bottom of my heart. I shall never forget it. Robert is still in Italy, and hopes to be sent to a more active sector.[8] I fear his wishes may be granted.

Much love to Charles.[9] Your respectful and grateful

Marcel Proust

1. Mme Anatole Catusse, a close friend of Proust's late mother. He had formed the habit of consulting her about his domestic affairs.
2. 'Comme Goethe sur son divan / À Weimar s'isolait des choses /. . . Sans prendre garde à l'ouragan / Qui fouettait mes vitres fermées / Moi, j'ai fait *Émaux et Camées*.'
3. Villa owned by Mme Catusse at Nice, where her husband was Préfet.
4. Allusion to his exemption from military service on medical grounds.
5. Normandy seaside resort, the height of fashion in the Belle Époque. Every summer from 1907 to 1914, Proust had re-visited Cabourg and its Grand Hôtel, the scene of childhood holidays with his mother and maternal grandmother, and the place which provided him with nearly all the settings for Balbec.
6. One of his principal sources of nourishment.
7. Étienne de Beaumont: see letter 17, n. 2.
8. See letter 13, n. 19.
9. Her son, Charles Catusse.

16 To Charles d'Alton[1]

[Tuesday 9 April 1918]

Dear Sir,

Yesterday, tidying up some papers, I found to my consternation and remorse a fourteen-page letter addressed to you which I thought had been sent at the time, received (and disdained) (and which I now enclose to prove my intent), having as I say come across this letter yesterday, I was about to write you another when I read with much sadness that it has been your misfortune and pride to have a nephew killed in action.[2] I learnt this from the *Figaro*. I had no idea that Madame d'Alton had a sister married to a brother of yours.

Thank God I knew that you didn't have a son, and only the charming Mademoiselles Colette and Hélène,[3] otherwise I can't tell you what a shock it would have been to read 'son of the Comte d'Alton and the Comtesse *née* La Roque Ordan'. Or rather, I can easily imagine it, for even knowing that you don't have a son, the sameness of the two names gave my heart a jolt. There are times when one is eternally grateful to God that those whom one loves (and I hope I may presume to tell you that, for me, you are among them) have only daughters.

I trust that Madame d'Alton is like me, in being indifferent to Gothas and guns. In my case, this indifference makes me very unpopular with my fellow tenants, for they interpret my being the only one not to go down to the cellars as a reproach to the rest. Yet it seems to me both natural and very sensible to be afraid of anything dangerous and, I'm capable of being frightened by less terrifying things, even if not of those particular ones. My only regret is that my charming maid feels it her duty to stay here with me, in the lowest building in the boulevard Haussmann, instead of going home, which is easily the best place for her.

I have received two souvenirs from your part of the world which touch me in inverse proportion to the social status of the senders. Robert de Montesquiou has sent me some magnificent violets from Artagnan,[4] and my former cook[5] writes from Lupiac offering to have me to stay, having got into her head the absurd notion that Paris is devastated. But I pay no more attention to the cannon than I do to the clock.

I'm out of touch with Cabourg, not having left Paris for two and a half years. Or rather, Foucart comes with each leave and it's Cabourg all over again. I hear from Guy Delaunay, Pierre Parent, Wessbecher, from time to time. As you know, poor Marcel Plantevignes nearly died; apparently, after spending two years between life and death, he has more or less recovered.[6]

Thanks to a lady who understands an invalid's timetable,[7] I've been able to leave my bed once or twice to dine with people all of whom you know: Mme de Béarn, Mme de Polignac,[8] Mme de Jaucourt,[9] the Étienne de Beaumonts, the Hinnisdaels,[10] Mme de Chevigné.[11] My brother is in Italy (unless he returns for the offensive)[12] where his wife is a nurse. I saw Guiche[13] before he left for his last visit to America, but it's a long time since I've heard from d'Albufera.[14]

I wonder whether, in the course of the war, you have come across a very close friend of mine, Clément de Maugny, Chief of Staff at Laval.[15] I'm about to write to him in the hope that he can make life a little easier for protégés of mine who have been called up and will finish their training at Laval and Dreux.

Kindly accept my sympathy in your glorious mourning, dear Sir, and share my respect with Madame and the Mademoiselles d'Alton.

Marcel Proust

1. Charles, Vicomte d'Alton (1857–1931).

2. William d'Alton, killed in action 31 March.

3. Colette and Hélène d'Alton, members of the group of Proust's young friends at Cabourg who were the origin of the 'little band' which the narrator encounters at Balbec in *Within a Budding Grove*.

4. The Château d'Artagnan, in Gascony, was the ancestral home of Robert de Montesquiou: see letter 41. Violets were the famous aesthete's favourite flower.

5. Félicité Fitau, cook to Proust's late mother.

6. These four young men were part of Proust's life in Cabourg before the war.

7. Allusion to Mme Soutzo.

8. Princesse Edmond de Polignac: see letter 23.

9. Marquise de Jaucourt.

10. The daughters of Comte d'Hinnisdael, Thérèse and Jeanne, had always held a special glamour for Proust; he was particularly impressed by their courageous behaviour during the Battle of the Somme, when the family château was caught in cross-fire.

11. Comtesse Adhéaume de Chevigné: see letter 75.

12. Allusion to the awaited German thrust on the Somme.

13. Armand, Duc de Guiche (1879–1962), heir to the Duc de Gramont. A distinguished scientist and expert in aerodynamics, Guiche was on a military mission to Washington. See also following note.

14. Louis, Marquis d'Albufera (1871–1963). Like Guiche, 'Albu' was one of the artistocratic quartet who modelled for aspects of Saint-Loup. He was also the source of some of the Duc de Guermantes's more absurd mannerisms. Proust's one-time role as go-between for him and his mistress, Louisa de Mornand, had provided the material for Saint-Loup's relationship with Rachel in *The Guermantes Way*.

15. Clément, Comte de Maugny: see letter 27.

17 To Madame Soutzo

[Tuesday 9 April 1918]

Princesse,

Do me the justice of not counting me among those people, I don't like to say those bores, who have tracked you down. You wrote me an enchanting letter before leaving Paris, but omitted to give me your address. Nor have I attempted to discover it. Because Céleste's husband is ill,[1] I've been dining almost every night at the Ritz. But not a single concierge, waiter, pageboy etc. have I questioned as to your whereabouts, and it was only in order to be able to satisfy the curious as to where you were not that decided me, three days ago, the day before I had your letter, to ask Lucien

Daudet, who is always at the Beaumonts',[2] where you were to be found. A question I found it rather humiliating to ask...

I haven't seen the Beaumonts, though we're so often invited to the same houses that I feel it augurs well for your friend's kidney.[3] One of these numerous dinners was given by Mme Scheikévitch, and I particularly regret not having gone as your brother[4] was there! These transpositions into another sex of a face one has loved fascinate me. That's why I would so much like to have known young Benardaky, who was killed at the beginning of the war and whose sister, perhaps without knowing it, was the intoxication and despair of my youth.[5]

Princesse, I can't talk to you about the war. It has become so much a part of me, alas, that I can no longer see it in isolation, can no longer talk about the hopes and fears which it inspires in me, any more than one can talk about emotions so deeply felt as to be indistinguishable from oneself. The war, for me, is less an object (in the philosophical sense) than a substance interposed between me and all objects. As people lived in God,[6] I live in the war. (You know those headaches that one is always aware of, even while talking about something else, even while asleep.)

As for guns and Gothas, I assure you that I never give them a thought; I'm afraid of far less dangerous things – mice, for instance – and, not being frightened by air-raids, and still not knowing the way down to the cellars (for which the other tenants cannot forgive me), it would be an affectation on my part to pretend to a fear of them. Unfortunately, their effect on Céleste is to make her nervous, a reaction which I find inexplicable but which I respect, and as she has a very comfortable home of her own to go to, I fear she may leave me. I'm too scrupulous to seek to influence her. But added to the inconvenience of losing Céleste would be that of taking back Céline.[7] Céleste is indignant because Mme Catusse (to whom you have often been kind) has offered me her empty villa in Nice and I choose to remain in Paris.

But it's quite different for you, Princesse, and since you're in a place which you don't specify (I much appreciated: 'letters will be forwarded') but which is a long way from Paris, it seems to me only sensible for you to stay there; after all, the longer your absence, the less urgent your return. I'm talking against my heart – but also for my heart, more so, in fact. For my happiness at being able to see you would be far outweighed by my fears for your safety and my awareness of your discomfort.

Unfortunately, I was unable to see Truelle[8] when he called yesterday, but with charming artlessness he handed Céleste, to give to me, a letter which he had had from Morand.[9] Now, for *imperatoria brevis*, this letter is the most dictatorial bulletin one could possibly receive.[10] Truelle probably didn't take it like that, and I'll be careful not to point it out to him. But to call it a bulletin is an exaggeration, it's a sort of 'idiot's guide'. And Morand proceeds by numbers, in order to make his explanations and instructions easier to follow:

1. Do this.
2. You were wrong not to have done that etc.

One whole sentence is in capitals. I doubt if even Napoleon used a more peremptory tone.

Princesse, I suddenly feel unwell, and what I wanted to say to you will have to wait. Kindly accept my most respectful regards.

Marcel Proust

The morning you left I sent you round a copy of Hermant's *Affranchis*.[11] Did they give it to you?

---

1. Odilon Albaret, his regular taxi-driver, had a throat infection which Proust was afraid of catching.
2. Étienne, Comte de Beaumont (1888–1956) and his wife, *née* Édith de Taine de Raimonval, lavish party-givers. Discreetly homosexual, a balletomane, Beaumont was Jean Cocteau's chief patron. He was famous for equipping and leading convoys of ambulances to the front.
3. Beaumont had a kidney infection.
4. Jean Chrissoveloni.
5. Allusion to Dimitri and Marie Benardaky, whose father had been a courtier of the Tsar. As a child, Marie had been one of Proust's playmates on the Champs-Élysees; she appears as Marie Kossichef in his abandoned novel *Jean Santeuil*, and became a model for the Gilberte of *Swann's Way*.
6. An old-fashioned piety: the sense of being engulfed in God's love.
7. Céline Cottin, the wife of Proust's former manservant, Nicolas Cottin. Proust had taken on this peasant couple in 1907. (Céline was responsible for the triumphant *bœuf à la mode* which Françoise cooks for M. de Norpois: II, 18, 33–4.) He took an intense dislike to her and was much relieved when, in 1913, she fell ill and left.
8. Jacques Truelle (1891–1945), lawyer and diplomat. He had lost a leg in the war.
9. Paul Morand, her fiancé: see letter 42.
10. Allusion to the bulletins issued by Napoleon.
11. Novel by Abel Hermant (1862–1950), follower of Zola and influential critic.

18   To Jacques de Lacretelle[1]

Paris, 20 April 1918, an end-of-season Paris-by-the-Sea, deserted after the guns and Gothas, and where I wish we were on our way together to the same Casino.[2]

Dear friend,
There are no keys to the characters in this book,[3] or rather, there are eight or ten to a single one; equally, for the church at Combray,[4] my memory borrowed several churches (or had them pose) as 'models'. I can no longer tell you which ones. I don't even remember if the paving is from St-Pierre-sur-Dives or Lisieux. Certain stained-glass windows are undoubtedly from Évreux, others from Pont-Audemer and La Sainte-Chapelle.[5]

My memories are more precise for the Sonata.[6] To the extent that I drew on reality, a very limited extent, in fact, the little phrase from this Sonata, and I've never told anyone this before, is, at the Sant-Euverte soirée[7] (to begin at the end), the charming but mediocre theme from a Violin and Piano Sonata by Saint-Saëns,[8] a composer I dislike. (I'll show you the precise passage, which recurs several times and was a triumph for Jacques Thibaud.[9]) At the same soirée, a little further on, it wouldn't surprise me if, talking of the little phrase, I hadn't been thinking of the Good Friday Spell.[10] Still at the same soirée, when violin and piano lament like two birds calling to one another,[11] I was thinking of Franck's Sonata,[12] especially as played by Enesco[13] (Franck's Quartet[14] appears in later volumes). The tremolo passages played[15] over the little phrase at the Verdurins' were suggested by the Prelude to *Lohengrin*, but the phrase itself at that moment by a piece by Schubert. At the same Verdurin soirée, it becomes a ravishing piece by Fauré.[16] I can reveal (soirée Saint-Euverte) that for M. de Saint-Candé's monocle[17] I thought of M. de Bethmann's[18] (not the German, though he may be German by origin, related to the Hottinguers), for M. de Forestelle's monocle that of a brother officer of a musician called M. d'Ollone,[19] for General de Froberville's monocle that of a self-styled man-of-letters, a real brute called M. de Tinseau,[20] whom I used to meet with the Princesse de Wagram and her sister.[21] M. de Palancy's monocle is that of poor, dear Louis de Turenne,[22] who can scarcely have thought that he would one day be related to Arthur Meyer,[23] to judge by the way he once treated him at my house. In *Le Côté de Guermantes*, I believe, the self-same Turenne monocle passes to M. de Bréauté.[24] Lastly, for Gilberte's arrival on the Champs-Élysées in the snow,[25] I was thinking of somebody who, without her ever having known it, was the great love of my life (or the other great love of my life, for there have been two), Mlle Benardaky,[26] nowadays (but I haven't seen her for years), the Princesse Radziwill. Naturally, the freer passages involving Gilberte at the beginning of *À l'Ombre des jeunes filles en fleurs*[27] have nothing whatever to do with the person in question, for I never had any but the most proper relations with her. For a moment, as Mme Swann walks past the clay-pigeon shoot, I thought of a wonderfully handsome cocotte of the day called Clomesnil.[28] I'll show you photographs of her. But Mme Swann is like her only for that moment.

I repeat, my characters are completely invented, and there are no keys at all. Thus, nobody is less like Madame Verdurin than Madame de Briey.[29] And yet Madame de Briey has the same laugh.

Dear friend, I'm thanking you very clumsily for the touching pains you took to get hold of this book by defacing it with these handwritten notes. There is no room for the passages you asked me to copy out, but if you like, I could do so on some loose sheets for you to insert. Meanwhile, I send you my friendly regards.

Marcel Proust

1. Jacques Lacretelle (1888–1985), novelist and critic.

2. Allusion to the Casino of the Grand Hôtel, Cabourg.

3. *Swann's Way*. Lacretelle had acquired a copy of the 1913 edition and sent it to Proust, who returned it with this letter of dedication.

4. I, 56–76.

5. In 1907, Proust saw these churches (except for La Sainte-Chapelle, Paris) in the course of being chauffeured round Normandy by his beloved Agostinelli, a tour which he described in an article for the *Figaro* ('Impressions de route en automobile': *CS-B*, 63–9). After the publication of *Swann's Way*, in an important letter to the critic Henri Ghéon explaining the 'little pieces of truth' in the structure of his novel, he wrote: 'Thanks to the passionate, and prescient, hours which I was privileged to spend in La Sainte-Chapelle, Pont-Audemer, Évreux, I assembled impressions from which I reconstituted a *stained-glass window*.'

6. Vinteuil's Sonata for Violin and Piano, the 'national anthem' of Swann's love for Odette, and which he hears for the first time at the Verdurins': I, 247–63.

7. The Vinteuil Sonata is played again at Mme de Saint-Euverte's, when it reminds Swann of his lost happiness: I, 414-24.

8. Sonata No. 1 in D minor.

9. Jacques Thibaud (1880-1953), French violinist. In *The Captive*, M. de Charlus compares Morel's playing with that of three celebrated violinists of the day, Jacques Thibaud, Georges Enesco and Louis Capet: V, 325.

10. I, 418-22. Allusion to the Faith Motif in Wagner's *Parsifal*.

11. I, 423.

12. Sonata for Violin and Piano, by César Franck.

13. Georges Enesco (1881-1955), Romanian violinist. In 1913, after hearing Enesco play the Franck sonata, Proust wrote to Antoine Bibesco: 'the mournful twitterings, the plaintive calls of his violin answered his piano as though from a tree.'

14. String Quartet in D.

15. I, 262, 317.

16. Proust summed up the ingredients of his sonata to Antoine Bibesco in autumn 1915: 'The Vinteuil sonata is not Franck's. [...] I shall tell you, with a copy in my hand, all the works (some of them mediocre), which "posed" for my sonata. Thus, the "little phrase" is a phrase from a sonata for violin and piano by Saint-Saëns which I'll hum to you (tremble!); the restless tremolos above it come from a Wagner prelude; the opening, with its plangent rise and fall, is from the Franck sonata; the more spacious passages from Fauré's *Ballade* etc.'

17. See the passage on the variety of monocles: I, 393-4.

18. Baron Hugo von Bethmann, who had the same name as the German Chancellor.

19. Max d'Ollone, composer, who had the same name as an army general.

20. Léon, Comte de Tinseau.

21. Princesse Alexandre Berthier de Wagram and the Duchesse de Gramont, Second Empire hostesses.

22. Louis, Comte de Turenne d'Aynac (1843-1907).

23. See letter 115, note 13. A social climber despised by Proust, Meyer had created a scandal by marrying, aged 60, Turenne's 24-year-old daughter, Marguerite. Proust alludes to an occasion in his parents' apartment on the Boulevard Malesherbes, where he used to entertain lavishly before his father's death in 1903.

24. III, 497.

25. I, 477-90.

26. See letter 17. Marie Benardaky divorced Prince Michael Radziwill in 1916. The other young woman was Jeanne Pouquet: see letter 177.

27. See the narrator's encounter with Gilberte behind the laurels: II, 76-7.

28. I, 503-5. The famous courtesan Léonie de Clomesnil, whose clothes Proust borrowed for Odette.

29. Comtesse Théodore de Briey.

19 To Lionel Hauser

Sunday evening [29 April 1918]

Dear friend,

My first thought on reading your book[1] was of something you once said to me when I had consulted you, retrospectively so to speak, about an investment I had already made. 'Another time', you wrote, 'you would do better to consult me before rather than after.' By the same token, if I was supposed to act the secondary-school master in respect of your book, the only job I know, and, like a conscientious monitor, advise you to modify an adjective or alter the position of a verb, it would have been better to send me proofs rather than the printed book. But as it happens, by some extraordinary miracle you have said all you had to say faultlessly and precisely, so that I would be hard-pressed to suggest such-and-such an alternative formula, as I've found myself doing even to writers who are masters of the pen. Having said that, before discussing your book, I'll answer your letter.

You are wrong to think of style as an embellishment, a sort of Sunday best. It's inseparable from thought and feeling. And that is why yours is so admirable. And I shall have two further compliments to pay you on the subject of your book. As Kant constructed a necessary universe, but one dependent on a suprasensible act of free will,[2] so you have pegged a utilitarian work, of necessity a little dry, to a higher doctrine, that of theosophy. In other words, your ethics and your logic stem from a metaphysical system. You are also to be complimented on having so clearly understood that any reform will be in vain unless it begins with the reform of the individual, unless it's a reform of the inner self. There I agree with you entirely.

I shall reproach you for going into sometimes pointless details about relatively commonplace things and then, without offering a shred of proof, proclaiming the dogma of successive reincarnations as self-evident. It's an article of faith, like belief in the Immaculate Conception. For myself, the constant study of interior phenomena, the ear cocked for inexplicable associations, might induce me to believe that our present existence is not indeed the first, and that the sponge of forgetfulness has not completely wiped out the memory of earlier ones. Even that might be more worthy of development than people's tendency to enter the Métro by the gate marked No Entry, or the disadvantage of living in unhealthy accommodation (an idea to which you add an ingenious twist by bringing in the employer's role and obligations).

But one of the nicest things about you, and it links you to Ruskin, is the way you imperiously proclaim truths which are not self-evident, declare them to be 'the key to the enigma'[3] and, having brandished the angel's flaming sword, conscientiously offer practical hints. Moreover, if I weren't so tired, I would show you a resemblance to Ruskin other than this mixture of imperious esotericism and purely practical exotericism. Even so, certain original passages might be more worthy of *italics* than rather banal statements which, even if not heeded, are too often made. But I realize that when, in writing, one sets oneself a practical goal, there is no need to be afraid of repeating what has gone unheeded. Ruskin liked to come down from Sinai to primary school and give us an idiot's guide to the Tablets of the Law. You merely hold them up from afar, but with a magisterial gesture, and the book is so perfectly structured that there is nothing one would wish to see left out. Of how many works could one say as much?

On the subject of Hell, you are at one with the Abbé Mugnier, to whom a scandalized lady said recently: 'But in that case, M. l'Abbé, there would be no Hell!' And the Abbé, to reassure the lady in her shaken orthodoxy, replied: 'Yes, yes, Madame, there is a Hell. Only there is nobody in it.' (She's that rather silly woman[4] who always talks about Mérimée as of a writer whom she had discovered. Whence the Abbé's remark: 'One mustn't forget that she lives on Christopher Columbus street' – where it's true that she has a house.)

As regards what is fundamental to your doctrine, my dear Lionel, we can agree to differ. There are Spinozists and Hegelians, and they think no less of one another for that. I don't deny that, a priori, the perfect equilibrium of the faculties, the health of mind and body, the fruits of a rational education, are excellent things. I'm even wrong to say a priori, for there have been times when physical and moral well-being was the very fount of pre-eminence in all things, and of genius. Plato's young disciples (who differed from yours in loving young men rather than women, but that was the fashion of the day) were certainly beings in whom body, mind and a sense of justice were developed in harmony through physical, intellectual and moral exercises. And there is nothing to say that this sovereign health, this moral perfection, cannot one day be reborn. Meanwhile, what strikes me most about the modern world is the opposite, alas. On the one hand, I see doctrinaires' sons, raised in the best traditions of public-spiritedness and moral integrity (natural heirs to the Broglies,[5] if you like), turning out to be academic duds of no use to anybody, and, on the other, the new language, which reveals a hitherto unknown part of the mind, an extra nuance to love, springing from the drunkenness of a Musset or a Verlaine, the perversions of a Baudelaire, a Rimbaud, even a Wagner, the epilepsy of a Flaubert. Either Bergson[6] or Boutroux,[7] I forget which, said that a thinking reed bends even more beneath the weight of thought than beneath the weight of matter.[8] But I believe that, if only through the creative value of suffering, bodily sickness is (in our degenerate times) almost a condition of intellectual power verging on genius.[9]

Above all, I believe that individuality,[10] to which moreover you devote much space, works to the benefit of others much less through a desire to do good than through a scrupulous fulfilment of its duty to itself. Naturally I'm talking only of the highest, in some way inspired, forms of activity. But in this category, all the good ever done in the world, by artists, writers, scientists, if not exactly done out of selfishness (their aim not being the gratification of personal desires but the clarification of some glimpsed inner truth), is done without regard to others. Altruism, for Pascal, Lavoisier, Wagner, was not a question of interrupting or perverting the course of a solitary task in order to perform charitable works. They made their honey like bees, and in fact this honey benefited everybody ('sic vos non vobis, mellificatis apes')[11] but could be made only on condition that, in the making, no thought, no consideration was given to others etc.

I completely agree with you about politics[12] (all that's very Ruskinian, by the way). As for politeness, I suspect you flatter the gallants of former times by supposing that, for them, it was an expression of magnanimity.[13] On the other hand, one could say a lot about politeness. It may emanate from a kindly nature that stops short of action, though brute frankness wouldn't serve either, and the kindly curmudgeon is a myth. For my part, I know that I belong to the ranks of the polite and, without wishing to boast, if I told you of the endless sacrifices I've made for curmudgeons who would never do anything for me, you would be amazed. On the other hand, Pascal's remark 'Go to church, take holy water, make yourself an idiot, the rest will come naturally'[14] could be applied to politeness. It's possible that politeness, in bending body and manners to a certain gentleness, inclines the soul that way; we don't notice anarchists being more hypocritical than great lords. Mind you, your own courtesy is so excessive (and I quite realize that it is purely a matter of form) that it cannot but deceive, if taken literally. One writes you the most trifling business letter, and you reply: 'I have read your letter of ... with the greatest interest and am giving it my closest attention.' Now, that is almost ironic, it usually being in response to 'Kindly sell so many Mexican Tramways on my behalf etc.' It doesn't mean that you are not the best and most sincere of men. The entire *habitus corporis* may be riddled with such courtesies without their necessarily being hypocritical.

While not even touching upon what I wanted to say about your remarkable book, I've exhausted my strength. To finish with, I'll come down from morality and Literature (in which you excel, believe me) to business, that is to say, from heaven to earth, to ask you the following: do you have a list of the shares which I sold in July 1914, the proceeds of which resulted in two cheques, the first cashed, the second uncashed?[15] If not, do you at least know the amount of the cheque that was cashed, that is, the first one? (I know the amount of the second.) I ask because I've found my June bank statement (plus several instructions to sell). So if I subtract the shares sold (those resulting in the two cheques) from the total that I had in the bank in June (*the list I've found*), the difference will be the shares which I still hold, and I can thus make the declaration required by law,[16] which is, I realize, long overdue, though I'll probably be excused because of my health. All I need to know is whether I should declare the second cheque, it being still uncashed. Obviously not the first, since I've cashed it.

Still marvelling to see you suddenly turn into law-giver and author, and with such charm, skill and authority, I send you, my dear Lionel, my warmest regards.

Marcel Proust

1. A theosophical tract entitled 'The Three Levers of the Modern World: skill, probity, altruism. An Essay in Social Reconstruction'.

2. Cf. Gilberte's tea-parties in *Within a Budding Grove*, whose 'ordered and unalterable design seemed, like Kant's necessary universe, to depend on a supreme act of free will.' II, 90.

3. Hauser, *op. cit.*: 'Here is the key to the enigma: the ills besetting mankind stem from a gross misunderstanding which in turn stems from ignorance. Indeed, the human race as a whole confuses individuality, the divine spark which every man has within him and which represents his true and everlasting self, with personality, which is transitory, and varies with each new reincarnation.' Hauser, *op. cit.*, 6.

4. The lady in question was the Comtesse Aynard de Chabrillan.

5. Ducal family which in four generations produced a marshal of France, a statesman, a distinguished historian and, in Proust's day, two notable physicists.

6. Henri Bergson (1859–1941), philosopher of the psychological dimension of time, Proust's distant relation.

7. Émile Boutroux (1845–1921), under whom Proust had studied philosophy.

8. See Boutroux, *Studies of the History of Philosophy*: 'The thinking reed bends beneath the effort of thought, but even more beneath the weight of matter.' Allusion to Pascal, in *Pensées*: 'Man is but a reed, the weakest in nature, yet he is a thinking reed.'

9. Proust elaborates on this in his critical essay 'Concerning Baudelaire': *AS-B*, 290.

10. See note 3.

11. 'Thus not for you yourselves, bees, do you honey make.' Lines attributed to Virgil.

12. 'Only a people sufficiently evolved as to be capable of self-government are worthy of a republican regime. It follows that the less evolved a nation is, the more it needs to be ruled by a firm hand.' Hauser, *op. cit.*, 81.

13. 'In its golden age, politeness was the external and tangible manifestation of the noble, exalted ideals by which individuals were inspired.' Ibid., 70.

14. Proust paraphrases Pascal, in *Pensées*: 'Take the road they took in the beginning; it lay in doing everything as if they believed, in taking the holy water, in having Masses said, etc.; that way, even naturally, you will come to believe and make yourself an idiot.'

15. In July 1914, believing that a falling stock market had brought him to the brink of ruin, Proust sold shares held by Warburg's Bank, Hamburg, raising FF 50,000. The ensuing delay in processing the second of the two resulting cheques through the Crédit Industriel, Paris, meant that FF 30,000 in cash, and his remaining shares in Hamburg, were blocked indefinitely by wartime legislation. Proust had enlisted Hauser, other bankers and even friends in an attempt to discount it at the Comptoir d'Escompte or the Rothschild bank, but without success.

16. French citizens were required to declare investments held abroad.

20 To Lucien Daudet

[Saturday 11 May 1918]

My dearest Lucien,
 On this saddest of days,[1] I think of you with a feeling of prayer and inexpressible communion. I know that one is supposed to hope for an end to the sufferings of those one loves. But no matter how great these sufferings, I've never been able to get used to the idea of hoping that a friend's life will end. Any more than I can get used to the idea that his life is over. It's not only the deaths of recent years, those of Fénelon[2] and Emmanuel Bibesco, which, every night, I go over sorrowfully in my mind, but of far longer ago. And sometimes the anguish of those who genuinely grieve even causes me to lament the deaths of people I never knew. Thus, the Duc de Chevreuse, whom I never met, lives on for me in the despairing but wonderful letters his father[3] wrote me.
 My dearest, I kiss you tenderly, with a very heavy heart. If you see Frédéric de Madrazo,[4] tell him how much I've been thinking of him, knowing all he did for Clary.
 Did I tell you about my being forced to lie to Joachim on my last visit to the rue Galilée (to lie about his state of health),[5] thus making it impossible for me to go back there because, only ever seeing him at times when he was alone, had I not given him the favourable explanation which I had promised him, my silence would have taken away his remaining illusions.

Your
Marcel Proust

1. Allusion to the funeral of Joachim, Comte Clary, former courtier to the exiled Empress Eugénie.
2. Bertrand, Vicomte de Salignac-Fénelon (1878–1914) a diplomat; one of the models for Saint-Loup. Proust, having allowed their intimacy to cool, had suffered acutely when, for three months in 1914, Fénelon's fate was unknown; he was finally reported killed in a futilely heroic action. See Saint-Loup's similar end: VI, 192 ff.
3. Honoré, Duc de Luynes et de Chevreuse (1868–1924), premier duke of France, whose son, a pilot, had recently been killed in action.
4. Frédéric ('Coco') de Madrazo, a painter.

5. Clary had been semi-paralysed and almost blind when Proust paid him several visits in 1915. See Charlus's Lear-like appearance in old age: VI, 207–10.

21 To Madame Soutzo

Wednesday [3 July 1918]

Princesse,

I wrote to you on Sunday. And remembering that your addresses in the South had a tendency to float, I had Céleste telephone the Ritz to ask if the Hôtel du Palais, Biarritz is really where one writes to you.[1] It was the address you gave me, the chief reason for supposing that it wasn't yours. Céleste returned to tell me that it was some other hotel, whose name she simply couldn't remember. Considering that she understood this name to be Eskualdunahendaye[2] (never having heard of Hendaye, she thought it was the name of an hotel in Biarritz), you will, I think, find her excusable (though not for having left me[3] without pen and ink, so that I'm struggling with a splayed nib which I dip into a sort of mud). And now, having discovered this by word of mouth, here is your letter![4] Joy at the sight of the handwriting (your other beloved face which, on a different plane, in a quite a different medium, portrays you almost as faithfully as the one in the flesh), sadness at the *tone* of the letter (gone are Marcel, my dear friend, valetudinarian etc.), melancholy, or rather, resignation, of which it's merely another form, at knowing you to be less far away than I thought, nearer to an absent friend[5] whose affection for you is, I'm glad to hear, abiding and requited, a more troubled melancholy in the case of 'all those friends' in St-Jean-de-Luz[6] who, without my being able to put a name to them, pierce my heart with unpredictable arrows.

Princesse, I feel that this last sentence, composed of nothing but moaning antitheses and redundant parentheses, is already longer than a sentence in *Swann*. So I finish by saying simply that I'm virtually certain not to come, that you mustn't look for a house for me, that I shall try to find peace and catch up on lost work in the boulevard Haussmann; above all, lady of the wonderful robes, I want to tell you that you are a rare and remarkable writer. Your description of sea breezes, Hendaye (which must be familiar to every conceivable authority, to judge by the number of stamps on the envelope), the Ritz, are ravishing passages which take off beautifully, truly soar, and make a perfect landing. You talk well but you write even better; indeed, when you write, it's as though you were talking. What beautiful conversation your letters make!

I don't need to tell you, Princesse, that I would have preferred the so-peaceful Hendaye you describe to a livelier Biarritz, and it doesn't follow that just because you have made me partly renounce my solitude, you should deny me my preference for its comforts and an appreciation of its worth. But to tell the truth, even if Céleste were well, I don't feel up to going anywhere at the moment, not even to Cabourg, nearer and yet so far. Misquoting, I could say of myself as I said of Swann: 'he had the heart to remain, but not the heart to go.'[7] My quoting this is quite absurd, for not only do the cases have nothing whatever in common, the very situation would be almost reversed, since to go to Hendaye would not be to flee you but to rejoin you. A stupid quotation, without the justification of truth. The adjectives most applicable to me are, I suppose, sore, sedentary and possibly scarred (the second implying a self-imposed state designed to make the third possible).

Farewell, Princesse, I would dearly like to be close enough to you to kiss your hand and for you to reassure me that my moustache hasn't left sugar on it. But I have no alternative except to resign myself to begging you to accept (what a lot of infinitives) my deepest respects.

Marcel Proust

If you write to Morand, or see him, tell him again that my tender friendship for him doesn't fade like a dead memory, but flourishes, like something deep-rooted, fruitful and living.

1. See letter 17.
2. i.e. the Eskualduna Hotel in Hendaye, a small seaside town near the fashionable resort of Biarritz.
3. Proust had no telephone: Céleste made and received calls from a nearby café.
4. She was recovering from 'flu at her home in the Cévennes.
5. Mme Soutzo's fiancé, Paul Morand: see letter 42.
6. Small fishing port near Hendaye.
7. 'No doubt Swann was assured that if he had now been living at a distance from Odette he would gradually have lost interest in her, so that he would have been glad to learn that she was leaving Paris for ever; he would have had the heart to remain there, but he hadn't the heart to go.' I, 425.

22 To Madame Hecht[1]

[Around September 1918]

Madame,

I have your letter and will naturally comply with your negative instructions.[2] All it means, in fact, is that I shall be spared much fatigue, as well as much pleasure. I say much pleasure because I'm almost sure that I would have been successful. But being only almost sure, and furthermore needing somebody else's consent, I didn't want to submit to you as definitive lines which might never appear. I preferred to surprise you with my success, rather than boast in advance about something of which I was almost but not absolutely sure.

And now that things have been settled negatively, kindly allow me, absurd though it is, with my eyes in this terrible state, to be writing an inessential letter when I have over fifty essential letters to answer, to give you my views on this in all frankness and sincerity. Above all, don't read my letter as a reproach, which would be insane on my part, and supremely ill-mannered. I know how exquisitely high-minded you are, and if there is anybody not in need of advice about the reverence due to the memory of her beloved dead, that person is you! But precisely because your sensibilities are of such a high order, I feel the need, ill as I am, to chat to you by letter, to tell you how surprised I am, whenever there is a question of a posthumous tribute, that the survivors, by whom I mean the most pious, the most nobly and painfully devoted to a memory, should be thinking not of the person who has died, but of themselves. I am certainly far from suggesting selfishness or neglect. The survivors, out of 'a sense of propriety', would be 'pained' by it, and no sentiments could be more high-minded, but should they not be asking themselves what does it matter if I'm wounded in the most delicate fibres of my being, it's not of myself that I should be thinking, but of the poor dead man who, could he speak for himself, would ask for only one thing, life!

I wouldn't dream of overvaluing the few lines of praise in my preface. It is execrable. But as the book itself is delightful, a great improvement on the same author's *Cahiers d'un artiste*,[3] which is dreary in the extreme, it would have been widely read, and as I mention *nobody*, not even very famous painters whose names (between ourselves) I was asked to omit, M. Hecht's name would have stood out. In fact, it's strange that I should have chosen to write about M. Hecht, whom I never knew, rather than M. Charles Ephrussi,[4] who was a dear friend. But I think that is because Charles Ephrussi, having written books on art, is sometimes quoted. Whereas M. Hecht left no book behind him that I know of, and it was a unique opportunity of keeping his memory alive in a setting worthy of him.

If I discuss these things with you retrospectively, when it's too late to do anything, it's because I believe that the noble instincts which you obeyed, instincts which, to be frank, I condemn and admire in equal measure, are shared by all the best people. I know, or rather, once knew, some admirable parents. Having had the misfortune to lose their son[5] at the beginning of the war, they arranged to have the letters he wrote them from the front printed for the benefit of a few close friends. I never met this young man, but his letters were so alive, and exuded such goodness and courage, such an artless ambition to make a 'name' for himself, that I couldn't read them without weeping. I advised his parents to publish them, and, although in a wretched state of health even then, offered to ask people like Barrès[6] and Hermant to quote a few passages from them. Without a doubt, this would have overjoyed a young man so full of life, so desirous of glory. The parents flatly refused, out of a 'sense of propriety' etc.[7] I didn't insist, but I had the distinct impression that they were putting their own grief (unquestionably sincere and inconsolable though it was) before the person whom they mourned. Perhaps they told themselves that they would make this young unknown's name known later on, by publishing the novel he had embarked on before the war. If so, they were blinded by parental love, for this young man had no 'talent'. The delightful nature revealed by his letters, the interest of the actions in which he was involved, all that, combined with a form and style that were pleasing without being enough in themselves, would have made the charm of any book. It is now unpublishable, I might add, too many war books having destroyed its appeal. Were his parents in the right? Or was I? I'm positive that Maman[8] would have thought as I did.

Manet having been the reason for our correspondence, would you permit me to come and see your Manets one evening, when I am better and you are alone (I mean either on your own or with your children or my aunt or Adèle?[9]) Unfortunately, my attacks never giving me any warning, I could have you telephoned only on the same day – on the off-chance, if that wouldn't be too inconvenient – to ask if I might call after dinner. It's over twenty years since I've looked at paintings.

As you are at Madame Cruppi's,[10] kindly give her and her husband my respectful regards. She is a link with those happiest of times when as a child I would hear her sing Mozart at home, evenings which themselves sing in my memory.

And I can still hear her voice when she acted in *Les Fourberies de Nérine*[11] (was it at Mme Baignères's[12] or Mme Aubernon's?[13] I forget the setting, but how well I remember her). She has more luck than me, for she must often see my dear Princesse de Chimay.[14] But friendships persist in solitude, without needing to be renewed by social intercourse. When I last corresponded with the Princesse de Chimay, about a common sorrow,[15] it seemed to me, on reading her letters and in writing mine, that I had seen her only the day before.

Believe me, Madame, I am very respectfully and
affectionately yours,
Marcel Proust

1. *Née* Mathilde Oulman, an elderly widow, a relation of Proust's by marriage.

2. Allusion to his preface for Jacques-Émile Blanche. This being full of references to Manet, at the last minute he had asked and been refused permission to write about her late husband, Alfred Hecht, Manet's patron, who is portrayed in the painter's famous *Bal masqué à l'Opéra*.

3. Blanche's *War Journals*.

4. Charles Ephrussi (1849–1905), distinguished Jewish patron of the arts and one of Proust's chief models for Swann.

5. Jean Bénac. In 1894, Proust and Reynaldo Hahn had spent a holiday with the Bénacs at Beg Meil, a resort which had served as an early model for Balbec.

6. Maurice Barrès (1862–1923), novelist, essayist and nationalist politician who had been a leading anti-Dreyfusard.

7. Cf. the 'sacred Pudor' which keeps Bloch from singing the narrator's praises: IV, 582–3. See also the narrator's memories of his mother's 'cult of grief' for her own mother: IV, 194–7.

8. Mme Adrien Proust, *née* Jeanne Weil (1849–1905), the beautiful, cultivated mother who had devoted her life to him and whom he had never ceased to mourn.

9. Mme Georges Weil, *née* Amélie Oulman (1853–1920), Mme Hecht's sister and Proust's landlady; her daughter, Adèle.

10. Mme Jean Cruppi, *née* Louise Crémieux, cousin of Mme Hecht and Mme Weil, married to a former cabinet minister.

11. Verse-play by Théodore de Banville. See Mlle Léa's forthcoming appearance in the same play at the Trocadéro: V, 157.

12. Mme Arthur Baignères: see letter 29.

13. Mme Georges Aubernon, *née* Lydia de Nerville, the Second Empire hostess who was one of Proust's models for Mme Verdurin.

14. Princesse Alexandre de Caraman-Chimay, *née* Hélène Bassaraba de Brancovan (1878–1929).

15. The death of Emmanuel Bibesco, Mme de Chimay's cousin.

23 *To Madame de Polignac*[1]

102, boulevard Haussmann
[First fortnight of September 1918]

Princesse,

Time and again, I've wanted to see you. But you are never in Paris. Recently, no longer seeing mutual friends who could have put me right, I had supposed that the silence of your telephone coincided with times when you were dining out. But now Reynaldo[2] tells me that you are in the Pyrenees.

I'm writing to you on the off-chance. It may already be too late for what I want to ask you,[3] the editor[4] having sent my book to press before leaving for America, and the printer having refused to make corrections which I considered essential. Still, it may be possible to add a dedication on a separate page, even to a printed book.

I therefore venture to ask your advice without being sure that I can profit from it; I counted on bringing out all the volumes of my *Swann* at once, and for reasons which I intended to explain to you, I saw no objection to dedicating it to the Prince's memory.[5] In reality, nothing could be more in keeping with the facts and spirit of the book. But you have a friend who is my enemy, and I a friend who won't remain a friend much longer[6] (for reasons which have nothing to do with you) with whom you have quarrelled (Robert de Montesquiou). Now, I feared lest they attempt to use this dedication to revive your former unjustified ill-will towards me. Not only that, one of them would have happily pretended to find some resemblance between a character in my book[7] (a non-existent resemblance, on any level) and the Prince. For once, it couldn't be said, as about a previous article of mine,[8] that it was to you that I was being unjust. In all five volumes of *Swann*, there isn't a single woman who has the slightest connection with you, however remote. Nor is there anybody who in the smallest degree resembles the Prince. But since one character – wholly different from the Prince, his very opposite – is a great nobleman with a taste for artistic things, the dedication, which is not open to misinterpretation, might nevertheless serve as a pretext, giving two people the opportunity for a bare-faced lie.

Now, my admiration for your character notwithstanding (I equate it with your mind, which says a good deal), I retain from the old days the perhaps mistaken impression, and if so, kindly excuse my frankness, that you sometimes let yourself be misled by malicious people. In short, for all these reasons, but less, perhaps, for the sorrow I would feel at falling out with you again than for the even greater sorrow of hearing the Prince's name spoken without due reverence, I thought it best to abstain.

In fact, there was no hurry; what with five volumes to correct, printers defaulting and proofs not forthcoming, I would have had plenty of time to chat to you. But now my editor wants to publish the second volume of *Swann* at the same time as some collected articles of mine,[9] and the other three volumes at a later date. Now, this second volume, *À l'Ombre des jeunes filles en fleurs*, doesn't seem to me, even trying for a moment to enter into the mind of the most brazen would-be slanderer, to offer the smallest pretext. The story opens with the description of a diplomat of the Cambon type[10] (M. de Norpois). Then the little boy of the first volume, now an adolescent, visits Mme Swann, loves Gilberte, is made unhappy by her; long passages about Mme Swann's salon, Mme Cottard, etc. Then comes Balbec, where we get a glimpse of M. de Charlus (the extract in the *Nouvelle revue française*)[11], and that's not even a sixth of the book. Lastly, the young girls in bloom, the sporty girls whom the boy meets at Balbec (this part not in the *NRF*), falling for each in turn. Truly, I don't see how the objections which I pointed out to you earlier could possibly apply to the volume in question.

On the other hand, it doesn't seem to me to be completely unworthy of being dedicated to the Prince. Naturally, I would have preferred to offer him, as well as to have written, *La Chartreuse de Parme*, or *Les Frères Karamasov*. But one can only give what one has. And of what I have, it's the least bad. I believe that when all five volumes have appeared, this second one, which at first sight has the effect of what in the military arts is termed a diversionary movement,[12] will take on a certain significance. Should it then be read and liked by people who never knew the Prince, and whose admiration would be worthy of him, for it to bear his name would mean a great deal to me. 'I give him these verses so that my name / Should safely reach the shores of time.'[13]

Princesse, I would be very grateful for an immediate answer (even immediate may be too late). Say yes or no, don't trouble to explain. Certainly don't say 'yes' to please me. What I mean to say is that, barely able to see, let alone write, I wouldn't be writing you a ten-page letter if I didn't attach great importance to it. But it's best that you ignore my wishes and come to your decision objectively. I haven't yet had occasion, and probably never will, to dedicate a book to Monsieur France (who wrote a preface for my first book),[14] nor to all those others who have shown me such infinite kindness. I mention this to show you that, should I choose to have them for a particular book, I wouldn't be 'short' of dedicatees, even were I to limit myself to those imposed by gratitude. So if you have the slightest objection to my dedicating this book to the Prince, don't hestitate, write and say 'no'; if it's 'yes', it might be safer to send me a telegram.

Another solution, perhaps the best, occurs to me as I'm about to close, namely, to let *À l'Ombre des jeunes filles en fleurs* appear without a dedication. You would read the book and, knowing all there is to know, when the time comes for the inevitable second edition (around the third impression), we can add the dedication if you think fit.[15] In fact, I have a set of fairly clean proofs which you can read at your leisure, for the book won't be out for some time, especially if I let a newspaper have extracts. But once the book is printed and bound, even if not yet out, it will be too late to change anything; it may be so already. I need to keep the proofs in any case, on account of this possible serialization.

Princesse, I've just noticed something written on the back of this page. So kindly accept this half-page with my most respectful regards.

Marcel Proust

1. Princesse Edmond de Polignac, *née* Winaretta Singer (1865–1943), a wealthy American (she was the sewing-machine heiress) who had a noted salon.

2. Reynaldo Hahn (1875–1947), composer and conductor, Venezuelan by birth. He and Proust had a passionate liaison in 1894, and thereafter kept up an intimate correspondence in their private language that lasted until the war (Reynaldo was

in the army). They were to re-find their old intimacy only as Proust lay dying.

3. At the last minute, seeking an illustrious dedicatee for *Within a Budding Grove*, Proust had settled on her late husband.

4. Gaston Gallimard: see letter 32.

5. Edmond, Prince de Polignac (1834–1901). The pomp in the church at Combray for Saint-Loup's burial was his: VI, 197.

6. Proust awaited with trepidation Montesquiou's reaction to his portrayal as the Baron de Charlus.

7. Allusion to the Prince de Guermantes, revealed in *Sodom and Gomorrah* as homosexual and Dreyfusard. The Prince de Polignac was both.

8. Allusion to one of Proust's pseudonymous high-society articles for the *Figaro*, his so-called 'salons', in which he eulogizes the Prince at the Princesse's expense: see *CS-B*, 464–9.

9. *Pastiches et mélanges*: see letter 10, n.12.

10. Allusion to Jules Cambon (1845–1936), an ambassador of the old school.

11. II, 382–4. The extracts appeared in the *NRF* in 1914.

12. See Saint-Loup's disquisition on strategy: III, 120–1.

13. 'Je te donne ces vers afin que si mon nom/Aborde heureusement aux époques lointaines': Baudelaire, 'Spleen et Idéal' xi, 1, *Les Fleurs du Mal*. Proust substitutes *lui* for *te*.

14. *Pleasures and Regrets*: see letter 10, n.14.

15. Mme de Polignac having refused her permission, *Within a Budding Grove* appeared without a dedication.

24 To Jean-Louis Vaudoyer[1]

[Between 18 and 25 October 1918]

Dear friend,

I had no idea, and I cannot tell you how painful the thought of your suffering is to me. You are so dear to me, my friend. Your sorrows are my wounds.

How grateful I am to you for introducing me to your wonderful Mother[2] at that Capet concert when they played the A-minor Quartet.[3] In the dreadful hours through which you are passing, when human beings matter only inasmuch as they are our link with what we have lost, and when we prefer an old housemaid who knew our mother to a gifted friend, I am comforted to think that you don't count me among those who never knew her. Did the music of the sublime quartet give me more profound insight into human nature that evening? But it seems to me that I understood and admired your Mother to the full. I would have given so much to see her again.

You will have the consolation of knowing, as you keep alive the cult of her memory, that you were her pride, her joy, and, at the beginning of the war, the solace of her broken heart.[4]

My dear friend, I embrace you tenderly. Kindly tell your family, particularly Mme Daniel Halévy,[5] with what sympathy and understanding I share in their grief.

Marcel Proust

1. Jean-Louis Vaudoyer (1893–1963), poet and art-critic. He and Proust had long shared a love of art, music and the Russian ballet, for which he wrote *Le Spectre de la Rose*.
2. Mme Alfred Vaudoyer, whose death had just been announced.
3. A concert in 1913, given by the string quartet led by the famous violinist Louis Capet (see letter 18, n.9), at which they played Beethoven's Quartet No.15, Op. 132.
4. Allusion to the death of Jean-Louis's brother, Michel, killed in action in 1914.
5. *Née* Marianne Vaudoyer, Jean-Louis's sister.

25 To Lionel Hauser

[23 or 24 October 1918]

My dear Lionel,

I won't disguise from you that I was dismayed (as well as deeply moved) by your letter. My dismay is not, as you can imagine, financially inspired. Its sole cause is your apparent feeling that I've disappointed you, that I've been inconsiderately unravelling, like an incorrigible Penelope, what you had so expertly woven for my own good. This has reduced me to despair. For in that case, as you say in your previous letter,[1] you cannot believe in my gratitude, since, according to you, I have destroyed the very thing that would prove it.

I don't doubt that this way of thinking stems from theosophy,[2] and the greater my detestation of this metaphysical system, the more I admire it. For I can see that, to the theosophist, love, *crudelis amor*,[3] is not a passion which takes little account of life, still less wealth, but knows, even in its worst lapses, how to remain rational, so to speak economical. And, naturally, I think the theosophist is right. And I shan't retort that 'the heart has its reasons which reason knows nothing of'.[4] For there is absolutely no merit in yielding to the promptings of passion, in being carried away by the only thing that counts for one at a given moment, whereas there is immense merit in putting a brake on the impulses of one's heart. Whatever this yoke may be that we have the courage to accept, it takes on a certain grandeur by virtue of all the powers for expansion which it holds in check, and to which it has an agonizing compulsion to submit. Call this yoke accountancy, it doesn't really matter. In such a case, there is a sublime accountancy, a Cornelian accountancy.[5] But, not to tax your patience and my strength, I shall leave the domain of feeling and of the profound regret I felt when I had the impression a) that I had let you down, at least in your eyes, and b) that you saw in my clear-sighted folly (consistent with the acceptance of fast-approaching death) only something at odds with your goodness to me. In which, moreover, you were right. But tonight, as I said, not to tax your patience and my strength, I'll simply restrict myself to the question of practical accountancy, and, purely from that standpoint, even consider your idea of a life annuity,[6] that is, inasmuch as it might prove favourable from the point of view of income, and not in order to substitute this external brake for human reason.

Now, regarding the pecuniary advantages of an annuity (my brother having married a very rich woman, he repeatedly advised me, not against an annuity but not to worry about him on that score, for example to get married etc. Anyhow, I need have no conscience about that, for reasons I prefer not to go into. So let's return to discussing the advantages). I have two observations to make regarding this. The first may well favour your idea. Is the 'France' an insurance company you recommend? I ask because my father,[7] when company doctor there, installed one of his pupils as his successor, a Dr Lafitte who, for reasons I could give you, owes a great debt of gratitude to Papa's memory and knows better than anybody that, whatever you say, my health is nothing like Voltaire's.[8] I therefore believe I could get 20 per cent (but that's pure speculation). As for the Company Director, he and Papa were on excellent terms. His name is Truelle, and he is a relation of that stockbroker who died the other day. But when I asked his son,[9] of whom I'm very fond and who is even fonder of me, if he was related to the director of an insurance company, young Truelle practically denied it. It must be to do with a family quarrel, for while snobbery was once this very young man's weakness, he has a very good heart (and mind). He has never ceased to uphold the most violently pacifist views to the very people most likely to be scandalized by them, even though, having lost a leg in the war, he no longer has anything to gain from the Peace. To return to the subject: as long as Dr Lafitte is still with the 'France', which I'll discreetly find out, and as long as he isn't put off by the fear of offending my brother, I believe I may count on good results from that quarter.

My second observation about your idea is that of the two policies we could have adopted after my ruin, in 1913,[10] the one advised by R. G. Lévy[11] seemed to me quite wrong, being to sell shares that had held up well and to hang on to the weakest, in short, to have an eye to capital gain.

The policy I followed, on the other hand, moreover embellished by the thousand ingenuities with which you adorned it, was concerned with income. (I compare the two purely for the purposes of discussion, by the way, for they obviously have many points in common.) Now, I suppose that to take out an annuity means selling shares, and thus those with the highest yield. Which doesn't of course preclude the sale of shares which yield nothing. But thanks to you, I have first-class investments, such as Government Bonds. The recent turn of events makes it likely that the market will see a rise, perhaps a large one. Wouldn't it be better to await this rise before selling capital to buy an annuity? Or would an insurance company accept stock at par, without my having to sell? Lastly, if the 'France' offers only 12 percent (I say only, I realize it's enormous), are there not shares like Royal Dutch which yield almost as much without my having to part with capital? Won't American shares, at present hit by a massive war tax, bounce back after the Peace? In short, since you have been good enough to show me so much kindness (I doubt if theosophy alone would account for it, without a warm heart), I'm examining with you the pros and cons of investing in an annuity from the point of view of income. As for not being able to touch the capital[12] (in fact, I don't know what it amounts to) (rubbish like Gold Mines represent a small outlay for a large income – land nowadays, I suppose, for a small income), we can, if you don't mind, out of pity for your patience, my eyes and my strength, go into that some other time.

With all my heart, and my increasing gratitude and friendship,
Marcel Proust

Many thanks for the authorization concerning the widow Blumenthal.[13] But there has been some misunderstanding. 1) I don't know her. I'm never rude about people I know in my books. 2) There is not the slightest possibility of her being heroine of a novel of mine (some heroine). She will be mentioned by name in *Pastiches et mélanges*.

1. 'Imagine how a doctor feels when he has fought like a fiend to snatch a patient from the jaws of death only to find him, still convalescent, tucking into choucroute. Well, that's how I felt on reading your letter. I make superhuman efforts to weave a blanket to keep you warm, and the moment my back is turned, you amuse yourself by cutting it to pieces and throwing it to the winds. And do you show the slightest remorse – no, as usual, you smile, thus blatantly demonstrating your utter irresponsibility.' Hauser, 20 October.
2. See letter 19.
3. 'Cruel love'. Proust had confessed to Hauser about his unhappy love-affair with 'a man of the people' (meaning Henri Rochat: see letter 11) and to 'attendant acts of philanthrophy' which had depleted his bank account by some 30,000 francs.
4. 'La coeur a ses raisons que la raison ne connaît point': Pascal, *Pensées*.
5. Allusion to the plays of Corneille, in which will dominates passion.
6. Hauser had recommended a *rente viagère*. Income is paid (often by a family member) in return for property or capital sum on death.
7. Dr Adrien Proust (1835–1903), an eminent physician renowned as a pioneer in hygiene.
8. 'Being destined to live a long life, you'll find it all the more advantageous. Your illness makes me think of Voltaire.' (Allusion to Voltaire's death at 74, despite a lifetime of chronic illness.) Hauser, *loc. cit.*
9. Jacques Truelle: see letter 17, n. 8.
10. See letter 19, n. 15.
11. Raphaël-Georges Lévy, economist, Proust's distant relative.
12. '[An annuity] will have a double advantage: on the one hand, part of your income will increase, on the other, you will be protected from the impulses of your heart.' Hauser, *op. cit.*
13. Mme Cécilia Blumenthal was a laughing-stock because, though remarried, she still styled herself Duchesse de Montmorency, her second husband, Louis de Talleyrand-Périgord, having inherited this Napoleonic dukedom. See the Duc de Guermantes's discourse on titles of pretension: III, 684–5. Proust had pretended to think that she was Hauser's friend.

26 To Madame Straus[1]

[Tuesday evening, 12 November 1918]

Madame,

What a beautiful letter! But I feel for you, knowing the fatigue of penning the words and marshalling the thoughts. A thousand thanks for the valuer.[2] I'll write to M. Sibilat[3] to say that my hideous jumble of dusty dining-room furniture can be seen on Saturday afternoons from three o'clock.

This afternoon, I went out and returned very ill, so I suppose that, on Thursday and Friday, I shall certainly have to do some fumigations.[4] I can't be sure of being up on Saturday, but Céleste is quite capable of showing the man around, though I would be grateful if he didn't mention his valuations in front of her, especially if they are on the low side. I'll explain why.

Your evocation of Shakespeare à propos of the present tragedy is so profound, so perfectly in tune with your Father's great literary tradition,[5] that one is instantly reminded that Sainte-Beuve called him the best-read man of his time, and that this scholarly man was Permanent Secretary to the Academy. Only in Shakespeare's plays are all the events crowded into a single scene, and only in one of his scenes could one hear: 'William II: "I abdicate."[6] The King of Bavaria: "I am heir to the world's most ancient lineage, I abdicate."[7] The Crown Prince[8] weeps, sighs, and is assassinated by his soldiers.'

One mustn't rail against Fate, especially when, with a shift in a timing mechanism one had thought jammed for the past four years, it has given us this final spate of triumphs. Yet even I, who am such a supporter of the Peace because unable to bear men's suffering, believe that if total victory and a hard Peace was what we wanted, it had been better to make a still harder Peace. The treaties I prefer are those which leave no bitterness in anybody's heart. But since it ceases to be a treaty of that sort from the moment it bequeaths a desire for vengeance, it might have been a good thing to make the wreaking of vengeance impossible. Perhaps that is the case. Yet President Wilson[9] seems to me a very mild man, and since a conciliatory peace is out of the question through Germany's own fault, I would like to have seen more rigorous conditions, being a little afraid of German Austria coming to reinforce Germany as compensation for the loss of Alsace-Lorraine. But all this is mere conjecture, perhaps I misread the situation and it's not so bad as it is. General Galliffet[10] said of General Roget[11] that he talked well but too much. President Wilson doesn't talk very well but says far too much. There are times in the lives of nations, as in those of men (I've had occasion to apply it to myself, alas), when the true motto is Vigny's line: 'Silence alone is strength; all the rest is weakness'.[12] You know it comes from 'La Mort du loup', and you remember all those blood-stained, stoical lines.

But at this very moment I myself am breaking the law of silence doubtless imposed by your doctor, and I must be tiring you. So I bid you goodbye and beg you to share with M. Straus my most grateful and sincere respects.

Marcel Proust

1. Mme Émile Straus, *née* Geneviève Halévy (1850–1926). Born into a cultivated, musical family, she had first married the composer Georges Bizet, then Émile Straus (1844–1929), lawyer and financier. Beautiful, sympathetic, a martyr to neurasthenia, she was very close to Proust; he had been an habitué of her salon even before it became the refuge of leading Dreyfusards, and had borrowed her brilliant conversation for the style and wit of the Duchesse de Guermantes.

2. Proust was raising money by selling family furniture (see letter 6, n. 2). The Strauses had already once displayed his best pieces for sale in their house.

3. René Sibilat, M. Straus's nephew.

4. Proust regularly inhaled the smoke from Legras powder for asthmatics.

5. Fromental Halévy (1799–1862), writer and musician, composer of *La Juive*. Sainte-Beuve devoted one of his *Lundis* to him on his death.

6. Kaiser of Germany from 1888 to 1918, deposed by revolution.

7. Ludwig III (1845–1921), last of the Wittelbachs.

8. Frederick von Hohenzollern (1882–1951), falsely reported shot as he made his escape.

9. Woodrow Wilson (1856–1924), President of the United States 1913–1921.

10. Gaston, Marquis de Galliffet (1830–1909), the minister for war who conducted the revision of the Dreyfus Case.

11. Gaudérique Roget, leading army witness against Dreyfus.

12. See letter 3, n. 10.

27   To Clément de Maugny[1]

[Shortly after 18 January 1919]

My dear Clément,

Forgive me for not having thanked you for your letter and those very pretty, very comical sketches.[2] (The ministering angel – what an enchanting apparition before she turns into matron!)

There's more than one reason for my silence, alas: laryngitis (which recurs as soon as I get up) accompanied by a temperature of over 30°, thus lethargy, which means that I don't answer or even open letters (yes, when I recognize your handwriting), haven't corrected a single proof of my book, receive frantic letters from my editor. I'm now better and might be able to work, provided that the roof-tiles don't come crashing about my head. My landlady,[3] without warning me, has sold the building where I live to a banker[4] who will doubtless turn it into a bank, meaning the likelihood of a move and, despite a verbal agreement with my ex-landlady, my having to pay all the rent owing from the war years at one fell swoop.

All that gives you a vague idea of my worries. I'll bear in mind what you say nevertheless, but among the few publishers I know personally, I can't think of one who might suit you. I've only done one illustrated book,[5] for Calmann-Lévy, who never did another (Mme Lemaire's[6] illustrations were the attraction for him). And he was always telling me what enormous sums he had lost on it, and that he would remainder it for a song unless I agreed to buy it back. Naturally, I refused to buy back thousands of books with nowhere to put them, and moreover couldn't care less what he did with a book so utterly different from what I'm doing now. I told him to do as he liked, even send them to Maugny[7] if he wanted to be rid of them and you had the room.

But apart from this unhappy experience, and not recommending you to go to them, I know no publisher of the kind you mention. My book is coming out with the Nouvelle Revue Française which has never done illustrated books and publishes only a small group of writers: Paul Morand, Claudel, André Gide, Péguy etc. I wrote a preface for a book by Blanche but haven't met the publisher, who drags his feet in any case, nothing having yet appeared. Still, it seems so exactly the right moment for Mme de Maugny's book that I'll try and see somebody about it. But who? Supposing I don't find anybody (and even if I do), where should I return the drawings to you?

Affectionately yours,
Marcel Proust

1. An ex-cavalry officer and old friend of Proust, now fallen on hard times.
2. Caricatures of wartime hospital life by Maugny's wife, Rita de Bussé.
3. Mme Georges Weil: see letter 22, n. 9.
4. The proprietor of the Banque Verin-Bernier.
5. *Pleasure and Regrets*: see letter 10, n. 14.
6. Madeleine Lemaire, *née* Jeanne-Magdeleine Coll (1845–1928). A painter of 'flower-pieces' and hostess of musical soirées, she combined elements of both Mme de Villeparisis and Mme Verdurin.
7. The family seat where Proust had spent much time in 1889, when accompanying his mother to the nearby spa of Évian-les-Bains.
8. Rita de Bussé's album was to be published in 1920, with a preface by Proust: see *CS-B*, 566–8.

28   To Walter Berry

Tuesday evening [21 January 1919]

My dear friend,

I have such a cascade of things to say to you and ask you that, what with a severe bout of fever as well, I hardly know how to order and classify my questions.

In any case, I must first explain why I was in such a hurry the other morning at the Ritz. I had not only just had several sleepless nights, but some painful angina attacks as well; I was on the point of having another, if I didn't take the cachets of caffeine I had in my pocket with a drink of some sort. You thus saw me in the state of a Dostoievskian epileptic who senses that he is about to have a fit.

When I ran into you that morning, I still hadn't answered your charming letter about the London Bank.[1] I had been about to do so when a problem as bad as if not worse than the Mexicos came crashing down about my ears. So much so that, overwhelmed by worries and work, I've come to see the London Bank directors as negligible. The unforeseen blow, of the sort against which I am so defenceless that it will excuse my silence and perhaps induce you to grant my prayer, is this: I learnt, on the evening of the day I met you at the Ritz, through a disingenuously affectionate note from my landlady, that she had just sold the building where I live.

Without going into unnecessary details, this has resulted in a double nightmare for me: as I don't have a lease, I shall probably have to move, if not immediately, then certainly in the near future (for a banker, and thus I suppose a bank, has bought the house, probably (?) for offices); as I had come to a verbal agreement with my ex-landlady (an aunt by marriage to whom I myself, as its previous owner, had sold the house for 20,000 francs less than it was worth,[2] a favour since forgotten), whereby my rent would be deferred till after the war and the recovery of the Warburg shares you know about,[3] and as the new owner has taken over all expired and unpaid leases, I shall be required, the moment he asks for it, to pay all the rent for '16, '17 and '18 at one go, that is, some 25,000 francs. True, the other tenants had their rent reduced for the duration. But as I was the only one not to ask for a reduction, the full amount will obviously be exacted from me.

The Warburg shares, and even the cheque for 30,000 francs on the Comptoir d'Escompte which represents the major part, not being recoverable at present (for anything to do with cheque and shares, Hauser, and M. R.G. Lévy, who endorsed the cheque at the time and, being unable to cash it, re-endorsed in my name, could give you more precise details than I can, especially Hauser; I could do so myself, perhaps with less accurate figures, but that would overburden an already long letter), the simplest way for me to raise the 25,000 francs which will certainly be exacted from me any day now seems to me to sell two large tapestries I have no use for, a period rug ditto, a magnificent period armchair, some wall-brackets and a period settee. I believe they should fetch considerably more than the 25,000 francs, for I was offered 5000 for the chair alone some time ago. But in order to sell, they must be seen, and I'm either asleep or trying to sleep at all times when they could be viewed. And here begins my prayer.

Could you possibly be so kind as to house, somewhere on your premises, for a few days, the tapestries, the armchair, the wall-brackets and the (very small) settee? By your premises, I mean the American Chamber of Commerce, or some such building at your disposal. Perhaps your friends might see them there, and buy them.

If that is too much trouble for you, I could send somebody like Jansen[4] to look at them. He would buy them for less. But as long as it's enough to pay my new landlord, I would be prepared to cut my losses, as I was with the Mexicos. We'll postpone that urgent question, for at any moment the new landlord may forbid his tenants to remove their furniture. And I'll be caught in a vicious circle; unable to pay because I haven't sold; unable to sell because I haven't paid.

Lastly, I would be grateful to know how to approach the French government for help in cashing my cheque for 30,000 francs and my Warburg shares. Perhaps, after I've given you particulars, you could ask M. Pams[5] what course to take, so as to avoid my having to deal with too many people in my state of health, for mine can't be the only case!

I have one last request to make of you (I've asked you quite enough as it is!). I would like to dedicate my new book *Pastiches et mélanges* to you (unlike Blanche's, mine would be a printed dedication).[6] If you prefer a *Swann*, I could dedicate *Le Côté de Guermantes* to you. But it won't be out for some time. The *Swann* which is to come out with *Pastiches et mélanges* (*À l'Ombre des jeunes filles en fleurs*) has no dedication, but as it's already printed and bound, if not yet in the shops, I cannot add one. Whereas *Pastiches et mélanges* is still in proof; but I would need to know at once. There is less hurry for *Le Côté de Guermantes* as it's still at the first-proof stage. In one way, it would give me greater pleasure to dedicate *Le Côté de Guermantes* to you, because it was through the Guermantes that we met.[7] But *Pastiches et mélanges* also has its advantages, in that I can testify to my gratitude and admiration for you all the sooner. It's for you to choose, always supposing that you would like to have a book of mine dedicated to you. And as far as I can see, it has to be one or the other. As for *Sodome et Gomorrhe*, which comprises three volumes, I intend to leave them undedicated, the subject seeming to me to exclude all possible dedications.

I've expressed what I had to say to you very badly; it would be so much nicer to invite you to the Ritz and explain it to you over dinner tomorrow, Wednesday, the first day when you said you would be free (and probably are no longer). But having this feverish cold tonight, can I expect to be up by tomorrow? I fear not. And even if I could, won't my fever take so long to come down that by the time I get to the Ritz it will be nine o'clock, that is, intolerably late for you? Perhaps, in case my letter isn't clear, you would let me call on you in the course of evening, always supposing I can get up (I doubt I shall be able to; I could have you telephoned). In any case, my most pressing need, apart from your reply about the dedication,[8] is to sell some objects. As for giving you details, where the cheque is concerned, Hauser could do this admirably (as I could). He knows nothing about the apartment. The sooner I can pay the new landlord the better, for a change of surroundings is often fatal to an asthmatic. That is why I hope he keeps me on, if he doesn't take all the floors for offices.

Very sincerely yours,
Marcel Proust

1. Proust's bank had sold his Mexican Tramway shares at a lower price than instructed; whereupon the price immediately rose. He had asked Berry's advice about suing the bank's directors for compensation.

2. The apartment building at 102 boulevard Haussmann had been the joint property of Mme Proust and her brothers, Louis and Georges Weil. On her death, in 1905, it was auctioned between the surviving heirs, Marcel, Robert and their aunt, Mme Georges Weil. Robert waived his interest and Marcel (who preferred to go to a party given by Robert de Montesquiou) let his aunt have it at a prearranged price.

3. See letter 19, n. 12.

4. An antique dealer in the rue Royale.

5. Jules Pams, minister of the interior.

6. One chapter of Blanche's *De David à Degas* had a (printed) dedication to Berry.

7. In 1913, after reading *Swann's Way*, Berry had discovered a nineteenth-century book stamped with the Guermantes arms, which he had presented to Proust at their first meeting, at Marie Scheikévitch's.

8. Berry accepted Proust's dedication of *Pastiches et mélanges*. It reads: 'To Monsieur Walter Berry, lawyer and man-of-letters, who, from the first day of the war, pleaded France's cause before a still undecided America, and, with incomparable talent and energy, won his case.'

29   To Mademoiselle Louise Baignères[1]

[Around 24 or 25 January 1919]

Dear Mademoiselle Louise,

Your letter (about which the first thing to say is that I shall of course obey it in every particular) truly astonishes me. And then, in addition, there are principles on which we disagree; this is why, despite eye-trouble which forbids my writing letters, I wish to answer you in detail.

1. Question of fact. Nowhere in this preface for J. Blanche, a preface which I doubt will appear, though it's possible, do I write of you all in the way you describe, and at the time I was writing it, I regretted not having the occasion to do so. I can't be positive about a preface written a year or more ago, not possessing so much as a draft to which I can refer, but I think I can safely say that the only allusions I make to your family are to be found in the following sentences, which I quote almost word for word: 1) 'At that time, I would meet Jacques Blanche at the salons of Madame Straus, Madame Arthur Baignères,[2] the Princesse Mathilde[3] and the Princesse de Wagram', and 2) a few pages further on: 'the pencil-sketch of my portrait[4] by Jacques Blanche was made at Les Frémonts,[5] then the residence of Madame Arthur Baignères, up to which would frequently ascend in all their elegance, almost indescribable today, as belles of the Second Empire, her cousins the Marquise de Galliffet[6] and the Princesse de Sagan.'[7] That's all. It's not much. Should the preface appear (but it's not my wish, I wrote to Jacques Blanche advising him to suppress it), I could, I suppose, omit your Mother's name while making very few changes. Instead of 'the salons of Madame Straus, Madame Arthur Baignères, the Princesse Mathilde', I need only put 'the salons of Madame Straus, Madame Baignères, the Princesse Mathilde'. As Madame Baignères without a forename implies the elder Monsieur Baignères, and as it was also with her (your Aunt Laure)[8] that I used to meet Jacques Blanche, who came to her house as often as he did to yours, it seems to me that this will satisfy you. In the other sentence, I need only omit Madame Arthur Baignères's name and residence altogether, and put: 'The sketch was made at Les Frémonts, up to which would frequently ascend in all their elegance, almost indescribable today, as belles of the Second Empire, the Marquise de Galliffet and the Princesse de Sagan, cousins of the mistress of the house'.[9] The readers, not knowing who is meant by the mistress of the house, will think, especially if they consult a telephone directory, that Madame Finaly[10] is related to the Talleyrands.[11] Will that do?

2. Question of principle.

Dear Mademoiselle Louise, what I'm about to say can have no bearing on this preface, since there, as you see, I make only the most commonplace reference to your Mother and her salon. Nor can it anger you if I point out the differences between your ideas and mine, for you know my admiration for you, not least as the incomparable Daughter of your dear and revered parents. But I don't believe that we should deceive ourselves in such matters and, for the sake of indulging our unconscious pleasure in that respectful silence which you describe so well and which is, moreover, very noble, consider what we ourselves would like when we ought to be considering only what would please those who are no longer with us, could they still read and know. Now, there can be no doubt that what they would wish, our poor Dead, is to live on. To take the example of your beloved and wonderful Father. His career was never fulfilled; his writings are little known; and those few people who can remember his wit in conversation and, if I may so put it, his heart in conversation, are themselves disappearing. Now, suppose I were less ill, capable of writing essays (which is hardly likely, alas), were I to try and pin down on paper so singular and sympathetic a 'figure' (something which I would never do without first submitting my essay to you, but I repeat, we are concerned here only with suppositions and unrealizable dreams, simply in order to discuss a point of doctrine), do you not agree that I would be acting more piously than I would by maintaining a respectful silence which may be more pleasing to the survivors but which, to the dead, smacks of cruelty and injustice?

The pleasure of having a salon frequented by the literary and social élite is certainly of a less exalted order, but it is one which we envy when, for example, we read the eighteenth-century correspondence of somebody like Mme Geoffrin.[12] It is that pleasure which your Mother not only felt but unaffectedly admitted to enjoying, in which she was perfectly right. Naturally, my humble mention of her salon in this preface is completely inadequate, but in spite of everything, it seems to me that as a means of keeping forgetfulness at bay, as a reminder of this salon, it would not have displeased her.

Friends of mine had the sorrow of losing a delightful and very talented son who was killed at the beginning of the war.[13] I advised them to publish the letters which this young man had written to his parents; they revealed such a warm heart, such vitality, so many fine gifts, that publication would have made the name of one who will now remain unknown, for he intended to write but was not granted the time. Publication would have kept him in touch with what the dead need above all: life. His parents, almost as if offended by the suggestion, replied that their 'sense of propriety' prevented them. In so saying, excellent parents though they were, I believe that they were thinking more of themselves (I mean, of their grief, in the best sense of the word) than of their son, who would have enjoyed being liked and admired. There are people who, on visiting a sick-bed, find the sight of blood so unbearable that they turn away, and those who, having overcome their nervous dread, care for the patient and do him good. I permit myself this analogy only because I know you to be among the latter.

The tiredness of eyes that can no longer see obliges me to bring to a close a letter in which all we have done is to discuss the precedence of one point of view over another, each having its claim to nobility. Whichever yours may be, it can only inspire me, as with everything touching you, with admiration and respect.

Marcel Proust

1. The 54-year-old daughter of M. and Mme Arthur Baignères.

2. *Née* Charlotte de Formeville, whom Proust had known as a spirited, ageing Second Empire belle.

3. Princesse Mathilde (1820–1904), Napoleon's niece, to whom the narrator is introduced by Swann and Odette as she walks in the Bois de Boulogne: II, 133–6. See also Proust's *Figaro* article of 1905, 'A Historic Salon': *AS-B*, 152–60.

4. See letter 3, n. 1. The sketch was done in 1891.

5. A villa near Cabourg, built in 1869 by the Baignères, Les Frémonts was the model for La Raspelière, the grand villa with magnificent views which Mme Verdurin rents from the Cambremers: IV, 176 ff.

6. See letter 26, n. 10. The Galliffets owned the nearby Manoir des Roches.

7. *Née* Jeanne Seillière (1859–1937), later Duchesse de Talleyrand, owner of the splendid Villa Persane. She appears as herself in Proust's novel, and also, attended by a negro page, as the Princesse de Luxembourg: II, 319–22.

8. Mme Henri Baignères, *née* Laure Boilay. A formidable hostess known for her repartee, she was the originator of Blanche Leroi's quip about love: 'I make it often but I never, ever talk about it.' See III, 220.

9. See 'Preface to Blanche', *AS-B*, 246–7 for the passage in question.

10. Mme Hugo Finaly, wife of a prominent Jewish banker, later the owner of Les Frémonts.

11. Allusion to the Princesse de Sagan, who would have been displeased at the very idea.

12. The comparison could have been found unflattering: Mme Geoffrin was a servant's daughter who married into the bourgeoisie and became a celebrated hostess.

13. See letter 22 to Mme Hecht.

30 To Madame Straus

Saturday [25 January 1919]

Dear Madame Straus,
I thank you with all my heart for your permission.[1] It gives me great pleasure to include this passage[2] in my pastiches, which I find so tiresome in other respects because of the purely literary necessity to speak ill of the Murats, the Fels,[3] the Cambacérès,[4] the Duchesse de Montmorency[5] etc. At least, what I say about you is ... not nearly enough (exactly the passage copied out word for word by Céleste).

Within hours, my pleasure in your letter was poisoned by a worry with which you'll sympathize.[6] My aunt has sold the house where I live without warning me, the new landlord will probably throw me out because I don't have a lease and, whatever happens, my aunt having failed to tell him about our verbal agreement whereby, since 1916, my rent has been deferred till I can cash my cheque for 30,000 francs, I'll soon have to pay the new landlord all the back rent at once, at least 20,000 francs, not an easy sum to come by these days!

I immediately set about selling more furniture, but don't worry, this time I shan't be pestering you.[7] I've sent tapestries, armchair etc. to my friend M. Walter Berry, President of the American Chamber of Commerce, who will take charge of them, just as, with indefatigable kindness, he takes charge of anything that worries or might exhaust me, and who eases my path in a multiplicity of ways. It's all the kinder of him since I only met him through *Swann*, that is, not so very long ago.

The only thing I *may* ask M. Straus is the following: so as not to bother him, I've arranged *to retrieve the famous cheque* and have it re-endorsed in my name by *M. Raphaël-Georges Lévy*. Monsieur Straus told me that the simplest way to cash it might be through Rothschild's. Perhaps, if he asked them (or, if it's a nuisance for him, if Guiche did, though I doubt if Guiche would have the necessary authority), they might agree to discount it for me. (I use a term which I don't really understand, but which may mean to buy at less than its face-value.) This face-value is 30,000 francs, plus five years' accrued interest (lack of funds was the reason why the Comptoir d'Escompte didn't pay R.G. Lévy). The delay was thus Warburg's fault, for sending the cheque without transferring the money, which amounts, I believe, to some 40,000 francs.

You will kindly refrain from speaking ill of my aunt, who has behaved very badly, but firstly, I feel badly about my rudeness to her in the past. Then again, now that I've discovered that she gave the other tenants a rent reduction during the war, which she didn't do for me, if I have a chance (very unlikely) of her asking the new landlord not to demand more from me than the rest (apart from Williams,[8] whose rent I don't think was reduced), that chance would vanish if she thought that friends I love as much as I do you were speaking ill of her. Still, I might add that her behaviour throughout has been such that I dare not even mention it to my brother, who has a violent temper, in case he goes round to tell her off. I've just received from her, in answer to my letter asking if it's really true that etc., a 'masterpiece' of a note in which she says that she prefers 'the sweet name of aunt to that of landlady', and that, once I'm better and we can meet again, the advantage of her decision will be that, from now on, we need talk only of literature, not the house!

Which reminds me that I'm always talking to you about extremely boring things! Don't dream of replying. I've told you all this only to give you an idea of my worries at a time when I'm behind with work because of laryngitis and receive letters from my editor telling me to hurry it up. But all this doesn't make it easy to work!

My devoted and most grateful respects, Madame, and to Monsieur Straus.

Marcel Proust

1. She had agreed to her portrayal in 'Dans les mémoires de Saint-Simon', which Proust was writing for inclusion in *Pastiches et mélanges*. An extended version of his parody of Montesquiou at Versailles (see letter 41), it is a masterpiece of social satire, mingling Proust's acquaintance with personalities of the Régence. See *CS-B*, 38–59.

2. The passage quoted in letter 60, n. 4.

3. See letter 42.

4. This was to offend Louis d'Albufera doubly: he too had a Napoleonic title and his mother was a Cambacérès.

5. See letter 25, n. 13.

6. Proust goes on to raise topics discussed in letter 28 to Walter Berry.

7. See letter 26, n. 2.

8. Dr Charles Williams, an American dentist.

31   To Madame Soutzo

Saturday evening [1 February 1919]

Princesse,

This is only a note, but the reply is urgent, as the publisher can't wait any longer for *Pastiches et mélanges* and I never see you alone. In any case, even if I knew you were to be at the Ritz tomorrow, I can't be sure of getting up, having yet again spent some days in bed with a sore throat and fever. So here is what I wanted to ask you.

As my Saint-Simon pastiche is already too long, rather than cut short people whom I was to portray in detail, I'm keeping them back for the second Saint-Simon pastiche, the one to come later[1] (thus, I don't write about Mme de Chevigné,[2] even though her name would do perfectly for the visit of her friend the King of England[3]). All the same, considering the place you've held in my life for the past two years, I wish to usher in my portrait of you in the second Saint-Simon by mentioning you in the first (the one about to appear). But I can't do so without being sure that the passage (far less eulogistic than I would like, than it ought to be, than it will be in the second Saint-Simon where you will be queen, but I've been at my wit's end for want of space) meets with your approval. It goes like this[4] (but I must have your consent by this evening, if possible):

I speak of Mme de Noailles, and continue: 'she was cousin to the Princesse Soutzo, the only woman, as is well-known to my cost, to have succeeded in tempting me out of the seclusion[5] wherein I have lived since the deaths of the Dauphin and Dauphine. Why she should have succeeded where so many have failed, I cannot say. She resembled Minerva as that goddess is depicted in exquisite miniature on the earrings my mother bequeathed me; and the Goddess of Wisdom[6] also lent her beauty. I was ensnared by her charms and bestirred myself only to visit her. But I shall wait for a later chapter in these Memoirs to speak at greater length of her, and of her husband,[7] who was renowned for his valour and one of the truest men I have known.'

Princesse, I need your answer by this evening if possible, and it would be very helpful if you could return this letter, even in the case of consent, so that I may have the passage in front of me.

You thoroughly offended me the other night, as well as diminishing yourself in my eyes, by behaving in a way that I would never dream of behaving towards you. An almost instantaneous reversal only made me feel it the more keenly.[8]

I beg you to tell me what you think of the passage. I may have to cut it a little, because of a last-minute muddle, but I would like to know that at least nothing in it displeases you. I shall also 'kick off' with Morand[9] in this Saint-Simon, but in a completely different passage, nowhere near you.

Kindly accept, Princesse, my respectful regards
Marcel Proust

1. See previous letter, n. 1. Although 'Dans les mémoires de Saint-Simon' ends with the words 'To be continued', no sequel has been found.

2. Comtesse Adhéaume de Chevigné: see letter 75, n. 1.

3. King Edward VII: see *CS-B*, 43, 48.

4. See the passage quoted in letter 33 to Mme de Noailles. Proust was to alter this passage, Mme Soutzo having pointed out that she and Mme de Noailles were not related.

5. Cf. Proust's avowal to Mme Soutzo in letter 21.

6. Allusion to Athena, often associated with Minerva. There is a photograph of Mme Soutzo as Minerva: see letter 161, n. 9.

7. In the published version, this ending refers to Mme de Chevigné and her husband: see *CS-B*, 46.

8. In her letter of consent, Mme Soutzo asked what she had done to offend Proust. He replied on 3 February: 'I'll give you the explanation you ask for, and which is your due, both insofar as it's specific (that is, offensive to me) and general (the most hurtful sense of all, the one which diminishes you in my eyes). But the remark itself is so insignificant in its terms (if extremely significant in its implications) that I feel it should remain in the domain of speech, where it began, and not solemnized in a letter.'

9. Paul Morand is depicted as the king's envoy.

32 To Gaston Gallimard[1]

[Around 22 May 1919]

Dear Friend,

I remain utterly unconvinced by your letter. And I'm particularly sad that mine (you must be thinking of the previous one, for I don't see what there could have been in the last to have produced such an effect, nor indeed in the one before that) drives you to 'despair'. My one desire is to make you happy, so I'm the one in despair.

You play with words when you say that you're a publisher, not a printer. One of an editor's principal functions is to get his books printed. You've been directing plays in America,[2] and that, it seems to me, rather than any distinction you make between publisher and printer, accounts for my having, in À l'Ombre des jeunes filles en fleurs, the most botched publication imaginable.[3] Supposing for a moment that all the misprints are my fault, proof-readers exist for a purpose. You say that you've gone from printer to printer, and I blush with gratitude, but if so, it was to end up where you began, his name being the same as the one I was given when we left La Semeuse in December.[4] He may have admirable qualities, but I beg you to keep copies of the extracts he made from À l'Ombre des jeunes filles en fleurs for the NRF.[5] We'll go over them together one evening, either here or at the Ritz, and you'll see what a prodigy he is. Allow me this satisfaction, and I promise you the shock of your life.

I gather, dear friend and editor, that you dislike my method of proof-correcting.[6] I admit that it complicates matters (though not the matter of the NRF!). But you were familiar with it when you asked me to leave Grasset[7] and come to you, for you were here with Copeau[8] when he exclaimed, on seeing the corrected proofs from Grasset: 'But it's a new book!' I can explain myself to you in two ways, first and foremost by stating that you cannot have moral quality without material change. Since you're good enough to see a certain richness that you like in my books, remind yourself that it is precisely due to the extra nourishment with which I re-infuse them through living,[9] and of which these additions are the material form. And remind yourself as well that if you gave me signal proof of your friendship by asking me for my books, it was also out of friendship that I gave them to you. This may have been to my advantage when I sent you *Swann* and you rejected it, in that the lustre of your imprint might have rubbed off a little on my book. Since appearing under Grasset's imprint, it has made so many friends, I can't think how, that I could have let him publish the sequels without fear of their going unnoticed. In taking them away from him and giving them to you, I was obeying the dictates of friendship.

Alas, you went abroad, since when I've received a constant stream of other people's books (for some publishers have printers, to judge by the pile of uncut books at my bedside) but not a single proof.[10] I think they're on the way. I'm not as strong as I was, and it may be my turn to be a little slow. As long as everything comes out in my lifetime, all will be well, and should it turn out otherwise, I've left all my exercise-books[11] numbered and ready for you, and I count on you to complete publication. I haven't dealt with the other points in your letter, but exhaustion overcomes me and I leave you with a warm handshake.

Marcel Proust

I still haven't received my royalties from Grasset.[12] I leave that to you. This letter would have gone off but for a charming note which I've just received from Grasset, asking me for an extract from my book for a review which he is co-founding with Jean Dupuy,[13] and which has a circulation of 200,000. I shall tell him that it's impossible, the book being about to come out. In fact, June seems a dreadful month to me,[14] but we had better not lose one more day.

1. Gaston Gallimard (1881–1975), head of N.R.F. Éditions, the publishing arm of the *NRF*.

2. Gallimard had accompanied the Théâtre du Vieux Colombier to New York: see n. 8.

3. Proust had repeatedly protested about the innumerable misprints, unreadably small type and compressed lines of *Within a Budding Grove*.

4. Gallimard had moved from La Semeuse to Louis Bellmand, who was in future to share the printing of Proust's book with Frédéric Paillart.

5. In its first post-war issue on 1 June, the *NRF* was to print 'The Quarrel with Gilberte', an extract taken from various pages of *Within a Budding Grove*: II, 185 *et seq.*

6. On each new set of proofs, Proust would correct and recorrect till the galleys wore thin, often pasting on long additional passages.

7. Bernard Grasset (1881–1955), the only publisher to accept *Swann's Way* in 1913. He had no sooner published the book (at Proust's expense) and agreed to take its sequels than he was called up and forced to close. In 1916, Gallimard reopened negotiations with Proust, who promptly broke his contract with Grasset.

8. Jacques Copeau (1879–1949), pioneer of the theatre. A co-founder of the *NRF*, he had launched the experimental Théâtre du Vieux Colombier under its aegis in 1913. In 1918, he was invited to take the company to New York for the winter season.

9. Cf. *Time Regained*, where the narrator envisages creating his book 'in the same way that Françoise made that *bœuf à la mode* which M. de Norpois had found so delicious because she had enriched its jelly with so many carefully chosen pieces of meat.' VI, 434.

10. Proust was impatiently awaiting proofs of *The Guermantes Way*.

11. See letter 4, n. 10.

12. Grasset had offered to waive Proust's penalty for breaking his contract if Proust would waive his royalties, which amounted to less.

13. Proprietor of *Le Petit Parisien* and similar large-circulation newspapers.

14. *Swann's Way* (in the new N.R.F. edition), *Within a Budding Grove* and *Pastiches et mélanges* were all scheduled for publication on 21 June.

33 To Madame de Noailles[1]

102 boulevard Haussmann
[Tuesday 27 May 1919]

Madame,

What a resurrection of joy after so many years to see that Handwriting, whose wondrous machicolations would seemingly suffice to protect the Garden of Eden, where the Angel (now redundant), bearer of the flaming sword, stands sentinel.[2] Your kindness in writing to me as you did,[3] and so promptly ('qui cito dat, bis dat'),[4] has revived those feelings which I had formerly, before you bruised them somewhat.[5] And it saddens me to think that just as this respectful affection is reawakened, within a week three books of mine are to appear in which chance has left you so little space: some lines in the Renan pastiche[6] which you know and a line in a new Saint-Simon pastiche[7] which you don't know (perhaps also a word or two in the *Mélanges*, I'm not sure, I didn't make the selection).

I won't forget today's kindness and, before too long, will have the opportunity to give my gratitude fitting expression.[8] But it grieves me to think that, had I solicited and received your note a month ago, I could have put in one book what I can now only put in another.

I also have to thank M. de Noailles[9] (how the war has enhanced his handsomeness!). I shall find a way. How good he was to have mentioned it to you. Kindly tell him (be sure not to forget to tell him) how touched I am.

Need I tell you that your wonderful letter is no more than an exquisite drawing as far as I'm concerned, and I can't make out a single word. Bernstein's[10] name alone stood out, and I knew why it was there. But I had had him telephoned months ago, long before I troubled you, and he, like me, had lost the address. But it doesn't matter because Guiche (who has been a tower of strength throughout this dreadful move, seeing directors, extracting money from them when I thought I was in their debt)[11] has got one of his engineers to inquire about firms that might be prepared to turn my suberine[12] into bottle-corks.

In respectful and admiring gratitude,
Marcel Proust

Having finished my letter to you, I'm gazing for the umpteenth time at the exquisite Moorish design and, lo and behold, I see the words Cité du Retiro,[13] an Elysian Elysium which, inscribed by you, becomes the 'Elysian Fields' blazing in letters of fire. Tomorrow I shall send round to the Cité du Retiro to discover what lies behind this mysterious address, and perhaps find a buyer for the cork that won't fit into the lodgings where I'm to go after leaving the boulevard Haussmann. (The house has been sold to a banker, who, Josse-like,[14] wants to turn it into a bank and, in so doing, evict all the tenants, unaware that he is killing at least one of them by uprooting him.) However, I suppose that fortresses, even ones made of cork,[15] have had their day. And it occurs to me that one would do better to carry the means of defence in one's ears.[16] Madame Simone[17] mentioned ivory ear-plugs (how I long to know more about them!), and the Duchesse de Guiche[18] cotton-wool pads with vaseline. But no doubt these ladies are less sensitive to noise than me, I'm dreadfully ill, dying.

1. Comtesse de Noailles, *née* Princesse Anne-Élisabeth Bassaraba de Brancovan (1876–1933), the prolific poet and novelist Anna de Noailles, formerly assiduously cultivated and panegyrized by Proust.

2. Allusion to Genesis, III, 24.

3. Proust had told her husband that he was looking for a buyer for the cork that lined his bedroom walls.

4. 'He gives twice who gives quickly.'

5. Their friendship had cooled in 1909 as a result of a *faux pas* on his part.

6. See letter 10, n. 11. Proust/Renan writes: 'If she is the author of the poems attributed to her, the Comtesse de Noailles has given us an extraordinary *oeuvre*, superior by far to the Koheleth [Ecclesiastes], to Béranger's songs. But how it falsifies her social position! As, indeed, she seems aware, living a bucolic life of utter simplicity and seclusion, if perhaps of a certain boredom, a little orchard her sole interlocutor.' *CS-B*, 37-8.

7. See letter 31, n. 1. Proust/Saint-Simon writes: 'I shall have occasion to speak of her at greater length as being more gifted for poetry than any woman of her time, one in whom the miracle of the celebrated Sévigné is renewed, if not enhanced. [. . .] Daughter of Brancovan, ruling Prince, or Hospodor, as they say there, of Walachia, her beauty is equal to her genius.' *CS-B*, 51. Allusion to the Brancovans' pretensions to the throne of Romania.

8. Allusion to the missing sequel to the Saint-Simon pastiche: see letter 31, n. 1.

9. Mathieu, Comte (later Marquis) de Noailles (1873-1942).

10. The playwright Henri Bernstein (1876-1953), who had originally suggested that Proust use cork as insulation against noise.

11. Guiche had obtained him FF40,000 in compensation from the Banque Varin-Bernier.

12. Laminated cork.

13. Apparently a firm with premises off the Champs-Élysées.

14. Allusion to the goldsmith in Molière's *L'Amour Médecin*, whose name has become a by-word for self-interest.

15. An untranslatable pun on the word for cork and the fortified medieval city of Liège.

16. See the description of the narrator's experiments with ear-plugs: III, 78-91.

17. Well-known actress.

18. See letter 144.

34 To Henri Ghéon[1]

[Early June 1919]

Sir,

You've written a very fine book[2] about which I'll talk to you when not quite so ill. It would be unintelligent of me to talk to you about it with intelligence; there are spiritual dilemmas which the intelligence cannot foresee, nor yet the heart.[3] It's not enough to say: 'Poor soul, that's it!'.[4]

Meanwhile, your book both delights and disappoints me. For we lose thereby our most exacting judge of literary matters (as you see, I bear no grudge).[5] You once reproached Jammes for disallowing to criticism what the Popes themselves allowed.[6] You must have deprived that same criticism of the prerogatives of reason to a far greater extent than Jammes ever did. But sad as one is to see you leave office, one knows that it is to assume a higher one. And it's a further consolation that not all ties between the two Ghéons appear to be severed. I don't say that as a criticism, believing that your faith is all the deeper for being attached to your primary roots, to that 'fibrous substance' which

> 'Can never desist
> From the quest for deep waters
> On which the summits insist'[7]

as Paul Valéry says, in lines that remind me of Racine's *Cantiques*, and where, in a poetry worthy of Malherbe, Mallarmé breathes his last.[8]

What also makes me believe that we haven't lost the old Ghéon, while confirming my belief in the sincerity of the new, is that your form, heightened, remains impeccable. I was much struck, after the disparaging article you wrote about my book, by its extreme difference from the letter which I subsequently received from you.[9] I quite realize that one praises more readily in a private letter than a printed review, but that didn't seem to me to account for the huge discrepancy between the two forms of attention which you graciously afforded me. You told me that because the book was so much to your taste, you didn't like to overpraise it. Now, I took you at your word. How uncommonly scrupulous, I said to myself, here we have a critic who adds a hair shirt to 'His quill of iron which is not without beauty'.[10] He hasn't the slightest reason for duplicity where I'm concerned, therefore he must be a man of scruple, and, despite what he writes about Jammes, a Christian. So I wasn't far wrong. And if I was, just a little, there would be no great harm done, and if your letter was partly prompted by goodwill, your article remaining the expression of your opinion, then we need only carry forward this tiny flaw in the absolute and, for the sake of posterity, add it to the rational thinker's account without unduly depleting that of the mystic. The latter, in any case, will get the credit and arouse all the greater interest from the fact that your conversion, being completely unorthodox, owes nothing to the neo-Catholic movement of recent years.

I haven't said any of the things I wanted to say to you, but I have a fever of 30° and you haven't heard the last of me.[11]

Your devoted
Marcel Proust

1. Henri Ghéon (Dr Henri Vangeon, 1875–1944), critic, dramatist and mystic. Gide's intimate friend, Ghéon was a co-founder of the *NRF*.
2. *The Man Born of War: a convert bears witness*.
3. See n. 11.
4. 'Pauvre âme, c'est cela!', final line of the poet's dialogue with God in Verlaine's 'Sagesse'.
5. See n. 9.
6. Reviewing Jammes's *Christian Georgics* in 1912, Ghéon suggested that since Jammes claimed divine inspiration, his works should be immune to criticism and answerable only to God.
7. 'La substance chevelue / Par les ténèbres élue / Ne peut s'arrêter jamais / Jusqu'aux entrailles du monde / De poursuivre l'eau profonde / Que demandent les sommets'. Paul Valéry, 'Palme'.
8. Proust explains this comment in letter 65.
9. Allusion to Ghéon's sarcastic, patronizing review of *Swann's Way* (*NRF*, January 1914) and his reply to Proust's lengthy riposte. (In which Proust had the satisfaction of citing an encomium from Jammes: see letter 36, n. 7. For Proust's significant remarks to Ghéon, see letter 18, n. 5, letter 55, n. 22, letter 82, n. 3.)
10. Allusion to Alfred de Vigny's 'L'Ésprit pur': 'J'ai mis sur le cimier doré du gentilhomme / Une plume de fer qui n'est pas sans beauté'. Vigny, no less vain of his noble ancestry than of his poetry, turns the patrician's feather in his helmet into a quill of iron, to which, Proust suggests, Ghéon, equally vain, adds the hair-shirt of faith.
11. This letter was never sent. See Proust to Ghéon, early July: 'A month ago, I wrote you a long (very admiring) letter about your book, and therefore talked a great deal about you. But it seemed to me so unwise to talk of a state (in the spiritual sense) through which one has yet to pass, which one merely anticipates with the intelligence and the heart, that, regarding this state, I feared sinning in my letter through want – or excess – of intelligence.'

35 To Jean Cocteau[1]

[Shortly before 19 June 1919]

My dear Jean,

I read and re-read *Le Coq et l'Arlequin*,[2] and I marvel. There is not a thought which isn't profound, not a sentence which hasn't an unbelievable felicity. It could be you speaking when one reads: 'The Source nearly always disparages the direction taken by the river.' The ideas underlying the subtitle 'Sense': 'What is displeasing is their good music'[3] are especially startling. I wholly endorse 'The orifice is unimportant',[4] for I don't believe that you direct it against longer works. That we should always think alike about Modern Art, supposing that you really have read *Swann* or merely something in *À l'Ombre des jeunes filles en fleurs*, proves it.[5] But you express these things better (having discovered them for yourself). I envy you your arresting formulations. I find all the background to the story of *Parade*[6] fascinating to a degree! Nijinsky's exit[7] is astonishing. Certain ideas are self-contradictory (for example, 'We must all shout "Down with Wagner" along with Saint-Saëns' and 'How can one not defend Strauss against those who prefer Puccini'). But that enchants me, for I like people to show me their different faces. I'm always contradicting myself.

Talking of Saint-Saëns, I confess that he has always bored me sick (Gounod, in *Faust*, even more so), and I couldn't believe my ears when Stravinsky called his C-minor Symphony a masterpiece, superior to anything by Franck. Still, it seems a little hard to lump him in with Charpentier and Bruneau.[8] Perhaps the only point on which I would disagree with you is that of 'everyday music',[9] at least when considered as the only lasting music. There are times (after 'The Temple that was'[10] How idiotically precious!) when it's necessary to prefer the even,[11] which doesn't mean (though I'm not an admirer of Verlaine) that there are not other times when it becomes necessary to prefer the uneven.[12] If I stop short of the 'bottle',[13] it's because that would be as much of an affectation on my part as to talk about 'amphorae', though the other way round, for I haven't had the opportunity, except during my military service, which I did when too young,[14] of coming across 'bottles'.

You know how down-to-earth I am in my life. I made no attempt at an 'artistic' décor, I had cork when it was noisy, etc. But for me to talk of 'bottles' would be to romanticize. Because of my state of health, I always had the people who use them come to the house. One last quibble, to prove sincerity of admiration. I detest Wilde[15] (I should say I don't know him), and am doing my best not to come round to Strauss.[16] But it's not a crime to have taken a risqué joke as the theme for a serious work. It has happened hundreds of times in Literature. In Art, it's often the opposite. Suppose one were to take the religious painting of the Renaissance as Gospel! Had Racine taken *Phèdre* from a Greek curtain-raiser, his play would have been just as great. What a beautiful statement about the original artist and the copyist.[17] What a joy to hear you speak of Chardin, Ingres, Manet.[18] Unfortunately, I've never seen a Cézanne. Where can his painting be seen?

Very affectionately yours,
Marcel Proust

1. Jean Cocteau (1889–1963). An early admirer of his versatile talents, Proust was later critical of his desire to shock and his appetite for social life. Cf. Octave in his later avatar as a flawed genius: V, 693–6.

2. A pamphlet which was to become the manifesto of the group of French composers known as 'Les Six'. For Cocteau's aphorisms in the original French, see *Le Coq et l'Arlequin* (Paris, Stock, 1978).

3. 'The bad music despised by highbrows is very pleasing. What is displeasing is their good music.' Op. cit., 50. Cf. *The Guermantes Way*, 518.

4. '*Short works.* IN CERTAIN WORKS DEPTH IS EVERYTHING – THE ORIFICE IS UNIMPORTANT.' Ibid, 59.

5. 'WHEN A WORK IS IN ADVANCE OF ITS TIME, IT IS TIME WHICH LAGS BEHIND.' Ibid., 47. Cf. Proust: 'The time [...] a person requires [...] to penetrate a work of any depth is merely an epitome, a symbol, one might say, of the years, the centuries even, that must elapse before the public can begin to cherish a masterpiece that is really new.' II, 120.

6. Cocteau's and Diaghilev's ballet, *Parade*, outraged a public witnessing the last murderous battles of the war: it was a burlesque; danced to jazz music, it had weird sound-effects (added by Cocteau to Satie's score) that led Apollinaire to coin the term surrealism; it introduced Cubism on a wider stage, in the form of Picasso's décor.

7. Allusion to the dancer's prodigious leap in Vaudoyer's and Diaghilev's *Spectre de la Rose*. See Cocteau, 85.

8. Opera composers of the Massenet school.

9. 'Enough of clouds, waves, aquaria, water-nymphs and night-scented air; we need an earthbound music, an *everyday* music.' Ibid., 61.

10. 'And the moon sinks over the temple that was': title of one of Debussy's *Images*

for piano which, Cocteau claims, brought about the 'Debussy-ist abuse' of music. *Ibid.*, 56.

11. *le pair*. i.e. Proust prefers classical form. See following note.

12. *l'impair*. Allusion to the first verse of Verlaine's well-known poem defining Symbolism: 'De la musique avant toute chose, / Et pour cela, préfère l'impair / Plus vague et plus soluble dans l'air, / Sans rien en lui qui pèse ou qui pose.' ('Let us have music above all things, / And to this end choose the uneven / More vague, more dissolving in the air, / Nothing to weigh it down nor to alight.') Cocteau, so as to reverse the message, deliberately misquotes. *Ibid.*, 60-1.

13. 'A Holy Family isn't necessarily a Holy Family; it's also a pipe, a bottle, a card-game, a tobacco pouch': *ibid.*, 62. Cocteau alludes to Cubist still-life painting. Proust means that he is unfamiliar with the litre-bottles of rough red wine issued to French soldiers. See following note.

14. Proust did a year's national service at the age of nineteen (just before the two-year term became mandatory) and was to look back on his time as an infantry soldier at Orléans as one of the happiest years of his life. Cf. the narrator's delight in the military comradeship of Doncières in *The Guermantes Way*.

15. After their only meeting, in 1891, it seems that Wilde, arriving to dine at boulevard Malesherbes and finding Proust's parents there, had turned and fled with a disparaging remark. Yet Proust writes about Wilde sympathetically, notably in his dissertation on the plight of inverts at the beginning of *Sodom and Gomorrah*. See also 'Sainte-Beuve and Balzac', *AS-B*, 65.

16. There is no reference to Wilde or the Strauss/Wilde opera *Salome* in *Le Coq et l'Arlequin*.

17. 'An original artist is incapable of copying. Thus he has only to copy to be original.' *Ibid.*, 77.

18. 'For the past decade, the Masters of French painting have been Chardin, Ingres, Manet, Cézanne, and the foreigner has come to join his talents to their school. I now predict that French music will influence the world.' *Ibid.*, 65-6.

36 To Jacques Porel

[Shortly after 15 July 1919]

[ ][1] I shall have left the rue Laurent-Pichat[2] by the time you get back. I'll miss the black-and-white flowers on the red background. But I've written a description of them[3] which I'll send you as soon as I've moved. Reynaldo Hahn told me of an apartment on the rue de Rivoli going for 3000 francs (I spend that in a week). The Princesse Soutzo saw one for 30,000 (she calls her morning outings promenades in search of an apartment for me!) and said: 'I agree that it seems very expensive, even for Céleste'. Kindly inform your Mother that I keep neither piano nor mistress at rue Laurent-Pichat. I'm not to blame for the noises that bring complaints from

every floor in turn. Whereas my neighbours on the other side of the partition make love with a frenzy which makes me jealous.[4] When I think that this sensation has less effect on me than a glass of cold beer, I envy people who are capable of uttering such cries that, at first, I thought someone was being murdered, but I realized what was happening when the woman's cries quickly resumed an octave below the man's, and was reassured. This racket, which must be audible over distances as great as the cry of those mating whales described by Michelet as rising like the twin towers of Notre-Dame,[5] is no fault of mine. All I know is asthma [. . .]

An article which the *NRF* assured me would be a bouquet of flowers turned out to be a cartload of excrement. A metamorphosis for which M. Vandérem[6] will have to answer at the gates of heaven. Mark you, I find it only natural that people should dislike *Swann* (myself in particular). But Vandérem (and this is the comic part) wrote to me a few months ago saying exactly the opposite in so many words. His is certainly not the most agreeable letter I have received about *Swann* (have you seen the wonderful letter I had from Francis Jammes?),[7] but, miraculously, it says the opposite in identical terms. For example: in Vandérem's letter: '*Swann* is exactly the sort of book I like, you have the art of putting in everything.' In the article by the self-same Vandérem: '*Swann* is exactly the sort of book I dislike, etc.'[8] I pity critics. [. . .]

1. Passage cut in the original.
2. Proust had been renting an apartment from Porel's mother, Réjane: see letter 12.
3. See the wallpaper in the narrator's room at Doncières: III, 95.
4. Cf. M. de Charlus's first encounter with Jupien, overheard by the narrator: IV, 10–11.
5. Allusion to Jules Michelet's *La Mer* (1861).
6. Fernand Vandérem (1864–1939), a reviewer on *La Revue de Paris*.
7. Proust treasured Jammes's encomium of *Swann's Way* in 1913, in which the poet compares him to Shakespeare, Cervantes, La Bruyère and Balzac.
8. Reviewing *Swann's Way* and *Within a Budding Grove*, Vandérem called Proust 'bizarre, undisciplined, abnormal', saying of the novels: 'they are the opposite of everything I like, namely, order, selection, sobriety. Technically speaking [they are] not books at all, but a ragbag of memories and impressions.'

37 To Daniel Halévy[1]

[Saturday evening, 19 July 1919]

My dear Daniel,

Tonight, when for so long I've had such worthwhile things to write to you (it has taken a state *approaching death* for me still not to have told you what I think of your *wonderful* book,[2] for the booklet[3] which you lent me still to be on my bedside table, for me still not to have resigned myself, after having searched in vain for weeks for first editions of my books (bought up by I don't know which bookshop) to sending you more ordinary copies, which will at least allow you to read me if you wish), I'm writing to tell you how much I deplore your *Figaro* manifesto.[4] Disapproval of a manifesto is no less futile than the manifesto itself. The excuse for this one, you say, is that it is in answer to another, the 'Bolshevik' manifesto.[5] I haven't read the latter, not knowing where to find it, and don't doubt that it's absurd. But if I were less tired, I could show you absurdities galore in the *Figaro* manifesto. No right-minded person would dispute that, by de-nationalizing a work, one deprives it of its universal value, nor that the general flourishes when the particular is at its height.[6] But isn't it a truth of the same order to say that one takes away a work's universal and even its national value by seeking to nationalize it? The mysterious laws governing the emergence of not only aesthetic but also scientific truths are distorted from the moment an outside argument intervenes. The scientist who does France the greatest honour through the laws he brings to light, will cease to do her honour if that is what he seeks, not the truth alone, and will no longer uncover the unique connection which is what a law *is*. I would be ashamed to state anything so simple, but I don't understand how it escapes a mind like yours.

One would weep with joy to learn that France had been appointed custodian of world literature, but it's a little shocking to see us assume that role for ourselves.[7] This 'hegemony', born of 'Victory', is an unconscious reminder of 'Deutschland über alles' and, for that reason, rather distasteful. To know how to temper such pride with modesty used to be one of the characteristics of our race (can it be good French, to talk of a French 'race'?).[8]

Nobody admires the Church more than I do, but it's a bit much to disassociate oneself from Homais[9] to the extent of saying that it has been the guardian of the human spirit for all time.[10] True, Catholic 'unbelievers' exist.[11] But these, chief of whom was, I suppose, Maurras,[12] didn't exactly rally to the cause of French justice at the time of the Dreyfus Affair. Why take such a peremptory tone with other countries in matters like literature, where one rules only by persuasion? Time and again, you say 'we mean' (in the sense of 'we intend, brooking no argument'). That doesn't have the ring of the 'Defenders of the Faith'. And even in a manifesto that is so resolutely French, you adopt a Germanic tone. Needless to say, were I to read the 'Bolshevik' manifesto, I would certainly find it a thousand times worse than yours. But yours makes the cardinal error of being a manifesto. No manifesto could ever do France as much honour, nor serve her as well, as any one of your own works.

Your admiring friend,
Marcel Proust

1. Daniel Halévy (1872–1962), historian and critic, son of the author and librettist Ludovic Halévy, Mme Straus's cousin. An ex-pupil of the Lycée Condorcet, he was a co-founder of *Le Banquet*, the magazine which had published Proust's early work: see letter 10, n. 14.

2. *Charles Péguy et Les Cahiers de la Quinzaine*.

3. A bound copy of Proust's essay, written for the *Figaro* in 1907, about the extraordinary case of an acquaintance who committed first matricide, then suicide. See 'Sentiments filiaux d'un parricide': *CS-B*, 150–9.

4. 'In favour of a Party of Intelligence', *Le Figaro*, 19 July. Drafted by the right-wing Catholic journalist Henri Massis, its signatories included Jacques Bainville and Charles Maurras of *L'Action française*, Jean Schlumberger of *Le Figaro*, the writers André Beaunier, Paul Bourget and Henri Ghéon and, surprisingly, Daniel Halévy, Edmond Jaloux and Jean-Louis Vaudoyer.

5. The Communist Party Manifesto appeared in *L'Internationale* of 7 June.

6. For example, doctrines such as racism, nationalism and reasons of State, invoked at the time of the Dreyfus Affair.

7. The *Figaro* called for 'the rebuilding of public morale in France by the lofty paths of the intelligence and the classical tradition, the intellectual federation of Europe and the world under the aegis of a victorious France, guardian of all civilization.'

8. 'We believe – and the world believes with us – that it lies within the destiny of our race to defend man's spiritual values. Victorious France must regain her sovereign place in the intellectual order, the sole order through which domination may legitimately be exercised.' *Ibid*.

9. The proverbially anti-clerical character in *Madame Bovary*.

10. 'One of the Church's clearest duties over the centuries has been to protect the human mind from its own aberrations, the human spirit from self-destruction, and doubt from eroding reason, thus preserving rational thought as the right and prerogative of mankind.' *Figaro*.

11. See Proust to Georges de Lauris, 1903, the year of the rigid enforcement of anti-clerical laws: 'Today (and it is to the shame of Catholicism to have accepted their support), the mainstays of the Catholic faction (Barrès etc.) are non-believers. And the clericals don't mind. Once [...] Catholicism is dead in France [...] there will be just as many clericals – more rabidly anti-Semitic, anti-Dreyfusard and anti-liberal than ever, and they will be a hundred times worse.' Letter 251, *Selected Letters Volume One*.

12. Charles Maurras (1868–1952), poet and esssayist, prominent monarchist and nationalist who, with Léon Daudet, had founded *L'Action française* with the aim of promoting anti-Dreyfusism. Proust alludes to the call for the revision of the Dreyfus Case in 1888, following Zola's revelations in his article of perjury and forged evidence.

38 To Abel Desjardins[1]

[July 1919]

When I was still almost a child, one joy lit up unhappy years: it was Abel Desjardins's gift of a photograph, on the back of which he had inscribed these words: 'To my best friend'. Sadly, for the next two years, my joy was blighted, for after the words 'To my best friend' there had followed the qualification 'after X' (I no longer remember his name). This X, whom it so happened I had never met, seemed to me the most enviable chap in the world. But, one day, without my ever knowing what had caused X to do me the infinite kindness of losing favour in his eyes, Abel asked me for the photograph back and returned it with the words 'after X' crossed out. And I hardly knew which of them to thank in my prayers, Abel for his good deed, or X for his misdeed.

So dead has everything related to those years become for me, that, recently, forced to leave the boulevard Haussmann, I set about burning precious letters, unique manuscripts, irreplaceable photographs. All of a sudden, I was confronted by a small boy with a pointed nose and a cheeky expression, and, perched on his head, a three-cornered hat; and I cried out to the person who was helping me by throwing the things I was pulling out of huge sacks on to the fire: 'No, not that one!' It was the photograph in which I was

Abel's best friend, after X, and then, without qualification, his best friend. And I couldn't burn that one, for it was still alive.

Marcel Proust

1. Abel Desjardins (1870–1951), Proust's former schoolfellow at the Lycée Condorcet, now a doctor. This letter accompanied complimentary copies of *Swann's Way*, *Within a Budding Grove* and *Pastiches et mélanges*.

39   To Jean de Gaigneron[1]

8 bis, rue Laurent-Pichat
[Friday evening, 1 August 1919]

Dear friend,

(You don't mind, do you, if I give my feelings for you their precise expression?) And may I in turn count on 'dear friend' from you? Your 'my dear M. Proust' immediately makes me think that I'm vice-president of some provincial Bonapartist committee, and that the signature will read 'Sincerely yours, Napoleon'.

Yet it goes without saying that a letter from Prince Victor[2] would be nothing to me, whereas a note from you is precious. My memory of the said Victor's brother,[3] who was more intelligent than the Pretender, and whom I met at the Princesse Mathilde's when I was little more than a boy, will always be associated with the sort of ice which freezes over when the temperature drops to zero, like the haughty reserve of Princes (for the affability of Highnesses who lack all reserve, see my grandmother's meeting with the Princesse de Luxembourg at Balbec[4] in *À l'Ombre des jeunes filles en fleurs*, or else wait for the Princesse de Parme[5] in its sequel).

Meanwhile, dear friend, I apologize, subject to reciprocity, for not having sent you the books about which you say, with a writer's talent of which I can at least be a judge, the painter's being unknown to me (not for long, I hope), the very things which touch me most deeply. Your intelligence goes so directly to the heart of things that you have read not only my printed book, but the hidden book I had intended to write. And when you talk to me about cathedrals, I can only be moved by an intuition that leads you to divine something I've never mentioned to anybody, and which I write here for the first time; it is this: I had intended giving each section of my book a title: 'West door', 'Windows of the apse' etc., to pre-empt the stupid criticism that my books have no construction, whereas, as I'll show you, their sole merit lies in the solidity of the tiniest part.⁶ I immediately dropped the idea of these architectural titles as too pretentious, but I'm touched that you should have retrieved it through some process of intelligent divination.

If my books haven't yet been sent out to you, any more than to Barrès, France, Madame de Noailles, my dearest friends, the leading critics, it's because first editions have been monopolized and hidden away by some bookshop whose name I don't know, and being unable to get out myself, I've had people scouring Paris without their having found any but copies from the second, third, fourth and fifth, which I couldn't think of sending out. Unfortunately, the first recedes with every day that passes. But if I can't find a first edition for you and few others, I'll send out the second or even the third. Before then, I shall have invited you to dine with me. If I haven't yet done so, it's because I've been so wretchedly ill since my moves. I've been up twice in two months. I keep expecting things to improve and they get worse. I haven't even had the strength to correct my proofs or write a letter. The length of this one having tired me a little, allow me to break it off here, with my grateful and friendly regards.

Marcel Proust

1. Jean, Comte de Gaigneron (1890–1976), a young painter.
2. Napoleon's nephew, Prince Victor-Napoléon (1862–1926).
3. Prince Louis-Napoléon (1864–1932), described in Proust's 'A Historic Salon': see *AS-B*, 152.
4. See II, 319–23.
5. See III, 494–6.
6. Cf. The narrator's reflections on his forthcoming book in *Time Regained*, 431–2.

40 To Daniel Halévy

[Shortly before 13 August 1919]

My dear Daniel,

You were justified, and it was sweet of you to have taken my letter 'in good part'.¹ I must say that yours only half reassures me. Precisely because it's 'a question of civic duty',² it is extremely dangerous to subscribe to wrong ideas because of the virtues of those who express them. For between subscribing to ideas (in that way) and allowing actions a free rein is only a short step. Your example makes it easy to understand that officers who were, if anything, Dreyfusards, should have been revisionists, for they recognized the virtues of General Gonse[3] etc., and had more faith in the General Staff than in the Anarchists. Moreover, I've read the names of those men whom you feel 'that over the years etc.'[4] Is there one among them who would stand up to anything like a searching test?

Your way of looking at things must be right, I hasten to add, to judge by my emotions on reading *Margaret Ogilvy*,[5] where the old lady says to her son: 'Go on, you vote for your Gladstone.' Besides, by 'names' I meant signatories. There's no doubt that the name of Francis Jammes is that of a great writer who has, or had, a happy gift for imagery. But his neo-Catholic stance means that (in a case like this) even his signature carries little weight. Whereas a wonderful letter he wrote me a few years ago[6] is valid because he wrote it *in spite of* his beliefs.

Don't imagine that my lot is a pleasant one. It's atrocious. All I weave is my shroud, and so slowly, so painfully.

Ever your
Marcel Proust

But you don't say where the Bolshevik manifesto is to be found, nor who signed it.[7] Do you happen to remember showing me a letter from a woman who was either English or American? It riled me because, misunderstanding the construction of *Swann*, she said: 'It's got a bit of everything, an old bird-cage etc.' You retorted that on the contrary, I should consider myself lucky to inspire such letters. I wish I could remember who it was from.[8] But I'm sure that you too will have forgotten.

1. See letter 37, on the subject of the *Figaro* 'manifesto'.
2. See Proust to Jacques Rivière, early September: 'Halévy [. . .] had already taken account of my objections and still finds them valid, but felt that he couldn't refuse his signature to men "who have stood up over the years for everything we hold dear". He decided that it was a question of "civic duty".'
3. General Gonse (1838–1917), leading prosecution witness at Dreyfus's first court-martial.
4. See n. 2.

5. Biography of his mother by James Barrie. In an article written after his own mother's death, Proust speaks of the 'the pure and exquisite *Margaret Ogilvy*'. See *AS-B*, 229.

6. See letter 36, n. 7.

7. See letter 37, n. 5.

8. Irène von Fleming, American by marriage. She compared the delights of *Swann's Way* to 'the contents of an old cupboard in the attic'.

41 To Robert de Montesquiou[1]

[Around end August 1919]

Dear Sir,

Pray don't get the impression that this covering note[2] is marked 'Qui accuse s'excuse'.[3] True, you cannot know what has prevented my sending you my books till now. You cannot know (and I'm sure haven't the least desire to know) that a bookshop has been hoarding my first editions like so much butter or coffee, though less palatable, with the result that, unable to discover its name (and not liking to send out less rare copies), I haven't yet sent my books to Monsieur France, nor to Barrès, nor to Madame de Noailles etc., etc. You cannot know either that the house where I used to live having been bought by a banker who has turned it into a bank, I have had to move out, like the other tenants, and that my search for permanent lodgings, so far unsuccessful, has nearly finished me off for good.

But even if unaware of all this, you must, I believe, have heard that, in the guise of Saint-Simon, I have portrayed you at length in a book called *Pastiches et mélanges*, and that this portrait is not a simple reproduction of the one in the *Figaro*,[4] but contains new passages in your praise.[5] And for that reason, even if you haven't received the books, I had hoped for a note from you.[6] It would have been my solace on days when I was in such pain that I found it almost impossible to turn over in my unfamiliar bed.

At long last, I'm about to send you my two books. I trust that the portrait published in *Pastiches* is to your liking[7] and that you deem it worthy of you and also, dare I add, of your faithful and admiring

Marcel Proust

1. Robert, Comte de Montesquiou-Fezensac (1855–1921), poet, aesthete, dandy and wit. Inordinately proud of these roles, as of his lineage, the Count cultivated an extravagant personality, recreated in print in Huysmans's Des Esseintes. For Proust, he was 'A Professor of Beauty' and, in his life-style, a sort of Louis XIV. But, most famously, his speech and manners were to be caricatured in Proust's greatest comic character, the Baron de Charlus. He and Proust kept up a lifelong, often hilariously acrimonious correspondence, but it had virtually ceased with Montesquiou's failing health.

2. This letter accompanied complimentary copies of *Within a Budding Grove* and *Pastiches et mélanges*.

3. *Sic*. Proust inverts the famous proverb.

4. 'Fête chez Montesquiou à Neuilly', Proust's first Saint-Simon pastiche, written in 1904, satirizing the Count's lavish entertainments at his 'Versailles', the sumptuous Pavillon des Muses. *CS-B*, 710–15.

5. 'Dans les mémoires de Saint-Simon': see letter 30, n. 1.

6. In fact, Montesquiou had written Proust a long letter about *Within a Budding Grove*, to which he had no reply. A stickler for etiquette, he was to explain to Mme Straus that he felt unable to write a second time.

7. Proust also felt that he was pleasing Montesquiou by including a portrait of his beloved amanuensis, the late Gabriel de Yturri.

42 To Paul Morand[1]

[Shortly after 10 October 1919]

Dear friend,

This note being written at one of those moments when I'm 'almost dead',[2] you'll forgive its shortcomings. I can't blame you for having published your 'Ode'. The sacrifice of every consideration to Literature, notably the obligations of friendship, is not a dogma I adhere to, but I wholly endorse it. Luckily, in my *Pastiches*, I was able to limit any nastiness to people I don't know, like Mme Blumenthal,[3] M. Vigier, M. de Fels[4] etc. I didn't consider myself bound to the Princesse Murat[5] for inviting me to soirées for thousands of people where one files past as at an Élysée ball. Still, she having lost a son in the war, I felt obliged to add a few friendly remarks, though I needn't have bothered, for apparently the lady is furious.

I would have found it a bloody sacrifice, I admit, had it fallen to me to write those lines (I don't have your text in front of me, and am incapable of going as far as the table to get it) about a friend whose mysterious terrors have seemingly left him pale for all eternity.[6] The obvious implication is that I had been caught in a police raid,[7] or left for dead by apaches. Your poem being very beautiful, you were probably justified in daring to write such things. But knowing your infinite delicacy of heart, what must they not have cost you to write, to publish! The same delicacy has always prevented me from discussing that side of your life with you, let alone with others. As for writing about it, and having it published, I'm not a coward, but truly, I could not have borne the idea of feeling or inflicting such pain.

> 'But this harsh virtue was unknown to me.
> Allow me to admire and not to emulate.'[8]

You were perfectly justified, since you had the stomach for it, and it was even crueller in your case, faced as you were with a friend who, disarmed by his very affection, is willing to respond to the provocations of a Frisch[9] by challenging him to a duel but too broken-hearted to fight you. Your only fault, perhaps, concerns the first (and totally innocuous) part of the 'Ode', not in having written it, but in having 'prattled' it. The other day, for example, there was an article on me by M. Giraudoux,[10] the same M. Giraudoux whose essay in the *NRF*, like his *Elpénor*, is a source of perpetual *enchantment* to me. You having told me what nice things he had said about me, I looked forward to finding them in an article which, delightfully witty and profound like everything M. Giraudoux writes, no sooner mentions me than it embarks on the same old jokes about the boulevard Haussmann, exercise-books, closed shutters,[11] all of which, I suppose, came from you. The article made me laugh till I cried. But about me, frankly, it held not a word of truth.

I didn't know any of the other poems in your book. The last being very good, it allows me to be a little severe on the rest (bar a few, such as the lovely 'Parc de l'ouest'). In fact, dear Walt Whitman of our time and country, you are justified a thousand-fold, and all we need do from now on is to let our subconscious dictate to us unhindered. And that's exactly my own aesthetic. But is it really letting the subconscious speak, simply to take note, with the eyes alone, without any real *sensation*, of ladies' press-studs etc.,[12] delighting the ladies, who must think it the height of originality, but you, dear friend, who are the personification of intelligence, must know that it's the merest notation. You should recite it in your lovely voice, when it would sound dramatic, and thus could only be very beautiful. But it is written, and your voice unheard.

I'll write you a longer letter about my vexation. For if it was necessary to your work to write your 'Ode', it has completely wrecked what is necessary to mine (to my work). For the second volume of my *Pastiches* was to revolve entirely around you and your accomplice in the 'Ode', the Princesse. Yet now I can't publish it, it being infinitely eulogistic, without looking like a coward.[13]

Dear friend, it consoles me nevertheless that, thanks to this Horror portrait with its unshaven face[14] which has known the prelude to death, details of my home life, even down to Céleste's name,[15] should find a place in a work like yours, should be familiar to your dear memory. Moreover, as I say, I fully acknowledge not only your Right, but your Artistic Duty. Truth is all. Still, don't think too badly of me if I tremble a little at what you've done by thus exposing me to public opprobrium, and without a single fact (apaches have always been sweet to me, and routs unknown). Greater men than me were no more philosophical. Degas never forgave Blanche for his portrait, nor Whistler Montesquiou for selling his; Hugo suppressed a name in one of his books; Maeterlinck tried to ban Debussy's *Pelléas*. Your friend is better, but what a bizarre idea, to think that it should be as a result of dreadful terrors. Terror shouldn't make one well.

Your devoted
Marcel Proust

Many thanks for your charming dedication.[16] But, being handwritten, not printed, it will be unseen by the public and do nothing to counteract the 'Ode' wherein you cast me into that Hell reserved by Dante for his Enemies.

1. Paul Morand (1888–1976), novelist, poet and diplomat; Mme Soutzo's future husband. Proust appears frequently in his *Journal d'un attaché à l'ambassade* (Paris, 1949).
2. Allusion to lines in Morand's 'Ode à Marcel Proust': 'I say: / You're looking very well. / You reply: / Dear friend, I nearly died three times today.' The 'Ode' was part of a new collection of his verse, *Lampes à arc*.
3. See letter 25, n. 13.
4. René, Vicomte Vigier and Edmond Frisch, Comte de Fels.
5. Either Princesse Joachim or Princesse Lucien Murat.
6. 'Proust, what routs do you attend at night / to return with eyes so heavy and so lucid? / What forbidden terrors have you known / to come back to us so

forgiving and good?': Morand, 'Ode'. Allusion to Proust's rare visits to a male brothel: see letter 11. There, he may have witnessed sado-masochistic scenes such as that watched by the narrator between Charlus and the brothel-keeper Jupien: VI, 147–84. (The real-life brothel-keeper was Albert Le Cuziat, an ex-footman with a passion for genealogy with whom Proust had struck up a friendship and whose hotel he had helped to buy and furnish. See Tadié, *Marcel Proust*, 788–92.)

7. Jupien's brothel is raided by the police: see VI, 155.

8. 'Mais cette âpre vertu ne m'était pas connue; / [. . .] / Souffrez que je l'admire et ne l'imite point'. Corneille, *Horace*, Act II, scene 3.

9. See note 4. Proust/Saint-Simon says of Frisch that 'he comes from the dregs of society'. *CS-B*, 57.

10. Jean Giraudoux (1892–1944), novelist, playwright and essayist. His article 'Du Côté de chez Marcel Proust' had appeared in *Feuillets d'Art* on 31 May, and his story 'Nuit à Châteauroux' on 1 July. See 'the new writer' in *The Guermantes Way* who has discovered 'the new relationships between things' III, 375–7.

11. 'What is one to make of an author who, one day, aged thirty, shuts himself up and thereafter writes without stopping in a cork-lined room, its windows shuttered against the sounds of the boulevard Haussmann.' Giraudoux, 'Du Côté de chez Marcel Proust'.

12. 'Ladies in gold lamé dressing for dinner, / Their tempers fraying over their press-studs.' Morand, 'L'hôtel contre la nuit'.

13. Presumably the reason why Proust never published his second Saint-Simon pastiche.

14. 'You hold out silk-gloved hands to me; / your beard is growing silently / deep in your jowls.' Morand, 'Ode'.

15. 'Céleste, / sweet for all her sternness, dunks me in the dark juices / of your bedroom / that smells of warm cork and the cold grate.' *Ibid*.

16. 'Marcel, unlike you, whose dedications are baskets of roses left on the thresholds of your books, I am no good at them. But kindly accept, with this, my tender affection and my admiration for your genius.'

43   To Emmanuel Berl[1]

Sunday [26 October 1919]

Dear friend,

Even to write two lines is beyond me. All the same, I want you to know that it gave me enormous pleasure to see the mysterious arabesques which you ironically call handwriting in the letter I received from you this morning. But either because of my eyes or because, this time, you have surpassed yourself, I couldn't make out *a single word*. I knew the letter was from you only because I recognized your particular brand of illegibility. I could tell from the style, as one says: 'this drawing is by so-and-so' without looking at the signature. By dictating your letters to me in future, you will be depriving me of the pleasure of gazing at signs which, though devoid of rational meaning, nevertheless conjure up your face. And at least I'll know what it is that you want to tell me.

Your devoted
Marcel Proust

1. Emmanuel Berl (1892–1976), a gifted young writer who had corresponded with Proust from the trenches. Later a prominent radical and polemicist.

44 To Paul Souday[1]

44 rue Hamelin
10 November 1919

Dear Sir,

I was most touched by the manner, so kindly disposed towards me, in which you discussed my views on Sainte-Beuve,[2] and would have thanked you immediately but for a prolonged bout of asthma which has left me incapable of the smallest movement for the past few days.

I was all the more sensible of your kindness for the fact that, since the calamity which befell you,[3] since I learnt of your heart-rending sorrows which resemble my own, you are, if I may say so, as close to my heart as you are to my mind. I don't believe that I weary you by recalling your loss, for no convention is so absurd as that whereby, once and for all, on a given day, one offers one's sympathy to somebody whose grief will last as long as he himself. Such a loss, so deeply felt, is always 'present', and one is never tardy in speaking of it, never repetitive in recalling it.

To return to Sainte-Beuve (and by the way, you'll find my views on him expressed in my *Pastiches*, perhaps less analytically, it's true, but I think justly),[4] I'm not saying that he is absolutely wrong in each of his 'Lundis',[5] taken on its own. I don't doubt that Comte Molé and Chancellor Pasquier were worthy men.[6] I believe them to be less of a credit to French literature than Flaubert and Baudelaire, in speaking of whom Sainte-Beuve let it be understood that personal friendship, his esteem for their characters, partly dictated the grudging praises he accorded them.[7] I don't think it's always a serious matter to underrate a work of art. Flaubert despised Stendhal, who in turn thought that certain towns in the South were disfigured by their sublime Romanesque churches. But Sainte-Beuve was a critic, and furthermore stated at every opportunity that a critic stands or falls by his judgement of contemporary works. 'It's easy to be right about Virgil or Racine', he said, 'but about a book that has just come out etc.'

In that case, the same judgement about critics who praise only the past may be applied to him! I was therefore dismayed to find my friend Daniel Halévy extolling Sainte-Beuve as the most reliable of guides.[8] Had I not already bored him to tears with reproachful letters for having signed that stupid manifesto on behalf of the Intelligence Party,[9] I would have replied to him in a newspaper.[10] But I was too ill, too weak to hold a pen.

Thank you for announcing your intention to write about *À l'Ombre des jeunes filles en fleurs*. Naturally, nothing would make me happier than to have an article by you, if it doesn't tire you. To live with your grief, to allow atrocious pain slowly to metamorphose into luminous, sorrowful meditation, that is what is most important for you, just now. If to wear yourself out by writing an article of such length, so full of passages of regret, retards by so much as an hour the blessed miracle whereby the memory at the root of all your suffering becomes the sweet companion of your every moment, then I prefer that you shouldn't write it.[11] Besides, I fear that the construction of *À la Recherche du temps perdu* is no more evident in this book than it was in *Swann*. I can quite see readers jumping to the conclusion that, trusting to fortuitous associations and arbitrary ideas, I'm writing the story of my life.

My method of composition is veiled, and all the less immediately apparent for taking shape on a wide scale (forgive this style, it's so long since I've had the energy to write even so much as a dedication that my first, interminable letter shows my fatigue), but to remind myself of its rigour, I need only turn to your review, ill-founded, in my opinion, in which you condemn certain scenes in *Swann* as obscure and unnecessary.[12] If what you had in mind was a scene between two young women[13] (which M. Francis Jammes implored me to cut),[14] it's true that it was 'unnecessary' to the first volume. But its recall is the mainstay of volumes IV and V (because of the jealousy which it inspires etc.). By suppressing it, I wouldn't have materially altered the first volume; on the other hand, because of the interdependence of the parts, I would have brought two entire volumes of which it is the cornerstone crashing down about the reader's head.

Fatigue overcomes me, and I'm greatly afraid of having been the cause of yours. Don't on any account trouble to reply, and kindly accept my admiring and grateful respects.

Marcel Proust

1. Paul Souday (1869–1929), literary critic of *Le Temps*.
2. Allusion to Proust's preface for Blanche, which Souday had reviewed on 31 October as follows: 'In a delightful preface, M. Proust calls M. Jacques-Émile Blanche's *Propos* "the *Causeries du lundi* of painting" [...] and reproaches him, as he does Sainte-Beuve, for "taking the opposite path to that travelled by the artist". In short, for M. Marcel Proust, man does not realize himself in the artist; he rises above himself.' *AS-B*, 252.
3. The death of Souday's mother.
4. Allusion to certain of the essays later collectively known as *Contre Sainte-Beuve*. See letter 10, n. 12.
5. Sainte-Beuve's famous literary articles, collected in *Les Causeries du lundi* and *Nouveaux lundis*, appeared every Monday from 1849 to 1868, first in *Le Constitutionnel* and then in *Le Moniteur Universel*, both organs of the Establishment.
6. Louis-Mathieu, Comte de Molé (1781–1855), Louis-Philippe's ineffectual prime minister, and Étienne Pasquier (1767–1862) ('Chancellor' is a sarcastic reference to the post which he held for a year). Both were eulogized by Sainte-Beuve for political reasons, and slighted by Proust, usually in the same breath, in his essays and novel. See 'The Method of Sainte-Beuve', *AS-B*, 18–22.
7. See *AS-B*, 36–9; 270–1: 278–9.
8. Allusion to 'La Mémoire de Sainte-Beuve' in the *Journal des Débats*, a reassessment of the critic's reputation on the anniversary of his death.
9. See letter 37, letter 40.
10. Proust was to answer Halévy in the *NRF* of 1 January 1920, in his important essay 'On Flaubert's Style': *AS-B*, 270–4. Halévy's reply is quoted in letter 57, n. 12.
11. As Proust feared, when Souday came to review *Within a Budding Grove*, he reiterated his criticisms of *Swann's Way*. See following note.
12. Allusion to Souday's adverse review of *Swann's Way* in 1913, where he criticizes Proust for the banality and irrelevance of his 'childhood memoirs' and the 'off-putting length' of his sentences.
13. The sado-masochistic scene at Montjouvain between Mlle Vinteuil and her friend: I, 190–8.
14. Francis Jammes had written to Proust that the scene was a 'perversion contrary to art'.

45   To Gaston Gallimard

[Shortly before 3 December 1919]

Dear friend,

Forgive me, one should never complain without giving one's reasons. The fact is, I've been so ill lately that writing a line or signing a book has been too much for this odious disease. Today I seem to be entering upon a period of calm, so can write a little. And yet, how difficult it is to embark on recriminations! I've always tried to keep up our friendship – our potential friendship, for unfortunately we've had neither the leisure (you) nor the health (me) to realize its force. It has survived so many little things – which loom large in the long run – (and you yourself have kept it up with so many kindnesses) – that I hesitate to allow the sudden crystallization of unresolved grievances to come between us. Allow me to adjourn the debate, perhaps *sine die*.

But I want to raise two points, one directly affecting me, the other not at all, though it presumably affects you, having been made to me some time ago by M. Boylesve. The first, the one directly affecting me, is this: do you not think (you don't, or you would put it right, so better say, are you not wrong not to think) that, on the question of reprints, you are being deceived by subordinates, printers, I don't know who? (By 'you', I mean you, Gallimard, and Tronche,[1] for I believe that Rivière[2] is concerned solely with the Review, and Copeau with the Theatre.[3]) This is why. I never expected *À l'Ombre des jeunes filles en fleurs* to be a success. If you remember, I told you that I was rather ashamed to bring out this languid interlude on its own. Yet by some extraordinary fluke, this book is a hundred times more successful than *Swann*. I was very touched by the cherished expressions of support which I received for *Swann*, but they were few and far between, and I learnt of them indirectly. In the case of *Les Jeunes filles*, it's completely different. I would appear to be copying my parody of the Goncourts if I told you that the book is on every table in China and Japan.[4] And yet it's partly true. And for France and the neighbouring countries, not just partly, but wholly true. I don't know a banker who hasn't seen it on his cashier's desk or a woman who on her travels hasn't found it in friends' houses in the Pyrenees, the North, Normandy,

Auvergne. I'm in daily contact with the reader in a way I never was in the case of *Swann*. And requests for newspaper articles are no less frequent. None of this makes me in the least vain, for fashion often favours the worst books. It doesn't make me vain, but I do expect it to make me some money. Now, this is precisely where I fear that your subordinates are deceiving you and Tronche. The number of reprints isn't the only test of a reputation, but it is a test, like a Stock Market quotation or a sick man's thermometer. Well, as the sales of *Les Jeunes filles* increase, so the number of reprints diminishes. Not a single copy of the first edition has been available since the beginning of June (or July, I forget which, July, I think), when we were already on the sixth.[5] It's now December, and the vast majority of copies on sale are from the third! Some from the fifth and sixth are also available, I grant you, as in July. But the point is that nothing has been done for five months, even though it was after the sixth reprint that we had reviews in every journal in England (*The Times*,[6] in your opinion the warmest, being the coolest), Italy, Spain and Belgium. All that, four articles by Hermant,[7] and much else besides, produced no reprint for five months, even though there had been six in eight days! I accept that you've always had the next in the shops before the previous one has sold out. But *everybody* is reading this book now, and even those people who haven't read it are buying it, on the pretext that it's all the rage. *This should be reflected in reprints*. Where are they? Grasset did six impressions of *Swann*[8] and, if you remember, you believed that that was well below the true figure, suspecting him of having printed a lot of copies, about double, you thought, without calling them reprints. I don't know whether Grasset would stoop to that, but I know perfectly well that neither you nor Tronche, any more than Rivière, Copeau or my great friend Gide, is capable of it, each of you being, in addition to his other merits, probity incarnate. But are you being deceived? What makes me think so is the inertia, the resistance, which greets anybody who asks for the book at the N.R.F. To go into too much anecdotal detail would overtax my strength. But the demand is there. Look into it, I implore you.[9]

While I think of it, let me know if you've found an English translator. It's vitally important. If nothing comes of the lady whose letter I sent you,[10] I could give you the name of the translator of *Jean Christophe*,[11] who might be a good choice. The English being fonder of books than the French, a translation should be a great success.

Now for the matter that doesn't concern me. I had a letter complaining about the N.R.F. from M. Boylesve, who incidentally finds it deplorable that a proof reader had not corrected the misprints in my book. What really riled him is an innovation I know nothing about called something like 'Original Editions'.[12] He sees it as a dubious business practice (this between ourselves, though he didn't ask me to keep it a secret) whereby a reader has to agree to buy a certain number of books in order to get a first edition of the one he wants. He says (I don't remember his exact words and figures, but have kept the letter): 'Your publisher has made me spend 156 francs to get a first edition of one of your books. In future, for the first time in my life, I shall take every review-copy he sends me apart from yours to the *quais*.'[13] Perhaps he hasn't understood this innovation (which doesn't affect me personally and is none of my business). But he is very annoyed. If you agree, I'll reimburse him (out of my own pocket, naturally, but pretending that it comes from the N.R.F.) the 156 francs (or whatever the sum is, I don't remember exactly) and, in exchange, ask you to promise him a first edition of all my future books.

I don't think I told you about Régnier's charming action on my behalf.[14] But I'm worn out, dear friend, I'm still very ill, and a sudden onset of weakness obliges me to break off.

Tenderly and devotedly yours,
Marcel Proust

Have you had proofs of *Le Côté de Guermantes*? Or a typescript of *Sodome et Gomorrhe*? If so, it would help me to catch up on lost time if you sent them to me immediately.

1. Gustave Tronche (1884–1974), business manager of the N.R.F.
2. Jacques Rivière, editor of the *NRF*: see letter 55.
3. See letter 32, n.8.
4. Proust/Goncourt writes: 'And the minister confessed to a passion for our books, swearing that when in Hong Kong he met a great lady from those parts whose bed-table held only two books: *La Fille Elisa* [novel by Edmond de Goncourt] and *Robinson Crusoe*.' CS-B, 25.
5. The one-volume editions of *Swann's Way* and *Within a Budding Grove*, published in June, each ran to six reprints of 3300 copies.
6. Allusion to (unsigned) reviews of *Pastiches et mélanges* and *Within a Budding Grove* in the *Times Literary Supplement* of 31 July and 14 August.

7. Articles in *Le Temps* and *Le Figaro*, two of which Abel Hermant devoted to *Pastiches et mélanges*, praising Proust as a parodist.

8. Grasset's reprints totalled 3500 copies.

9. Within a week, *Within a Budding Grove* had won the Prix Goncourt (see following letter) and the N.R.F. were to print 13,200 copies of a new two-volume edition (correcting the misprints), and 8000 copies of a new two-volume edition of *Swann's Way*.

10. A Mrs Gertrude Joakes had proposed herself as Proust's translator.

11. The translator of Romain Rolland's novel was Gilbert Cannan.

12. An N.R.F. bookclub: *Swann's Way* and *Within a Budding Grove* were among the books on offer.

13. Second-hand bookstalls along the Seine.

14. Henri de Régnier: see letter 63. He had been campaigning to obtain the French Academy's Grand Prix de Littérature for Proust.

46 To Jacques Boulenger[1]

44 rue Hamelin
[Saturday 20 December 1919]

Dear Sir,

Your wonderful article[2] gave me profound joy. I found it untrue and unjust here and there. But that made no difference to my joy, and this is why: I have an immense liking for your writing, and was convinced that you disliked mine. With your article, a misunderstanding is cleared up, and my liking for you, freed from constraint, can now be expressed. That is the reason for my joy.

I'm so ill at the moment that writing a letter is very difficult. To give you one example in a thousand: since the summer, and even before, I've been too weak to send my book to Barrès and Mme de Noailles (among others). They wrote to congratulate me (?) on the Prix Goncourt just the same. And I still haven't thanked them. But once in every two weeks or so, I get up and go out (very late in the evening). If you're on the telephone (I'm not, but I can have you telephoned from a nearby bar), could I not invite you to dine with me, one evening when I'm better?[3] I could then reply in person to your unjust accusations of lack of 'composition' etc.[4] Had I not been so ill tonight, I would have tried to show you that, on the contrary, I set out to 'compose' with an unbending rigour, however veiled. But I was too anxious to thank you.

I'm delighted to have this Prix Goncourt, since it has brought us together. Your article is my confirmation that I've obtained it, I having thought, when Léon Daudet, M. Bourges,[5] Rosny[6] etc. brought me the news, that they were joking, for I had seen the following advertisement in the press: 'Prix Goncourt: Roland Dorgelès.[7] *Les Croix de bois.*' True, underneath, in small print, it said: 'four votes out of 10'. Even in the Chamber, where they're pretty 'free and easy', that would be almost enough to cost a deputy his seat. I say this without the slightest ill-will towards M. Dorgelès, whom I don't know, and who is, it seems, very gifted. But I strongly object to his 'communiqués' to the press. I must admit that, to judge by my press-cuttings, my publisher, too, has had advertisements printed (after the Prize, naturally) saying: 'Prix Goncourt: Marcel Proust'. His excuse is that *Les Jeunes filles en fleurs* having sold out prior to the Goncourt, and the demand for copies having far outstripped the supply, he very kindly wished to compensate me. Copies are now beginning to appear in the shops again, but who remembers the Prix Goncourt? Besides, in putting 'Prix Goncourt: Marcel Proust', my publisher was stating no more than the truth. M. Dorgelès's electoral manoeuvre was deliberately misleading. It's not at all the same thing.

Does your brother[8] know that I thanked him for his book and sent him mine? I've changed addresses so often in the last six months that letters could have gone astray. My present address (but don't tell too many people, because I'm so ill) is 44 rue Hamelin.[9]

I thank you again from the bottom of my heart.

Marcel Proust

1. Jacques Boulenger (1878–1944), influential literary critic and editor of the periodicals *L'Opinion* and *La Revue de Paris*.

2. 'M. Marcel Proust's work is of such obvious importance that nobody could reproach the Goncourt Academy for having honoured it. In my opinion, it reveals the most independent, powerfully original writer (along with M. Jean Giraudoux) to emerge for many a year.' Boulenger, *L'Opinion*, 20 December. Allusion to the controversial award of the Prix Goncourt to Proust for *Within a Budding Grove* on 10 December.

3. Unlike other critics, Boulenger, to preserve his independence, was to refuse this and all subsequent invitations from Proust.

4. 'This psychological novel [...] reveals a mind little concerned with organization, or, if you prefer, composition. In fact, M. Proust's work is hardly composed at all. [...] On the one hand, the reader won't fail to admire the accuracy of character-drawing, the quality of landscape, the acuity of feeling and impression, the depth and finesse of analysis; on the other, he will deplore the absence of composition and anything resembling a "plot".' Boulenger, *op. cit.*

5. Émile Bourges (1852–1925), Academician, novelist and Goncourt judge.

6. Rosny *aîné*: see following letter.

7. Roland Dorgelès (real name Lacavelé: 1886–1973), young ex-soldier, runner-up for the Prix Goncourt and considered by many critics the more suitable laureate: *Les Croix de bois*, a novel about life in the trenches, reflected the new social realism.

8. Marcel Boulenger (1873–1932), author and critic.

9. Proust had now moved to his final address, a spartan apartment on the fifth floor of a house near the avenue Kléber. For want of space, many of his belongings, most notably his books, remained in store; in place of cork, carpet was nailed to the walls and the concierge warned not to make any noise.

47 To *Rosny* aîné[1]

[Shortly before 23 December 1919]

Dear Sir and Master,

Even before I express my deep gratitude to you for your kind thought, I'm going to answer your questions[2] point by point, holding nothing back, after which you can decide whether we need address them all. For the past fifteen years, I've lived in bed, I mean literally in bed, in my room, not getting up for a minute. This bedridden state due to incessant attacks of asthma being interrupted every two weeks or so by an evening when my attacks subside, I will get up and go out (for once I'm able to get up, I can go out) for my room to be cleaned. And when I can, there being, alas, no art-galleries or concert-halls open at those times, I still sometimes go about in society. Over the past few years, my state of health, worse in other ways, has nevertheless improved in that I can now get up not once every two weeks, but once or twice a week. There was even a period before my moves when it was three times a week. Now it's back to once or twice. I go out at about half-past eleven and knock on the door of a friend who is still up, but social life is the exception. It would take too long in this letter to explain the complex psychological state which has given rise to this bleak existence. Its compensation would be work, if the necessity of performing several fumigations[3] for several hours a day, did not force me to spend nearly twenty hours to get seven of sleep (with goodness knows how much veronal etc.). I could go into more detail if you wish. But to bare all that in an article hardly seems desirable.

I remember that, when I went to the banquet for M. de Goncourt's cross[4] (for I knew M. de Goncourt!), Alphonse Daudet, whose frailty didn't allow him to stand up for the toast, said that he would drink it sitting down 'to put people at ease'. There seems to me something very courageous, and very graceful, in dissembling illness in that way.[5] From that standpoint, I would prefer it if you didn't talk too much about my health, saying at the most that for the past fifteeen years I haven't gone about in society except at rare intervals (à propos of bedridden periods alternating with days when I seem to be fit and well, I'm suddenly reminded that, a long time ago now, I fought a duel with a member of the Goncourt Academy whom I didn't know, and indeed saw only that once, at a distance of twenty paces: M. Jean Lorrain[6]).

Second question. My political and religious opinions. I haven't been to Mass since my First Communion, over thirty years ago.[7] I would rather not pick a moment when Léon Daudet has been so good to me[8] to declare that the only political party in which I was briefly active happened to be in opposition to his.[9] But Léon Daudet knows better than anybody that I signed the first of the petitions on behalf of Dreyfus, and that I was an ardent Dreyfusard, sending my first book to Picquart[10] in his Cherche-Midi prison. Needless to say, I resisted saying that in answer to newspapers who claim that I got where I am 'via the font and the forces of reaction'![11] In fact, I've kept quiet, having formed a poor opinion of the Press for the following reason. Reporters came to interview me, licking their lips, found me asleep, were very rudely received by my publishers (which I deplore) and departed, furious. There ensued this comedy: one paper (but don't quote me or it will recognize itself) let me know that its three leading columns were at my disposal for a story, an article by a friend, whatever I wished. I had nothing for them, I was exhausted, I was most unsatisfactory. Vengeance was swift. Its three leading columns were devoted to me all right, but for a savaging. I'm told that this has been followed by more rubbish, spiteful and moreover absurd, none of which I've read.

I gather that M. Dorgelès is very talented, and if I still have my sight after not having been well enough to visit an oculist for five years, I'll gladly read his book,[12] which I'm told is very good. But I find my silence the more dignified attitude, he having turned down the Vie Heureuse, saying that he wanted the Goncourt or nothing, failed to get it, ran straight to the Dames Heureuses and, once having obtained the Prix de la Vie Heureuse,[13] had himself interviewed in (I think) *Le Petit Parisien*, saying that he was thankful not to have had the Prix Goncourt!

Lastly, regarding the period during which I composed my books (I mean *Swann* and the *Jeunes filles en fleurs*, for as you know, on leaving school I published a book called *Les Plaisirs et les jours* with a Preface by France, and then two Ruskin translations), I can't be absolutely precise because my poor manservant,[14] who used to look after my exercise-books and could have given you the exact dates, has died. I must have begun *À la Recherche du temps perdu* around 1906,[15] and finished it about 1911. For all the books have been written (the last chapter of the last was written immediately after the first chapter of the first). When *Swann* came out in 1913, not only had *À l'Ombre des jeunes filles en fleurs*, *Le Côté de Guermantes* and *Le Temps retrouvé* been written, but also a large part of *Sodome et Gomorrhe*.[16] But during the war (without it making any difference to the end of the book, *Le Temps retrouvé*), I added something about the war that fitted in well with the character of M. de Charlus.[17]

The reason why the entire work didn't appear in 1913 is that *Swann* came out in December (I had endless trouble finding a publisher, five in succession[18] having kept my manuscript for months and months and eventually rejected it, and I had to resort to having it published by Grasset at my own expense, which happened in December 1913). The sequels were about to appear. By June or July 1914 (or May and June), to atone for having turned down *Swann*, the *Nouvelle revue française* had printed huge excerpts from *Le Côté de Guermantes*.[19] Then war broke out. Grasset having closed down, I moved to the Nouvelle Revue Française, but the printers had been called up etc., and I couldn't get proofs. Eventually, after a fashion, we brought out *Jeunes filles en fleurs*.[20] Now it's just the opposite. Proofs arrive by the cartload and I'm too ill to correct them. I hope to overcome my tiredness and get down to work. But the thought of having nearly five volumes to correct! For I want it all to appear at once in order that its structure may be understood, a structure to which I've sacrificed everything only for it to be so badly misconstrued that it's taken for a haphazard collection of memoirs! This structure, this rigour, is precisely what I wished to demonstrate to you, with some very striking examples. But I'm so exhausted by this letter that I can't write another line, and despite noticing a stray one crossing this page, the vestige of a letter I had started to you, rather than begin afresh, sensing that I haven't the strength to write another word, I beg you to accept my abiding and admiring gratitude.

Marcel Proust

But I haven't thanked you for suggesting this article! I can't tell you how touched I am. And another thing, don't you find it comic that I should have aged eight or nine years in five days, like a character in a pantomime who has grown a white beard by the last act. The socialist press said that I wasn't eligible for the Prize[21] because I was over 47 years old. I had no sooner received it, than I gained two years a day: 50, 51 and, finally, 56! Naturally, I didn't put them right.

And now, with eight hundred letters of congratulation to answer (including ten from Academicians to whom I haven't sent my book), whatever am I to do!

1. Joseph Boëx-Borel (1856–1940), the elder of two brothers who had collaborated on novels as 'J.H. Rosny'. The survivor, Rosny aîné, had been one of Proust's supporters on the Goncourt jury.

2. Rosny had proposed a biographical article for *Comoedia*.

3. See letter 26, n. 4.

4. Edmond de Goncourt (1822–96), was awarded the Cross of the Legion of Honour in 1895.

5. Cf. Proust's moving tribute to Daudet's stoicism after his death in 1897: *AS-B*, 140–3.

6. See letter 3, n. 11. Lorrain had contributed apocrypha to the *Goncourt Journal*, but was never a member of the Goncourt Academy.

7. Proust's Jewish mother was non-practising; his Catholic father had him baptized.

8. Léon Daudet, a member of the Goncourt Academy, had orchestrated the campaign for Proust's prize.

9. Dreyfus's plight briefly united politicians and intellectuals from various parties: see *Selected Letters Volume One*.

10. Georges-Maris Picquart (1854–1914), the army intelligence officer who was held incommunicado in Cherche-Midi prison to prevent his revealing the document which would have proved Dreyfus's innocence. Reinstated with Dreyfus in 1906, he later became minister of war.

11. Allusion to an article in *l'Œuvre*, 12 December: 'M. Proust is said to be a man-about-town, an invaluable asset at a time when writers make instant reputations over five o'clock tea, and an author out for money and glory must assiduously dip his pen into tea-pot and font.'

12. *Les Croix de bois*: see previous letter.

13. The Prix de la Vie Heureuse, better known as the Prix Femina, is awarded annually by an all-woman jury.

14. Nicolas Cottin (1873–1916). See letter 17, n. 7.

15. The year when Proust, having embarked on his essays of literary criticism attacking Sainte-Beuve (see letter 45, n. 4), had also begun writing the isolated

passages of fiction which were to become the embryo of his novel. These significant fragments are collected in *By Way of Sainte-Beuve* (Chatto & Windus 1984; tr. Sylvia Townsend Warner).

16. In fact, by 1922 his additions, in particular to the Sodom and Gomorrah sequence, were to expand his original novel by two-thirds.

17. See Proust to Gallimard, 1916: 'conversations about military strategy [...] between Robert de Saint-Loup and his officer friends [...] have led me to make a connection at the end of the book, not to introduce the war as such but a few of its episodes, and M. de Charlus incidentally gets his due in this motley Paris filled with exotic soldiery reminiscent of a Carpaccio landscape.' *Selected Letters Volume Three*, letter 217. Allusion to the narrator's meeting in the street with M. de Charlus, who is following two Zouaves during an air-raid: VI, 90–1.

18. Four publishers, not five, turned down *Swann's Way*: Fasquelle, Mercure de France, Ollendorf and the N.R.F.

19. These extracts also included parts of what was to become *Within a Budding Grove*.

20. See letter 32.

21. The left-wing press was antagonistic to *Within a Budding Grove* partly because of Léon Daudet's championship of it.

48 To the Abbé Mugnier

> 44 rue Hamelin (address semi-confidential so as not to be disturbed during my horrific attacks.)
> [Last days of December 1919]

Monsieur l'Abbé,

You've written me an adorable letter. Like Chateaubriand, you mingle the flowers of apple and hawthorn.[1] You might have heard from me a long time ago, for I think of you constantly. But it happens that, firstly, the house where I lived having been transformed by a banker into a bank, I've been forced to move three times in six months, and my health suffered to the point where I was unable to open a newspaper for weeks on end; secondly, that, owing to some bookseller's manoeuvre which I don't understand, first editions of *À l'Ombre des jeunes filles en fleurs* and *Pastiches et mélanges* proved unobtainable during the period of my moves. That hasn't prevented my spending several months searching for a first edition of one or other book for you. In the meantime, if you could make do with one of each which won't be the first, I'll send them to you at once, with a modest inscription.

If it was Monsieur Descaves[2] who told you that I was to receive the prize, he was better informed than me (which is understandable, since he is a member of the Academy), for when Léon Daudet came to awaken me with the news, I wasn't even aware that it was to be awarded in December, let alone to me. In any case, I'm sorry that you heard it from Monsieur Descaves, for he doubtless accompanied this very unimportant piece of news with snide comments. Indeed, he waged what amounted to a campaign against me, and greeted the outcome with these words: 'M. Proust has the prize, M. Dorgelès the youth and originality. One can't have everything.'

I even wondered if I had had the prize, for M. Dorgelès placed ostentatious advertisements in the press: 'Prix Goncourt. Roland Dorgelès'. True, it said underneath, in microscopic print: 'four votes out of 10'. In the Chamber, such electoral tactics would be enough to cost a deputy his seat. 'My lesson is drawn from very small animals.'[3] Don't think that I bear Monsieur Descaves the slightest grudge. Those who dislike my books share my own opinion. Apparently, the work that Monsieur Descaves wanted is truly remarkable. Had my general state of health not prevented my consulting an oculist about spectacles for the past five years, I would read *Les Croix de bois*. I shall ask somebody to read this fine book aloud to me. If I haven't thanked Monsieur Descaves (or Monsieur Bergerat)[4] or other hostile members of the jury, it's not because he didn't vote for me, which is perfectly understandable, but because, not having been present at the luncheon,[5] he didn't sign the address brought to me by Léon Daudet. Under those circumstances, I had nothing to thank him for, and could hardly do so on the pretext that he had voted against me.

Forgive my having talked so much about something as unimportant as the Prix Goncourt. Don't believe that it has altered me physically as much as one might think from the reports of journalists who, because I was unable to receive them, made me age overnight like a character in a fairy-tale. The day before the Prix Goncourt I had no chance of winning because I was 47 years old. The day after, I was unworthy because I was 'pushing' 50. Twenty-four hours later, I was 'past it', having now reached the age of 58! 'Quo non ascendam'![6] My age rises as fast as the Seine.[7] Don't be disappointed when you next see me if I lack the white locks with which it pleases a wishful-thinking press to crown my brow. I even dare confess to you that I haven't turned 'clerical', as they say, and that, far from being anti-Dreyfusard (for the spite is even retrospective), I was the most fervent, and possibly the first, of the Dreyfusards. M. Arthur Meyer[8] has never forgiven me.

With my grateful respects, dear Monsieur l'Abbé,
your admiring friend,
Marcel Proust

1. See letter 10.
2. Lucien Descaves (1861–1949), novelist and critic.
3. Proust paraphrases La Fontaine in 'The Dove and the Ant': 'The next lesson is drawn from smaller animals'. *Fables*, Book II.
4. Émile Bergerat (1845–1923), writer.
5. Members of the Goncourt Academy formally confirm their award over luncheon, and sign a letter notifying the laureate.
6. 'To what heights might he not ascend', motto inscribed beneath the image of a squirrel on the arms of Louis XIV's Superintendent of Finance, Nicolas Fouquet, who had amassed a fortune.
7. The *Figaro* reported dramatic floods on the Seine, measuring its rise by the statue of the Zouave on the Pont de l'Alma. Proust had turned 48 in July.
8. Proust's 'bête noire': see letter 114, n. 13.

49   To Jean de Pierrefeu[1]

44 rue Hamelin
[Sunday 4 January 1920]

Sir,

Will you do me the honour of dining with me at the Ritz Hotel next Thursday (8 January, I think), together with a few friends I intend to invite for you? The explanation for such an unforeseen invitation is this. I had a sudden urge to chat to you (something that is very difficult for me except, very rarely, over dinner, as I'm very ill). But at that moment your article on the Prix Goncourt appeared.[2] You will appreciate that it made, if not a duel inevitable, at least a friendly gesture impossible. Nevertheless, I was much struck by 'deep-sea diver of the self'[3], and my ill-humour having passed, was about to try again when I heard that you were writing an article attacking me: 'Le cas de Marcel Proust'.[4] My goodwill gesture was thwarted yet again, for it would have looked as if I wanted you to tone down your article. But now your article (not as nasty as all that) (and very well-written) has appeared. You won't have another chance to write about me, for all my forthcoming books are to appear at once, and are far too 'indecent' ever to be reviewed in the *Débats*. So, now that I can't be accused of trying to influence you, I would be glad to clear up a literary misunderstanding, retrospectively, over a chat. But at the same time I don't want to bore you stiff by talking aesthetics, so I'll be inviting Guiche, Boni de Castellane,[5] Pierre de Polignac[6] – and some charming writers whom you know.[7] Only, tell me at once if you're not free, it being so tiring for me that I don't want to make the effort for nothing.

If I fail to convince you that my novel (I don't mean the *Jeunes filles en fleurs* but the work as a whole) has no merit apart from structure, if I fail to acquit myself of having treacherously led my readers into the shadows of the subconscious (whereas my aim – or one of my aims, it's a complex work – is to bring this tenebrous subconscious into the full light of the intelligence), at least I shall have avenged my poor manservant who died during the war for the stupid (and invented) slur that some 'wit' repeated to you.[8]

In case you prefer to bring me your answer in person, you'll find me at rue Hamelin till about eleven o'clock tonight, Sunday, with Polignac and Gaigneron (and perhaps, though less congenial to you, I fear, the editor of *Comoedia*[9]).

I'm obliged to squeeze together these lines (as in my book)[10] because I see that I've begun something over the page. Lastly, don't count too much on my death, which you seem to see in your *Débats* article as the only possible termination of my book. The final word was written in 1914. So all is complete. True, it means five volumes to correct, and I may be prevented by illness. However, as it doesn't prevent my having you to dinner at the Ritz, I much look forward to seeing you, and also perhaps this evening, at 44 rue Hamelin.

Yours faithfully,
Marcel Proust

Kindly don't talk about this dinner for the moment.
P.S. (there is a fifth page after all) when handing the bearer your answer, kindly tell him whether it's yes or no. Because, rather than returning here to wake me as I sleep during the day, he could go on to invite Guiche and Castellane, for example, so as to have a better chance of finding them free on Thursday.

1. Jean de Pierrefeu (1883–1940), critic on the *Journal des Débats*.
2. Pierrefeu wrote in the *Débats* on the award of the Prix Goncourt to *Within a Budding Grove*, 12 December 1919: 'This compendium of sleepless nights by a voluntary recluse will please suffering souls. To the present generation, celebrating the glories of the struggle and the virtues of the light, it will be irrelevant, according ill with the classical revival which alone, the Party of Intelligence declares, is compatible with the greatness of a victorious nation.' Allusion to the *Figaro* manifesto: see letter 37, n.4.
3. 'A deep-sea diver of the memory, he has descended to the very depths of his being.' Pierrefeu, *loc. cit.*
4. 'Pierrefeu says he intends to discuss "The Case of Marcel Proust" in the *Débats*. If so, I'll answer him in *L'Opinion*. You see, I'm your champion.' Jacques Boulenger to Proust, 29 December 1919.
5. Boniface ('Boni'), Marquis de Castellane (1867–1932), a descendant of Mme de Sévigné.
6. Pierre, Comte de Polignac: see letter 56.
7. Jacques and Marcel Boulenger.
8. According to Pierrefeu, Nicolas Cottin had retorted to a visitor who suggested that the fug in Proust's bedroom was unhealthy: 'On the contrary, Sir, it does wonders for Monsieur's ideas.'
9. Georges Casella: see letter 195, n.1.
10. See letter 32, n.3.

50 To Jacques Boulenger

Night of Saturday to Sunday
[10–11 January 1920]

Dear friend,
(Can we honestly address one another otherwise, when I love your books and you carry indulgence to mine to unreasonable lengths.) My last letter was to say: 'Stop writing about me!' How nice of you not to have listened! You can't imagine my pleasure just now, on reading your wonderful article in *L'Opinion*.[1] One is rather ashamed to have written such fat books as I have, when, in two pages of a review, one sees somebody cover practically everything worth knowing under the sun, cut the Gordian knot, decapitate the Hydra of Lerna so that it cannot regrow and, in sketching the model from life (me), create, thanks to choice tones, to original accents, a portrait of himself, that of an incomparable St George of Literature,[2] resembling Carpaccio's St George whom you may have seen in Venice, at full tilt on his horse.[3] Hitherto, whenever

an 'unknown friend' pleased me at a distance, I would turn to Sully Prudhomme and reply to the said friend, who was not necessarily a nobody:

> 'Dear reader, take only a part of me,
> The part you liked for resembling you,
> But do not let us vow to meet;
> True friendship lies in feeling alike,
> The rest is fragile, let us spare ourselves adieux.'[4]

It was the standard p.p.c.,[5] even before we had met. But it's not at all the same thing when it comes to the extraordinary Jacques Boulenger, who seems to be saying to me: 'I've showered you with gifts, I mean to overwhelm you with them.'[6] The desire to meet him (I've never so much as laid eyes on you) would deprive me of sleep, had I any to lose. What a pity you didn't come to the dinner I gave here, when Polignac and Gaigneron must have missed you to the point of hating me for it, nor to that at the Ritz, so hilarious that we must talk about it again, when Castellane and Beauvau[7] would have carved up Austria for you.[8] We can do all that again, of course, only, you see, I made a colossal effort in order to meet you (colossal for me) and need time to recover. Now, next week, some dear reprobates to whom I'm greatly indebted have insisted that we 'make a date' (that's very badly put, I mean the date in question falls next week). Till then, I shan't be getting up except for today (Sunday) and don't like to ask you to dine here alone with me and my secretary[9] (needless to say, he isn't writing this, or it would be a great deal better), you would be too bored. Then again, I have a feeling that on Sundays there are obstacles in the form of Chantilly,[10] and if it chanced that you could come and I was asleep, Céleste would say that it was too late, she would never find crayfish at that hour on a Sunday. (But don't let that stop you, if you would like to come, come, and you and I will dine alone at the Ritz, which need not prevent us from dining with 'people' in a week or two. So, tonight, if you wish) but on Monday, Tuesday and Wednesday I must stay in bed, and it irks to think that it will be so long before we can meet, for the outings for which this rest is a preparation will themselves be followed by enforced rest. Don't be too alarmed by this desire to know you, by the way. I'm very undemanding, being constantly ill. Before the revelation of Jacques Boulenger, I would see my closest friends once every ten years. You've turned my life upside down. Besides, I'm seldom well enough to get up. Once in a blue moon, I may go out for dinner, or for a duel. It's twenty years since I've been to the Louvre.[11]

You're extremely nice to say that I'm very rational.[12] At bottom, I believe that it's true. My one aim is to clarify things. Admittedly, quite obscure things. But there would be no merit in it otherwise. I don't know why people so resent my having had the Prix Goncourt, I never asked for it; M. Dorgelès's friends can't forgive me, although I didn't know that he was a candidate. If anything, they should be grateful to me, for he has had the second prize,[13] and benefited more than I have from the first. But what distresses me is their way of showing their antipathy. For instance, I happened to come across, in the *NRF*, a summary of *Le Crapouillot* for 1 January. There was to be an article on me by M. Marx.[14] They had it suppressed.

I mustn't go on chatting to you or I'll never stop, and writing letters exhausts me. As I say, you can dine here very late tonight, Sunday, but alone. And once the fatal outings are over, 'I'll give you a ring', as Mme Cottard[15] would say (by you, I mean you and your brother, for you take such an unaffected and endearing pleasure in one another's company).

With my warmest regards,
Marcel Proust

Souday's article appeared not on 3 January, but on the 1st. There was also one by him in *Paris-Midi*[16] about my Flaubert, very friendly, considering that I don't cite him in an article on Flaubert.[17] I can't agree with him about the *Letters*. It would be truly galling for Flaubert to have taken all that trouble over his books only to have them thought inferior to his letters.[18]

1. 'On M. Marcel Proust', Jacques Boulenger, *L'Opinion*, 10 January.
2. See Boulenger's offer to be his champion: letter 49, n.4.
3. Allusion to a panel in the Scuola di San Giorgio degli Schiavoni, which Proust would have seen on his visit to Venice in 1900.
4. 'Cher passant, prenez de moi-même qu'un peu, / Le peu qui vous a plu parce qu'il vous ressemble; / Mais de nous rencontrer ne formons pas le voeux, / Le vrai de l'amitié c'est de sentir ensemble, / Le reste en est fragile, épargnons-nous l'adieu.' Sully Prudhomme, 'Aux amis inconnus'. Proust substitutes *lecteur* for *passant*.
5. *pour prendre conger*: to say farewell; a formula signifying prolonged absence.
6. Proust adapts lines from Corneille's *Cinna*, Act V, scene 3: 'Tu trahis mes bienfaits, je les veux redoubler; / je t'en avais comblé, je t'en veux accabler.'

7. Louis, Prince de Beauvau-Craon (1878–1942).

8. Allusion to the treaty of St-Germain-en-Laye, September 1919.

9. Henri Rochat: see letter 11.

10. Allusion to the elegant Sunday race-meetings at Chantilly.

11. See parenthesis in the following note.

12. 'One couldn't hope to find a mind in better health than that of this sick man, who possesses critical faculties of a rare vigour (see, alongside his psychological insights, his views on art) and who is, at bottom, the most rational man alive. I can think of nothing less debilitated than M. Proust's critical sense. [...] I cannot agree that this most lucid of men is "hermetic"; as for being "boring", I read his book with as much pleasure as I once read *The Three Musketeers*. [...] M. de Pierrefeu [...] cites in corroboration the readers' letters he received after his articles on *In Search of Lost Time*: "You've avenged us", they say, congratulating him on "having at last sided with the bourgeoisie". It seems that it's not "bourgeois" (in the Flaubertian sense, naturally) to like M. Proust. It's a consoling thought.' Boulenger, *l'Opinion*.

13. The Prix Femina: see letter 47.

14. Pseudonym of Madeleine Paz; her article in praise of Proust was to appear in *La Revue mondiale* of 1 October.

15. The good-natured woman who wonders at the novelty of the telephone: II, 211.

16. 'Flaubert and Marcel Proust', Paul Souday, *Paris-Midi*, 8 January.

17. Proust's critical essay 'On Flaubert's Style' had appeared in the *NRF* of 1 January. See *AS-B*, 261–74.

18. 'What is alone surprising in such a master is the mediocrity of his correspondence. [...] The abrupt and obvious heightening a writer's talent undergoes the moment he improvises [...] should be visible in Flaubert's correspondence. But rather it is a lowering that one notes.' Proust, *loc. cit.*, 266–7.

51 To Fernand Vandérem

44 rue Hamelin
[Thursday evening, 15 January 1920]

Dear Sir and friend,

I'm too ill tonight to write to you except to say ... that I can't write to you. But you'll hear from me soon. Meanwhile, I didn't want to let another day pass, whatever it cost me to write today, without telling you that your article[1] comes as a profound relief to me. That of last summer[2] caused me what at first I took for resentment but now realize was grief. That swelling of the heart, that 'inflation', as you would say, has been lanced, and it gives me great joy. Last summer's grief, which I thought it more dignified to conceal, contenting myself with not writing to you, was not just a result of having been ill-treated by somebody who till then had treated me amicably. I acknowledge that people kind enough to like me personally also have a perfect right to dislike my books. And when these people are Critics, to say that they dislike *Swann* is not merely their right, it's their duty. Only that wasn't the case with you; one evening at the *Figaro*, you were nice enough to say that you had what you kindly called a predilection for my book. Five years later, in a letter that came out of the blue, the vicissitudes of life (in my case, a state approaching death) having prevented our meeting, you kindly assured me once again, of your own volition, of this predilection. I'm sure that you are absolutely sincere, and say so not only because you have nothing to gain from me, but because you are one of those people who, not caring about privilege or position, speaks his mind 'fair and square' to anybody, be he all-powerful. Knowing you to be like that, I was especially touched by these repeated marks of literary friendship that reinforced our long-standing and cordial relationship. Thus, I was truly devastated when, the moment you had a chance to write about me, (puzzle!),[3] it was to give me what you yourself call, in your review, 'a savaging'.[4] Unluckily (I mean unluckily for me), you used the very same words to say the exact opposite to what you said in your letter to me. E.g., in your letter: '*Swann* is just the sort of book I like, I know of no higher praise'; in your review: '*Swann* is just the sort of book I dislike'. Note that I reap no advantage from these contradictions, alas. Doubtless they can be readily explained. You may have wished to discuss different qualities and defects in comparable terms. *Swann* may be the sort of book you like in some ways and detest in others. See the lengths to which I take an author's objectivity, and how I act as your advocate, not mine. Then again, you probably pay less attention when writing a letter to me than I do when reading a letter from you, it being so much more important to me. But this time, perhaps more out of sympathy for the underdog than for my book, the generous things you say are everything that I could wish.[5] Alas, as is your wont, you precede your praises with criticisms that discourage the reader in advance.[6] Personally, I read your articles (even when not about me) from beginning to end. A less attentive reader, noting that the author in question is diffuse, formless etc., will skip what you say about the *Jeunes filles en fleurs*, deciding that, even in the column of a much-read critic, it's not worth wasting time on an unreadable writer, and pass on quickly to the *Jeunes femmes en fruits*.⁷ I only wanted to give you a word of thanks, yet I'm on the tenth page of this letter. I must stop. But don't imagine that you've been let off lightly. I shall express my keen gratitude in person, while at the same time defending myself against the charge of a convoluted style, lack of structure, Sagan-ism.⁸ Tonight, it's the gratitude that I wish to express, and trust that you will accept its sincerity.

Marcel Proust

1. Vandérem, in the *Revue de Paris*, 15 January, acknowledged that Proust had been shabbily treated in the press over the Prix Goncourt.

2. Allusion to Vandérem's review of the previous July: letter 36, n. 8.

3. 'His style, though almost always correct, is so convoluted, such a jigsaw puzzle, that even the most attentive reader will have to read and re-read each phrase.' Vandérem, *Revue de Paris*, 15 July 1919.

4. 'After this savaging, you'll be surprised to hear me say that M. Proust's works are among the most interesting, captivating, not to say important, of recent years.' *Ibid*.

5. 'But it's rather for its tone, its psychology, its sensibility, that this book is accused of decadence. Yet, on these counts, who, writing today, is more modern, more in touch with our times, than M. Proust?' *Ibid*.

6. Vandérem begins with a catalogue of stylistic defects.

7. 'The transition from *L'Ombre des jeunes filles en fleurs* to *L'Ombre des jeunes femmes en fruits* seems entirely appropriate.' *Ibid*. The pun alludes to certain mature women writers.

8. Vandérem invoked the Prince de Sagan, whose name was synonymous with Second Empire elegance, to suggest that Proust's work was dated.

52 To Madame Greffulhe¹

44 rue Hamelin
[Monday 19 January 1920]

Madame,

I had begun answering a few letters of congratulation (!) on this prize. I then fell so ill that I'm left with 800 unanswered letters and no strength to begin again. Yours gave me both pleasure and pain. Having been relegated from Dear Friend, to Dear Sir and Friend, then to Dear Sir, then to Sir, I had thought that, with the addition of 'yours faithfully', I could descend no lower. I was wrong. This time, you inform me in the third person that the Comtesse

Greffulhe etc. Should I ever receive another prize, I expect that you won't write at all, and that one will read that the Comtesse Greffulhe is happy to learn etc. in a note in Gabriac's column.[2] *Sic transit gloria mundi.*

I'm too ill to write at greater length, but may I remind you of my request for a photograph (even if only of a Laszlo portrait).[3] When you refused me once before,[4] you gave me a very lame excuse, namely, that a photograph immobilizes and arrests a woman's beauty. But isn't that precisely the point, to immobilize, or rather, immortalize, a momentary radiance? A photograph is the effigy of eternal youth. I may say that the photograph of you which I once saw in Robert de Montesquiou's house[5] seemed to me more beautiful than the one of the Laszlo portrait. As for the photograph of the Helleu portrait, I already have it, in Montesquiou's book.[6] But it's nothing like you.

Forgive me for breaking off my letter here, and for my vain request. I'm so ill that writing letters is an effort I *must not* make, what with two books to finish and, more realistically, the prospect of an early death, not that that would matter, as long as my books are ready. I am!

With respectful regards to the Comte Greffulhe,[7]
I remain, Madame,
Yours faithfully,
Marcel Proust

---

1. Comtesse Henri Greffulhe, *née* Elisabeth de Caraman-Chimay (1860–1952), a model for both Guermantes ladies: the Duchesse for her style and dress, the Princesse for her beauty and social position.

2. Alexandre, Comte de Gabriac, society columnist on the *Figaro*.

3. Philip Laszlo (1869–1937), society and court portraitist.

4. In 1904, Proust had asked Guiche, as Mme Greffulhe's son-in-law, to help him obtain her photograph. With equal lack of success, the narrator begs Saint-Loup to help him obtain a photograph of his aunt, the Duchesse de Guermantes: III, 84; 107–11.

5. Mme Greffulhe had been deeply offended to learn that Proust had tried to borrow her photograph from her cousin Montesquiou.

6. *Paul Helleu. Peintre et Graveur*.

7. Henri, Comte Greffulhe (1844–1952), banker.

53   To Louis Martin-Chauffier[1]

44 rue Hamelin (address confidential)
[Around January 1920]

Sir,

I'm extremely ill, I have 800 letters to answer. If I make an exception for you, and answer yours by return, you will, I imagine, draw the right conclusion. It is this: your letter enchanted me, your pastiche made enchantment complete.[2] That is no small compliment. I'm very severe on pastiches. In particular, those which I've read purporting to imitate me seem to me extremely weak.[3] Yours is a rare and fine exception. I find fault with the general spirit (in fact, I'm too ill to explain. Perhaps if you were to tell yourself: he looks through a telescope rather than a microscope,[4] you would divine my meaning), and this basic flaw causes the pastiche to flag a little here and there. But what astonishing insights! You have hit upon, and parodied with infinite drollery, certain pecularities of syntax known, I suspect, only to the two of us. You have an exquisite way of mocking my similes. The old boy decorated by his ally the minister, the resemblance between father and son, a woman's different veils, the positive and the negative, all that is priceless.

Sir, there may come a time when I shall need your advice on etymologies.[5] I wrote to M. Dimier[6] (whom I don't know), who in turn kindly offered to put me in touch with M. Longnon.[7] In fact, I don't lack for people able to provide me with all the etymologies I need. But I would find it much more amusing if it could be you, now that I have an idea of your wit from your letter and your pastiche. In any case, there's no hurry. I'm too ill to try to remember the names I gave M. Dimier. However, there is an historical query (I'm in a furnished apartment and don't have my books) to which the answer is urgent. True, it comes long after the Carolingians.[8] It is this: I recall reading in the *Débats* some time ago (was it in an article by André Hallays?[9] I no longer recall) that a Montmorency, or rather, I believe, a Montmorency widow, ended her days as an abbess.[10] Was she not a Condé? Which abbey was it? I think it was in Richelieu's time. Kindly write to me if you know the answer. Otherwise, don't bother. In any case, please don't think that I wrote to you just for that. Letters are a terrible strain for me just now. I have essential ones which will never get written. Had it been merely a question of Mme de Montmorency, or Condé, I could have managed easily. A friend would have found the information for me. But your letter was so charming, and your modesty so excessive, that I made it a point to thank you for the one and cure you of the other. Good luck with your Carolingians. Whether they or others are destined to monopolize your literary talent, I don't know, but it is undeniable and delightful.

Yours sincerely,
Marcel Proust

Naturally, which *Débats* article is immaterial. What I need to know is whether a Montmorency etc.

In fact, if you knew of an abbess of any period who belonged to a Chapter as exclusive as that of Remiremont[11] and wasn't related to the Haussonvilles,[12] it would suit me as well as the Montmorency widow. The idea is to give Mme de Villeparisis (I almost put Ville-tournois)[13] an opportunity to show off the portrait of an abbess and surprise her guests a little.[14]

1. Louis Martin-Chauffier (1894–1980), historian.
2. In a special number of the magazine *Le Disque vert*, produced in memory of Proust in December 1952, Martin-Chauffier recalls his astonishment at receiving this reply: 'I didn't realize that all Paris knew Proust's confidential address, and that he wrote daily to at least seven people, maintaining that, although at death's door, he felt bound to make an exception in their case.'
3. Allusion to a pastiche of Proust entitled 'À l'ombre d'un jeune homme en boutons', in the satirical review *Le Crapouillot*, 1 October 1919.
4. Cf. the narrator's reflections at the end of *Time Regained*: 'Even those who commended my perception of the truths [...] congratulated me on having discovered them "with a microscope", when on the contrary it was a telescope that I had used.' VI, 442.
5. See Brichot's hilariously pedantic monologues on etymologies for the benefit of the habitués of 'the little train': IV, 330–4.
6. Louis Dimier (1865–1943), art historian.
7. Probably Auguste Longnon (1844–1911), authority on French place-names.
8. Subject of Martin-Chauffier's thesis.
9. André Hallays (1859–1930), critic.
10. Allusion to the widow of Henri II, Duc de Montmorency, later Mother Superior of the Convent of the Visitandines at Moulins.
11. Abbey in the Vosges, described by Chateaubriand in his *Mémoires d'outre-tombe*.
12. The family appealed to Proust for their ancient nobility and their literary

credentials as connections of Mme de Staël: VI, 47; 347. Comte Othenin was supposed to have inspired the Duc de Guermantes as 'a magnificent ruin': VI, 410. His wife was the subject of one of Proust's 'salon' articles: *CS-B*, 482.

13. A name figuring in Martin-Chauffier's pastiche.

14. See *The Guermantes Way*, where Mme de Villeparisis displays her inherited portrait of the Duchesse de Montmorency, 'abbess of one of the most famous chapters in the east of France': III, 224–5.

54   To Marcel Boulenger

[Shortly before 24 January 1920]

Dear friend,

I rasp so continually (incessant attacks of asthma for days) that it's far from easy for me to write to you. Yet I must try and find the strength to tell you that I've just received a cutting, forwarded from boulevard Haussmann and 'held pending' at rue Laurent-Pichat; it's an article by Marcel Boulenger,[1] and it was so sweet of you to write about me, and to say such nice things, that I wanted to give you my warmest thanks.

But I must tell you when we meet that this article, so full of poetry and wit, is, inasmuch as it's about my work, as wrong as it's possible to be.[2] It seems to me that the sole justification you could plead (in the logical and intellectual sense, naturally) is that you know, assuming you've read them, only the first two volumes of *Temps perdu*. Now, as my recall of two books written years ago is very poor (veronal etc.), and as I haven't attempted to re-read them (small print, inferior spectacles etc., etc.), I may be wrong in placing in these two volumes passages, scenes and characters to be found only in those yet to appear. And you are not Madame de Thèbes.[3] But I find it almost inconceivable that, in the early volumes, the tone of the rest hasn't already made itself felt. Now, despite my great desire to be equitable, to be impersonal, it so happens that in *Temps perdu* the calumniated social class, which is always in the wrong, which utters nothing but stupidities, the vulgar, tasteless class, is the nobility, is so-called 'high society'. It may be that this impression becomes irresistible only with *Le Côté de Guermantes*, but it seems to me that already, in *Les Jeunes filles en fleurs*, M. de Cambremer is the height of vulgarity, Saint-Loup 'intellectual' but a complete ninny, the guests at the Saint-Euverte soirée second-rate, the Marquis de Norpois absurd, Mme de Villeparisis cultured but at bottom totally lacking in judgment, and not nearly as nice as my grandmother, whose origins were so modest.[4] And the snob Legrandin hardly sympathetic. And M. de Forcheville (who I'm certain has already appeared in *Swann*, at the Verdurins')[5] grotesque. And the Duc de Guermantes, in the *NRF* of 1914 (extracts from forthcoming volumes), equally grotesque. There remains only Charlus. But he is first and foremost a lone wolf, such as is to be found in every social class.

Dear friend, I'm too tired to go on, goodbye, and thank you.
Marcel Proust

1. 'The Magic Nobility', *Comoedia*, 12 January 1920.
2. Proust objects to the following: '. . . such are the powers of this incomparable listener [. . .] that we believe in dowagers who possess every merit of sensibility and intellect [. . .], in their young descendants who, through some hidden virtue of their race, aspire to the highest level of mind, body and senses; in men and women of leisure, with no obligations other than to dress better than Beau Brummell and [. . .] discuss the finer points of literature and philosophy.'
3. A famous clairvoyant.
4. Proust's greatly loved maternal grandmother, Mme Nathé Weil, *née* Adèle Berncastel (1824–90).
5. See the 'newcomer' introduced to the Verdurins by Odette: I, 301.

55   To Jacques Rivière[1]

[Monday 26 January 1920]

Dear friend,

For once I regard it as purely accidental that I should have been robbed of a great happiness. After my 'outing' the other night, I was so ill that your splendid article[2] appeared to me only as a sun veiled in mist. Or rather, my intelligence grasped every word. But such was my pain that happiness – even the most fleeting pleasure – could not find 'the path to my heart'.[3] I have no regrets, for my suffering will pass, and then, no longer content with understanding, I can reap my rightful share of its joys with each beauty perceived. I shall have read you twice, once with the head and once with the heart. As I say, I have no regrets because concerned only (only!) with admiration for your work, and as if not I but another were its subject. And the interval between my having 'plumbed its depths'[4] and my enjoyment won't be so prolonged that I risk suffering the same fate as those pupils who, at an age when incapable of understanding him, learn Racine by heart so well that, later on, when old enough, they have known him too long to love him. You can see from this how objective I am. Otherwise, were it only a case of my personal pleasure at being praised by my dear friend the great Jacques Rivière, I would, once better, no longer have what General Nivelle[5] would call the 'benefit of surprise', and, worse still, I would be like those children who have known about and seen their New Year presents so long in advance that, at the solemn, candle-lit hour on the first of January, they are almost indifferent to them.

Where I become very self-interested, and not merely in my own interest, extremely exiguous, but real enough, but also in that, rather more important, of the *NRF* and its 'holy egotism',[6] is when I stoop momentarily to complaining about the article's presentation. From the readers' point of view, too many coincidences over recent weeks have made me look a deadly bore.[7] It didn't matter that, in January's *NRF*, you talked of a predominantly hostile press. I didn't even bother to point out that this wasn't quite accurate, the *Figaro*, the *Gaulois*, the *Petit-Parisien*, *L'Action française*, Rosny and Binet-Valmer, Boulenger, Charasson etc. (and on the same day Miomandre) having rather made up for the rest.[8] True, Souday had yet to appear.[9] On the contrary, as it turns out, to have drawn attention to it was important and useful, since it enabled you to deduce in such splendidly fortifying terms – a 'Leibig'[10] of human language – the value you place on my book.[11] But there are many passages in which the word 'patience', the words 'unpleasing', 'nothing new', won't be understood in the sense you intended, and will discourage a reader whose interest isn't already aroused. If, momentarily, I can see these things from the point of view of the *NRF*, it's because I rejoiced in my prize only for its sake. When it comes to my book, self-interest reviving, I can no longer see things in the same way. And when I come to think not of my book but of your article, I can see it only in terms of eternity and would die a thousand deaths were you to change a single word, all of which I say only because it's too late for changes which I trust you wouldn't grieve me by making for whatever reason. All I ask is that, there also being an article on *Les Croix de bois*[12] (I must tell you what Morand said about that), the *NRF* doesn't make it look as though it is copying *L'Action française* (Daudet is probably immersed in politics, unless there are other reasons) and dropping me for Dorgelès.

Dear friend, I've only just begun and yet I'm overcome by fatigue. I think I'm being impartial (and I could be partial only the other way round, by being my own enemy) when I say that I know nothing by you as remarkable as the article which you left with me the other evening. The Rimbaud essay,[13] fine though it is, is confined to a single, extraordinary, almost supra-human case. In this article, you hover over a century – I use hover to imply height, but no verb could be less exact, for there are also apprehension, capture, total grasp; ah!, no sick man ever wrote with such force. And the confusion of politics with literature![14] How many times have I not told Cocteau that he was wrong in both thought and word when he said: 'in art, I always lean to the Left'. Petrus Borel[15] probably considered Stendhal old hat, and Racine even more so, Gautier having claimed that that there is only one acceptable line in Racine: 'The daughter of Minos and Pasiphaë'.[16] As a child, I heard the same thing from the grandest Parnassians, who said that there were only two lines in Musset: 'The white Oloossone to the white Camire' and 'The snow falls peacefully on your bare shoulders'.[17] I confess that this disgusts me, not because I have the least liking for Musset, but because of the irresponsibility of the Parnassians who neglected what Musset sought to achieve (which wasn't much) and went out of their way to find the exact opposite of his aims in his work. The rules have changed, but not for the better. Nowadays, for Mme de Noailles, Musset is the greatest poet of the nineteenth century, as he is for Régnier and Mme de Régnier, who heard their father and father-in-law[18] say that he was the worst. But what they admire in Musset is so unlike him (for example: 'More dreary even than Milan / where once or twice yearly / Cerrito dances')[19] that their infatuation doesn't have the force of justice.[20]

Dear friend, I fear for you. For if it's really the case that only a masterpiece acquires a united chorus of enemies,[21] then you had better watch out! For if ever there was a masterpiece, it is your article. As I say, I haven't talked to you about its substance. I believe that you may come to change your mind about me, just a little. Certainly not to like me better, nor, please God, to stop liking me altogether! I don't believe that you are yet fully aware of my design, my 'volume', my 'psychology in space'.[22] Plane psychology, that was certainly how you thought of it, to judge by your choice of extracts for the *NRF*.[23] And I hasten to add that what I later asked you to include was very stupid, for while intended to disclaim the kind of praise I didn't deserve, it wasn't evidence for that which I did.

Dear friend, I'm so tired, I must stop. I don't know if I've told you that nobody could have a greater admiration and affection for you than your grateful

Marcel Proust

We must talk about the *number* of extracts you want for the *NRF*, so that I can give you first choice, before filling orders from others.

The taxi-strike means that this letter couldn't be taken round to you yesterday, so I had you telephoned to apologize, once at a quarter to five, when you hadn't yet arrived, and once at a quarter to six, when you had left.

1. Jacques Rivière (1880–1925), author, critic and editor of the *NRF* from 1913 till his premature death (he suffered from undiagnosed leukaemia).
2. 'Marcel Proust and the Classical Tradition', to appear in the *NRF* of 1 February.
3. Arguing that Proust resembles Racine in his search for psychological truth, Rivière cites Phèdre's declaration: 'Aricie a trouvé le chemin de mon cœur'; Act V, scene 6.
4. See La Rochefoucauld on self-love in *Maxims*: 'Its depths cannot be plumbed, nor its dark abysses pierced.'
5. Robert Nivelle (1856–1924), the general notorious for the Chemin des Dames offensive.
6. *Egotisme sacré*: Daniel Halévy's translation of the term *Selbstsucht* in Nietzsche's last letter to Lou Salomé: 'I see in you the holy egotism that obliges us to serve our highest interests.'
7. Allusion to criticisms of Proust's style in recent reviews of his work and in articles about his Prix Goncourt.
8. Articles by Robert Dreyfus, Abel Hermant, Gaston Rageot, Jacques-Émile Blanche, Rosny *aîné*, Jean Binet-Valmer (*Comœdia*), Henriette Charasson (*Le Rappel*), Francis de Miomandre (*L'Événement*).
9. See p.s. to letter 50.
10. Allusion to Liebig's Extract of Meat Company, in which Proust held shares.
11. 'Had I had doubts as to the importance of *In Search of Lost Time*, they would have been dispelled by the outcry we have just witnessed. Only a masterpiece is privileged to acquire, at its first appearance, such a united chorus of enemies.' Rivière, *NRF*, 1 February.
12. Allusion to a long article on Dorgelès by the critic Roger Allard.
13. *NRF*, July 1914.
14. 'It's no accident that the majority of those ranged against Proust should be

the believers in "revolutionary art" who, confusing politics with literature, imagine that boldness is the same in both domains, that [. . .] the only direction in which to go is *forward*, and the only innovator he who goes furthest – all those who equate literary innovation with emancipation, and greet every discarded rule [. . .] as another step towards Beauty.' Rivière, *loc. cit.*

15. Petrus Borel (1809–59), Romantic poet, leader of the *bousingos*, the revolutionary literary group to which Théophile Gautier belonged.

16. *Phèdre*, Act I, scene 1.

17. From 'La Nuit de mai' and 'La coupe et les lèvres' respectively.

18. In the person of José-Maria de Heredia: see notes to letter 63.

19. 'Plus ennuyeuse que Milan / Où au moins deux ou trois fois l'an / Cerrito danse'. Alfred de Musset, 'À mon frère, revenant de l'Italie'.

20. See Proust in his essay 'À propos de Baudelaire', *AS-B*, 202–4.

21. See note 11.

22. Cf. Proust in his riposte to Ghéon (letter 34, n. 9) in 1914: 'By showing the different attitudes of a group of people towards one another in the course of their lives, the aim is to do for psychology what geometry might achieve [. . .], to pass from plane psychology to space geometry, to practise psychology in Time.' See also Proust in *Le Temps* in 1913: 'For me, the novel is not only plane psychology, but psychology in time': 'Swann explained by Proust', *AS-B*, 234.

23. Proust considered that Rivière, in his choice of the fragments which made up 'The Quarrel with Gilberte' (see letter 32, n. 5), had put narrative before depth.

56 *To Pierre de Polignac*[1]

[Early February 1920]

Dear friend,

Your engagement[2] causes me great joy and profound heartache. When I was first drawn to you, you were leaving for China; now that liking has turned into great friendship, you are leaving for good. I master this sadness to share your happiness. Moreover, this sadness has already found its consolation in art, for with that clairvoyance which takes all the interest out of my life (because it lags behind my books), I wrote about your marriage (in one of my forthcoming volumes)[3] a year ago (naturally without mentioning you or anything connected to you).

In fact, the other day, when I read of your engagement, I had to rush to look at my proofs, for I had given the girl in question the name of Vermandois, which is too like Valentinois; it might have been thought that I was writing about you and the Duchesse de Valentinois in a way that you would not have liked.

Luckily, the proofs were still here. I changed Vermandois throughout, replacing it with Oloron.⁴ Oloron is so different from Valentinois that nobody would dream of a resemblance which was present only in the names. What a narrow escape!

[unsigned]

1. Pierre, Comte de Polignac (1895–1954). He and Proust had met in 1917.
2. Polignac's fiancée was Charlotte Grimaldi, Duchesse de Valentinois. The only child of Prince Louis de Monaco (from a liaison with a laundry-maid), she was adopted as Crown Princess by her grandfather, Proust's old acquaintance Prince Albert. It was announced that Polignac was to take the title of Duc de Valentinois.
3. See *The Guermantes Way*: the Comte de Nassau, through his marriage to a Luxembourg princess, takes the title of Grand Duke of Luxembourg: III, 378. Cf. III, 474; 617; 622–4.
4. See *The Fugitive*. Jupien's niece, Marie-Antoinette, having been adopted by Charlus, is introduced to society as Mlle d'Oloron, under which name she marries Léonor de Cambremer; as the narrator remarks: 'after all, she's the adopted daughter, and in the Cambremers' eyes, probably the real daughter – the natural daughter – of a person whom they regard as a Prince of the Blood. A bastard of a royal house has always been regarded as a flattering alliance by the nobility of France and other countries.' V, 756–7.

57 To Jean-Louis Vaudoyer

44 rue Hamelin
[Early February 1920]

Dear friend,

Forgive me if I dictate this letter tonight.¹ In the state I'm in today (in which I am almost every day), you wouldn't be able to read it if I wrote it myself. Now, I've been wanting to write to you for days, to thank you for your charming lines in *L'Opinion*² about the article in the *Nouvelle revue française*. Among other things temporarily postponed, I wanted to tell you this: you have never written better. I couldn't read without a secret envy the harmonious, scintillating passage where you speak of the reciprocity that goes with an imaginative approach to painting.³

A few days ago, I received your questionnaire about the Louvre.⁴ Dear friend, I sense my caffeine working, so can continue this letter on my own, and it's so pleasant, if only for a few lines, not to have a 'third party' between us. Now I long to give you my answers, but it's over fifteen years since I've been to the Louvre. I'll be going as soon as I can get up, but quite see that you can't wait till then. So, may I say in reply that, without expressing an opinion on galleries I haven't visited (I won't say for reasons of health, that being of no interest to anybody), I'm not really in favour of Art going out of its way to meet the art-lover rather than the other way round. (Naturally, there are exceptions; but between two extremes, I prefer the exacting demands of a *Rheingold* that one has sat through without pausing for dinner[5] to the condescension of musicians who are afraid, if a piece lasts more than five minutes, of tiring an audience whose staying-power is on the contrary increased tenfold by the beauties in prospect, and who think that nobody can listen to Beethoven's last quartets.) While praising its management, I would advise against turning the Museum into a sort of Hôtel Porgès.[6] In case an answer along these lines doesn't suit you (I can't find the actual questionnaire, it's buried beneath all the 'Surveys' to which I haven't replied, nor ever will), I could simply confine myself to listing the eight paintings, which would be, I think: *Portrait de lui-même* by Chardin,[7] *Portrait de Mme Chardin* by Chardin, *Nature morte* by Chardin, *Le Printemps* by Millet, *Olympia* by Manet, *Les Falaises d'Étretat* by Monet (if in the Louvre). A Renoir, or else *La Barque de Dante*[8] or *La Cathédrale de Chartres* by Corot. Either *L'Indifférent* by Watteau or his *L'Embarquement*.[9]

May I say, *supposing* we were to ask the Austro-Germans for pictures, that, rather than a second Watteau, I would prefer the Vermeer from Dresden or the Vermeer from Vienna?.[10] And, while on the subject of Vermeer, I would like to ask that his *La Dentellière*[11] be hung as a masterpiece in its own right, instead of with other Dutch pictures. (This doesn't mean that I prefer Vermeer to Watteau, as I would explain.)

If you see Daniel Halévy, tell him that exhaustion has prevented my writing to him, that I'll be doing so, that I was very touched by the respectful way in which he spoke of me in the *Minerve française*, even if only to criticize me.[12] Tell him that I'm not profligate. Rivière being ill, and his Review still incomplete, I wanted to save him a trip to Bruges[13] by writing him a long and simple letter on Flaubert's style. He went anyway; and, in correcting my proofs at the printers, turned my letter into an article;[14] his misreadings compounded my own errors of fact, notably in the passage on Daniel.

Ever yours,
Marcel Proust

1. From now on, Proust frequently dictated letters to Rochat, who took them down in longhand, often making grammatical and spelling errors.

2. 'Among the extraordinarily lucid, sensitive and stimulating passages to be found in M. Marcel Proust's article on Flaubert's "style", we find the following: "Moreover, we have only to read the masters [...] with a greater simplicity. We shall be astonished to find how alive they still are, at our side, offering us countless triumphant examples of the endeavour we ourselves have lacked."' Vaudoyer, 'The Lesson of the Louvre', *L'Opinion*, 24 January.

3. 'Ten minutes in the Louvre's Salon Carré, and we forget the habits and constraints of memory. Not only that, we see the paintings afresh [...] in a mysterious exchange akin to falling in love, which felicitous harmony is probably the true secret of their power.' Allusion to the re-hanging of the Salon Carré with masterpieces of the Italian Renaissance. *Ibid.*

4. *L'Opinion* had invited celebrities to choose eight masterpieces of French painting from the Louvre. The newspaper was to print part of Proust's letter on 28 February.

5. Wagner's *Das Rheingold* lasts 2 hours, 35 minutes without interval.

6. Allusion to the palatial house on the Avenue Montaigne built in 1892 by the Dutch banker Jules Porgès to house his art collection.

7. See Proust's essay 'Chardin and Rembrandt': *AS-B*, 122–31.

8. Probably Delacroix's *Dante and Virgil*.

9. *The Casual Lover* and *The Embarkment for Cythère*.

10. Respectively, *Lady reading a Letter at an Open Window* and *The Art of Painting*.

11. *The Lacemaker*, the Louvre's first Vermeer, acquired in 1870.

12. See 'Sainte-Beuve has failed his re-examination as a critic [...]. It took M. Marcel Proust a mere two or three pages, written, so he tells us, without his books to hand, to make up his mind. I wish he would be less profligate with the authority of a superior taste.' Daniel Halévy, *La Minerve française*, 1 February. Allusion to Sainte-Beuve's anniversary: see letter 44, n. 8.

13. The *NRF* was printed in Bruges.

14. Rivière printed 'On Flaubert's Style' in its epistolary form.

58 To Madame Soutzo

44 rue Hamelin
[17 or 18 February 1920]

Princesse,

I'm more than grateful to you for your thought, for your invitation (which I'm unable to accept), but I can't describe the melancholy it awakens in me. True, nothing could be kinder than an invitation to join you in that grand, glittering box, to listen in your company to the works of that gifted composer, M. Darius Milhaud, as part of an entertainment devised by my dear friend M. Jean Cocteau.[1] But how bitterly it makes me feel 'The dying of the light, the drawing in of days'.[2] A year ago, to be alone in your suite, Morand joining us, or rather, my joining you both, was my greatest happiness; and often, you would give one of your ravishing dinners which, for me, were merely the stage and limelight for your entrances, never twice the same. I would compliment you on your frock, and you would say 'I'm so glad you like it' with a smiling trustfulness that in anyone else would have seemed naïve, but which I found so deeply touching because it never crossed your mind that I was merely being polite and didn't like it all that much. But there was such openness between us that distrust was unthinkable, and, to me, your exclusion of all other hypotheses never seemed complacent but rather the tenderest of tributes to the sincerity of my admiration. All that was blighted (I couldn't possibly tell you why) about the time you invited the Queen of Romania to dinner at the Ritz,[3] a dinner which I didn't accept, though not, I swear, to prove my indifference to queens. Moreover, such an affectation would have been absurd, not to say a pure waste of time, for I knew by then that you wouldn't have noticed my absence any more than M. Stoïcesco's[4] or M. Astier's.[5] Those were the days when, not having been to bed, I would sometimes breakfast at the Ritz at teatime, then hurry upstairs to your suite to hear you berating your brother, and you would say that my eyes looked tired.[6] Now, it's a year since I've been out before half-past eight in the evening, there being no point as I no longer see you. I've put on weight, my eyes are no longer tired and, in consequence, now that it no longer matters, I don't look so old.

Yet by some incredible coincidence I receive a letter from you saying (quite wrongly) 'I know that you sometimes go out in the evening about five' on the day after an afternoon when, unable to sleep, I had in fact got up at five o'clock to go to the Nouvelle Revue Française. My sole daytime outing for a year, and you 'divined' it. Returning exhausted, I was hoping to lie down when Céleste started a chimney-fire in my room, and we couldn't lay a proper fire to warm me up until the accidental one, which lasted all night long, had burnt it itself out.[7]

Princesse, it's because of my extreme fatigue that I break off here. For despite not having answered an urgent letter for months, I can't end this one, which might go on for ever; indeed, I'm not writing it, I'm *weeping* it. Read it between tear-drops, if you are glad to have been loved.[8]

Adieu, Princesse.
Marcel Proust

Apologize to Morand for me, I owe him a letter. Tell him that everybody at the N.R.F. thinks *very highly* of him. As for the matinée, I had better refuse. I'm not saying that I'll never again go out during the day, but it's very unlikely to be that particular day and I wouldn't want you to waste a seat.[9]

1. A private dress-rehearsal of *Le Boeuf sur le toit*, Cocteau's new burlesque ballet at the Théâtre des Champs-Élysées; one of Étienne de Beaumont's famous Spectacles–Concerts with décor by Raoul Dufy.
2. 'La fuite des jours, le retour des soirées'. Unidentified quotation.
3. A dinner for Queen Marie of Romania, Queen Victoria's granddaughter, in March 1919.
4. Georges Stoïcesco, Romanian diplomat: see letter 247.
5. Baron Maurice d'Astier de la Vigerie.
6. See Morand's 'Ode to Marcel Proust': letter 42, n. 12.
7. Central-heating being bad for his asthma, Proust relied on coal fires.
8. Cf. the end of the narrator's love for Mme de Guermantes: III, 431.
9. In fact, he was to attend the dress-rehearsal.

59 To Robert de Flers[1]

44 rue Hamelin
[Sunday 22 February 1920]

My dearest Robert,

I can't tell you the joy, on reading your article this morning, suddenly to see your beautiful blue gaze turned towards me, your hand outstretched. What you say about me is magnificent, far too magnificent; I don't deserve such praise. But I make allowances for the happy blindness of friendship, and my joy is not diminished but increased.

I've been unable to see *The Winter's Tale*,[2] or anything else for that matter, so I was delighted to enjoy this play, thanks to you, from a bed rather than a seat in the stalls. But I didn't expect to be mentioned, as when Gide gives his lecture[3] ('portants étroits'[4] is marvellous, and couldn't be more true. I'm very fond of the people at the *Nouvelle revue française*, but we have little in common. Even when they praise me, their praises, while excessive, don't seem to me to be quite those I deserve). He came to dinner the other night on his way through Paris. I would have 'given you a ring', as one says in the 'best circles', but one feels that you'll never come, that you won't reply, and one gets discouraged. But one loves you. Ah! how I would like to see you again! Perhaps, even before you get this note, I shall have succeeded.[5] But with me, alas, everything is so uncertain, so exhausting.

With best wishes to Madame de Flers,[6] and my affection and gratitude,
Your admiring friend,
Marcel Proust

1. Robert, Marquis de Flers (1871–1927), editor of *Le Figaro*; co-author of light comedies with Gaston de Caillavet. He had helped found *Le Banquet* at the Lycée Condorcet with Proust.

2. The first post-war production at the Théâtre du Vieux Colombier. Fler's review alludes to the N.R.F. connection and congratulates them on having also produced 'M. Marcel Proust's much acclaimed novel, justly awarded the Prix Goncourt and, in its scope and power, a lasting monument to French fiction.'

3. Unfinished sentence. Gide sometimes gave lectures and readings from the stage.

4. Untranslatable pun on Gide's novel *La Porte étroite* (*Strait is the Gate*) and *portans*, the framework supporting stage flats etc. Flers's pun refers to the alleged 'Jansenist élitism' of Copeau's production: 'Clearly,' he writes, 'the dogmatism of his pronouncements [...] being no accident, he seems, so to speak, to be dreaming of a stage with *portants étroits*.'

5. Proust went to the *Figaro* that same evening, but missed seeing Flers.

6. *Née* Geneviève Sardou, daughter of the playwright Victorien Sardou.

60   To Madame Straus

44 rue Hamelin
(address confidential)
[Shortly after 15 March 1920]

Dear Madame Straus,

Alas, you were so ill and I had no idea! Did my body know, perhaps, so mysteriously linked to yours ('And we are still entwined, the one with the other'[1] despite our never having shared sleep, not even at the same times, and in my case scarcely having slept at all), for I was unaware that my 40° of fever, not nearly high enough in retrospect, had followed on your horrifying 41°. All I knew was that you had been bled and were in need of the peace which my visits and letters would have denied you; moreover, I only come to life for an hour every two weeks or so (I now understand the meaning of what you call 'living death').[2]

If anything could add to the horror of the dreadful months I've been through as a result of my moves, it's the knowledge that you were in pain. And I can tell from your letter that you were suffering.[3] What a blessing that you're cured! And what a blessing it will be, when you permit it, to come and sing hosannas with you. You don't know what you mean to me. My few friends do. Pierre de Polignac, a charming fellow who has become engaged to the Prince de Monaco's granddaughter, said to me: 'Perhaps this means that I shall meet the woman with the hassock at Versailles who made that pretty retort to M. de Noyon'.[4] I didn't realize that he meant you at first, having forgotten pastiches which my friends know better than I do. And, in *Le Côté de Guermantes*, they'll find those witticims of yours which made them laugh so much when I repeated them and which I've given to the Duchesse de Guermantes (whose red shoes you won't find till the second volume)[5], but without naming you, for you asked me not to put you in a novel but to keep your name for pastiches and essays, present and future. But your witticisms are so well-known that your name will be on everybody's lips. What irks me about this *Côté de Guermantes* is that, accidentally, thanks to its leading characters, it gives the impression of being very anti-Dreyfusard. True, the suceeding volume is so very Dreyfusard that it makes up for it, for the Prince and Princesse de Guermantes are Dreyfusards, though not the Duc and Duchesse, and so too is Swann.[6]

I'm prattling on about myself like a child. But I'm afraid of aggravating you by talking to you about yourself. Tell Monsieur Straus, who has always been so good to me about my money worries, that I've got no further with the cheque, but have discovered 12 Royal Dutch I didn't know I had, which means that Céleste has some hideous bird-of-paradise feathers in her hat. Above all, tell me when I may come, and kindly share with M. Straus my grateful and respectful regards.

Your
Marcel Proust

1. Victor Hugo, 'Booz endormi': 'Et nous sommes encore tout mêlés l'un à l'autre. / Elle à demi vivante et moi mort à demi'. Mme Straus had quoted the same lines in the letter to which Proust replies.

2. See the second line quoted above.

3. Proust ignores the chief object of Mme Straus's letter, which was to reproach him for his long silence towards Montesquiou.

4. Part of Proust's portrayal of Mme Straus in his Saint-Simon pastiche: see letter 30. Proust/Saint-Simon writes: 'She had her hassock in the chapel at Versailles, and she it was who, when asked by M. de Noyon, in the exaggerated and outlandish parlance peculiar to him, whether she had not found the music octagonal, made the reply: "Ah! Monsieur, I was about to say the same thing", for all the world as though his had been the most ordinary of remarks.' *CS-B*, 52–3.

5. i.e. at the end of the second volume of the first edition of *The Guermantes Way*. Proust alludes to the chilling scene where the Duc de Guermantes, interrupting Swann's announcement that he is mortally ill, orders the Duchesse to change her shoes because they don't match her red ball-gown: III, 688–90.

6. The Prince and Princesse de Guermantes are converted to Dreyfusism in *Sodom and Gomorrah*, Part Two, Chapter One. See Swann's conversation with the Prince, IV, 121–9.

61 To Lionel Hauser

[Shortly after 8 April 1920]

Dear Lionel,

How could you think that I've 'put up' with you![1] I fully appreciate all your remarkable qualities, and to have perceived a weakness among them has done nothing to lessen my affection, though it sometimes adds a touch of melancholy. Let me explain about the Prix Goncourt,[2] I misunderstood, thinking that that was what you meant by my being drunk on glory.[3] On the other hand, you are wrong about Henry James, whom I never met.[4] I was very surprised to learn, long after his death, that I had come so high in his esteem, having no reason to suppose that he had ever seen a line I had written.[5] Another error: the Crédit Industriel has on the contrary always said that the cheque for 30,000 francs was unfunded, a view shared by the adjudicator. Moreover, I intend to take the matter up with Warburg's. I spoke to the German Assets Bureau about it only because the 'competent' authorities keep changing.[6]

As for the moral debate that forms the substance of our correspondence, forgive me if I don't reopen it. The very fault I identified in you would prevent your profiting from my criticism (the wrong word, in any case) and have the effect of making me totally obnoxious to you, or at least the memory of me unbearable for its associations with such statements. At all events, since my feelings of gratitude and attachment remain completely unchanged, I beg you to be content with that assurance, and believe that I'm your very loving and grateful

Marcel Proust

You tell me that you prefer salons where one works to those where one chats.[7] I admit that I can't share your opinion, for a reason. Not frequenting them, I have no views on salons where one chats. As for salons where one works, I'm sure nobody frequents them, for the simple reason that they cannot exist. Salon life seems to me incompatible with work. Historically, they were said to be compatible;[8] but as I doubt whether the laws of the mind have changed, it follows that I can't believe in this former so-called compatibility.

Regarding politeness and rudeness, it's certainly true that if the first is a mask and the second a consequence of frankness, then the second is infinitely preferable to the first. But sometimes politeness springs from a good source and rudeness from a bad one. In that case there is a reversal of values. It goes without saying that I'm not talking about you. But you must have known men who were unpleasant or even violent for reasons which did them no credit. We're too quick to assume that sincerity and rudeness go together. The most abusive and slanderous newspapers are often the least sincere and the last to believe in what they say. But we've strayed a long way from our subject!

1. 'Having put up with me all these years, you suddenly tell me that my kindness is impenetrably clad in amour-propre, that I've sinned against you out of pride.' Hauser, 8 April.

2. 'You accuse me of assuming that you made a lot of useful business contacts through the Prix Goncourt. Yet [...] my actual phrase was: "Now that you're more famous than ever, pampered, fêted, receiving thousands of letters from your admirers etc." I think you'll agree that it says nothing about making new contacts.' *Ibid.*

3. 'I feel justified in resigning. [...] I regard you as a spoilt child who sulks when he can't get what he wants. [...] I'm very much afraid, my dear Marcel, that you may be drunk on glory.' Hauser, 1 April.

4. 'In your letter [...] you say: "with your usual lack of psychology". Is it really for nothing, I ask myself, that Henry James, one of the greatest of all psychologists, [...] spent the last year of his life annotating *Swann.*' Proust, 1 January. 'I dare

not claim that you lack insight because, to impress me, you'll only invoke the testimony of your friend Henry James once again.' Hauser, 8 April.

5. Proust would have learnt this from Walter Berry, whose friend Edith Wharton introduced *Swann's Way* to Henry James.

6. 'It makes me dizzy to think of the number of people involved in your affairs.' Hauser, 10 March.

7. 'You adore polite, well brought-up people. I have a horror of them, not for their politeness and upbringing, but because their politeness is a mask. [. . .] I therefore gave up going to salons where people chat in favour of those places where, instead of chattering, they work.' Hauser, 8 April.

8. Possible allusion to the Duchesse d'Abrantès's *Histoire des salons de Paris*, 1837.

62 To Robert Vallery-Radot[1]

[Shortly after 10 April 1920]

Dear Sir,

I was deeply touched by your article,[2] for which I have the keenest admiration. It is, I think, the most remarkable article I have read on *Les Jeunes filles en fleurs*. And nowhere have I seen the structure of the book (not that of the complete work, which has in fact only just begun to appear) so clearly and subtly felt.[3] Why does something which gives me so much pleasure have to be spoilt by a criticism that no work of literature could withstand?[4] I don't want to make myself ridiculous by comparing myself to great writers, but it's less a question of comparison than of seeking justification in one's betters. Think of the number of secular plays Racine had to write before he was worthy of creating *Esther* and *Athalie*. Don't you think that to stick to one's feelings, to one's beliefs, to be true, in the strictest and narrowest sense of the word, is the essential preparation for any kind of higher life? And isn't that what I've done, with an honesty, a devotion to everything we see around us, which doesn't deserve censure. I'm putting this very badly, I'm extremely ill, incapable of writing a letter, and not having your article in front of me, may be making too much of it; I haven't the strength to show you my design, but it will emerge little by little from my books, each being a leaf detached from one and the same work; all I wanted was to thank you for having read me so well, and for having so well described what you read.

Your grateful
Marcel Proust

1. Robert Vallery-Radot (1885–1970), Catholic scholar.

2. A review of *Within a Budding Grove* in the *Revue des jeunes*, a Catholic magazine for young people.

3. 'Closing this book, and murmuring its Japanese title, one seems to see the two panels of a screen, finely-woven in multi-coloured silks. On one, in the background, the Paris of our childhood [...]. On the other, a changing iridescent sea, and, strolling across the foreground, a group of young girls, a mysterious youth, an enigmatic prince, an ageing marquise, a princess [...]. And below, where the panels meet, the youth of the hawthorns once again, nonchalantly reclining, blowing bubbles on his clay pipe[...]. And as one lingers among the characters, and wanders through landscapes and interiors, one realizes that the creator of this marvellous décor is also a moralist in the best tradition.' Vallery-Radot, *loc. cit.*

4. 'yet we never see either his subject or his heart escape from this touching but puerile domain of romantic sensibility; not for one moment, it seems, does he conceive of a more spiritual life, an anguish greater than that of being scorned by Odette or by Albertine; in short, of the existence of God. And thus, at the same time as our minds are being seduced by so much ingenuity, so much mischievous and subtle observation, we have a sense of claustrophobia, of a path leading to a dead end.' *Ibid.*

63 To Henri de Régnier[1]

44 rue Hamelin
[Wednesday evening 14 April 1920]

Dear Sir and friend,

I can't tell you how deeply your letter touched me, it moved me to tears. The vote you offer me[2] – a unique vote, its uniqueness, practically speaking, being no substitute for the requisite number – means more to me than you may realize. I may have Guiche telephoned, to ask him to join us. But I'm too tired to write to Barrès, to Bordeaux,[3] to so many others. I happened to write to Boylesve the other day, but at the time (although it was less than a week ago) I had no academic ambitions. So I didn't mention it. In any case, he is someone to whom I can always drop a line. There are so many drawbacks to my candidature. Take Hanotaux,[4] for example. You may remember that I saw a great deal of him at one time, it being at my parents' house that he, and you too, I believe, first met that great genius, as he will always remain for me as long as there is a French language, José-Maria de Heredia.[5] Yet excesses of pain and fatigue have meant that I've never sent Hanotaux my books. He hasn't heard from me for almost twenty years. That doesn't make it very pleasant to write and ask him a favour. Naturally, I'll visit him, and everybody else, if I stand. I cite his example (I could also cite Loti's,[6] as someone I hardly know but who has shown a liking for me) to show you what a poor 'academic subject' I am in this respect. But then, to await a vacancy.... It's much more likely that my own vacancy will come first! At least it's not indispensable to have been a member of the Academy, and not having been an Academician, one can die without immense regret! If I had somebody the equivalent of Léon Daudet at the Goncourt Academy, who hadn't seen me for twenty years but canvassed tirelessly on my behalf, forming my scattering of supporters into a solid block, producing others out of thin air and defending me 'unguibus et rostro',[7] as he put it, through every round of voting, perhaps I would enter the fray. But it doesn't seem as though I have anybody like that at the French Academy. But I may talk to Guiche. I doubt if he can tell us much.

Often, when faced with a problem of literary conscience, I think of you. For instance, I see that you have written an article on Moréas,[8] though I shan't get it till tomorrow or the day after. If it accords the author of *Stances* the place given him by a literary circle which has treated me so generously, and to which I'm extremely grateful, I doubt that it will convert me. While admiring *Stances* (without really knowing it), I fail to see why writing purely should be considered praiseworthy when one has so little to say.[9] Yet one feels that words might fail him at any moment if he didn't rely on pastiche. Now, I believe one resembles great masters only by doing what they do differently (take the 'scandal' of Manet's *Olympia*).[10] I've been your admirer too long for you to suspect me of self-seeking flattery if I tell you that I would give the whole of Moréas, and much else besides, for 'We're on our way to town where there is singing on the streets', even just for the 'silence of swooning dances'.[11] Moreover, your later verse is written in the form in which Moréas probably thought he was writing. But in your case, the purity and simplicity of the lines doesn't exclude invention and feeling. I can say all this because I never met Moréas; knowing his work so little, I ought not to say it, but the little I know is enough to 'confirm me', as he would have said, in my doubts. I don't expect this revival of his reputation to last very long.

I don't know how often you see Madame Muhlfeld.[12] But should you have the chance, kindly tell her (I'll be writing to her in any case) that a wicked genie must be intercepting her letters to me and vice versa, for as at a séance, we never seem to be aware of the other's previous communication.

To return, after this long digression, to the Academy election. I believe that General Mangin,[13] whom I don't know, but he is my brother's *close* friend and also, I hear from another source, a friend to my books, might be helpful to me. Also Madame de Pierrebourg,[14] who is good enough to have a great liking for me. To put myself forward now, always supposing I have the time left to await a vacancy, seems to me to have the disadvantage that, being little known, my name will quickly be overshadowed by candidates more in the public eye. But naturally I don't understand these things.

Dear Sir, kindly give my humble greetings to the Queen of the Canaques,[15] and share with her my grateful admiration and undying friendship.

Marcel Proust

1. Henri de Régnier (1864–1936), leading Symbolist poet, also a novelist.

2. Proust was contemplating standing for election to the French Academy: one of the so-called 'Immortals' had died, leaving a vacancy.

3. Henry Bordeaux (1870–1963), novelist and Academician.

4. Gabriel Hanotaux (1853–1944), French statesman, historian and Academician.

5. José-Maria de Heredia (1842–1905), Cuban-born poet, first and most famous of the Parnassians. Proust alludes to a dinner at boulevard Malesherbes in 1885; as well as Régnier and Hanotaux, then foreign minister, the guests included Félix Faure, President of the Republic, with his two daughters, friends of Proust, Robert de Montesquiou and the Heredia family.

6. Pierre Loti (1850–1923), author of romantic, exotic novels.

7. 'tooth and nail'.

8. Jean Moréas (1856–1910), poet, Greek-born Symbolist turned Classicist, best known for his eight-volume work *Stances*.

9. Allusion to Moréas's style. Proust thought him short-winded, with an unfortunate penchant for archaic language. See *AS-B* 100.

10. Allusion to the Paris Salon of 1865. The Louvre acquired Manet's painting of a nude courtesan from the exhibition, but didn't dare show it until 1907. See *The Guermantes Way*: III, 484–5; 604.

11. Proust quotes from Régnier's 'Scène au crépuscule': 'En allant vers la Ville où l'on chante aux terrasses / Sous les arbres en fleurs comme des bouquets des fiancées, / En allant vers la Ville où le pavé des places / Vibre au soir rose et bleu d'un silence des danses lassées [. . .].'

12. Mme Lucien Muhlfeld, wife of the editor of *La Revue Blanche*.

13. Charles Mangin (1866–1925), hero of Verdun and leader of the 1918 Marne

offensive, 'A genius', according to Saint-Loup (III, 123). Mangin had mentioned Robert Proust in his dispatches for courage in operating under fire.

14. Baronne Aiméry Harty de Pierrebourg (1872–1963), alias the novelist Claude Ferval, a member of the Prix Femina jury.

15. Mme Henri de Régnier, *née* Marie de Heredia (1875–1961), alias the poet Gérard d'Houville. Marie was the most striking of Heredia's three daughters, all of whom had inherited an exotic Cuban beauty and whose admirers called themselves 'Canaques' or slaves.

64   To Jacques Rivière

[Shortly after 20 May 1920]

Dear friend,

If I haven't written before this, it was to leave you in peace.[1] Now I'm so ill in my turn that, as you see, I'm obliged to dictate this letter. As you're due back shortly, we can have a chat about possible collaboration on the *NRF*.[2] But in my opinion, the main thing is for me to devote my strength, such as it is, to finishing *Swann*. I delivered the next volume[3] to Tronche a few days ago and would have done so sooner but for an event which forced me to start all over again.[4] Anyhow, it having gone to press, I'm ploughing my furrow once again and making slightly better progress.

I've returned the Sainte-Beuves[5] to Tronche. In fact (just as well, in my opinion), you misunderstood my reply about the Sainte-Beuve. It was exactly the same as for the Flaubert.[6] Only my fear of not doing it well made me hesitate to accept the commission. It's now too late, but what I could do is to write an informal letter, off the cuff, addressed to Jacques Rivière, explaining why I can't be drawn into the Sainte-Beuve controversy just now.[7] And my refusal to reply would amount to a sort of reply, but you must allow me the 'My dear Rivière' formula. Let me know if you publish a book by Baudelaire, Balzac etc., and I'll gladly do you a 'note'.[8]

An English newspaper has sent me what appears to be an extremely kind article by your friend Monsieur Thibaudet.[9] À propos, how wrong Gaston is to procrastinate over translations. There have already been eight or nine articles in *The Times* alone (Thibaudet's wasn't in *The Times*, I forget the name of the newspaper). Obviously, people who read these articles and don't know French would be glad of a translation. I can't repeat indefinitely what I've been saying for the past year about the *Pastiches* etc. But why do badly what it is in everybody's interest to do well.

My dear friend, this is strictly between ourselves: would it be acceptable or unacceptable to the *NRF*, advantageous or disadvantageous to my books, if I stood (with a chance of success, otherwise I wouldn't do it) for election to the Academy? Dear friend, I can't tell you how fond I am of you and what a pleasure it will be to see you again.

With my respectful regards to Madame Rivière,[10]
Ever yours,
Marcel Proust

1. Rivière was convalescing in Gascony.
2. Proust's frequent criticisms had led Rivière to suggest this idea.
3. *The Guermantes Way*, Part One.
4. Presumably Pierre de Polignac's engagement: see letter 56.
5. Proust had borrowed copies of Sainte-Beuve for his essay 'On Flaubert's Style'.
6. i.e. a similar essay in epistolary style.
7. See letter 57, n. 12.
8. Proust was thinking of putting together a book of literary criticism; meanwhile, he was renewing his attack on Sainte-Beuve in a preface he was writing for Morand, and in his essay 'Concerning Baudelaire' for the *NRF*, also in epistolary form: see *AS-B*, 278–81; 299–301.
9. Albert Thibaudet (1874–1936), the critic whose article on Flaubert in the *NRF* had prompted Proust's own essay. His essay 'Marcel Proust and the Analytical Novel' appeared in the *London Mercury*.
10. *Née* Isabelle Fournier, sister of the writer Alain-Fournier.

65 To Maurice Montabré[1]

[Around June 1920]

Sir,

You make a distinction between the manual and intellectual professions to which I find myself unable to subscribe.[2]

As our good Chardin said (better), one paints not only with the hand but with the heart. And the great Leonardo said of painting that it is *cosa mentale*.[3] Much the same applies to other forms of physical exercise, such as making love. That's why it is sometimes so tiring.[4] Let me invoke this collaboration of hand and mind in order to tell you that, were I to find myself in the situation you specify, as manual labour I would take precisely the same job as I have at present, that of writer. If the supply of paper dried up completely, I would, I think, be a baker. It is an honourable thing to give men their daily bread. Meanwhile, I endeavour to bake that 'Angels' bread' of which Racine (whom I quote from memory and probably quite inaccurately) said:

> 'Our Lord himself bakes it
> From the choicest of his wheat
> The one bread so delectable
> That the world which we obey
> Does not serve at its table
> Then I to my disciples say
> Draw near: do you wish to live?
> Take it, eat it, and live.'[5]

Do you not think that here Racine resembles M. Paul Valéry, who in turn rediscovered Malherbe via Mallarmé?[6]

Believe me, dear Sir and colleague, yours faithfully,
Marcel Proust

1. Journalist on *L'Intransigeant*: see letter 68, n. 1.

2. The newspaper had asked prominent writers the following question: 'If for some reason you were obliged to take a manual job, what job would you choose as best suited to your tastes, talents and abilities?'

3. Allusion to Leonardo da Vinci's *Trattato della Pittura*: 'If you say that non-mathematical sciences are things of the mind, then you must say the painting is a thing of the mind.' Cf. *Within a Budding Grove*: 'Happiness [. . .] was a thing I had never ceased to think of, a thing wholly in my mind – as Leonardo said of painting, *cosa mentale*'. II, 84. See also the passage on Chardin and Elstir in *The Guermantes Way*: III, 483–5.

4. Remarks cut when this letter appeared in *L'Intransigeant* on 3 August.

5. Proust quotes, with minor inaccuracies, from Racine's *Cantiques spirituels*, Book IV: 'Dieu lui-même le compose / De la fleur de son froment / C'est ce pain si délectable / Que ne sert point à sa table / Le monde que vous suivez / Je l'offre à qui me veut suivre / Approchez: voulez-vous vivre? / Prenez, mangez, et vivez.'

6. See letter 34, n. 8.

66 To Jacques Porel

[Wednesday 16 June 1920]

My dear Jacques,

    Only since yesterday evening have I been able to weep with you.[1] On the evening of the day before the shock was too sudden, and so physical that, like those beasts which stand stock-still, as if paralysed, I was unable to budge. The release, and the sobbing, came only in the morning. Eye-strain prevents my reading the papers, yet I read Bidou,[2] and your Mother meant so much to me, I hardly knew how much, that a simple tribute to her acting,[3] a professional comment, made me weep with a relative's grief.

    Store up, against the day when you may find them helpful, the things I said to you the other night.[4] These words hold no meaning for you at present; are even, perhaps, repudiated by bitter thoughts. But once this journey from bereavement to Memory is completed, a journey from whose terrible twists and turns you cannot, alas, be shielded, you will find them true and sweet and fortifying.

    Give my deepest respects to Madame Porel, and allow me to embrace you.

Marcel

1. His mother Réjane had died at home of a heart attack on 14 June.
2. Henri Bidou (1873–1943), 'Réjane', *Journal des Débats*, 16 June.
3. See letter 12, n. 4.
4. Proust had heard the news while at the opera and had left immediately for the rue Laurent-Pichat to be with Porel.

67 To Jacques Rivière

[Shortly after 2 July 1920]

Dear friend,

    I add a postscript to my letter in order to thank you, and also to reassure you on the subject of the 'psychological aspects' of my novel.[1] As it is a construction, it naturally has walls and pillars, and, in the space between two pillars, I give myself up to minutely detailed painting. The entire volume on the break with Albertine, her death, the forgetting, leaves the quarrel with Gilberte far behind. Thus you will have three sketches of the same subject, all very different (separation of Swann and Odette in *Un amour de Swann*[2] – quarrel with Gilberte in *Les Jeunes filles en fleurs*[3] – separation from Albertine in *Sodome et Gomorrhe*,[4] the best part).

Dear friend, it so happens that literary journals in France and abroad never stop talking about *Jeunes filles en fleurs*. But I didn't like to ask you to mention it (not you, Jacques Rivière, the *NRF*). Yet you had an enormous 'Review of Reviews' in your last issue. If you have another in the next, you'll be obliged to single out, as it's almost the lead, Pierre Lasserre's stupid article 'Marcel Proust, humorist and moralist' in the *Revue universelle*.[5] If so, I would be grateful for the courtesy of a few lines in which to refute it (anonymously, of course) or preferably under the by-line of whoever writes the Review of Reviews (if this is signed). In that case, kindly let me know in advance so that I have time to draft ten lines or so. And I would also like you to have them re-typed (or I will myself), so that not even the person who reviews the Reviews will know that these ten lines were written by me, and will think that they come from you.[6]

Affectionately yours,
Marcel Proust

1. 'On the train from Paris, I began reading the proofs of your book [*The Guermantes Way*, Part One] and was at once irresistibly carried away [...]. You are a great writer, and in this beginning to your new book, which is rather more poetical than psychological, or at least richer in long descriptive passages than its predecessors (as I write, I wonder if this is really true, or if my impression comes from not having found any sustained psychological developments, such as the quarrel with Gilberte, or the growing love for Albertine), you reveal qualities of style even more astonishing than those you have already demonstrated.' Rivière, 29 June.
2. Part Two of *Swann's Way*.
3. See letter 32, n.5.
4. 'Grieving and Forgetting', V, 477 ff., a chapter in the fourth volume of *Sodom and Gomorrah*, as yet untitled (later *The Fugitive*).
5. A long essay by Pierre Lasserre (1867–1930) attacking Proust for decadence appeared in the new literary review edited by Jacques Bainville of *L'Action française*.
6. Rivière was to reply to Lasserre himself in the *NRF* of 1 September.

68 To L'Intransigeant[1]

[End July or early August 1920]

Gentlemen of the Thirteen,

Since you are good enough to invite me to make a fourteenth,[2] I give you my opinion forthwith: people with very little money, as well as those with a lot, are unable to buy books, the first through poverty, the second through greed. Instead, they borrow them. Lending libraries would therefore merely regularize an existing situation, but with this quaint innovation, that books, once borrowed, would have to be returned. On the other hand, how convenient, how advantageous for publishers who cannot sell their books. Hiring them out will be more profitable (look at cars). Editors will be permanently relieved of the necessity for that increasingly rare thing: the reprint. But Sirs, I embarked on this letter forgetting that I am an author. And, for authors, it would be disastrous. For it's not a case of the good, old-fashioned reading-room, sole repository of books found nowhere else, like the novels of Céleste Mogador[3] or the Comtesse d'Asche,[4] or the occasional copy of Balzac's preface to *La Chartreuse*,[5] books that one dared read only when wearing kid gloves. The new reading-rooms, being very 'modern', will enable our contemporaries' books to earn a publisher money without his having to pay royalties to his authors. But I've forgotten something else, which is that I like my publishers, who are charming and generous men. Don't you think that they may wish to open their own reading-rooms? I shall now give you some excellent arguments in favour of cirulating-libraries (as I believe they are called). When, I would like to know, has one ever heard of an acquired taste leading to restraint rather than overindulgence? To take riding-lessons gives one the desire to own a horse. To borrow books will eventually lead to the desire to buy, if not to read them. All these arguments are self-contradictory, I hear you say, yet each seems very sensible to me. In the hope that they also seem so to you, I remain, yours faithfully,

Marcel Proust

1. Journal founded in 1880 by the Nationalist politician Henri Rochefort-Luçay for the purpose of promoting anti-Semitism and anti-Dreyfusism.

2. Writers were asked whether or not they were in favour of the proposed new lending libraries in a survey entitled 'A Little Investigation by the Thirteen', an allusion to the secret society in Balzac's *Histoire des Treize*. Proust's answer was to appear in *L'Intransigeant* of 20 August.

3. Pseudonym of the Comtesse Lionel Mobreton de Chabrillan, nineteenth-century actress and literary hostess.

4. Pseudonym of the Vicomtesse de Saint-Mars, nineteenth-century memorialist of aristocratic morals.

5. Balzac's study of Stendhal first appeared in *La Revue parisienne* before being published as the preface to the 1846 edition of *La Chartreuse de Parme*. See the narrator's discoveries in country-house libraries: III, 636.

69   To Paul Morand

[Towards the end of August 1920]

My dear Paul,

Many thanks for your note. I haven't yet received your novellas,[1] but I hope it won't be long now. Did I tell how annoyed I was that this preface should appear before *Guermantes II*?[2] But I suppose it can't be helped. Moreover, everything is late.

As for Giraudoux, if I needed anything (which I don't in fact, this business never having looked like coming to anything, and I don't know what possessed me to tell you about knocking people up with my cane),[3] he is the last person I would turn to. The reason is that I've just finished reading *Adorable Clio*.[4] Can it be that till now I thought I had read Giraudoux when I hadn't? I see no other reason why *Adorable Clio* should have come as such an extraordinary revelation to me. I admire this book so much that I'm going to write and tell Giraudoux. Now, to follow that by asking him a favour might make him think, in retrospect, that my praises had been self-interested, which would horrify me. (Besides, as I say, I don't need anybody, it's not a crime to make a noise, I was only trying to get the concierge to let me in and, should she lodge a complaint, I'll appear in my own defence, confident of having a good case.)

Not a line in Giraudoux's book but I find something to admire in it. It has minor stylistic defects, and a seeming lack of breadth which comes from this perpetual criss-crossing of innovations. But it's breathtaking. I like *Nuit à Châteauroux*[5] even better on second reading. I dare not ask him in my letter if he really meant Pavel to make those spelling mistakes ('Rucian' for 'Russian').[6] I should be sorry to learn that Giraudoux was spiteful. Not that it's incompatible with having talent. But it's a pity not to be able to like unreservedly. You couldn't possibly be nicer, but you're not *good*. (For instance, it was your idea to hypnotize Beaumont.)[7] The most beautiful sentence in the book, in my opinion, is where the young men are leaving for the front and become their parents' elders, being nearer to death. I found the soldiers with space to the side of them (sea, Switzerland),[8] and the piano-teacher who drums on his kit-bag to keep his fingers supple etc. absolutely hilarious. Perhaps my first impression will change. At the moment, I'm extraordinarily excited by his way of picturing a thing, anything. All is reflected in an eye so original as to seem barely human. I may be exaggerating. What a bore that the three of us couldn't dine together because of my four beards.[9] In my opinion, what Giraudoux's admirers say (you excepted) about his talent doesn't do him justice.

I found a barber eventually, so this evening I was able to dine, alone, in the restaurant at the Ritz. My table was near M. Paderewski's.[10] He thought he was thanking the French nation by telling the Swiss manager[11] that it was victory for France.[12] And the things that were said to him by complete strangers who came up to his table were unbelievably comic!

Ever yours,
Marcel Proust

1. *Tendres Stocks*, a book of three novellas, for which Proust was writing the preface. See 'Preface for Morand': *AS-B*, 275–85.

2. Proust's preface was to appear in the *Revue de Paris* on 15 November and *The Guermantes Way* Part Two in May 1921.

3. 'Last night, about 10.20, I went to a friend's Montmartre hotel (nothing like Charlus!) to collect some antiquarian books. [. . .] The concierge refused to open up, saying that it was too late for visitors. [. . .] I persisted, offering her 10 francs through the shutters; she told me to keep my money and go to hell. In a fit of rage, I banged on the door with my cane so loudly that my friend heard and came down. [. . .] I'm told that the concierge (I never saw her, she shouted at me through the shutters, calling me a drunk, a brute etc.) has threatened to take me to court for disturbing the peace. [. . .] Do you know anybody who might put in a good word for me with the Préfecture or the Police Superintend of Montmartre?' Proust to Morand, *c*. 18 August.

4. Collection of Giraudoux's war stories.

5. The first story in *Adorable Clio*, see letter 42, no. 10. Proust talks about *Nuit à Châteauroux* in 'Preface for Morand': *AS-B*, 284.

6. Proust sympathizes with Pavel: he himself often spelt names phonetically.

7. Allusion to a séance at a party given by the Beaumonts at the Ritz in 1917.

8. See Giraudoux, *op. cit.*, 232: 'At dawn, of all the soldiers in line, only two, one stretching his arms out to sea, the other to Switzerland, had space to the side of them.'

9. See letter 42, n. 14.

10. Ignace ('Jan') Paderewski (1860–1941), Polish statesman and world-famous pianist.

11. Camille Wixler: see letter 219, n. 6.

12. Paderewski had taken part in the disarmament conference held at Spa, Belgium, in July.

70 To Madame Sert[1]

[1 September 1920]

Madame,

I was very touched that you should trouble to write and inform me of this marriage that has the awesome perfection of all wonderfully unnecessary things.[2] What wife could Sert have found, and you what husband, as pre-ordained, as uniquely worthy the one of the other? I knew Sert when you, I believe, were unknown to him, and I thought to myself: this, this and this appeals to him. Yet all these things are united and reach their perfection only in Madame Edwards. To my mind, she is already his wife. And vice versa. That is why I never saw one of you without speaking of the other. You say that St Roch must have had something to do with it. The Scuola di San Rocco brought you together.[3] It is fitting that the Church of Saint-Roch[4] should have blessed you, as do an incalculable number of people among whom none is more warmly admiring of you, and of Sert, than your respectfully devoted

Marcel Proust

To see your beloved Poland safe made me very happy.[5]

1. *Née* Maria Godebska (1872–1950). In the 1890s, as Mme Thadée Natanson, she befriended Mallarmé, Bonnard and Vuillard; then, with her second marriage to another magnate, Alfred Edwards, Stravinsky, Diaghilev and Picasso. Proust portrays her, unflatteringly, as the Princesse Yourbeletieff, patroness of the Ballets Russes: IV, 165; V, 267.

2. She had married the Catalan painter José-Maria Sert (1876–1945) after living with him for ten years. They were on honeymoon in Venice.

3. See Proust to Walter Berry, *c.* 1 September: '[In Venice] you doubtless enjoyed the company of Tintoretto himself (alias Sert) and his lovely Dogesse. In telling me that their marriage was blessed by St Roch, I think she confuses the sacred and the profane, as in the Renaissance, and means the Scuola di San Rocco.' Proust alludes to the magnificent San Rocco murals by Tintoretto, Sert being famous for his huge murals for the Ballets Russes. See V, 421–2.

4. Parish church in Paris.

5. Allusion to Poland's victory over the Red Army in the Battle of Warsaw, establishing her eastern boundaries for the next twenty years.

71 To Sydney Schiff[1]

44, rue Hamelin
[1 or 2 September 1920]

Dear Sir (Do we use 'and friend'? I don't have your letter in front of me. But friend seems to me both pleasant and true),

Your wonderful letter[2] leaves me in despair as it forces me to answer you. It enchants me, infuriates me, etc.

Enchants me: thanks to its gallery of portraits, which is a marvel, and your enjoyable, pugnaciously profound views on humanity.[3] You don't mince your words! A little hard on Louis, perhaps.[4] I think he is nobler in spirit than you say. He may talk about film-stars but unfortunately has eyes not for Mlle X and Mlle Y but only for their motor-cars. (I'm overtired, or I would edit what I'm saying a little.) I envy him his capacity for non-reaction. I'm ill, and yet I feel I could fight a duel every day for what remains of my life. You can't imagine my nervous energy (except for work). Everything passes him by like a whiff of roses, and he finds even that a little strong. What I reproach him with is telling lies. He lied in order to get to know me and has hardly stopped lying since.[5] But there is no harm in him, only sweetness, understanding, and a yearning for culture.

I'm infuriated (not with him, with you) by your criticism of the sale of de-luxe editions.[6] Are authors supposed to starve to death? True, I'm writing my *Swann* in a garret, but because of the housing shortage, this garret costs me 2600 francs a month. (And my secretary has left me.) The philistinism of readers reminds me of something in Ruskin which you may know.[7] And you must know Whistler's story of entertaining the richest men in England to luncheon. They (the bailiffs) come to seize his belongings. A quarter of the unsold pictures there would have served to get rid of the bailiffs, but it doesn't occur to a single one of these art-lovers to buy so much as a 'Harmony in Grey and Silver'.

That said, I entirely agree with you, not having the slightest interest in either de-luxe editions or autographs. But not for the same reason. You feel that there is something sacred about them (a beautiful idea of yours, beautifully expressed);[8] but while that may be true for the lover of an author's books, it isn't so for the author himself, who never even sees them (cf. the Goncourts' will, which stipulated that the collection they had so lovingly assembled be auctioned, so that, rather than moulder away in the indifference of a museum, each object might be acquired by a person who genuinely desired to possess it).

Your remark about people in general, their boringness, made me die with laughter. It's so like me! Only I'm closer to Madame Schiff[9] (I adore the touchingly tender way you speak of her) when it comes to choosing my company. I mean that I do my intellectual work within myself,[10] and once among my fellow men, it doesn't much matter to me whether they are intelligent, as long as they are kind, sincere etc.

Were you Dreyfusard in the old days? I was, passionately. Yet it so happens that *Le Côté de Guermantes*, because I'm totally objective in my books, gives the appearance of being anti-Dreyfusard. But *Sodome et Gomorrhe I* is wholly Dreyfusard and makes up for it. Naturally, I'll send you *Le Côté de Guermantes* as soon as it comes out.[11]

You are so nice to have ordered a de-luxe copy of *Les Jeunes filles*. I only hope you manage to get one. To find out, I would have to write to the N.R.F. And it's so much more enjoyable writing to you. In any case, there's no point, for you tell me that you're writing to them, and they're bound to write back. To finish with, for tiredness overcomes me, I was astonished that you should have attributed my silence to disappointment.[12] That's like Robert de Montesquiou saying that I hadn't replied to any of his letters because I was 'fashionable' (!) and feared that he might dedicate his next book to me! How could you think that I hadn't immediately liked you both. There is nobody I would rather see when you are next in Paris.

No, I shan't be going to Monte Carlo.[13]

As for *Richard Kurt*,[14] tiredness has nothing to do with my not having read it properly, it's because I no longer know a word of English. A friend who speaks very good English[15] will soon be back, and will translate while reading it aloud to me. Did you know that a lot of English newspapers are being very complimentary about *Swann* and talk about it so familiarly and in such minute detail that it shows a real knowledge. What a pity it isn't translated. Much to tell you about the Asquiths (the daughter[16] is unbelievably intelligent, did you know?) but as you see from this disjointed ending, I can't go on.

Once more, heartfelt thanks for the de-luxe copy. My deepest respects to Madame Schiff.

Your friend,
Marcel Proust

1. Sydney Schiff (1868–1941), English man-of-letters with whom Proust had corresponded regularly since April 1919. He was later to translate *Time Regained* under the pseudonym Stephen Hudson.

2. Schiff wrote to Proust in a flowery, somewhat inaccurate French.

3. Schiff had given Proust a caustic description of his sister Edith's four stepchildren by her marriage to Comte Albert Gautier-Vignal.

4. Louis, Comte Gautier-Vignal (1888–1982), wartime pilot, source of much of Proust's information about aviation in the Albertine story.

5. Cf. Nissim Bernard's perpetual lying: II, 410–11.

6. Allusion to the limited edition of *Within a Budding Grove*, hand-bound, with autograph passages etc. Fifty copies were printed at 300 francs each.

7. See Ruskin's remark in *Sesame and Lilies*: 'What do we, as a nation, care about books? How much do you think we spend altogether on our libraries, public or private, compared with what we spend on our horses?'

8. 'I'm disgusted by the commercial exploitation of an author and his most personal things [...]. The few books I love passionately are sacred to me [...] and it seems like sacrilege to turn them into fashionable gewgaws.' Schiff, 20 August.

9. *Née* Violet Beddington (1875–1962).

10. Cf. the narrator's reflections on solitude and society in *Time Regained* and his allusion to 'the timeless man within me'.

11. *The Guermantes Way* Part One was to be published in October.

12. The Schiffs had met Proust for the first time in May.

13. 'I'm sure to die without seeing the place I hate most: Monte Carlo. But that may change, now that one of my best friends has married the Prince's adopted granddaughter.' In fact, Polignac was to snub Proust after his marriage. (Proust hated Monte Carlo because it was to Monaco that his beloved secretary Agostinelli had fled with his wife and died in a plane crash.) Proust to Schiff, *c.* 30 August.

14. Novel by Schiff under his pen-name Stephen Hudson.

15. Antoine Bibesco.

16. Elizabeth Asquith (1897–1945), daughter of the late prime minister, had recently married Antoine Bibesco.

72   To Lucien Daudet

[15 or 16 September 1920]

My dearest Lucien,

You're a thousand thousand times too good, but you greatly exaggerate. I'm not happy with my book,[1] and furthermore it's totally disfigured by misprints, several hundred at the very least, to count only the most glaring. In your indulgence, you not only overlook the author's errors, you overlook the printer's! I admit that, at moments, there is a little of the Contades daughter[2] in Mme de Villeparisis, a little of Walewski as opposed to Cholet in Borodino,[3] and that I took into account (infinitesimally) the identical stupid remark made to me by Montholon[4] and Félix Faure,[5] the first about the Duc d'Orléans, the second about the Prince of Wales. Neither, in their opinion, being suitably solemn or majestic. I'll give your brother chapter and verse if it interests him. Lastly, there is a touch (the merest touch) of the Brissaud type of doctor, more rhetorician and sceptic than clinician, in du Boulbon.[6] But I'm letting myself get carried away by your sweet letter and, naïvely, beginning to look for keys, as if that could interest anyone! Besides, there are so many to every door that, in reality, there are none.

Only in succeeding volumes does the work become almost good, and I am very embarrassed to dedicate to your brother a book so unworthy of him and of your great name. But as the coming volumes involve Sodom and Gomorrah, I felt that the title might displease. And I was too impatient to show him my gratitude to wait for the ones after that. Moreover, in my precarious state of health, I didn't want to put it off for too long.

I'll tell you about the *NRF* another time.[7] I'm searching everywhere for Gide, so as to talk to him about Rivière[8] (nothing to do with you) and for Rivière so as to talk to him again about you. Yet I can discover the whereabouts of neither. In Gide's case, it's 'somewhere in England', which is a little vague! It reminds me of Jean's[9] reply when I asked him for Cendrars's[10] address (he must be the tenth person I've asked this year, for having written Cendrars a very long letter of appreciation at a time when I thought writing would kill me, I wanted him to know of my gratitude) and Jean replied: at last, I have it: 'somewhere between Bordeaux and Aix'.

In any case, I think I told you that I caught a glimpse of Rivière on his way through Paris and talked to him about you and about what you said about Lasserre.[11] He was very touched and sends you a thousand thanks. He is sure to come and see me on his return and I'll write to you. I have no news of Reynaldo, except that he has found lodgings in the rue St Honoré. I didn't realize his brother-in-law's[12] condition had worsened, but it must be him, for he has been ill for almost twenty years. It's a good fifteen or twenty years since Chauffard[13] condemned him to death and was indignant, having rather brutally informed Madame de Madrazo of his verdict, when he failed to die.

My dearest, I've had enough (which doesn't meant that I don't care about Madrazo), so give my grateful respects to Madame Daudet,[14] Madame Léon Daudet[15] and, in case she is with you, Madame Chauvelot,[16] and share my loving gratitude with your brother.

Marcel

1. Proust had sent the Daudet family proof-copies of the *The Guermantes Way* Part One, dedicated to Lucien's brother, Léon Daudet.

2. In later life, Comtesse de Beaulaincourt, who lived down scandal to become an influential hostess; maternal grandmother of 'Boni' de Castellane.

3. Comte Walewski, who bore an Empire title, and the aristocratic Comte de Cholet were Proust's captain and lieutenant at Orléans. In *The Guermantes Way*, the Prince of Borodino, an officer at Doncières, is jealous of Saint-Loup, a popular NCO, and suspects that his title, too, is 'touched-up': III, 142.

4. Tristan, Comte de Montholon, an ambassador. Cf. M. de Norpois's 'manoeuvrings' with the German premier, 'Prince Von', at Mme de Guermantes's party for the Prince of Wales: III, 292–300.

5. Félix Faure, President of the Republic 1895–9.

6. Dr Edouard Brissaud was a colleague of Proust's father; du Boulbon is the physician who attends the narrator's grandmother: III, 344–53.

7. Proust had promised to review Daudet's latest book for Rivière.

8. Allusion to his and Gide's efforts to obtain a literary prize for Rivière.

9. Jean Cocteau.

10. Blaise Cendrars (1887–1961), Swiss avant-garde poet.

11. Daudet had praised Rivière's reply to Lasserre's attack on Proust: see letter 67, n. 5.

12. Raymond de Madrazo: see following letter. Daudet had read a report that could have referred to his son Frédéric.

13. A Dr Anatole Chauffard.

14. Mme Alphonse Daudet, *née* Julia Allard (1844–1940), poet. Proust had been a member of her influential salon in the 1890s.

15. See letter 86.

16. *Née* Esmée Daudet, sister of Léon and Lucien.

73   To Madame de Madrazo[1]

[Shortly after 15 September 1920]

Dear and unhappy friend, a thousand times more dear for being unhappy.[2]

I've seen you in mourning,[3] I've seen you lavish upon your Father a strength greater than that of any man, I'm aware of the confinement in which love and a fearful vigilance kept you at Versailles, I know the horror of final separation; but as I've just written to Frédéric,[4] I knew nothing, and no longer reading the papers because of failing eyesight, nothing warned me of your plight.

Dear friend, I seldom saw, but fully admired for his sensitivity, the man to whom you gave the strength of your tender devotion and youth. Beside him, other people seemed either stiff-necked or vulgar. This great artist was the simplest and noblest of men. I felt that he must have found the world irksome, and that he gave me the impression that he wasn't bored in my company out of kindness.

Dear friend, I've often thought of the miracle whereby you prolonged his life, and dreaded the inevitable hour when its memory would be your only reward. For you have held off that hour, to everybody's admiration, for so long. I no longer have Reynaldo's address, so kindly tell him from me, with all my affection, that my heart shares in the sadness of you all.

Your
Marcel Proust

1. *Née* Maria Hahn (1865–1948), Reynaldo's sister.
2. Allusion to the death of her husband, the Catalan painter Raymond de Madrazo (1841–1920).
3. Allusion to the death of her parents, Carlos and Elena Hahn.
4. Her stepson, Frédéric 'Coco' de Madrazo.

74 To Robert Proust

[Shortly after 18 September 1920]

My dearest brother,

Many thanks for the extremely nice letter I've just had from you. Don't worry: knowing that he was a friend of yours, I would never under any circumstances have allowed General M.[1] to be approached till I had heard from you. By which I don't mean that we couldn't have acted independently in this particular case, the general's interest in me being confined to my books. All the same, I wouldn't dream of troubling your friends without your approval. And you say that you would rather he were asked nothing. Rest assured, your wish is my command, I shan't ask him a thing, nor allow anybody else to do so.

I'm all the more grateful for your offer regarding General Manoury[2] (though I fear his blindness might prevent the victor of the Ourcq from taking part in the proceedings) because, whatever happens (if he is in fact an active member of the Council), it could be *very helpful* to me. Not that anything in the dossier itself (unless it's falsified!) could hinder my decoration. But for example: volumes are being advertised with the title *Sodome et Gomorrhe*. Members of the Council might conclude (with some displeasure) that these books are pro-Sodomite and pro-Gomorrhean, as Barrès and the Abbé Mugnier did, only to be rather disappointed to find them on the contrary anti-Sodomite and anti-Gomorrhean. In fact, I would have preferred them to be neither 'pro' nor 'anti', and merely objective. But it was the fate of the characters, the protagonists, to be anti. But that's not in the title. Moreover, even this 'anti' comprises portraits which, no matter how cruel and harsh, will appear horribly crude to people who have forgotten the language used by the Church Fathers and are accustomed to a more saccharine literature. Now, it would be truly absurd if, having been decorated, I were to be prosecuted for writing obscene books.

However, none of this may arise. The Fourteenth of July Honours have been so long delayed (probably a lot of string-pulling on behalf of really unacceptable candidates) that I think I'm hardly likely to be decorated this time round. Yet by next July, *Sodome et Gomorrhe* will already be out, and so recently that it will, I think, remain an obstacle. But I shan't retard my book by a single day for that reason, any more than for the Academy, as I said to Barrès and Régnier, both of whom said that I was right. I don't despise honours, but they are a luxury one can do without. I must get on with the book; the rest is secondary, and may or may not follow.[3]

I wish I could prolong this letter with chat about all sorts of nonsense, funny and sad. But various complications have worsened my debilitated state, already bad enough. As you foresaw, my earplugs[4] had not been removed properly. I had a little pain in one ear, waited, and then, Bize[5] still being away, asked Gagey[6] for a specialist (he seemed to prefer Castex) and chose Wicart[7] (I don't know if that's how he spells his name, I must have told you about him, he looks after Reynaldo and Clemenceau). He found my ear completely blocked, unblocked it and departed on holiday. Unfortunately he said he would be back to finish the job, which seems to consist not merely in unblocking my ear but in curing my asthma etc. He is charming, but too clever for me. Ah! the restfulness of doctors like good old Bize, who hasn't listened to my chest for ten years.

My book *Le Côté de Guermantes* comes out the first week in October (but I've probably already told you that, I no longer remember, having written this letter in two parts). Even though it's half the length of the others, I know you won't read it. In any case, nothing about it seems to me to justify the Daudets' enthusiasm.[8] (I sent them proof-copies, as it's dedicated to Léon.) On the other hand, one day when you come to see me, I must force some of my pastiches down your throat. I'm sure that you would find them amusing. And they're very short!

Thank you again, my dear boy, and should they be with you, share my brotherly embraces with Marthe and Suzy.[9]

Marcel

---

1. General Mangin: see letter 63, n. 13. Friends were campaigning to obtain Proust the Legion of Honour.

2. Michel-Joseph Manoury (1847–1923), hero of a battle on the Argonne, where he had lost an eye. Robert had offered to write to Dr Gabriel Manoury, the general's brother.

3. Proust was to be made Chevalier of the Legion of Honour on 25 September, his brother carrying out the investiture at the rue Hamelin on 7 November.

4. See p.s. to letter 33.

5. Dr Maurice Bize, the Proust family doctor.

6. Dr Émile Gagey, a former tenant at 102 boulevard Haussmann with whom Proust had fought a running battle about noise.

7. Both Dr André Castex and Dr Alexis Wicard were ear, nose and throat specialists.

8. See letter 72.

9. Proust's niece: see letter 243.

75 To Madame de Chevigné[1]

44 rue Hamelin
[October 1920]

Madame,

I don't write to you but I write only about you.[2] The whole of my next book is about you. And the memory of our least conversation so haunts me that on the very day of the Prix Goncourt I added to a story in *Le Matin*,[3] so that it would bear your stamp, a remark you once made to me about Madame de Beaulaincourt[4]: 'She has eaten him out of his last farm rent.'[5] How much less bad my books would be, if I saw you more often! At least they are always full of reminders of you, like that church at Brou where, with tender monotony, each pillar is entwined with the 'initials' of the beloved.[6] Thus, as in the poetry of Lamartine, I can write nothing that does not echo the name of 'Laure'.[7] That's not to say that I take myself for Petrarch,[8] alas, but I preserve the ineffaceable trace of enchanted moments.

Kindly accept, Madame, my respectful regards,
Marcel Proust

1. Comtesse Adhéaume de Chevigné, *née* Laure de Sade (1860–1936). Distinguished by birth, wit and elegance, she was the earliest incarnation of the Duchesse de Guermantes: for Proust, as for his youthful narrator, she was the unattainable great lady whom he would wait to see pass in the street: III, 59–60, 70–2, 159–61, 440. Proust wrote to Reynaldo Hahn in 1895: 'I shall come and wish you good evening after dinner. [...] I shall be delighted to walk that little way, which was my "road of hope", and always has been, come to think of it. In the days when I would go to the Avenue Marigny every morning to see Madame de Chevigné pass [...] I always took the same itinerary.'

2. She had written to ask if it was true that she was to appear as the Duchesse de Guermantes in *The Guermantes Way*.

3. 'Mme de Villeparisis in Venice'. See V, 715–54.

4. A model for Mme de Villeparisis: see letter 72, n. 2.

5. *Fermage*, a pun on *fromage*. This Balzacian phrase appears only in *Le Matin*, but it alludes to Mme Sazerat and her piteous desire to see Mme de Villeparisis, 'the beautiful aristocrat responsible for her father's ruin': V, 727–8.

6. Flamboyant Gothic abbey church near Bourg-en-Bresse containing the magnificent tombs built by Marguerite d'Autriche in memory of her husband Philibert le Beau. See 'Swann in Love', I, 356.

7. Allusion to doomed platonic love, and to Lamartine's poem 'To Elvira': 'Yes, the Anio continues to murmur / The sweet name of Cynthia to the rocks of the Tiber. / And Vaucluse has preserved the dear name of Laura.'

8. Petrarch's hermitage at Fontaine-de Vaucluse is near Avignon, where his beloved Laura lies buried with her husband Hugues de Sade, Mme de Chevigné's ancestor.

76 To Madame Straus

[18 October 1920]

Dear Madame Straus,

40° of fever doesn't make it easy to write. But I wanted to send you my book[1] before it comes out and didn't want it go off without a word (don't give it away as it's a very rare edition, despite the arbitrary number on the copy). Anything witty in it is yours.[2] You wouldn't let me credit you with your 'witticisms' as it's a novel. I'll take my revenge in the second *Pastiches*,[3] that being a 'genre' you're prepared to tolerate. Above all, don't think that I've become anti-Dreyfusard. I write at the dictates of my characters and many in the present volume are anti-Dreyfusard (already were, in 1913, when the short extracts from the book appeared in the *NRF*). As, tentatively in the next volume, and wholeheartedly in the one after that, my anti-Dreyfusards become Dreyfusards, and others whom one thought anti-Dreyfusards extremely Dreyfusard, balance will be restored. This to show you that by the time I'm better (?), you'll find me unchanged.

I recommend an *enchanting* article by Léon Daudet which appeared about ten days ago in *L'Action française*: 'A new novel by M. Marcel Proust'. Apart from an unjust remark about Hervieu[4] which pained me, you'll find it very amusing. I'm also sending my book to Montesquiou.[5] If you see him, tell him that having had 40° of fever for ten days like the King of Greece,[6] and it having attacked someone who lives like the Mayor of Cork,[7] I can appear neglectful while remaining the soul of fidelity.

With my devoted and grateful respects, dear Madame Straus, to you and Monsieur Straus,

Marcel Proust

1. *The Guermantes Way* Part One.
2. See letter 60.
3. i.e. in the second Saint-Simon pastiche, which was never published: see letter 42, n. 13.
4. Paul Hervieu (1857–1915), dramatist and novelist. See Léon Daudet, *L'Action française*, 8 October: 'I have moments of hilarity when I recall the superiority with which society, the bores, the snakes-in the-grass, the show-offs and other imbeciles in white tie and tails, treated the unfailingly deferential, diffident, awkward and excessively polite Proust. How, I ask myself, did Marcel heroically endure [. . .] those silly, malicious, haughty silences typical of a pompous toady like Paul Hervieu.'
5. See Mme Straus, 15 March: 'After the Prix Goncourt, Montesquiou came to see me. He was dying to congratulate you but was awaiting your reply to a long letter he had written you about *Jeunes filles en fleurs*. Given his age, his habitual formality etc., he felt he couldn't write again till he had heard from you.' See also letter 60, n. 3.
6. King Alexander of Greece had recently died from the bite of his pet monkey.
7. Terence MacSwiney, an IRA sympathizer on hunger strike in Cork gaol; he was to die on 25 October, after a record 75 days of fast.

77 *To Paul Souday*

[Around 6 or 7 November 1920]

Dear Sir,

Let us not confuse life (and the deferential sympathies which it engenders) with literature.

So, firstly, Life:

Were you not told that about ten days ago, having an evening's respite from illness, I sent a taxi round to enquire if you would care to dine with me that same evening at the Ritz, a taxi which, after the rue Guénégaud, went to various districts in search of fellow-guests I wished to invite for you. When I can, I shall try again. And can you give me the 'Open Sesame' for success?

Secondly, literature.

Three or four days ago, I had what people call 'a bad Souday'.[1] There was a time when I too would have seen it as such. But now that I've come to know you, to sympathize with you in your grief,[2] to like you, all that matters to me is the vexation of not seeing you, that of a 'bad Souday' being minimal. I would welcome fifty worse if we could dine together from time to time.

Only, common sense loves to reason. And therefore I cannot help asking you this: how is it, when you must be aware that I've known Guermantes duchesses all my life, that you haven't understood the effort I had to make in order to put myself in the place of somebody who has never known any and longs to do so?[3] There, as in the case of the dream etc. etc., I tried to see things from within, to heed the imagination. The snobbish novelists are those who, from the outside, ironically depict the snobbery they practise. Since you are friendly with the Princesse Lucien Murat,[4] she can tell you at what age I became familiar with Guermantes of all kinds. I might add that if Mme de Guermantes utters a 'witticism' (no, that would take too long for me to write and you to read). Anyhow, society people are such imbeciles that I was faced with this: fed up with Saint-Simon's endless talk of the Mortemarts' 'unique turn of phrase' while never telling us in what it consists,[5] I was determined to try and create a 'Guermantes wit'. Yet, for a model, the only woman I could find was not somebody 'well-born', but Mme Straus, Bizet's widow. Not only are the witticisms quoted in the book hers (she didn't wish to be named), I even parodied her conversation.[6] I'll tell you something stranger still. In *Guermantes II*, which you don't know, my hero receives an invitation from the Princesse de Guermantes (the Duchesse's cousin). He thinks this so smart that he suspects a hoax.[7] Yet this trait was not my invention. M. d'Haussonville (the father), in his *Mémoires*, relates that he and his friend M. d'Aramon so longed for an invitation from Mme Delessert[8] that when it came, unable to believe their good fortune, they set out independently to discover if it was genuine. These are perhaps the only two instances in my entire work when I haven't 'invented' out of whole cloth. Lastly, Mme de Guermantes isn't unkind to my hero because he is bourgeois, but because she knows she is loved. Once she is no longer loved (in *Guermantes II*, in print, not yet out), she flings herself at her former admirer and never stops inviting him to dinner.[9]

Thirdly, the relationship of literary criticism to life.

One thing hurt me where you certainly intended no malice! Just when I'm about to bring out *Sodome et Gomorrhe*, just when, because I talk of Sodom, nobody will have the courage to defend me, you pave the way for every mischief-maker (without malice, I'm sure) by referring to me as 'feminine'.[10] Anybody who has acted as my second at a duel can tell you whether I show the spinelessness of an effeminate. I repeat, I'm sure that you said this without premeditation. Dear Sir, this long letter (wholly private and confidential, naturally, and not for publication) comes with my warmest admiration and gratitude. You'll be receiving the books in question in May,[11] but I very much hope that we see one another before then.

Marcel Proust

1. Souday's review of *The Guermantes Way* Part One in *Le Temps* of 4 November.

2. Proust is inhibited by his sympathy with Souday over the death of his mother.

3. 'Not one of Balzac's social-climbers ever dreamt more ardently of this mysterious country, this Land of Canaan. To belong there is the sole aim of this outsider who briefly imagines he is in love with Mme de Guermantes but is really in love with this Olympus, this dwelling-place of Gods who are the cream of society, the height of unattainable elegance.' Souday, *op. cit.*

4. *Née* Marie de Rohan-Chabot, daughter of the Duc de Rohan.

5. For example, Saint-Simon observes: 'It is worth remarking on the death of the abbess of Fontevrault; the daughter of the first Duc de Mortemart and sister to the Duc de Vivonne [...] and Mme de Montespan, she was even more beautiful than the last and exceeded them all in wit, which is to say much, possessing that turn of phrase which none but they had mastered.'

6. i.e. in his Saint-Simon pastiche: see letter 60, n. 4.

7. See III, 657–61.

8. The model for Flaubert's Mme Dambreuse in *L'Éducation sentimentale*.

9. See III, 431–6.

10. 'His style, overwrought but often shimmering and sparkling, has brought comparisons with Saint-Simon [...]. Essentially though, M. Proust is a highly-strung aesthete, a little morbid, feminine almost, and thus far at least, lacks [Saint-Simon's] outbursts of passion and rage, although these may await us at the end of the Guermantes way, in the land of Sodom and Gomorrah.' Souday, *op. cit.*

11. *The Guermantes Way* Part Two and *Sodom and Gomorrah* Part One were to be published on 2 May 1921, as one volume.

78 To Jacques Rivière

44 rue Hamelin
[7 or 8 November 1920]

My dear Jacques,

Perhaps my second sight is at fault, but it seems to me that you alone could have penned those ravishing lines in the Review's pink pages.[1] If I'm wrong, and it wasn't you, please thank for me whoever it was among your colleagues who, in writing about *Le Côté de Guermantes*, proved himself not only so very benevolent but also brilliantly inspired. But does he exist, this colleague of yours, or might each line not as well be signed Jacques Rivière? My hypothesis, my virtual certainty, rests on two facts which I separate with difficulty. The less important, for all its worth, is that the enumeration of spiritual truths is very characteristic of you. I remember an article which, I think, appeared in *Excelsior* (for you've spoilt me!) where you list, with a similar grace and incomparable lucidity, the emotions aroused by too beguiling a face[2] (that's not it at all, I ruin it by trying to quote from memory) and much, much more. Now, here again I find that same calm assurance in the accumulation of clauses, and this time it gives the enumeration, which I would never have thought possible, the form of synthesis. And this brings me to the second fact. Who else but you could have painted in a few lines, in all its diversity, literally leaving nothing out, the whole of *Le Côté de Guermantes*? One is never satisfied with one's own portrait, nor even with somebody else's, it being too fragmentary. Yet here, for me, is the finished portrait of *Guermantes*. Perhaps, scrutinizing it, I shall find that it lacks one or two touches. But no, they are there. I hope it's not by somebody else, for I enjoy admiring you too much. And I know that I shall never discover the secret of your transparent, tranquil art

> 'Alike to those waters which flow without force
> Pure and lovely, from their natural source'.[3]

Your friend,
Marcel Proust

My dear Jacques, the Jericho roses,[4] the aquarium at the Opera,[5] no, I would be truly sorry were these marvels not yours. And the cadences, the phrase about the characters, you must reassure me when we meet, you cannot allow me either to transfer my gratitude to another or to divide my favours.

1. Allusion to the blurb advertising *The Guermantes Way* in the *NRF* of 1 November.

2. 'The portraits of women in Marcel Proust! Who can contemplate them without a tender, tacit pang of complicity, without becoming embroiled in that compassion, that desire, that wonderment, that rebellion, that rapt disillusion which together flood the heart when it is beguiled by too charming a face.' Rivière, *L'Excelsior*, 11 December 1919.

3. 'Et pareil à ces eaux si pures et si belles / Qui coulent sans effort des sources naturelles!' Molière, *Don Garcie de Navarre*, Act I, scene 1.

4. 'In succession, Françoise, Saint-Loup, the Duchesse de Guermantes, the Marquise de Villeparisis, Monsieur de Norpois, Bloch and Monsieur de Charlus, reveal aspects of their characters and their lives that are totally unforeseen. Putting out new shoots, they unfurl before our eyes, like those Jericho roses one thought dried and ready for pressing but whose vegetal instincts are revived by a single drop of water.' Allusion to a desert plant with the ability to lie dormant until revived by rain. Rivière, *NRF*, 1 November.

5. '[...] amid the innumerable character-sketches dotted about the landscapes of the book, one delights in pages where the author [...] evokes the amazing aquarium of the Opéra house where, in transparent shadow, white nereids, attracted by the spectacle, swim to the surface.' See the narrator's vision of the auditorium of the Opera as part of a marine underworld: III, 37–41. *Ibid.*

79 *To Madame Soutzo*

[Around 8 November 1920]

To Madame the Princesse Soutzo[1]

It is an artist's privilege to place a blessed memory where he pleases, to put, on his book's most secret page, the sad thoughts, still mauve and livid like an evening sky after a passing storm, that he has for so long clasped to his breast. Any disguise suits his purpose; sometimes he turns a shepherdess into a queen. Elsewhere, the better to mislead the reader, he transports the salon of a princess to the most mediocre setting. You cannot have failed to recognize your own, dear and incomparable Friend, in the one I depict here beneath the spell of the Parsifalesque miracle of the guelder-rose snowballs.[2] Swann instead of Soutzo is a deliberate mistake, just as sable instead of ermine is an involuntary lapse.[3] At most, two or three friends, those with the power to give me pleasure or pain, will pass through the pages of *A la Recherche du temps perdu*. Perhaps you alone, from the depths of your 'Divans deep as tombs',[4] can revive – I dare not say 'joyously' but I hope 'loyally' – 'The tarnished mirrors and the lifeless flames'.[5]

Your respecful and grateful
Marcel Proust

1. Mme Soutzo having bought a de-luxe edition of *Within a Budding Grove* (see letter 71, n. 6), Proust wrote her this dedicatory letter.

2. See Odette's salon on a wintry Easter day: 'It was enough [...] that, overhanging the loose snowdrifts of the muff in which Mme Swann kept her hands, the guelder-rose snowballs [...] should remind me that the Good Friday Music in *Parsifal* symbolizes a natural miracle which one could see performed every year if one had the sense to look for it.' II, 244–5.

3. Allusion to Odette's sable muff and cape in the above scene; Proust was to change it to ermine in later editions, the better to evoke the whiteness of snow.

4. 'Divans profonds comme des tombeaux', line from Baudelaire's 'La mort des amants' in *Les Fleurs du Mal*.

5. Proust quotes from the last verse of the above: 'Et plus tard un Ange entr'ouvrant les portes / Viendra ranimer, fidèle et joyeux, / Les miroirs ternis et les flammes mortes.'

80   To Henri de Régnier

[Sunday, 28 November 1920]

Dear Sir and friend,

(I believe that to be the formula whereby I attempt to reconcile my profound friendship for you with my no less profound respect.)

I was extremely touched by the exquisite kindness with which you spoke of me in this morning's *Figaro*;[1] you know what praise from you means to me. Since even the most flattered authors are never completely happy with their portrait, allow me to say (while taking nothing away from my immense gratitude) that I cannot agree with you when you say that you see Memoirs, Recollections,[2] in a body of work so constructed that I wrote the words 'The End' on the last page of the final volume (not yet out) before I had written the volumes just published. The 'I' is a pure formula, and the phenomenon of memory that triggers off the work, a deliberate device,[3] similar, if you like, to the song of the thrush heard at

Montboissier that reminds Chateaubriand of Combourg.⁴ M. Bidou's review of the selfsame *Côté de Guermantes*, in which he gives its 'structure' due prominence, seems to me exactly right.⁵

In the belief that admiration should avoid imitation – except in the case of deliberate pastiche⁶ – I've always tried to distance myself in my writing from your wonderful books. It is none the less true that in composing *Du Côté de chez Swann* (and the comparison doesn't flatter you, I fear) I unconsciously reflected the arrangement of my favourite novel, *La Double Maîtresse*.⁷ True, I never dreamt of doing so! But I now realize that the first part devoted to the young man, the second (*Un amour de Swann*), harking back to a distant past the young man knows only from hearsay, and the third, returning to the young man, testify (very clumsily, and quite unconsciously) to the indelible impression made on me by M. de Galandot's adventures between the first and third episodes of *La Double Maîtresse*. In sensations like the little 'Madeleine'⁸ – but you must long since have forgotten my *Du Côté de chez Swann* – isn't there something of the grapes,⁹ and doesn't the 'peripeteia' in my book, as in yours, hang upon the sudden recall of a sensation? Lastly, features symmetrical to other features in my book (I'm no longer talking of *Du Côté de chez Swann* but of *À la Recherche du temps perdu* as a whole) are generally to be found in different volumes, because its scale is so vast. But it would be no trouble for me to show you, unless it would be to talk about myself too much and unless, by telling me that you never go out in the evening, you give me no hope of seeing you and Madame de Régnier, that deferred explanations (such as that you give in *Le Bon plaisir*¹⁰ for the significance Louis XIV attached to a face) are constantly to be found in my books.

Needless to say, this speech for the defence is not intended for the *Figaro* but simply to show you that in addition to being infinitely touched by your kindness, I have a sound and enthusiastic comprehension of your books.

Kindly give my affectionate regards to Madame de Régnier, and share with her my grateful admiration.

Marcel Proust

I much appreciate your tact and consideration for having so kindly and flatteringly singled me out in your article beside a great writer like Duhamel,¹¹ instead of leaving me to drown in the current flood of second-rate publications.

1. Régnier's review of *The Guermantes Way* in the *Figaro* of 28 November.

2. 'As we know, M. Marcel Proust has embarked upon a series, part autobiography, part novel, in which, with an undeniable evocative power and outstanding analytical skill, and by taxing his memory to the utmost, he recounts a past youth that has every appearance of being his own. [. . .] In fact, rather than writing confessions in the manner of Rousseau, or memoirs in the manner of Casanova, he has set out to make a sort of novel of his past.' Régnier, *loc. cit.*

3. See *Time Regained*: VI, 216–33. Proust has rehearsed his arguments to Régnier in 'On Flaubert's Style', *AS-B*, 272–3.

4. In *Time Regained*, the narrator asks himself: 'Is it not from a sensation of the same species as that of the madeleine that Chateaubriand suspends the loveliest episode in the *Mémoires d'outre-tombe*': VI, 283–5. Proust also appreciated the fact that the episode at Château de Montboissier in the Perche had taken Chateaubriand back to holidays spent at Combourg in Brittany.

5. 'Imagine a block of stone hewn out of life, revealing its disparate strata, rather as a cross-section of a cliff reveals the non-conformities, the intrusions, of its juxtaposed rocks. In fact, the book is composed of four parts [. . .] in two tableaux, it shows us the aristocracy. And before and after these tableaux, two scenes of bourgeois life. [. . .] Thus a book which seems at first to follow events at random [. . .] turns out to be composed, consciously or not, with an unerring artistry and sense of symmetry.' Henri Bidou, *Les Annales politiques et littéraires*, 21 November.

6. See Proust's pastiche of Régnier: *CS-B*, 21–3.

7. Régnier's best-known novel, a historical saga.

8. The famous episode in *Swann's Way*: I, 53–5. See note 4.

9. In *La Double Maîtresse* a girl throws grape-pips at her cousin, the young M. de Galandot, arousing his desire; when, in his old age, a courtesan does the same, it triggers desire and he becomes enslaved.

10. Régnier's 'memoirs' of a courtier at Versailles.

11. Georges Duhamel (1884–1966), whose novel *Civilisation* had won the 1918 Prix Goncourt.

81 To Émile Henriot[1]

[Thursday 2 December 1920]

Sir,

I believe that all art is classical but that the laws of the mind often prevent it from being recognized as such at its first appearance.[2] Art, in this respect, is like life. The language of unhappy lovers, party politicians, sensible parents, automatically carries an irresistible authority. Yet those to whom their words are addressed are not noticeably convinced: if a truth is to impose itself on minds from outside, it must first have moulded them to a likeness of the mind wherein it originated. Manet could insist for all his worth on the classicism of his *Olympia*, telling onlookers: 'See, it's no different from what you admire in the Old Masters'; all the public saw was something to be jeered at. But today we get the same kind of pleasure from looking at *Olympia* as we do from looking at the other masterpieces in its vicinity[3] – and the same from reading Baudelaire as from reading Racine. Baudelaire was unable, or unwilling, to finish a piece, and yet perhaps nothing he wrote contains all the truths that are crowded, in swift succession, with such richness, into Phèdre's declaration alone.[4] But the style of the banned poems, which is exactly that of the tragedies, perhaps surpasses it in nobility.[5] Great innovators like these are the only true classics, and they form an almost unbroken series. At their best, imitators of the classics merely gratify a pleasure in our own erudition and taste that counts for little. That innovators worthy of one day becoming classics should obey a rigorous interior discipline, should be builders first and foremost, is unquestioned. But precisely because their architecture is new, it takes us a long time to recognize it. These still unrecognized masters, and those of the past, practise the same art, to the extent that the former remain the best critics of the latter. Preferably, their criticism should not run counter to an artist's tendencies, to his line of development. Nothing is stupider than to say, like Théophile Gautier, a third-rate poet, moreover, that the finest line in Racine is 'The daughter of Minos and Pasiphaë'.[6] But in Racine's tragedies, in his *Cantiques*, in Madame de Sévigné's letters, in Boileau, we have the chance to enjoy beauties which are there to be found and were barely perceptible to the sixteenth century.

In short, it is those great artists who were misunderstood to the point of being dubbed romantic, realist, decadent etc. whom I would call classics – had M. Charles Maurras not warned us, in the magnificent essays which he signs Criton,[7] of the dangers in thus multiplying such more or less arbitrary denominations.

Marcel Proust

1. Émile Henriot (real name Maigrot: 1889–1961), writer and critic.

2. Proust replies to a survey entitled 'An Inquiry into Romanticism and Classicism'. It was to be published in *La Renaissance politique, littéraire, artistique* on 8 January 1921.

3. After fifty years, the scandal surrounding Manet's *Olympia* died down; the Louvre finally exhibited it in 1907, hanging it alongside another nude courtesan,

Ingres's *La Grande Odalisque*, and causing the Duchesse de Guermantes to remark: 'Nowadays nobody is in the least surprised by it. It looks just like an Ingres!': III, 604.

4. See *Phèdre*, Act II, scene 5.

5. Allusion to the six poems in *Les Fleurs du Mal* which were banned in 1857 for 'offending against morality and decency'. See Proust's comparison of Racine's tragedies and Baudelaire's banned poems in 'Concerning Baudelaire', *AS-B*, 295–302.

6. See letter 55.

7. Maurras's by-line in *L'Action française*.

82   To Jacques Boulenger

Saturday evening [4 December 1920]

Dear friend,

You know how I like you. I should have thanked you this morning. But what happened was this. Yesterday at five o'clock I had a terrible attack (by seven, I couldn't even be told that Gallimard and Rivière had come, so they went away again). During the night, I didn't even remove the wrapper from the *Débats*, something almost unheard of for me. Consequently, I didn't see the summary of *L'Opinion* (I couldn't have suspected that you would be talking about *Guermantes*, but *L'Opinion* doesn't have to talk about me for its contents to interest me). This afternoon, calmer, and having slept thanks to a good deal of veronal, I didn't so much as glance at letters, newspapers, *L'Opinion*. By now, unless they are in bed, Antoine Bibesco and the Princesse Murat must be wondering why I hadn't told them I wouldn't be coming to dinner.

At last, the little death receding, I opened *L'Opinion*, to read the finest, most profound article that you have ever written.[1] I don't say this to encourage you to talk about me, to suggest that I 'inspire' you. I would say the same if the article were about Bourget.[2] Parts of it are truly astonishing in their depth, and express the nearly inexpressible with bewildering felicity. There were a few things with which, selfishly, I wasn't happy. For I see a rift opening up, on two points at least.[3] Naturally, I'm delighted with the rest. But I don't want to talk about myself now, about where you are certainly mistaken. I'm thinking of you, of this amazing leap in your talents, these heights which, at least to my knowledge, you have scaled for the first time.

Now, not wanting to overtire myself by writing you a ten-page letter, a plea. I sent round for Rivière at about ten o'clock tonight, and he had the goodness to come. I told him that I wanted to buy two de-luxe copies of *Jeunes filles* and needed them for tomorrow, Sunday. What I didn't tell him was that they were for the Boulenger brothers. Some day, I shall. But first give me time to think up a reason for this predilection for friends I've never met. Rivière (whom I adore) would be sure to think 'Why doesn't he give me one', and the same thought would occur to Léon Daudet, who hasn't had one either, to Régnier, Barrès, Bergson, my sponsors at the Academy, friends who call every day to ask how I am. But there cannot be many copies left, only fifty having been made. So if you would kindly keep yours in a cupboard for the time being, like those bookshops who hope to sell them on, I'll come round one evening and write in it whatever you wish. Give the other one to your brother for me, telling him that I have many nice things to say to him and will, moreover, write him a long dedication for his copy, but that I'm very tired. Meanwhile, I would be very grateful if he didn't mention it to *anybody*. I'll be sending this letter in the morning, saying that it's to go as soon as Rivière has dropped the books off, so you should receive both together. However, as it's Sunday, it's possible, though unlikely, that Rivière won't have been able to break into 37 rue Madame,[4] in which case you'll receive just the letter (I shan't know till later as I'll probably be asleep by the time it goes off) and the books not till Monday. Moreover, you yourself, with your Chantillys like Louis XIV's Marlys,[5] may not be there on a Sunday (my lines keep being held up because here on page 8 I see a couple of lines where, an hour ago, I had begun a letter to you which I was too tired to continue).

I'll write to you another time about the frock-coat,[6] the leave-taking,[7] the snobbery,[8] the structure,[9] but tonight, truly, it's beyond me.

My warmest thanks to your brother for having given me so much pleasure by mentioning me in the company of such eminent writers in *L'Avenir*. I saw the piece only very belatedly, but I was most touched.

One more thing. Do you and your brother possess *Les Plaisirs et les jours*? Let me know, if not. I would gladly send it to you, if only to prove that I'm capable of writing purely (as you very kindly say that you believe I am in your article).[10] I don't know which of your colleagues will be writing about this year's Prix Goncourt. But whoever it is, I don't expect him to say, like Léon Daudet, that never since its foundation has the Goncourt Academy honoured a work the equal of *Les Jeunes filles en fleurs*.[11] Any more than I would want him to say (unless it gives him especial pleasure, in which case I wouldn't mind in the least): 'This verdict makes a change from last year, when that ghastly Proust, a hundred if he is a day, made off with it by wangling, scheming and using every vile trick *Le Populaire* was sure would easily fool Émile Bourges and Rosny, triumphing over fine, wholesome young men from the trenches and from whose works one could have picked a masterpiece, instead of that soporific etc. etc.' Perhaps 'soporific' will send me to sleep.

On that note, my heartfelt thanks for your article, and above all, dear unknown and much-loved champion, for those magnificent pages.

Marcel Proust

1. 'Du Côté de Marcel Proust', *L'Opinion*, 4 December. Boulenger was shortly to publish this article, together with two others on Proust, in his book of critical essays *Mais l'Art est difficile*.

2. Paul Bourget (1852–1935), middle-brow novelist.

3. Boulenger states that 'nothing could be more Bergsonian than his art'. Cf. Proust, in *Le Temps*, 1913: 'To say "Bergsonian novels" [...] would not be accurate [...] for my work is dominated by the distinction between involuntary and voluntary memory, a distinction which not only does not appear in M. Bergson's philosophy but is even contradicted by it.' *AS-B*, 235. See also Proust to Henri Ghéon, 1914: 'Your saying that I wanted to make a novel out of M. Bergson's philosophy left me aghast. It's the last thing I thought of!' For the second point, see n.9.

4. Address of the N.R.F.

5. Allusion to the royal hunting-forests at Marly, which Proust compares to the Sunday race-meetings at Chantilly: see letter 50, n.10.

6. 'Would anybody, even in Dreyfus's time [...] have worn a frock-coat (and thus a top hat) to go the country before returning for luncheon in a Paris restaurant?' Boulenger, *L'Opinion*. Allusion to the narrator's excursion with Saint-Loup and Rachel: III, 171.

7. 'Has anglomania triumphed in high society [...] to the point where one leaves a social gathering without so much as a word to those to whom one hasn't been introduced.' *Ibid*. Allusion to the comedy of Bloch's farewells at Mme de Villeparisis': III, 246 ff.

8. '[...] he identifies himself with his protagonist to a surprising degree [...] (one might believe he is indeed Marcel Proust, had he not been given the vice which so colours his outlook on life, a vice which one may be sure without even knowing him would never infect a man of M. Proust's intelligence: snobbery).' *Ibid*.

9. 'I believe his books will last for their richness and quality, but that is not to say they will last as perfect books. I said last year – perhaps rashly, since we know

barely half of it – that his works seems almost completely lacking in structure, and I see nothing in this latest fragment to make me change my mind.' *Ibid.*

10. 'Time and again, M. Proust exhibits such purity of style that we don't for one moment believe that his grammatical "faults" are involuntary; he is, after all, the author of the wittiest and most ingenious parodies ever published.' *Ibid.*

11. Comment by Daudet in *L'Action française* on 12 December 1919.

83 To Harry Swann[1]

[10 or 11 December 1920]

Sir,

It's nothing short of a miracle that I can answer you. I've been very ill, and thousands of letters have piled up unanswered. What chance has given yours a different fate and me a moment's strength to answer it, I cannot say. In fact, that I should have read this particular letter is rather unlucky for us both. For I'm unable to give you the details you wish. By the time I had brought out my *Du Côté de chez Swann* eight years ago (having written it twelve years ago) (it was published in 1913), I was already very ill, and for most of the names I simply used, like Balzac, real names belonging to existing people. But it was different in the case of my hero, for I didn't know, and had never heard of, anybody by the name of Swann. The prototype for Swann was M. Charles Haas: Haas the friend of princes, the Israelite of the Jockey Club.[2] But he was only the starting-point. Naturally, my character evolved differently. The main thing was to find a name that would look Anglo-Saxon while at the same time giving my ear the *blank* sensation of the double 'a' preceded by one consonant and followed by another (I tell you this in the strictest confidence because, although there's nothing secret about it, after a lapse of twenty years I might be mistaken about the special chemistry which takes place in the brain when we invent a name). The double 'n' replacing the double 'a' was supposed to avoid any association between Mme de Guermantes and a swan (a wise precaution, as it turned out, for one of the King of England's sisters,[3] who is either a wit or a simpleton, remarked: '*Du Côté de chez Swann*, why, that's the story of Leda from the standpoint of the swan'). I could go on telling you funny things about that for ever if I wasn't so tired. But the one reflection that springs unbidden to my mind, not without melancholy, is the littleness of what we call fame (to which, I confesss, I'm totally indifferent). Here is a book that came out nearly eight years ago. Before, I didn't know a single Swann; after, even though, not knowing them, I hadn't in fact thought of giving them the pleasure they claimed to feel, several Swanns had themselves introduced to me (for I still occasionally went about in society in those days). The book was reviewed all over the world, even in China.[4] I was decorated for it and, even more flattering to an author who had been thoroughly spoilt, Swann clubs were founded in Belgium and England where readers (modesty forbids my saying admirers) could meet and discuss my work. Every leading English, French and Italian newspaper returns to it constantly. Yet this book which, if I were vain, I might have thought well-known, is, I see from your letter, unknown to a man who, tempted to see himself in it or not, is clearly literate (your letter is proof of that) and whose name happens to be Swann. Alas, Monsieur, you have no sooner made the acquaintance of my Swann than he is about to die, and not even his name will survive in the final volumes, for his widow is to marry a M. de Forcheville, and her daughter will also change her name.[5] Luckily, a hero's death has no effect on the people who bear his name in real life and continue to be in the best of health. I trust that is so in your case. It isn't in mine, alas.

Yours faithfully,
Marcel Proust

1. A stranger.
2. Charles Haas (1832–1902), elegant clubman and patron of the arts, of whom the narrator's reflections after Swann's death are a faithful portrait. See V, 222–3.
3. The Princess Royal, Princess Louise.
4. See letter 45.
5. In *The Fugitive*, Odette enters society by marrying her lover, Swann's friend the Marquis de Forcheville; Gilberte takes his name and marries Saint-Loup. The young Marquise de Cardaillec, *née* Forcheville, whom Proust describes in a charming sketch in 'Sainte-Beuve and Balzac', is an early version of Mademoiselle de Forcheville, Gilberte's daughter: *AS-B*, 84–5.

84 To Antoine Bibesco

Saturday morning [11 December 1920]

Dear Antoine,

I'm worried because I'm having a terrible attack and don't know when I can go to bed and sleep. And once asleep, I may not wake till late this evening, probably not before midnight (though I hope it will be earlier). And if you're off tomorrow, I shan't see you again unless you take a chance on tonight about half-past eleven, but who knows what state I'll be in. Whatever happens, in case I don't see you.

1. Tell me when you leave so that I can have Mme de Noailles's letter (the one you sent me addressed to you) taken round to you, for it's probably not very safe to send it by pneumatique. I could hardly read a word of it so didn't understand why you should have sent it to me.

2. I had received her book[2] the previous day with a long covering letter, this time almost wholly legible and extremely nice about me. I still haven't answered it, finding it very awkward to thank her wholeheartedly for all her delightful compliments when you tell me that she says quite different things about me behind my back.[1] On the one hand, I bask in her letter, in her evocation of the past when we used to meet,[3] in her wish that we (she says Hélène[4] and me) should meet again, in her beauty, so fresh in my mind (naturally that's not her speaking, it's my recollection of a fortnight ago),[5] in her genius, in the things she says about my book – and on the other, I'm inhibited from expressing my feelings in case hers are insincere. But I can't understand why she should say all these things, not only in such magnificent words but with such delightful friendliness, if she doesn't mean them. I don't see the point. Our hearts must be very different. Personally, I tell the people I love best 'Your book is no good' if that's what I think. And nobody takes umbrage.

Affectionately yours,
Marcel

1. It seems that Mme de Noailles had said or written uncomplimentary things about *The Guermantes Way* to Bibesco.
2. *Les Forces éternelles*, her latest book of poems.

3. In the autumn of 1899, Proust spent some of the happiest days of his life visiting the Brancovan family at Féterne, their villa on Lac Léman near Evian-les-Bains; Féterne was the name he gave the Cambremers' magnificent house near Balbec.

4. Her sister Hélène de Chimay, his favourite; see letter 22, n. 14.

5. Mme de Noailles had been Proust's guest at a dinner he had given at the Ritz on 27 November.

85 To Madame de Noailles

[Shortly after 12 December 1920]

Madame,

Having been incapable of writing these last few days (what you took for improvement was death's grip on my entire being),[1] I couldn't thank you for your immortal Vedas,[2] nor for a letter so heavily laden with honey and flawless wax that, reading it, one sees only that the younger you grow, the richer and more abundant your store of nectar. Were I capable of writing to you, I would explain all that better. And I would also tell you that you are two Madames de Noailles, the one who writes books that will take their rightful place beside those of Hugo, Baudelaire, Vigny[3] – and another whom I can't pretend not to know without lying to you. But I don't seek a place in the Chorus, nor yet in the Heart.[4] How Illimitable[5] your heart would be if it weren't fickle, and for those who love you, isn't that fickleness the harsh ransom demanded for fidelity to your genius? For myself, I feel that I've paid dearly for reading such a book and receiving such a letter. 'And I want no other Paradise',[6] as Verlaine says.

I would have written all this to you, and much else besides (having first thanked you for that magical presence the other night) but for a state of health that still, this evening, prevents my prolonging this rambling letter. All I would say to you, assuming that I had misread, is what Madame Valmore wrote to Lamartine: 'Oh! was glory the word you said / The very word I never heard.'[7] Lamartine, to whom I was glad to see Régnier compare you yesterday, with fitting warmth.[8] My sole advantage over M. de Régnier, to whom I defer with a modesty born of the liveliest admiration, is to have been the first, when, twice in the selfsame *Figaro*, I placed you on a level with, and higher than, our greatest poets.[9] I'm certainly not comparing myself to him, I would no more be capable of writing his *Double Maîtresse* than I would his *Bon Plaisir*.[10] I measure the range and grant him an immense territorial advantage. But in your case, on at least two occasions (I don't keep count of such trifles), I was the one with the better aim, the one who fired the first shot. I'm honoured that he should so generously endorse an admiration that has never faltered.

Kindly accept, Madame, my deepest respects,
Marcel Proust

The other night at the Ritz, talking to you about your poems on your son, I was thinking of those sublime early ones in your *Premières Méditations*.[11] Since the day before yesterday, I think I admire even more those you address to him in your *Recueillements*.[12] Alas, I see the Vine but cannot enter the House.[13] I'll write and tell Gans[14] what wonderful things you say about him.

Kindly remember me to Monsieur de Noailles, he is always so good to me.

1. Mme de Noailles had written, on 8 December: 'I only wish I might die as you are dying – by getting better and better!' Cf. Proust's personification of death as 'a stranger [who] has taken up residence in my brain' in his 'Preface to Morand', written about this time, *AS-B*, 275.

2. Hindu poems. An allusion to *Les Forces éternelles*: see previous letter.

3. Cf. *The Guermantes Way*, where Mme de Noailles is described as 'a young Eastern princess who was said to write poetry quite as fine as Victor Hugo's or Alfred de Vigny's': III, 116–17.

4. Play on the words *choeur* and *coeur*. See following note.

5. Allusion to her first book, *Le Coeur innombrable*.

6. 'Et vraiment je ne veux pas d'autre Paradis'. Proust hints at his disillusion by quoting the last line of Verlaine's 'La Bonne chanson' IV, a love-poem written to his fiancée before their disastrous marriage.

7. 'Mais dans ces chants que ma mémoire / Et mon coeur s'apprennent tout bas, / Doux à lire, plus doux à croire / Oh! n'as tu pas dit le mot gloire? / Et ce mot je ne l'entends pas.' From 'À Monsieur Alphonse de Lamartine' by Marcelline Desbordes-Valmore (1786–1859).

8. Allusion to Régnier's review of *Les Forces éternelles* in the *Figaro*.

9. Allusion to Proust's review of her book *Les Éblouissements* in 1907, and to his Renan pastiche of 1908: see letter 33, n. 6.

10. See letter 80, n. 7, n. 10.

11. By allusion, Proust compares her early work to Lamartine's *Méditations poétiques*.

12. Allusion to her latest work and to Lamartine's *Recueillements poétiques*.
13. Allusion to Lamartine's nostalgic poem 'La Vigne et la maison'.
14. Henri Gans, a young banker also present at Proust's dinner at the Ritz.

86   To Madame Léon Daudet[1]

[December 1920]

Dear Madame,

Your letter is as much a proof of my crass ignorance[2] as it is of your sweet nature. Indeed, I've been meaning to read *Les Mystères de Paris*[3] for over fifteen years; I haven't done so. And now eyes that can no longer see will be reserved, should I ever be well enough to visit an oculist, for works that I'm even more curious to read. Thus, I knew of only one Archduke Rudolf, the son of the Empress Barrès wrote about. There being no trace of either Austrian or German blood of whatever rank in my family, I thought that rather than to me, this referred to those society people who even in wartime pride themselves on being related to Archdukes. How I should love to tell you some funny stories about that! But after forty-eight hours of uninterrupted suffocation I barely have the strength to write you this note. The only actions I was capable of were to read your very charming letter and to look at some proofs of *Guermantes* (*Guermantes II*); now, by some happy chance at the printers', the first galley begins at these words (I quote from memory, it having slipped beneath a pile of *Actions française*): 'one of those purely French cookery terms one hardly ever comes across except in the delicious Pampille'.[4] When I tell you this, I'm not pretending that it's great praise, it doubtless flowed from my pen all those years ago as naturally as a conjunction or an adverb. I wouldn't mention anything so trifling, were it not for the happy coincidence of your living letter superimposing itself on my dead prose.

Similarly, in a church in Normandy, I once saw a dog-rose flowering over a porch whose pillars were decorated with the self-same eglantine, as if the living plant had wished, through this juxtaposition of corollas, to show how faithfully the stonemason had sculpted the native vegetation.[5] I can't now remember the name of the church (it lies in a green hollow somewhere between Caen and Ouistreham). But its name doesn't matter any more than the name of my book. Its charm lay in the flower, as it will lie in your dear husband's name in the dedication to be re-printed in the next *Guermantes*.[6]

An extract from this second *Guermantes*,[7] very badly cut, is to appear in the *NRF* of 1 January. But they can't include the dedication (it's not their policy, but at least they'll keep 'To Léon Daudet'). Besides, it's too long (exactly the same as for the previous volume, unless there are changes that any of you would like to make). But it will appear on the fly-leaf of the book (*Guermantes II*).

I'm going on too long about too little. But I wanted to tell you the story of the dog-rose so that you won't exile my bouquets. One doesn't have to be an Austrian archduke in order to send flowers. Before gathering the bouquet of *Lys dans la vallée*,[8] some very French writers had found *La Guirlande de Julie*.[9] And your having forbidden me to send you flowers more than once a year makes me impatient for next December. I'm making hardly any alterations...[10]

1. *Née* Marthe Allard, Léon Daudet's second wife.
2. A ludicrous misunderstanding: in thanking him for flowers, she had compared them to 'Archduke Rudolf's bouquet', to which Proust, associating this with Rudolf of Bavaria and the double tragedy at Mayerling, replied: 'The very thought of Archduke Rudolf's bouquet send shivers down my spine.'
3. Best-selling novel by Eugène Sue (1804–57) about an Archduke Rudolf and his daughter, the recipient of the bouquet, and his adventures in the Paris underworld.
4. Mme Daudet had written cookery books under this pseudonym. Mme de Guermantes's vocabulary is described as being 'as richly flavoured as those dishes which it is possible to come across in the delicious books of Pampille': III, 580.
5. Cf. the sculpted foliage on the porch of St-André-des-Champs on the Méséglise way: I, 182.
6. *The Guermantes Way* Part Two and *Sodom and Gomorrah* Part One were to appear as one volume in May 1921.
7. 'A Death-bed', taken from passages leading up to the death of the narrator's grandmother: III, 359 ff.
8. Balzac's novel of the same name.
9. Seventeenth-century poems and madrigals, the subject of each a flower, written for Julie d'Angennes by habitués of her mother's salon at Rambouillet.
10. The rest of the letter is missing.

87   To Madame de Chevigné

[December 1920]

Madame,

It's true that much time has been lost through my having wanted a book in which there is so much of you to be printed on unique paper, and in a copy made especially for you.[1] And moribundity[2] having set in again, I've been unable to deal with such printers' matters.

Moreover, I felt that the present (in the sense of the gift) lay in my having done this book for you. And that its outward form, and whether it was bought by you or by me, hardly mattered. There, we disagree. So, since you attach greater importance to reams of paper than to memories of the heart, here is a copy (alas! there were only these hideous ones left, but I'll go on looking). The infernal part of this misunderstanding, one that results from your tendency to fall into traps, is the word 'snobbery',[3] echoing down twenty years like the 'Clerical Peril'[4] etc., etc. To how many duchesses who shrieked 'But that's not a duchess, it's a society woman for little Jewish salons' have I not retorted: 'She shows more breeding than you.' An odd form of snobbery, that consists in never accepting an invitation. (All too long to explain here.)

It was necessary to show that, in reality, Places and People diminish as one approaches them. Balbec in the case of places, Guermantes in the case of people. I'm too tired to demonstrate for you the steps whereby I arrived at this logically, but it was perfectly well understood, not long ago, by the leading Danish newspaper *Politiken*.[5] But you have seen only the petty side of things. I prefer to keep the beau role, though it gives me infinite pain.

Your respectful
Marcel Proust

---

1. This letter accompanied a copy of *The Guermantes Way* Part One. Mme de Chevigné seems to have expressed her surprise at his having neglected to send her one. Cf. letter 75.

2. *moribondage*: her word (a mixture of *moribond* and *marivaudage*, meaning banter) for his constant announcements of impending death.

3. Merely seeing a form of snobbish persecution, and because she never read his

books, Mme de Chevigné had completely failed to understand Proust's (and his narrator's) attitude towards her and Mme de Guermantes. See the passage beginning 'I was genuinely in love with the Duchesse de Guermantes': III, 70. See also the Duc de Guermantes: 'People in society are too apt to think of a book as a sort of cube one side of which has been removed, so that the author can at once "put in" the people he meets. This is obviously rather underhand, and writers are a pretty low class.' IV, 77.

4. Term dating from the enforcement of anti-Clerical laws.

5. An article entitled 'A new French mega-novel' by Christian Rimestad in the *Politiken* of 7 August.

88 To Madame de Clermont-Tonnerre[1]

44 rue Hamelin (address confidential)
[30 December 1920]

Duchesse,

Your letter[2] is a veritable Watteau, a *Fête galante* by Verlaine[3] (who was particularly susceptible to footmen in blue velvet).[4] I must return it to you and will keep it here at your disposal, for you should publish it, if not on its own, then in one of your books. This 'pastoral' would be its gem. Your guarantee that I don't flatter you is that I put it far, far above anything you have yet written. It sometimes happens that in a letter – if one knows that one has an appreciative and demanding correspondent – things come naturally that one might not have written. A perfect, exquisite page is a rarity; be sure not to lose this one.

I'll have endless comments for you when we meet. I'll tell you about my 'Ruy Blond'[5] (Montesquiou's appellation) (definitely not recruited for the use to which Prince Constantin put his[6]) who, for that very reason, and because he was immune to all temptation, I found far superior to your Polish neighbour's footmen. He made an indelible impression on the Comte Greffulhe, who saw him at Cabourg in 1914 and never forgot him, which I believe is very unusual for Comte Greffulhe where footmen are concerned (needless to say, his admiration was merely that of a master for the professional qualities of a servant. I'm too well aware of the enormous number of Charluses in the world to make ridiculous insinuations about one of the few men who is precisely not one of them).

I have a Ruy Brown as my secretary at the moment (greatly

inferior to Ruy Blond, whom I would have sent with this letter had he not been in America, so that you would be confronted by a reminder of the 'blue statues'). I know a few of the latter,[7] very dilapidated and low class. Where their former master is concerned, they knew only one scandal to speak of (and I don't advise you to repeat it to the Duchesse de Doudeauville[8] for a very special reason which I'll explain). The liaison which gave rise to this scandal was not, as you might think, that between Prince Constantin and one of the blue statues, but between him and Lady Pirbright.[9] The footmen in blue velvet worshipped their Master.[10] One resisted, unused to his ways, and was on the point of throwing him out of the window when the Princesse Radziwill intervened, displaying what seems to me exceptional wisdom in a madwoman: 'My good man, if you don't want to, you have only to say so.' She told the recalcitrant footman, 'But one can't go about killing people just for that.' A maxim that would prevent many a war.

You don't say whether you authorize me to cite the impressive rigidity of your asparagus in my *Guermantes*.[11] It happens to be rather urgent, as I'm correcting the final proofs.

I wouldn't have been able to write to you but for an unexpected hour's respite in the middle of one of my terrible attacks. For I can't write letters any more, not even essential ones.

Kindly accept, Duchesse, my admiring respects.
Marcel Proust

1. The ex-Duchesse de Clermont-Tonnerre, *née* Elisabeth de Gramont (1875–1954), Guiche's half-sister, recently divorced. She became notorious as one of the so-called 'amazons', women artists and writers of post-war Paris who defied sexual convention.
2. All but a fragment of the letter is missing. It evidently described the celebrations surrounding the baptism of the Guiches' infant daughter, to whom Montesquiou, as a cousin, stood godfather.
3. Allusion to Verlaine's sophisticated pastoral poems of 1869.
4. 'Blue' is associated with the slang phrase *ballets bleus* for orgies with young men.
5. Allusion to Victor Hugo's eponymous valet, Ruy Blas, and to Proust's former secretary-cum-manservant Ernest Forssgren, a handsome young Swede.
6. Prince Constantin Radziwill (1850–1920) of whom Montesquiou wrote: 'For Constantin Radziwill / Talk of women is uncivil'.
7. One of Radziwill's former footmen was Albert Le Cuziat: see letter 42, n. 6.
8. The doyenne of formal society: see IV, 71. Her son, the Duc de Bisaccia, was a notorious homosexual.

9. Proust alludes to this incident in a letter to Reynaldo Hahn from Cabourg in August 1911.

10. Cf. M. de Charlus's favours to his valets: III, 639.

11. Allusion to an entry in her *Almanach of the good things of France*. She was to allow it to be quoted by the Duc de Guermantes: 'green asparagus grown in the open air, which, as has been so quaintly said by the charming writer who signs herself E. de Clermont-Tonnerre, "not to have the impressive rigidity of their sisters", should be eaten with eggs.' See *The Guermantes Way* Part Two: III, 582. This is one of many references to asparagus in Proust's novel.

89 To Madame de Clermont-Tonnerre

44 rue Hamelin
[1 or 2 January 1921]

Duchesse,

Here is the masterpiece so justly reclaimed.[1] Acute bronchitis prevents my writing to you at length. I couldn't read the name of the marquis who was an ancestor of the Luynes. Chambrun? Hardly likely.

In returning your letter, may I ask that you destroy mine. Not so much because of Ruy Blas (I'm told that Mme de la Béraudière[2] claims authorship of this nickname, which is Montesquiou's) or the number of dukes compromised, as for a quite different reason, namely my absolute insistence (I shall state it publicly at the front of *Swann*) that none of my letters should be kept, let alone published.[3] Don't think for one moment that I wish to conceal my tributes to you. If this ban on my correspondence wasn't total, there is no exception I would more willingly make. Moreover, I hope I can do better than to quote a single line about asparagus. None the less, awaiting something better (and much longer), I am delighted to cite 'E. de Clermont-Tonnerre' and thank you for your permission, albeit for so little.

With my admiring and respectful regards,
Marcel Proust

You may meet (along the Bois Boudran way)[4] a charming old friend of mine called François de Pâris.[5] He was supposed to send me the etymology, motto and arms of the Guermantes, all of which are essential to me. True, I have the book stamped with the Guermantes arms that Walter Berry gave me, but it's in store. I don't think there was a motto. Anyhow, I don't need be too precise, for my Guermantes are invented, and nothing like the simple *famille de robe*[6] related to Pâris. Still, it would be nice if the motto turned on the name. I made up some rather pretty ones in my last book[7] (not yet out). But best of all are those invented by Balzac. You must know those glories (for Beaumont, 'Pulchre sedens melius agens'[8] and Mortsauf[9] etc.). It was a Gramont[10] (I know he wasn't really a Gramont) who found that for him.

1. See previous letter.
2. Comte Greffulhe's mistress.
3. According to Céleste, Proust was horrified to think that he was powerless to prevent the publication of his letters. See Albaret, *op. cit.*, 201–2.
4. Bois Boudran was the Greffulhes' vast sporting estate about fifty miles east of Paris.
5. François, Vicomte de Pâris (1875–1958); Proust took the name of Guermantes from his modest family seat near Bois Boudran.
6. Term applied to pre-Revolutionary titles conferred on members of the judiciary.
7. See the devices stamped on books bound for Morel by M. de Charlus: IV, 538–9; also the motto of the moribund Comte de Crécy whose patronym was Saylor, 'Ne sçais l'heure'. IV, 562.
8. Roughly, 'The finer the seat, the more gracious the act'. Presumably Beaumont is a slip for Beauséant, a recurring name in Balzac (but see letter 145). Cf. Proust's M. Montsurvent, who inhabits a windy, hilltop castle: IV, 562.
9. 'Safe from death'. Balzac's Mortsaufs belong to the provincial nobility; an ancestor, hanged for adultery and revived in the bed of a spinster (whom he married) was created Sieur de Mortsauf by Louis XI.
10. Allusion to Mme de Clermont-Tonnerre's maiden name. Balzac's secretary. Ferdinand, styled himself de Gramont.

90 To Madame Léon Daudet

[Early January 1921]

Madame,

If I have waited twenty-four hours before answering your delightful letter, it is because I was torn between two totally conflicting decisions. It was cruelly hard to part with this marvel, coming as it does from you, and from two men I had so much admired.[1] Alas, it has to be faced, and the book returned to your library. It would be a crime to keep it here, for any fine book is blackened, then destroyed, by the smoke I inhale for my asthma. Such as I possess are thus sacrificed. Where a book has no material value, I feel that it is a sacrifice I must accept, for a book is made to be read and that the author would consent to its gradual decay, to its eventual destruction, on condition that it was held 'in spirit and in truth'.[2]

The same cannot be said of the work of art you have offered me with such magnificent generosity, and which is a treat for the most blasé bibliophile. I know them by heart, these marvellous *Contes du lundi*, given fresh meaning and an even greater poignancy by the war. (How wonderful it would be if you and your dear husband were to write 'La Première classe'!)[3] It is thus not merely a question of a work by Alphonse Daudet, but of his most precious copy of it. Let us think of the dead. What would Jules Lemaître say, what would Alphonse Daudet himself say, were this enchanting jewel to come here only to be blackened, lost for ever, thanks to the effects of a powder I cannot do without and whose appalling ravages I have noticed only since living in an apartment so small that the smoke doesn't disperse as in my former abodes. To keep it would be to consign to a factory chimney the ornaments with which Jules Lemaître's exquisite taste embellished Alphonse Daudet's genius. You would not, I'm sure, wish us to conspire in such an act of double impiety. My gratitude is all the greater for knowing the unique worth of what you were offering me by this exquisite gesture. For one whole day, I allowed my gaze to linger over what I may not have with those looks which say, better than 'Carpe Diem', 'Love what you will never see twice'.[4]

If I were not so tired, I would give you yet more reasons. Above all, you mustn't think of giving me anything. My greatest joy is to be allowed to send you flowers occasionally. Yet I dare do so only very rarely, when the yearly Festival permits, that is, half as often as Chénier allowed: 'Twice yearly, by thy hand tended lovingly, / Let roses be thy garden's crowning glory'.[5]

Note how discreet I am in not following poetic ritual and keeping it to once a year. At least let me do so every year, but to send precious objects, books, into captivity in my hovel would be massacre. Only give me leave to send you flowers from time to time and I'll be eternally in your debt.

Allow me to express to you and husband, Madame, together

with my wonder at your letter, in itself a most magnificent, sumptuous and subtly-blended bouquet, my admiration and gratitude.

Your respectful friend,
Marcel Proust

1. Alphonse Daudet's own richly-bound copy of his *Les Contes du lundi*, originally from the library of Jules Lemaître.
2. See 'The Gospel according to St John', IV, 24.
3. Allusion to 'La Dernière classe', a patriotic story from *Les Contes du lundi*, and to the return of Alsace-Lorraine to France: set in Alsace in 1871, it is about a schoolboy whose future lessons will be in German.
4. 'Aimez ce que jamais l'on ne verra deux fois', a line from Alfred de Vigny's 'La Maison du berger'.
5. 'Que sous ta soigneuse main / Les roses, deux fois l'an, couronnent ton jardin', a line from 'Néère' in André Chénier's *Poésies antiques*.

91 To Gaston Gallimard

[Tuesday 11 January 1921]

My dear Gaston,

Not wanting to put you to unnecessary trouble, I'm sending you a pneumatique. The thing is, despite an attack of bronchitis which has lasted over ten days, I got up this morning for my room to be cleaned and immediately lost such voice as I had, so I'm going to try and rest this afternoon, telling them not to wake me, and in case I've managed to get to sleep by this evening, I would be extremely sorry if you were to come in vain.

This pneu is not the place to discuss topics already several months old. It was precisely because we had so much to talk about that I ruled out the alternative, a letter, as being too tiring. But in view of my recurring bronchitis, and the likelihood of our meeting being postponed, I'll confine myself to two purely practical points. The first concerns my book (*Le Côté de Guermantes II* / *Sodome et Gomorrhe I*) (it's one book, but being so long it will be in two volumes, to be sold together, like the two-volume *Les Jeunes filles*.[1] *Le Côté de Guermantes II* will take up the whole of the first volume and about half the second, *Sodome et Gomorrhe I* the rest of the second volume). With this book, whose ending will herald what is to come, we shall be finished once and for all with worldliness, digressions etc. (the point of which will emerge later), and the four long volumes to follow at fairly long intervals (if God grants me life),[2] *Sodome II*, *Sodome III*, *Sodome IV*[3] and *Le Temps retrouvé*, should give you an idea of what might then be termed my talent, and will not, I hope, give you cause to regret having included me among your authors.

For the moment, therefore, to get these *Guermantes* out of the way as quickly as possible, the next book to appear will be *Guermantes II* and *Sodome I*. But the text has been so corrected (you having sent the proofs I had counted on using to the printers) that I prefer to make my final corrections on a new set of proofs which I'll pass for press myself. Now, all this is enormously long, and remember that *Sodome I*, to come out simultaneously, is still in manuscript and not even at the first proof stage. An overlap would be disastrous. So I think it would be best if I waited to get *Guermantes II* back before sending off *Sodome I*, but all that will take time! So we must hurry the printer. We said we would come out in February. That being a practical impossibility, we had better set a date which, however late, we shan't overrun by a single day, rather than give wrong dates which would lead to reviewers jumping the gun etc. I therefore suggest that you bring the book out on the first of May: the first, not the second.

The other point: our friend Tronche told me in June that he would send me something in advance against royalties, the rest to follow shortly. He did indeed send me a down-payment.[4] I then asked him, so as to know where I stood, and how best to budget on what seems horrifyingly little: 'Tell me when I can expect the rest. I'm not hurrying you in the least. It's so that I know. But give me a definite date.' The date he gave me was mid-September at the latest. It's now January, and I've still had nothing. I didn't want to press him because I assumed that he was following your orders and it seemed best to talk to you. But should this state of affairs continue, I see it causing a number of problems.

1. Accounts already overlap (a headache), for in addition to the sums outstanding, there are those which I should be receiving (according to our contract)[5] from the reprints of *Guermantes*. And the de-luxe edition on top of that. Yet I haven't had a sou since the famous down-payment in June. It's not as if these complications can be justified. But as a friend[6] said to me, he having been so indiscreet as to ask if I had received anything for *Guermantes* and I having stupidly replied that no, I hadn't, wouldn't it be simpler

if M. Gallimard were to pay his authors before opening a new bookshop[7] etc. the costs of which are largely borne by them? It all adds up to an impression of muddle. Another inconvenience: having to sell shares I've only just bought.

There are a thousand things I wanted to talk to you about, had I not completely lost my voice, such as the farcical stories people make up in order to set me against you, even telling me that you went around Normandy during the war sporting a false beard![8] You can imagine with what rage and hilarity I greeted that! But since one should never repeat a slander, however ludicrous, to a single person, I didn't even mention it to dear Jacques Rivière, although he adores you and would have greeted it the same way as I did. I preferred that you alone should know the unbelievable depths of human perfidy. And as you see, I've ended up, tired or not, by putting more or less all I had to say to you in a letter, purely for the pleasure of chatting with you.

Letters! I must be over a thousand behind, alas. And I still haven't written to Grasset about your refusal to let him have the 'selected pieces'.[9] Naturally, if you're against it, I shan't give his proposal a second thought. That goes without saying. Still, he probably ought to be told. But my decision to back you up is final.

Don't you agree that the gutter-press goes rather too far with its lies? I never issue denials, and there are a hundred reasons why I don't want to do so in this case; but don't you find it incredible that *Aux Écoutes*, a paper that prints invariably crazy rumours about me (invariably the opposite of the truth, not necessarily malicious), such as reporting my attendance at M. René Boylesve's soirées when I've never set foot in his house,[10] should now go so far as to say that I've done the décor for an entire Montmartre theatre.[11] Yet I can't even draw, and have never heard of the theatre in question! But even though it's invention pure and simple, I prefer not to correct them, nor to complain (unless you feel it would be useful to take them to court, in case it saves our having to do so when the *Sodome et Gomorrhes* come out).

Dear friend, I'm too tired to go on; forgive this torn page which I've noticed too late and am too exhausted to begin afresh.

Warmest regards,
Marcel Proust

1. See letter 45, n. 5.

2. Proust was to live to see the three-volume *Sodom and Gomorrah* Part Two published in April 1922. The two remaining parts, and *Le Temps* retrouvé, were to be published posthumously, in 1922, 1925 and 1927.

3. Volumes III and IV, as yet untitled, were to become *The Captive* and *The Fugitive*.

4. Gustave Tronche had sent him 10,000 francs.

5. See *MP–GG*, 645–6.

6. Paul Morand.

7. The Librairie Gallimard had opened in October 1920, at its present address on the boulevard Raspail.

8. See letter 94.

9. 'Morceaux choisis'. Proust was eager, for financial reasons, to be included in Grasset's project. Gallimard himself was to bring out *The Best of Marcel Proust* in 1928.

10. The paper had implied that Proust had picked up a footman.

11. Described as a male cabaret 'decorated by M. Marcel Proust'.

92 To Jacques-Émile Blanche

[Sunday 16 January 1921]

Dear friend,

Need I tell you that since the announcement of *Dates* I haven't stopped sending people round to Émile-Paul? Today, at last, they returned with the long-awaited book.[1] I hesitate to tell you that I've begun reading it in the throes of terrible bronchitis, which I've had for the past three weeks – for as you've already talked about my asthma, insomnia, bad eyesight etc.,[2] I'm afraid lest you also talk about my bronchitis.

Dear friend, in general, let me be absolutely frank about this *admirable* preface. It does me far too much honour,[3] and I'm *eternally in your debt*. But at the same time, for a number of reasons, it upsets me greatly. First, and don't be angry at my frankness, that you, a man of your education and refinement, the son of parents like yours,[4] should do something that no journalist, however unscrupulous, would stoop to. What was written to you in a private letter (and, alas, what was not written to you), what it is tacitly understood that a correspondent will keep to himself, you print, blatantly, without so much as by-your-leave. It's quite true that in my opinion, given the defects long ascribed to you and against which (in conversation, and also in the very preface I wrote to *De David à Degas*)

I've always defended you, you were wrong in your determination to answer Forain's insults with redoubled politeness.[5] My rebuke was addressed to you and you alone, and came under the heading of friendly and well-considered advice. The problem is not my stupefaction at seeing you print it. For I accept full responsibility for my opinion. But it's the first time in my life that I've seen anybody, even some little gossip-columnist, make a private opinion public in that manner,[6] let alone when it was bound to embroil me in a deadly quarrel with the selfsame Forain, with whom I've been back on speaking terms these past two years. Tiredness prevents my going into all the personal remarks that will be twisted (like the 'he' that could be read as 'she' etc.).[7] In fact, exhaustion forces me to stop. But I want you to know that you were always the one guest I longed for. You appear to think otherwise; your memory plays you false, I'll refresh it.

Just now I must nurse this bronchitis, and can neither move nor speak. But I hope it will be cured and that, over a chat, I can convince you that I have *never* given a 'feast'[8] without asking you to be its most illustrious ornament. *Never.* If you have seldom come, you have only yourself to blame for refusing, or cancelling.

Dear friend, these magnificent pages fill me with pride and gratitude. I'm very proud to have inspired what a friend's indulgence mistakes for admiration for my work, and what certain traits in your character (which I tried to gloss over in my preface by speaking only – the actual words escape me – of the 'unvarying expansiveness of a kind heart and the serenity of a just one')[9] prevent your recognizing as a malicious tease.

I thank you, I admire you, I like you. Forgive the clumsy style of a letter from a man with a temperature of 40°.

Marcel Proust

I add a postscript, feeling that you might have found my gratitude half-hearted, although it's immense, and my rebukes too harsh, although the warmth of a tête-à-tête would show them in their true light. Furthermore I'm very pleased, objectively speaking, to have been the unwitting cause of this preface, one of the best things you have ever written. The quasi self-portrait which emerges as you do mine – it's characteristic of Old Masters – Rembrandt's *Burgmeister Six*[10] is both him and Rembrandt – and of our times – and our aesthetic – is your masterpiece. I hope you will never publish a book without letting me have the proofs. Your style tending towards the centrifugal, a specific subject, or the portrait of a painter, brings it back to its centre. Your Venice is much more sparkling.[11] But that's the nature of Venice, where everything is bathed in reflections.

My first outing will be to visit you. But my hours are now worse than before my bronchitis, alas. (Before I had bronchitis, I gave a few little dinners at nine-thirty at the Ritz, but never without having you telephoned first. Not long in advance, I admit. But you can ask my guests, like Mme de Noailles, who came even though invited on the same day).

1. *Propos de peintre: Dates*, the sequel to Blanche's *Propos de peintre: De David à Degas*: see letter 3 ff.

2. Allusion to Blanche's preface to *Dates*, in which he addresses Proust directly: 'Your biographers will find pages and pages from you in my desk [but] my pleasure in reading them (despite your spidery hand) was spoilt by what you had told me of the pain they gave you to write, so bad was your eyesight, so excruciating your asthma.'

3. In his preface, Blanche compares Proust to George Eliot, Bergson and Einstein.

4. Dr Antoine-Émile Blanche was a distinguished psychiatrist.

5. See letter 3.

6. On the subject of his eulogy of Forain, which he had reinstated in *Dates*, Blanche writes: '[. . .] you, who flatter yourself on being so Dreyfusard, begged me, for the sake of the pacifist, post-war reader, not to reprint my essay on the Nationalist Forain, yet your own genius is fêted in *L'Action française* [. . .].'

7. 'It seems to me that you sometimes give one sex the traits of another; that in some of your portraits there is a partial substitution of "gender", such that *he* could be read for *she* and masculine adjectives for feminine.' Blanche, *loc. cit.*

8. See letter 95, n. 2.

9. See Proust in 'Preface to Blanche': *AS-B*, 246.

10. Rembrandt's *Portrait of Jan Six*. In *Sodom and Gomorrah*, the Duc de Guermantes's melancholic manner is said to have 'that gentle gravity which constitutes the broad and unctuous charm of certain portraits by Rembrandt, that of the Burgomaster Six, for example': IV, 91–2. On the subject of Proust's 'portraits', Blanche writes: 'And perhaps most characteristic of your genius and, together with your vocabulary, your chief originality, is this duality of artist and model.'

11. An exhibition in Venice was the subject of one of Blanche's essays in *Dates*.

93 To Paul Souday

[Shortly after 15 January 1921]

Dear Sir,

I owe you a letter (and you also owe me one. For I still don't know if you received a copy of my 'de-luxe' *Jeunes filles en fleurs*). If I were less ill, I would write you a long letter ('felix morbus!')[1] to thank you with all my heart and to defend myself on the subject of 'style'.[2] As you'll see, we happen to think exactly alike where metaphors are concerned.

I feel certain that, disliking lines that are contrived, however brilliantly, as much as I do, you nevertheless agree that Baudelaire, if he intended devoutedness to fly up to heaven, had to provide her with wings.[3] The Wright brothers did no less. Renan's death's wing is another matter.[4] And it requires all your ingenuity to justify the apostles' barque setting sail for Greece, given the fact that the apostles were fishermen (freshwater fishermen) on the Sea of Galilee.[5]

I offer you this book[6] to show you that at the age of sixteen, when I wrote it (not when I published it), I had certain stylistic gifts. A benign oracle might have said: 'Tu Marcellus eris'.[7] But the 'aspera fata'[8] intervened.

Together with a book which never expected to have the honour of ending up in your hands ('habent sua fata libelli'),[9] kindly accept my respectful and devoted admiration.

Marcel Proust

1. 'O happy illness!', an echo of 'O felix culpa!' in St Augustine's Easter hymn.
2. Souday had written an article in the *Revue de Paris* of 15 January taking issue with Proust's views on metaphor in 'Preface to Morand', the essay which had appeared in the *Revue de Paris* in November. See letter 69, n. 1.
3. Allusion to a verse from Baudelaire's 'Les petites vieilles' in *Les Fleurs du Mal*, in which the old women implore devoutedness, who had lent them her wings: 'O mighty Hippogriff, fly us up to heaven!' See 'Preface to Morand', *AS-B*, 277–8.
4. Allusion to the phrase 'Death struck us both with its wing' in Renan's dedication to his sister in *La Vie de Jésus*. See *AS-B*, 277.
5. Allusion to Renan's *Les Apôtres*. See *AS-B*, 277.
6. This letter accompanied a copy of *Les Plaisirs et les jours*.

7. Virgil, *Aeneid*, Book IV: 'Thou shalt be Marcellus!' Anchises to Aeneas, pointing out the young Marcellus among the heroes of the underworld.
8. 'The cruel fates'.
9. 'Books have their destiny', a tag favoured by Brichot: see VI, 127.

94 To Gaston Gallimard

[Between 14 and 19 January 1921]

My dear Gaston,

Although completely incapable of writing a letter, I have some very important things to say to you.

But first I acknowledge receipt of 7500 francs for *Guermantes*[1] and wish to say that if you're short of money just now I can easily, once I've cashed the cheque, lend you 3000 francs (of the 7500). I'm not an author who seeks to harass his publisher, being on the contrary extremely fond of him. Far from exploiting the situation, you saw that when I had the Prix Goncourt, I didn't ask for Grasset's terms to be bettered in any way, and if I occasionally mention the harm you unwittingly inflict on yourself, it's purely out of affection for you and because I know that things I hear,[2] which you wouldn't otherwise know about, could be useful to you.

Not for one second, as you seem to think, did I dream of bringing up the 'mistress' question.[3] I'm neither so foolish nor so indiscreet as to meddle in my friends' private lives! I mentioned the false beard only to show you the extent of some people's imbecility and the sort of vipers we live among. I hasten to add that not everybody is a viper, thank God. I know that you are blessed with many good and faithful friends. Jacques Rivière loves you like a brother. I believe Tronche's loyalty as a colleague to be absolute. And there are many others.

Since I've brought up the subject of Rivière, permit me to meddle for a moment (although exhaustion and a trembling hand must make me barely legible) in what is certainly none of my business. He has talked to me about the Gide epistle he is about to publish.[4] I haven't read it. But as far as I can judge, to print it seems deplorable. I'm very fond of Gide and greatly admire him; of you all, he is the one I know best (though not well enough) and have known for longest. But at a time when Rivière is literally working himself to death on his Review, and also at a moment when new reviews like the *Revue universelle* etc., are presenting the *NRF* with a very real challenge, to choose such a moment to publish in the *NRF* itself a statement that it's boring to read, and has been since Rivière became editor, and that this statement should be reinforced by the prestige and authority of Gide's name, really upsets me. Is to say that the Review is boring supposed to make it more attractive? Tiredness forces me to stop when I've only just begun, and without having said any of the things I wanted to say. But since Rivière doesn't want me to talk to Gide, nor, where he is concerned, even want it to look as if I'm in the know, it seems to me that you, as managing director, have the right to ask Gide to retract his disloyal remarks.[5] Don't suppose from this that I have the least animosity towards Gide! Between ourselves (and I would say as much to Rivière), I admit to not being a fanatic *NRF*-ist. But for dog to eat dog is too absurd. I cannot possibly be accused of self-interest in saying this, never writing for the *NRF*! I'm thinking of the three of you and your common interest. Forgive me for interfering in what is none of my business. I'll adjourn this conversation until an evening when I'm in better health.

Very sincerely yours,
Marcel Proust

Don't forget my first editions, I need them urgently.[6]

---

1. Part payment of royalties for *The Guermantes Way* Part One (henceforth to be paid off at 2500 francs a month).
2. Such as the 'false beard': see letter 91.
3. Gallimard, 14 January: 'What haven't people said about me, what won't they say next! They say I keep mistresses, even my brothers' wives...' *MP–GG*, 312–13.
4. Allusion to one of Gide's 'Billets à Angèle'. These ironic articles, subtitled 'epistles to a literary lady', appeared regularly in the *NRF*.
5. Gallimard got Gide to tone down his article.
6. Proust needed first editions of *The Guermantes Way* to send out as complimentary copies.

95 To Jacques-Émile Blanche

[Second fortnight in January 1921]

Dear friend,

Thank you for your letter. I'm glad that you wrote it. What made the previous one so painful to read was that I might unconsciously have imagined that your response was so violent because I was so loving, and that you were keeping your meekness for the spiteful. Yet had this unfortunate suspicion occurred to me, your last letter would be enough to dispel it. For my friendly words met with such friendliness in return! Thus, your second letter[1] acts retrospectively on the first, giving it a nobler meaning.

I'm too tired to write at length. But till we meet, I can tell you firstly that (as far as I remember) the only person (or one of the only people) who could have said that she had dined with me was the Princesse Lucien Murat (which isn't to say that I haven't dined with others). Yet I haven't seen her for over a year. It must be thirteen or fourteen months since we last dined together. In her, you have a true and warm friend who speaks of you in your absence as though you were present, which is the most that any of us can hope for. Moreover, it's very likely that I wrote to you after having been very ill, the disruption of my sleeping habits always having that effect on me. Whoever it was who saw me at the Ritz[2] (so unkindly described – the Ritz, I mean – in your splendid recent book about which I have yet to write to you properly) cannot know how many bedridden days (and nights) without so much as a half-hour's respite had preceded and followed that two-hour outing.

Dear friend, I hope that what you say about your portraits of Americans doesn't mean that, like me, you've reached a point where you have to sell armchairs, tapestries etc.[3] (this between ourselves). But regarding these portraits, can I not help through my friend M. Walter Berry? I couldn't ask him for anything for myself, but would you not like me to talk to him? Don't trouble to reply if you think it would do no good.

As for humility, your letter is ample proof of that! And it being, after all, an arrogant humility, and simply an assessment seeking to be 'objective' about the 'situation' in terms of dealers etc. (something which naturally has nothing to do with talent), it may, alas, have a basis in truth, a truth that will however be purely temporary. As far as I can tell what goes on beyond my cork-lined walls,[4] it seems to me that your experience in the making of a reputation is almost unparalleled (and yet, if one were to study the lives of certain painters, La Tour,[5] for example, I believe that one would find many another case). It seems to me (but again, this is the tentative response of an hysteric who reads despite bandaged eyes through extra-sensory perception) that after you had been a 'delightful amateur' in the eyes of society for so long, suddenly, with supersaturation, the invisible droplets of admiration crystallized and, lo and behold, you were a great painter. But rather than this state being permanent ('Such as into himself at last eternity changes him'),[6] there was a third phase, marked by a temporary reflux (of reputation). It only needed somebody to hit upon the word 'pasticheur'. But as this reflux won't last, the second phase being definitive, I saw no point in even alluding to the third in my preface, and stopped at the second (naturally, I'm talking about reputation, not worth). It seemed to me kinder, more just and less complicated to spare us the 'round trip'.[7]

    Finally, dear friend, for my eyes are tiring, regarding those whom you call the XYZs, I can assure you that not one bears you any ill will. What I said to you at the Théâtre Astruc[8] has nothing to do with it. But nobody who spoke to me about the Preface intended the slightest malice towards either of us. Somebody or other very kindly told me what you had thought of it (or what they thought you had thought of it), none of it disobliging to me. I was the one who said to myself that, all things considered: 'If this aspect bothers Blanche, and that somebody else, then I don't want to be a nuisance.' You tell me that there's no question of that, and I'm delighted. But all I wanted, quite simply, was to put you 'at your ease', just as, in the old days when I could still leave Paris, if I heard that somebody who had invited me to stay in the country dreaded the smell of my fumigations, I thought it kinder to cancel my visit, or at least offer to do so. We have known one another for so long that it seemed absurd not to talk to you quite openly. You misunderstood me and that I found hurtful. But I don't regret it, for your second letter is so kind that (speaking for myself, at least) I feel we are better friends than we were before, and that I may congratulate myself on having given you the opportunity, in this second letter, of unconsciously painting what is to me the most sympathetic of all your self-portraits, and one in which the features I had cherished long before the first are confirmed in all their force.

Believe me, dear friend, your affectionate and grateful admirer,

Marcel Proust

1. Neither of Blanche's letters has survived, but he seems to have pursued the subject of Proust's response to *Dates*: see letter 92.

2. 'You wouldn't like even Morand to portray you alone at your table at the Ritz after the other customers have gone to bed, surrounded by a swarm of waiters who, grown rich on your extravagant tips, scurry back and forth to place a poached egg in front of M. Proust's pelisse. One should draw Proust before and Proust after the Victory, resuming at the Ritz the cosseted feasts he gave at his parents' house in the old days.' Blanche, preface to *Dates*. Allusion to Morand's 'Ode to Marcel Proust' (see letter 42) and to the dinners Proust gave at his parents' apartment in the boulevard Malesherbes.

3. See letter 28.

4. Proust is thinking of his years at the boulevard Haussmann.

5. Quentin de La Tour (1704–88), fashionable portraitist described in *Time Regained* as a painter 'despised by revolutionaries': VI, 238.

6. 'Tel qu'en lui-même enfin l'éternité le change', opening line of Mallarmé's 'Le Tombeau d'Edgar Poe'.

7. Cf. Mme de Surgis's social predicament in *Sodom and Gomorrah*: 'she had had to set to work to reconquer laboriously, inch by inch, what she had possessed as a birthright (a round trip that isn't uncommon).' IV, 123. See also 'Preface to Blanche': *AS-B*, 251–2.

8. See letter 8.

96 To Louis Martin-Chauffier

[3 or 4 February 1921]

Dear Sir,

Jacques Rivière will describe for you my present pitiable state of health. It prevents my writing to thank anybody. But for you, I can, can I not, make an exception dictated purely by my heart. The article I've just read in the *NRF*.[1] (as I immediately told Jacques Rivière who by some happy chance has just been to see me, though I hardly ever see him), your article, is astonishing in its profundity, its richness, its infallible accuracy of aim. This accuracy in selecting the real from an infinitude of possibilities – with the certainty of a carrier-pigeon travelling invisible pathways – is what impresses me the most. Make no mistake, by accuracy, I don't mean the plaudits (they touch me deeply but are prompted by friendship), I mean the insights. I would be quite impartial (since it's not about me) if, as an example, I were to cite the criticism of Montesquieu's advice.[2] I believe that I'm no less so, even though it touches me directly, in citing what you say about the transition from fiction to reality,[3] and it is so exactly the answer I was making to a critic that I'll have to alter the words, though not the sense, for it to remain mine. Likewise the parallels between Balbec and Guermantes.[4] Take the best critics of the past: can you name one who you think could enter so wholly into an author's intentions? You uncover my secrets, you play hide-and-seek in my chiaroscuro, you are my medium.

This article truly surprised me. I hesitated to say so before, for fear of influencing you, but your style, notably in your letters but also in your articles, seemed to me, on account of archaisms and a certain over-refined abstraction, to run the risk of becoming dry and congealed. And now my fears have been well and truly dissipated! There is not a sentence which does not live, is not justified by a new and profound idea. The phrase grows, it blossoms, and it acquires, as you express it so well (as you express it too rarely in your articles and letters) 'the veils of petals and leaves'.[5]

We are never sufficiently ceremonious in our manners. We are always too much so in our descriptions ... I'm too weak to talk to you about yourself any longer (I say yourself because not for one moment in this letter did I stop to think that you were writing about me). But I thank you again from the bottom of my heart and, in the hope of seeing you soon, give you the warmest of handshakes.

Marcel Proust

Jacques Rivière, a friend whom I hold in the highest intellectual and moral esteem, spoke very warmly of you, in a way I've seldom heard him speak of a writer. To revert to my own opinion: remember to avoid the pitfalls of overlong sentences (so funny in the pastiche you did of me)[6] when in the abstract. Avoid seventeenth-century formulations, retaining from that admirable epoch only its sense of reality, its underlying vigour, its strongly-felt impressions of which an apparent solemnity should never lessen our awareness.

1. A review of *The Guermantes Way* Part One in the *NRF* of 1 February.

2. Having quoted Montesquieu's dictum: 'no subject should ever be treated so exhaustively that the reader is left with nothing to do', Martin-Chauffier makes the point that Proust may be exhaustive but leaves readers a vast field of discovery: 'the domain of our inner lives'.

3. Alluding to *Within a Budding Grove*, and to the criticism that Proust lacks structure and design, Martin-Chauffier cites the way in which 'he contrasts the poetry of Balbec's name with the banality of the landscape', concluding: 'One could say, therefore, and not only of *The Guermantes Way* but of every book that has appeared so far, that the significance lies in the transition from fiction to reality.'

4. '[. . .] the name of Guermantes, far from being the magic word that unlocks a faery kingdom, becomes the term designating a certain type of society woman, and then a certain type of family [. . .].' Martin-Chauffier, *loc. cit.*

5. 'One might justly compare him to a botanist whose inquiring mind goes far beyond the limits of botany and uses all the scientific knowledge at its disposal. Studying a branch of blossom, he shows us not only the interlacing of the fibres, the material of the wood, the veils of petals and leaves [. . .].' *Ibid.* Cf. II, 330–1.

6. See letter 53.

97 To Jacques Rivière

[Monday evening 7 February 1921]

My dear Jacques,

Alas, I'm going to give you the advice that you say you don't want. I advise you to publish your book.[1] I'm having an attack of such violence that it's hard for me to explain why I find it so admirable. (You are however singularly devoid of those weaknesses you imagine you have.)[2] Your illusion has various causes, some of them physical. Apart from the fact that, your marvellous gift being of the kind known as 'natural', your exaggerated amour-propre makes you fear that it might not be enough. If I haven't written to you before, it's because 1) I started copy-editing your text line by line and realized on page 25 that I was being 'dotty'. Listen, I'm in too much discomfort (they've turned on the central heating etc.)[3] to go on with this letter for the moment, I'll write again in a day or two. I shall advise you to cut certain things which would be all right in a revised edition but in a first, when one has yet to appreciate that such innocence is as precious as that one finds in Rimbaud, would seem too simple. And there are grammatical errors. Ah, if only I had such a severe critic, if only you were to tell me cut this, cut that! Tiredness stops me.

Tonight or tomorrow, when my attack is over, I'll write to Gaston about translations etc. You didn't finish your letter, there's a page missing.

Affectionately,
Marcel Proust

1. Rivière's first novel, *Aimée*, inspired by his platonic love for Gallimard's wife, Yvonne Redelsperger.
2. 'I wrote it as a prisoner of war in 1915, but wanted to enrich it with what I've learnt and come to understand since. I've completely rewritten the first two chapters, which was agony. Now I can get no farther (tiredness, self-disgust, disenchantment with life and a general sense of futility).' Rivière, 1 February.
3. See letter 58, n. 7.

98 To Jacques Boulenger

[Saturday 5 March 1921]

Dear friend,

I'm writing you a note which in any case is certain to arrive too late. But I've long been 'as good as dead', thus physically incapable of writing to you.[1] Here is the note. In the *Revue hebdomadaire*, not the latest one but the one before that, which I enclose, Mauriac has done an article, on me, 'l'Art de Marcel Proust',[2] in which he tries to shield me in advance from the attacks which I suppose I must expect with the publication of my next book, *Guermantes II/ Sodome et Gomorrhe I*. He says, notably, that in my case questions of morality and immorality don't arise.[3] I would have been very pleased if 'Sayings of the Week' (I don't in fact know what it's called in *L'Opinion*) could have quoted this judgement of his (not the remark about morality on its own, which might have looked too tendentious, but together with one or two of those coming before and after). Only, as it's the issue before last, it may be 'too late to speak of it now'.[4]

One 'dodge' might be to omit the date of the *Revue hebdomadaire* and simply put 'In the *Revue hebdomadaire* etc.'. Anyhow, if it's the slightest trouble, we won't talk about it, it's not important.[5] What really worries me is having to leave so many letters, invitations, books about me,[6] unanswered. Lamartine was quite right to say that it's a nuisance to die more than once.[7] I only wish that the final coming, the real one that gives us the courage 'to fare on till nightfall',[8] could at least be postponed until after I've met you. I can't tell you how glad I am to think that you'll see no more Guermantes in my book, but people who are very different from them; they crop up once more in *Guermantes II*, but you'll be pleased with me for all that.

Warmest regards,
Marcel Proust

Did I write to you about your wonderful article on the Haiku? Ah! that pimento![9]

1. Proust's bronchitis had now lasted three months.

2. Allusion to François Mauriac's comments (*La Revue hebdomadaire*, 26 February) on two pre-publication extracts in the *NRF* from *The Guermantes Way* Part Two: 'The Kiss', taken from Albertine's visit (III, 407–27); and 'A Foggy Evening', taken from the narrator's outing with Saint-Loup (III, 459–78).

3. 'What people call M. Marcel Proust's snobbery is merely curiosity about such fine distinctions. And moralists will doubtless note with displeasure that religion plays no part in his re-created world. Perhaps M. Proust thinks it is none of his concern; but is he not colluding with the moralist, in fact, by giving us an "abstract" of "modern sensibilities"? [...] What they yield up, these myriad observations assembled [...] by this patient visionary, is Truth, which is the ultimate quest of Art. Henceforth, in discussing his work, let there be no talk of immorality; the examination of conscience lies at the root of all moral life, and the pitiless light shed by Proust penetrates to our very depths. His art is as dispassionate as the sun: all is dragged out from the shadows, including that which nobody before him has dared to name.' Mauriac, *loc. cit.*

4. See Alfred de Musset in 'À la Malibran': It may be too late to speak of her now; / Two long weeks have passed since she is no more.'

5. Boulenger was to quote from Mauriac's article in *L'Opinion* of 12 March.

6. Possibly an allusion to Boulenger's 'Mais l'Art est difficile': see letter 82, n. 1.

7. Proust appears to confuse Lamartine with de Musset: see letters 100, 101.

8. Allusion to the first verse of Baudelaire's 'La Mort des pauvres' in *Les Fleurs du Mal*: 'It is Death, alas, that consoles us, and keeps us living. / Death is the aim of life, the only hope of all. / Like an elixir, enkindling, uplifting, / It gives us the courage to fare on till nightfall.'

9. In *L'Opinion* of 29 January, Boulenger had quoted two versions of a haiku about a dragonfly alighting on a pimento.

99 To Gaston Gallimard

Sunday evening [6 March 1921]

My dear Gaston,

(or my dear Tronche, if Gaston is away), I beg you to pay the greatest attention to this letter. It's vital, urgent. Gaston, if it's you I'm talking to, because you wrote to me in mid-Lent, I didn't get your letter till the evening of Good Friday, hence a delay that isn't my fault. In any case, against all the odds I've just provided you with a colossal amount of work, and so that we can come out, let's take the plunge without more ado and pass the lot for press (the enclosed packet contains the whole of *Guermantes II* and *Sodome I* except for the proofs which Tronche took away with him). For it is not, as you thought, the beginning of *Sodome I* that is to appear with *Guermantes II* but the whole of *Sodome I*, which is very short (shorter than the other *Sodomes*); thus what is to come out in May is a two-volume work without a dedication and entitled *Le Côté de Guermantes II – Sodome et Gomorrhe I*.

Redouble your attention at this point; Tronche said that he would have fresh proofs made from those he took away and that I should put the headings for chapter two of *Guermantes II* on to these proofs. Yet I've had nothing from you except your letter about passing it for press (there we completely agree, and having promised not to ask you for an errata slip this time, if there are any errors I'll say that they're mine) so, on galley one, which I think is the one Tronche took away, where my grandmother's death finishes with roughly these words: 'Death, like a mediaeval sculptor, had laid her to rest in the form of a young girl',[1] after these words, and before 'It was a Sunday in autumn', you should put

Chapter II

Albertine's visit – Prospect of a rich marriage for some of Saint-Loup's friends – The Princesse de Parme has a taste of Guermantes wit – My strange visit to M. de Charlus, I understand his character less and less – The Duchesse's red shoes.[2]

The printer shouldn't forget to number the first page 1, the second 2, instead of, as at present, something like 26, 27 etc.

For *Sodome et Gomorrhe I*, he should start again with 1, 2, 3 etc.

I don't agree with putting the line from Vigny[3] on the jacket.

I've put it in the second volume, after the title and subtitle.⁴ That's enough.

In haste, with warmest regards,
Marcel Proust

Keep this letter.

1. See III, 397.
2. See letter 60 to Mme Straus, n. 5.
3. 'Woman will have Gomorrah and Man will have Sodom' ('La Femme aura Gomorrhe et l'Homme aura Sodome', Alfred de Vigny, 'La Colère de Samson').
4. Proust's subtitle for *Sodom and Gomorrah* Part Two reads: 'First appearance of Men–Women, descendants of the inhabitants of Sodom who were spared the fires of Heaven'.

100   To Lionel Hauser

44 rue Hamelin
[Shortly after 7 March]

My dear Lionel,

You cannot imagine (as well as the pleasure of having a letter from you)¹ the droll effect on somebody who has spent weeks close to death, incapable of turning over in bed or opening a letter (much less answer one), to read in yours the formula: 'Trusting that you are in the best of health'. Especially when one knows that the reality expressed in Lamartine's beautiful lines on the tedium of 'dying more than once here below'² is as much of a nuisance to others as to oneself. And as it so happens that your letter arrives at a moment when my brain is clear and my hand mobile, I hasten to set aside this presentiment, before you reproach me for not having realized it quickly enough, and to answer you cheerfully.

Speaking of 'realizing', I'll confine myself to the other sort. First let me say that I believe I've inherited from my dear Maman, along with a lot of faults she didn't possess, enough discretion and tact never once to have brought up your name with Warburg's on the many occasions when they wrote to me at this address, which they know perfectly well (disorder must reign in that office), nor did I ask them to send my share-certificates to you. When they told me, ages ago now, that they were holding these Japanese etc.,[3] I asked Henri Gans[4] if he would allow me to have them sent to him. He having given his unqualified consent, I did so, and Gans sold the Japanese to meet my living expenses. I feel tiredness overcoming me, and won't go further into all that. If at the time of the Comptoir d'Escompte,[5] I ventured to ask your advice, it was following a letter from M. Neuburger and, he having expressly asked me not to, it didn't seem worth mentioning to you. But as I was one of those who took your side when, years later, people sought to make those stupid accusations against you,[6] you can well imagine how careful I would be not to run the smallest risk, however infinitesimal, of reviving them in the slightest degree.

You're going to have to answer this letter (if you would be so kind). Since we last wrote, my vagaries of health have been such that I couldn't even draft or sign the order to sell my Government Bonds for the London County bank. Now, writing to you, I receive a letter from them (that may sound contrived, but it's the exact truth) saying that my overdraft is 47,000 francs and that so as to answer a query from their head office in London, they need to know whether I intend to keep it or pay it off. A perfectly understandable question (even without the query from London) considering that a few months ago I asked them to sell in a sudden feverish urge but my order was never sent, my illness having tightened its grip on me. Yet I wish to repay them. But I'm afraid that to repay them by selling Government Bonds would be like repaying them in a year's time. So I think it might be more practical to ask them to sell my Suez (which I think are in deferred shares and thus pay no dividends), paying them back like that, and depositing my other shares with, say, Rothschilds', getting them to proceed with the sale of my Government Bonds. It's partly the London County's own fault if my Government Bonds weren't sold, firstly because, in good faith or not, they had kept some hidden from me, and because, despite their stubborn refusal to learn my address for over a year, I had asked them to make out the order to sell for me, feeling rather too 'Schlemihl-like'[7] to do so myself. Yet they did nothing. Even so, I feel that to say I intend to repay them, but in Government Bonds, is rather like saying that I'll repay them when I'm dead. Moreover, still feeling 'Chamisso-like', I would have to exhaust myself drafting orders to sell etc.

As for depositing the share-certificates with them even after having paid them back, since I bear them no grudge for their

Mexican behaviour,[8] I could, once in the black, leave the Government Bonds with them rather than with Rothschilds'. It makes no difference to me either way.

With my warmest regards, my dear Lionel,
Marcel Proust

Your dear Father,[9] who in a letter to you once made the only intelligent suggestion about my illness that any doctor has ever given me, namely, that my asthma attacks must be partly due to my liver, is probably the only person who could tell what it is that I'm dying of now (something quite different). I am full of gratitude and respect for an all-seeing clairvoyance exercised quasi-mediumistically over such a great distance and on a subject unknown to him apart from your description.

1. Allusion to a formal business letter from Hauser on 7 March, expressing his displeasure that, even though he was now retired, he continued to receive letters and share certificates from Proust's bank.

2. In fact, a reference to Musset's 'Letter to M. de Lamartine': 'And here below we are dying more than once, / For how else to term the necessity / On this earth to change misery for misery?' Cf. letter 98, n. 7.

3. Japanese Bonds on which Hauser had offered his advice.

4. Mme de Noailles's young banker friend: see letter 85, n. 14.

5. See letter 19, n. 12.

6. In 1918, wartime hysteria had led to Hauser's being denounced as a German spy; Proust and Walter Berry had been among those who had used their influence to allay suspicion and prevent a prosecution.

7. Allusion to Peter Schlemihl, the hopelessly unwordly hero who sells his shadow to the devil in the story by Adelbert von Chamisso (1781–1838).

8. Allusion to the bank's sale of Proust's Mexican Tramway shares. See letter 28, n. 1.

9. Philippe Hauser (1832–1925), physician to the Spanish royal family in Madrid.

101 To Rosny aîné

[Shortly after 8 March 1921]

Dear Master and friend,

I've just passed through yet another period of death (I can still barely move in my bed). I'm aware that if it's tedious for the patient to have to 'die more than once', as Lamartine puts it, it's no less so for those exasperated by these announcements of death postponed, the postponement moreover being of little benefit to a man who is no better than a corpse. 'For how else can we term on earth' etc.. You know those 'Novissima Verba'.[1]

But I wanted to muster my remaining forces (if force is not too ironic!) to express my deep gratitude for the way in which you spoke of me in *Comœdia*.[2] In fact I have much else to say to you, for on the one hand, if you don't know the comic background story, certain things in the Preface must have seemed inexplicable to you, and on the other, you must find it odd that, feeling it so strongly and regardless of my tokens of it,[3] I have never expressed my gratitiude to you publicly.[4] But all this is beyond the first attempts at handwriting by somebody who cannot even call himself convalescent, nor, like Beethoven in his sublime fifteenth quartet, give thanks for the return of health,[5] since there can be no more health for me. But perhaps, one of these days, I may be able to chat with you nevertheless; meanwhile I offer you my unbounded gratitude, admiration and respect.

Marcel Proust

1. Once again, Proust confuses Lamartine, in his poem 'Novissima Verba', with Alfred de Musset: see previous letter, n. 2.
2. Rosny had discussed Proust's 'Preface to Morand' on 8 March.
3. Proust had evidently sent presents to thank Rosny for his 'profile' in *Comœdia* (see letter 47) and his support on the Goncourt jury.
4. A roundabout way of saying that he couldn't dedicate a book to Rosny.
5. See letter 25, n. 8. The slow movement of Beethoven's quartet is inscribed 'Thanks to the Godhead by one recovering from illness'.

102 *From Robert de Montesquiou*

22 March 1921

Marcel,

Somewhat shop-soiled, dragging its feet, there arrives this very ordinary copy of a book[1] which you brought out over six months ago and had sent to all and sundry.

If that's what you call deference,[2] then I no longer know the meaning of the word, nor do I wish to in this *topsy-turvy* world.

As you have always treated me very kindly, I find this volte face, this change of tone, completely incomprehensible. The only excuse that I can see (if it is one) is that a sign has entered the lower half of your Zodiac which may well be called Cancer.

The *reading time* that I had long set aside for you, and which I flatter myself is both *receptive* and *exceptional*, could certainly have been put to better use; but I shall return to it.

And you must admit that, for somebody who is said to be *cantankerous*, I show great *good nature* in overlooking your moods and fits.

Be happy
R. Montesquiou

1. *The Guermantes Way* Part One.
2. Proust had written in November to explain that he had failed to send Montesquiou a copy of his book 'out of deference', having been unable to find a suitably rare edition.

103 To Gaston Gallimard

[22 or 23 March 1921]

Important letter: to be read to the end.

My dear Gaston,

It's very difficult to write, I've just had a relapse! I have no luck.

About the addition, Céleste tells me that you'll be taking it to the printers yourself. That's ideal, as long as you have other reasons for seeing the printer. But to go just for that would be pure folly, especially for something almost unimportant.

If you have to see the printer (*but only if*), this addition should be inserted in the Duchesse de Guermantes's dinner-party, at the point where the Princesse de Parme's lady-in-waiting insists on seeing a relationship, purely imaginary, between me and the Admiral Jurien de la Gravière.[1] It (the insert) follows immediately after. I'm reluctant, having spent the last few days writing things about doctors for *Sodome II*[2] that will amuse you, to send you this comparatively boring addition that you will find stupid. But you'll see the point of it eventually. It is no more than useful, and totally charmless, but if you have to go to the printers, it might as well be for something useful. Indispensable it is not, and not worth two kilometres of anybody's journey.

Although it's extremely difficult to write to you in my present state, I want to tell you something very useful indeed. In my opinion, *Sodome II* (not the one coming out in May but the one after that) is the only *Sodome* that will need actual resetting. As for the other volumes, I could be dead and they could come out as they are, more or less.[3] Consequently, the sooner I have galleys of *Sodome II* the better, while I'm still able to work (?). It won't mean your coming out any earlier, but it will mean (on the best hypothesis) that I can give you *Sodome II*, which you can then bring out when you think fit. As for the next, and final, volumes, little remains for me to do, and if necessary, should the worst come to the worst, once certain things have been explained to you, or to Jacques, my exercise-books could appear as they stand. This isn't the case with *Sodome II*. So try and hurry the printer in charge of it (I don't mean hurry him because he is late, for he can only just have received my manuscript).

I wanted to ask Jacques, because I think it's too slipshod to reflect on such things in a few lines, if I might reply to Paul Valéry in the Review.[4] But this relapse means that I'm not ready. And should it be only temporary, I would do better to concentrate on my books. Forgive me for talking so much about myself, only remember that it's in order to talk to you about yourself, and out of an author's scrupulousness. I'm sorry to hear that Jacques has the 'flu.[5] I don't think he looks after himself properly. I could tell him how to avoid catching it. Anyhow, since he is better and suffering mainly from fatigue, he would do well (provided that he doesn't have *hypertension*) to ask Dr Roussy[6] if it might not be a case for adrenalin injections. They're the best possible remedy for fatigue (as long as there are no contrary indications, as in the case of hypertension, for instance).

There's nothing to stop him continuing with a little phytin,[7] which, though less efficacious, is not to be despised.

Yours,
Marcel Proust

1. See III, 574. The addition concerns the false idea that people often have of us.
2. See IV, 47–9; 127–8.
3. This remark (which Proust reiterates) was to convince Jacques Rivière and

Robert Proust that they were justified in relying on the exercise-books when, after his death, they edited his penultimate volume – which they entitled *Albertine disparue* – for publication in 1925. The 1954 Pléiade edition was based on their text, but, following Proust's preference, re-titled *La Fugitive*. In any case, neither set of editors had a complete typescript. This turned up only in 1986, when it was discovered that in the weeks before his death Proust had secretly been working on a parallel version of the Albertine story, making major changes in its development and dénouement: see letter 263.

4. The *NRF* had printed extracts from Valéry's essay on La Fontaine in the *Revue de Paris* on 1 February. On 1 June, in the *NRF*, Proust was to take Valéry to task for his 'air of lofty detachment' in his own critical essay 'Concerning Baudelaire': see *AS-B*, 290.

5. There was a recurrence of the post-war 'Spanish 'flu' epidemic in 1921.

6. Professor Gustave Roussy, recommended to Rivière by Proust.

7. Tonic derived from plants, indicated for depression, anaemia etc.

104 To Robert de Montesquiou

[Shortly after 22 March 1921]

Dear Sir,

I have received your letter.[1] I read it with sad bewilderment. I could understand neither what had inspired it, nor rediscover your former benign tone. You say that my book was shop-soiled. Now, that astonishes me, for it was a completely new copy which, by the way, I am quite prepared to exchange. You go on to say that it's very ordinary. I know that only too well, alas! During these long weeks when I have been constantly at death's door (though not as a result of *cancer*, as you so obligingly assume), I became obsessed, as one is with a flower on a patch of wallpaper,[2] by the desire to obtain two 'first editions' if it was the last thing I did; one not for you but for an old friend of Maman who has been like a second mother to me,[3] and the other for you.

Somehow, between injections, at a time when the least movement costs me dear and gives me nausea, I found the strength – ill-rewarded – to write to my publisher, without success. He was unable to find a first edition anywhere. You see a contradiction between this fact and the fact that I sent first editions to several people. No such contradiction exists; to begin with, I had anticipated receiving many more than the few parsimoniously doled out to me. And as and when people dropped in to ask how I was, I signed them from my bed. You may be sure that had I known I wouldn't be getting any more, I would have sent you yours at once. You may also be sure that had I known how you would greet the result of my daily efforts over six months, I wouldn't have bothered. If your letter strangely clouds my affection, it does nothing to alter the deference I spoke of, nor an admiration which, fervently expressed to the very few people I see but who are luckily those best able to appreciate its timbre and amplify its echo, cannot have failed more than once in recent years to titillate you pleasantly or rather, as the saying goes, make your ears burn.

Respectfully yours,
Marcel Proust

1. See letter 102.
2. Cf. letter 36, n.3.
3. Probably Mme Catusse.

105 To François Mauriac[1]

[Second fortnight in March 1921]

Dear friend,

You must, I suppose, have guessed that I've been gravely ill since your visit.[2] If not, how could I have failed to write to you, despite your request[3] and even without waiting for your letter. This note is written at a moment when I'm still unwell. But I didn't want you to think my lengthy silence meant that I had taken you at your word.

When we meet again, if we meet again, I beg you to be what you tell me is your usual self.[4] I can't see why the 'admiration'(!) which you so kindly say you have for me should change anything, for you must know that it is balanced by an equal admiration on my part. Thus, it cancels itself out, and we need only see ourselves as two jolly gentlemen with a love of life (even the one who has one foot in the grave) who when apart and alone, think profound thoughts, but when together, genuinely partake of all the pleasures enjoyed by those honest folk who are not artists and not given to mutual admiration, pleasures which, furthermore, do not necessarily exclude that of literary conversation. I'm so tired that I'm putting this very badly, and with the sort of pedantic air I abhor, as though you didn't know as well as I do, indeed, far better than I do, what goes to make the charm of an open and simple friendship.

Warmest regards,
Marcel Proust

1. François Mauriac (1885–1970), soon to become famous for his religiously-inspired novels set in the region of Bordeaux.
2. Mauriac had dined at Proust's bedside on 28 February; it was their first meeting.
3. Mauriac wrote on 1 March, in a letter full of warmth and admiration: 'Prove your friendship for me *by not replying* to this letter.'
4. 'With people I don't admire I feel I can let my hair down, let my imagination roam. But admiration makes me unsociable.' Mauriac, *loc. cit.*

106 To Lionel Hauser

[Around 7 April 1921]

Dear friend,

It makes me miserable not to be able to write to you,[1] for your letters are such masterpieces of wit that one would like to 'go the distance' with a rival of your calibre. Unfortunately, since we last wrote, although I've been up only once (as you must have heard, it was with the intention of having you to dinner, but you were away for Easter) and haven't even once left my apartment (which would easily fit into your office), this unaccustomed rising has added rheumatic fever to my usual delightful complaints, meaning that I can't move without crying out and deserve some credit for writing you a letter as proof of my unswerving devotion.

My excellent doctor[2] subjects my body to morphine, aspirin, adrenaline, euvalpene, sparteine,[3] in short, every medicament you can – or rather, I hope, cannot – imagine. So far the effect has been minimal, other than total exhaustion, which may induce you to forgive the squalid banality of a letter whose sole virtue is to mean well, and to believe nevertheless in the affection, more sensitive than its gross expression, of your devoted and grateful

Marcel Proust

1. Proust replies to Hauser's long answer, partly practical, partly personal, to his letter of *c.*7 March: see letter 100.

2. Professor Joseph Babinski, neurologist. Proust's nervous troubles had recurred: see letter 13.
3. Poisonous alkaloid used in cardiac medicine; euvalpine is unidentified.

107 To Robert de Montesquiou

[18 or 19 April 1921]

Dear Sir,
How kind you are to have written me that magnificent letter![1] I could receive no greater honour. To distract you with some frivolities, I reply to what you say about the spurious keys in my book. There are two or three at most in the entire work (I don't mean in individual books, but the ensemble), and they unlock only for an instant.

Thus, there are none for Saint-Loup, but for the passage that appeared in the *Revue hebdomadaire*[2] from an as yet unpublished part of the book, I had in mind the circumambulation of banquettes[3] once performed in a café by my poor friend Bertrand de Fénelon, who was killed in 1914. Apart from that, they had nothing in common.

Should you have a vague recollection of *À l'Ombre des jeunes filles en fleurs* (forgive my referring to my forgotten works like this, but it was you who encouraged me), for the scene where M. de Charlus fixes me with a distracted stare outside the Casino,[4] I thought momentarily of the Baron Doäzan,[5] an habitué of the Aubernon salon[6] and a fairly typical example of that genre. But I then dropped him, and I constructed a Charlus on an infinitely vaster scale, and entirely invented. As for Bloqueville, Janzé etc.,[7] I knew them only by name, and my Madame de Villeparisis is more like Madame de Beaulaincourt (with a touch of Madame de Chaponay-Courval);[8] I even said she painted flowers rather than made them, for Madame de Beaulaincourt having made artificial flowers, the resemblance would have been too close. My Charlus doesn't quite come off in the next volume, but later on (I flatter myself) I believe he acquires a certain amplitude.

People think that Albufera is Saint-Loup; it hadn't occurred to me. I imagine he thinks so himself; it's the only explanation I can find for his having quarrelled with me,[9] and the fact that he had just done me a favour grieves me all the more. Strangely enough, your letter happened to arrive just as I had written (I, who can never write letters) to the editor of an important, or fairly important review, saying among other things: 'What a pity that serious art criticism should not be entrusted to the best art critic of our time, Monsieur de Montesquiou'.[10]

Dear Sir, what a peculiar idea you have of my life! I gave a rueful smile at 'fat dividends',[11] for I earn nothing from my books. And it would make no difference if the opposite were true, for what pleasure can there be for a man who can't even pronounce his words. I ventured into a restaurant the other day and had to repeat Contrexéville[12] six times before I could make myself understood. I've never had syphilis, so this dreadful affliction is inexplicable. It doesn't necessarily prevent our meeting, as it responds, for a few hours, to days on caffeine and adrenalin. Poison, my brother says: his patients must be reassured by bedside manner. Turning my face to the wall, I can only repeat after Baudelaire: 'Sleep the sleep of the beasts'.[13]

Dear Sir, I send you all my good wishes for a prompt recovery (you don't say what is the matter with you)[14] and my grateful and respectful thanks for having sent that bouquet of praises to a sick man 'who lacks bitterness'.[15]

Marcel Proust

1. A long, witty and subtle appraisal of *The Guermantes Way* Part One. Montesquiou makes no mention of his portrayal as M. de Charlus.

2. 'A Foggy Evening': see letter 99, n. 2.

3. III, 475-9.

4. See II, 383-4.

5. Baron Albert Agapit (1840-1907), otherwise known as Jacques Doäzan, a notorious homosexual; like the Baron de Charlus, he was stout, with pomaded hair and a waxed moustache.

6. See letter 22, n. 13.

7. Montesquiou's former cronies, the Marquise de Blocqueville and the Vicomtesse de Janzé.

8. With the above, the Marquise de Chaponay-Courval made up the trio of dowagers portrayed as the three 'Parcae' (fallen godesses) at Mme de Villeparisis's party: III, 222-4.

9. Proust's old friend 'Albu' must have recognized the parallels between Saint-Loup's liaison with Rachel and his own with Louisa de Mornand (see letter 16, n. 14), and had also taken offence at the portrayal of his Murat relations in Proust's Saint-Simon pastiche.

10. See Proust to Jacques Boulenger, *c.* 18 April: 'I'm always giving you advice

about *L'Opinion* even though it's none of my business! I consider that Robert de Montesquiou is the best critic writing on art today, yet nobody ever asks him for an article [. . .].'

11. '[. . .] everybody will buy it, this person for delectation, that out of indignation, and each *to know what's going on*, according to the *repulsive* and *seductive* convention [. . .] whereby one may say *anything* so long as it earns one *fat dividends*.' Montesquiou, 17 April.

12. A brand of mineral water.

13. Proust quotes a line from 'Le Goût du néant' in *Les Fleurs du Mal*: 'Résigne-toi, mon cœur; dors ton sommeil de brute.'

14. Montesquiou was dying of nephritis.

15. Proust adapts a line from Montesquiou's *Le Chef des odeurs suaves*: 'Ne portez pas de fleurs aux malades aigris' ('Don't take flowers to the sick and embittered').

108   To André Gide

[Saturday 23 April 1921]

Dear friend,

If you have ever had the desire to bewitch a child (albeit a very old child), I don't say by filling a Christmas stocking (for it's not exactly the season and we're closer to the suns of the Resurrection than to the snows of the Nativity), but by sending him a huge, miraculous Easter egg, you have never succeeded better than by writing the article of which Rivière has sent me a proof.[1] I would like to have waited, not till I was cured (which would mean being dead), but at least till my terrible rheumatic fever, the result of a chill, had abated. For I sensed this present to be so beautiful, so unexpected, that I kept it beside me, like the unbearably exciting things which, as a child of five, I would decide not to open till in exactly the right mood. What changed my mind was Venice.[2] I arrived there long ago in such pain that I could take nothing in; but Venice etched herself in my mind notwithstanding, and, whenever I think of her, I still feel the enjoyment of a pleasure deferred.

Dear friend, every sentence came as a revelation to me. I'm not so vain that being their sole subject impairs my critical faculties. Happy are the Poor, if, at moments, you mistake your purity for poverty.[3] It surpasses the treasures of the earth. From the first, no such voice has been heard since Malherbe!

I wish to be ignored if . . . etc.[4] Aside from all the other powers you possess, you endow me, under the illusions of friendship, with your own bewitching ability to turn a simple walk with my parents into a fairy tale,[5] and what fresh delights you have found, as I never could, in the dissection of a spray of flowers.[6] With each line, I said to myself: 'It's impossible that he should have still more treats in store for me.' But in the next line the sorcerer brought me new gifts, and in what form! the most beautiful, the most technically perfect, the most natural that I know.

Dear friend, I still can't write a long letter without tiring (even though your 'Billet' meant more to me than an Easter egg, it was Easter itself! 'Dic nobis Maria quid vidisti in via?'[7] Mary Magdalene thought it was the gardener, Thomas (my doctor) persisted in doubt and denial. But won't my pierced feet force him to believe?).[8]

Gaston and Jacques Rivière must have told you how often of late I have begged them to send me your preface to Baudelaire,[9] it being unknown to me. I would have valued it at any time, for it must be the best thing ever written on Baudelaire. But there was a special reason. I've been asked to do a 'Baudelaire' for the next issue.[10] Fever has prevented me from doing more than scribble a few lines, with the weakest, most superficial discourse imaginable (when I think of your 'to convey'[11] in the 'Billet à Angèle', so knowledgeable, so beautifully-written, what a boon your preface would have been to me!). But neither Gallimard or Rivière could have had it, since I never received it despite repeated appeals. Speaking of Baudelaire, have you read the *very good* articles on him by Léon Daudet?[12] I shan't have a chance to quote them, since I shall quote nobody if I can't talk about your preface. But you'll find them worth reading. This morning (Saturday), he has an article in *L'Action française* on the Dutch painters,[13] inferior to those on Baudelaire, but still very good.

Believe me, my dear friend, I am full of admiration and grateful affection. It is your 'Billet', far more than my book, that enables me to regain lost Time.

Marcel Proust

1. Gide had made Proust the subject of one of his 'Billets à Angèle' (see letter 94, n. 4). It was to appear in the *NRF* on 1 May, the day before the publication of *The Guermantes Way* Part Two and *Sodom and Gomorrah* Part One – neither of which Gide had read when he wrote his article: see letter 110.

2. Proust visited Venice once, in the spring of 1900, with his mother. See 'Sojourn in Venice': V, 715–64.

3. 'I try to fault his style, and cannot. I seek its dominant qualities, and cannot

find them either; he doesn't just possess this quality or that: he has them all [...], and all at the same time; his flexibility is so disconcerting that, beside him, all others seem stiff, dull, imprecise, crude, lifeless. Must I confess? Whenever I happen to plunge into this lake of delight, I go for days not daring to pick up a pen, convinced – as always happens when a masterpiece holds us in its sway – that this is the only way to write, and seeing only poverty in my so-called "purity of style".' Gide, *NRF*, 1 May.

4. 'I wish to be ignored, if it's the case that, within two generations, names like Curel, Bernstein, Bataille, are more highly regarded than even that of Mendès.' Reference to Catulle Mendès (1841–1909), poet and playwright, and to his lesser-known contemporaries. *Ibid.*

5. 'What extraordinary books! it's like entering an enchanted forest; a forest in which you are lost from the first page, but happily lost; soon, you have forgotten where you came in, or how far it is to the next clearing; [...] you no longer know where you are or where you are going, then: "Suddenly, my father would come to a standstill and ask my mother – "Where are we?"'. *Ibid.* See *Swann's Way*, 136.

6. 'Proust dissects each spray with care. But it is not enough for him to show us the flower, he shows us the stem, right down to the delicate root-hairs.' *Ibid.*

7. 'Tell us, Mary, what saw you on the road?' From an eleventh century Easter hymn.

8. Proust paraphrases 'The Gospel according St John', XX, 15–24. Cf. Gide, *Journals*, 14 May 1921: 'Proust [...] complains that his life is nothing but a slow agony and [...] asks me if I can enlighten him on the teaching of the Gospels, someone having told him that I talk particularly well on the subject. He hopes to find in the Gospels some support, some relief from his sufferings.'

9. Allusion to Gide's preface to an illustrated edition of *Les Fleurs du Mal* published in 1917.

10. 'À propos de Baudelaire' was to appear, in epistolary form, in the *NRF* of 1 June. See 'Concerning Baudelaire', *AS-B*, 286–309.

11. '[...] to convey what is beyond words, he has recourse to imagery; he deploys a treasury of analogies, equivalences and comparisons so precise and exquisite that one wonders which imparts the more life, light and gaiety to the other, the sentiment underlying the image or the floating image awaiting the sentiment to alight upon it.' Gide, *loc. cit.*

12. *L'Action française*, 3 and 14 April.

13. There was an important exhibition of Dutch painting on loan to the Jeu de Paume: see following letter.

109   To Jean-Louis Vaudoyer

44 rue Hamelin
[Sunday 1 May 1921]

Dear friend,

    I write, very badly (but in what a condition! where a letter, requiring a prior injection, is a real torture), to say what I've long wished to tell you. It is that I've never known an Ascension to be sustained as successfully as yours, in article after article. When it came to the Watteau, had I not been half dead (my publishers had to correct the proofs of my books themselves), I would have congratulated you on a masterpiece. The things you say about comparable geniuses dying young are so true![1]

    Yesterday, I read the Vermeer,[2] where perhaps you had less opportunity to spread yourself, but which I found the most moving of all. When I saw *A View of Delft* at the Museum in The Hague, I knew that I had seen the most beautiful picture in the world.[3] In *Du Côté de chez Swann*, I couldn't resist making Swann undertake a study of Vermeer.[4] I dared not hope that you would do so much justice to this extraordinary master. For being aware of your (very sound) views on hierarchy in art,[5] I feared that he might be a little too Chardin for you. What a joy, therefore, to read that page. And I still know practically nothing by Vermeer. A good fifteen years ago, I remember giving Vuillard[6] a letter to Paul Baignères,[7] so that he could go and see a copy of a Vermeer I didn't know at his house.

    Tiredness brings me to a stop. I've been meaning for some time to tell you that I didn't think you were very nice to say those things about me à propos of Blanche's preface to *Dates*.[8] I share your opinion. But it's not my fault if somebody sees fit to print things I would regard as excessive in a telephone conversation or a *pneu*.

    Because of my state of health, I could do nothing about my plans for the Quartets;[9] still less for going to the Jeu de Paume.[10]

    Kindly give my respects to Madame Vaudoyer, and believe me when I say that you never cease to amaze your friend

Marcel Proust

1. See Vaudoyer on 'Eighteenth-century painting in the Louvre', *L'Opinion*, 25 December 1920: 'The works of a genius doomed to die young [...] have an indefinable quality that is lacking in a healthy man who may live almost as long as his century. Take the work of a Watteau, a Mozart, or a Musset, compared to that of a Chardin, a Bach, or a Hugo [...].'

2. Allusion to Vaudoyer's article 'The Mysterious Vermeer', *L'Opinion*, 20 April, on Dutch paintings from the Mauritshuis in an exhibition at the Jeu de Paume.

3. Vermeer's panorama of a waterfront lit by the evening sun, a painting which Proust had seen at the Mauritshuis when on a solitary visit to the Netherlands in October 1902. See the narrator's conversation with the Duchesse de Guermantes: III, 605–6.

4. Modern art historians agree with Swann's claim that another painting in the Mauritshuis, *Diana and her Companions*, then attributed to Nicolas Maes, was in fact by Vermeer: I, 425.

5. Vaudoyer criticizes the 'hierarchy of genius' at the Louvre whereby Chardin is automatically preferred over artists with equal but different virtues.

6. Edouard Vuillard (1868–1940), possibly Proust's inspiration for Elstir.

7. Louise Baignères's brother.

8. In *L'Opinion* of 21 February, Vaudoyer had deplored Blanche's personal remarks about Proust: see letter 92.

9. Proust had hoped to repeat the occasion when, earlier that year, he had had the Poulet Quartet play for him at rue Hamelin. See Albaret, *op. cit.*, 129–30.

10. Three weeks later, accompanied by Vaudoyer, Proust was to visit the Jeu de Paume and see his favourite Vermeer once again. Céleste describes his exalted state on his return: see Albaret, 277. (This visit, and certain passages from Vaudoyer's articles on Vermeer, quoted in letter 213, n. 4, were to play a significant part in Proust's novel.)

110 From André Gide

Tuesday [3 May 1921]

My dear friend,

Last night, I finished reading No. IV (in my impatience, I had bought two copies from the N.R.F. the day after it came out, one for myself, to thumb through and 'manhandle' as I like – I have a passion for reading on walks, on métros, trains etc.); but I soon had to admit that you are best read in the comfort of an armchair – and the other for my nephew, who was off to Warsaw the next day with the 'bag'.[1]

Ah! how glad I am that I wrote my article[2] before the book came out! Not that I don't think it hasn't the qualities of its predecessors – but glad not to look as if I was waiting for it, and glad not to have to qualify my praises with non-literary concerns. I'm rehearsing in my head what I want to say to you, but it will come out right only in a conversation which I entreat you to make possible.

Roughly speaking, here is what I would say had I written a different article. Although he is impartial, adopting the standpoint of a true naturalist, M. Proust paints a picture of 'vice' that is more damning than any invective; by branding the subject he speaks of, he does more to encourage entrenched attitudes than the most forceful moral tract. Almost incidentally, tucked away in a parenthesis (p. 276),[3] he offers a brief word of reassurance: he avers that in certain cases inversion is curable. If anything could cure an invert, it would be to read these pages, for they will induce in him feelings of self-reproach infinitely greater than the author's reproach.

From which, from all of which, you will gather that, in congratulating you, I would have been guilty of a certain hypocrisy.

Because of the great intelligence and cunning (in the best sense of the word) that I sense in you, I can readily persuade myself that you were right to present uranism in its most repellent guise, thus effectively ridding the public mind once and for all of any suggestion of complicity on your part.

Ah! When shall I see you again?[4] Knowing how difficult it is for you to predict a day when you will be feeling better, I sometimes wonder if it wouldn't be best to go and ring at your doorbell daily, in the hope that, for once, Céleste will say: 'Yes, M. Proust is better this evening, he can receive you for a moment...'

Your very devoted
André Gide

A pederast (in the purely Greek sense) would never dream of recognizing himself in the picture you paint of 'inverts'; do you not see any essential difference between him and them? Or are they all, in your opinion, merely variations of one and the same genre?

1. i.e. the diplomatic 'bag'.

2. His 'Billet à Angèle' of 1 May: see letter 108.

3. See the parenthesis (IV, 29) in the long meditation on 'the race of inverts' at the beginning of *Sodom and Gomorrah* Part One: IV, 17–38.

4. Proust was to invite Gide twice. Describing these visits in his *Journal* for 14 and 17 May, Gide records his surprise at Proust's insistence on his own homosexuality, and his efforts (in the context of Gide's preface: see letter 108) to persuade him of Baudelaire's.

111 To Paul Souday

[Wednesday evening, 11 May 1921]

Dear Sir and friend,

Your fine article[1] gave me much pleasure, and it was very good of you to attach so much importance to a book of mine, albeit a 'less substantial' one.[2] Now, once again, alas (it dates from the far-off days of *Du Côté de chez Swann*), you return to the charge that I write sentences in 'chapter-headings'.[3] The one you quote (word for word, from *Guermantes II*)[4] is, I admit, completely unintelligible. But as if my own proof-correcting wasn't already bad enough, when a book like this comes out having been printed directly from my indecipherable drafts, the first edition, despite my publishers' best efforts to supervise it, is a dreadful mess.

In so saying, I'm not trying to defend myself against the well-deserved reproach that my sentences are too often overlong, too closely intertwined with the meanderings of my thought. 'It's crystal clear' gave me a good laugh.[5] But I think you are over-generous when you suggest that it becomes clear on a third reading; speaking for myself, I find it incomprehensible. You can imagine how honoured I felt at seeing my name bracketed with Bergson and Einstein.[6] Come to that, there are a thousand other things to touch me in this article. What I would reproach you with is your habit of beginning a review with criticisms or quotations that discourage the reader in advance from embarking upon a book of the kind. But all the profound insights and over-generous remarks that follow so touch the author that, persuaded that it is a fine article, he ceases to ask himself whether it is a good one, or whether the critic's kind heart has not prompted him to give praise where reason alone might perhaps have withheld it.

Regarding the ending, I would have hoped that as you had accused my N.C.O. Saint-Loup of extreme naïvety for losing his temper over being 'propositioned',[7] you might have been less evasive about my Baron de Charlus. But I realize that in addressing the general public from your elevated platform, you are obliged to watch your words, which is not the same as being pusillanimous. Anybody who doubts that need only recall your rare courage in staying loyal to Wilde in his misfortune in order to be enlightened.[8]

But in literary terms, you appear to congratulate Saint-Simon for showing such 'restraint'.[9] Naturally, I'm not so insane as to put myself on a level with the genius of the *Mémoires*. I'm only too aware of the thousands of metres separating me from his Altitude. But in those places where Saint-Simon is restrained, I believe another author fulfils his duty by trying to delve more deeply. I don't know if I've ever told you this,[10] but the reason for my having been driven to writing, like a schoolboy his lines, all those retorts for the Duchesse de Guermantes, into creating a 'Guermantes wit' that is at once coherent and consistent, was my disappointment at not finding in Saint-Simon, who never stops telling us about the 'Mortemart wit' and the 'special turn of phrase' unique to Mme de Montespan, Mme de Thianges and the Abbesse de Fontevrault, one word, the slightest hint, that might help us to grasp what it was that was so singular about the Mortemarts' manner of speech. Unable to reconstitute the 'Mortemart wit' of the past, I attempted the impossible by inventing the 'Guermantes wit'. Alas, I lack Saint-Simon's genius. But at least my readers will know in what the Guermantes wit consists, which is, when all's said and done, a little harder than simply saying 'this so-special wit', without offering the smallest clue.

Ah well, not realizing that I was supposed to 'show restraint', I dealt with M. de Charlus as I had with the Duchesse de Guermantes. But I sense that I'm tiring myself, and certainly boring you, and merely ask you to accept my admiring and grateful friendship.

Marcel Proust

1. A review of *The Guermantes Way* Part Two and *Sodom and Gomorrah* Part One in *Le Temps* of 12 May.

2. 'Indefatigably, M. Proust pursues his Search for Lost Time; here we have the fourth volume, a little shorter, and perhaps a little less substantial, than its predecessors. There are only two hundred and eighty pages, but [. . .] being very long, wide and dense, they might have been invented, in their typography alone, before one has read a single line, to give the precise image and physical impression of M. Proust's literary style.' Souday, *loc. cit.*

3. As he had in his review of *Swann's Way* in 1913 (see letter 44, n. 12), Souday accuses Proust of stringing together parentheses in a single sentence in the manner of an old-fashioned chapter-heading or *phrase du chapeau*: cf. letter 99. Apparently, the term was sarcastically applied to the speeches of Henri Patin, a famously long-winded Permanent Secretary to the Academy: see following note 5.

4. The 133-word sentence beginning: 'Is it because we relive our past years . . .'. III, 459.

5. 'It is crystal clear. And would be more so if everybody had the benefit of M. André Gide's informed discourse, which would probably clarify even M. Patin's famous "phrase du chapeau".' Souday, *op. cit.* Allusion to Gide's comment, in his 'Billet à Angèle' on Proust: 'Only let me read these interminable sentences aloud: how everything falls into place! how the scaffolding rises.'

6. 'And now I myself am in danger of becoming as unclear as Marcel Proust, who is the Bergson or Einstein of the psychological novel and finds, almost inevitably, that his rather too subtle ideas require a rather too abstruse vocabulary.' *Ibid.*

7. See Souday to Proust, 26 November 1920, probably in response to letter 77, where Proust objects to his use of the word 'feminine': 'Such morals are an anachronism these days, but one doesn't have to have read Plato to feel genuinely insulted, like your aristocratic sergeant Saint-Loup.' Souday alludes to Saint-Loup's assault on the 'impassioned loiterer' who propositions him outside the theatre: III, 205-6.

8. No trace has been found of Souday's defence of Oscar Wilde.

9. 'In the final chapter, I might add, the story takes a direction that is hard to follow. Saint-Simon tells us that men like M. Proust's Baron de Charlus were to be found even in royal circles; but the author of the *Mémoires* indicates this with more restraint.' Souday, *loc. cit.*

10. Proust had elaborated the point in letter 77 to Souday.

112 To Robert de Montesquiou

[Shortly after 17 May 1921]

Dear Sir,

In sending you my parcel,[1] and in thanking you for yours[2] on this humble sheet of paper, which I hope you'll excuse as it's all I have beside my bed, I would like to offer you some eminently practical advice. Firstly, your style being this wondrous open lacework which, with its paradise flowers and firebirds, reveals the 'points'[3] of a France increasingly forgotten with each day that passes, what charm there would be in a lexicon[4] where, for example, one might find under the letter R: 'Ratafia (preserve of), made from.... Consumed by M. Robert de Montesquiou as a child at the house of M. and Mme etc.' and so on.

On the other hand, whereas a novel has no keys (I'll come to that in a minute), an essay (which can, moreover, be superior to a novel) has a great many. Why amuse yourself by so distorting them as to make them unusable, when the whole of society might appear? True, those with inside knowledge, as Mme de La Moussaye[5] would say, can work it out for themselves. I had no hesitation about Chabert, Rodier and M. de Béhague[6] – and it was as clear as daylight that the Satyres de Trente concealed dear Mme de Brantes (C.S.B.).[7] (Speaking of whom, don't get the idea that I've pirated your book in one of my forthcoming volumes. Mine, written long ago, was inspired by a Mlle Aron whose mother having married M. de Faucompré, found a husband as Mlle de Faucompré.[8] Moreover, the story being quite different from the one you recount, you cannot for one moment (I can't find the paper I was using so am starting afresh, this time on a page of headed stationery) suspect me of plagiarism.) But how to identify Floris and Fanfan? Comte Chamois, I take it, is the Comte Chevreau, now d'Antraigues.[9]

Regarding my own keys, since you are kind enough to ask, there aren't any, other than these.[10] At Mme de Villeparisis's party, Mme de Bloqueville, whom I never knew (except through *Brelan de Dames*)[11] and Mme de Janzé are equally absent. But it was Mme de Beaulaincourt (in this particular volume, not in its predecessors) who gave me the idea for Mme de Villeparisis; but she having made flowers, I had her paint them to make it less obvious. That's my only portrait, unless you count a Baron Doäzan, an habitué of the Aubernon salon, where I dined with him a few times, who served as my model for M. de Charlus on his first appearance in *À l'Ombre des jeunes filles en fleurs*, when he stares at me me while pretending not to see me.[12] But this experience is as fugitive as a memory that brings back a 'view' to a painter. My character, being pre-fabricated and wholly invented (despite what you say about Vautrin),[13] and also, I believe, on a grander scale, contains far more of human diversity than if I had limited him to a likeness of M. de Doäzan. And even for non-living things (so-called), I drew on the sum of a thousand unconscious memories. I can't tell you how many churches 'sat' for my Combray church in *Du Côté de chez Swann*.[14] People are entirely invented, the churches emerge piecemeal, one lending its spire, another its paving, another its dome.

Dear Sir, I'm too tired to go on, I can't talk to you about your second book, which is finer still; in parenthesis: I talked about it to Gide, so that he should know the nice things you say about him in connection with Mallarmé.

As a good commoner, I don't share your opinion of coronets. Society people (naturally, I except those who are serious artists) have no other means of reminding us of their sole *raison d'être* than by having their letter-paper stamped with the equivalent of 'Pulchre sedens melior agens'.[15] And I would be sorry were the 'good sisters'[16] (superior to others of their milieu, moreover) to have Leuchars[17] stamp theirs with a monogram, like Madame Porgès,[18] rather than an informative coronet. I would dearly like to know the connection between Mallarmé and the Duchesse d'Uzès.[19]

Goodbye, dear Sir, I hope that you are quite better, and that your resurrection will come at the same time as my death, that is to say, soon.

Your affectionate and grateful admirer,
Marcel Proust

1. This letter accompanied the two volumes of *The Guermantes Way* Part Two and *Sodom and Gomorrah* Part One

2. Montesquiou had sent Proust his latest works, *Les Délices de Capharnaüm*, a book consisting mainly of anecdotes about real people with fictional names – the principal subject of this letter – and an art-book, *Diptyque de Flandres, Triptyque de France*.

3. *Points*, both in the sense of aspects and of stitches in needlepoint lace, as in *point d'Alençon*.

4. Montesquiou had concocted a lexicon of traditions falling into disuse, its first entry being *Les Dentelles* or 'Types of Lace'.

5. Comtesse Eugène de La Moussaye, a Second Empire hostess.

6. Montesquiou's contemporaries.

7. Montesquiou's late cousin: *née* Cessac (C), who had married a M. de Sauvage (S), who had added de Brantes (B) to his name.

8. In *The Fugitive*, Gilberte Swann is adopted by her stepfather, takes his name for snobbish reasons and marries Saint-Loup as Mlle de Forcheville. See V, 644–8; 654–6; 670–5. Cf. letter 56 to Pierre de Polignac.

9. *Chamois* and *chevreau* are types of goat. Comte Urbain Chevreau had upgraded his name to d'Antraigues on his marriage.

10. See letter 107.

11. Montesquiou's satirical essays on blue-stocking dowagers: see letter 107, n. 7.

12. See letter 107, n. 5.

13. On 17 April, Montesquiou had written to Proust, alluding to Balzac's master-criminal: 'Vautrin is all the rage, now that your Charlus admires him'. Balzac is an author whom Charlus 'knows by heart': III, 567.

14. See letter 18.

15. A Balzacian motto: see postscript to letter 89.

16. Montesquiou's soubriquet for the Hinnisdael sisters: see letter 16, n. 10.

17. Smart Paris stationer.

18. Mme Jules Porgès. Evidently, for Proust, the Porgès family epitomized the *nouveaux riches*: cf. letter 13, letter 57.

19. Montesquiou was to explain that he had been introduced to Mallarmé by the Duc de Chaulnes, a distant relative of the Duchesse d'Uzès.

113 To Louis de Robert[1]

[Shortly before 26 May 1921]

Dear friend,

Your dedication,[2] which I've seen only today because I've spent weeks unable to turn over in bed and without opening my eyes, is very distressing to me. You say: 'who *was* my friend'. Evidently I am so no longer. And yet, since the onset of this death worse than death which I endure, you are the only one of my friends, or one of the very few, whose books I have read and acknowledged. And for which I've thanked at length, for you must remember the long, admiring letter I wrote you a few months ago. If there are books of mine which haven't reached you, you have only to tell me and I'll see that you receive them. Although I have reservations about sending you my *Guermantes*. I recall that, in *Swann*, about which you were so helpful, there were passages that revolted you by their licentiousness.[3] What won't you think about *Sodome et Gomorrhe*! And on the other hand, you felt that I was wasting my time in striving to reproduce passages of conversation that were not worth the effort. Rightly or wrongly, my *Guermantes* will attract even more blame in that respect. Lastly, if you have time, tell me why I am no longer your friend. Bear in mind that, having for so long been unable to go upstairs, I'm now unable to go downstairs, and that, proof-correcting being far, far beyond my strength, my publishers were obliged to have *Sodome et Gomorrhe* printed from my original draft, without the benefit of a single proof.

A hellish existence must excuse my silence (observed in the case of all my friends, even my brother's, but never in yours).

Regards,
Marcel Proust

---

1. Louis de Robert (1871–1937), novelist and fellow-Dreyfusard to whom Proust had turned for help in publishing *Swann's Way*. He had been both officious and critical. See *Selected Letters Volume Three*.

2. 'To Marcel Proust, who was my friend', inscription in a complimentary copy of Robert's novel *Reconnais-toi*.

3. Allusion to the sado-masochistic scene between Mlle Vinteuil and her friend at Montjouvain: I, 190–8.

114   To Émile Mâle[1]

[Wednesday 1 June 1921]

Dear Sir,

    I've just spent long years literally in the tomb, where I still am. I don't even have the strength to correct the proofs of my books from my bed.

    But I've just taken some caffeine in order to be able to tell you with what joy I read you (with eyes that can no longer see) in the *Revue de Paris*.[2] Your essay on Romanesque Art is superb. If I had only known it when, from Avallon, I climbed the hill to Vézelay.[3] Few pages in the French language, I believe, can equal your description of the porch. I know of nothing more striking than the expression on the faces of the missionaries all agog to be on their way to evangelize the heathen.[4] Barrès, who once wrote to me that Vézelay was the most beautiful thing he knew in France, would certainly regret not having read this essay as much as I would, so I shall have it sent to him.

    This vitality which you discover everywhere in the scenes at Vézelay is above all what animates your own pages. Just one thing puzzles me, but only vaguely. I seem to remember your having written that this scrolling, this uplifting of Byzantine draperies[5] was a question of textiles (maybe even of starching). But my recollection is as hazy as a dream. And probably this remark (which in any case wouldn't stain your magnificent essay) didn't come from you but from Mérimée.[6]

    Even I, who love your books so much, wouldn't place any one of them on a level with, let alone above, these pages. Exhausted or not, that is what I wanted to tell you.

    Should you ever have occasion to write to me (most unlikely), the safest address would be the Nouvelle Revue Française, 37 rue Madame. The building where I used to live on the boulevard Haussmann was bought by a banker, who not unnaturally wished to turn it into a bank. At the time, I was unaware of the existence of those plugs which, when inserted into the ears, more or less cut out noise. And the thought of the courtyard being dug up, the staircase rebuilt etc., made me flee a house which had become inhospitable. As apartments are very difficult to find, I couldn't get what I wanted and was forced to move three times in two years, which is why I think that the safest address is that of my publisher (the Nouvelle Revue Française) who will be apprised of my latest move, always supposing that I'm in a fit state to be moved.

Thank you again, dear Sir, for the joy which your superb essay has given me, and kindly accept my admiring and devoted respects.

Marcel Proust

1. Émile Mâle (1862-1954), the leading authority of the day on Christian art and architecture. Proust had sought Mâle's advice about suitable churches and monuments for his novel, and, in his descriptions of medieval sculpture, was clearly influenced by Mâle's studies.

2. Published on 1 June, the first of two essays.

3. Proust was in Burgundy in the summer of 1903, when he visited the basilica at Vézelay, a masterpiece of Byzantine Romanesque.

4. Speaking of the flame-like qualities of the sculpted figures on the great tympanum, and of the expressions on some of their peasant faces, Mâle remarks: 'One can sense the enthusiasm of the Christian missionary ready to give his life to save the soul of the most degraded savage.'

5. Mâle describes the Apostles flanking the figure of Christ, with 'their tunics uplifted by the great wind that entered the Tabernacle'.

6. As Inspector-General of historical monuments in France, the writer Prosper Mérimée wrote numerous reports on church art and architecture.

115 To Armand de Guiche[1]

[Friday 17 June 1921]

Dear friend,

There is a certain merit, when one thinks one has something very witty to say, in holding one's tongue. It's so in my case. My little gem was prompted by your letter about the play you saw.[2] But I thought to myself: only let this game continue for another week, and Guiche will be beaten hollow. (Seemingly, that shows a lack of modesty on my part. But only seemingly, for I have a very deep, very sincere regard for large areas of your knowledge, quite apart from the *terra incognita* of science where I know that you reign supreme. But it's not very arrogant of me to say that on the solitary and very minor point of the rather unpromising début in pseudo *Lettres Persanes*[3] you have just made in writing to me, I wouldn't exactly have to sweat my guts out, to use a common expression, in order to 'wipe the floor' with you, to use an even commoner one.) Now, a man who is beaten fair and square hasn't much love for his opponent. And your friendship is far more important to me than my petty triumph of wit. So, if you, for your part, feel as warmly and sincerely about it as I do, let us not stray outside the bounds of true friendship, which excludes unequal contests or, indeed, any contest at all. Speaking for myself, I love you with all my heart.

Two further points, the one purely theoretical, the other to do with a remark made the other night. The theoretical point concerns telepathy. Bergson finds nothing extraordinary in the fact that, on the day a woman dies in Cape Town, her daughter in Paris should have a vision of her death; what he finds extraordinary is that such phenomena should occur so rarely. Consciousness not residing in the brain, it's quite natural, according to him, that any number of different consciousnesses should be in communication.[4] Now, all during the war, military matters aside, I recorded a whole series of events in my books which I invented, which I couldn't have known about, which in many cases had yet to happen and which, in real life, proved to be accurate down to the last detail. I'll give you a few examples when I see you (they have nothing to do with you, by the way, there being nothing of you in my books apart from the pastiche where you are prominent,[5] and you know about that). But far from attributing this description of events I couldn't have known about to telepathy and Bergson's theory, I believe it to be a logical consequence of true premises. Isn't there a theorem stating that when two equal triangles etc.? Well, I believe that this geometry is also true for human beings, and that by not straying from the lines of correct reasoning, one arrives naturally, and with the most delicate precision, at what life later confirms, to the unthinking surprise of a reader in possession of the facts.

The remark that was made at Mme H.'s[6] the other night (and here we abandon the processes of reason, telepathy etc. as no longer relevant) is this: either you or Mme H., I forget which, claimed that Madame Greffulhe[7] is Mme de Guermantes in my book. I objected most strenuously. Yet, in the end, I conceded that for a moment, in *Guermantes I*, there is a flash of elegance and beauty at the Opéra[8] which is certainly not unlike Mme Greffulhe. But never dreaming that a reader, man or woman, might care about the details of a book, I forgot to say that the Mme de Guermantes who for five lines resembles Madame Greffulhe is not the Duchesse de Guermantes in whose salon people gossip for an entire volume, but her cousin, the Princesse de Guermantes. Moreover, if we can glance at the book together for a moment, you'll see that there is no possible room for doubt; the two are poles apart. The Duchesse de Guermantes is the exact opposite of the Princesse de Guermantes. Except that she is chaste, she (the Duchesse de Guermantes) is a little like the tough old hen whom I once took for a bird of paradise, and who, when I tried to capture her beneath the trees of the avenue Gabriel, could think of nothing to say to me,[9] but kept repeating like a parrot: 'Fitz-James expects me'![10] By turning her into a mighty Griffon,[11] I have at least saved her from being taken for an old crow. These harsh words are all talk, by the way, for I'm as heartbroken today as I was then that she misunderstood me.[12] I haven't set foot in her house for I don't know how many years, and the words I write to you now I would go and say to her face, with all the pain that I feel, were I not afraid of exposing myself to the risks of a salon lorded over by Arthur Meyer,[13] he of the bald pate like a sugar-loaf, looking for all the world like the chief augur in that delightful *Belle Hélène*[14] of the Empire that must remind him of his great age, he being in his second childhood. As for my books, I don't send them to her. She having met Croisset[15] in my house, and grabbed him for a son-in-law, it seems to me that he can supply her literary needs.

I leave you, my dear friend, after having bored you with far too many pages.

Believe me, I am your truly devoted
Marcel Proust

By a strange coincidence, I have no sooner finished writing to you than I receive a marvellous 14-page letter from R. de Montesquiou. It's just like the previous one.[16] What a fund of talent he has, this epistolary genius, what drollery, what self-righteous bitterness, what noble melancholy! I feel genuinely ashamed when he talks to me of his lack of success, so undeserved, and of my own success (!), equally undeserved. I can't explain in a letter how heartbreaking I find all that.

Second P.S. Do you know Mme Gérard de Rohan-Chabot? To whom, without my having realized it, I have reason to be eternally grateful.[17] When I say 'Do you know', don't think I mean 'Can you introduce me' or 'Mention my name to', which is what people usually mean in such cases. Alas, I don't need anybody to mention me to her, having discovered belatedly that she wants to talk to me. But I'm afraid of being too ill to visit her, let alone have her visit me before she leaves (and as I don't even know her by sight, we're back in the realms of telepathy).

Another woman (not in the least like Mme de Chabot) has thoroughly annoyed me with her lying inventions. First she claimed to have seen me at the Duchesse de Clermont-Tonnerre's soirée, where I couldn't go for the same reason that prevented my going to your sister's,[18] alas. Thus far, the lie was trivial. But she went on to say that, while there, I quarrelled with you, the thought of which horrifies me. Fond as I am of a duel, I'm much fonder of you!

Letter written 'tit for tat', as M. de Norpois would say, but Céleste forgot to post it.

1. Armand, Duc de Guiche: see letter 16, n 15 *et seq.*
2. The contents of Guiche's letter are unknown.
3. Allusion to Montesquieu's satire of the same name, the subject of a parody by Proust: see *CS-B*, 424–7.
4. See Bergson's presidential address to the London Society for Psychical Research in 1913.
5. Allusion to Proust's second Saint-Simon pastiche.
6. Mme Jean Hennessy, *née* Marguerite, Comtesse de Mun. On 15 June, Proust had attended her dinner for the engagement of the American heiress Gladys Deacon to the Duke of Marlborough.
7. Mme Greffulhe was Guiche's mother-in-law.
8. III, 52–9.
9. Allusion to Mme de Chevigné. See letter 75, n. 1. Mme de Chevigné had always seen Proust's habit of lying in wait for her along the avenues of the Champs-Élysées as a form of snobbish persecution.
10. The Duc de Fitz-James and the Comte de Chevigné were fellow courtiers of the exiled Comte de Chambord, Henry V of France.
11. In *The Guermantes Way*, the young narrator sees the Duchesse de Guermantes as a predatory bird: III, 63.
12. See letter 87, n. 3.
13. Arthur Meyer (1844–1924), editor of the society paper *Le Gaulois*, a 'scamp' and a snob, according to Proust's narrator: see VI, 88, 200. Proust's bête-noire, Meyer was a professed anti-Semite and anti-Dreyfusard. His wife, thirty years his junior, was the Duc de Fitz-James's granddaughter: see letter 18, n. 23.
14. Offenbach's operetta, first produced in 1864.
15. Francis de Croisset (real name Franz Wiener: 1877–1937), writer of light comedies.

16. In his second long letter to Proust in the course of a week, Montesquiou had returned to the subject of 'keys'.

17. Apparently, Mme de Chabot had let Proust know that her son had had *Swann's Way* with him when he was killed in action on 16 July 1918.

18. Comtesse Hélie de Noailles, *née* Corisande de Gramont.

116 To François Mauriac

[Around 25 June 1921]

Dear and admired friend,

I only wish my health permitted me to talk to you about these amazing *Préséances*,[1] certainly the most original, the most remarkable book that I've read for a long, long time, quite different from what I had expected. If I can readily respond to the discriminating mind that differentiates between a John Martineau, a Freddy Durand a Maucoudinat, to the painter's (sometimes extravagant) gifts that make one detest Hourtinat, even to the dramatist's resources deployed to bring about Augustin's return, mixed in with all this, or rather, acting as the substructure to all this, there is an interior life which I'm not so sure of understanding yet long to enjoy most of all. Since being exposed to Augustin's remorseless gaze, I've tasted the incorruptible salt and lived with its bitterness on my lips.[2]

Dear friend – and this has no direct bearing on what I've just said – I don't usually care for the talking side of books, not being convinced that the transposition works. But when I hear the way you speak, even when shocked, outraged by Hourtinat's atrocious behaviour at the theatre, I bless you for reviving in my mind the lineaments of that evening when I had the pleasure of getting to know you (I mean the evening when you were good enough to come here and very kindly dined in my little room with me and my one and only Henri, who departed today for some faraway country where I've found him a 'situation').[3] True, your gaze, your voice, the things you said, your letter the following day, have never been out of my thoughts; but you brought all that back to life, and with the greatest exactitude, when behind your printed words – especially in the Hourtinat scene – I recognized that particular way you have, forceful and charming, of delivering your words. Your Chateaubriand quotation, in all its sublimity, came at just the right moment to make me see why it is that I'm so attached to certain consonants on certain pages.[4] 'To break with real things is nothing. But with memories!'[5]

Dear friend, I haven't broken with your memory, and may even be granted the chance to be with you other than in spirit and in truth.[6] I've been so mortally ill (I think I told you that I couldn't even correct my proofs and that the N.R.F. were kind enough to print my last volume from my original draft, with the result that this book has fewer misprints than the others, for as you rightly say, I don't know how to correct a proof) that I can neither write a letter nor overtax myself by asking you the meaning of this or that page of your book. The less I see of myself in a book, the more I like it. We must be strangely different, you and I. Today, when everything is the same, how your book stands out. I may not know how to correct a proof, but you should have sent me yours. I would have suggested removing a few minor blemishes.

If you see Francis Jammes, tell him that it's more than illness, mortification, to be exact, which has prevented my thanking him for *Saint-Joseph*.[7] I'm suddenly reminded that when I was doing my military service at Orléans at the age of 17 (which I believe is unique),[8] a lieutenant in my regiment, short, dark, slender, very good-looking, extremely sweet and well-mannered, used to walk around Orléans with a very large missal under his arm. That took courage in those days.[9] I was told that he died that same year. I wasn't in his company, nor even his battalion. Men wept when they spoke of him. I believe he may have been related to Francis Jammes. Let this great poet commend me to his favourite saint, through your intercession, so that he may grant me an easy death, not that I don't feel well armed with the courage to face a very cruel one.

Very sincerely yours,
Marcel Proust

I've started to get up again occasionally, and to go out, despite the ill-effects of a recent experience. Could we perhaps take the opportunity to meet? The trouble is, I never know till the last minute if I can get up, and whether I can reach you at that hour. I see that Francis Jammes is standing for the Academy. I was told what your friend Arthur Meyer had to say about it, and I was shocked, having forgotten the imbecility of society people. I could just see the editor of the *Gaulois*, the image of the great augur in *La Belle Hélène* with his pink, sugar-loaf skull[10] and his nape covered in curls like a lap-dog's, pontificating in his nasal tones. The child Arthur must be reminded in his dotage of those distant days when *La Belle Hélène* was first performed. I don't really know why I make fun of him. I was 'Guermantizing' the other night, and my hosts, though nicer than he is, seemed to me to be just as stupid.[11]

Dear friend, one simply cannot make up one's one's mind to leave you.

Your
Marcel Proust

1. Mauriac's latest novel.
2. In Mauriac's novel this remark is addressed to Augustin, the hero.
3. Henri Rochat had left for Buenos Aires, where Proust had found him a post in a bank owned by a friend.
4. i.e. pages which Proust had dictated to Rochat.
5. Quotation from Chateaubriand, in *La Vie de Rancé*. Proust alludes to a passage in Mauriac's novel where the narrator parts with Augustin: 'I even felt a strange need to be alone again, to reassure myself that this wretch, this pathetic man, had not destroyed my inner image of the adolescent Augustin [. . .].'
6. See letter 90, n. 2.
7. Francis Jammes's *Le Livre de Saint-Joseph*.
8. See letter 35, n. 14.
9. i.e. in the days of anti-Clericalism.
10. See previous letter, n. 13.
11. Allusion to Mme Hennessy's party: see previous letter, n. 6.

117 To Jacques Boulenger

[End of June 1921]

Dear friend,

I believe I wrote to you saying how sickened I was by the Martin-Chauffier affair.[1] And now, what am I to reply to Jacques Rivière, when he says (alluding to my having pressed him on certain questions, such as whether the Martin-Chauffier note would do)[2] 'When I wrote to you, the sentence that offended Boulenger had escaped my notice' (not my, Marcel Proust's notice, for I didn't know about it until too late, but his, Jacques Rivière's)? And he is so obviously telling the truth that one can't help thinking of his fatigue, his illness, however much one disapproves.

You refer to the change in my feelings for you;[3] well, there are two aspects to this, one of which I hadn't even wanted to hint at, because, not being in a position to talk to you about it for a very, very long time, it seemed stupid not simply to keep quiet about it.

The other is nothing, quite simply that, as I told you the other evening when you were here,[4] you were not as I had imagined. That alone shows how much I've thought about you over the years, and, as always with any person, any place, any object that one has long thought about, one is surprised, on seeing them, to find that they are not as one expected. So one quickly changes direction, starting from the real as opposed to the imaginary, and one restores to the person, the place etc., all the feelings one had previously invested in them, which then merely pass from the world of dreams to that of experience. I therefore believe that what is not my disappointment but my 'change' has made a very promising start. And I'm sure that if we saw one another regularly you would sense my true friendship for the new Jacques Boulenger (don't suspect anything of Charlus in that, I beg you!).

Tired as I am, I have a favour to ask you, not for myself, naturally, but for somebody I haven't seen (don't tell him that I see people occasionally) for a good many years, somebody who is so cantankerous (not with me, I'm one of the few people with whom he hasn't quarrelled) that it wouldn't take much for him to make a grievance out of my good intentions, even though I would, I think, have given him great pleasure and, in so doing, myself. It's Robert de Montesquiou. The world has enveloped his old age (impoverished, what's more, I gather) with a thick blanket of silence which is most unjust; for as an art critic, as a marvellous essayist, he knows better than anybody how to paint, in prose, the work of an artist or sculptor whom he admires. And yet think of this (everything that follows is confidential): I was eighteen years old, a callow youth under my parents' thumb who had written nothing but *Les Plaisirs et les jours* (much better written than *Swann*, in fact) when I met Robert de Montesquiou, who believed himself to be on the path to glory and treated me so much as a child that, to this day, he remains for me what children call a 'grown-up'. That's evident, for example, from the fact that (irrespective of the huge difference in age between us) I never end a letter to him without using the epithet 'respectful',[5] as I would never do with somebody equally my senior but whose acquaintance I had made later in life, and not, like him, as a visitor to my parents' house.

Thus, saddened to see him the victim of what is a form of ostracism, every time a newspaper mentions my name, I think to myself: 'How galling it must be for him'. And I long to see his name reappear. As he truly deserves it, I thought that perhaps you would ask him for some essays on artists.[6] Even if it never comes to anything, I'm sure that your simple request would comfort an old age which must be cruelly hard. If you don't know him personally, you could write to him: 'We were saying the other day, Marcel Proust and I, what a pity it is that you are so stingy with your essays on art etc.', but preferably 'we were saying', not 'Marcel Proust was saying to me', for he would hate the thought of being patronized. And of being pitied. So it would be more tactful to treat his abstinence as voluntary. This is only half of what I had to say to you about him, but I'm too tired, and it will be enough, I think, should you ever have room for him in your review and like to use him. I've taken to corresponding with him again, going out of my way to be friendly because of the absurd rumour that I have portrayed him as Charlus. What makes it worse is that, although I've known a very great many inverts in society whom nobody else suspected, in all the years I've known Montesquiou I have never, ever seen him, at home, at a party, anywhere at all, show the smallest sign of being that way inclined. All the same, I think (?) he believes that I meant to portray him. But being infinitely intelligent, far from giving me that impression, he was the first to congratulate me most warmly on *Guermantes* and *Sodome*. But I think he believes it none the less. Consequently, the kindness of his letters is a torture to me. Especially as I would grossly insult him if I gave him the impression of being aware of the rumour and of apologizing for it. He is a malicious man, and his folly caused his parents much suffering. But in his sad old age, deprived not only of the glory which he thinks is his by right, but also of simple justice, he breaks my heart.

Adieu, Jacques Boulenger.
Marcel Proust

In a recent letter, he said, speaking of how he is ignored: 'These days when, O ineffable heights!, people talk of an *underrated* Croisset'.[7]

His address, should you need it, is Palais Rose, Le Vésinet, Seine-et-Oise. I've never been to the Palais Rose. That shows how long it is since I've seen him. Our last meeting goes back to a visit he paid me at the boulevard Haussmann in the first year of the war, when, having promised not to stay longer than five minutes so as not to tire me, he stayed at my bedside for seven hours.

That's why you mustn't tell him that I can be visited at rue Hamelin, an address he knows perfectly well but where he never comes because I've told him that I'm too ill.

Burn this letter, for its contents are enough to enrage to the point of damnation this Count whom I wish so much to please.

1. Allusion to Martin-Chauffier's review, in the *NRF* of 1 June, of Boulenger's book of critical essays, *Mais l'Art est difficile*. Proust had persuaded Rivière to give the book to Martin-Chauffier (it contained Boulenger's articles on *Within a Budding Grove* and *The Guermantes Way*) and was thus embarrassed when the review seemed to accuse Boulenger of pandering to certain writers out of self-interest.
2. Backed by Proust, Boulenger protested to the *NRF*, whereupon Rivière proposed printing an editorial note: 'While we regret having offended M. Jacques Boulenger, we also regret that [. . .] he saw fit to take such a high-handed tone with a critic whose balanced and courteously-expressed views are appreciated by all our readers [. . .]. Evidently, these days, criticism is no less difficult than art.'
3. 'Knowing my feelings for you (feelings which have changed just a little, though they remain as affectionate as ever), you can imagine the effect on me of Martin-Chauffier's article.' Proust to Boulenger, *c.* 6 June.
4. Their one and only meeting had taken place just before the letter quoted in the above note.
5. Proust could have added that he always replied with 'Dear Sir' to Montesquiou's 'Dear Marcel'.
6. He has asked Boulenger this before: see letter 107, n. 10.
7. '*Solitude* is suffocating my *output* and my *Life*, and my *pride* takes a knock when I see insights of modern taste such as – ineffable heights – the notion that a *Croisset* can be underrated.' Montesquiou to Proust, 7 June. Allusion to Francis Croisset: see letter 115, n. 15.

118 To Walter Berry

2 July 1921

Dear Sir and friend,

In passing on my invitation to you this afternoon, Céleste omitted to tell you that, at first, I had been unaware of yours to me. I ought never to put aside anything American (I should realize that it might contain your dear name) without careful examination. But the other day, faced with the maximum of post and the minimum of strength, I had allowed anything printed, typed etc. to pile up. And when you told Céleste (not today, the other day) that you had just sent me an invitation, I had supposed a letter inviting me to dine at your house, or at the Ritz. It was only yesterday (as I was hoping to explain over dinner this evening) that a chance search for a letter brought the drowned pearl to the surface. I can't tell you how touched I am that you should remember my desire to attend the commemoration of this glorious event.[1] It means more than a thousand dinners to me, for I have never heard you speak and, to judge by my emotion whenever I read a speech of yours, your eloquence being superior to any Frenchman's, it would be like seeing a painting that I had admired only in a photograph. This will give you an idea of the temptation and the honour. But I have to think of the open windows at the Palais d'Orsay, of the ludicrous possibility of providing the morning papers with a tidbit about your magnificent celebration: 'Yesterday, in the middle of M. Walter Berry's speech, a certain M. Proust collapsed with a stroke.'[2] Coming so soon after this evening's outing, it hardly seems practical. It might be wiser, in case I can get up, to await you at Bailby's.[3] But unfortunately he too has a garden. I'll try and see you soon whatever happens, having much to tell you.

Did Céleste mention that it was several hours after her first telephone calls before she managed to talk to you? You were out. In spite of your predilection for thin women (whom you soon fatten up, moreover, purely as an excuse for inconstancy, in my opinion), I trust that, like me, you noticed the deliciously plump arms of the young 'Faisanderie' the other night, so incomparably Paros-like that her Helvetius ancestor would have raved about them.[4] But, leaving her aside, how true it is, this perversity in women that leads them to lose the characteristics for which one loves them! One would like to apply to them (in the feminine) Mallarmé's line: 'Such as into himself at last eternity changes him'.[5]

But we should make excellent accomplices in that case, for I would be your ideal successor, never, unlike you, finding any woman too fat for my taste.

Your grateful friend
Marcel Proust

What also makes me hesitate about coming on Monday is that all Hennessys assuming that 'very ill' automatically means temporary inhumation in the cellar, they would take my presence at the

Independence Day dinner as a sign that they had been duped about the state of my kidneys, if not my heart.⁶

1. An Independence Day dinner at the Ministry for Foreign Affairs.
2. Cf. Bergotte's thoughts just before his fatal heart attack in the Jeu de Paume: 'All the same, I shouldn't like to be the headline news of this exhibition for the evening papers': V, 208.
3. Léon Bailby (1867–1954), editor of *L'Intransigeant*.
4. Allusion to Mme Jean Hennessy, and to her dinner at the rue de la Faisanderie: see letter 115, n. 6. Proust compares her arms to the white marble of Paros in the Cyclades The ancestor referred to is Claude-Adrien Helvétius (1715–71), philosopher of the Enlightenment and advocate of sensualism.
5. See letter 95, n. 6.
6. Cf. the passage on 'those barbarian festivals that we call dinner-parties' in *Time Regained*, where 'nothing but death or a serious illness is an acceptable excuse for failing to attend': VI, 440–1.

119   To Sydney Schiff

[Saturday 16 July 1921]

Dear Sir,

Only today am I sending you *Guermantes II* and *Sodome et Gomorrhe I*. I would have done so sooner, but I've been on my death-bed. I kept thinking of you, and my moans of Schiff, Schiff were rather like Tristan's awaiting the barque.¹ Madame Schiff's delightful note quickened my desire to write to you both (being unable to separate you). But I was literally incapable of movement. And furthermore incapable of correcting a single proof of the book in question, and it was the editors at the N.R.F. themselves who corrected my draft at the office, without my being involved. Thus there are rather fewer misprints than when I have a hand in things. I gather that nice Louis Gautier,² unjustly a recurring theme in our correspondence, has been looking for me in all sorts of places. So I'm pleasurably threatened, one of these evenings, by the prospect of his entry into my bedroom, whose small, very narrow door is ill-suited to the dear fellow's acrobatic contortions, and he does hate to 'fluff his entrances'. However, all that, together with the regal tilt of his head to add to his dignity, is merely a little circus act lasting barely four minutes. After which, he lays aside his mask and is as good as gold, chatting in the nicest possible way, but unfortunately larding his conversation with lies which harm nobody but himself. If I were less tired, I could quote you a typical example of his completely paralysing my desire to do him a favour through his own fault. But he put the 'whopper' in his letter so artlessly and categorically that I thought it must be true.

I believe I told you, as you're kind enough to take an interest in my life, that I had a secretary who was to marry a concierge's daughter.[3] He has broken off his engagement, and being afraid that, without this distraction, he would get bored here alone with me, I have found him a very good post in America,[4] a considerable feat on my part, I may say, considering what he is like. I always bungle the things I want for myself, but sometimes, very rarely, I succeed in doing something for others.[5]

I long to know when you intend to come to Paris, and the unbelievable thing is that I, who never miss anybody, am constantly bored without you. And now that you have so many villas everywhere, I have little hope of your coming to Paris. But you know that I think of you, and of Madame Schiff, to whom I send my humble respects and also, to share with you, my deepest affection.

Your devoted
Marcel Proust

1. Alusion to Wagner's *Tristan and Isolde*, and the dying Tristan's repeated utterance: 'Das Schiff? Siehst du's noch nicht?'
2. Louis Gautier-Vignal: see letter 71.
3. In *The Captive*, Morel is briefly engaged to Jupien's niece, thus transforming his relationship with M. de Charlus. See V, 45–51.
4. Henri Rochat had gone to Buenos Aires: see letter 116, n. 3.
5. Cf. letter 4 to André Gide.

120 To Léon Daudet

[Shortly after 15 July 1921]

Dear friend,

On no account answer this, *it's not of the slightest importance*. The other day, in *L'Action française*, I saw a long extract from Fernand Vandérem's review of Pierre Benoit[1] in the *Revue de France*. I was very pleased, especially for Vandérem, but also for Pierre Benoit whom I greatly admire without knowing him. (What a wonderful review you wrote of *Le Lac salé*.)[2] Only I can't help wondering by what mysterious process Vandérem, unmentionable in the case of *Guermantes II*,[3] becomes laudable in the case of Pierre Benoit. But it's not worth discussing, as the only person who would mind is Vandérem and, in all likelihood, he won't have noticed.

Dear friend, your article about Auto-suggestion,[4] if correct, opens up a vast field to medicine. I can't help having my doubts. When I had hay-fever as a child, I remember being told that cauterization, by destroying the nasal erectile tissues, gave total protection against pollen. Such was my faith that I let them do more than a hundred cauterizations, rather unpleasant to say the least. 'Off you go to the country,' Dr Martin said to me, 'you'll never have hay-fever again.' I left with my parents. At the first flowering lilac, guaranteed harmless, I had such a bad attack of asthma that by the time they got me back to Paris, my hands and feet had turned blue from asphyxiation. I could cite you twenty similar examples. True, one could say that I was insufficiently 'self-aware', that it was my ego protesting. I don't mean to dismiss your 'Novum Organum',[5] nor can I bear the kind of doctor who takes blood samples etc. But it occurs to me to wonder, without caving in to Widalism,[6] that if auto-suggestion (in my case, that I wouldn't have asthma every spring) cannot work with a patient so malleable, so suggestible that he reminds himself, even in his sleep, that he is due for an attack at twenty past midnight – whether it can work with a more recalcitrant, organically ill patient. These are the simple doubts of an ignoramus, affectionately submitted to the great savant: you.[7]

Your friend, who has pledged you his gratitude and admiring affection,
Marcel Proust

---

1. Pierre Benoit (1886–1962), author of 'escapist' novels.

2. Benoit's latest novel, praised at length by Daudet in *L'Action française*.

3. Vandérem's review of *The Guermantes Way* and *Sodom and Gomorrah* had been banned from *L'Action française*; to Proust, Daudet blamed Maurras's objection to the subject-matter, but the true reason was that Vandérem was Jewish.

4. Daudet's article (*L'Action française*, 15 July) entitled 'La Guérison par la Persuasion' ('Cure by Auto-suggestion'). It advocated the use of Émile Coué's 'self-help' method, popularized in the United States by the slogan 'Every day in every way I get better and better'.

5. Francis Bacon's philosophical work describing inductive methods of scientific inquiry.

6. Allusion to the immunologist Dr Fernand Widal (1862–1929), whom Proust had consulted in 1914.

7. Léon Daudet had trained as a doctor.

121 To Joseph Gahier[1]

[Shortly after 18 July 1921]

To Monsieur Gahier

Sir, I have received your magnificent article.[2] You are a truly original, powerful critic such as I admire. You have few equals. This fine piece contains a few inaccuracies,[3] but these seem only to enhance the penetrating gaze you turn upon the whole. When you ascribe to me something I never wrote, when you place one of my characters a little outside his sphere, you still remain so truthful, so profound, that it is I, it seems to me, who am mistaken.

Yours sincerely,
Marcel Proust

1. Joseph Gahier (1890–1948), literary critic of *La Nouvelliste de Bretagne, Maine et Normandie*.

2. 'M. Marcel Proust is a prodigious artist, a painter of incomparable portraits, a collector of sumptuous, unfamiliar images. An exuberant life flows from his novels, linking them to the works of classical writers, to a La Bruyère, a Saint-Simon, a Balzac [...]. He discerns the indiscernible, setting down in harmonious prose, fully, vividly, the nuances of our sensibilities, the infinite aspects of our inner world, the world of the soul whose mysterious recesses alone it is worth our while to explore.' Gahier, *La Nouvelliste*, 18 July.

3. Gahier refers to the Duc de Guermantes as the main character, to his brother as the 'Duc' de Charlus, and to Swann as a banker.

122 From Jacques Rivière

Paris, 20 August 1921

My dear Marcel,

I've received your packages. Many thanks. I'll try and extract something from them.[1]

In any case, in the September issue, you'll have Allard's[2] review of *Sodome*. Gide returned it to me without offering any objection. So you see, my having consulted him didn't have the disastrous results you feared.³

I was sorry not to have been able to dine with you last night, but it so happened that I had been invited to dinner by Madame Gallimard.

My dear Marcel, disregarding all my faults, accepting me as the unreliable fellow I am, do me the immense pleasure of giving me the most beautiful fragment of your next volume for the *NRF*.⁴ I'll see to it that it has as impressive a presentation as possible. Don't refuse me this.⁵

Your very affectionate friend,
Jacques Rivière

1. Proust was in the habit of sending Rivière cuttings which could be used to publicize his books in the *NRF*.
2. See letter 127.
3. Proust must have thought Gide would object to the following passage in Allard's review: 'This first chapter on Men–Women is an historic date in literature. [...] These pages brim with such eloquence, such harsh and noble poetry, that they break the aesthetic spell by which sexual inversion has for so long bewitched the arts and literature.' Cf. letter 110.
4. Rivière, ill, and about to leave Paris to convalesce, was counting on extracts from *Sodom and Gomorrah* Part Two for his November issue. In particular, he wanted the magnificent passage later to be entitled 'The Intermittencies of the Heart': IV, 174–209.
5. 'It's possible that I shall be unable to give you an extract from *Sodome II*. But you should be pleased, for if I keep it for somebody else I might, in order to appear even-handed, have to give you a much longer, more varied fragment than the one you want. So you are much better off if I give you nothing.' Proust to Rivière, *c*. 4 September.

123 To Jacques Boulenger

[Early September 1921]

Dear friend,

As I must often have told you, for I'm always telling myself, you're a (nice) beast! A beast in the affectionate sense that Léon Daudet meant by comparing me to a lion, as well as to a stick of dynamite, in this week's *L'Action française*.¹ Alas, the poor suffering lion has been too unwell (euphemism) to thank you for your kind letter and to express his astonishment that you should imagine a coolness between us about ... Flaubert!² What an idea! But you had a duty to challenge me if that's your opinion. And I'll explain why we'll never convince one another about this (about Flaubert). But I see no particular reason why we should.

I'm too tired for words. Adieu.

Yours,
Marcel Proust

I re-open this because I've just been handed a – charming – letter from M. Duvernois.³ As I doubt whether it will come to anything, kindly don't mention it to Gallimard just yet, he is always so touchy whenever one plays truant. It will help to 'pacify' him if I tell him myself. Renewed thanks, regards as always, and one more thing: how could you have imagined that I thought you had 'pinched' the 'vices of Alexander' etc.⁴ from me. It's not mine to pinch, alas! Supposing that, one day, I were to quote 'Ariadne, my sister,'⁵ which you, too, may have quoted; it wouldn't occur to me that I had pinched it from you.

1. 'Jean Lorrain [...] can hardly have known that he was playing with dynamite, or teasing a lion ... the best and friendliest of lions, I hasten to add, but one who knows his strength, as well as the range and power of his literary reflexes.' Allusion to Proust's duel: see letter 3, n. 5. Daudet, *L'Action française*, 1 September.

2. Boulenger had criticized Proust's 'On Flaubert's Style' in *La Revue de la semaine*. Proust was eager to reply in the *NRF*, but Rivière, still smarting from the Martin-Chauffier 'affair', refused to allow it: see letter 117, n. 1.

3. Boulenger had suggested that Henri Duvernois, editor of *Les Oeuvres libres*, might pay more than the *NRF* for pre-publication extracts from *Sodom and Gomorrah*. This accounts for Proust's hesitation over Rivière's request for extracts: see previous letter, n. 5.

4. In 'On Flaubert's Style', Proust had quoted the line from Montesquieu's *Lysimaque*: 'Alexander's vices were extreme like his virtues; he was terrible in his wrath; it made him cruel', See *AS-B*, 262.

5. Allusion to *Phèdre*, Act 1, scene 3: 'Ariadne, sister! From what wounded love / Do you die abandoned on these very shores!'

124 To Lionel Hauser

[2 or 3 September 1921]

My dear Lionel,

I can't tell you how touched I am by your letter. It's extraordinarily nice of you to worry about my health. Alas, when the leading specialist in his field[1] asks one to say 'Constantinopolitan' and 'artilleryman in the artillery', one knows only too well what it implies, even if he thinks one doesn't.

The amiable Warburgs have become rather less so. As for Cox's,[2] I take it all back, for no sooner had you given signs of your displeasure from your telephonic Sinai than my cheque-book arrived with the speed of a *pneumatique*. Ah! what it is to be a man of influence! Do you still see my friend Walter Berry? Naturally, I haven't been out of bed for months. But he was the last person I saw, about five months ago. I think of you with loving gratitude.

Marcel Proust

1. Professor Joseph Babinski, neurologist. Proust was convinced that he had a brain tumour.
2. The Paris branch of Cox & Co., Proust's new bankers.

125 To Gaston Gallimard

Saturday evening [10 September 1921]

My dear Gaston,

Today I received a telegram that gave me profound pleasure and a letter that vexed me. The telegram was from Jacques. As he had seemed so frantic in his letter of yesterday about my not giving him an extract for the *NRF*[1] (obviously not because he wanted it, but because he had a gap to fill and finding a substitute for me was getting on his nerves), I sent him a telegram at the crack of dawn to stop him worrying himself sick and to reassure him that the extract was already with Paulhan.[2] I hardly like to repeat to you the telegram I received in return, it was so full of joy, testifying to a new-found calm that touched me to the core.

The letter that vexed me (received only this evening, Saturday) was yours,[3] and you know quite well that if it upsets me it's because I can tell that you are upset. But my dear Gaston, since you are upset, and since I had told Duvernois that the deal was *subject to your approval*, why not say 'don't do it' in time? I committed myself to it only after having seen you. You say, and I quite understand, that you said nothing in order not to disappoint me, but I would prefer not to have upset you. I'm sending Duvernois a note suggesting we call it 'Une Jalousie'[4] instead of *Sodome et Gomorrhe II* (I won't ask him to put Extract from *Sodome et Gomorrhe* etc., for with two titles, imagine the subsequent confusion. A reader might come into the N.R.F. and ask 'Let me have "Une Jalousie" by M. Proust.' 'Oh but we know of no such book by him here.'

Your letter also vexes me (but this is secondary) because I see that I must give up hope of publishing other extracts from other volumes in *Les Œuvres libres*.[5] Now that you've told me, belatedly, that you disapprove of my giving them this first one, that avenue is closed to me for good. I know better now, it's not your wish, thus I could never re-offend,[6] for the last thing I want is to go against your wishes. It's difficult to know what to say to you about the money, as I can't follow your logic. In a word, if I've understood correctly, this collaboration may earn M. Proust a little money, but M. Fayard[7] infinitely more.[8] But remember that by forbidding me to take M. Fayard's money in future (naturally, I'll obey you and never mention *Les Œuvres libres* to you again), you put me in an extremely awkward position, in that I shan't be receiving any money from the N.R.F. either. At the moment (according my calculations, but I could be wrong), the N.R.F. owes me about 60,000 francs. How can they ever expect to pay me (in my heart, I sincerely hope that they can and will)? This is far from being a reproach, and, as you know, I myself agreed to your method of paying me, at 2,500 francs a month. But it doesn't always function. And what I receive one month is 'chargeable' to previous months. On the other hand, all the time N.R.F. is unable to pay me and I am delivering them new books, the debt mounts up. It's Sisyphean. Believe me, I say this to you with the utmost affection, which is certainly not the tone I use when talking about it to myself. It's neither criticism nor ultimatum but quite simply regret that you won't allow others to make up for it a little.

You know, when it comes to 'rubbing shoulders',[9] unlike you, I've never thought it does an author much harm, however underrated he may be. Otherwise I might as well have refused the Prix Goncourt because it had been given to Claude Farrère, and to so many like him. And it's not as if the N.R.F. themselves publish nothing but masterpieces, beginning with the works of your faithful servant and friend

Marcel Proust

I repeat, read this in the spirit in which it's written, that is, in all friendship.

N.B. I've left three pages blank – my mistake, so follow the page numbers.

---

1. Proust having repeated his hesitation about giving him extracts for his November issue, Rivière had replied: 'With the lack of foresight that always accompanies extreme fatigue, before leaving Paris I hadn't arranged for a substitute in case you should refuse me. [. . .] If you don't give me the extracts I was counting on, I'll be very awkwardly placed and will probably have to return to Paris.' In the meantime, having decided on the extract he would give Duvernois, Proust had sent the *NRF* the passage that Rivière had wanted: see letter 122, n. 4.

2. Jean Paulhan (1884–1968), critic and essayist. He was acting as editor of the *NRF* in Rivière's absence.

3. Gallimard's letter was written more in sorrow than in anger after a meeting at which Proust confessed to having agreed a lucrative deal with Duvernois. See *MP-GG*, 9 September, 384–6.

4. 'A Case of Jealousy'.

5. A new monthly, edited by Duvernois; its purpose was to print unpublished work or pre-publication extracts.

6. Proust was nevertheless to give *Les Œuvres libres* a further extract.

7. Arthème Fayard, publisher of *Les Œuvres libres*.

8. '*Les Œuvres libres* are books in disguise (same format – same design – same price – same distribution). Thanks to the vulgarity of this "station kiosk" collection, in which Maurice Rostand rubs shoulders with Sacha Guitry, Claude Farrère etc., Fayard can print 40,000 copies. [. . .] If you calculate your royalties on the basis of his offer, you'll find them derisory. [. . .] But truly, should you receive similar offers in future, I assure you that I would somehow find the means to give you the same advance.' Gallimard, 9 September, *MP-GG*, 385.

9. See n. 8. Claude Farrère was the author of 'escapist' fiction.

126 **To Henri Duvernois**[1]

[Saturday evening, 10 September 1921]

Dear Sir,
This business letter requires clarification. The day before yesterday I had a meeting with Gallimard, the consequences of which are both happy and unhappy. The happiest and most important consequence is that I shall be bringing out the extract in *Les Œuvres libres*. The unhappy consequence is that Gallimard, having changed his mind, has written me a long letter (he exonerates you, by the way, as he did in his conversation with me, saying how much he likes you) as a result of which I can never again give you extracts, nor collaborate in any way with *Les Œuvres libres*. The other annoying result is that this interview (lasting from six o'clock in the evening till one in the morning) has left me so exhausted (for all my pleasure at seeing Gallimard, to whom I'm devoted) that I shall have to postpone my meeting with you.

I enclose my extracts,[2] having cut pages 143 to 198 (I think) for fear that it might be too long. Seeing me determined to go ahead, Gallimard wishes it to be as short as possible. My own wishes are *diametrically opposed*, as they say, to his. Let us stick to our arrangement. Especially as, being doomed to 'Serfdom' from now on, I wish to make to the most of my moment of 'Freedom'.[3] Let the 'advance' not be a consideration. It's quite unnecessary that understandable impatience on my part to send you my manuscript should entail a similar rush on yours to send off the 'advance'. I'm not in need of money and can easily wait a month or two.

There have also been indirect consequences. 'M. Proust is too tired, after copying out a novella etc. for *Les Œuvres libres*, to attend such-and-such a reception for H.M. the Queen,[4] or any future engagement.'

I've entitled the extract 'Une Jalousie', adding a string of subtitles. If you would rather something else, it's up to you.

Having had a moment's respite this evening, I wanted to ask you to come and dine at my bedside. But in the squalid district where I live (44 rue Hamelin was the *sole* vacant apartment in the whole of Paris), the poulterers close for 'the weekend'. (And as I take nothing but milk, the cupboard was bare.) So I sent my taxi-driver to search other districts, whence he returned with a minuscule melon and a scrawny chicken. But at least we could have 'rustled up' a meal for you. Only, to avoid the risk of your dying of hunger, I didn't want to have you telephoned till we had these modest supplies, And, by then, it was half-past eight. I assumed that you would have dined. And I was miserable to think that, but for so little, I would have had the chance to get to know you and to thank you.

The extract I'm sending you ends with (and includes) the episode of the young girl who watches the others in the looking-glass.[5] All things considered, I think it makes a good ending. I attached particular importance to it, since it sets in train all that follows. Now that I am forbidden its sequel, it's less important. Nevertheless, as an ending, it's not bad. And if the extract is too long (I haven't counted the lines), it would be best if you make any cuts you wish in the middle. If you see Gallimard, he may ask you to put 'Extract from such-and-such a book'.[6] Don't commit this folly, he knows that I'm against it. 'Serfdom' and 'Freedom' was how I put it to him.

With grateful and friendly regards,
Marcel Proust

P.S. *Very important.* When they send me proofs, kindly ask them to return the enclosed manuscript.

I also enclose a telegram from Jacques Rivière[7] to show you how demented people become when they want extracts for themselves but not for others.

---

1. Henri Duvernois (real name Simon Schabacher: 1875–1937), novelist and critic, editor of *Les Œuvres libres*.

2. Passages taken from the Princesse de Guermantes's reception and the beginnings of the narrator's jealousy of Albertine: IV, 39–160; 218–38.

3. *œuvres serves* and *œuvres libres*: Proust puns on the title of the magazine.

4. Doubtless a reception given by Mme Soutzo for Queen Marie of Romania: see letter 58.

5. See the episode in the Casino at Balbec, where Albertine observes Bloch's sister and her girl cousin in the ballroom mirror: IV, 232–3.

6. Proust's extract, now entitled 'Jealousy', was to be billed as 'a complete unpublished novel by Marcel Proust' in *Les Œuvres libres* No. 5, November 1921.

7. See the opening sentence of the previous letter.

127 To Roger Allard[1]

[Shortly before 13 September 1921]

Dear Sir,
Had I not been so deplorably ill these last few days, I would have thanked you for your article[2] without delay. It's a great pleasure to be so profoundly understood, down to one's least intention. I couldn't have explained better myself what it is that presages M. de Charlus's attitude,[3] and this paragraph makes an altogether remarkable opening to your article. No less remarkable is everything you say relating to *Dorian Gray* etc.[4] I'm extremely touched to see what a profoundly inquiring intelligence you have brought to my story. If I haven't understood the sentence about Freud,[5] it's because I haven't read his books;[6] that being the case, it could appear ill-intentioned. But in a sentence that comes from you, such an intention is unthinkable. After my misinterpretation of your article on *Les Croix de bois*,[7] which we cleared up to our mutual satisfaction, there can be no more misunderstandings between us.

With renewed thanks, yours very sincerely,
Marcel Proust

1. Roger Allard (1885–1961), poet, essayist and critic.
2. Allard's review of *The Guermantes Way* Part Two and *Sodom and Gomorrah* Part One in the *NRF* of 1 September.
3. 'M. de Charlus's first appearance at the Grand Hotel, Balbec, his moods, not so much changeable as of a piece with his abrupt manner, his mysterious behaviour and, last but not least, the author's care in depicting this new character in the sharpest physical relief, all have led to our premonition that this strange figure was reflecting the light from a source invisible to us but whose existence we divine, emanating from an as yet unexplored region that lies beyond those landscapes through which we happily follow M. Proust in the search for lost time.' Allard, *loc. cit.*
4. 'Thanks to M. Marcel Proust, the whole climate of opinion, from *The Picture of Dorian Gray* to *The Martyrdom of St Sebastian*, will be better understood and appreciated. For this magician anticipates the very work of time; upon an epoch, that of Alfred Dreyfus, he invents and imposes his own colour and style until it seems that it must be his creation alone.' *Ibid.* Allusion to Wilde's novel, first published in 1895, and to the music–drama by D'Annunzio and Debussy, first produced in 1911. See also the quotation from Allard's review in letter 122, n. 3.
5. 'In the wake of Professor Freud, one school considers dreams to be an effort

on the part of the physical being to realize shameful desires by offering them a symbolic object. It could be said that every work of art is the product of a similar velleity. Thus, stripped of its normal veneer of false motives, it appears to us in a new form. According to M. Proust's simple and profound statement that "reason opens our eyes to the truth", one can say that an error dissipated endows us with an extra sense.' *Ibid.*

6. Freud was not to be translated into French until 1926. In May 1921, Gide had drawn Proust's attention to articles by Freud in the *Revue de Genève* in December 1920 and January 1921.

7. See letter 55, n. 12. Proust had taken a derogatory remark about obscurity in Allard's review of Dorgelès as applying to him.

128   To Jacques Rivière

[12 or 13 September 1921]

My dear Jacques,

I sent you a telegram[1] because I sensed that you were under a strain and didn't want to add to it by one iota. Rest assured, *not one word* of what I sent Paulhan could be called improper (never mind free). I don't know if it corresponds line for line with what you wanted. Anyhow, it comes to the same thing. It's the fragment in question.[2] In case it's too long (I don't think it is), Gaston has been told to ask Paulhan to keep two extra pages in case.

I shall continue to be 'frank'. Everything in your letter the other day shocked me. Your advice to avoid anything indecent was utterly misplaced.[3] If you remember, I was the one who said (ages ago) that to avoid harming the Review, I wouldn't be giving you the Men–Women. On the other hand, I find it deplorable that when I had closed the Boulenger incident with an extremely forceful letter to him, and his only fault lay in being a little impertinent, you should consider it 'ignominious' (after three weeks, for that wasn't your attitude before the September issue) for me to reply to him.[4] By developing Flaubert, I could have made a critical book. Duvernois's *Œuvres libres*, more liberal than the *NRF*, wanted an extract and some [. . .][5] novellas, and, with Gaston's leave, I agreed. Unfortunately, once it was settled, Gaston wrote to say that he was very annoyed but hadn't liked to stand in my way. I was doubly upset, as I wrote to him, firstly that I had annoyed him and next, since I could have earned a fortune by doing the same with later books, that this first fee should be my last. Anyhow, as far as you are concerned, the extract I've given them is nothing like yours, and won't even be called *Sodome et Gomorrhe*.

I hate to feel that you're under a strain, and would like to hear that *Aimée*[6] is going well. Morand, who thinks nothing too good for me, finds Allard's review 'fair to middling'. Being of the opposite opinion, I wrote him a very warm letter. Thibaudet still hasn't sent me the results of his mythological research.[7] I've also written very warmly to Paulhan.

Did I tell you that it took me an hour, via the oddest literary by-ways, to track down Allard's review? It was virtually impossible to find. Did I send you Daudet's article comparing me to a lion (!).[8] You never use anything I send you in any case,[9] and instead of the review of my book by the man from Rennes (I forget his name),[10] I found a sixth or seventh article by Allard (from the *Revue universelle*) on Fragonard.

Dear Jacques, all this is only a joke between friends. What matters is your health, and that your book is completed with the utmost success and without its having tired you. The rest isn't even literature.[11]

Affectionately yours,
Marcel

Give my regards to Madame Rivière if, as I believe, she is with you. I beg you not to judge my book by this faulty typescript. Anything nearly good is missing. You can read it in the book, if you are not tired, when it comes out, which will be in May, I think.[12]

1. See letter 125.

2. The chapter from *Sodom and Gomorrah* Part Two later entitled 'The Intermittencies of the Heart'. See letter 122, n. 4.

3. 'In putting together your extract, I ask only that you avoid scenes where M. de Charlus is the hero. People complain so much about the Review's growing licentiousness that while it doesn't bother me, at the moment, for commercial reasons, I would prefer not to give them the opportunity.' Rivière, 6 September.

4. 'Regarding your reply to Boulenger, naturally I'm very keen to have it, above all for its content. Can't you find some other way of developing your ideas without putting me in the rather ridiculous position made inevitable by your tone towards him [...]. His recent remarks in *L'Opinion* would add insult to injury by making my climb-down appear more ignominious than it was at the start of this affair.' Rivière, 8 September. Allusion to the Martin-Chauffier affair: see letter 123, n. 2. Proust had now expanded his reply to Boulenger into a long epistolary essay

about Flaubert; meanwhile, Rivière's reluctance to print it had been stiffened by a gibe by Boulenger at the *NRF*'s expense.

5. Missing line(s).
6. Rivière's novel: see letter 97.
7. Rivière had promised to ask Albert Thibaudet to recommend suitable examples from mythology for the scene where M. de Charlus is riveted by the beauty of Mme de Sturgis's two sons: IV, 99–100.
8. See letter 123.
9. Allusion to the press-cuttings supplied by Proust: see letter 122.
10. Joseph Gahier: see letter 121.
11. Proust adapts the last line from Verlaine's 'Art Poétique', *Jadis et Naguère*: 'Et tout le reste est littérature.'
12. *Sodom and Gomorrah* Part Two was to be published on 29 April 1922.

129 *From Jacques Rivière*

Cenon, 11 September 1921

Dear Marcel,

Yes, you have saved my life,[1] and furthermore given me great pleasure by letting me have these pages. The idea that you might refuse me ended by giving me writer's block, and I could no longer work. Now I am liberated. Thank you again.

My one regret is that, if what Paulhan tells me is correct, you haven't given me my favourite passage (moreover, it seems to me indispensable to an understanding of the rest): it's where the hero, through cardiac fatigue, suddenly finds himself confronted by the image of his grandmother.[2] If you thought it too long, you could have cut some pages out of Mme de Cambremer's visits.[3] But it really is a pity to sacrifice anything about the grandmother.

Is it too late to add these pages? I imagine that Paulhan could still manage to fit them in.

I'm not sure how far you mean to go in this issue. Paulhan writes that what he has received goes up to 'It was a day in Spring'.[4] Obviously, that doesn't constitute an ending; moreover, to break off there would make it far too short. But whatever your intentions, we could hold over the ending to the next issue if the additions I suggest make it too long. I know that you're not afraid of an abrupt break.

Thank you again, my dear Marcel. My gratitude knows no bounds. I wish I could express it more fully, but somebody is waiting to take this letter to the post.

I hope you're feeling better. I give you a friendly handshake.

Jacques Rivière

1. This letter seems to have crossed with the previous letter.
2. See IV, 179 ff.
3. See IV, 190 ff.
4. See IV, 209: 'But [the apple-trees] continued to hold aloft their pink and blossoming beauty, in the wind that had turned icy beneath the drenching rain: it was a day in spring.'

130   To Jacques Rivière

[13 or 14 September 1921]

Dear Jacques,

Your letter drove me completely crazy. I've given you everything you asked for, more, in fact, for you weren't to know that before the image of my grandmother comes back to me, my arrival at Balbec begins with a long conversation with the hotel manager.[1] If you're missing a single word, tell me. I cut the part about the Balbec page-boys[2] because I thought it rather too indecent. The main thing is that you shouldn't get the idea from the letter I wrote you yesterday (it may not have gone off yet, Céleste being crazy as well) that I've let *Les Œuvres libres* have your extracts. What I've given them is completely different.

You're wrong to think that 'it was a day in spring' isn't an ending. You can't have read it properly. It's raining, it's muddy, it's a typical spring day. If I hadn't thought it was the ideal ending, I wouldn't have asked for two extra pages in which to reach it. What are you missing (can Paulhan have mislaid it)? I entreat you not to spread it over two issues. You're right to say that I like abrupt breaks. But I like to choose both my abruptness and my break. If you would like the Verdurins' dinner[3] with M. de Charlus for the next issue, it's yours in advance. But that *is* what I call indecent.

When do you get back?

Your
Marcel (very ill)

1. See IV, 174 ff.
2. See IV, 199–201.
3. A comic tour-de-force: the Verdurins entertain at La Raspelière, some of their guests arriving by the 'little train': see IV, 304 ff.

131 To Gaston Gallimard

[Monday 19 September 1921]

Important letter: to be read with care.

My dear Gaston,

While it's not very pleasant to be writing a letter so soon afer having had a fall in my bedroom,[1] it would be dishonest not to express my reasons for dissatisfaction with the N.R.F., and as this fall (nothing serious, by the way) will probably preclude both visitors and outings (it's now four months since I've been out), I'm obliged to write to you, especially if you are going to Brittany as usual. The N.R.F. has two directors whose job it is to torment me, one of them being you, the managing director. He is always out, in a meeting etc., at any rate, somewhere I can't find him when I need his advice. And even when he is at the Review, he gets somebody to say that he isn't (it takes me back to the days when *Swann* was turned down, and I would naïvely telephone two or three times a day in vain). The editor of the Review, my very dear Jacques Rivière, has got it into his head for I don't know what reason that he hasn't had the whole of the extract he asked for, whereas he has had it all, and more besides. The result has been weeks of letters, telegrams, and anxiety enough to drive me mad. (My sincere apologies to M. Paulhan; but for my fall, I would have tried to thank him in person.) Anxious that Jacques might have needed still more, I gave him the Cambremers' visit in addition. But apparently it was too long. Finally, for the November issue, I offered him the entire ending. But it would need cuts. There I draw the line (kindly send him this letter, it's too tiring to write to you both).

You fear that an extract in *Les Œuvres libres* will discourage people from reading the book. But with a different title,[2] there's at least a chance that it will be the other way round. In the *Nouvelle revue française*, however, whose readership is my readership, everybody will realize that it's the sequel and if I made cuts, I would be mutilating my own work, for nobody will turn to the book. So you can tell Jacques that I shan't be giving him anything for November, and, for October, only what he asked for plus a little extra. I've given up the idea of replying to Jacques Boulenger in the *NRF* because he refuses to budge[3] (not Jacques Boulenger, Jacques Rivière). While not admitting the principle that an extract in *Les Œuvres libres* is harmful to the book, I confess, or rather, fear (for I still haven't had proofs) that the fragment in question may be too long and, from the point of view of the book, very badly chosen. I would have consulted you at the time, had you not slipped through my fingers like the proverbial eel. (You didn't even answer my letter.)

I saw Duvernois after seeing you, before he left for Brussels where he is now. He immediately sent me an advance of 10,000 francs; he believes that I could get as much again from sales. I told him of your liking for him, by which he seemed greatly touched, and also that he would never get another line from me for *Les Œuvres libres* because I was afraid of upsetting you. He seemed very put out, and said that I shouldn't give up hope, but my decision, however reluctantly taken, is final. I shan't be writing for *Les Œuvres libres* again (and wouldn't have done so in the first place had you said not to, the evening you were here). And now, my dear Gaston, I wish to warn you against something *very important*. Do not (naturally, questions of goodwill and rights don't enter into it, I have complete trust in you), in order to prove to me that Duvernois is wrong and that *Les Œuvres libres* will harm *Sodome II*, take any less trouble over the distribution of this book (it may be two books) than with its predecessors. For one thing, it would be absurd, since I've already promised you not to write for *Les Œuvres libres* again. For another, it would be a grave error. This book (*Sodome II*) is the richest, in terms of psychology and range of feeling, that I have given you yet. The part I've given Duvernois is by far the least good (and if I'm sorry I did so, in fact, it's because it's the most detrimental to the book). So, put all the more effort into launching this volume (or these two volumes, it's very long)[4] to counter any harm its pre-publication in a magazine might cause, and also to compensate me for my sacrifice in refusing to collaborate further with them.

Regarding the title of Jacques's extract, I suggest something like 'La perte après coup de ma grand'mère'.[5] You can put in a note that it's an extract from *Sodome II* (not that the passage chosen by

Jacques is likely to encourage people to read it). In any case, as this fragment contains nothing of Sodom or Gomorrah, those two names would be out of place in the main title. Kindly tell Paulhan so, with my compliments. Tiredness – exhaustion, rather – forces me to stop.

Your affectionate and devoted
Marcel Proust

Before I could seal this letter, the proofs arrived from the *NRF*. They 'fall' (like me!) at the worst possible moment. I'll correct them nevertheless, but would like them back when you've finished with them because my corrections (there are a great many misprints) will be useful for the book. A better title for the extract would be 'Les Intermittences du Cœur'.[6] It's the best, without question. I see to my joy, glancing at the proofs, that everything Jacques asked for is there. Tell him nicely, as a joke, that he has been making my life a misery for nothing.

Dear Father Superior, I think it's very good of me to have renounced *Les Œuvres libres* for ever and ever, Amen, there being no mention in our contract of vows of celibacy, chastity or poverty. Let me warn you once again to take particular pains over the launch of my new book, upon which I unhesitatingly heap as many praises as Balzac, with equal naïvety but also with genius, did upon his in his letters. And its successors being even better (!), we mustn't allow a limitation on the number of reprints to give the impression that I'm 'finished'. As it is, M. Souday seems to prefer Binet-Valmer.[7] A proof of his political independence, no doubt.

P.S. I see that I've spilt a drop of coffee on the first page of this letter. But to begin seventeen pages all over again is unthinkable.

1. Proust had had an attack of giddiness.
2. See letter 126, n. 6.
3. See letter 128, n. 4.
4. In fact, *Sodom and Gomorrah* Part Two was to take up three volumes.
5. 'My grandmother: a belated sense of loss'.
6. This was to be retained as a chapter heading. The extract was to appear in the *NRF* of 1 October.
7. Jean Binet de Valmer (1875–1940), penname Gustave Binet-Valmer. His explicitly homosexual novel *Lucien* (1912) had been mentioned by Souday in connection with *Sodom and Gomorrah*.

132   *To Madame de Chevigné*

44 rue Hamelin
[Around September 1921]

Madame,

Reynaldo admits to having told you that I was 'festering'. I didn't ask him to tell you that. But I can't blame him for doing so, it's the truth.

In that regard, the only thing that irks me (secondary, it's true) is to be reminded that this 'festering' had the result, a few months ago, of making me too unguarded in things I said when portraying you in a letter to Guiche.[1] In fact, no great harm was done as I don't think he recognized you (I'll ask him). All the same, if one writes harshly about a woman (even when the harshness stems from misunderstood affection), one should tell her at once. My letter to Guiche had no sooner gone than I wanted to write out my sentence again and send it to you. Then, being in a state beyond mere illness, I was forced to put it off, along with everything else.

And I now feel that I should do so. But I also feel that in saying certain things to a woman about herself, one is being indelicate. In that sense, Reynaldo's frankness has embarrassed me, and about a mere aside, moreover, nothing to do with the book. Alas! when it comes to the book, I know the eternal story of Petrarch and Laura takes every possible form and still remains true.[2] I'm not now thinking of the extent to which you are the Duchesse de Guermantes of my novel. But even if it's to a lesser extent than you imagine, it's none the less true that every newspaper in England, America, Switzerland etc. . . . has published essays on the Duchesse de Guermantes, inasmuch as you and she coincide; inasmuch, that is, as you are unanimously praised and, indirectly, the subject of theses in Sweden and lectures in Holland and Switzerland, and inasmuch as I've had over 800 letters about you[3] to which I haven't had the strength to reply, while the only person to whom it hasn't occurred to write to me happens to be you. It was a safe bet, and my first steps along the Marigny way[4] were unlikely to leave me with grand illusions as to their continuation, purely literary this time, along the Guermantes way. Yet it so happens that to be misunderstood, after twenty years, by the same person, and in a fashion so incomprehensible that the tittle-tattle of malicious rivals cannot excuse it, is one of the few great sorrows still capable of afflicting a man at the end of his life who has renounced everything.[5]

This futile letter, when I'm incapable of writing to anybody, is unfinished, but I haven't the strength to continue with it this evening. I shall try and write again in a few days. Meanwhile, Madame, I remain yours respectfully,

Marcel Proust

1. Proust had likened Mme de Chevigné to a 'tough old hen' and a parrot: see letter 115.
2. See letter 75, n. 7.
3. Allusion to his letters of congratulation on the Prix Goncourt.
4. Avenue off the Champs-Élysées. See letter 75, n. 1.
5. See letter 67. Because she never read his books, Mme de Chevigné continued to misunderstand her role in them and in his life, not even allowing Cocteau to read her the complimentary passages Proust had written about her.

133 To Jacques Boulenger

[Friday 14 October 1921]

Dear friend,

I was badly poisoned yesterday.[1] I'll tell you what happened another time. But for this accident – which was almost the end of my continued liking for you – I mean of my life – I would have returned the letters[2] there and then. I intend to keep your secret, I consider it a favour. Oddly enough, though nobody had told me about it, I knew what your letter would say. Novelists see beyond walls.

Your
Marcel Proust

1. A locum pharmacist having misread his prescription, Proust had taken ten times his usual amount of caffeine. His letter is dictated to Céleste.
2. Presumably Boulenger's dossier on the Martin-Chauffier affair.

134 To André Lang[1]

[Second fortnight of October 1921]

Dear Sir and colleague,

I don't much like the term 'analytical novel'. It has come to mean the study of minutiae, a term itself falsified in common speech, microscopic things certainly not being – as medicine teaches us – devoid of importance. Personally, I prefer the telescope to the microscope as a working tool.[2] But because I had the misfortune to begin a book with the word 'I', people jumped to the conclusion that, instead of seeking to uncover laws in general, I was undertaking 'self-analysis', in its most personal and detestable sense. Therefore, if you don't mind, I shall replace the term 'analytical novel' with that of 'introspective novel'. As for adventure stories, it being obvious that real life, external life, also has its general laws, the story that can reveal them is the equal of an introspective novel. All that can help uncover laws, shed light on the unknown, deepen our knowledge of life, is equally worthwhile. Only, such an adventure novel is nothing but an introspective novel under another name. What is the external, if not what we discover within ourselves? Leonardo da Vinci's *cosa mentale*[3] can be applied to all works of art. Although it must be said that the adventure story, even when not aiming very high, more readily reflects the quality of the mind that directs it. Stevenson, who wrote great masterpieces, also wrote simple adventure stories of a peculiar charm. They revolve around Prince Florizel of Bohemia,[4] and to rid his story of the slightest trace of any stupid snob-appeal, the author has him end up selling cigarettes in a London tobacconist's shop. To say a final word on the so-called analytical novel, it certainly ought not to be a purely intellectual novel, in my opinion. It's a matter of wresting from the subconscious to bring it within the domain of the intelligence, while trying not to mutilate it but to keep it alive by preserving it as far as possible from degradation, a truth which, seemingly, the pure light of intellence would be enough to destroy. To succeed in this task of salvage takes nothing less than all the forces of the mind, even of the body. It's not unlike the prudent, docile, audacious effort incumbent on a sleeping man who wishes to make a conscious study of his sleep without waking himself up in the process.[5] Care is needed, but the task, though at first sight embracing a contradiction, is not an impossible one.

Lastly, you ask about 'Schools'. These are merely the outward symbol of the time it takes for a great artist to be recognized and placed among his peers, the time it took for the despised *Olympia* to be hung alongside an Ingres,[6] for Baudelaire to be allowed to fraternize with Racine (to whom he is closest in form).[7] Racine is the richer in psychological insights, Baudelaire in the laws governing recollection, which for me are in fact more vividly revealed by Chateaubriand and Nerval.[8] In Baudelaire, the recollection is there, in a static state, already in existence when a poem begins ('When with both eyes closed' etc.,[9] 'O fleece curling' etc.[10]). Final and negligible difference: Racine is the more immoral.

No sooner is the innovator recognized than the School, now redundant, is disbanded. Furthermore, its taste, while it lasts, lags far behind that of the innovators. Hugo brandished the romanticism of his school while at the same time appreciating Boileau and Regnard[11] to the full. Wagner was nothing like as severe on Italian opera as the Wagnerians.

With my warmest regards, dear colleague,
Marcel Proust

---

1. A journalist preparing a book of interviews with contemporary writers. Proust having refused to see him, Lang sent him two written questions: 'Are there still Schools of Literature? What, if anything, is the point of the distinction made between the analytical novel and the adventure story?' Proust's reply was to be printed in *Les Annales politiques et littéraires* in February 1922.

2. See VI, 442. See also letter 53.

3. See II, 84. See also letter 65, n. 3.

4. Allusion to 'The Rajah's Diamond' from the collection of stories in Robert Louis Stevenson's *New Arabian Nights*, translated in 1885 and a great favourite with Proust.

5. See the famous opening passage of *Swann's Way*. See also its reprise in *The Guermantes Way*: III, 161–3.

6. See letter 81, n. 3.

7. See letter 81, n. 5.

8. See the examples cited in *Time Regained*: VI, 284–6.

9. From the first line of 'Parfum éxotique' in *Les Fleurs du Mal*: 'Quand, les yeux fermés, en un soir chaud d'automne'.

10. From the first line of 'La Chevelure' in *Les Fleurs du Mal*: 'O toison moutonnant jusque sur l'encolure'.

11. Jean-François Regnard (1655–1709), dramatist, closest successor to Molière.

135 To Jacques Boulenger

[24 or 25 November 1921]

Dear friend,

Before I ask Gallimard to give me 'leave', I need to know if one of your reviews (*L'Opinion* or *La Revue de la semaine*) would like to have an article by me – extremely dithyrambic – on Léon Daudet (eschewing his political writings, naturally, bar certain set pieces à la Saint-Simon showing deputies dithering over whether to stand up or sit down for the censorship vote or what colour paper to put in the ballot box, and ending up by abstaining. Wonderful articles, irresistibly funny. But mine will have no political colour whatsoever, for I'm not and never have been involved in politics, unless you count my having signed a petition for the revision of the Dreyfus case twenty-five years ago a political act). If, for reasons of principle or other reasons, *L'Opinion* and *La Revue de la semaine* wouldn't take such an article, there would be no point in my tiring myself by writing it, at least for you, nor in my asking a Gallimard still barely convalescent after *Les Œuvres libres* for an authorization he is quite likely to refuse me, for as he so charmingly puts it (which doesn't prevent my loving him dearly): 'exclusivity, though not written into your contract with the N.R.F., exists in the mind of the contracting party.'[1] Presumably his use of the singular implies its existence in his mind rather than in mine. In any case, I won't do it if it upsets him. I've taken a solemn vow never to write for *Les Œuvres libres* again.

Above all, dear friend, don't get the idea that I had this article in mind when, partly to tease you, I put your name on my latest, terribly long extract.[2] No, it was on receiving a book dedicated to me by Léon Daudet,[3] and thinking of his tireless propaganda on my behalf, that the idea, long present, resurfaced in my mind. I'm aware that Léon Daudet is detested and that, by praising him, I shall offend the few friends I have left. But gratitude and admiration are powerful emotions which need to be expressed. If the idea appeals to you, I shall find my material in his *Souvenirs* since I cannot discuss his novel. I never write articles, it's like opening a wound and letting my last blood flow away. But I can't bear it that nobody ever writes about him, that a journalist of his calibre should be ignored, or treated as a mere Rochefort.[4] True, I don't share his views. But just as, in the old days, he overlooked the Dreyfusism with which I plagued him, I can be equally impartial and simply be the literary critic.

Tell me frankly if the idea irritates or embarrasses you. In many ways, it would be a relief not to have this article hanging over me.

Your devoted friend,
Marcel Proust

It goes without saying (it's all the same to you, I know, but I absolutely insist) that I won't accept a sou for this article. It's a present, if a very modest one. But some presents can be unwelcome. So I beg you not to say yes just to please me. Give me a straightforward no. But spare a thought for the fact that, at a time when the entire press has deserted me on account of *Sodome et Gomorrhe* (with the exception of Binet-Valmer),[5] Léon Daudet has never let a day pass without springing to my defence, and furthermore in a newspaper (*L'Action française*) whose prudishness is a joke. Thus, as he never reads his own paper, while he was praising me beyond my deserts on page one, on page three, one could read: 'This book whose title we dare not even name' (a title taken from Vigny). Naturally, I didn't draw his attention to this difference of opinion, and he'll never know to his dying day that his own newspaper had its 'reservations' (to quote the American Senate)[6] about me.

1. See Gallimard, *MP–GG*, 26 September, 405.
2. Allusion to the extract from the Verdurin's dinner-party, 'The Little Train to La Raspelière' ('En tram jusqu'à La Raspelière') due to appear in the *NRF*: see letter 137, n. 6. By dedicating it to Boulenger, Proust was supporting him over the Martin-Chauffier affair and also teasing Rivière.
3. Léon Daudet had dedicated his latest novel, *L'Entremetteuse* (*The Go-Between*), to 'Marcel Proust / master of introspection, biologist of the inner life'.
4. Henri Rochefort-Luçay (1831–1913): see letter 68, n. 1.
5. In the latest of his arch commentaries for *Comœdia*, Binet-Valmer praises Proust for his fragment 'Jealousy' but ends: 'You're a good advocate, but give me the simple love between boy and girl any day. I'm nauseated, my dear! Marcel Proust's heroes love one another, and the promiscuous Albertine swoons in the arms of Mlle Andrée. It's embarrassing!'
6. Allusion to the US Senate's refusal to ratify the Treaty of Versailles.

136   To Robert Proust

[Monday 28 November 1921]

My dear boy,

1. You can imagine my feelings the other night! But it was nobody's fault.[1] While I'm no worse, my present attacks often mean that I have to do my fumigations until eight or nine o'clock at night. Then, unless I get a few minutes rest etc. (I won't go into details because of fatigue, changes in the weather like today's fog etc.).

2. Céleste got it all wrong when she telephoned you about Morand. In case Vaquez[2] refuses, as seems likely, telephone Morand at the ministry with the name of any doctor you like (particularly a kidney specialist). He leaves it up to you. His one stipulation (probably as a result of some stupid society chit-chat) is that it shouldn't be either Widal or Abrami. I smiled, they being the best. But that makes it easier, as they're probably hard to get. The main thing is, the recommendation has to come from *you* as he trusts you unreservedly. So, if you suggest Bize, don't bring me into it. I'm sure that Cottet[3] wouldn't refuse you. He might refuse a fee (because of Evian) but I get on too well with him for that to matter. But somebody I don't know, an 'authority', seems to me preferable in the present case.

3. (I must break off for a second. I need to collect my thoughts. I'll continue in a minute.)

(Breakdown over.) I wanted to tell you how horrified I was to discover, after your visit (the time when I saw you), that you had been called in. My dear boy, do you imagine that I would have bothered you when you're so tired – or even when you're not tired – for something as trivial as rheumatism and a fever! Or even for something more serious. Always go by me, not by over-zealous people who don't know what they're talking about. Truly, the thought that you came round for a mere indisposition *breaks my heart*. While we're on the subject, you would *do me a favour* if you could *suggest* in advance – in case I ever fell into the fireplace and burnt myself, or had one of those painful attacks Maman used to have, obliging her to call out Landowski or Lafitte,[4] I forget which, in the middle of the night – if you could suggest, as I say, one of your pupils who makes night calls. Anyhow, my random conjectures are precisely those which will never happen, the future lying invisible in the lap of the Gods. But in case I had an accident (which I'll do my utmost to avoid), it would be useful to know somebody who wouldn't leave it till morning before dressing my burns.

Apparently, Reynaldo came that same evening, and Céleste told him the same thing as she told you. I'm full of remorse, for he had written to me and, moreover, since he has a rehearsal or a performance every night,[5] he had gone to a lot of trouble to come. As soon as I can, I'll write to him.

I wonder if you've seen some of the charming articles being written about me these past few days, notably Léon Daudet's overgenerous words in yesterday's *Action française*.[6] On the other hand, my self-imposed rule of never replying to the press seems a little too rigid when I see a paper of the *Canard enchaîné* type[7] putting this sort of thing in its announcements: 'New Swan pen from the Marcel Proust factory' or 'M. Marcel Proust has written to point out that he is not related to the Captain Proust accused of espionage and theft. We are happy to print the distinguished novelist's denial.' Naturally, I hadn't written to say that I wasn't related to Captain Proust. But there would be no end to it if one were forced to deny everything. It's accepted that 'M. Proust spends his time at M. and Mme Boylesve's soirées' whereas, although on excellent terms with the Academician in question, I've never set foot in his house.

Evidently, Léon Daudet's praise doesn't win one friends. Au revoir, my little brother, my good brother, I'm boring you with all this chat. I hate to stop when writing to you. And I'm probably wrong, for in all likelihood you never read long letters like this to the end.

A thousand kisses, to be shared with Marthe and Suzy.

Your loving brother,
Marcel

---

1. Robert Proust had arrived to see his brother, having been summoned by an anxious Céleste; but on finding Proust asleep, she had sent him away again.

2. One of the specialists recommended to Morand by Robert Proust.

3. Dr Jules Cottet, who had looked after Mme Proust when the family had visited the spa of Évian-les-Bains in 1899.

4. Pupils of Dr Adrien Proust: see letter 25.

5. Hahn was conducting Mozart's *Die Entführung aus dem Serail* at the Opéra before taking up a post as musical director of the Winter Casino at Cannes.

6. 'If only we can annoy as many people as we did when we crowned Marcel Proust's book and launched into circulation the name and work of this magnificent writer, this master of analysis! But that is too much to expect [...].' Daudet, *L'Action française*, 26 November. Allusion to the Academy Goncourt who were about to make their award for 1921.

7. *Le Merle blanc*, a satirical weekly.

137 To Jacques Rivière

[Tuesday 29 November 1921]

My dear Jacques,

Since writing to Gaston, I've been ill yet again. (Naturally, no question of cause and effect!) So it's an effort to write this note in reply to yours (just this minute received).[1]

1. Regarding Porel (whom I haven't seen), I had Céleste warn him of your decision and pass on your praises, which she may not have remembered exactly. Only in his case can I save you the trouble of a reply.

2. Regarding Algot Ruhe,[2] if I may give you a word of advice which you are quite at liberty to ignore (my saying that is laughable, a pleonasm, as if I could grant you a Liberty when I count for nothing at the *NRF*), I wouldn't submit his French to a group of people for their opinion, as seems to be your intention. Bergson (who put me in touch with Ruhe, and who is his sole translator, commentator etc.) is the obvious person to polish these little poems, if you like them. If you would rather not bother Bergson (who would certainly go out of his way to help Ruhe but is so wrapped up in Einstein that he has given up teaching), I would gladly polish them myself. (I hope the eminent Swede won't recognize himself as the Norwegian philosopher in *Sodome et Gomorrhe*,[3] but I'm on tenterhooks.) Or, if you prefer, give them to sombody else to polish, but don't let a committee usurp your editorial judgement about poems that you yourself have read.

3. Regarding Bugnet,[4] I think the trouble is that you had met him before you read him. For there are some beautiful things in what Fargue[5] sent me. But I can't quarrel with your verdict. I myself (the only time I met him) failed to recognize the born poet in him. But I would rather not be the one to inform him of his sentence, especially after what he wrote to me about you.

4. I don't know if you intend to publish my fragment on 1

December or 1 January.[6] Your letter (the one before last) seems to exclude either possibility (I'll explain when we meet). But my body was so racked with pain that I didn't think to ask you when it was to be. Anyhow, don't trouble to reply. We're nearly in December (two days away, in fact) so it's pointless for you to write to me when I can easily see for myself in the Review.

Don't imagine that my sending this letter through the post implies a cooling-off in our relations (never warmer or more tender on my side, and your kindness allows me to believe that the same is true of you). But I am so afraid of physical cold because of my rheumatism that I avoid asking people to deliver letters etc., for the moment anybody opens the front door the house turns into an ice-box.[7]

Yours,
Marcel Proust

1. A letter turning down poems which Proust had undertaken to submit to him.

2. Algot Ruhe (1867–1944), Swedish writer, author of *Henry Bergson: His Life and Philosophy*.

3. After a recent meeting with Ruhe, Proust had written him into the Verdurins' dinner-party at La Raspelière: 'At this moment the meal was interrupted by an eminent Norwegian philosopher who spoke French very well but very slowly, for the twofold reason that, in the first place, having learned the language only recently and not wishing to make mistakes (though he did make a few), he referred each word to a sort of mental dictionary, and secondly, being a metaphysician, he always thought of what he intended to say while he was saying it, which, even in a Frenchman, is a cause of slowness' (IV, 380).

4. Captain Charles Bugnet, a young war poet.

5. Léon-Paul Fargue (1876–1947), poet.

6. 'The Little Train to La Raspelière' was to appear in the *NRF* of 1 December. The dialogue between Mme Verdurin's guests in this extract, both in the 'little train' and at La Raspelière, involved a wide range of Proust's characters. See IV, 295 ff.

7. Proust not only refused central-heating because of his asthma but, fearing a repetition of the chimney-fire (see letter 58), had forbidden Céleste to light a fire in his room. See Albaret, *op. cit.*, 325–6.

138 To Jacques Boulenger

[Thursday 29 November 1921]

Dear friend,

Nothing could be nicer than your letter, *but*... I'm very fond of you. Therefore I take the idea that I might stir up resentment against you very seriously. I'll have another think, to see if I can't give it a more lenitive form.[1] But I doubt if I can come up with one because what applies to resentment also applies to love, for which Theocritus says there is no remedy.[2] In any case, until we have reached a mutual decision, I would be grateful if you didn't tell this 'excellent writer' that I had asked for your authorization to write about him, and that you had given it. For in case I defy your authorization, I would appear guilty of an act of hostility when my intention, as you know, is the opposite

I don't quite understand about Benda,[3] but if you think that he would like one or other N.R.F., I can easily act as go-between. Without knowing him, I think him very talented. Personally, I have no cause to like or dislike him; he wrote about me in the *Figaro* as if I were an ultra-Romantic,[4] and as far as I remember, it was to reproach me. But he placed me in 'noble company', as they sing in *Le Pré aux clercs*.[5] Moreover, his error – very courteously expressed – stems from his assumption that I write without a plan, hit or miss, whereas structure is all I care about. But having had the misfortune to begin my book with 'I', which I couldn't then change, I'm 'subjective' in aeternum.[6] Had I begun instead: 'Roger Beauclerc, who lived in a country house etc.', I would be considered 'objective'. I'm rather too ill to explain all that to you in detail. In any case, it seemed pointless to reply to M. Benda. But you needn't even tell him that I'm involved, I'm only too happy to make it easier for him (if it's really what he wants – I would have thought he was too 'established' for either publisher to tempt him) to approach N.R.F. Éditions or the *NRF* Review where, to tell the truth no one can help, but if by chance anyone can, I suppose it would be me.

I know nothing about M. Crémieux.[7] I imagine (perhaps quite wrongly, it's pure supposition) that he is very touchy. In one review, differentiating between my book and *Les Croix de bois*,[8] which he in fact praised, he said that mine was 'something new in the evolution of the novel'. That deserved a note of thanks. But I was ill and overworked. Two months later, Morand's *Tendres Stocks* came out, for which Gallimard had asked me to write the preface. Every single newspaper in France and abroad devoted more space to the preface (I'm sorry to say) than to the book. With one exception: M. Crémieux's review in the *NRF* made no mention of the preface, even in the heading. I don't hold it against him in the least! and doubt if I would remember it now but for you (not that I would dream of comparing you to M. Crémieux!). For no sooner had I built up a picture of you in my mind as, firstly, a man of the most delicate, inexhaustible, exquisite sensibility, the most profound and many-sided intelligence, the broadest scholarship – you must realize that it was solely to avoid wasting your time that I didn't quiz you about etymologies which I've now done on my own, after a fashion – and, secondly, as a teaser ('Teaser Augustus', Mme de Guermantes would say,[9] with justice for once), than he immediately makes his presence felt. For instance, this month I've been bombarded with 'cuttings' because the papers are all talking about me à propos of the Prix Goncourt[10] (not that I'm a candidate!) and Daudet's dedication of *L'Entremetteuse*. Only *L'Opinion* has been out of step. 'Jalousie', which appeared in *Les Œuvres libres* thanks to you,[11] was mentioned in every single publication, Binet-Valmer devoting an entire article to it; only *L'Opinion* quoted from all the magazines except that particular issue of *Les Œuvres libres*, thus depriving me, at least in *L'Opinion*, of the supreme accolade of having my name bracketed with that of Victor Margueritte.[12]

And I sincerely believe that all these coincidences and others, at least the first – I'm beginning to tire and I abbreviate – are the work of your colleagues, and that you don't even read 'What People Say' – 'The Reviews' – 'Rising share prices' etc. I believe it, but I prefer to think otherwise, because it would fit in with my conception of the Teaser I cherish and admire, who isn't teasing me at all. Your article on *L'Épithalame*[13] – like you, I prefer *Épithalame* – is wonderful. I don't think you've ever written better. And between ourselves (or rather, not between ourselves!), what good publicity for the book! Ah! the 'slice of life',[14] it takes talent to correct that naïve misconception.

Ever yours
Marcel Proust

Your fragment[15] will appear on 1 December, I think. In any case, whether it's December or January, I'll send it to you. And then beware, for one of these days you'll have a book, once I'm out of the sulphurous valleys whose stench you tend to exaggerate. Not that I go as far as Mme de Régnier, who says it's what she likes most of mine. But I've saved my friends embarrassment which, out of politeness, they would have called pleasure, by not dedicating a single volume of *Sodome et Gomorrhe* to them. What I ought to have dedicated to you is 'Les Intermittences du coeur' (which has no dedication, by the way, I never dedicate things), for it has landscapes, and you like landscapes; but it's too late now, my apple-trees having shed their blossom.[16] I pass over the question of money for the possible article. There'll be time enough for that, should I return to the idea.[17] And in that case, no money, or else I would have to send you a Cartier tie-pin, which is hardly within my means. Besides, it's supposed to put an end to friendship.

Listen, good-bye, I'm too tired for words.

Marcel Proust

1. Allusion to Proust's proposed eulogy of Léon Daudet: see letter 135.

2. 'I say there is no remedy for love, Niklas, no ointments, no powders, merely that which the Muses have to barter.' Theocritus, 'The Cyclops', *Idyll XI*.

3. Julien Benda (1867–1956), uncompromising critic – notably in his recent work *Belphégor* – of 'emotionalism' and 'intuition' in contemporary literature, and of the desertion of their principles by the intelligentsia, eventually the subject of his famous pamphlet *La Trahison des clercs*.

4. In an essay attacking Pierre Lasserre's *Le Romantisme française*, Benda had bracketed Proust with Giraudoux.

5. Proust alludes to Benda's contempt for *les clercs* and to Hérold's operetta. The aria is quoted by the Duc de Guermantes: III, 567.

6. See letter 134 to André Lang.

7. Benjamin Crémieux, regular contributor to the *NRF*: see letter 152.

8. Proust is mistaken: Crémieux's comparison was not with his old rival Dorgelès but with the 1920 winner of the Prix Goncourt, Ernest Pérochon.

9. See the Duchesse de Guermantes's much-admired pun in *The Guermantes Way*: III, 536–7. Hearing M. de Charlus called a 'teaser', Mme de Guermantes exclaims: 'Teaser, teaser? Then he must be "Teaser Augustus!"', which her husband proudly explains is 'an allusion to Augustus Caesar, the Roman Emperor'. This was the translator's solution to an untranslatable pun: Proust, in his letter, as in his novel, has her say: *Taquin le Superbe*, a pun on *taquiner*, to tease, and Tarquin, King of Rome.

10. See letter 136, n. 6.

11. See letter 123, n. 3.

12. Victor Margueritte (1866–1942), middle-brow novelist who had had a story in the same issue of *Les Œuvres libres*.

13. A saga. The title means The Nuptial Song. The author was Jacques Chardonne.

14. Boulenger compares the haphazard roles allotted to Chardonne's vast range of characters with Tolstoy's precision in *Anna Karenina*, concluding: '*L'Épithalame* is a "slice of life"; M. Chardonne completely confuses "life" with art. In my opinion he is wrong.'

15. See letter 135, n. 2.

16. See letter 129, n. 4.

17. Proust's article on Léon Daudet, 'An Illimitable Wit and a Genius', remained unpublished in his lifetime: see *CS-B*, 601–4.

139 To Gaston Gallimard

[4 or 5 December 1921]

My dear Gaston,

I return the manuscript.[1] But I can't wait to see it in print. And you still don't say if it is to be 1 May or 1 October. If it sits in a corner of your office in the rue de Grenelle it will be never. Five months may seem a long time, but you'll see that it's very little and thus *high time* that we got going.

I'm ashamed to say that I cannot authorize you to discuss the grievances we mentioned.[2] Ashamed, because one should never say things that cannot be repeated. I shall try to meet your demands by asking the person concerned to make his complaints to you himself. And I believe that I shall succeed. I can't leave it to you (how to explain this to you?) because it sometimes happens in life that a friend will tell you six things, two of which honour demands should not be divulged. And if you admit to having repeated the other four, the friend imagines that you have repeated all six. That's not very clear. But to be more precise would exacerbate my offence, of which, although it was committed solely out of my great friendship for you, I feel somewhat ashamed.

Here are the letters from Germany and Italy.[3] Don't you think that to ask *nothing* is going rather to the opposite extreme?[4] The little madeleine dipped in the cup of lime tea, or the moment when Swann realizes that Odette has lied to him about everything (*Du Côté de chez Swann*), or the young ladies of the telephone (*Guermantes I*), or my grandmother's death-bed (*Guermantes II*), or the hawthorns (*Du Côté de chez Swann*, the white and the pink), or even the very end of *Swann* (finishing with the avenues as fugitive as the years) seem very good to me (as well-chosen fragments, I mean).[5]

Regards,
Marcel Proust

I have no hesitation about using larger type. As it's in two volumes, I don't even think that the shorter lines (which is what you want, I think?) will mean fatter books.[6]

As for the reprints, I don't think it's a good idea, unless it's useful to you. Obviously, it's absurd to go into battle empty-handed when everybody else is carrying a sword.[7] But it's Blériot all over again.[8] We can talk about it later, since there's no rush. (What we should do now, however, is to include Grasset's nine (I think) with the reprints of *Swann*, you having started with no. 1 instead of no. 10.)[9]

So that we shouldn't seem too easy-going where the *Nouvelles de la Bourse de Berlin* is concerned, I've dictated a note to M. Gold saying that, as it's complicated, he should write to you. I think a response is urgent, as it's for their Christmas number. I enclose his letter, together with the Italian one. As for Fayard, I don't know how to answer him, nor if I should involve you.[10] I'll take your advice and ignore *Le Merle blanc*.[11]

---

1. The first chapter of Part Two of *Sodom and Gomorrah*, the book which Proust had been virtually rewriting.

2. One of Proust's objections was that Gallimard asked so much for foreign rights that publishers were put off. (Evidently he had forgotten that the N.R.F. had already negotiated various translations, including the English translation.) Gallimard, rightly suspecting that this came from Morand, had asked Proust's permission to confront his informant.

3. A Berlin newspaper wanted extracts, and an Italian publisher to reprint, 'Jealousy'.

4. Gallimard had said that, in view of of Proust's reproach, he intended to waive reproduction fees: see *MP-GG*, 433.

5. Respectively, I, 51–5; 331–9; III, 146–52; 391–7; I, 164–9; 506–13.

6. Proust wanted the larger typeface of Grasset's *Swann's Way*: see *MP-GG*, 424. Cf. letter 32. Gallimard agreed, but pointed out that it would mean shorter lines, thus increased size and cost: see *MP-GG*, 427.

7. Proust had also objected that the number of reprints claimed by the publisher of the 1920 Goncourt winner far exceeded the figure for *Within a Budding Grove*. To which Gallimard retorted that he was prepared to lie on a similar scale if Proust so wished: see *MP-GG*, 429–33.

8. Possible allusion to the fact that Blériot threatened to close his aircraft factory unless the government waived the taxes on his wartime profits.

9. See letter 45.

10. Proust was unclear about the rights to 'Jealousy': see letter 125.

11. See letter 137. Gallimard had advised Proust to ignore such 'organs of blackmail': see *MP–GG*, 428.

140   To Gaston Gallimard

[7 or 8 December 1921]

My dear Gaston,

Forgive me if a slight worsening of my condition tonight obliges me to dictate this short note.[1] I wanted to say that, since you're ready to come out on 1 May (*Sodome II*), perhaps, for *Sodome III*, which may well be a very short book (something we'll decide by mutual agreement depending on where we break it off), you could have everything prepared in case we can bring it out in October. I don't promise that it will be possible, but it doesn't seem to me entirely impossible. Now, for *Sodome III*, why don't we proceed as follows. (I'm writing the rest of this letter myself, for the wailing woman to whom I'm dictating it is uttering cries so like a woman in labour that should she remain in the room with me, I fear there may soon be two wailing creatures instead of one.) We make a typescript of *Sodome III*, I correct it (hardly at all, I think) and we use it as the definitive text for the printer. In this way, you save on the costs of both proofs and type-setting. Moreover, I propose reducing your expenses still further by relieving you of the typing. That is to say, I would engage a typist and have the work done here. Am I not an accommodating author? (It compensates for being the expensive author you apparently say I am.)

Another thing. I'm not sure how inconvenient it would be for you to let me have (there's no hurry) two or three *Jeunes Filles* (de luxe)[2] and debiting them from my account. I think that would be best, for if you remember, our figures didn't agree the last time I bought some from you. However, if you find it a nuisance, I can do without these 'Luxes'.[3] I don't really need them.

I so enjoy chatting to you that having made the effort to begin this letter (at four in the morning, and on top of a hideous day and evening of asthma attacks), I would love to talk to you about the four worst things, in terms of literature, that I've read for a long time. But I want to keep my strength (!) for work, not waste it in literary gossip.

Your very affectionate
Marcel Proust

I learn from reading a column by the eminent writer to whom Jacques entrusts drama criticism,[4] that the dialogue in *Amants* is more realistic than that in a play by Porto-Riche.[5] An argument which, if taken to its logical conclusion, sets Claudel's plays beneath all others. But then what could be less realistic than *Phèdre*, which seems to me to pullulate with truth. And Jarry[6] showed himself to be pretty good at deforming natural speech, even finding it necessary to add that extra 'r' to the word *merde*.[7] True, the song by Jarry[8] quoted by M. Boissard is realistic enough (at least, I think it's by Jarry, I don't have the review in front of me). Yet this so-called 'realism' is obvious only to a few initiates. And even M. Boissard is obliged to explain it in a 'note'. I can be be quite impartial in saying all this, having always been careful (mistakenly, in my opinion) to model my dialogue on everyday speech.[9] What a lot one learns from drama criticism like M. Broissard's. Music criticism can be equally instructive, and in his column in *L'Opinion*, M. Bidou shows a mastery of technical jargon worthy of one of M. Jourdain's professors.[10]

1. The first part of this letter is dictated to Céleste.
2. See letter 71 ff.
3. *Sic*.
4. Maurice Boissard, pen name of Paul Léautaud (1872–1956), a critic whom Proust detested for his cynicism. Boissard's column in the *NRF* of 1 December discussed revivals of Maurice Donnay's *Amants* (1895) and Alfred Jarry's *Ubu Roi* (1896).
5. Georges de Porto-Riche (1849–1930). Proust much admired his innovative psychological dramas about love.
6. Alfred Jarry (1873–1907), Symbolist poet, dialectical wit and, as creator of Ubu, hero of his scatological farce, precursor of Surrealism and the Theatre of the Absurd.
7. 'Merdre', rendered as 'pschitt' by Cyril Connolly in his translation of *Ubu Roi*.
8. Allusion to a song in Act II, scene 5.
9. Cf. letter 116 to François Mauriac.
10. Allusion to Molière's *Le Bourgeois gentilhomme*.

141 To Walter Berry

[Thursday evening, 8 December 1921]

Dear Sir and friend,
(Such, I believe, was the measure of deference to affection in times which I relive daily in my heart but probably seem, alas, quite remote to you.) This evening, after six months in bed, I went to ask the good Olivier[1] to give me dinner at midnight, and I thought how pleasant it was, when I used to come here with M. Walter Berry! And I asked myself: 'Am I past the time for loving?'[2] (La Fontaine without a hint of Charlus.) How I long to see you again! My appalling state of health seems none the worse for this outing (but I've only just returned). I'm simply rather tipsy, having finished an entire bottle of Ritz port on arriving home. But don't ascribe my tender effusions solely to the '345' (that's the bin number).[3] It's sad to think that I met the man in whose company I take the greatest pleasure at the moment I entered upon this night of pain. The day you came to dinner with Mme Scheikévitch (whom I've never seen again, and who constantly reproaches me for having preferred you. Cf. *Pastiches et mélanges*),[4] I didn't see my Destiny! I thought you very nice for having brought me *Guermantes*.[5] I didn't yet love you (no hint of Charlus!) ... And then, I still went out from time to time. Could we not find some way of meeting again before we die (speaking for myself), of telling one another things the seeds of which will, perhaps, germinate in Eternity? Apparently, your compatriots on the other side of the Atlantic are very well-disposed towards me, and never stop asking to be lectured on *Sodome et Gomorrhe*. But I prefer the Parisianized American, despite intermittencies of the heart (from what I hear). For once, I have no pain in my back and chest (rheumatism?) and can share with you what may amount to an hour's relief. It's a long time since I saw Guiche (he wrote to me, but I didn't have the strength to reply). His Destiny (you can tell him from me) is written in these words: 'Cut down on the pleasures of the flesh, and stop intellectualizing golf.'[6] He can't believe that clairvoyant eyes see through walls.
You have strange compatriots. An American woman who assures me that she is very beautiful and twenty-seven years old (I forget her name, but as she lives in Rome, at the Villa Wolkonski, I

couldn't care less) has written to tell me that she has done nothing but read my book morning, noon and night for the past three years. I wouldn't repeat this (I never repeat such things) were it not for her conclusion which, unless she exaggerates, mortifies me: 'And after three years of reading you non-stop, I've come to the conclusion that I understand nothing, but absolutely nothing. Dear Marcel Proust, don't be a poseur, come down from your ivory tower for once. Tell me in two lines what you're trying to say.' That being something she hasn't managed to understand, nor I to explain, in two thousand lines, I decided that it was pointless to answer her. And she'll think that I'm a poseur. Have you any idea who she might be (not that it matters)? I'm flabbergasted to hear that your friend Mme G.[7] (who has spared you the sorrow of parting since fat women don't appeal to you, which is where we differ, and she has become not merely fat, but enormous) is making films and appearing on the cinema-screen. You're so Parisian that you must find this as incomprehensible as I do.

Your compatriot, the one who asks me to tell her in two lines (perhaps she means telephone her) what she has failed to understand in two thousand, doesn't sound very Parisianized. She says: 'Your great writers, France, Baudelaire, G., Loti, Renan'. G. is M. Constant Say's idea of a writer (do you know if one should sell Say Refineries?[8] I was told not to sell Egyptian Oil and they immediately fell from 1600 to 500). I never see anybody from that world, for when I dine at the Ritz I get them to heat up a room for me so that I needn't dress for dinner at eleven o'clock at night, which, for me, though approaching midnight, is the hour when I take my café-au-lait, having only just got out of bed.

Does Mme H. still have dimpled arms?[9] That would be indispensable. I'm afraid that our great orator Briand didn't make much of an impression your countrymen.[10] Still, I don't like it when, very often in the same article, he is described as a pimp and I as a genius.[11]

Dear Sir and friend, one longs to show you that you are not forgotten, that on my side there are no 'intermittencies of the heart'; one gives vent to one's feelings (no hint of Charlus) and there gushes forth this great epistolary outpouring from your friend who, ninety days out of a hundred, cannot put his name to a book or a cheque. But at least this friend, unlike our cause,[12] which seems to be on the wane, is yours for ever! And he is not very demanding. For he doesn't go out, doesn't entertain and, apart from this voluminous screed, which comes to you with all my love, doesn't write letters.

Marcel Proust

P.S. Is Mme de S. slimming to please you, or is that another [...]? Once you have fallen for a woman who is slimming, you must recite, with some slight alteration, Mallarmé's lines: 'Such as into herself at last Eternity changes her'.[13] (Furthermore, he said it about an American: Poe.) And it's kinder to put up with their slimming than to reduce them to ashes, like Landru.[14] But, perversely, they get fatter! 'And thereafter, an eternity of pain' (Sully Prudhomme).[15] I think this may be the first time in my life that I've written a fifteen-page letter.

1. Olivier Dabescat, head waiter of the restaurant at the Ritz. He is portrayed in Proust's Saint-Simon pastiche: see *CS-B*, 55.
2. 'Ai-je passé le temps d'aimer?', 'Les Deux pigeons', *Fables*, Book IX.
3. Cf. M. de Cambremer's confession over dinner at La Raspelière that he would prefer 'a good glass of old brandy or even 345 port', IV, 416.
4. The book that Proust had dedicated to Berry.
5. The book that Berry had presented to Proust: see letter 28, n. 7.
6. Proust had heard that Guiche was studying golf manuals.
7. Mrs John Garrett: see letter 1, n. 7.
8. Say was a sugar magnate, and Raffineries Say shares are among those recommended by M. de Norpois and sold by the narrator 'in a rash moment' after Albertine's death. V, 734.
9. See letter 118. Philip Laszlo was painting Mme Hennessy's portrait.
10. Aristide Briand, the French prime minister, had gone to the disarmament conference in Washington with the aim of encouraging reconciliation with Germany.
11. Attacking Briand's mission, Léon Daudet had called him a pimp, among other things, in *L'Action française* of 27 November.
12. i.e. reconciliation with Germany.
13. See letter 95, n. 6.
14. Henri Landru, who was to be guillotined in 1922, was awaiting trial for the murder of eleven fiancées. See the narrator on the subject of M. de Charlus's sexual depravity: 'Irresponsibility aggravates faults, and even crimes, whatever may be said. Landru (assuming that he really did kill his women) may be pardoned if he did so from financial motives, which it is possible to resist, but not if it was from irresistible sadism', V, 229.
15. 'Et de là, des douleurs infinies', from *L'Art sauveur*.

142 *To Armand de Guiche*

Friday to Saturday night [9 or 10 December 1921]

Dear friend,

1. What makes you think it would bore me to dine with Mme de La Béraudière?[1] This first part of the message to Céleste surprised me, for I have nothing against Mme de La B., she was perfectly nice to me in the old days.

2. I had you telephoned at eleven o'clock this evening to say that Walter Berry and I were here on our own, and would love it if you came round. But I was told that you had guests and were not to be disturbed.

3. I can't help putting two and two together; last year, you invited me to a party two days after it had taken place; this year, you politely brush me off via Céleste. If we go on like this every year...

It occurred to me, given the sodomites' annoyance at the way I vilified them (*not on purpose, purely for artistic and literary reasons*) in *Sodome et Gomorrhe*, that you had one or two with you this evening, such as the Duc de Bisaccia,[2] or the Duc de Le (not being very good at genealogy, I won't go on for fear he is a distant relation of yours). I trust that you haven't fallen among the Gourgauds, Salas and Sturgesses.[3] At least, so I'm told, you have houses to rent at Vallières,[4] which might give us a chance to meet.

Dear friend, I wouldn't have written all this to you in my present state of fatigue and unspeakable physical pain if I didn't have something to say. It is this: Walter Berry thinks it would be amusing to dine at the Ritz on Sunday fortnight to watch the dancing, which is apparently quite a sight. We thought of you at once, and would get one or two ladies to join us. It's difficult for me to know in advance if I'll be well enough to get up, but Berry is only free on that Sunday, so 'in principle', as Bibesco would say, would that suit you? I'm very sad to feel that you are distancing yourself from me. I don't expect you to write, like the president of the Swedish academy: 'You accelerate and decelerate the rotation of the Earth at will; you're greater than God', that's going a bit too far! But still, I seem to have sunk in your estimation. If friendship didn't forbid it, I would envisage a corrective in a second pastiche, which would begin thus: 'The Duc de Guiche, as we have seen, cultivates the Sciences. They quite fail to cultivate him.'

How I would love to talk to you about Einstein![5] No matter how many people tell me that he is an influence on me, or I on him, I don't understand a word of his theories, being ignorant of algebra. And I doubt if he, for his part, has read my books. Apparently, our ways of distorting Time are analogous. But I can't see it in my case, because it's me, and one doesn't know oneself, any more than I can in his, because he is a great scholar in sciences of which I know nothing, and I can't get beyond the first line without being brought up short by some 'sign' I don't recognize. But it's not only because you popularize (only for me, and only in this, because otherwise you've nothing of the popularizer) scientific truths that I like you. I like you for yourself. And I think it's high time that you cleared up the slight distrust that has arisen between us over nothing, at least nothing to do with me, for I have never ceased to be your blameless friend

Marcel Proust

1. The mistress of Greffulhe, Guiche's father-in-law. Céleste had misunderstood (or Proust perhaps pretends): Guiche had invited him with a Mme de Lariboissière.

2. The Duc de Doudeauville's son: see letter 88, n. 8. See the conversation between M. de Norpois and Mme de Villeparisis: V, 805.

3. Allusion to Baron Napoléon Gourgaud (a descendant of Napoleon's companion on Elba) and Comte Antoine de Sala. 'Salaism' had long been a code-word for homosexuality among Proust's friends. The third man is unidentified.

4. Guiche's family seat, a vast nineteenth-century château. He was to reply that he had no idea what Proust meant by this statement.

5. Einstein had just received the Nobel Prize for Physics.

143 *From Walter Berry*

58 rue de Varenne
13 December 1921

Dear friend (without measure and in all affection),[1]

Yes, alas! they are far off, those happy days when we used to meet again and again beneath the smiling gaze of Olivier the Provident (not once did you agree to dine with me at home, because of the stairs: today, my elevator awaits you), and I would smoke

Havanas the length of a greasy pole while you drank extra-strong black coffee 'for six' . . .

What painful months you have been through! Sometimes, on my way back from tennis (not a game I intellectualize, myself), I would stop and ask the concierge for news of you, and she would always reply that things were not too good, that you never went out any more. I didn't write, not wanting your long, sleepless nights to be haunted by the thought of yet another letter to answer. But now, if you go out, even if it's at eleven o'clock at night, why not have me Céleste-phoned and we can share a bottle of the 345? It would show you that intermittencies are nothing but suspensions, like those experienced by Indian fakirs who are interred, eyes tightly shut, tongue rolled back, to be disinterred six (or even seven) months later, thinner but unchanged.

Personally, during this suspension, I was able to dream of going about in Society, of being invited to the Prince de Guermantes's to renew old acquaintances (the Duc, especially; ah, that Duc, always putting his foot in it); that I was awaiting the Albertine for whom we all wait in life and who never comes when you expect her; that I was trundling along in the little train, on my way to the so smart Verdurins' . . . The other day, when an American woman, the image of yours in Rome (yes, I'm bound to know her, for I've met hundreds like her), asked me if I liked your books, I replied: 'Yes, but they have one serious fault: they're far too short.' And the poor woman fled, speechless. I might have added that they have an even more serious fault: having read them, one can no longer read a book by anybody else.

Down La Faisanderie way, the arms are as dimpled as ever. Laszlo has just served them up in oils, to thunderous applause from the regular diners. The other ladies are still in circulation, but I'm no longer in their orbit. As for Mrs Garrett's fatness, they say it was a myth; at any rate, it has melted away and she is as svelte as ever!

Dear friend, let's put an end to intermittencies, don't you agree?

Ever your
Walter Berry

---

1. Allusion to Proust's opening remark in letter 141, to which Berry refers throughout.

144   To Madame de Guiche[1]

[Sunday 18 December 1921]

Duchesse,

    I won't say, like Hugo to Saint-Victor: 'one would write a book for the sake of receiving a page from you';[2] such a compliment would be quite baseless, for I hardly know you. But I will say it in the sense that, if I allowed myself to draw on the infinitude of my memories, and if illness did not prevent me, I could indeed write you a volume on M. de Montesquiou[3] in reply to your few lines, the subject being inexhaustible. I have only one thing to say to you, which will tell you nothing and may, at first sight, seem a little ungrateful on my part, even though it is infinitely the reverse. It is that, of all the people about whom he spoke to me, there is no memory upon which he dwelt with more pleasure than he did on yours, and with an admiration which, being unique, seemed to me biased, for I had so seldom met you that I could hardly discern its reasons. However, this access of frankness on my part must not go so far as to make me lie in the opposite sense. Naturally, I never expressed my mild surprise at his unique predilection. I loved the gentleness with which he pronounced the name 'Élaine', and the tender smile that then lit up his eyes with wonder. I thought that, by telling you this, I would be of more comfort to you in your grief than I would by telling you of mine, or by relating countless stories in his praise. You must know just as many, though different, our lives having never overlapped. And I was so young myself when I met him that, for me, he has always remained what a child calls a 'grown-up'. It's a miracle that during all those years when I watched one 'Olympian' after another turn into 'old brutes' overnight, with the bewilderment of one who hasn't been warned that Summer Time had started the day before[4] and can't understand why his watch doesn't synchronize with others – that during all those years, no cloud ever came between us, and that he always suffered me to reproach him for his conduct towards countless people with a smile. I say there were no clouds, at least as far as I knew, but he wasn't a man to conceal them, being more inclined to hurl down thunderbolts. In any case, his memoirs will decide that for me. Yet it's hard to believe that he didn't feel some anger (and right up to the last weeks of his life, despite his repeated protestations) at the disproportion, indeed absurd, between the modest success of my books and the appalling obscurity into which his were allowed to fall.[5] It is one of the great injustices of our time, and he felt it sorely. He never knew of my efforts to put a stop to this conspiracy of silence, for which, perhaps, to begin with, he himself was partly responsible. But two things give me hope where he is concerned. Firstly, I don't believe (in spite of all the telegrams he sent me last year from his clinic) that he is dead in the literal sense of the word. Was he ever really ill? Or if he was, his illness must have given him the idea of a faked death, at which, like Charles the Fifth,[6] he would be present for the sake of surprising us later. He has stage-managed more ambitious productions than that. Apart from anything else, if he was dying, his departure for Menton is inexplicable.

If, alas, his death was not faked, but real (which I refuse to believe), he will make a come-back nevertheless. There will be an end to injustice. And he will be reborn, at least in spirit and in truth.[7]

It was so as to learn a little more about his illness, and his end, real or otherwise, that I asked your husband to dine here, alone except for Walter Berry, whose presence would not have hindered our conversation, on Saturday last, my first day up for seven months. Unfortunately, the first time I had him telephoned, he was out hunting, and the next, 'dining out' (not with me, to my sorrow, for you know how fond I am of him).

If you see your Mother, the changeless Egeria of the departed Poet (who published your poems before life interrupted them),[8] kindly tell her with what respect and sympathy I share in her grief. I cannot write to her, being forbidden to write letters. I would have defied this ban, drawing momentary strength from an injection, had I thought a letter from me wouldn't displease her. The fact that I hear much testimony to the contrary in no way lesssens my grateful devotion to her.

Yours respectfully,
Marcel Proust

Kindly give my grateful respects to your Father.

1. Duchesse de Guiche, *née* Élaine Greffulhe (1882–1958).

2. Phrase from a letter from Victor Hugo to the drama critic Paul de Saint-Victor in *Correspondances 1836–62*.

3. Robert de Montesquiou had died of nephritis on 12 December, at Menton, on the Riviera. He had alienated family and friends; the handful of mourners at his funeral didn't even include his cousins the Guiches.

4. Official Summer Time was inaugurated in June 1916. See the narrator's evening stroll through the streets of wartime Paris: VI, 88–9.

5. Montesquiou reportedly said: 'I should have liked a little more fame. For that, I needed only to call myself Montesproust!'

6. The Holy Roman Emperor Charles V (1500–58), Charles I of Spain, who allegedly celebrated his own Requiem Mass at the Monastery of Yuste.

7. 'The Gospel according to St John', IV, 24.

8. Élaine Greffulhe's childhood poems had been privately published by Montesquiou.

145 To Étienne de Beaumont[1]

[Shortly after 17 December 1921]

Dear friend,

Allow me to say 'forse che si'[2] etc. And even that is more than my state of uncertainty warrants. 'Non' is more probable, alas! And yet, with the coming New Year, I would like to dispel your injurious doubt (in the Latin sense, in which Malherbe still used the word injurious.[3] And Roman law: 'Summum jus, summa injuria'.[4]) Last night, I was reaffirming my affection for you with our friend Monsieur Faÿ,[5] who was good enough to come and spend a moment at my bedside at two o'clock in the morning (where I'm sorry to say I kept him, with bookish chat, till four). But he was leaving for America that morning, and couldn't have seen you. And only the other day, I was exchanging similar compliments about you with Walter Berry.

I would like (not to put them in a book! but out of a love of order, and of evoking the past) to sort out a few things about your family. 1. Are you directly descended from the Comtesse de Beaumont *née* Jeanne de Castries whom Montesquiou described so well at a Gaudinière ball, 'dressed in a silver sheath like one of the Germain Pilon Graces'?[6] And is there a portrait of her at rue Duroc? If so, perhaps you would permit me to come and see it one evening. As I rarely make use of such permits, one may grant them with little risk of being troubled.

2. The memory of another description – this time, of the wonderful, and truly regal, Mademoiselle d'Harcourt, now Madame de Boisgelin,[7] written by a woman friend of hers, makes me associate her name with that of a very young man[8] to whom you introduced me – for a split second – at a soirée at the Ritz given by our dear Princesse Soutzo about four years ago (Auric etc.).[9] The young man had the same name and seemed *extremely nice*. Is he her son? I can't believe she has a son of that age, although he looked very young (I don't remember his face). Or her brother-in-law?

3. I shan't ask you about the cross (which Céleste tells me isn't a cross but a fleur-de-lys) beneath your coronet. As my next books are full of devices etc., I prefer not to risk confusing them with yours.[10] *So don't tell me*. For that matter, don't tell me anything. None of my questions requires an answer, and is put (in case I'm unable to do so on the 31st, but perhaps I may come) for the pleasure of chatting to you and gossiping about the old days with a Friend 'retrouvé'.

Le Temps retrouvé won't be out this year, but you'll be receiving two fat volumes in May (*Sodome II*). Before *Le Temps retrouvé*, alas, I must stay awhile, guarded by the Angel, in these valleys of brimstone and pitch.[11]

Au revoir, dear friend, I never write letters, so you can see that I've made a long exception. And, inexcusably, I haven't used a blotting-pad, which will probably make the letter unreadable. Read my affection in it none the less, and give my humble respects to Madame de Beaumont.

Marcel Proust

Will it be warm? And how late may one arrive?

I don't think my p.s. is legible. Up to what time may one come? The guests have warmed up the room when one arrives late, which is perfect (for me). In any case, it's most unlikely that I'll be able to come.

1. See letter 17, n. 2.

2. 'Perhaps yes'. Allusion to D'Annunzio's novel *Forse che si, forse che non*, and to the Beaumonts' forthcoming New Year's Eve ball.

3. Allusion to the last verse of Malherbe's 'Ode au feu Roi', in which the words '*trépas injurieux*' ('unjust death') appear.

4. 'Extreme law, extreme injustice'. Cicero, *De Officilis*, I, x, 33.

5. Bernard Faÿ (1893-1979), Professor of American Civilisation at the Collège de France.

6. Allusion to Montesquiou's *La Divine Comtesse*, where he compares Mme de Beaumont (at a ball at the Château de la Gardinière, the Doudeauville family seat) to one of the 'Three Graces' by the sixteenth-century French sculptor Germain Pilon.

7. Comtesse Bruno de Boisgelin; Beaumont's mother was *née* Henriette de Boisgelin.

8. Henri de Boisgelin, Beaumont's cousin.

9. Allusion to the composer Georges Auric.

10. See p.s. to letter 89.

11. See the story of the destruction of Sodom and Gomorrah, where the Angel says to Lot: 'Escape for thy life!' Genesis, IX, 17-24.

146 To Étienne de Beaumont

[Saturday 31 December 1921]

Letter not written by me, my hand still being too shaky.[1]

Dear friend,

I'm the most troublesome of guests (but I must begin by telling you that I very much hope to come).

I'm feeling rather sprightly at the moment.

But in my fear of not being able to come, I've been swallowing drugs with such abandon that you'll have a man who is semi-aphasic and above all unsteady on his legs through giddiness. All the same, I'm determined to come to this ball (it will make me a lot of enemies among those I've refused, but that's a consideration only in so far as it makes me all the keener to bring you my good wishes and see the New Year in with you). I might ask you for a cup of boiling-hot tea on arrival (lime tea, anything), hot enough to burn the throat, not simply very hot. And also not to introduce me to too many intellectual and fatiguing ladies. In the hope of seeing you shortly, dear friend, very affectionately yours,

Marcel Proust

I had just finished dictating this when I was handed a delicious note from Madame de Beaumont. Please thank her with all my heart.

1. Letter dictated to Céleste.

147   To Gustave Tronche[1]

[Early January 1922]

Very dear friend,

You're a monster, not of selfishness but of generosity. This time we shall quarrel for good, unless you solemnly swear that never again shall I receive the pride of your farm chickens, of anything 'of whatever nature', as it says in writs. And to add to my embarrassment, you've accompanied it with an old master etching. The next thing you know, I'll be asking you for an aeroplane, or a transatlantic liner.

I can't write you a longer letter because I've had a dreadful day, my physical sufferings being compounded by an unspeakable mental anguish. The doctors can try every trick in the book, my terrifying clairvoyance sees through their contradictions and deprives me of hope.[2] What a pity that doctors should be 'conscientious' and that one can't say to them 'kill me' instead of 'treat me', since they can't cure one. But let's drop the subject of doctors, there will enough of them in *À la Recherche du temps perdu*, and return one last time to my categorical ban on your absurd munificence, designed to turn me into a collector the envy of every connoisseur of etchings, and a Lucullus. I have always thought honey the most diabolical of inventions.

Kindly give Madame Tronche my respects, and beg her to curb your extravagance! Having scolded you (in all sincerity), I want you to know that I was extremely moved, touched to the core.

Your grateful
Marcel Proust

1. See letter 45, n. 1. Tronche had now retired from the N.R.F.
2. Cf. Bergotte's experiences with doctors, and his nightmarish symptoms leading up to his death: V, 204–6.

148   To Walter Berry

6 January 1922

Dear Sir and friend,

You mustn't be cross (I'm so very grateful to you) but I'm going to have Céleste return the book,¹ the book that is too magnificent for my hovel, the book that will be blackened by my fumigations but will brighten the day at rue de Varenne. And if I delay for twenty-four hours it's merely because Céleste insists on looking at the pictures with a curiosity I find touching in somebody who, since living in Paris, has known only one Louvre, not the one with *La Dentellière*,² the one where they sell all that fake lace.³

Nothing could have given me greater pleasure, but it's too beautiful for me.

The other evening,⁴ when, against my better judgement, I was doing The Lancers with ladies from Poland, Russia, Belgium, Romania, and gentlemen from Mexico etc., whereas the dear citizen of France and America had abandoned me, that same greatly beloved friend had told me that he had something to say to me about Gallimard. Could this not be put in writing (I would return it at once, you needn't fear that it would lie around beside my bed)?

I would also like to ask your advice about something. A Franco-American lecturer⁵ tells me that the American public has a 'taste' for anything to do with the French aristocracy. And you yourself told me that American magazines pay very well. As I've known Robert de Montesquiou since I was eighteen years old, perhaps an anecdotal, worldly article about him would go down well over there. I wouldn't tire myself by writing it unless you could give me an idea of what I might be paid (I can also ask Bibesco, who writes to me regularly).⁶ À propos, do you have an address for his cousin Marthe, I have a six month-old letter for her.

I can see why Cocteau is with La Sirène,⁷ for he looks just like a siren himself with his thin, bony nose and those fascinating eyes. And he also looks rather like a seahorse. He is very sweet, and I still haven't answered a cross letter from him. So don't tell him that he looks like a siren and a seahorse, I only say that to you because you like him.

Marcel Proust

1. A New Year present, evidently a book on the Louvre.
2. *The Lacemaker*, then the Louvre's only Vermeer.
3. Allusion to Les Grands Magasins du Louvre, the rue de Rivoli department store.
4. Allusion to the Beaumonts' New Year's Eve ball.
5. Bernard Faÿ: see letter 145, n. 5.
6. Antoine Bibesco was *en poste* in Washington.
7. Cocteau's publishers.

149   To Louisa de Mornand[1]

44 rue Hamelin
[Tuesday 10 January 1922]

Dear friend,

I was deeply touched by your letter. Alas, the postmark on the envelope aroused the faint hope of a telephone conversation with you this evening, had I felt able to get up, let alone talk (for I have a tiresome speech problem). Unfortunately, the boulevard Saint-Denis address makes this impossible, since it means writing *in advance*.[2] And I never know anything in advance. Should there be a place where you sometimes go late at night, I would join you there, once I'm well enough. Last year's dreary lassitude is a thing of the past for the moment, and I still (once again) have a few good evenings when I can stay on my feet thanks to adrenalin.

In your kindness and consideration as a friend, and I fully appreciate the delicacy of the thought, you would have me write to Louis.[3] I don't like to, having already done so several times, in the most pressing and affectionate terms, and he has never replied.[4] Don't imagine that some stupid pride prevents my renewing my efforts to rekindle his dead affection. It's simply that I don't want to bother him. There can be no such thing as pride between you and me and him. For I place you both, in my memory and my heart, on a pedestal so high that it is out of reach to pettiness or touchinesss. Even in the case of people I don't care about, such feelings are alien to me. All the more reason why it would be unforgivable and shameful of me to give way to them in the case of a friend like Louis, of whom I always think with the most grateful affection. Not to recall with emotion and gratitude all those happy times at the rue Edmond Valentin,[5] at Évian,[6] at the Mathurins,[7] at the rue de Courcelles,[8] would be to uproot from my memory all that is best and most irreplaceable about the past.

Believe me when I say this, tell him to believe it, and accept my tenderest memories.

Marcel Proust

1. Stage-name of Louise Montaud (1884–1963), the minor actress who modelled for Rachel and for whom Proust had once pretended love. See *Selected Letters Volume Two*.
2. Evidently a poste-restante address.
3. Louisa's former protector Louis d'Albufera, for whom Proust had acted as go-between, as the narrator does for Saint-Loup.
4. See letter 107, n. 9.
5. Louisa's address from 1903 to 1908.
6. The three of them had visited Évian-les-Bains together in 1903.
7. The Théâtre des Mathurins, where Louisa had made her début.
8. The Proust family's address between 1900 and 1905.

150 To Clément de Maugny

[First fortnight in January 1922]

My dear Clément,

A thousand, thousand thanks for your wishes. You have mine, from the bottom of my heart, for your double happiness. You never wrote back, last summer, when I had somebody from the Ministry of Foreign Affairs come round to discuss the question of your inheritance from your poor mother's estate.[1] It can only be dealt with in Romania for the moment. And although barely able to hold a pen, I wrote to put you in touch with him. But neither he nor I heard from you again.

You are looking for a post in Paris, I take it. If you like, I'll see what I can do, but I'm not the best person to ask as I never see a living soul. At any other time of year, I would have asked my old friend Reynaldo (his efforts on behalf on his own friends have come to nothing, but it doesn't follow from one setback that all will fail), but these hard times mean that he is obliged to waste his energies and talent in Cannes, as musical director of the Winter Casino. He left without saying goodbye, and I don't think he returns till April or May. What sort of job would suit you, now that you're demobilized?

Thank you for your praises, but if I've had a modicum of success, at least in England and America, I cannot savour it, for I live in constant pain, relieved now and again only at sunset, like a pink glow on the snow near Mont Blanc on evenings when I would go to meet you with so much joy.[2] How happy I would be, if I could find you what you want!

With admiring respects to Madame de Maugny,
your ever-loving friend
Marcel Proust

1. The penniless Maugny having been unable to touch his mother's estate in Poland, Proust had consulted Morand.

2. Allusion to their meetings at Évian-les-Bains, described in Proust's preface for Mme de Maugny: 'What evenings we spent together in Savoie, watching the sun go down and, fleetingly, before being shrouded in night, the Mont Blanc become the Mont Rose.' *CS-B*, 566–7. See letter 27, n. 8.

151 To Gaston Gallimard

[Wednesday 18 January 1922]

My dear Gaston,

I've been hoping to see you from one day to the next, hence my otherwise inexcusable delay in thanking you, and asking you to thank your brother,[1] for your great kindness in sending me a cheque for 1360 francs[2] for a collaboration which I had assumed was voluntary. But I stayed awake every day in expectation of your visit, and for reasons it would take too long explain as well being too boring for you, unless you come this evening, Wednesday (which I don't think you will, it being your day for receiving visitors), I shall go to a musical soirée given by my ex-landlords, the Porels, and consequently pay for my outing on Thursday and the following days with severe attacks that will prevent my seeing anybody. That being so, I didn't want to delay further the acknowledgement and thanks I so wished to give you.

My dear Gaston, two things on the subject of *Sodome II*, somewhat contradictory. The first is that two deaths, notably that of a prelate of the Church,[3] enable me to enrich the character of M. de Charlus with certain traits which, by diversifying him, will not only make this book more interesting but, in its sequels above all, add to his complexity. Because of this, and despite my fatigue, my 'added bits' will be rather more numerous than I said, for I hadn't foreseen an event[4] that allows me, without causing embarrassment to anybody, to give you a better work, in terms of its psychology, than I had expected.

Now (and this is my second point), I can see you taking this slight increase in length (perhaps a page and a half in total for *Sodome II*) as an excuse for splitting it into three volumes, something I assumed was an error in the *NRF* advertisement but which your letter indicates as a possibility. I believe such a split would be disastrous. First of all, I consider it unnecessary. You want to use the type-face (or if that's the wrong technical term, then the same printing method) as Grasset.[5] Now, Grasset's *Swann*, like yours, fits into one volume (far less handsomely, I may say! but that doesn't concern us for the moment) and because of the larger print, is much easier to read. I think we even exaggerate the split by dividing *Sodome II* into two volumes published simultaneously. Nevertheless, I have no objection. However, to launch three volumes of *Sodome II* on to the market at once would put the reader off and at the same time, given the subject matter, offend him morally. To both these objections, you will retort that whether it's in three volumes or two, the reader won't have to read a single extra line. That's perfectly true. But he won't give a damn about that. He'll say: 'Three volumes at one go!' You listen to only one voice. I listen to others. Not one (to my regret, for I like them immensely) is raised in favour of Salmon[6] or Mac Orlan.[7] Because of their prolific output, publicized in advance, they are associated, wrongly, with literary stratagems designed to deluge the public with books. The length of my book may earn me the same criticism. To launch two volumes of *Sodome II* already seems to me excessive. I think that three would be badly received. Note that I'm not putting myself in the place of the author, and his fragmented composition. But you're too shrewd not to be aware of commercial risks which, it seems to me, we should avoid. Not only that, if people were somewhat shocked by the advertisement for a *Sodome II*, a *Sodome III*, a *Sodome IV* (and I'm almost sure that there was a *Sodome V* and a *Sodome VI*), when they see that *Sodome II* alone has three volumes there will be some disquiet about the volumes to come, even though, I may add, their disquiet will prove unfounded. For after these two volumes, I intend to make *Sodome III* rather short (like the first *Côté de Guermantes*). Again, we must talk about that, for I'm not sure that, in the case of *Sodome III*, it won't be possible to publish two parts together. But *Sodome III* not being for now, let's forget about it. My last word on the subject is that, although deeply touched by your offer of collaboration[8] (it reminds me of the Studios of old masters in the golden age of Art, when the Artist wasn't afraid to be thought an artisan), I must refuse. So it only remains for you to decide, and *the sooner the better*, whether you want to have the manuscript typed at the Nouvelle revue française, or whether I should engage a secretary-cum-typist to work here.[9]

A final word before I see you again, my dear Gaston. Should the somewhat vast proportions which the *Recherche du temps perdu* has assumed cause you to regret your decision to publish it, don't worry about offending me, or leaving me in the lurch. In that case, I would take shelter elsewhere, while still remaining your friend if not one of your authors. I say this purely as a precaution, so as not to risk becoming a burden to you, otherwise I shall remain a homing pigeon, more than content to lay my eggs in the literary 'dovecot' which is your publishing house.[10] Don't trouble to answer me on this point. If the day comes when you've had enough of me, I can always migrate. I merely wanted to put your mind at rest.

Do any of your colleagues read English? I'm anxious to get the sense of two or three articles. (For that matter, I can perfectly well ask Morand to do it rather than bother you.) I see that I haven't dealt with the question of the American translation.[11] But for now, my letter being so long, I don't want to risk exhausting your patience by adding that complex subject to the rest. It involves several different people, and I've taken up quite enough of your time as it is.

Till we meet, your devoted friend
Marcel Proust

1. Raymond Gallimard, who had taken over from Tronche at N.R.F. Editions.
2. Payment for extracts published in the *NRF* in 1921.

3. Cardinal de Cabrières, for whose name Brichot supplies the etymology: see IV, 562.

4. Proust alludes, of course, to the death of Robert de Montesquiou.

5. 'Don't be alarmed by the *NRF* advertisement for *Sodome et Gomorrhe* in three volumes. It's aimed at subscribers to our Original Editions collection. [...] Yet with the new format you want, as well as the larger type-face, I don't see how it will be possible to fit the text into two volumes [...].' Gallimard, 13 January, *MP–GG*, 453.

6. André Salmon (1881–1969), poet and successful novelist published by the N.R.F.

7. Pseudonym of Pierre Dumarchey (1882–1970), best-selling author of realistic adventure stories published by the N.R.F.

8. 'I fear that the worsening of your condition may be due to overwork. Your health comes first, and if you're worried about work, and it suits you, I am willing to come and help you every evening.' Gallimard, *loc. cit.*

9. Proust was to employ Yvonne Albaret, Céleste's husband's niece. She was to type the whole of the volumes later entitled *The Captive* and *The Fugitive*.

10. Play on words on the association between the N.R.F. and the Théâtre du Vieux Colombier.

11. Gallimard had been discussing a separate American translation of *The Guermantes Way*. In the event, American publishers were to take the Chatto & Windus translation of all Proust's books.

152 To Benjamin Crémieux[1]

[18 or 19 January 1922]

Dear Sir,

A word only, writing being a physical impossibility. Rivière didn't tell me that you would be writing about me.[2] Had I known, I would never have sent you my book. It makes it look as if I wanted to bribe my Judge (very cheaply!). He will confirm that I knew nothing about it.

No, I haven't received *Premier de la classe*.[3] But don't send it to me. It's for me to send it to you, for your signature, once I've read it. Thank you for comparing my book to a city[4] (despite your modest predictions, I'm sure that you'll be more than a match for me in the matter of urban architecture, and that it won't diminish our pleasure in visiting one another's cities).

Meanwhile, you've gone 'one better' with your 'Passage des Favorites'.[5] The mystery of this delightful name enchants me.

It is indeed too little understood that my books form a structure, but the compasses being opened wide, the composition, which is *rigorous*, and to which all else is sacrificed, takes some time to discern. Although nobody will be able to deny it, once the last page of *Le Temps retrouvé* (written before the rest of the book) comes full circle to meet the first page of *Swann*.

With renewed thanks, yours very sincerely,
Marcel Proust

I can't give you a precise answer about the Preface to Morand, for I'm so tired tonight that I haven't the strength to look out the number of the Review[6] – nor to restart this letter which I've just noticed is written on a page where I had begun another. I have no idea to whom.

1. Benjamin Crémieux (1878–1944), author and critic.
2. In a book review in the *NRF* of 1 January, Crémieux had written: 'It may be that such legendary heroes are incapable of the minute-by-minute existence, meticulously detailed, amazingly lifelike, of Marcel Proust's characters.'
3. Crémieux's latest novel.
4. In his memoir *Du Côté de Marcel Proust* (1929), Crémieux states that, thanking Proust for *The Guermantes Way*, he had written: 'I wandered, lost, through your great work, as through a forest, or an unknown city.'
5. Crémieux's address in Montparnasse.
6. The *Revue de Paris*, November 1920.

153 To Clément de Maugny

[January 1922]

My dear Clément,

I had thought of asking you to come and be my secretary, but didn't like to suggest it, even supposing you could have put up with the hovel where I now live. I inquired about the restaurants where you would have to eat (for you know I take nothing but café-au-lait), there never being any food in the house ... and it struck me as very inconvenient and hardly practical that you should always eat out.

As you know, I've completely lost touch with the Mathieu de Noailles. But they have a high regard for me and know how fond

I am of you. Now, Mathieu likes you very much,¹ and his wife is on good terms with politicians of the Viviani type.² I'm not well enough to write them a personal letter, but if you wrote to Mathieu, who is very discreet, my friendship for you would be more effective than if I were able to write to him myself. And perhaps, through his wife, he could get you attached (or she could) to the League of Nations. That seems to me the best solution.

Another, less good, but still not bad, would be for me to put the matter into the hands of Jules Cottet³ (not for the League of Nations, where he can probably do nothing), telling him that it concerns you (you know how much he likes you, and how discreet he is) so that he can look out for something for you. Being a doctor in Évian, he sees a great many people.

Very affectionately yours,
Marcel Proust

1. Maugny and Noailles had been fellow cavalry officers.
2. Allusion to René Viviani (1862–1925), French representative on the Council of the League of Nations in Geneva.
3. See letter 136, n. 3.

154 To Gaston Gallimard

[Saturday 28 January 1922]

My dear Gaston,

Once again,¹ apologies for this writing-paper; truly, my stationery-box has fallen prey to a witch.

I'm *very* sorry to hear that your little boy is so ill,² be sure to tell his mother that I sympathize with you both in your anxiety. I shall keep myself informed of his progress.

I'm very upset (although it's less serious) that my letter should have displeased you. But in that case you can't have read it. As you'll see, when we examine it together.

To turn to practical matters. Let us not be *Cornellian* and go back on what has been agreed.³ I questioned the number of reprints,⁴ I explained my queries to you at the time and then fell in with your wishes. Don't now say 'let's give up the idea'. That's the way to make life a misery.

By the same token, I've arranged it in three parts. If, after mature consideration, you've changed your mind,[5] so be it. I'll restore it to two, but don't do it to please me, now that I've done the necessary work. Do *whatever you think best*. What is *urgent* is that I should know if it's to be two volumes or three. Feelings don't come into it. Precisely because there is feeling on both sides, let's keep it in its proper place. Also *urgent*: the printer says that several passages are duplicated, probably as a result of the extracts in the *NRF*. How much (what sum) should I give somebody like your friend Gabory[6] for reading the book in two days and marking the duplications (which it was the printer's job to point out to us!)?

I've finished the additions for the part I've had so far, and corrected such misprints as I spotted. But for headings and chapters, I need your decision on two volumes or three. I don't have to see M. Gabory. Having read the book, he has only to write to me: 'Sir, the same passage occurs on page 110 and page 17' (I pick these numbers at random). I make the changes and the book goes off to the printer.

After my month in bed, I'll probably get up tomorrow feeling much worse, for my niece celebrates her eighteenth birthday tonight, and as she knows that I went to the Beaumonts' on New Year's Eve, she might hold it against me if I don't put in an appearance between three and four o'clock in the morning in order to catch cold all over again.

I'll have you telephoned for news of your son.

Fargue[7] isn't involved (that I know of). I'll try and see Morand.[8] But that's not the point. No matter who it is, you must talk to me first.

I have the impression (no pun intended) that *Sodome II* won't be out before October, we are 'dithering' so much. I hope I'm wrong. There's nothing to tell you about *Sodome III*. I'll have you telephoned tonight about your son. What's the matter with him?

Ever yours,
Marcel Proust

P.S. I keep thinking about your son's health, and can't help worrying.

As you see, I have lost no time. And all in one night. And with a fever.

1. Proust refers to a missing letter; he had evidently written again to Gallimard about the split of *Sodom and Gomorrah II*.
2. Eight-year-old Claude Gallimard had fallen victim to 'Spanish' 'flu.
3. Allusion to the plays of Corneille.
4. See the end of the following note.
5. 'As far as the division into three volumes is concerned, say no more; having failed to convince you, I won't accept what you call "a further capitulation". We shall therefore do it in two volumes. What would it profit me to make you "capitulate"? Whose interests do I have at heart, if not yours, that is, the sale of your books. [. . .] And you mustn't regard as a capitulation your having authorized me to increase the figures for reprints as much as I liked. [. . .].' Gallimard, 27 January, *MP-GG*, 463. Cf. letter 139. Gallimard evidently also refers to the missing letter: see n. 1.
6. Georges Gabory (1899–1978), a struggling young writer, regular contributor to the *NRF*.
7. Léon-Paul Fargue: letter 137, n. 5.
8. Allusion to a (false) rumour that N.R.F. Éditions was going bankrupt. See Gallimard, *loc. cit.*: 'I hope that Paul Morand isn't also among the rumour-mongers; it would be the purest hypocrisy on his part, considering his friendly behaviour towards me and mine towards him.'

155 To Paul Morand

[Saturday evening, 28 January 1922]

My dear Paul,

I'm extremely cross because, yesterday, I found 100 francs on my table, which makes me think that you accepted only half Vaquez's consultation fee,[1] and that you treacherously profited from a moment when my back was turned to add 100 francs. Just in case, I enclose 100 francs, and you must tell me the truth.

Have I your permission to tell Gallimard your opinion of the various criticisms being made?[2] For my having passed them on without mentioning you, he suspects Fargue, whom I've absolved. I think that if I named you, liking you as he does, he would take it like a lamb.

I've been to a ball for my niece this evening. It's the first time in my life that I've attended a medical reception that didn't stink of iodine. With the possible exception of the Dieulafoys',[3] who always had people like Montesquiou and the Greffulhes. But in their case it was hardly medical. Whereas at my brother's it was medical, military and mundane. On the whole, my presence didn't cast the chill of the Resurrection of Lazarus. True, I shall return to the tomb. 'Yesterday, white tie and dissipation at the ball. / Tomorrow, Dial Ciba, Veronal and Luminal' (Casimir Delavigne.)[4]

Your Marcel

Very medical: two people in succession insisted on offering me their chairs, the Comtesse Treilhard and Dr Bouffe de Saint-Blaise.[5] *Sicissime*, as Antoine would say.[6]

1. See letter 136.
2. See previous letter, n. 8.
3. Professor Georges Dieulafoy (1839–1911), society doctor. Having been recommended by the Duc de Guermantes, he attends the death-bed of the narrator's grandmother: III, 387–8; 394–5.
4. Opiates (CIBA is a brand name). Proust parodies a poet often quoted by his mother.
5. The obstetrician whose fame M. de Cambremer compares to that of Cottard: IV, 415.
6. Antoine Bibesco's coinage for what is unbelievable but true.

156 From Paul Morand

Sunday evening [29 January 1922]

Dear Marcel,

I left 100 francs because Vaquez only charged me 100 francs. Should medicine also profit the sick? I am cross that you should put me to the embarrassment of accepting.

Being sure that you had been out dancing last night, I didn't come to disturb you this evening.

In case you read my novella in *Mercure*,[1] I want you to know that the letter quoted in it is authentic. It's the key to the whole story.

I entreat you to say nothing to Gallimard about what I told you (I've tried to remember what it was and can't), but I'm so outspoken that it must have been pretty dreadful. Gallimard wasn't mistaken, it must have been Fargue.

When can I bring Maurice Martin du Gard[2] to see you? This evening, passing the Lycée Carnot on my way home, I worked out that it's been seven thousand evenings since I left school. I ask you: where have all those evenings gone?

With love,
Paul M.

1. *La Nuit de Charlottenberg, Mercure de France*, 19 January. (The title is in homage to Giraudoux's *Nuit à Châteauroux*.)
2. Maurice Martin du Gard (1896–1970), editor of the avant-garde literary review *Les Écrits nouveaux*. Morand knew that Proust had good reason for wishing to avoid a tête-à-tête with him: see letter 184, n. 3.

157 To Gaston Gallimard

[Wednesday 1 February 1922]

My dear Gaston,

I acknowledge receipt of and send you all my thanks for your cheque for 2,500 francs of 29 January (chargeable to I don't know what month). Kindly thank your brother for always being so prompt with his remittances.

You haven't told me if we're to come out in two volumes or three. Don't forget that the overall size will be greater than might appear from the proofs, on account of my long additions. I'm positive that you won't be ready for 1 May, so we had better postpone it till 1 May 1923, October not being the ideal month. But it's a disaster. Since I for my part want to do everything in my power to be ready to come out this May (1922), tell me just in case where I should have the corrected proofs sent to M. Gabory, since he is willing to re-read them and to mark the 'duplicate passages'[1] which the printer mentioned without, diabolically, telling us where they occur. (100 francs seems too little, I'll make it a little more.) Sometimes, since the printer has put 'Sodôme' at the head of each galley, I've written 'no circumflex', but not always, thinking that he will come to realize that the spelling of the biblical city isn't optional.

My dear Gaston, I'm so glad that your son is better. Please thank Madame Gallimard for letting me know, and give her my best wishes. I shan't trouble her again because, apart from anything else, Jacques Rivière has confirmed that the improvement is definitive.

Very affectionately yours,
Marcel Proust

1. See letter 154.

158 To Gaston Gallimard

[Friday 3 February 1922]

P.S. to my letter.

My dear Gaston.

My letter not having been taken round to the N.R.F. yesterday or the day before, as it should have been, I'm adding an *essential* p.s.

The proofs hadn't arrived by Wednesday, nor by Thursday 'at the latest', any more than by the previous Saturday 'at the latest', let alone by any other, prior, date. Alas, I'm not a machine which can be oiled day-in day-out to make it work at full capacity; and it's time that I gave my drugs a rest. Consequently, I shall have less strength for work while having to make a greater effort, since the longer the proofs are delayed, the less time I shall have left for them. I say the less because I shall continue to work *as if* we are to be on sale on 1 May, a date you considered far too late, wanting to make it much sooner, but which, however distant, I judged, using a modicum of common sense, to be the only practical and attainable one. So I'll carry on *as if* we are to be in the bookshops on 1 May.[1] The effort I shall put in won't be one second the less. But I'm still convinced that we shan't come out before May 1923. And as I have so many books for you which, if I die, will never appear (*À la Recherche du temps perdu* has scarcely begun), and as my characters will be even more forgotten by May 1923 than they will by May 1922, it will be a disaster. And this disaster, compounded by many others, won't have happened through any fault of yours, my dear Gaston. It will be due (oh! the last thing I want is to vex you, in vexing you I vex myself infinitely more, ask Jacques, he knows how fond I am of you) solely to this: you have *no authority whatsoever* over your printer. It's obvious in so many ways that he doesn't take us seriously, if only from the fact that the first part (of which I've had proofs), though covered in corrections to virtually every word, was done *prestissimo*, once you had made up your mind to send it to him. Whereas the proofs of the second and final part, on which he had to make scarcely any corrections, fail to arrive. Furthermore, we can't accuse him of not taking us seriously because, desperate to come out, we have too much to lose by upsetting him. All in all, I think that, from a commercial point of view, your system (the additions having made it longer) of three volumes rather than two may be the more practical. So tell me if I should adopt it. I shall do so gladly.

2. Warn M. Gabory, so that, my work finished, I shan't lose so much as an hour before he starts his reading. What is his address?

3. Don't copy-edit, with or without Jacques. It will save that much more time. In any case, the misprints are so glaring that the reader can correct them for himself. Only we must put *Sodome*, not *Sodôme*.

I'm so pleased that your son is better, and that you and his mother can stop worrying.

Your very loving friend
Marcel Proust

When I see all the publicity surrounding the stupidest, worst-written book I've ever read, *Saint Magloire*,[2] it saddens me to think that people will assume I've taken two years over *Sodome II*. If *Saint Magloire* sells ten copies, the glory, no pun intended, will be the publisher's. Should he be you, you are unforgivable for having gone to so much trouble over something so inept, so unworthy of the fine, moving, serious, truthful *Croix des bois*.[3]

1. In fact, *Sodom and Gomorrah* was to come out two days early, on 29 April.
2. Dorgelès's second novel, published by Albin Michel.
3. See letter 46 *et seq.*

159 To Madame Soutzo

[Sunday evening, 5 February 1922]

Madame,

As in those happy, far-off days when Antoine Bibesco warned you that I never knew in advance how I would be, may I come, but only later in the evening? In case I'm too ill at the last moment, I wouldn't want to upset your table by accepting an invitation to dinner.[1]

The person you mistook for Fernandez[2] and is nothing like him, was Mlle d'Hinnisdael,[3] who unbent sufficiently to dance a few numbers for me.[4] For in an hour's benevolence, this person who used to petrify me and doubtless will do so again, condescended to give me some lessons in choreography. And I was surprised and charmed to see how, with the utmost naturalness, she could throw herself into the very latest dances[5] while still remaining an heraldic unicorn emblazoned on a coat of arms.

As for Madame Landowska,[6] you insisted on asking her and now you blame your machinations on me. In the excellent end-of-year Revue,[7] when, the worse for wear, I came on as a stumbling, agoraphobic compère (without the pirouettes about to be inflicted on us two seconds later by Gautier-Vignal), you gave me no chance to greet you but dragged me off to meet Mme Landowska, who was engaged in biting Mlle Vacaresco[8] in the buttocks; and, all this time, hugging my lime tea and having in my agitation addressed Madame Vial as 'Madame Scheikévitch', not realizing that she had gone back to calling herself that the day before,[9] I was bewailing my gaffe. And everything seemed to me so little changed that I was inclined to doubt your nation's profound wisdom (but is your nation not rather France?) in saying that all is flux. And, simultaneously, I realized that this παντα[10] was no exaggeration, for *you* had changed (I mean towards me). By your charming letter, you very sweetly show me that, on the contrary, you haven't changed, and that I might still be as happy as I was in the days when, in order to persuade me to come, you would say: 'You'll find General Averescu',[11] whom I hadn't lost, and 'You can chat to Madame de Chabrillan', as if to promise me the moon, not to mention the loss of my voice.[12]

Your 'list' is dazzling, and I feel hardly worthy to be on it, though that in itself is unlikely to prevent my coming, there being an element of falseness in the most genuine modesty. For precise reasons which you may consider invalid, they being unverifiable, I would have liked to see young (Henri?) de Boisgelin.[13] If you had rather Beaumont didn't arrive hand-in-hand with his cousin, he could at least bring along in his pocket his great-aunt's photograph (the photograph of the Mme de Beaumont who was Gambetta's friend) (he has promised to show it to me) (Mme de Beaumont *née* Castries). And I could ask him a few more questions about defunct Beaumonts, not that I intend writing a monograph. But what could be more Ciro's,[14] and the early days of the Ritz, than these evocations of old ladies. In addition to young Boisgelin, I would like it if Morand could bring his friend (Morand's friend) Martin du Gard, for he asks if he can bring him here and I can't see when. But let's forget all that, for I probably won't come, and if I do, I shall have, I can have, eyes only for you, as is happily always the case, except when, three hours after having said to me 'I'm off', you vanish into some invisible room in order to show me that, if you had stayed on, it wasn't for me. Not that I needed to be shown, for it was obvious, and I knew it already, alas.

Goodbye Princesse. Till Tuesday, perhaps.[15] And if another evening, before or after, should suit me better – I'll have you telephoned to ask if you would care to receive me, with the heating on (the Beaumonts were very good about that).

Adieu Princessse, from your respectful and grateful admirer
Marcel Proust

1. Mme Soutzo was giving a ball on the following Tuesday.
2. Ramon Fernandez (1894–1944), author of *Philippe Sauveur*, a novel about homosexuality.
3. Thérèse d'Hinnisdael: see letter 16, n. 10.
4. The occasion was the Beaumonts' New Year's Eve ball.
5. i.e. the latest jazz and negro-inspired dances imported from America.
6. Wanda Landowska (1877–1959), Polish composer and famous harpsichordist.
7. Probably a series of elaborately-costumed tableaux.
8. Hélène Vacaresco, well-known literary journalist.
9. Mme Scheikévitch's brief second marriage had just ended in divorce.
10. *Panta thei*: law enunciated by Heraclitus.
11. General Alexander Avarescu, former prime minister of Romania.
12. The Comtesse de Chabrillan was deaf. See letter 19, n. 4.
13. See letter 145.
14. Fashionable restaurant where, according to Françoise, 'the main dishes are the ladies of the world': II, 66.
15. Proust was to attend her dinner and ball.

160 To Madame de Clermont-Tonnerre

44 rue Hamelin (address semi-confidential)
20 February 1922

Madame,

I'm told that you were almost the only one of his friends at poor Montesquiou's funeral.[1] I say poor Montesquiou, though everything convinces me that he is not dead, and that at his funeral, as at Charles the Fifth's,[2] the coffin was happily empty. It's that which makes me postpone the essay I intend to write on him.[3] I hadn't seen him for a long time, but he wrote me some extremely nice letters, and having learnt from him that he was ill, I tried to do something to please him. This was to arrange for a magazine to publish pieces which he rightly felt were unjustly neglected. Unfortunately, he was the most difficult man in the world to please. The next day, he suddenly changed his mind, and wrote me a letter which, though charming about me, was appallingly rude about the magazine editor to whom I had gone down on my knees, begging him to be as deferential as possible. Then he sent me his last book;[4] I was too ill to write and tell him how much I liked it, and if, against all expectations, he really is dead, can only regret that I didn't have the chance. But then, I had every reason to believe that this supreme man of the theatre had brought off a final, masterly coup.

Goodbye Madame, I have too much to say and too little strength to write more.

Very sincerely yours,
Marcel Proust

1. Cf. letter 144, n. 3. Other mourners were Mme de Noailles, the Emile Strauses, Maurice Barrès and Paul Helleu.
2. See letter 144, n. 6.
3. Proust was also apprehensive about Montesquiou's memoirs.
4. *Élus et appelés*. It included some ironical judgements of Proust's work.

161 To Madame Soutzo

[Tuesday 28 February 1922]

Madame,

Forgive me for not having thanked you before this.[1] But I was hoping to so do in person. Yet I haven't once been able to go out, apart from last night when I dined alone at the Ritz. There was no point in letting you know as you weren't free (Beaumont). I never dreamt of asking you to do me a *translation*! I merely thought you might cast an eye over it, to see if it was favourable or unfavourable.[2] For nothing is hidden from you. I've received a long essay by the great Curtius of Munich.[3] And it saddens me to discover that I no longer know a word of German. On the other hand, since all the quotations are in French, I think the Germans must be quite familiar with our language. In fact, the quotations were the only part I could understand. From time to time, the names of Molière and Racine suggested something to me. But not daring to hope that he was comparing me with them, I assumed that they were there to mock me. It's not always easy to know what people are talking about. There was a rather muddled conversation at your party, all about Popes, and overhearing one of your very charming guests say 'a most remarkable man', I assumed that he was talking about Leo XIII. Yet his words referred to my friend Olivier of the Ritz.[4] And he was speaking French. Goodness knows what I would have assumed, had it been Romanian, or German.

The day before yesterday, I had Morand telephoned to ask him to come and see me, but he wasn't interested. It's to do with an Italian journalist who has written to me. True, it's not of much interest to Morand, since he wanted to ask him questions about me. I don't know this journalist. But I was very taken with the following sentence in his letter: 'Personally, I like all your books, but my wife's favourite bit is the meeting between M. de Charlus and Jupien,[5] though she also particularly likes M. de Charlus hailing the cab.'[6] Yet I don't think he was trying to be funny. Anyhow, in case I can't see the author of *Tendres Stocks* in the next few days (I'm in a bad way tonight), kindly tell him how much I admired the way he danced with the woman in mauve. His many other glamorous qualities apart, Morand has the physical grace peculiar to certain portly young men. He can slim himself down at will. He dances with that chastely flirtatious air of his, and all the while his eyes are fining down his nose and his nose is slimming down his hips, and one has to admit the great charm of this choreographic phantasmagoria, since, for me, it adds to that of a man who I thought already possessed the maximum. I am so pleased with the truth of my appraisal that I would like you to show it to him. If I could draw, I would be just the person to render that smile, designed simultaneously to reduce his present paunch and, in this dance with a lady whose attire belonged with Mme de Castiglione's violets,[7] to put the clock back by a century.

I thought I was making a particular gesture of friendship to the Beaumonts (matched by theirs) by staying up all night at their New Year's Eve ball. They seem to have thought otherwise, for I wasn't invited to the party where you were in charge of a tableau that 'didn't allow you to be yourself'. (I suspect that you went to too much trouble in the expression of this universal preoccupation with dressing-up.) Anyhow, I can always make believe that they invited me. For my concierge having sprained her arm, she sends my letters up with a two-year-old little girl, and the other day, this child handed me an envelope whose contents she had allowed to fall out, never to be found. Thus I pretend that it held an invitation from this or that person in turn, to whom I would like to feel grateful. One day I say to myself: 'Goodness, how nice of the Xs to have thought of me', and the next: 'What a pity I couldn't go to the Ys'. Needless to say, the Beaumonts came in for their share of this alternating gratitude. Still, if I hadn't happened to have been up the day before, I would have loved to see you make the 'entrance' over which (though I doubt it) you were so agitated, and if, as I suppose, it was a fancy-dress ball, then even had the envelope not come from the Beaumonts, I could always have disguised myself as a well man and gone unrecognized!

I still have my typist, and as Céleste's family seems fated to multiply around me,[8] shall no doubt be keeping her. But tonight I was able to dispense with her and her machine, and, as you see, when I write a letter myself, at least if it is one to you, I become tiresomely garrulous, especially when, as at this very moment, I have a certain photograph beside me in which your arms are bare.[9]

Adieu Princesse, know that I shall pick a quarrel with eleven people next week, it making the writing of literature easier. The trouble is, some of them are your close friends, and you'll be obliged to choose between them and me, with the inevitable result.

You were very kind to have signed the book on my behalf at the residence of the Princess of Greece.[10] I failed to do it for the Grand Duke Dimitri,[11] though I meant to. But some trivial reason made me prefer abstention.

    Kindly accept, Princesse, my most admiring respects.
                 Marcel Proust

It wasn't M. Sosthènes de La Rochefoucauld[12] but M. Stanislas de La Rochefoucauld,[13] hence the rather pointless misunderstanding.

Kindly don't mention this letter to anybody except Morand, or else, my having written you thirty pages when I'm no longer supposed to write a single line, only dictate, you'll embarrass me vis-à-vis those who merely receive something typed (or printed).

I haven't talked to you in this letter about what you did to upset me, as well as wrong me.[14] It's as complicated as it's trivial, and the spoken word is preferable, supposing that I'm still capable of speech.

1. Allusion to her party on 7 February.
2. Unidentifed article in a foreign journal.
3. German critic: see letter 164. From now on, Proust was to badger Gallimard for a translation of his essay.
4. See letter 141, n. 1.
5. The scene where Jupien, observed by the narrator, flirts grotesquely with M. de Charlus whose true nature is revealed: IV, 3 ff.
6. The scene where M. de Charlus pounces on the cab driven by the half-tipsy youth: III, 339–40.
7. Allusion to Napoleon's III's mistress, Montesquiou's 'Divine Comtesse' (see letter 145, n. 6), famous for the violets that decorated her fans.
8. Céleste's sister, Marie Gineste, had now joined her, her husband and his niece, typist Yvonne Albaret, in Proust's service.
9. A photograph by Nadar shows Mme Soutzo with bare arms, dressed as Minerva.
10. Better known as Marie Bonaparte, the distinguished psychiatrist who worked with Freud and became his translator.
11. Dimitri Pavlovitch, Grand Duke of Russia, cousin to the murdered Tsar Nicolas II.
12. Patronym of the Duc de Doudeauville, whose forename Proust had borrowed for the single appearance of Sosthènes de Guermantes in the scene where he adds the final touches to his false eyebrows: VI, 143.
13. Grandson of the above, and son of the notoriously homosexual Duc de Bisaccia.
14. Cf. letter 31, n. 8.

162 To Camille Vettard[1]

[Around March 1922]

My dear friend,

I would gladly answer your questions at length, but as I'm virtually on my death-bed, my replies will be more in the nature of a dying wish. What I would like people to understand about my book is that it emerged fully fledged as a result of the application of a special sense (or so I believe) almost impossible to describe (like the sense of sight to a blind man) to those who have never exercised it. But that not being so in your case, you'll grasp my meaning (you'll certainly find something better yourself) when I say that for the present at least the (very imperfect) image which seems to give the best idea of this special sense is that of a telescope trained on time,[2] for a telescope brings into focus stars invisible to the naked eye, and I have tried (I'm not at all wedded to my image, by the way) to make visible to the conscious mind those unconscious phenomena which, completely forgotten, are sometimes located in the distant past. (Come to think of it, it's probably this special sense that has caused me – or so it's said – to be associated with Bergson, for as far as I'm aware there has been no direct influence.)

As for style, I've deliberately rejected anything dictated purely by the intellect, anything imprecise, rhetorical, prettifying, images that are forced, used for effect (the images I expose in my Preface for Morand),[3] so as to give expression to my deep and authentic sensations and respect the natural progression of my ideas.

I'm putting this very badly, being obliged to dictate with an incredible difficulty[4] that leaves me with just strength enough to assure you again of my admiring and grateful affection.

                                                Marcel Proust

1. Camille Vettard (1877–1947), mathematician; a pre-war literary critic on the *NRF* (notably of H.G. Wells); now a civil servant. He was engaged on an essay for the *NRF* to be entitled 'Proust and Einstein', and on a long, eulogistic dedication to Proust intended for his unpublished novel.
2. See letter 53, n.4.
3. See letter 93 to Paul Souday.
4. Allusion to his speech problems.

163   To Paul Helleu[1]

44 rue Hamelin
[Around March or April 1922]

Dear friend,
There is no special reason why I should write to you today rather than yesterday to express my tender and fervent admiration, unless, perhaps, it is the fear of not being able to do so tomorrow ... Already, it's a mortal effort for me to dictate, let alone write, a letter. Yet I don't like to use my typist's hideous 'machine' when writing to you. Quite simply, not having managed to see you for several years (twice you were in America), and keeping more and more to my bed (I go for months without rising but not without pain), I wanted, while my hand is still capable of forming a few characters, to remind you of an admirer who would so like to have enjoyed more of your company in his life.
Kindly give my respects to Madame Helleu, and to your daughter.

Your grateful friend,
Marcel Proust

1. The portraitist and etcher: see letter 5, n. 1.

164   To Ernst Robert Curtius[1]

[7 or 8 March 1922]

Sir,
I'm so gravely ill at present that only my deep sense of the honour you do me[2] could have induced me to write to you myself, such few letters as I have the strength to write being dictated to a typist. So kindly permit me, just for today, and only because of my painful and feverish state, simply to give you my heartfelt thanks. When I saw your magnificent knowledge of French literature, and the facility with which you quote me in French, I wished I could have answered you in German. Alas, I fear the discrepancy between your French and my German is too great. I have the highest regard

for German philosophy and literature, but am less familiar with your language (though I place it, with Greek, among the richest). I was about to add music (it's the word I've crossed out – not the thing!), in which Germany is literally unsurpassed. And, on laying down your essay, it is to Beethoven's A-Minor quartet that I shall turn, in the hope – extremely uncertain – of recovery from illness.[3]

With my respectful gratitude and admiration,
Marcel Proust

1. Ernst Robert Curtius (1886–1956), leading German literary critic.
2. Allusion to Curtius's long, detailed appreciation of Proust's work in the February issue of *Die neue Merkur*. See letter 161, n. 3.
3. Allusion to Beethoven's inscription. See letter 101, n. 5.

165 To Rosny aîné

44 rue Hamelin
Paris, 10 March 1922

Dear Sir and Master,

A thousand thanks for thinking of me, even when it was to distance yourself from me.[1] I'm not so idealistic as to go farther than John Stuart Mill,[2] for whom objects are nothing but possibilities for permanent sensation (although, to my mind, this permanence leaves the notion of space rather too indeterminate. It seems very solid to me, this space of Mill's, since, in the Forest of Fontainebleau, if I take a particular path, I am sure of always finding the same quality of greenness;[3] true, he wouldn't say if I take a particular path, and instead, if I feel a certain degree of muscular sensation,[4] but it comes to the same thing). Unfortunately, my seeing greenness of any sort, whether in the Forest of Fontainebleau or the Champs-Élysées, is out of the question at the moment, for I'm nailed to my bed, unable to write, and this excuses my dictating this typewritten letter in which, being too tired, I can't attempt to demonstrate why there is no disagreement whatsoever between my ghost-writer and you (or rather, you and my ghost-writer).[5] The way in which the survey was conducted, and the way in which I responded to it, are probably the causes of a misunderstanding between us which, in reality, is non-existent.

Kindly accept, dear Sir and Master, my undying gratitude, my respectful admiration, and also, if I may say so, something akin to an *imperiously* tender affection.[6]

Marcel Proust

1. In 'M. Marcel Proust's Ghost-Writer', *Comœdia*, 28 February.

2. John Stuart Mill (1806–73), the study of whose philosophy Mme de Cambremer 'abandons only for that of Lachelier': IV, 372.

3. See the discussion on the sensations and attributes of colour in Mill's *System of Logic*, Book I, chap. II, 4.

4. 'My conception of the table at which I am writing is compounded of its visible form and size, which are complex sensations of sight; its tangible form and size, which are complex sensations of our "organs" of touch and of our muscles; its hardness, which is a sensation of the muscles [...]. [A body is], in short, a set of sensations, or rather the possibilities of sensation, joined together according to a fixed law.' Mill, *op. cit.*, chap. III, 7.

5. 'However, the ghost-writer rather oversimplifies when he has M. Proust write to M. Lang [...] "What we think of as external is what we discover in ourselves". [...] But it doesn't follow that we cannot write great works without having recourse to introspection.' Rosny, *loc. cit.* Allusion to Proust's response to André Lang in *Les Annales politiques et littéraires*, 26 February. See letter 134.

6. Allusion to Rosny's novel *L'Impérieuse bonté*.

166 To Louis Martin-Chauffier

[Shortly before 22 March 1922]

Dear friend,

I propose to answer your letter with the utmost precision and in complete sincerity.[1]

1. One fact is paramount. For the past seven months, I've been bedridden with attacks of uremia alternating with (excuse the two 'withs') other, equally serious problems. It's been three months since I've been able to open a letter.

2. When I received the letter announcing your engagement, on the other hand, I was lucid, and if I hadn't given up all correspondence of the sort a long time ago for reasons of health (!), there is certainly nobody to whom I would more willingly have written. Indeed, I almost did so (even though I was expected everywhere for dinner and not having had the strength to reply, was more upset than my hosts, who merely thought me rude). Two reasons

prevented me. Firstly, in my need to be honest about the least thing, I would have felt compelled to challenge one particularly odd sentence in your otherwise innocuous letter. And that would have led to endless repercussions. Secondly, I had precisely wanted to recommend Jacques Boulenger's book to you, and having learnt at that very moment that you were about to marry, I felt you had enough on your mind without worrying about a review, and that it would be rather ill-mannered of me to reply to you with a 'business' letter.

3. I can't possibly blame you for your article on Jacques Boulenger. It's true that, later, I suffered a good deal of distress as a result of this affair. But it wasn't your fault, nor anybody else's for that matter; my distress stemmed from my having appeared to mislead Jacques Boulenger. It happened like this. I had met Jacques Boulenger once in my life, for five minutes, but this sufficed to give me a great liking, I may even say a great affection for him, and in an excess of zeal I asked Rivière if your review of *Mais l'Art est difficile* was favourable, in which case it would be my pleasure to give the author the good news. At the time, Rivière was very overworked. The offending passage having escaped his notice, he gave me to understand that the review was very favourable and that Boulenger would be happy with it. I thus gave Jacques Boulenger a false report, unintentionally, and without any intention to deceive me on Rivière's part. But knowing me so little, Boulenger would have been justified in thinking that I had made a fool of him. He thought nothing of the kind. But I was unhappy about it none the less, for I hate to appear to be less than candid with somebody I don't care about, let alone with a friend. You mention an offensive letter from Jacques Boulenger, whereas I remember only an offended one. Besides, he wrote to Rivière offering to withdraw it, and left the task of rectification to you (or him, I forget which). But Rivière never answered him (I learnt this only much later, and I don't think I've had the chance since, or rather, alas, the physical possibility, given my terrible state, to see Rivière and discuss it with him). I doubt if I would have done so in any case. For Jacques Boulenger, being extremely open and fair-minded by nature (naturally I don't mean as opposed to Rivière, for whom you know my deep and admiring affection, or as opposed to anybody else for that matter), has long considered the incident closed and forgotten.[2] I have no idea what you mean by talking about his rudeness, there must have been some misunderstanding . . . I trust this controversy

has done nothing to cloud your happiness, in which I share with a grateful heart!

With warmest good wishes, my dear friend, and my respects to Madame Martin-Chauffier,
Marcel Proust

Naturally, to avoid raking over the ashes, this letter is confidential. Not that I would have the least objection to your showing it to Rivière, from whom I have no secrets. But I don't think it would do any good.

Don't worry about those dreadful etymologies I asked you for.[3] I managed as best I could on my own, which is to say, very badly. Anything too improbable or inaccurate will be put down to ignorance on the part of my characters. Although I've been meaning to write and ask François de Pâris for the etymologies of Cambremer and Guermantes for over a year. But writing a letter is beyond me. Having made this exception for you, it will probably be weeks before I can go for an hour without adrenalin or caffeine. But I have too great an esteem for you not to answer your courteous accusations, and to show you that my behaviour has, I believe, been irreproachably correct.

Marcel Proust

P.S. Kindly excuse not just the style but also the grammar of this ten-page letter. While not being the Mayor of Cork,[4] I haven't eaten for ten days, during which I've slept some three hours in all.

---

1. This letter is missing, but it evidently called Proust to account for his behaviour over the Martin-Chauffier 'affair': see letter 117 *et seq*. See also letter 133.
2. Boulenger had been pacified by Benjamin Crémieux's review of the second volume of *Mais l'Art est difficile* in January's *NRF*.
3. See letter 53.
4. See letter 76, n. 7.

167 To Jacques Boulenger

Paris, 22 March 1922

Dear friend,

With your permission, I use the machine to thank you. We'll talk about this double article[1] another time, its prospects seeming rather uncertain. but I was very glad to have your agreement since I was able to read it to Léon Daudet, who was duly grateful. (I enclose an article by M. Curtius. Only if you are writing to me anyway, tell me about these 'Hommes du jour',[2] and if they are the sort of people one thanks.)

M. Martin-Chauffier (for that still drags on), whose letter I don't enclose because it would only be a pretext for more futile discussion, thinks I'm still cross with him because I can neither see him nor write to him and has sent me a sort of disavowal of the article about you. Anyhow, it exonerates you completely, leaving us to disagree over my insistence that he was offensive and his that he was offended, but truly, we can't go on like this for ever, life is too short.

I think I must be in my second childhood, for I have the feeling that I wrote you a long letter all about the Duc de Luynes, fortresses and dungeons; yet as so often when my thoughts turn to you and are prevented by fatigue from taking epistolary and postal form, it can only have been addressed to you in spirit.

Believe me, dear friend, your very grateful
Marcel Proust

1. Proust had asked Boulenger to print Vettard's dedicatory essay (see letter 162, n. 1) in *L'Opinion* above his encomium of Daudet: see letter 135.
2. A résumé of Curtius's essay had appeared in a weekly, *Les Hommes du jour*.

168 To Léon Daudet

[Wednesday 22 March 1922]

Dear friend,
 I'm sensible of the absurdity, when your articles reveal your preoccupations with the affairs of the nation, of bothering you with a matter of complete indifference to you. Yet, for both our sakes, I want to explain the enclosed letter from Jacques Boulenger[1] which, without my comments, you would find incomprehensible. The main thing is, he promises to go ahead with my article on you, and he is a man of his word.
 I suggested it to Jacques Boulenger over a year ago.[2] He replied with a letter full of admiration for you but also pointing out to me that 'friends of mine' who are also his friends and contributors, Régnier, Hermant etc., might be offended at my tone in speaking of you. But, having said that, in the same letter he promised to take the article, putting me on a footing with Bourget, the Bourget who writes for his Review (Paul, not the J.M. Bourget who has just done an article in the *Débats* to show that Painlevé was telling the truth and that Mangin had lied.[3] What cheek! He must have had it from Pierrefeu. Pure guesswork, but based on his views on the matter). So Boulenger's letter is all that one could wish, and not without merit, considering that he earns his living from his Review etc. Only he is so busy with his jobs, his fencing and his boxing (the one thing he has in common with his brother Marcel Boulenger) that I haven't heard from him again. (He pays so little attention to what he reads that when I begged him to stop writing about me in *L'Opinion* he thought I meant the opposite, as you'll see, if you read his letter.)
 Don't think that when he says Doumic's lectures are incomparable it means that he thinks highly of Doumic.[4] I think by that he means to flatter me, finding no comparison in terms of literary merit between a lecture by Doumic and an article by me (forgive me, it's not me speaking), but that since it brings him readers etc.
 The dedication he mentions, now past history, refers to an old article of mine.[5] I dedicated it to him because it had looked as though I had been responsible for a dirty trick which the *NRF* had

played on him and I was anxious to show him my support. In fact, he subsequently discovered the truth and, despite having met me once for five minutes in his life, had never doubted me. I don't know if you read the series of truly profound articles he wrote about me.

Speaking of the *NRF*, I have their solemn word that there is to be an excellent article on you. But ever since they turned down my article on *Vers le Roi*[6] (I nearly put *Secret du Roi*,[7] thinking of *L'Action française*), since all that trouble I had with *Comœdia*, who promised, then reneged, I'm no longer certain of anything. To go through the fatigue of getting oneself up, just for that! How lucky you are to have your own newspaper! A letter kills me, I'm so weak; it's true that I now have a typist, but I don't like to use her when writing to you. Letters kill me, and yet (*unless you tell me not to*, for you are the Law and the Prophet,[8] ask Barrès – if he remembers) I'm about to write a completely pointless one. In the days when M. Philippe Berthelot[9] was at the height of his power, I was invited to at least twenty parties for him and always refused. I met him only once, at your Mother's (an evening when you were dining),[10] when he completely ignored me. But it's a failing of mine, once somebody 'comes unstuck', to want to express my sympathy (and, conversely, to ignore honours, sometimes to the point of exaggeration). True, the few pronouncements M. Philippe Berthelot made that evening struck me as singularly devoid of sympathy. But the question is, do we think that only those who feel pity deserve to be pitied, or shouldn't we rather be tender to the hard-hearted in their misfortune? But I might add that this sympathy (it would seem appallingly Tolstoyan to Jacques Boulenger, the best of men, but hardly sentimental) has its limits. And, for example, the horror which somebody like Paul Meunier[11] inspires in me stifles all compassion.

The things I could tell you about A.R., by whom, I take it, you mean Albert Robin,[12] a man whom Papa treated like dirt to his face, without my understanding why. And I wanted to ask you if drinking port makes one an alcoholic, or if it's considered a wine.[13] And much else besides. But it's a week since I've had a minute's sleep, and fatigue prevents my finishing a letter which I doubt you will have read to the end in any case.

Kindly give my respects to Madame Léon Daudet, and share with her my profound and admiring gratitude.

Marcel Proust

I have an idea that I've made a spelling mistake (in the tense of a verb) but am too tired to re-read my letter.

1. Referred to in the previous letter.
2. See letter 135.
3. Allusion to a dispute between Paul Painlevé, prime minister of France in 1917, and General Mangin over German reparations.
4. René Doumic (1860–1937), an Academician whose lectures had been mocked by Daudet.
5. See letter 135, n. 2.
6. A book of Daudet's essays, published the previous year.
7. Title given to the secret correspondence between Louis XV and his diplomatic spies, published in 1878 and evoked in *The Fugitive*: V, 620.
8. See Matthew, VII, 12.
9. See letter 170 and its n. 7. The following references to Berthelot and compassion could thus be read as a veiled reproach.
10. The occasion was a dinner in honour of Francis Jammes in February 1908.
11. Paul Meunier (1871–1922), deputy. After a vicious campaign by Daudet, Meunier was arrested for spying in 1919 and held on remand until found not guilty in 1922.
12. Professor Albert Robin (1847–1928), distinguished but eccentric physician, also a writer, who had a notorious liaison with the courtesan Liane de Pougy. See the scene described in the Goncourt *Journal* for 7 June.
13. Allusion to an article by Daudet entitled 'Les Ennemis du vin', *L'Action française*, 15 March. See Proust's confession to Berry that he had drunk a whole bottle of port: letter 141.

169 *From Léon Daudet*

CHAMBRE DES DEPUTES
Thursday [23 March 1922]

My dear Marcel,

I return the letter from your Olibrius.[1] I beg you not to write anything about my little book, either in the *Revue universelle*[2] or elsewhere, it would only tire you, to the detriment of your own admirable writings. These suffice for my pleasure, and for that of any man or woman interested in the workings of the human mind. You are unique and, as such, you must look after yourself, behave ruthlessly.

I know your friendship for me. I don't need you to prove it to me in an article. I have a profound affection for you too, Marcel, and want you to be strong and well. Probably very little stands between you and health – which lies in your work – if you could only see it.

'Léon has gone soft in the head!'

Not at all. Once a doctor, always a doctor. But you never would listen to any advice from me which you thought might disagree with you.

On Saturday evening, I leave with my tribe for Brittany. But my wife and I will read you on the seashore, for you too are πολυφλοοβοιος,[3] and the tritons will hear tell of our joy.

Affectionately,
Léon

The good J. Boulenger is a nice chap, and very young. He believes in the existence of Régnier and Doumic. I don't.

1. Olibrius the Gaul, commonly invoked to signify a swashbuckler.

2. The journal favoured by right-wing intellectuals to which Proust had first offered his encomium of Daudet; it was turned down because it praised the editor Jacques Bainville.

3. *polyphlosbios*: poetic epithet having the sense of 'ceaseless roaring', as in waves breaking on the shore; it occurs in *The Iliad*, Book 1, line 34. Daudet probably also alludes to his comparison of Proust to a lion: see letter 123.

170 To Philippe Berthelot[1]

[Shortly after 22 March 1922]

Sir,

It's a strange undertaking, to be writing to you. My health forbids my writing a single letter by hand. The nature of this one scarcely permits me to have it typed without indiscretion, and I'm risking mortal fatigue for the sake of somebody to whom that will be a matter of total indifference. For you probably don't even remember who I am, having ignored me when we dined together at Madame Alphonse Daudet's[2] and then apparently failed to recognize me, a few days later, at the Opéra. For a year or two after that, we were often invited to the same houses, but I was never able to accept. If I write to you now, it's because things have changed. I feel that a man of the highest integrity, you, has been the victim of a grave and cruel injustice.[3] This idea being insupportable to me, I felt the need to write and tell you so. I don't attach the least significance to the sanctions taken against you. I know that such courts are habitually biased. And it so happens that I once knew one of your judges quite well.[4] He never did me any harm personally, but I take him for a man lacking in judgment and, moreover, blinkered by passing infatuations and lasting grudges, one in whom an aptitude for doing ten things badly cannot, whatever people say, be the same as excelling in one.

'I pity you for falling [or rather, having been pushed] into his fearsome hands.'[5] Moreover, your judges must be very foolish to believe that they can rule you out for the next ten years. At a time when everything is called into question every three months, do they really imagine that their judgment alone will last?[6] Besides, you cannot be prevented from exercising your considerable talents in another field. You must already have said all this to yourself, but I thought it might be more reassuring to hear a sympathetic echo from an outsider. I need not tell you that I would be devastated were you to publicize this letter in any way (not that I write to you in secret, having already told Léon Daudet[7] of my intention to send you a note), but I know so little about this whole affair that it would be ludicrous of me to proffer my incompetent testimony when all I wanted, as a simple bystander, was to give you a sense of human solidarity.[8]

Kindly give my regards to Madame Berthelot, next to whom I was sitting at that same dinner at Madame Alphonse Daudet's almost three years ago, and accept my heartfelt sympathy.

Yours faithfully,
Marcel Proust

---

1. Philippe Berthelot (1866–1934), diplomat, until recently, chief adviser (*Secrétaire générale*) at the Quai d'Orsay.

2. See letter 168, n. 10.

3. Allusion to a scandal involving the Industrial Bank of China of which his brother was President. Berthelot, accused of nepotism, had been placed on the retired list for ten years.

4. Allusion to Camille Barrère (1851–1940), Ambassador of France. A regular guest of the Prousts at boulevard Malesherbes, he considered himself the model for M. de Norpois. See letter 236.

5. Proust cites Racine. 'Je te plains de tomber dans ses mains redoubtables', *Athalie*, Act II, scene v.

6. In fact, Berthelot was to be reinstated after three years.

7. This seems to imply that Daudet had campaigned against Berthelot.

8. This letter was never sent.

171   To Pierre-André May[1]

Paris, 26 March 1922

Dear friend,

I was just about to write to you; I meant to do so the day after you visited me here but have been constantly ill ever since. Much as I dislike sending you a typed letter, I can see that there's no help for it.

What I wanted to say to you was that, quite unintentionally, I was most inconsiderate in letting you return at nine o'clock at night for nothing. I had absolutely no idea that you were coming back, or I would have sent somebody to the rue de Phalsbourg to warn you that, for some time now, I haven't rung before one or two o'clock in the morning. Had she not gone out, my maid would have explained that to you, and prevented your return. The person you saw was her sister,[2] who was standing in for her and expected me to ring at about nine o'clock. I was vexed, having wanted to meet you.

The question of extracts seems to me to be fraught with difficulty. The whole of the first part has been published in *Les Œuvres libres*, and two long fragments have appeared in *La Nouvelle revue française*. Moreover, in the interests of the book (which has to be in the shops by 30 April, whatever happens), I feel that there should be something left unpublished for the reader. My main concern, however, is that the extract should be integral and meaningful. Provided that this presents no problem to you, which I trust will not be the case, I can suggest two fragments to you: either the scene in the brothel, but in its entirety, that is, from the newcomers' gaffe in taking it for an hotel and wanting to take up residence, Morel's visit there and subsequently to the Prince de Guermantes, where M. de Charlus's photograph stares at him from the chimney-piece;[3] or else another fragment which would consist of the whole of the end of the book, that is, from Albertine's return, when she talks to me about Mlle Vinteuil, right through to the end, without omitting a single word.[4] As I have refused them to everybody else, I trust that you will feel privileged rather than annoyed at being restricted to the choice of these two fragments, but only on the understanding that they are to be published in their entirety.

Yours sincerely,
Marcel Proust

1. Editor of *Intentions*, a new monthly magazine. May had asked for a pre-publication extract from *Sodom and Gomorrah* Part Two.
2. Marie Gineste: see letter 161, n. 8.
3. See IV, 551–8.
4. See IV, 594–615, the chapter ending with the words 'I absolutely must marry Albertine'. May was to publish it in the April issue of *Intentions*.

172 From André Gide

5 April 1922

My dear Proust,

I can't resist the pleasure of copying out for you these few lines from a letter I have just received from Curtius.[1]

'... I have been deeply moved, and also delighted, to receive a letter from M.P. that is marked by a charm, a grace, a goodwill and a sorrowful humanity (not to say tragedy) – impossible to describe. I always keep this letter on me, to re-read it, and to relive the joy it gave me. I haven't yet written to Proust to thank him, though I shall. Meanwhile, should you see him, kindly thank him on my behalf.'

And so I do – invisible friend – but by letter, alas. I often think that if you could imagine a fraction of the joy it would give me to receive a letter from you saying: 'come and see me on such-and-such a day'... then you would write me that letter, would have written it long ago. I always have a horror of intruding, on you above all, and you can be sure that I wouldn't dream of doing so, despite my longing to see you, unless you sent for me. But if I thought I shouldn't be a nuisance, I would come post haste.

Ever yours,
André Gide

1. See letter 164.

173 To Paul Souday

[Saturday 7 April 1922]

Dear Sir and friend,

Many apologies for the men-only dinner the other night.[1] I had understood that you were not free, and by the time I knew that you were, it was too late. A further reason for apology is this. As bad luck would have it, till now, on the rare occasions when you have been my guest, it has been within a fortnight of your having written an article on me, thus giving the dinner the air of a particularly stupid thanks-offering, since, by dining with my friends, you were making me a second present on top of the first. Now, this time, it's the reverse, and even more ridiculous. (When I saw you the day before yesterday, I hadn't corrected a single proof, and to tell the truth, I don't even know if there were proofs, for I believe that my publishers, realizing the task was beyond me, had had the book printed straight from the actual manuscript. Still, whereas I take a year, they took three weeks, and no doubt fearing to clash with political events,[2] they write to say that the book will already be out next week.) With the result that not only do books (*libelli*) have *sua fata*, but I, *Marcellus eris* (which I haven't been, having failed to cheat my cruel destiny),[3] am fated to have my invitations take on the air now of thanks-offerings to my critic, now of inducements to him. I'm proud to be a man-of-letters, but not to that extent. I would prefer it if our relations were man-to-man (as they are, in reality, but for the vexatiousness of what Jacques Blanche calls 'Dates'[4] making it appear otherwise), with agreeable ladies *sub rosa* and, except on days when, as on the day before yesterday, I am semi-apathetic, literary chit-chat.

Sincerely yours,
Marcel Proust

A thousand thanks, dear Sir, for your kind information. As for 'Sesame', there is absolutely no need to write for it again.

Ever yours,
Marcel Proust

1. A last-minute dinner which Proust had given at the Ritz on 5 April.

2. See Proust to Gallimard, early April, on the subject of the publication date for *Sodom and Gomorrah*: '[. . .] our correspondence is plagued by politics, not only do you want to go to Genoa, you want to revise our treaty. [. . .] But before 1 May, all eyes will be on the Genoa Conference.[. . .].' Allusion to the European Economic Conference, 10 April – 19 May: see letter 178.

3 See letter 93 to Souday.

4 Allusion to the title of Blanche's book: see letter 92.

174 To Sydney Schiff

[7 to 8 April 1922]

Dear friend,

You'll see the full tragedy of it, as the German critic Curtius says of my predicament.[1] Your letter said: 'We're here.' I took here to mean 'arrived in Paris'. Despite being very feverish, I immediately began a course of injections so that I could get up and go to the Ritz, where you had told me you would be staying. I didn't want the bother of dressing for dinner, so I took a room where, I thought, we could meet, Room 12, to be precise, which had been taken by new arrivals from 7 a.m. on Saturday but left me the whole of Friday evening to see you before returning to my bed at rue Hamelin. I arrive at the Ritz to find no Ellès,[2] and no Olivier, whose day off it is. I go up to my No. 12 and ask the floorwaiter to find out which suite is occupied by Monsieur and Madame Sydney Schiff. Half an hour later, he returns: 'M. Schiff has arrived, without his wife.' Somewhat surprised, I send him back downstairs, where a commissionaire is in charge, the concierge being ill (the Ritz is a desert without oasis[3] at present, the staff useless). I begin to be consumed by anxiety and foreboding. At last, the waiter comes back: 'Yes, Monsieur Schiff is here, M. Mortimer Schiff.' But not, alas, my dear (forgive the familiarity) Sydney Schiff. Soon afterwards, I leave and return home. There, I re-examine your letter and notice that the envelope is stamped Restaurant Foyot. Even if I had noticed it in the first place, I would probably have assumed (your 'We shall be at the Ritz' was so definite) that you had written from Foyot's but were staying at the Ritz. (Moreover, Olivier kept telling me that you were 'expected'.) But there was no point in my wondering whether or not I would have taken the address to mean Foyot's the refreshment-stop on the way to the Luxembourg

Gardens, or the hotel, for I hadn't looked at the envelope. On the one hand, I open my post, if at all, with my eyes closed, because I've been in the state of torpor from which my injections wrenched me for a few hours this evening for some time, and on the other, I avoid touching the envelopes, because the concierge's daughter has either measles or whooping-cough. If I managed to find yours with Foyot on it just now, it's because, this very day, we have acquired a box of Formol[4] into which all my letters are plunged for two hours at a time, and yours was among those taking a dip. Alas, if only Foyot's doubly prestigious name, which evokes memories of the delicious luncheons I had there in my youth, when I was sitting the Concours Général,[5] or my exams for the licence,[6] were a good omen. I hardly dare believe it. Firstly, how soon can I get up again after tonight's vain outing at the Ritz! A week's rest is the minimum required, always supposing things go well, which looks unlikely (Céleste is talking to me, causing my writing to change the last line, not my thought). And will I be able to restart my injections in a week's time? Secondly, it's always very late by the time I arrive (if I see M. Ellès, and say: 'What are you doing up so late?', he always replies: 'But it's very early for you'). Now, I fear that Foyot's, delightful though it is, and infinitely superior to the Ritz, is too 'sleepy' to open up for me late at night. Perhaps you could very kindly find out when they close.

I'm taking advantage of your arrival in Paris to write and shake up the *NRF*, for Jacques Rivière had still not discussed the matter of Sydney Schiff, and has used that as a pretext for hanging on to my copy since the moment I received it.[7] They have just done the dirty on me for the twentieth time, which is why I hope that, on the twenty-first, they'll jump at the opportunity not to please me but to come clean. In any case, my letter will force them to make up their minds.

Have you read Curtius's fine essay on me in the Munich *Neue Merkur*? Not only that, Gide has received a letter from him about me which he copied out for me (it's because Curtius applied the word tragedy to my life that I cited him at the beginning of this letter). And awaiting me, bathed in Formol, is a letter from Curtius himself which I have yet to read. I still haven't managed to write to M. Middleton Murry.[8] In any case, I can't write letters any more unless I dictate to my typist (Céleste's niece). But I didn't like to do so with you.

Dear friend (who said he wasn't coming before May, otherwise

I would have started my treatment earlier), I still have a thousand things to say to you. But let one suffice, fatigue overcoming me. Don't mention my state of health to Ellès, Olivier etc. I dislike people feeling sorry for me, and you are the only one, or almost the only one, to whom I confide such things. And even then I probably wouldn't do so if I didn't want you to know that, but for my terrible state, my affection for you would often bring me to London to spend the day with you. But in general I dislike talking about my health.

> 'To pray, to weep, to moan, all are craven,
> Stick bravely to thy short and heavy task,
> Then, like me, suffer and die in silence.'[9]

Dear friend, kindly give Madame Schiff my warmest regards, and share with her my grateful admiration.

Your loving friend,
Marcel Proust

1. See letter 172 from André Gide.
2. Henry Ellès, manager of the Ritz.
3. Allusion to a line from Baudelaire's 'Le Voyage': 'Une oasis d'horreur dans un désert d'ennui'.
4. Brand name for a powerful disinfectant containing formalin. See Albaret, *op. cit.*, 341.
5. A prestigious examination, by invitation only, for pupils selected from Lycées throughout France. Proust was invited to sit his, in history, in 1887.
6. In 1892 and 1893.
7. Proust had undertaken to ask Rivière to read Schiff's novel *Elinor Culhouse* (written under his penname Stephen Hudson), with a view to serialization.
8. Schiff had put Proust in touch with the English critic and editor John Middleton Murry: see letter 182.
9. 'Prier, pleurer, gémir, est également lâche, / Fais régulièrement ta courte et lourde tâche, / Puis après, comme moi, souffre et meurs sans parler.' Alfred de Vigny, 'La Mort du loup'.

175 To André Gide

44 rue Hamelin
11 April 1922

Dear friend,

I was very moved by your thoughtfulness, and your letter[1] afforded me much pleasure, to give that word the meaning it once held for me when I knew what it was to be happy, or at least to suffer less. You say that I cannot imagine the joy it would give you (you are far too kind and generous) to see me again etc.... You should rather imagine the immense joy it would give me to see you, reminding yourself that if I denied myself this joy, it could only be that I found myself up against a physical impossibility.[2] Suffice it to say that I haven't spent so much as an hour out of bed for seven months. True, there were moments even so, once a month, say, when I could receive a friend at my bedside. And, when I did so, it wasn't always to see my dearest friends, but those whom I knew I could reach, in the unexpected event of a brief remission lasting a few hours at most, either by telephone or by some other means. Alas, you are not among them, to judge by your letter (marked by an exquisite goodness of heart in which I felt I could recognize the noblest side to your charm), for you not only omit to give me a time, or any other practical detail that might help bring about the meeting I so greatly desire, you go so far as to leave off your address, so that even if I did feel better one evening I wouldn't know where to send for you. Last time we met – an epoch-making event in the sad emptiness of my daily life – you were about to move. But where to? You never said. As for talking of *intrusion*, that is a cruel word, for it seems to suggest that I don't know what I'm missing through being in this dreadful state. I shall have lived through the same epoch as you, and, except for a look, a smile, a word, well-remembered but too infrequent, all I shall have known of you is your books. It's already enormous; but not being everything, it's not enough. (À propos, since we owe the truth we hold dear to Plato,[3] I felt that you were very patronizing towards Wilde.[4] I don't much admire him. But I don't understand reticence and harsh words towards a person who is down on his luck.)

Dear friend, I'm able to write to you only thanks to an injection, the effects of which are now wearing off (I didn't like to dictate to my typist), leaving me without the strength to talk about the real reason for this letter, namely, M. Curtius. It is he, not I, who deserves to hear the things he says about my letter of thanks, for I found his letter to you moving and delightful[5] (and what delicacy it gains, superimposed on yours, when transcribed by you with such exquisite thoughtfulness!). But I'm ashamed that he should find my letter adequate. I was too ill to say any of the things on my mind (and mean to write to him). It was a torture for me to write those stupid words, yet I wrote them nevertheless, as a temporary measure, not knowing when I would be well enough to thank him properly. And yet he doesn't think the worse of me for that; he guesses; he understands; how kind and good he is!

Affectionately,
Marcel Proust

Forgive these torn pages which, alas, will have obliged you to follow the numbering.

1. See letter 172.
2. The Duchesse de Guermantes's favourite excuse: see IV, 189.
3. Allusion to the proverb 'Amicus Plato, sed magis amica veritas' ('Plato is dear to me but dearer still is truth'). Cf. *AS-B*, 157. Proust also alludes to Gide's reproaches of hypocrisy at their last meeting: see letter 110.
4. Allusion to an anecdote about the last meeting between Gide and Wilde in *In Memoriam: Oscar Wilde*, the memoir Gide published after Wilde's death.
5. Proust cites Curtius: see letter 172.

176 To Émile Henriot[1]

[Thursday 13 April 1922]

Dear Sir,

I've just been very seriously ill (on top of my habitual state of ill-health). Thus, it being very difficult for me to write letters or receive visitors (to give one example among thousands), you'll see that I'm the only writer in M. Lang's book[2] not to have sat for his portrait because I was unable to receive the artist. That doesn't mean I wouldn't make a greater effort for you. Beginning with this note: I feared that you might find a letter dictated to my typist too impersonal. Still, I must get up for an injection one of these days. On that day, having had you telephoned earlier in the evening, I could join you for a meal that would qualify as my dinner and your supper (for I expect you'll have dined long before), around midnight, in a room at the Ritz. Since I prefer not to show myself in the Ritz dining-room nowadays (for fear of draughts and invitations, and also because of the lateness of the hour), it's true that, room for room, you could equally well dine at my bedside. But at the moment I live in a veritable hovel, 44 rue Hamelin, and I'm afraid lest you, who notice external things (which doesn't prevent you from delving into things of the mind), might be repelled by the ugliness of the only rooms I could find. The Ritz is hideous, but in a different way, and at least doesn't pretend to be anybody's 'home'. My friend Guiche says that it's 'almost as ugly as Vallières' (V. being the château belonging to his father, the Duc de Gramont). It all depends on whether you're in a hurry for the information you require for the article you mention.[3] If so, perhaps it would make sense for me to give it to you in a letter, and for us to meet later, in rather less inhuman circumstances. I only wish I had at my disposal the study in which the distinguished mathematician M. Vettard makes a link – as often happens in England and America – between my way of seeing Time, volume etc., and Einstein's. On the other hand, if you read German, I could send you the remarkable essay by Curtius that was published in Munich. Come to that, why don't I give you the details you ask for in a few words, while I'm about it. The book is entitled *Sodome et Gomorrhe II* (I wished to shelter my somewhat explicit portrayal of certain traits beneath the chaste Vigny's couplet from *La Colère de Samson*: 'Woman will have Gomorrah and Man will have Sodom etc.'). But in actual fact, this particular part (to come out in three volumes) (or this particular volume, to come out in three parts: I don't know the exact terminology) is mainly about my love for Albertine, one of the *Jeunes filles en fleurs*, and the book ends with a desolate dawn and a jealous scene, just as I'm about to take her to Paris and make her my wife. That is the part (*Sodome et Gomorrhe II* in three volumes) to come out in two weeks' time (April 30). Next year, *Sodome et Gomorrhe III* will tell the story of my life with Albertine and the outcome of my projects for marriage. M. de Charlus will reappear often in the present book, and so too, Einsteinian or not, will studies of sleep, and of dreams. And the Verdurins at Balbec, the Princesse de Guermantes etc.[4]

Only none of this (which you're welcome to use or not as you please, I don't know why it is that I always write to you when I never write to anybody) gets us any further with the vital question of how we are to meet and get to know one another. I can't visualize you at all. True, there are some privations I have to accept, having cut myself off from humanity for so long. As the Duc de Luynes wrote to me the other day: 'You have built a veritable fortress around yourself, and you never lower the drawbridge for me.'[5] (On no account put that in your article!)

Very sincerely yours,
Marcel Proust

I'm often haunted by the scene of possessiveness that you describe so well.[6]

I've come to feel a strong sympathy with you through your writings. I believe that you are a close friend of Jean-Louis Vaudoyer, whom I like immensely. Perhaps we could all meet, when I'm better. It's been an age since I heard from him.

1. See letter 81.
2. The book of André Lang's collection of interviews, illustrated by Don, for *Les Annales politiques et littéraires*: see letter 134, n. 1.
3. Henriot had requested an interview on the progress of Proust's novel.
4. As ever, Proust was in the throes of drastic revision: see Tadié, *op. cit.*, 886. Part Three of *Sodom and Gomorrah*, later entitled *The Captive*, was to be published posthumously, in two volumes, in November 1923.
5. Cf. letter 167.
6. Allusion to a scene in Henriot's recent novel, *Les Temps innocents*. His article was to be published after Proust's death, in *Le Temps* of 19 December.

177 *To Madame Maurice Pouquet*[1]

44 rue Hamelin
[Wednesday 19 April 1922]

Dear Madame,

No, I don't have a friend with me, and in any case wouldn't have been well enough to receive one. True, I have a typist (my maid's niece) whom I never see, being too ill, but as she lives here and never goes out, I could have dictated this note to her tonight, which would have tired me less than writing.[2] But even though you seem to give me leave, I don't like to write to you by machine, and will summon the young woman who knows how to use it only if my strength lets me down. Forgive my talking so much about myself, but I wanted to explain (in confidence, as I dislike talking about my health) why I hadn't written to you before this.

No, I didn't know Gaston[3] at school. He may have attended the same lycée as me (Condorcet), but it wasn't there that I met him. I no longer know who introduced me to Gaston's mother,[4] but I remember that I was about to do my military service, which I did very young, it being the last so-called voluntary year.[5] I don't know if the same applied to Gaston. In any case, he was about to finish just as I was starting, and, during my brief 'leaves', I would catch sight of him in his mother's salon. But he was so sweet to me that we immediately made friends. I would dearly like to know whether, in some depository or other where my belongings are in store, there are not some of his letters to me, dating from that period (1889, I believe) when he scarcely knew me. His letters were not only admirable in sentiment, he took great pains with their composition, having at the time a respect for my 'intelligence' which I didn't deserve. A page on the science of numbers in music[6] (and possibly somewhat inspired by M. France)[7] particularly impressed me. For a long time, he kept up this friendship thus born out of correspondence with a sweetness, an infinite kindness, that I shall never forget. There were no such things as taxis in those days, and it's amazing to think that every Sunday, when I had to catch the 7.40 train back to Orléans, he came to drive me to the station. For him, it meant leaving before seven and not getting back before half-past eight, in other words, missing dinner. Once, he even came to Orléans.[8] One's heart melts at such memories; how can one relive them without weeping? He was all the more admirable for persevering with our friendship because, at least for a time, I was loathed by nearly all his comrades. A certain Lévi-Alvarès wouldn't even speak to me, nor would Grunebaum (avenue de Messina). Whereas the other Grunebaum (Paul) was very nice to me, but it didn't last. Louis de Koenigswarter and Fernand Prévost were decent enough, and so was a certain Schuhmann, and a future theatre-director whose name escapes me (he married Mlle de Soria).[9] When I saw him at Cabourg a few years ago (probably the year before the war), I was very touched by the way he spoke of Gaston. This man (I think his name is Franck), physically rather unattractive but certainly good-hearted, behaved very well towards Gaston, even better, perhaps, than Gaston knew. Being immensely fond of Gaston, I talked of nobody else in the barracks, until my batman, the corporal etc., seeing him as a sort of god, sent him a respectful address for the New Year. Goodness knows what it said! This was before Gaston met Robert de Flers, and he took rather a dim view of my affection for his future collaborator. My friendship for Gaston had an unexpected effect on me about this time. Acting as a sort of vaccine, it immunized me against the unbearable pangs I suffered for the love of Mademoiselle Pouquet. Knowing them to be practically engaged, I couldn't allow myself to hope. You may have been less beautiful than you are now but you were completely different, you were limpid as a spring. I can feel myself becoming over-tired, I must break off this letter, kindly remember me to Monsieur Pouquet, whom I only glimpsed at your dear Mother's[10] in those days at the rue de Miromesnil. He gave me the impression of being extremely nice, but he won't remember me, for I hardly saw him.

With my deepest respects,
Marcel Proust

1. *Née* Jeanne Pouquet (1874–1961), the other 'great love' of Proust's youth who modelled for the Gilberte of the Champs-Élysées: see letter 18, and its n. 27. In 1919, as a widow, she had married her cousin, Maurice Pouquet.

2. Mme Pouquet had written, out of the blue, to ask for Proust's recollections of her former husband as she was writing a memoir of his mother (see following notes), suggesting that he could dictate them to a friend or a secretary.

3. Gaston de Caillavet (1869–1915), writer of light comedies, notably in collaboration with Robert de Flers. After his marriage to Jeanne Pouquet in 1893, they had a daughter, Simone, who was also shortly to reappear in Proust's life: see letter 247, n. 6.

4. Mme Armand de Caillavet, *née* Léontine Lippmann (1844–1910), a renowned hostess and an early model for Mme Verdurin.

5. See letter 35, n. 14.

6. The theory of numbers and proportion, usually associated in music with Debussy. Baudelaire had remarked: 'les notes musicales sont les nombres' in his essay 'Du vin et du haschich', *Les Paradis artificiels* (1851).

7. Anatole France was the 'lion' of Mme Armand de Caillavet's salon.

8. In fact, both Gaston and Jeanne, when secretly engaged, visited Proust at Orléans: see Tadié, *op. cit.*, 131–2.

9. Her husband, Franck de Soria, like Paul Grunebaum, was an early collaborator of Gaston de Caillavet.

10. Mme Eugène Pouquet, *née* Marie Rousseau.

178 **To Robert de Flers**

[Saturday 29 April 1922]

My dear Robert,

Heartfelt thanks for the way in which you presented an extract from my book in the *Figaro*,[1] it was extremely nice of you. I don't know what made Gallimard choose that meaningless passage[2] (about Mme Jacques de Waru[3] and Mme Legrand[4] combined). But your little preamble made me literally overflow with gratitude and affection. I express the one and the other to you without delay, despite not having been in a fit state to write for the past four days. But to delay thanking you *after*, when I had written to you at such length *before*,[5] would be a moral agony for me. Not only that, you are unaware of the terrible vagaries in my health; and just when my heart is so full of you, you might convict me wrongly of ingratitude. I well know from my regular reading of the *Figaro* how easy it is to reach the wrong conclusion through being kept in ignorance of fresh developments in a case under review. I much enjoy Capus's[6] articles, in which, it seems, things are seen clearly and in depth, as within the sharp, decided contours of a piece of rock-crystal. Except that, he having demonstrated on the front page, *more geometrorum*,[7] why the Bar-le-Duc speech has cleared the air and reconciled Mr Lloyd George to us once and for all, we learn from the Stop Press in the same issue that this very minister rudely dismissed M. Poincaré's speech and nearly came to blows with M. Barthou.[8] Unfortunately, the beautiful rock crystal can no more change its lines than can the immutable dry-points of M. Helleu, whom you don't want to see retrace my features.[9] And a different clear-cut, deeply faulted mineral must be found for the morrow. Which isn't to say that another can do better than Capus, but that perhaps events, especially current events, above all when distant, with Genoese complications,[10] don't lend themselves to being reduced to the translucent beauty of a decisive art-form with finite lines. And in this nonconformity between the facts and the editor's pellucid 'copy', it is the facts, in my opinion, which are at a disadvantage. I don't want that to happen to me, and for you to make sweeping judgements without taking into consideration the unravelling of a state of health which, like the Conference, worsens daily. That's why, though incapable of writing, I wrote to you without delay.

I wish I saw more of you. Having been proved right, down to the last detail, in everything I wrote to poor Deschanel,[11] I could have done you a living portrait of this man now, alas, dead. I'll send you my book as soon as Gallimard deigns to 'release' it. Not that I wouldn't willingly buy you a copy. But I prefer you to have a special edition.

With my deepest affection and gratitude,
Marcel Proust

1. To coincide with the publication of *Sodom and Gomorrah* Part Two, Gallimard had placed a short extract in the *Figaro*, choosing it himself as Proust had failed to read his letters on the subject. See *MP–GG*, 506–7.

2. The comedy resulting from the ambiguous social position of the Princesse d'Orvilliers: IV, 139–40.

3. Comtesse Jacques de Waru, like Proust's Princesse d'Orvilliers, was said to be the natural daughter of the Duke of Parma.

4. A model for Proust's absurdly snobbish Blanche Leroi.

5. Proust is embarrassed because, a few days earlier, he had written to Flers complaining about problems with his subscription to the *Figaro*.

6. Alfred Capus (1857–1922), right-wing political columnist.

7. Allusion to the geometrical method adopted by Spinoza, notably in *Renati Des Cartes Principiorum Philosophiae Pars I et II. More geometrico demonstratae.*

8. In a 'keynote' speech, the incoming prime minister, Raymond Poincaré (soon to preside over the occupation of the Rhineland) stated France's new hard-line policy towards German reparations, thus pre-empting discussions to be held at the European Economic Conference: see note 10. As the minister accompanying Poincaré, Louis Barthou had the job of pacifying Lloyd George.

9. Paul Helleu was to draw Proust's death mask. Cf. letter 163. See also Proust's mention of his *Figaro* obituary: letter 268.

10. Allusion to the current international conference at Genoa set up by Lloyd George and the outgoing French prime minister, Aristide Briand, to discuss post-war economic problems in Europe.

11. Paul Deschanel (1855–1922), elected President of France in 1920 on a wave of dissatisfaction with the Treaty of Versailles. In *Time Regained*, Proust refers to the symptoms that led up to his unexpected death: VI, 354–5.

179 To François Mauriac

[End April or early May 1922]

Dear François,

With what admiration and gratitude (above all, admiration) I was going to write to you! But I was dead. And, Lazarus-like, I arise *de profundis* still swaddled in my grave-clothes. I hope to see you soon. I couldn't write to Jammes about a single one of his books, and you know how much he means to me. I shall try and send him this book of mine.[1] But life returns only drop by drop.

Your friend,
Marcel Proust

1. This letter accompanied a complimentary copy of *Sodom and Gomorrah* Part Two.

180 To Binet-Valmer

[Tuesday 1 May 1922]

Dear friend,

I apologize for having obliged you to answer me, since letter-writing tires you. And please don't hesitate to use the machine whenever you need to write to me. I find it only natural! I merely read something into your letter that wasn't there. Now that you mention it, I'm certain that I missed the Martel incident,[1] for I couldn't have forgotten anything so extraordinary. But I can go for weeks without opening a newspaper. Alas, one can be an intermittent observer, however meticulous. (I object to meticulous, by the way. If you're thinking of my books, all I seek to do in them is to bring out very general laws. But a universe that one is trying to observe, if very distant, may be no more than a pinprick of light. Therein lies the essence of astronomy, and its task has nothing to do with 'nit-picking' or 'hair-splitting'. But I'm a fool to talk about myself like this. And one cannot be a judge of oneself. If I give the impression of observing minutiae rather than of bringing the obscure into the light, then it's for want of skill. Intentions are not what count in art. If, on the other hand, by meticulous you mean my having remarked that your letter wasn't hand-written, that wasn't meticulousness but a friend's protective solicitude.)

A pile of volumes arrived just now. Copies of my book, believe it or not.[2] My publishers doubtless have the best of intentions. But to mean well is not enough in their case either, and their negligence depresses me. And then, when I complain, they say I'm never satisfied, and that I make their lives a misery. Added to which, by implication, though unwittingly, I made some very strict vows.[3] To have given Duvernois the occasional unpublished episode would have made my life easier financially, and wouldn't have required any effort on my part. But for me to write for *Les Œuvres libres* would drive the N.R.F. to despair. And I don't wish to drive anybody to despair. I greatly envy you your good work (the Legion)[4] and the fact that you are rewarded by so much love. I believe my old regiment had something of the kind. I was so well-liked, and felt that I could be so useful, that when the time came I didn't want to leave. Nothing could be less like my situation. Not that I lead a selfish life, but my activity, being immobile, secretive, unseen, is not, like yours, rewarded with all those hearts which belong to you.

I'm glad that it didn't come to a duel between you and Thierry de Martel,[5] whom I remember, twenty-five years ago, as a charming man. My real friend was his brother Aymar, the incarnation of gallantry, candour and loyalty. He was killed very young, in the colonies. Though still a child, he was truly a man. When I compare him to some of the people I've fought, like Lorrain! I was barely twenty years old, and found it a huge joke. And I still can't help laughing, despite my respect for a noble memory, when I think of Paul Adam,[6] Lorrain's second, overcome with emotion, giving way to hysterics.

I'm boring you, my friend, in my delight at having an hour's lucidity in which to chat to you after the pleasure of your letter.

Your admiring friend,
Marcel Proust

1. 'The Vicomtesse de Martel wasn't attacking you, she was covering you with praises [...] while insulting me (*Comœdia*, *Le Gaulois*) to the point where I had to send my seconds to call on Thierry Martel. The result was a police inquiry which was widely reported and couldn't have escaped the notice of so meticulous an observer as you.' Binet-Valmer, 30 April. Allusion to a row in the press about the reputation of certain French novelists; Mme de Martel, in her *alter ego* as the

fiercely nationalistic satirist 'Gyp', had referred to Binet-Valmer, who was Swiss, as 'a foreigner who writes kitchen French'.

2. Gallimard seems to have delayed sending out complimentary copies of *Sodom and Gomorrah* Part Two.

3. See p.s. to letter 131 to Gallimard.

4. French equivalent of the British Legion.

5. See note 1. Thierry de Martel's seconds were obliged to insert an apology in *Comœdia*: 'MM. Maurice Barrès and Jean-Louis Faure are pleased to acknowledge the ancient French origins of M. Binet-Valmer's family, and congratulate themselves on the happy conclusion to an incident between two Frenchmen both of whom fought with distinction in the war [. . .].'

6. Paul Adam (1862–1920), well-known novelist of the day.

181   To Henri Bergson

[Early May 1922]

To Monsieur Henri Bergson[1]

To the first great metaphysician since Leibnitz (and greater still). His creative system may evolve but will always bear the name of Bergson.

A loving and grateful admirer asks pardon for having been spoken of, without rhyme or reason, as the author of 'Bergsonian novels' etc. But all newly-minted coinage is stamped with the effigy of the indisputable reigning monarch.[2]

Kindly give her cousin's humble respects to Madame Bergson.[3]

Marcel Proust

1. This letter accompanied a first edition of *Sodom and Gomorrah* Part Two.

2. Proust used this image in an article on Ruskin, written in 1900, soon after the critic's death. See *AS-B*, 182.

3. *Née* Louise Neuburger, Proust's mother's first cousin.

182 To John Middleton Murry[1]

[Early May 1922]

To Monsieur J. Middleton Murry

In admiring and grateful homage, from a writer whom you have always protected and supported, and who wishes he had an hour's good health in which to thank you less briefly.

Marcel Proust

I send this book[2] to the address supplied by our mutual friend Sydney Schiff.[3]

1. John Middleton Murry (1889–1957), writer and critic; from 1919 to 1922, editor of *The Athenaeum*, where Proust had been favourably reviewed.
2. This letter accompanied a complimentary copy of *Sodom and Gomorrah* Part Two.
3. Schiff had sent Proust advance proofs of Murry's article 'Marcel Proust. A new sensibility', to be published in *The Quarterly Review* in July.

183 From François Mauriac

[Early May 1922]

Dear friend,

I use this little card so as not to have to write to you at length about your book. *My immense admiration* you already know. But it makes very painful reading ... Your accursed cities lack the ten righteous men; admittedly, the Lord failed to find them there....[1] For want of these ten righteous men, your book suffers from a lack of proportion; one feels that Sodom and Gomorrah have become merged with the Universe. *A single saintly figure* would have put everything to rights. Also, I prefer the allusiveness of the portrait of Charlus in *Jeunes filles en fleurs* (cab episode).[2]

But where that's concerned, I must admit that your Sodomite is as they say 'telling': living, terrible, eternal. I admire you more than any of my contemporaries, but as to the *choice of subject* in your work, much remains to be be said ...

Do we choose our subjects?
Have you read *Le Baiser au lépreux*?³
My dear friend, I shake your hand and wish you were better.

Your
M.

1. See Genesis, XVIII, 32.
2. In fact, in *The Guermantes Way*: see letter 161, n. 6.
3. Mauriac's latest novel.

184 To Gaston Gallimard

[Wednesday 3 May 1922]

My dear Gaston,

You must admit that I have no luck; yesterday, apart from all my other medicaments, I accidentally swallowed, undiluted, a very dangerous drug that burnt my gullet like vitriol,¹ causing me three hours of real torture. And although not nearly as bad as it was, the pain is such that I can neither eat nor drink, and my stomach will have to be 'plastered' to seal the ulcerations.

I dislike talking about my health, but I wanted to tell you so that, given my enfeebled state, you will forgive me for being a little slow.

In the enclosed April issue, I've marked the place where, despite your refusal to believe me, 'À ne pas laisser lire aux jeunes filles',² or something like that, occurs beneath Clauzel's review of Morand. While bearing in mind what you tell me, I shall write to M. Martin du Gard.³ I won't say anything you wouldn't say. But it's too tiring to explain in a letter. When I'm not quite so weak, I'll tell you why I think the Boulengers (particularly Marcel) are a bad choice for the *Figaro* article. On the other hand, I think that somebody like Schlumberger⁴ would do it very well. If you see M. Malexis,⁵ apologize to him for me, and tell him what happened to me. His copy is ready for him, dedicated and packaged, but since yesterday I haven't been able to be left, and my new books are still in my room, waiting to be sent off. I expect to get them off any minute. Does publicity material inserted by hand, whatever you call it, have the slightest value?⁶ Why does the card, for which a thousand thanks, have *Swan* in capital letters (with one 'n')? The N.R.F. are the last people who should make a mistake like that.

My dear Gaston, I feel my strength deserting me, like Phèdre,[7] and can say no more than all my love,

Marcel Proust

If you happen to know M. Robert Kemp,[8] tell him that but for my condition I would have thanked him for what was certainly a very well-intentioned article (though dreadful, between ourselves).[9]

1. Proust had swallowed undiluted adrenalin. This was his second accidental overdose of a drug: see letter 133.
2. 'Unsuitable for young girls', an advertisement that Gallimard had placed in *Ève* for Morand's last book, *Ouvert la nuit*. He was to place the same advertisement to coincide with a review of *Sodom and Gomorrah* in *Ève* of 28 May.
3. Maurice Martin du Gard: see letter 156. In July 1921, his magazine *Les Écrits nouveaux* had published a venomous review of *The Guermantes Way* in which the reviewer had called Proust 'an elderly governness to the aristocracy who has become the valet's mistress'. Proust was to decide against writing a letter, although he feared the same fate for *Sodom and Gomorrah*.
4. Jean Schlumberger (1877–1968), novelist and critic, co-founder of the *NRF*.
5. Charles Malexis, deputy editor of *Ève*.
6. Gallimard had sent Proust a package of publicity material, including a card listed as 'une prière d'insérer'. See *MP–GG*, 515.
7. *Phèdre*, Act I, scene 3: 'Je ne me souteins plus; ma force m'abandonne'.
8. Robert Kemp (1879–1959), critic and essayist.
9. In *La Liberté* of 8 May, Kemp hints at the length and difficulty of Proust's work, announcing his intention of reading him only after having caught up on all the passages he had skipped in Thomas Aquinas, Montaigne, Plato etc.

185 To Roger Allard

44 rue Hamelin
[Shortly before 8 May 1922]

Dear Sir and friend,

My heartfelt thanks for the fine article you have devoted to me, it is far too kind.[1] What you say about the flowers which blunt the point of too sharp a thought is ravishing, and very true.[2] I dare not hope that somebody who sees and judges so many *painted* scenes as part of his unique and illimitable labours,³ could have given a moment's thought to the scenes of the sea, and above all, to the sky resembling a tank in a white-walled courtyard,⁴ with which I have varied this book here and there. But they vindicate what you say.⁵

I am not of the opinion that homosexuality, at least in our time (in Plato's time, it was a matter of conforming to custom, and a 'gynophile' of those days took a 'lover' out of philosophical snobbery, as a homosexual keeps a dancer today, as 'the pious man will be an atheist under an atheist prince'⁶), is not a perversion. A perversion compensated for by superior gifts.⁷ The most one can say is that, in these volumes, the question of morality doesn't seem to apply to this wholly neurotic perversion.⁸ But in future volumes there will be no more such partitioning-off of morality.

When Jacques Rivière brought up your name as a critic who might review *Sodom II*, I objected out of tact. I remembered your review of *Sodome I*⁹ too well not to feel that to trouble you a second time would be an imposition. You have very kindly implied that you didn't find it so. Thus there is nothing to cloud the honour and pleasure you have done me.

Believe me, your grateful friend,
Marcel Proust

As for what constitutes inversion, I would formulate it like this: 'Homosexuality is the illusory, aesthetic, theoretical aspect under which inversion appears to itself, and chooses so to consider itself.'

P.S. (after page 4). I keep re-opening this letter, but it behoves a grateful author to be thorough, as critics so seldom are. That being so, I forgot to tell you how very much I enjoyed your passages on M. de Charlus's comicality,¹⁰ and Albertine's telephone call.¹¹ But I'm too tired to go into it.

---

1. Proust had received an advance proof of Allard's review of *Sodom and Gomorrah* Part Two.

2. 'What underlies the tolerance one senses in M. Marcel Proust is not scepticism, but rather a reflection of the moralist's private satisfaction at having the safety of his diagnosis confirmed. [. . .] In this respect, nothing is more revealing than the graceful strokes of the pen, like flowers, with which M. Proust chooses to blunt the point of too sharp a thought.' Roger Allard, *NRF*, 1 June.

3. Allard also wrote art criticism.

4. See IV, 454–5: 'Maman's bathroom, festooned by the sun with a dazzling,

Moorish whiteness, appeared to be sunk at the bottom of a well, because of the four plastered walls on which it looked out, while far above, in the square gap, the sky, whose fleecy white waves could be seen gliding past, one above the other, seemed (because of the longing that one felt) like a tank filled with blue water [...].'

5. 'Everything that Proust paints, everything that he says, is seen as it were reflected in the eyes of his characters. Sites or faces, they are not described, they are revealed.' Allard, *loc. cit.*

6. Proust cites La Bruyère in *Caractères*, XIII, as he does in the very similar passage in *The Captive*: 'he [Brichot] did not understand that in their day to love a young man was the equivalent (Socrates's jokes reveal this more clearly than Plato's theories) of keeping a dancing girl before getting engaged to be married in ours. M. de Charlus [...] refused to see that for nineteen hundred years ("a pious courtier under a pious prince would have been an atheist under an atheist prince," as La Bruyère reminds us) all conventional homosexuality [...] has disappeared' (V, 229).

7. See M. de Charlus's surprising gifts as a pianist: IV, 407–8.

8. See note 2. See also Proust's allusion to Mauriac's review in letter 98.

9. See letter 127.

10. Allard writes that Proust's care in making M. de Charlus seem somehow lovable is comparable to that which Molière takes with the character of Alceste in *Le Misanthrope*.

11. According to Allard, nothing in earlier psychological novels – such as Constant's *Adolphe* or Fromentin's *Dominique* – is as fine as the passage where Albertine's voice blends, over the telephone, with the sounds of her surroundings. See IV, 151–2.

186 From Madame Straus

Saturday 13 May [1922]

My little Marcel, so very dear,

Setting aside all notion of fatigue, at least for a few moments, I must tell you about a phenomenon which occurs every time that I receive one of your books.

It goes like this:

I pick up the book, I cut the pages, and I say to myself: I'll just read for a quarter of an hour, and the quarter hour duly passes ... I read ... I read on and on. Dinner is announced, I say: 'I'm coming' ... and then continue with my reading. The servant returns, hesitant, and stands there ... finally, embarrassed by his reproachful presence, I go downstairs. After dinner, we go back upstairs and, surreptitiously, with a nonchalant air, I edge the precious book towards me ... and there I am, absorbed in my reading once again, until there comes a moment when the intemperate lawyer[1] you know so well cries out, with a vehemence that you will also recognize: 'But it's insufferable, the woman never stops reading, she reads and reads, morning, noon and night!'

This little scene from my life for the past two days will be more telling than all the compliments in the world, and also serve as my excuse for not having thanked you sooner for sending me those precious three volumes of the last *Sodom et Gomorrhe*. Today, I have time to do so because I'm alone and have decided not to go out, a sensible decision in any case, for I didn't sleep last night and am feeling very ill. *But that's not the real reason.* The real reason is that I want to go on with the end of Book II and start on Book III ... perhaps even finish it – with regret.

Marcel, my little Marcel, how I long to see you! We have so many things to talk about! But that would be at once too gay ... and too sad, for it seems to me that it will never happen again. Never! what a cruel word! I don't want to get used to the idea that I shall never see you again; however, I take a little hope from the lovely Céleste, who tells me that you might come one day before I leave for Versailles (early in June, if the weather is fine).[2]

Au revoir, my dear little Marcel; I can't bring myself to say goodbye. I'm very sorry to hear that you are still unwell. Anyhow, I'm following your example, which is as it should be.

Thank you again for the immense joy you have given me. I love you tenderly.

Your old and faithful friend,
Geneviève H.S.[3]

Hermant[4] isn't yet back in Paris; he should be here tomorrow or the day after.

Thank you for remembering the words from *La Juive* so well.[5] I am touched.

The number of questions I have for you about your books! but we should talk, not write.

1. Her husband, Émile Straus.
2. They were never to meet again; she was to outlive Proust by almost four years.
3. The initials stand for Halévy Straus.

4. Abel Hermant: see letter 17, n. 11. Proust wanted to know where he should send him a complimentary copy of his book.

5. Allusion to a passage near the end of *Sodom and Gomorrah* Part Two, where Nissim Bernard's amorous adventures in the Grand Hotel put the narrator in mind of Fromental Halévy's opera: IV, 282. See letter 26, n. 5.

187 *To Paul Souday*

[Around mid-May 1922]

Dear Sir and friend,

I don't know if you heard about the accident[1] that has prevented me from thanking you sooner for what I personally, unlike people harder to please, consider a very good article,[2] its very length – as I see it, at least – implying a tribute to the author. Were you and I not linked by the common bond of a glorious memory,[3] how I should like to have answered you with something like this, which I would have turned into a pastiche of M. Souday's chronicle:

M. Souday, chronicler of the work of M. Proust, has treated us to a new episode. It takes up no fewer than five columns. Of these five, at least two are devoted to considerations of the book's length, the number of its pages, its parallels with the most interminable and discredited seventeenth-century novels.[4] The third is entirely taken up with poking fun at M. Proust, who doesn't know a word of French grammar.[5] One lapse, which M. Souday finds particularly 'amusing', concerns Bélise's rule.[6] Yet, on this point, it seems that M. Proust is not to be criticized. He said from the first that Bélise's rule is not very strict, and that the lift-boy takes it too far.[7] Admittedly Molière states it very badly. An analysis of both sentence and grammar would demand the complete revision and re-setting of the offending lines. They are no less marvellous for that, and who would stop, given the verve of the piece as a whole, to consider a clumsy turn of phrase? Which only goes to show that a critic shouldn't be too much of a grammarian. But there's more. Firstly, the rule itself, wrongly stated or not, would still be absurd. It's all very well to say that two negatives are one too many, but what about one on its own? In that case, are we to deny nothing?[8] And then, is nothing a negative? I once heard somebody argue the contrary 'res'.[9] But above all, the lift-boy is no more at fault than is Assuérus, when he says: 'Of what are you afraid, Esther? Am I not your brother?'[10] People often spoke like that in the seventeenth century, and without "poetic licence". M. Benda,[11] who prides himself on writing good French when he can be bothered, has been known to put in a newspaper article: 'Have we not seen that Europe etc.?', 'Is it not strange that etc.?'

Lastly, without going as far as Flaubert, who said: 'The moods and tenses of verbs are so much bunkum, it doesn't matter what one writes, as long as it's good',[12] might one remind M. Souday that it was none other than M. Proust who showed that Flaubert, by violating the rules of agreement, produced his best effects, not of literal correctness, but of living, grammatical beauty? 'In Brittany, they now had a garden, and every day would climb the hill that *affords* a view of the sea.'[13] Does not the mood of the present where one was expecting the imperfect (I cite Flaubert's sentence loosely, but that present tense in 'affords a view of the sea', discovered by me, is clear in my mind) explain at a stroke the contrast between the permanence of the hill 'that affords a view of the sea' and the fleeting existence of those climbing it? Montesquieu and La Fontaine are full of such lapses which, thanks to the flouting of a grammatical rule, give a phrase its delightful variety.

We are reliably informed that M. Proust was particularly touched by the fourth column. Indeed, how could he be insensible to the tactful warmth with which M. Souday vouches for him to the over-puritanical reader, declaring, with all the authority that his high status commands, that M. Proust never disgraces his pen.[14] Moreover, this column is the best of the series. The first half of the final column comes to the defence of society people[15] into whose mouths M. Proust puts words that are too coarse, but truer to life, it must be said, than those which M. de Goncourt gives to the aristocratic Mme de Varandeuil: 'O Paris! Filthy rotten pig of a city, to deny a patch of earth to your penniless dead.'[16] One half-column remains. This M. Souday has raised to the honour of M. Proust, whose works he sums up with a benevolence and a broad understanding for which, it is to be hoped, he will soon be thanked in person, in those words from the heart which alone can reach the heart,[17] by his ever-loyal and grateful friend

Marcel Proust

1. See letter 184, n. 1.
2. Souday's review of *Sodom and Gomorrah* Part Two in *Le Temps* of 12 May.
3. Allusion to the deaths of their mothers: see letter 44.
4. 'Here we have the fifth tome of his great work, destined to have eight, but this fifth tome alone has three volumes; one wonders anxiously about the number of volumes that will be required for the remaining three tomes. M. Proust is likely to break all records, including those of Romain Rolland, La Calprenède and Scudéry.' Souday, *loc. cit.* Allusion to the prolific novelist Gauthier de Costes de La Calprenède (1610–63), and Madeleine de Scudéry (1607–1701), literary hostess, author of romances.
5. 'Some sentences, frankly limp, defy syntax. There is much use of the subjunctive, not always when necessary and sometimes when unnecessary. M. Proust is at odds with moods, tenses and grammar in general, a temperamental incompatibility that leads him into some amusing lapses.' *Ibid.*
6. In *Les Femmes savantes*, Molière's play ridiculing the prevailing cult of grammar, Bélise, in response to the remark 'Ne servent pas de rien', states the rule: 'De "pas" mis avec "rien" tu fais la récidive / Et c'est, comme on t'a dit, trop d'une négative.' ('Put "not" before "nothing" and you are re-offending / And as we told you, that's one negative too many' (Act II, scene 7). In other words, to make a negative, French requires *pas* (literally, 'step') after *ne*; the *rien* is superfluous.
7. See the narrator's irritation with the pretentious speech of the lift-boy at the Grand Hotel: IV, 220–3. In the translation, 'Bélise's rule' doesn't appear, the rule not applying to English. In order to render the comic dialogue with the lift-boy, the translator, Terence Kilmartin, was obliged to substitute a similarly pedantic rule.
8. See note 6.
9. Latin for 'thing'; the French *rien* is derived from the accusative *rem*.
10. 'Que craignez-vous, Esther? Suis-je pas votre frère?' Racine, *Esther*, Act II, scene 7. The fact that *ne* is missing is not apparent in English.
11. Julien Benda: see letter 138.
12. Proust invents from various remarks in Flaubert's letters.
13. 'Ils habitaient maintenant en Bretagne un jardin et montaient tous les jours sur une colline d'où l'on découvre la mer.' Proust cites the same sentence (this time correctly) from *L'Éducation sentimentale* in his long discussion of grammar in 'On Flaubert's Style': see *AS-B*, 263–6.
14. 'M. Proust's treatment of his twin subjects is certainly not for use in educational establishments of either sex. But while he lacks Balzac's reserve [...] M. Proust doesn't disgrace his pen and is not to be compared with "the divine Marquis."' Souday, *loc. cit.* Allusion to the Marquis de Sade.
15. 'M. Proust is bent on letting us know that he regards society people as irrelevant, ignorant and utterly stupid. It's difficult to believe that the young Comte de Sturgis hasn't heard of Balzac, or that the Duc de Guermantes doesn't know if Ibsen and D'Annunzio are dead or alive.' *Ibid.* See IV, 77; 112–113.
16. Proust quotes from the Epilogue to *Germinie Lacerteux*: see letter 12, n. 4.
17. 'Cette voix du cœur qui seule au cœur arrive'. Alfred de Musset, 'À la Malibran', *Poèsies nouvelles*.

188   To Jacques Boulenger

[Around 15 May 1922]

Dear friend,

I'm too weak to write more than a few lines, and I apologize for their lateness. 'What on earth is this?', I hear you say. 'This', I imagine, is Camille Vettard's absurd letter.[1] You may even have forgotten his name, which is that of a very gifted writer, a profound mathematician and ... a sous-Préfet.[2] I've never met him, but I've read him. And as he had written a very nice piece about me, when you kindly offered me the hospitality of the *Revue de la semaine* for an article on Daudet,[3] I asked you if it might not serve to 'introduce me' to your readers; with the generosity that so endears you to me, you immediately agreed to its preceding my article. An article which, so far, I've been too ill to give you. Vettard, who didn't regularly receive my letters in his Pyrenees, and who strikes me as an impulsive melancholic given to black moods, may well have thought better of his dedicatory article and decided to rewrite it; I have no idea, as the lines between the Pyrenean hermit and the Parisian invalid have been cut. In any case, I was shocked by the tone of his letter to you, by his apparent belief that one thinks only of him. That not being one of my failings, I feel entitled to try to remedy it in people who are worth the trouble, and yesterday, I wrote giving him a 'piece of my mind'. I said there was no point in his apologizing for his letter, as you hadn't a spare moment to give it your attention, and that you probably wouldn't remember his name, it having no doubt been wiped from your memory by the torrent of your multiple tasks. Don't hold a neurotic melancholy that has the deceptive appearance of vanity against him, and, when my article is written, I'll send you his dedicatory preface which will, I think, please you.

Dear friend, I have a million things to say to you. Have you had the copy you wanted? Being too ill to see anybody from the N.R.F., I didn't know how to tell which copies were on 'linen paper'. (Moreover, owing to unbelievable vagaries in my health, I've had to stop sending out copies for the moment.) If your copy (whatever else, it's a first edition) isn't on 'Lafuma',[4] and if 'Lafuma' is what you would prefer, you have only to say so. 'It's charming'

(?), you tell me, speaking of my book, which is very charming of you. At least your morality will be satisfied, for you'll see that, at the end of the book, my hero, the denigrator of Sodom, is about to marry. Future *Sodoms* will be almost entirely about my hero's passions for women; moreover, I mean to give them titles less inspired by Vigny. I had thought of calling the next *La Prisonnière*, but I'm not sure that isn't a little banal. Before bringing it out, I'll ask you for your advice. I'm no good at titles. I should like to have a title of which you approved.

In all admiring affection,
Marcel Proust

1. Vettard had written forbidding Boulenger to print his eulogy of Proust: see letter 162, n. 1.

2. Civil servant in departmental administration. Vettard was sous-Préfet of the department of Hautes Pyrénées.

3. See letter 135.

4. Hand-made paper, used for twenty copies of the first edition of *Sodom and Gomorrah* Part Two.

189   To Francis Jammes

[Shortly after 15 May 1922]

Dear Sir,

I met you – you, the greatest poet ever revealed to me – at a time when my illness, having suddenly taken a turn for the worse, began to go downhill, since when its descent has gradually become steeper and more rapid. Although, on the very rare days when I can allow a friend to visit me in my bed, where I always am, I have always begged him (for, more often than not, he is a friend of yours also)[1] to give you fervent messages of my increasing admiration, nevertheless, after having been unable to write a letter, correct a proof or utter a syllable, I wanted my first words to be for you. Your *Mémoires* in the *Revue universelle*,[2] even on days when I could scarcely open my eyes for five minutes at a time, have been my link with the outside world, invisible to me, but sensed through all those inspired images which, from now on, will always be associated with the colour of a stream, the high-stepping trot of a carriage horse, the Caribbean sea,[3] with all the things you describe and thus make beautiful for our benefit. I hesitate to send you my latest book, lest you should be disturbed by 'a perversion contrary to art'.[4] And yet the ending would prove to you irrefutably that I wasn't lying when, in a correspondence which you – not I – will certainly have forgotten,[5] I said that I couldn't suppress an episode in *Swann* of which you disapproved without entirely destroying a future volume of the work, for which its sudden recall would act as the trigger.[6] I wasn't lying then, and now you would have the proof.

Reading your marvellous portrayal of Brissaud[7] at Orion, after Castétis and its streams abounding in the flower whose name rhymes with it so well, and whose colour tints your eyes after the desert,[8] I was reminded that when I was a young man he wanted to take me to Orthez. Much as I enjoyed his company, the sort of cures you witnessed had the slightest effect on me. While I didn't portray Brissaud in the book I sent you two years ago, *Le Côté de Guermantes I*, he partly inspired my description of Dr du Boulbon.[9] He is the doctor who explains with such eloquence that my hero's grandmother has nothing whatever the matter with her and that she should go for a walk, at which she takes her grandson to the Champs-Élysées and is felled by a stroke.[10] Your descriptions of eyes, whether Brissaud's, Heredia's or Rodenbach's,[11] are unforgettable. You have reason to be proud, for in your book you parade more different eyes than a peacock in its ocellated tail. And the young girls' eyes, like scarabs, are the most beautiful of all.[12] When I wasn't so ill, early on in your memoirs, where there are those wonderful similes of the peacock-blue rivers,[13] I would amuse myself by doing little pastiches of your meetings with the sous-Préfet, and your departures on hunting mornings. But I decided not to publish them. Pastiches make one smile. And, however affectionately, one shouldn't smile at the things one loves.

Believe in my immense admiration, and, in your prayers to Saint Joseph,[14] ask him to grant me in death a greater peace than I have known in life.

Your grateful
Marcel Proust

1. Apparently an allusion to their mutual friend François Mauriac.
2. The *Revue universelle* was serializing Jammes's second volume of memoirs.
3. Allusion to Jammes's description of Marie de Heredia on her wedding day:

'She exuded exotic charm, completely enveloped in spirals of old lace reminiscent of cliff-side waterfalls beside the Caribbean sea.' Jammes alludes to her Cuban origins: see letter 63, n. 15.

4. Jammes's own phrase for the sado-masochistic scene in *Swann's Way*: see letter 44, n. 14.

5. Allusion in particular to Jammes's letter panegyrizing Proust: see letter 36, n. 7.

6. The scene foreshadows the narrator's crucial discovery of the truth about Albertine's relations with Mlle Vinteuil: see IV, 596ff.

7. Dr Edouard Brissaud, who had an establishment near the Pyrenean spa of Orthez.

8. 'One practical result of my Algerian travels was that I returned with blue eyes. [...] It was six months before the Saharan skies gave way to the forget-me-nots. A rhyme for the name of these delightful flowers came spontaneously into my head, reminding me of Castétis, a charming village near the town of Orthez.' Jammes, *Revue universelle*, 15 May. (The rhyme is *Myosotis*, from the Latin for forget-me-not.)

9. See letter 72, n. 6.

10. III, 341–59.

11. Georges Rodenbach: see letter 200.

12. 'There, I watched long-limbed, lissom girls at play, picking flowers. [...] Their eyes, blue or black, shone like scarabs on pink and matt-white roses.' Jammes, *loc. cit.*

13. In his first volume, Jammes uses a variety of similes for the blue-green of North African rivers.

14. Allusion to Jammes's *Le Livre de Saint Joseph*. Cf. letter 116 to François Mauriac.

190 To Madame de Saint-Marceaux[1]

44 rue Hamelin
[Shortly after 16 May 1922]

Madame,
    The first miracle is that I should have received a letter addressed to the rue Laurent-Pichat, given that it had made the pilgrimage, melancholy for me, to my various former lodgings.
    The second miracle is that I should have found the strength to write to you in my present state of health. For I would never presume to dictate a letter for *you* to a typist. Alas, I very much doubt if these two miracles will be succeeded by a third, the most important for me, which would grant me the two things I want most in the world, to see Monsieur de Saint-Marceaux's maquettes,

and to chat with you once more. Unfortunately, I'm confined to bed, pitifully ill. Last year, I didn't get up for *seven months*. Lately, thanks to certain injections, I've been able to get up about once every three weeks. When I can, I'm strongly advised to go out. But it can only be after my attack is over, that is, generally very late, long after you have gone to bed. Thus, willy nilly, I am oblivious to the interval between lying in bed and arriving like a revenant when the ball is over.[2] And it is precisely on the very rare occasions when such is my fate that I find myself thinking of Monsieur de Saint-Marceaux (not that I don't think of him in the interim). Indeed, one day, when we had both taken the same train at Dieppe,[3] he was good enough, young nobody though I was, to talk to me wonderfully, irresistibly, about the ballet. At the time (I was twenty years old), Cléo de Mérode[4] was living in Dieppe. I was rather smitten. All of a sudden, I wanted to talk of nothing but dancers and dancing. I can't tell you the beauty of listening to Monsieur de Saint-Marceaux. He was not only a very good sculptor, he was like a living, deeply-chiselled statue himself. I never dared tell him, but I can tell you, how much he made me think of a young archangel on the cathedral at Reims.[5] And this cathedral's statues being so very Greek, while he talked ballet to me, I could see him in my mind's eye presiding with smiling majesty over a graceful procession of Panathenaean maidens.[6]

You see the miracles you have wrought – I haven't so much as glanced at the proofs of my latest books, let alone corrected them. Yet I'm writing you a long letter just as if I were not ill, and probably tiring you. I admit that, were you here in person, I would take even more pleasure in this conversation 'in spirit and in truth'.[7] Should I see the smallest possibility of that, at a reasonable hour, don't worry about a car. My maid's husband is a taxi-driver and his entire family has gradually adapted themselves to my routine, so I can be sure of always having him at my disposal in the evening.

I'm very grieved to hear that Madame and Mademoiselle Lemaire,[8] who, against all the evidence, have never believed in my illness, imagine that I've 'dropped' them! I don't say this in the hope of convincing them otherwise, indeed, I should be very upset were you to mention it. Their preconceived idea is too strongly held, and I haven't suffered an invalid's existence at its most terrible for so long only to be reproached for being a malingerer. For them, it's 'settled', I'm a successful (?) author who spends his evenings in the Faubourg Saint-Germain. There's nothing I can do about it, and I've given up trying to convince them. The other day, I had a charming letter from the Duc de Luynes (he is just the sort of person I hardly ever see despite having known him for so long), asking me if I mean to spend the rest of my life fortifying the the walls of my keep, and if I won't lower the drawbridge for him.[9] I might have sent his letter to Madame Lemaire, as a certificate of non-snobbishness. It would have been no use. Besides, I dislike references.[10] I seldom have to write them, almost never changing servants.

Madame, I can sense your tiredness from my own. Never writing letters, I pretend to myself that, on the rare occasions when I do, it gives pleasure, even though I know at bottom that it's not true. Please give my regards to your sons, and kindly accept my admiring and grateful respects.

Marcel Proust

1. *Née* Marguerite Fred-Jourdain, widow of the sculptor Charles-René de Paul de Saint-Marceaux (1845–1915).

2. Allusion to the story of Cinderella, and to the Petipa ballet of that name, first staged in 1893 at the Russian Imperial Court.

3. It was 1895, and Proust was on his way to stay with Reynaldo Hahn at Mme Lemaire's villa.

4. Cléo de Mérode (1881–1966), a famous ballerina. Proust had met her when he was staying in Dieppe.

5. There are references to the statues of Reims cathedral in *Within a Budding Grove*: see II, 41, 367–8, 555.

6. Allusion to the Athenian festival portrayed on the friezes of the Parthenon.

7. See letter 90, n. 2.

8. Madeleine Lemaire's daughter, Suzette.

9. See letter 176.

10. In fact, Proust had recently provided Céleste with a reference, knowing that she would need it after his death.

191 To Jacques Benoist-Méchin[1]

[Wednesday 17 May 1922]

Sir,

Thank you for your letter, and for the amusing and kind things you say. My thanks are rather belated because I'm very ill and have had an accident which, though unrelated to my illness, makes everything impossible. I have nevertheless written to Gallimard to ensure that you or your colleagues (not having your letter in front of me, I don't know who would translate and publish these extracts)[2] will have no rights to pay, either to him or to me. I was astonished to have negotiated this trivial matter so easily. He (Gallimard) waives all rights, asking only that you acknowledge the Nouvelle revue française as the publisher. He would also like three copies (I suppose in order to satisfy himself that this is done).

I recall once meeting your Mother.[3] I didn't know her, but I remember her well. She was superb, and very tall. Are you like her? I shall probably never see you, but if you were to send me a photograph of yourself I would return it at once. I'm always fascinated by the reincarnation in another sex (as you may have gathered from the reflections on Gilberte Swann's resemblance to both her father and her mother in *Les Jeunes filles en fleurs*)[4] of a type that one admires.[5]

Thank you again for having read me with so much goodwill and understanding.

Marcel Proust

If there is anything more you need, the safest addresses for me are, bizarrely enough, either the Nouvelle revue française, 3 rue de Grenelle, or care of M. Olivier Dabescat, Ritz Hotel. I'm very jealous of my privacy, so the Ritz address is confidential, for you alone.

P.S. The fragments you suggest seem to me to be the best (the least bad). But given your intelligence (the proof: your letter), the best would be ... whatever you choose. Or none at all, if you prefer. I couldn't be less of a man of letters and I usually throw all my letters into the waste-paper basket. Don't feel committed, should you have changed your mind.

1. Jacques Benoist-Méchin (1901–83).
2. Benoist-Méchin hoped to be the translator of extracts from Proust's published work for the *Tägliche Rundschau*.
3. See following letter.
4. See II, 159–62.
5. Proust makes the same remark to Mme Soutzo in letter 17.

192 To Gaston Gallimard

[17 or 18 May 1922]

My dear Gaston,

I return the request from Hellens[1] (I enclose another along the same lines but can't lay my hands on the rest). The board isn't very exciting, but congenial,[2] and since you advise me to agree, I do so willingly (and gladly). I wonder if we shouldn't keep anything unpublished for French magazines, for nobody here will know what has appeared in *Le Disque vert*.[3]

Regarding the *Neue Rundschau*, I've written to M. Benoist-Méchin, telling him of your generous concession. I left it rather late, I'm afraid. It might be as well not to mention the magazine to your other inquirers (whose letters I enclose). Especially as I don't even know if my reply will reach M. Benoist-Méchin.[4] I'll let you know as soon as I hear from him. As he seems extremely intelligent and has a certain intellectual prestige over there,[5] it's better to leave the choice up to him. I don't know him; I once met his mother, the Baronne Benoist-Méchin. How little the generations resemble one another![6]

Do you still have some unnumbered copies (I don't mean first editions)? I would find it very useful to have a few.

I fear I may have offended Régnier[7] (and have absolutely no intention of finding out). I hope not, firstly because I like him, and secondly because it will undermine my authority with the Blumenthal jury.[8] For various reasons, I don't feel I'm in a very strong position at the moment, and Paulhan badly needs my support.[9] Morand urges other candidates on me, very interesting, I don't doubt, but there's a limit to the number of prizes! With Paulhan in mind (and in any case he was deserving), I've had first editions sent to Mme Blumenthal, Mme Muhlfeld, Jaloux,[10] Bergson etc.

I don't see a single Brussels newspaper on your list. Yet several have been consistently charming about me. I don't remember which. In any case, it seems a mistake to leave out *L'Indépendance belge*. Ditto the M. Gahier[11] (reactionary Breton press etc.) who always gives Gide and me such excellent reviews. I seem to have lost Mme Fitzgerald's address.[12] A thousand apologies for asking you for it yet again (it's all right, isn't it, to send her one of the

'11th edition' copies that I've bought?) Have you sounded out Schlumberger[13] and Flers? If need be, I can always ask Jacques Boulenger. (Is it true that Marcel Boulenger is standing for the Academy?) My brother says he knows of a bookshop which in spite of the price[14] is selling 50 copies a day of *Sodome II*. I don't know if that's a lot or a little. Anyhow, he seems to think that we haven't printed enough.

Au revoir, my dear Gaston, fatigue alone stops my chatter, which shows you what a lot we would have to say to one another if we met more often. How I would love N.R.F. life in the little literary convent where, once a day, I could ask Frère Jacques (Jacques Rivière) not, are you asleep? but have you slept well? He would ring the bell for Matins, and I, as befits me, the evening Angelus. Don't you find it sad when old friends never meet any more?

With all my love,
Marcel Proust

A woman I loved thirty years ago has written me a furious letter to say that she is Odette and I am a monster.[15] It's letters like that (not to mention having to answer them) that kill all desire for work. I won't say for pleasure. I've long since renounced that.

Have you read Souday's supposed indictment of my grammar?[16] Talk about bad French! As for his defence of society people! What a devastating reply I could make, if only we didn't get on so well.

1. Franz Hellens, editor of *Le Disque vert*, a new Belgian literary magazine.
2. Jean Paulhan was on the editorial board.
3. *Le Disque vert* published nothing by Proust. But see letter 53, n. 2.
4. Benoist-Méchin was doing his military service in the Ruhr.
5. Ernst Robert Curtius had recommended Benoist-Méchin. In fact, nothing came of it.
6. Evidently, Benoist-Méchin had sent Proust his photograph: see previous letter. It turns out to have been a question of mistaken identity: see letter 202.
7. Proust rightly anticipates Régnier's reaction to an article he had just written for *Le Gaulois*: see letter 198.
8. Proust was a judge for the Prix Blumenthal, a biennial literary prize founded by Mme Georges Blumenthal that offered two bursaries of 6000 francs each. Rivière had been a laureate in 1920: see letter 72, n. 8.
9. Paulhan was one of Proust's two candidates for the Prix Blumenthal.
10. Edmond Jaloux: see letter 197.

11. Joseph Gahier: see letter 121.
12. Ellen Fitzgerald, American critic. Her review of *The Guermantes Way* had appeared in translation in the *NRF* of 1 March.
13. Jean Schlumberger, the critic Proust wanted for the *Figaro*: see letter 184, n. 4.
14. The price of the three-volume *Sodom and Gomorrah* Part Two was 6FF, 75.
15. See following letter.
16. See letter 187.

193 To Madame Laure Hayman[1]

[Tuesday evening 18 May 1922]

Madame,

After having had an accident last week (I swallowed a medicament neat, not realizing that it should be diluted, and was in such pain that I lost consciousness), I had hoped to be left to suffer in peace, without having to write a single letter. But since some people whom you don't name have been spiteful enough to reinvent this fairy-tale, and you credulous enough to believe them (which, in you, astonishes me), I'm obliged to protest yet again, with no more hope of success but as a point of honour. Not only is Odette de Crécy not you, she is your exact opposite.[2] That, it seems to me, is patently obvious with every word she utters. It is indeed strange that no hint of you should have insinuated itself into the portrait of the other. Of all the characters I have invented out of whole cloth, she is perhaps the only one where some memory of this or that person, having nothing to do with the rest, has not crept in to add its touch of poetry and verisimilitude. For example (in *Les Jeunes filles en fleurs*, I think),[3] I filled Odette's salon with the particular flowers which a lady of the 'Guermantes set', as you call it, always had in hers.[4] She recognized them, she wrote to thank me and it never occurred to her for a second that it made her Odette. You tell me that, in this context, your 'gilded cage' is Odette's. That shocks me. Your taste is so sure, so uncompromising, that had I needed the name of a furnishing, or a material, I would have come to you in preference to any artist. Now, very clumsily, perhaps, but to the best of my ability, I set out to show that, on the contrary, Odette had no more taste in furnishing than in anything else, and that (except in her dress) she was always a fashion, a generation, behind. I couldn't describe your apartment in the

Trocadéro, or the house in the rue La Pérouse,[5] but I remember them as being the *exact opposite* of Odette's house. Even if there were details common to both, it wouldn't prove that I was thinking of you when creating Odette, any more than ten lines reminiscent of M. Doäzan,[6] when intermingled with the life and personality of a character to which I've devoted several volumes, mean that I intended to 'paint' M. Doäzan. In *Les Œuvres libres*, I made a point of the stupidity of society people who imagine that a 'real person' is 'put' into a book in this way.[7] I might add that they usually pick on somebody the exact opposite of the character in question. I've long ago given up saying that Mme Greffulhe, being her opposite, 'isn't' the Duchesse de Guermantes.[8] But I shall never convince somebody who is as gullible as a goose. That's the bird to which you compare yourself, but it's rather as a swallow, for your volatility (I mean quickness), a bird-of-paradise for your beauty, a dove for your loyalty as a friend, a tern or an eagle for your dash, a homing pigeon for your sure instincts, that I remember you. Alas! do I over-praise you? You read me, and you see yourself in Odette! It makes one despair of writing books. Mine are not very clear in my mind. Yet I can tell you that when Odette goes for a drive in the Allée des Acacias in *De Côté de chez Swann*,[9] I was thinking of the clothes, the gestures ... of a woman known as Clomesnil[10] and, here again, although she was very pretty, her type of elegance, her trailing skirts, her stately walk beside the clay-pigeon ground, were the very opposite of yours. Moreover, apart from that moment (perhaps half a page), I never gave Clomesnil a second thought. In the next book, Odette marries a 'nobleman', and her daughter, having acquired a grand title, becomes a close relation of the Guermantes.[11] Society women haven't the faintest notion of what literary creation involves, with a few honourable exceptions. Your letter came as a great disappointment to me. I haven't the strength to go on, and in bidding farewell to the cruel correspondent who writes only to cause me pain, I lay my humble respects and my tender memories at the feet of the other, who once held a better opinion of me.

Marcel Proust

1. Laure Hayman (1851–1932), a famous cocotte. Witty, clever, artistic (she was a talented sculptress), she had been the mistress of Proust's great-uncle, Louis Weil. See Uncle Adolphe and the 'lady in pink': I, 89–93. She and Proust had had a long, flirtatious friendship.

2. Yet Proust had acknowledged to others that she was the principal model for Odette.
3. See II, 244–5.
4. Mme Straus. See also letter 79 to Mme Soutzo.
5. See I, 263–5. Thus, Laure Hayman and Odette de Crécy had an address in common.
6. A model for M. de Charlus: see letter 107, n.5.
7. The extract in *Les Œuvres libres* included the Duc de Guermantes's thoughts on authors: see letter 87, n. 3.
8. As Proust explains to Guiche, in letter 115.
9. See I, 501–11.
10. Another famous cocotte, Léonie de Clomesnil: see letter 18, n. 28.
11. See letter 112, n. 8.

194 To Gabriel de La Rochefoucauld[1]

[Shortly after 18 May 1922]

[...][2] Alas, little did I know that when, irked by people saying 'Don't deny it, Madame G. is the Duchesse de Guermantes' (whereas the Duchesse de Guermantes is everybody and nobody and in any case the exact opposite of Madame G.), I said in *Les Œuvres libres* that people have so little idea of literary creation that they imagine one puts them into a book just as they are, a woman (who is not in society) would claim to be Odette de Crécy while being her exact opposite etc., etc. Such absurd assimilations infuriate me. Inevitably, memory will provide a trait for some totally dissimilar character. For instance, the Duc de Guermantes has nothing in common with the Marquis de Lau,[3] of whom I was thinking when I had the Duc shave in front of his window.[4] There is nothing of Madame Swann in my dear friend Madame S.,[5] and she is far too nice to think anything of the kind. But I filled the salon of Madame Swann with the beautiful guelder-roses of Madame Straus, and she thanked me without imagining that I identified her with Odette.

1. Gabriel, Comte de La Rochefoucauld (1875–1942), one of the quartet of young aristocrats who modelled for Saint-Loup at the time when Proust was embarking on his novel.
2. Only a fragment of this letter survives.

3. The nobleman whom Gilberte longs to meet: V, 672-3.
4. An episode illustrating the Duc's arrogance and vanity: III, 27-8.
5. Mme Straus: see previous letter.

195 To Binet-Valmer

Wednesday [24 May 1922]

My dear, infinitely dear friend,

I find writing a letter very difficult, but my sorrow at Casella's death[1] (which I read about only yesterday, having been more or less unconscious for forty-eight hours) and my admiration for your offer to give him your blood (which I read about at the same time) makes it imperative. You may not know that until the evening of the Prix Goncourt, when he came to ask me for something, probably a photograph, I hadn't seen Casella for thirty years, not since the day we spent together on the beach at Dieppe, where I had gone between trains to watch a storm at sea.[2] I had gone there with a schoolfriend, older than Casella; we never saw the storm. It had passed. But I was charmed by Casella, and by his poems, some of which he recited. We didn't meet again. But, thirty years later, he was to remind me of something I had completely forgotten (something his kindness had prompted him to write and tell me, and then to repeat to me in person). A few years after we had missed the storm at Dieppe, Casella, who was very young at the time, asked if I could get his poems printed in a magazine where I knew somebody or other, I forget who. I undertook this all the more willingly because I sincerely admired the poems he had sent me. It couldn't have made a scrap of difference to his literary career! But thirty years later, in his goodness, his modesty, he said to me: 'Do you remember that it was you who launched me?' (Needless to say, there wasn't a word of truth in this speech, made in an outburst of goodwill touched by mischief.) I saw him several times in 1920, before my illness took a sudden turn for the worse. I remember an evening when he came to dinner with some friends of the 'Guermantes set'.[3] Never shall I forget that evening, when there was so much talk of you, of him, of me. Remind me to tell you about it. The beauty of what was said would go straight to your heart. Too weak to write just now, I feel my letter coming to an end. It was my last, my only enjoyable evening – enjoyable and so solemnly moving in retrospect. Every word takes on a sense of eternity.

Later, there seems (?) to have been a misunderstanding, which I stupidly failed to clear up at once. My one consolation is this. Three weeks ago, owing to a serious accident, I had to stop sending out my books. By an unbelievable stroke of luck, the first book I had sent out – before my accident – had been to Casella. I had had it taken round to his office. The misunderstanding, if there was one, was resolved. It doesn't in any way lessen my grief, my eternal regret at his loss, but had I felt that we had parted with a disagreement, this grief would have been for ever marred by an unbearable, nagging remorse. The first thing my maid said to me, on learning of Casella's death, was: 'Oh my God, what a terrible thing, but at least Monsieur will have the comfort of knowing that he asked us to take the first copy round to Monsieur Casella.'

Dear friend, my heart grieves for you.
Marcel Proust

1. Georges Casella (1881–1922), poet and dramatist, editor of *Comœdia*, had died suddenly on 20 May.
2. See the storm at Balbec: I, 464–5.
3. Doubtless one of the dinners described in letter 49.

196   To Walter Berry

[Shortly after 23 May 1922]

Dear sir and friend,

I had hoped to come and thank you today, but cruel fate has decreed otherwise. Yesterday, for the first time in ages, I went to the Ritz (don't mention this passing visit, I'll explain why). Odilon goes there night and day to collect ice-cream for me, it being the only thing I can swallow.[1]

As always, your letter was wonderful, just as your speeches are always wonderful. Therein lies the argument against the exclusivity of nationalism. I consider you to be a Frenchman of American origin, and I very much doubt if the language, in a Frenchman of purely French origin, ever attains the delicious savour of yours. It's probably a result of what happened when the English, demoralized, crossed the Atlantic. Their 'one-way' voyage to the United States turned out pretty well! But the return voyage, with a stop-off in France and Walter Berry as sole passenger, had even more dazzling results. When I read your speeches – and your letters, whose eloquence is yet more elliptical and moving – I like to think that I'm tasting the supreme fruits of this double import–export trade. But for an accident that struck like lightning just as my book came out, I would have sent you your copy myself. But it's not too late. Tell me what kind of copy you have received, and I'll send you another, or else some page-proofs.

In grateful friendship, dear Sir and friend,
Marcel Proust

My use of the phrase 'exclusivity of nationalism' is certainly not aimed at Léon Daudet, whom I idolize and who gives me a new reason for idolizing him every day.[2]

1. The consequence of his having taken neat adrenalin: see letter 184.
2. Allusion to a front-page article in *L'Action française* of 21 May containing many references to Proust, and concluding: 'For the past twenty years, I've been "Marcel's" intimate, his comrade and his confidant. Apart from Elstir, who doesn't exist, I alone am capable of painting the portrait of this great novelist for posterity.' Daudet's article, 'Les cent portraits', was about an exhibition that included Blanche's portrait of Proust.

197 From Edmond Jaloux[1]

3 rue de Valois
Friday [26 May 1922]

Dear friend,

I have longed to write to you. Forgive me if I cannot do so. There is too much to say. But you shall have it all in time. Thank you for your latest books, and the dedication. I don't read them, I *live* them; you will know what I mean.

But at least this stupid note has a purpose: to my great pleasure, Middleton Murry and Katherine Mansfield[2] are to dine with us on *Monday evening*, 29 May. You know their admiration for you; they would be overjoyed to see you. We shall be dining at the Bœuf à la Mode,[3] rue de Valois, at 8.30. If you could join us, we should *all* be delighted. But I know how careful you have to be; I would be very pleased to have your acceptance, but you mustn't go to any trouble.

We shall expect you without expecting you, and if, at the last minute, you can't come, don't worry. As we shall have a small private room you can feel quite at ease. Should you be late, that won't matter either. We shall be *four,* and we shan't dress, so you are completely free to do as you wish! But if you are able to come, our joy will know no bounds. Dear friend, I hope it will be yes.

Dear friend, I will write you a proper letter soon.

With all affection and admiration,
Ever yours,
Edmond Jaloux

1. Edmond Jaloux (1878–1949), novelist and influential critic.
2. Katherine Mansfield (1888–1923), short-story writer, married to John Middleton Murry.
3. Can the choice of the Bœuf à la Mode have been pure coincidence? (See letter 32, n. 9.)

198 From Henri de Régnier

27 May 1922

Dear friend,

I've just read your very interesting piece on Goncourt in the *Gaulois*.[1] My admiration for him hasn't wavered since the far off days of the banquet.[2] As in the toast on the evening to which you refer, and recreate with such exactitude, he will always be 'Monsieur de Goncourt' to me.[3] Forgive my delay in thanking you for your latest book, but I suffer from very bad rheumatism and, being rather unwell, must keep my reading to a minimum.

Yours sincerely,
Henri de Régnier

1. *Le Gaulois* had invited Proust and other 'avant-garde' writers to discuss Edmond de Goncourt on the anniversary of his birth.
2. The banquet for Edmond de Goncourt's Légion d'Honneur in 1896: see letter 47.
3. See Proust, *Le Gaulois*, 27 May: 'A crack developed between the more ephemeral aspects of his work and the forms of art that came after. I felt this most sharply

during the banquet [. . .]. The "naturalists" present had unceasingly proclaimed "Old Goncourt is a jolly good fellow", and every toast had opened with the words *Maître, cher Maître, illustre Maître*. It came to M. de Régnier's turn, who was to speak in the name of symbolism. We know how everything he does in life is governed by an infinite delicacy, and how this can sometimes be wrapped in a glassy frigidity when he speaks. Indeed, it must be admitted that the overheated atmosphere [. . .] was suddenly chilled when M. de Régnier stood, turned to M. de Goncourt and began: 'Monsieur'. He went on to say that he wished he could toast him from one of the Japanese bowls so beloved of the master of Auteuil. The ravishing and perfect phrases with which M. de Régnier alone could decorate the bowl may be imagined. Nevertheless, that icy "Monsieur" gave the impression, even in the succeeding phrases, less of a bowl being held out than of a bowl being smashed. This, I felt, was the first crack.' See also 'The Goncourts', *AS-B*, 312.

199   To Edmond Jaloux

[Saturday 17 May 1922]

Dear friend,

    Never was an 'alas!' more sincere. When I'm less frail I'll explain to you why Monday is a physical impossibility for me.[1] I don't even know, my sole nourishment for a month having been some ice-cream and (once, in thirty days) some asparagus, how it is that respect and admiration have given me strength to reply. My desire to meet your guests (which is known to M. Middleton Murry, to whom I owe a letter) only adds to my regret (I would so much enjoy a chat with him). I'll write to you in a day or two or, if I'm strong enough, come to see you; otherwise, if the prospect of sweating in a boiling hot room doesn't put you off, you can dine here with anybody you choose, such as Léon Daudet or Gide (I say 'or' because the room is so small that with both of you there, and me facing you, I fear you would find it too hot, nothing ever being too hot for me) or Berry, or Morand, or Gabriel de La Rochefoucauld; in short, anybody you wish.

    Thank you for thinking of my books as I think of yours. I would be most grateful if you could give me Miomandre's[2] address, for want of which his copies of my latest books (even last year's), though dedicated, have still not been sent.

                           Allow me to say, yours affectionately,
                                              Marcel Proust

What pleasure your letter gave me!

1. See letter 197.
2. The critic Francis de Miomandre: see letter 55, n. 8.

200 To Henri de Régnier

[Sunday 28 May 1922]

Dear Sir and friend (that, I believe, is the ritual formula I adopt when addressing you, friend expressing deep feeling and Sir tempering it with deference), it has taken my fear of being misunderstood[1] to induce me to answer you, for since a severe setback to my health a month ago I have lived (?) exclusively on ice-cream and *once* (once in thirty days) asparagus-tips. I am therefore very weak. Had the request from the *Gaulois* not followed me from pillar to post (for I've had a succession of lodgings), so that by the time I opened the envelope the deadline had expired, I would have first submitted to you this very indifferent article (rendered even less intelligible by cuts) even though, every minute counting, it could not then have appeared. Now, I thought that, between two evils, the lesser was the better, and that it was worthwhile, in that it gave me an opportunity to mark an act in your life that few people comprehend but whose significance you explained to me so well at the time that I believe I have faithfully reported your deliberate action that evening. I merely tried not to make it look like an act of hostility towards M. de Goncourt. I would express all this better (in terms of the ousting of Rodenbach[2] and Montesquiou) if I were less ill. The only thing I would add, and having told me that you dislike him, you may think it unsympathetic to you (whereas it's very sympathetic, and proves to you that I deny nobody before my Masters – among whom, perhaps, you stand alone for *La Double maîtresse*,[3] as you'll discover one day, at length)[4] – is that but for a deplorable cut made at the newspaper,[5] I would have praised Léon Daudet (anything less would have been despicable on my part) for his admirable study of Goncourt,[6] and all the more joyfully for being able to write at long last about somebody whose goodness to me since I've been ill (despite my having been unable to receive him), and yet again recently,[7] has been truly sublime. (That is between ourselves – between the three of us (Madame de Régnier) – for I don't like to brag about people's kindness to me.) I haven't seen him since the Prix Goncourt, and I find his polemics, and those of Maurras etc., against people like Briand[8] or the directors of the Bank of China,[9] men I've never met and don't suppose ever will but who are, after all, human beings, almost too cruel to bear. But where he is concerned, and in spite of disagreements that go back to the time of Dreyfus, his goodness to me, expressed not only in words but *in deeds*, and underlined by charming attentions, is such that the burden it imposes on me won't be lifted until I can shout my admiration for him from the rooftops.

Naturally, I couldn't write about you yesterday, except obliquely, making the banquet an excuse to praise you; thus far, I have no 'literary criticism' to my credit, alas. If I permitted myself the word 'frigidity' (essential, moreover, it describing the crack developing between the idiotically fervent naturalists and symbolism),[10] it was because, without of course saying so, I associated it in my mind (but I'm so tired that I don't see how I can finish this letter) with personal memories of which I have never spoken to you, a lifetime of your infinite kindnesses to me having blotted them out; but, for example, I remember a time when, a mere youth excited at the prospect of his first duel,[11] I came to ask M. Heredia to be my witness, and you, of whom I was such an ardent proselyte that I would beg my father daily to paint you to M. Hanotaux[12] as the only writer who would be truly meaningful Academician (it's a good twenty-five years since M. Hanotaux heard from me), you exhibited that very same frigidity, remarking with a sarcastic laugh: 'Well, Proust, you had a good roasting in today's *Écho de Paris*.[13] A charming article, I thoroughly enjoyed it.' I went home with a heavy heart. Don't imagine that I held it against you for a single second. On the contrary, I have never ceased to remember all that you have done for me. Even if I hadn't known you, to have read your books would still have been one of the greatest boons of my life. But I did know you, I knew you before your marriage, I still know you, and if I had to list all your kindnesses to me they would more than fill a volume of 'small print with no blanks' (as the critics say of my books). It is therefore out of a sense of gratitude and, if I may say so, affection, that I permit myself a frankness which, to my mind, is a further proof of my tender sincerity. I've already had to pull myself together three times in order to finish this letter, so I'll just say a word on the subject of your comments on the book I sent you. The day it went off, books were piled up at my bedside. Gallimard had warned me that only ten were on linen-paper.[14] I fingered them all, but not being a bibliophile, I didn't know which was which. I sent you one on linen-paper (or what I thought was linen-paper). I don't know if it was from an unnumbered edition (specially made for me) or a first edition. I particularly wish to know so that I can send the other to Madame de Régnier. True, I said (as far as I can remember) that, because of the work's indecency, I would send her a copy only if she claimed it. But that was merely a Canaque's respectful joke,[15] for she enjoyed *Sodome I* and it was far more indecent than the present one. Only then came my accident, I was constantly feverish, I couldn't turn over for the terrible pain everywhere the medicament had touched,[16] and I had to interrupt the despatch of my books. I have now started again (the despatch of my books) on my better days. And if what I sent you was a first edition, I would prefer to send Madame de Régnier either an author's edition (which would at least have the advantage of adding variety to your library) or, if that is what I sent you, a first edition. In short, whichever you choose, with or without variety. Your wish is my command.

Her humble subject sends the Queen of Canaques his respectful regards, and begs you to share with her, dear Sir, his admiration and gratitude.

Marcel Proust

1. Allusion to Proust's article in *Le Gaulois*: see letter 198 from Régnier.
2. Georges Rodenbach (1855–98), Belgian Symbolist poet who figures in Proust's pastiche of the Goncourts: see *CS-B*, 26–7. (Evidently he suffered a rejection similar to Montesquiou's: see letter 117, n. 7.)
3. See letter 80, n. 7.
4. Allusion to an essay which Proust intended to publish on Régnier.
5. *Le Gaulois* cut all references to Léon Daudet.
6. 'Edmond de Goncourt's attic', *La Revue universelle*, 15 March 1921.
7. Allusion to Daudet's article of 21 May: see letter 196, n. 2.
8. See letter 141, n. 10, n. 11.
9. See letter 170, n. 3.
10. See letter 198, n. 3.
11. Not his famous duel with Jean Lorrain, so presumably an earlier, abortive affair.
12. See letter 63, n. 4.
13. A mystery, unless Proust has mistaken the newspaper.
14. See letter 188, n. 4.
15. See letter 63, n. 15.
16. See letter 184, n. 1.

201 To Sydney Schiff

[Tuesday evening 30 May 1922]

Dear Sydney,

I answer your second question first[1] (I'm sitting down all alone to a huge dinner I had sent out for to the Ritz and had counted on sharing with you, but as you had forty-five guests, I thought better of it, and also of dining tonight at a friend's house with some very agreeable people[2] and the Princesse de Polignac, or yesterday with Jaloux or with Diaghilev.[3] I'm loyal and obedient, but I find you a tyrant[4]).

So, to answer your second question first. My dear friend, of course I think the N.R.F. should publish these stories, and said as much to Gallimard this afternoon. I think it would have been wiser for me to say nothing. For as they know from everything I've said about you and asked for on your behalf that nothing could give me greater pleasure, my recommendation won't have done any good and may have done harm (for cruel fate dictates that since refusing *Swann*, they now refuse me everything). But that's the situation, I've spoken to Gallimard; so send them to Rivière and, if you wish, I'll write to him. Send him one to start with. Being ill, he'll read it with greater attention.[5] You've certainly taken your time to come round to my idea that your immediate need is for some publicity.

2. In replying to your second question, I would much rather stick to its actual wording, for I don't want to fall out with the man I'm fondest of, namely you. And once before, while you were in England, you acted towards me in a way that, while perfectly friendly, similarly excluded things which seem so natural to me, of which no true friend will defraud his friend. In any case, regardless of what I may think on that point, you have shown me such immense kindness, even if not in accordance with my theory and practice, that it would be churlish of me not to adore you for what you are, reminding myself that, in an imperfect world, even he who does the most cannot think of everything,[6] otherwise there would be perfection, which is impossible. So, without further ado, I'll deal with your first question by saying this: if you wish to question somebody who understands me, nothing could be simpler, just ask

me. There is no such person as the friend who fully understands me. And if there were, I hope he would be worthy of the name, and refuse to answer any questions whatsoever without my prior consent. I know everything there is to know about me, and will gladly tell you all; so there's no point in my nominating a less well-informed friend who, inasmuch as he could tell you anything, would no longer deserve the name of friend if he replied to your questions.

Dear Sydney, I was so sorry to inflict a Turkish bath on you the other night.[7] Somehow or other I've managed to catch cold (having got up *for you*, and having sent out for this dinner to the Ritz where I believe I owe several thousand francs!) so don't know when I shall be up again. Kindly lay at the Angel Violet's[8] feet, more beautiful than Leonardo's, kindly lay at the feet of the Angel Violet, whom I've never once seen in the same *dress* but whose *character* is always the same, being that of an integral, unalterable sweetness, the humble and respectful feelings which you and I both share for her.

Marcel Proust

1. The letter to which Proust replies is missing, thus the questions to which it refers can only be surmised.
2. Allusion to an invitation from Mme Soutzo.
3. Allusion to the invitation from Jaloux for 29 May (see letter 199) and possibly to another from the Schiffs, who had just given a grand party for Diaghilev and the Ballets Russes.
4. Schiff had accused him of accepting too many invitations: see letter 224.
5. Jacques Rivière was never to publish anything by or about Schiff in the *NRF*.
6. Proust adapts the French dictum 'Qui peut le plus peut le moins' ('He who is capable of the most is capable of the least').
7. Allusion to Proust's specially-heated room at the Ritz.
8. Proust's nickname for Mme Schiff.

202 To Jacques Benoist-Méchin

[End of May 1922]

[. . .][1] Don't apologize, the mistake was mine. I should have checked my facts before writing to you. But as it is, things turn out to be more interesting than you might think, for your photograph has confirmed the validity of my hypotheses about love. So it's not surprising that I should attach great importance to it. I don't believe, in fact, that a man loves this or that woman by accident, he falls for a certain type to which he always remains faithful.[2] If a man loses the woman he loves, through divorce or bereavement, he will consistently, and often unconsciously, seek out and pursue the same type of woman. If your father chose your Mother as his second wife, it was because she was the incarnation of the particular type he favoured above all. She must in some way have resembled his first wife.[3] It is therefore not surprising that, in your photograph, I should rediscover the features of a woman who wasn't your mother and whom you probably never knew. Through her, a reflection of the type of woman your father loved has superimposed itself on your face, creating as it were a likeness at second-hand. This confirms all my ideas, and, as you see, it turns out that I wasn't so wrong after all. In any case, we'll talk about it when you come to see me, for I trust you'll give me that pleasure when you are next in Paris on leave. [. . .].

1. The beginning and end of this letter are missing.
2. Cf. VI, 270.
3. See letter 191, letter 192.

203 From Jacques Rivière

Thursday evening 8 June 1922

My dear Marcel,

When I think of all the trouble you take, ill as you are, to see that Paulhan succeeds,[1] I'm speechless. I'll tell him what you say. And I know he will be profoundly touched.

I'm writing to Crémieux,[2] to ask him to send you the necessary details. At the same time, I'll warn him of the need for *absolute discretion*.

You can rely on Paulhan's discretion.

I'm sorry if all this canvassing has tired you out. And I was so pleased to have found you a little better!

One thing you said upset me. Why despair of finishing your book? I know that you will finish it. Our need of it is too great, it's unthinkable that it should go unsatisfied. That's mysticism, if you like! But it's true.

In warmest friendship,
Jacques Rivière

Thanks for the photograph. I'll send it to the *Semaine Littéraire*.[3]

1. Allusion to Paulhan's candidacy for the Prix Blumenthal: see letter 192, n. 8.
2. Benjamin Crémieux was Proust's candidate for the other bursary.
3. A Geneva weekly.

204 To Walter Berry

Saturday midnight [10 June 1922]

Dear Sir and friend,

I have this minute been handed a note that has just been delivered by Mme Blumenthal's chauffeur. I can't tell how grateful I am to see that you had the infinite kindness to intercede with Mme Blumenthal as I asked. She refuses to accept Paulhan as a candidate. She says that the rule excluding candidates over the age of thirty-five is strict, and must be followed to the letter. I must admit that the reasons she gives are perfectly sound. I had thought, in case Mme Blumenthal should turn down Paulhan (as has in fact happened), that I might excuse myself from Tuesday's meeting,[1] the time (four o'clock in the afternoon) being particularly tiring for me, and going instead to Mme Hennessy's soirée on Monday, where I would see you at last! It's ages since I've accepted an invitation, and I thought that as Mme Hennessy is certain to have asked hundreds of people whose warmth will revive me, as Baudelaire says,[2] I could safely risk making an exception for Monday. But yesterday, having eaten some ice-cream and drunk some iced beer in bed, where I was too hot, I developed a sore throat, and am now not sure of being well enough to go out for the first time on Monday. Furthermore, Mme Blumenthal is ignorant of the mechanisms of my routine and my attacks, and if she found out that I was at Mme Hennessy's on Monday night (where she may be herself) she will think that I should rather have come to her the following afternoon. Especially as she was good enough to say that she was looking forward to my surprising her again this year, as I did two years ago, by arriving at the last minute when everybody had given me up. I've been weighing up the pros and cons, while cursing the ice-cream (for which the Ritz has charged me 850 francs this month, which seems excessive) and taking my pulse. And I keep seeing the same image, that of you at Mme Hennessy's, you, probably the being whom I love most in the world. I wouldn't have made that declaration to you the day before yesterday, just as I was about to ask you a favour. But now that it has been granted (to no purpose, alas) I dare do so, in sincere affection, and admiring gratitude.

Marcel Proust

1. A meeting for the judging of the Prix Blumenthal. Proust, however, understood it to be merely a preliminary meeting.
2. Proust alludes to Baudelaire's 'Chanson d'après-midi', *Les Fleurs du Mal*: 'Et tu connais la caresse / Qui fait revivre les morts!'

205   To Madame Hennessy[1]

[Tuesday 13 June 1922]

Madame,

To thank you to the best of my poor abilities for a most enjoyable evening at your house yesterday, I noted down for your benefit a long and particularly inane conversation, a mere half of which I enclose.

Yours respectfully,
Marcel Proust

I wouldn't like anybody except you (and Berry and Guiche) to know about this little piece of buffoonery because, although written in the hope of making you smile, it might, on account of the proper names, appear malicious if divulged.

Inane conversation overheard at a distinguished lady's house

'My dear, it's dazzling, quite simply the most beautiful residence in the whole of Paris.' 'And so it should be, if it's to be worthy of the mistress of the house.' Discreet murmurs of approval from everybody within earshot. 'Why does that woman keep singing

"We must get away from here"? I never felt less like leaving in my life.' The singer continues, but after 'We must get away from here', the speaker, being deaf, hears:

> 'Where I'll catch my death
> Save me from this terrible fate'.[2]

'It's pretty music, but the words don't make sense.' 'Sybille[3] is as lovely as ever.' 'You know she's Chateaubriand's great-niece?' 'My dear, that's impossible, he didn't have any children.' 'Oh, but I thought she was called after one of his novels.' 'No, it was that novel by Octave Feuillet.[4] Another great writer.' 'Speaking of great writers, can you guess who's here?' 'No, who?' 'Do you see Berthe de Ganay?'[5] 'Berthe, Berthe, wait a minute ... Oh, now I know who you mean. Where can that icy draught be coming from?' 'It's the Princesse de Polignac. She has rather a look of Dante, don't you think?' 'Ah, now I see your great writer. His hair is standing on end.' 'Don't you realize that you're pointing at the American Ambassador!'[6] 'That sort of buffalo who came in just now and went to take refuge behind Thérèse Murat,[7] the one who's shaking himself all over, who can it be?' 'But it's Gustave Schlumbec!'[8] 'So where's your great writer?' 'He's the man with the uncombed black hair, the one who looks so ill. Gracious, he's talking to Boni!'[9] 'Ah, I see him! I knew he wasn't one of us the minute I laid eyes on him.' 'Hush, he's a genius. He suffers from hay-fever.' 'Really? How interesting. But who is he?' 'He's the famous Marcel Prévost[10] who wrote *Les Don Juanes*.' 'Oh, if only one could meet him! He's talking to some woman now, lucky thing. Have you read *Les Don Juanes*?' 'Have I read it! I drank in every word. It's true what they say about heredity. Élie de Gaigneron and Charles-Louis are terribly alike.' 'Only when they're sitting down. Heavens! we mustn't make so much noise, we're interrupting the music.' 'Keep your voice down. If we whisper, we can have a really good talk.' 'The mistress of the house looks as if she's had enough of her party.' 'Heavens! The singing has gone on for two hours. Who's the woman getting up to sing now?' 'She's His Serene Highness's sister.' 'Which Serene Highness?' 'Pierre.'[11] 'Ah, you're right, she's singing Monegasque songs.' Etc. Etc. Etc.

Guiche leaves with His Serene Highness's sister. A car door slams. A feeble cry of protest can be heard. From which of them, it is impossible to tell.

1. Mme Jean Hennessy: see letter 115, n. 6.
2. Proust parodies an aria from Gounod's *Romeo and Juliet*: 'Il faut partir hélas! Il faut quitter ces bras.'
3. Comtesse Jacques du Durfot, *née* Sybille de Chateaubriand.
4. Octave Feuillet (1821–90), author of popular romances.
5. Marquise Jean de Ganay, née Berthe de Béhague.
6. Myron T. Herrick.
7. Comtesse Joachim de Murat.
8. Gustave Schlumberger (1844–1929), historian. Proust had never forgiven him for his treacherous desertion of the Dreyfusards.
9. 'Boni' de Castellane. See letter 49, n. 5.
10. Marcel Prévost (1862–1949), author of popular society novels specializing in feminine psychology.
11. Pierre de Polignac, now Duc de Valentinois of Monaco: see letter 56, n. 2. He had two sisters.

206   To André Gide

[Tuesday evening 13 June 1922]

Dear friend,

    I've been through a terrible day, physically and morally. When I rang at six o'clock, just before going to sleep, I was given a note from your candidate, who is also mine.[1] Even if I had dressed there and then, I couldn't have been there in time. In any case, we were only supposed to be naming our candidates today.[2] And Madame Blumenthal knows from all the letters I've written to her over the past few days that Monsieur Gabory is my candidate for one bursary and (failing Paulhan, who is too old by two years) Monsieur Benjamin Crémieux for the other. I told her to go to you for any additional information about my candidate (Gabory). I did so (in Monsieur Gabory's interests) at the suggestion of somebody whose name I'll give you when I see you. On the other hand, I didn't ask her to try and rally you to Monsieur Crémieux's cause for the other bursary as you had told me that you were committed to voting for Monsieur Genevoix.[3] (My badly constructed sentence doesn't of course mean that that was what I told Mme Blumenthal, not having the slightest reason to talk to her about your other vote.) What I mean is that you yourself having told my maid that you were obliged to vote for Monsieur Genevoix, I didn't want to influence you to switch to Crémieux. Moreover, I understand that he has several supporters on the jury because Crémieux made sure that I knew (not that I know him). I trust that he and Gabory will be successful when it comes to the vote. I'm sure to be summoned; but in order that I have time to prepare, I would be most grateful if you could send me a pneumatique in any case, telling me when we are to vote (or let me know through Monsieur Gabory). Kindly thank him warmly for his note, and tell him that Madame Blumenthal knows that my support for him is unshakeable.

Yours very sincerely,
Marcel Proust

1. Proust had transferred his vote for the Prix Blumenthal from the disqualified Jean Paulhan to Georges Gabory, the young writer who had worked on *Sodom and Gomorrah*: see letter 154. Gabory's note had begged Proust to to be sure to attend the meeting that afternoon, but Proust, whose routine had been disrupted by Mme Hennessy's party, had received it too late.

2. Proust had been misinformed by Walter Berry, who was also on the Blumenthal jury.

3. Maurice Genevoix (1890–1980), later awarded the Prix Goncourt for his novel *Rabollion*.

207 From André Gide

Wednesday morning [14 June 1922]

My dear Proust

I found your pneumatique of this morning deeply moving – typical of your exquisitely sensitive nature. Alas, it's too late. Last night, I had to take Gabory the sad news that he had failed.[1] A few of us are therefore to try and help him – for he has absolutely no private means and, in addition, is also (partially) responsible for supporting his ailing parents. He is a person of great charm, intelligent, full of curiosity (I mean full of that interest in people which is the mark of the true novelist). Of all the 'young' I have come across, he is certainly one of the most talented, and even those who didn't vote for him yesterday paid tribute to his remarkable poetic gift. One argument against him even went like this: 'Somebody as talented as that will always get by' (direct quote). Meanwhile, without our help, he could easily starve.

The assurances I was given, in particular by Mme Muhlfeld and

Mme de Noailles, made me far too confident of his success. Mme de Noailles had promised me to vote for him – on condition that I voted for Genevoix – only to let me down at the last moment. Crémieux skilfully employed last-minute tactics, intriguing, writing letters, getting Thibaudet to write to Bergson. I kept my word, and voted for Mme de Noailles's candidate; mine turned out to be the sacrifice. Of course I wish Crémieux well; we publish him, as you know, and do what we can for him on the magazine; but he is still better-off than Gabory: Crémieux has a guaranteed salary of 1000 francs a month – on top of what he earns from his articles; Gabory has nothing, and the very nature of his talents doesn't make it easy for him to earn his living by them. Nobody took the slightest notice of your letters; they were not even mentioned – and not being supposed to know about them, I thought it more discreet for your sake to say nothing.

I know that you will be as saddened as I am, and I'm sorry to have to tell you all this – not that I have any choice, you had to be told – in all friendship, knowing that I have your profound sympathy.

Ever yours,
André Gide

1. The previous afternoon, in Proust's absence, the Blumenthal Committee had cast its votes in favour of Maurice Genevoix and Benjamin Crémieux.

208   To Benjamin Crémieux

[Thursday morning 15 June 1922]

Dear friend,

A line. 1. Things didn't happen in quite the way you imagine.

2. Had I known that we were to vote, and had I not been well enough to attend, I would have said to you: 'I'm not well enough to go', not 'there isn't to be a vote'. I'm better than I was, but on the eve of the vote I went to a party, something I would never have done had I known we were to vote the next day.

3. To corroborate my word, since you don't know me, I'm sending you two letters from Walter Berry (but I need them back straightaway) in which he mentions you, and says that there isn't to be a vote. True, I had a third letter from him, saying that we

might be voting, but I didn't receive it till midnight on Tuesday.

4. Indeed, if I have any influence on this jury, it's because I keep my word, whereas others who are more talented but less strong-minded than me, have none.

5. I was sad to learn of the failure of Gide's candidate (Gabory), who was also mine for the other bursary. If he failed, it was because he was competing against you. That was not my intention. Had I been there, I would have insisted that we vote first on one bursary, then on the other. That's how I achieved unanimity for Rivière, two years ago. I'm very upset for Gabory, but whatever people think, I was acting in good faith when I said that since we were not to vote, I need only attend on voting day. Luckily, I had sent your biographical details to Madame Blumenthal in time.

With warmest congratulations, dear friend, and please thank Madame Crémieux for her kind thought.

Marcel Proust

209 To Jacques Boulenger

[Around 15 June 1922]

My dear Jacques Boulenger,

I have Vettard's riposte[1] to an article by Allard (all this must be Greek to you) which I may 'communicate' to you later, as he talks a lot (and very nicely) about you. I wouldn't write to you about anything so trifling if I didn't remember having written to you the other day, and if I didn't have the impression that, in the confusion of the 'better days' and 'worse days' ('better', for the moment) which have been causing such wild fluctuations in my health lately, this letter may not have been taken round to you. My recollection of it is vague, but you will know from what follows whether or not you have received it. It seemed not only exhausting but quite unnecessary to 'explain' my book, so I didn't attempt it. But I said that I found it deplorable (unless we've quarrelled without my noticing, or knowing why) that *L'Opinion* should have found the courage to talk about me again merely to say that all my characters are tainted by 'shameful vices' (I quote),[2] something which has given a deplorable impression generally, even of *L'Opinion* itself – (not to say of me).

If I've said this already, it's superfluous, and if I haven't it's probably superfluous in any case. 'Silence alone is strength'.[3] But the main purpose of this letter is to ask you whether all your Doumics[4] etc. have fallen silent, and whether, before your pages become cluttered up, or I should say, happily replenished, with more 'celebrities', you have room for the column on Léon Daudet, preceded or not – preferably preceded – by Vettard's foreword[5] (what Mallarmé called: *avant-dire*).[6] I wanted to write to your brother, who has misunderstood my book and, more to the point, appears to have no conception of what my youth was like, but I would have wearied him as well as myself. Not only that, it meant putting myself forward, and being seen in a worldly, and displeasing, light. I find it more decorous to appear as a 'vagabond' in my books, as if to say: 'I'm not sure I'm invited'.[7] It seems to me more becoming, even if I have never experienced that kind of insecurity. Stevenson didn't hesitate to have his Prince of Bohemia end up as a London tobacconist.[8] I was amazed to discover how many Guermantes have read my books without realizing how shocking they are. Guermantes ladies, the soul of virtue, flock to me. Either they haven't understood what they've read; or, perhaps, looking about them, they see that the proportion of those tainted by 'shameful vices' in society is marginally greater than in my books, where at least people like Cottard, Elstir, Bergotte, Norpois etc., etc. maintain the tradition of what used to be deemed 'normal'. I really ought to correspond with Monsieur Thérive.[9] I've been telling myself that for the past two years.

Regards,
Marcel Proust

Prévost has asked me for a contribution to the *Revue universelle*. What do you think?

1. Proust had received a proof of Vettard's epistolary essay to appear in the *NRF* of 1 August, entitled 'Proust and Einstein': see letter 162, n. 1. Allusion to Allard's review of *Sodom and Gomorrah*, which had appeared in the *NRF* of 1 June: see letter 185.

2. Allusion to comments in an unsigned review of current books: 'By this time M. Proust's characters have become tainted by shameful vices (and I'm not talking of snobbery but of what is evident from the title of the book). He never wearies of describing, nor we of regarding, these monstrous, minutely-observed curios, more intricately carved than any Chinese ivory. And while admiring the book, one wonders about its increasing influence on young people.'

3. See letter 23, n. 10.

4. See letter 168, n. 4.
5. Vettard's dedication to Proust: see letter 167, n. 1.
6. Title of an introduction by Mallarmé which the poet had read before a Reynaldo Hahn concert in 1894.
7. Cf. III, 660-1.
8. See letter 134, n. 4.
9. André Thérive (1891–1967), author of society romances.

210 To Abel Bonnard[1]

[15 June 1922]

Dear friend,

    I took up a copy of the *Revue de Paris* for the doubly frivolous pleasure of reading Mérimée's letters to the Princesse Mathilde. And what should I see but your name! for so long nothing but a cherished memory, it having ceased to dispense that beauty of which you alone know the prescription essential for our well-being. It's almost absurd that somebody as ill as I am, unable to write a letter, however urgent, should greet your 'come-back' (or rather, the first thing of yours I've read for a very long time,[2] but then it's been so long since I've been able to read that I've lost touch with the world of newspapers and magazines) with anything other than one of those 'silences' you depict so well,[3] and which assume the dignity of the marble you describe as being affronted by the gesticulations imposed on their subjects by the sculptors of today.[4] I wish you would collect your *Figaro* articles, so often my *panis angelicus*:

> 'The one bread so delectable
> That the world which we obey
> Does not serve it at its table
> Then I to my disciples say
> Draw near: do you wish to live?
> Take it, eat it, and live.'[5]

    I should like to compare my present impressions with those I had then. In these brilliant summer days – beyond my ken – the familiar, curling smoke of your initials is missing. It is a relief to discover, beneath such a title (it occurs on the cover of a book by Verlaine which, though repellent enough, is less so than his *Hommes*),[6] these very different delicacies. Although I don't agree with all the things you say, this disagreement instantly makes me think that I'm in the wrong. (I refer in the main to the assertion that a feeling for nature is necessary to a woman; its utility, is, I grant you, implied in my ill-chosen title, *Jeunes filles en fleurs*, and certainly in the text; but not, I think, its necessity. Nor do I agree with you about the different fruits of trees.[7])

Sick men are frivolous. A word from you (for my part, I promise secrecy) as to the identities of the first lady, the mistress of M. d'Autrefois, and the second (Ritz, Biarritz, St Moritz) would cheer me up.[8] I would love to know them all; but I respect the mystery of poetic creation.

Your devoted,
Marcel Proust

After many months, I can at last pronounce, faultlessly, even very fast, the word Palmacamini. An over-dose of drugs and not, as I thought, my illness, had interfered with my speech.[9] It happened just after we met, alas, so I was unable to chat to you about books which are as fresh in my mind as on the day I read them.

I only have to read a line by you to know that we would agree about the dreadfulness of modern writing. I fear that you may feel the same about my books, alas. I suppose that we can at least, with so many different genres to choose from, still choose whom we read among our contemporaries. And our choices would scarcely differ. But nobody knows how to read or write any more – or almost nobody.

1. Abel Bonnard (1883–1968), poet, novelist and essayist, later minister of education in the Vichy government.

2. An essay by Bonnard entitled 'Femmes'.

3. See Bonnard on the subject of a young girl of twenty-two: 'I believe she finds us all terribly frivolous, and that if she says so little it is because, feeling the full weight and value of words, she expresses her respect for them through silence. [...] some silences are merely gaps, holes, absences. Whereas others mean more than the sentences between which they occur, completing their meaning, and, in conversation, their presence is truly impressive.'

4. Allusion to Bonnard's comment on the statues in the Tuileries gardens.

5. From Racine's *Cantiques spirituels*: see letter 65.

6. Allusion to Verlaine's books of pornographic poetry, *Hombres* and *Femmes*, published respectively in 1891 and 1890, what Proust called 'sad little poems': see 'Concerning Baudelaire', AS-B, 299.

7. 'Human beings have as many different ways of keeping silent as trees of producing fruit.' Bonnard, *op. cit.*.

8. Bonnard's Mr 'Old-fashioned' contrasts two types of society women, one haughty and conventional, the other smart, modern and associated with 'luxury trains and palatial hotels'.

9. Allusion to the title of Bonnard's novel *Le Palais Palmacamini*, and to Proust's fear that he might have had a brain tumour: see letter 124.

211 To Jacques de Lacretelle

[Friday 16 June 1922]

Dear friend,

My warmest thanks for your beautiful card, with its ingenious allusions to friendship. And I deserve a pat on the back for replying, having been at death's door for seven months and, at the time of writing, having eaten nothing and slept for a total of three hours for the past ten days. I often think of you, and of the cruel fate that deprives me of a much-cherished friendship; tell Brach[1] about the state I'm in, so that he will forgive my silence. I try a new remedy every day, no longer, of course, in the hope of victory, but I want to get out again, and above all, to work.

I was very sorry to see the Academy dishonour itself by turning down Hermant.[2] I don't know about you, but despite the perfection, often a little superficial for my taste, of the novels (Hermant's), and however accomplished they are, I far prefer the delightful Oxford stories.

I'm full of admiration for Porto-Riche's *Passé*, and his *Vieil Homme*. But as for M. Madelin!![3] At any rate, I wanted Hermant (as he knows), and however disloyal to Porto-Riche it may seem, I think he should have got in. It wouldn't have added to his stature. But his absence certainly reflects badly on the Academy. And how about you, dear friend, are you happier than me, are you working, enjoying life?

Ever yours,
Marcel Proust

I've written to you twice, but I never know if you get my letters.

1. Paul Brach (1893–1939), a young writer who had become one of Proust's regular night-time visitors.

2. Two of Proust's friends, Abel Hermant and Georges de Porto-Riche, were candidates for a vacant chair. Hermant was to be successful in 1927, Porto-Riche in 1923.

3. Louis Madelin (1871–1956), a historian, was to become an Academician in 1927.

212 To Paul Morand

Friday night [16 June 1922]

My dear Paul,

My letter and Céleste's give such a contradictory impression that I beg you not to suspect duplicity on my part. She told you that I would be resting today. Now, I was so ill that I was dressed by midday, went to my brother's, the Ritz etc., and after having gone so long without food or sleep, am wondering what the next few days will bring. This is to excuse myself in case you should call tomorrow and I'm unable to receive you. I've had a pneumatique from your friend,[1] telling me that he has moved since his last letter (yet I've had nothing apart from his pneumatique) and wanted to see me only to express his admiration. I never answer letters from admirers, especially unknown ones, but I had the impression (from what, I don't know, for his pneumatique hinted at nothing of the kind) that what lay behind these sentiments was not grinding poverty (I wouldn't jump to that conclusion without first checking with you), but a desire to be secretary to the Blumenthal Committee, or something of the sort. So assuming my admirer to be humble, I answered his letter at once, while refusing his request for a meeting. Alas, if, as you say, the poor boy has been thrown out yet again, he won't have received my letter at the last address he gave me (a bookshop on the avenue Lowenthal, I think). Tell me what you would like me to do (and I think it's best done through you) and I'll do it. The circumstances you describe, the lack of a roof over his head, are heart-rending; if they are less so me, it's because at the moment I have three friends, none of whom, including the poor Comte de Maugny whom you know about (I tell you this under seal of the strictest secrecy), has any idea from one day to the next where their next meal is to come from. Which isn't to say that I'm any the less sorry for your protégé, far from it. But I don't feel for him in the same way as I do for Maugny, whom I know and love, who is married and whose wife, an angel, far better than he deserves, can't find work at the League of Nations despite speaking six languages. Since they prefer to starve to death at home rather than come here and let me help them, I shall make one last attempt to get them to write to Mathieu de Noailles, Maugny's old comrade-in-arms, who knows the Vivianis[2] etc. well – or at least allow me to tell M. de Noailles the truth. As you don't know them, I feel I can talk about them to you in a way I cannot to M. de Noailles without their permission, for they are so absurd as to wish to keep up that most fragile of appearances, wealth. Anyhow, I'm talking to you purely out of a need to sob over so much misery, not with any practical aim in view, for I'm well aware that the ministry can do nothing where the League of Nations is concerned, and I beg you to believe that, had I thought otherwise, I wouldn't have been so underhand and despicable as to seem to equate the Péret affair with the Maugny affair, and go on to ask you a favour. But I can talk to you with a clear conscience because I know there's nothing you can do, the poor things having refused all our offers of help because they were 'counting on the Genoa Conference to stabilize the Polish currency'![3]

Dear Paul, the words 'I only want to express my admiration' don't tell much about 'quo, quomodo' etc.,[4] so tell me what I should do for M. Péret, and don't get it into your head that I'm one of your 'fat cats', for I've had nothing to eat for three weeks except a plate of asparagus, and couldn't keep even that down. Unless I've reached my grandfather's[5] stage (but at least he was eighty-five years old) who, on seeing that he had kept nothing down for two days, allowed himself to starve to death within the week, during which he insisted on being carried thrice daily to his bath, where Papa, terrified, never stopped taking his pulse, my powers of resistance – though virtually non-existent – would end up by making me believe that I have some kind of vocation.

> 'Booz did not know that a woman was there
> And Ruth did not know what God wanted of her.'[6]

But don't worry, you won't see me suddenly succumb to that strange form of pride. I don't believe in vocations, I don't really believe in God, alas.

Ever yours,
Marcel

I need the Swede's address urgently.[7] Until he has received his copy, I don't dare send a single book to any of those countries.

Some consolation, rare enough at any time, has come in the form of letters from Mme Gabriel de La Rochefoucauld[8] and her husband[9] which betoken an affection, an understanding and, dare I say, an admiration that has overwhelmed me. Don't mention this to anybody, not even to them, I'll explain why. I didn't think I was still capable of being so moved by a sign of affection.

1. Benjamin Péret, a young poet.
2. See letter 153.
3. The Genoa Conference (see letter 178, n. 10) had addressed but not solved either this problem or that of Russian bonds (see letter 6 to Mme Scheikévitch, n. 9).
4. Allusion to a hexameter from a discourse on rhetoric by Quintilian, first century AD: 'Quis, quid, ubi, quibus auxiliis, cur, quomodo, quando?' ('Who, what, where, by what means, why, how, when?')
5. Proust's maternal grandfather, Nathé Weil (1814–96), whose death-bed Proust had attended. Cf. letter 54, n. 4.
6. From from Victor Hugo's poem about spiritual destiny, 'Booz endormi': 'Booz ne savait pas qu'une femme était là / Et Ruth ne savait point ce que Dieu voulait d'elle'. Cf. 'Concerning Baudelaire', *AS-B*, 288.
7. Allusion to Algot Ruhe, the 'Norwegian philosopher' portrayed in *Sodom and Gomorrah*. See letter 137, n. 2.
8. Odile de La Rochefoucauld was the daughter of Proust's old friend the Princessee Albert de Monaco, a model for the Princesse de Luxembourg.
9. See letter 194.

213 To Jean-Louis Vaudoyer

[Shortly after 17 June 1922]

My very dear friend,
I'll tell you some other time about the strange accident[1] that befell me the other day, leaving me marooned farther from port than ever. From that moment, I had to stop sending out my books. I'm not yet ready to start again, but my first exception is for you.[2] Although you still haven't 'acknowledged receipt' of *Guermantes II / Sodome I*, and I had it taken round to you at the time you said and to the address you said.

I wish I had been well enough to write to you after each of your Watteaus, Vermeers etc.,[3] so wonderful did I find them. I hope you still write for Boulenger's *Opinion*. You haven't appeared in recent numbers. I have a shining memory of the morning and when you tenderly guided my faltering steps towards that Vermeer in which the gables are like 'priceless specimens of Chinese art'.[4] I've since managed to get hold of a Belgian art-book,[5] and its numerous reproductions, studied with your article in hand, have enabled me to recognize the identical accessories in different paintings.[6]

Dear friend, have I told you how good your colleague M. de Traz[7] has been to me, and sometimes how cold. I wouldn't say this to anybody else, but you're too fond of him for it to seem like criticism when kept between the two of us (and him, naturally). Extremely moved to hear of his wife's death, I dictated a letter to him telling him of my feelings. He thanked me so touchingly that I thought I had made a friend. He then sent me his handsome book on Marquet with the following dedication which, I swear, is unique in my experience of writers who send me their books: 'To Marcel Proust from F. Fosca'. It's the sort of thing that drains the strength from arms and legs, from arms opened ready to enfold a suffering friend, from legs braced to take a step towards him. And now, having written you in my parlous state a dedication the length of one of my books, here I am with arms and legs so drained that when ready to start sending out the rest, I, too, can envisage confining myself to 'from M. Proust'.

Au revoir, dear and admired friend,
Your grateful
Marcel Proust

1. See letter 196, n. 1.
2. This letter acompanied a copy of *Sodom and Gomorrah* Part Two.
3. The series of articles on painters which had appeared in 1921: see letter 109, to Vaudoyer.
4. Allusion to their visit to the Jeu de Paume in May 1921: see letter 109, n. 10. Afterwards, Proust rewrote the scene in *The Captive* in which Bergotte, too, on the strength of 'an article by an art critic', decides to visit the Jeu de Paume, where he will collapse and die in front of *A View of Delft*, 'a picture which he adored and imagined he knew by heart, [in which] a little patch of yellow wall (which he could not remember) was so well painted that it was, if one looked at it by itself, like some priceless specimen of Chinese art, of a beauty that was sufficient in itself'. V, 207. Cf. Vaudoyer, *L'Opinion*, 7 May 1921: 'these brick houses, painted in a substance so precious, so dense, so deep, that if you isolate a small patch, forgetting its context, you might as well be looking at porcelain as paint.' And on 14 May: 'Vermeer brings a Chinese patience to his art, a skill in concealing his modus operandi that one finds only in paintings, lacquers and gems from the Far East.'

5. *Jan Vermeer of Delft* by Gustave Vanzype, mentioned by Vaudoyer in one of his articles.

6. Cf. the narrator's monologue to Albertine on the authentic proof of genius: 'You told me you had seen some of Vermeer's pictures; you must have realized that they are fragments of an identical world, that it's always, however great the genius with which they have been re-created, the same table, the same carpet, the same woman, the same novel and unique beauty [. . .].' *The Captive*, V, 430.

7. Georges de Traz, Swiss novelist, painter and art critic who wrote under the name F. Fosca; he had proposed doing a guide to Proust's characters. See *MP-GG*, 361–2.

214 To Edmond Jaloux

[Shortly before 23 June 1922]

Dear Edmond Jaloux (and the day you wish to dispense with Proust after Marcel, I'll dispense with Jaloux after Edmond, and nothing will make me happier), dear and close friend,

I must first talk about a practical matter, it being the privilege of the poetically minded to be more matter-of-fact than others about practical things. I got up for a moment today to change rooms, thinking that you might be too hot in mine. Now, I had to go back to bed with problems which make my doctor suspect I may have uremia, and as he comes tomorrow or the day after to take a blood-sample and I must stay where I am till it is analysed, our little dinner will have to be postponed. As soon as I can, I'll explain why the Ritz might be preferable.

Dear friend, I've received the incomparable *Escalier d'Or*.[1] With each step, you hurl defiance at every sage who has ever lived. You take from each his finest speech, the one most loaded with meaning, his purest ingot, and this, which nobody but you could have discovered in the hidden recesses of some celebrated work, you place on one tray of a pair of scales, which then sinks beneath this marvel of dense metal. And then, when it seems that, after these sacred texts, nothing remains to be said, you throw your wisdom, your own poetry, on to the second tray, and the first, for all that it contains Nietzsche, Firdausi,[2] Schopenhauer, rises, yielding to the greater weight. Yours are joyful and enchanted mansions,[3] and one feels that nobody can have lived a more wonderful life, even though probably woven by you continuously from a poetry that we ourselves would never have discovered in the same things, were we to see them in real life. In search of the eternal Françoise, we should find only Madame Agniel.[4]

Dear friend, how moved I was to see that among the great names you call upon in *assaying* your soul, you have, on a friendly whim such as will always prompt a great artist, included mine. Thanks to you, a sentence of mine may endure.[5] I cannot say of my books: *Habent sua fata libelli*.[6] Mine aren't slim books, they are interminable tomes. But I love the beautiful Destiny (*fata*) you shape for them ... How right you are, in your wonderful ending about the earth 'matted with roots and corpses'[7] (if I quote you correctly from memory), to say that one doesn't reach the truth by a golden stairway. Yet there are some fates that are perhaps too cruel, or would be, had a poet in his friendship not lent them his aura, his halo; take pity on your friend who, in his ever more rapid descent into the abyss by a hard ladder of iron, nevertheless regrets not having climbed the golden stairway.

Ever yours, dear friend,
Marcel Proust

1. Jaloux's latest novel (*The Golden Stairway*), each chapter of which is headed by a quotation from a famous writer or thinker.
2. Tenth-century Persian poet and historian.
3. Allusion to 'The Gospel of St John', XVI, 1.
4. In Jaloux's novel, the guileless, romantic Françoise ends up as a middle-class housewife married to the lawyer Agniel.
5. Jaloux heads one chapter with the sentence from *Swann's Way* beginning: 'And this malady which Swann's love had become ...' See I, 371–2.
6. 'Books have their destiny.' See letter 173.
7. 'A sacred poetry, a religious lyricism, arose from this hard, burning earth matted with roots and corpses. [...] I knew then that wisdom was not to be attained by climbing the golden stairway, and that all that matters in this world is the truth.' Jaloux, *op. cit*.

215 To Camille Vettard

[Shortly after 24 June 1922]

Dear friend,

Forgive this atrocious paper, but it's all I have within reach and I'm in the grip of a painful rheumatic fever, with the added misery of a constant 39°, having had a few days of feeling so much better that it felt almost like a semi-cure. However I tried to throw it off when I had your letter, so as to send Rivière your essay[1] and ask him to put it in the July issue. (Failing which, I would have sent it to Robert de Flers.) Rivière vacillated for so long that it now won't appear till August. But I don't want it to sound as if I'm grumbling about the *NRF*, having already complained to them with a vigour and comprehensiveness which, to be honest, I regret, and Gide, who came to see me and isn't all that keen on the *NRF* himself, said that I was being monstrously unfair and ungrateful. Which is untrue. (If you like, and you promise to keep it a secret, I'll let you see two fascinating letters on the subject from Jammes.) One way and another, it seems that I've been behaving badly all round (don't believe a word of it), having somehow managed to get on the wrong side of Jacques Boulenger. None the less, I wrote to him saying that I would send him your essay to read because of the nice things you said about him. As you rightly say (not that I repeated it to the *NRF*), Allard's article is very 'slapdash'. However, even though I don't know him, he very kindly wrote to apologize.[2] Some other time, I'll tell you the incredibly involved story of the Curtius essay which I wanted to have translated for you.[3] Anyhow, I believe the *NRF* are to print extracts in July. But it won't add up to much, because I don't think it's possible to give an idea of such a long and detailed essay in an extract.[4]

If they make changes in your article, don't blame me. I haven't touched so much as a comma.

I wish you could be a regular contributor to the *NRF*. Your influence would then be infinitely greater than that of somebody like me, who writes only very rarely, on the spur of the moment. Still, I suppose I am the most useful go-between you could have in the meantime. God knows, Rivière, overworked, worn out, distrait, would never get anything done if I didn't nag him. And the Vieux Colombier path[5] seems to me the worst of all.

I abbreviate my close out of exhaustion.

Your great friend,
Marcel Proust

1. 'Proust and Einstein'. See letter 209, n. 1.
2. On 8 May, Allard had written to Proust admitting that his review had been 'incomplete' and 'unworthy of its subject'.
3. See letter 161, n. 3.
4. The extract was entitled 'À propos de Marcel Proust'; the following passage

gives a flavour of Curtius's essay: 'From the reader, Proust demands a suppleness and an adaptation of his aesthetic perceptions which, at first, requires effort, but which later – like a series of physical exercises – results in a revitalization beneficial to the whole organism. He has something new to say, and to achieve this effect, I repeat, he had to invent new means of expression.'

5. Allusion to Jacques Copeau: see letter 151, n. 10.

216 To Gaston Gallimard

[Sunday night 25 June 1922]

My dear Gaston,

1. Not remembering your having told me anything about book-shops in countries with an unfavourable exchange-rate, I have no idea what you're talking about.[1] The likeliest explanation is not that you didn't write telling me what you wanted, but that I didn't read your letter, or hadn't understood it and let it slip my mind. At all events, to spare you the trouble of writing to me again on the subject, I accept your decision in advance. You're the expert in such matters and I'm a total ignoramus. Only, when you have a chance, even if it's in a year's time, let me know what you decide so that I don't look a fool if I'm asked about it. Also, if you have a chance, tell me if my book has been or is about to be translated into English,[2] as I've had various requests (I don't know what a *guinea* is worth).[3]

2. Gide and I were singing your praises for your goodness to Gabory – and also for your many kindnesses to people at the *NRF* whose names escape me. Despite my irritation with Gabory every time I open my book and see it riddled with misprints[4] – but it's not a crime in a young man to be unconscientious, merely very annoying for the author – I intend to help him myself, as I may have told you, and Mme Blumenthal has also done so, as well as Gide. He would be no good as my secretary (which seems a pity), being far too slapdash.

3. Some review or other pokes fun at us: 'this work contains 2,700,000 characters'. I told you that was absurd.[5]

4. There's nothing to tell you about my book. As you know, I've been in constant pain since my accident around 2 May (the medicament swallowed neat). I had an interval of two very good days. And then my rheumatic fever came back (it seems? much better now). I have a complete manuscript of this volume and the next, or rather a typescript (in addition to the manuscript) for, if

you remember, I engaged a typist for the purpose. But the work of correcting this typescript, making additions throughout, changing everything, has scarcely begun.[6] True, there is a carbon copy. But what's the point of your going to the expense of galleys when I can just as well correct on the typescript. À propos, I may say that Tronche told me some time ago to vary my titles, people being so silly as to say to themselves, when they pick up a book called *Sodome et Gomorrhe* like its predecessors: 'But I've already read that' (I thought he was exaggerating, but I'll give you an example that seems to show he was right). Therefore, having reflected on Tronche's remark since being tempted by Prévost's proposals,[7] I'm thinking of calling *Sodome III La Prisonnière* and *Sodome IV La Fugitive* (even if it means adding 'sequel to *Sodome et Gomorrhe*').

If you had a moment, a pneu telling me whether or not Régnier is to review my book would be helpful, indirectly. I ask only because Flers must have mentioned it to you when you saw him.[8] True, I need to write to Flers, he having asked me for an article on Shelley[9] (which I'm incapable of doing). But it would save me time (for something else) if you already knew (otherwise, don't bother to ask him). I must leave you, I can't go on. I had hoped to see you yesterday evening, to spare me this letter. I had Jacques Rivière telephoned to find out where you were, but he didn't know, at least, not officially.

All good wishes, my dear Gaston. Gide tells me that *Saul* has got off to a good start. Naturally, I didn't tell him that we had discussed it. A critic whom I don't know but who has always been very kind about me, had given it a very good review in *L'Opinion*.[10] What about Doucet?[11]

[Unsigned]

1. Gallimard was distributing books at cost price to East European countries with an adverse exchange rate.

2. Proust had evidently also forgotten that, as long ago as April 1921, Gallimard had signed a contract with Chatto & Windus for C. K. Scott-Moncrieff's translation of *Swann's Way* and its sequels. See *MP-GG* 360.

3. 21 shillings sterling was then worth FF51,70.

4. In fact, Georges Gabory was only supposed to find duplicated passages: see letter 157.

5. 'If I announced that *Sodom* contains 2,700,000 characters, it's because publishers often put that sort of thing on wrappers. People will always mock, but some feel that it justifies the price.' Gallimard to Proust, *MP-GG*, 548.

6. It is possible that Proust is disguising from Gallimard the fact that he has embarked on a completely new version of the Albertine story: see letter 103, n.3.

7. See letter 209.

8. Flers had told Gallimard that, as Proust wanted, Jean Schlumberger was to review *Sodom and Gomorrah* Part Two for the *Figaro*. See letter 228.

9. To mark the anniversary of Shelley's death.

10. Allusion to the first production of Gide's early play at the Vieux Colombier, and to a review by Gérard Bauër.

11. Jacques Doucet (1853–1929), wealthy art-collector and bibliophile. He had offered to buy proofs of *Sodom and Gomorrah* with Proust's corrections, for which Proust wanted 700 francs, a sum which Gallimard rightly surmised that Doucet would be unwilling to pay. Eventually, Doucet was to acquire a considerable number of Proust letters.

217 To Jacques Rivière

[Shortly after 1 July 1922]

My dear Jacques,

I despair, for there is nobody whom I like, whom I esteem, whom I admire more than I do you.[1] And in my blundering way I always manage to vex you, even, you say, to 'discourage' you, you, the one being I would love to see endowed with courage and to spare. I'm too ill to go into your quite unnecessary excuses.[2] Regarding *Sodome III*, wait till you hear what I have to say. There's no danger, I'm not committed to anything. But when you've weighed up my arguments, I think you'll come down on my side. I can't promise to keep extracts for you because the text doesn't really lend itself to them. But for all that I can perfectly well arrange not to be absent from the *NRF* in 1923, by giving you extracts from succeeding volumes. The reader, seeing a title (which we'll decide on together for the review), won't care in the least if the fragment he is amused by or touched by, depending on whether you want something comic (or at least meant to be comic) or moving (inasmuch as I'm capable of being moving), won't give a damn if it has come from *Sodome III* or *Sodome V*. Besides, I repeat, nothing is settled. Prévost has offered me long-term serialization over which I would have complete control. I didn't agree to a thing, and took the opportunity to say that I was an *NRF*-ist first and foremost, which he understood perfectly. In any case, I'll give you our conversation verbatim. For now, having left it vague, I would prefer you not to talk about it to anybody, except for Gaston. Being too exhausted to write to him, I would be grateful if you could pass this letter on to him, or least its substance. And even though you never pass on my messages, could you kindly tell Paulhan that for some mysterious reason my letters from the day before yesterday having remained unopened (or rather, unnoticed), I have only just spotted an envelope with his handwriting, and that, while I shall read his letter, I may not answer it immediately (unless it contains something urgent) for I'm at the end of my tether. I hope you won't deprive me of the July number in order to prove that the review is easier to obtain when one's on holiday than it is in Paris,[3] but that you'll send it to me anyway. When are you back? *What a lot I have to say to you!* not least to tell you how fond I am of you.

Marcel Proust

Are you aware that Jaloux has written a most remarkable preface to Mérimée's *La Double Méprise*? I'm not sure that I would say as much about *La Double Méprise* itself. But I have no reservations about Jaloux's preface.

1. Proust is replying to Rivière's letter expressing sorrow and outrage that Proust was tempted by Prévost's offer of serialization in the *Revue de Paris*. (Nothing was to come of the project.)

2. Rivière had explained why he had been unable to find room for Vettard's 'Proust and Einstein' in the July issue.

3. Rivière had contested Proust's opinion that the *NRF* went unread in summer because people on holiday would find it unobtainable.

218 *To Edmond Jaloux*

[Shortly after 1 July 1922]

Dear friend,

At this very moment, caught unawares, I don't see what I could 'give' you, but I use the word deliberately to indicate that, exactly like a lover, I have a desire, a need, almost, to make you a present. You allude to the intermittencies of the heart,[1] and it was probably something of the kind that determined what Stendhal called the 'crystallization', the term you yourself use à propos of what would have happened had Julie loved Châteaufort and not Darcy.[2] Moreover, after the supreme intellligence of everything you say about the triple mirror,³ the oblique approach to the story,⁴ the black spot,⁵ I admit to finding *La Double Méprise* rather lightweight. Just the same, it's marvellous. But how odd it is (and, I'm sure, deliberate) that this novella should have – on every page – a grammatical error, a jarring repetition, an assonance that sounds like repetition. I don't think one would find as much charm in the delicious scene at the Opéra were it not so 'dated', with its bouquets of flowers whose scents the women inhale.⁶ But one mustn't complain, for it's not just a line or two in Musset's 'La Mi-Carême', and the balls of those days,⁷ which benefit from this 'datedness', it's the whole of Balzac. Profound as he is, Mérimée appears stupid at times. The unsupported statement, uttered deadpan, like some witticism, that mothers whose daughters have good teeth are grateful to anybody who makes them laugh⁸ – a squalid cliché even in Molière's day – is astonishing, placed here like some rare pearl. The phrase about the art of worldly people in being watchful while appearing distrait⁹ is precisely (if one replaces worldly people with 'dukes' or the 'Faubourg St Germain') one of those phrases in Balzac which one finds ridiculous but is in fact so true. It's also an art common to Charlus and his kind.¹⁰ What I find utterly and inexplicably negligent (and it's the only example) is the treatment of Julie's illness. It's a waste of time to tell us so long in advance, in order to explain her accident, that her husband has left her an unserviceable carriage unless one takes equal pains to tell us that she has tuberculosis, or whatever it is. For no woman spits blood because she has given herself to a man the night before, even if she has caught cold into the bargain. Nor does anybody die in three days.¹¹ Which doesn't mean that it's not a marvellous story. I said just now that Mérimée puts one in mind of Balzac. I would define Mérimée's art by taking the closing sentence from a story by Balzac (the one that gains most from being dated: *Les Secrets de la Princesse de Cadignan*).¹² Balzac says something like: 'Is that the end of the story?' (or the explanation, I forget which). 'Yes, for those who have the wit to understand; no, for those who insist on knowing everything.'¹³ If I were less ill, I would make a copy of this letter, for I'm naïve enough to find a rightness in my modest remarks. And if I felt I were morally justified in doing so (I'll explain what I mean another time), I would send them just as they are to the *NRF* as a short review (naturally, I would suppress the opening, which might appear rather sodomist).

I'm doubly impatient for Morand's return, and to know how

long you are to remain in Paris.[14] Speaking for myself, it's been eight years since I've been able to leave Paris, even for an hour. There seems little chance of a turn for the better this year. And I take no pleasure in the fact, not sharing Darcy's opinions on the subject (how Flaubertian his landscapes are).[15] Besides, it was easy for him to talk, he had travelled so much. For my part, I don't even get to see Paris. I see nothing but my hideous bedroom walls, and never by daylight.

Affectionately yours,
Marcel Proust

1. Jaloux, in his preface to *La Double Méprise* by Prosper Mérimée, writes: 'If one wished to sum up *La Double Méprise*, one might say that it gives us a first glimpse of what Marcel Proust calls *Les Intermittences du Cœur*.'

2. The leading characters in *La Double Méprise*.

3. 'Thus Julie is revealed to us thrice, by her husband, by Châteaufort, and by Darcy. Each facet of this triple mirror reflects the identical image.' Jaloux, *loc. cit.*

4. 'Few stories have been treated so obliquely; the subject is approached back to front.' *Ibid.*

5. 'There is thus in all his best stories what might be termed a "black spot", something Mephistophelian, disturbing.' *Ibid.*

6. 'Several times, Julie inhales in turn from her *casolette* and her bouquet of flowers.' *Ibid.* A *casolette* is an old-fashioned scent-bottle.

7. Allusion to the traditional balls of mid-Lent.

8. Allusion to a party scene in chapter 7 of *La Double Méprise*: 'Whenever he would whisper to the young girls, causing them to laugh aloud, their mothers were unperturbed, and those whose daughters had good teeth even remarked on M. Darcy's particular civility.'

9. Allusion to a scene between Julie and Darcy in chapter 8: 'Quickly recovering her presence of mind, she returned his look with that gaze, absent yet watchful, which worldly people can adopt at will.'

10. See M. de Charlus's visual encounter with the narrator outside the Casino: II, 383–4.

11. In chapter 2, Julie's husband complains about the state of her carriage-horses; in chapter 11, her carriage overturns, and her rescuer, Darcy, seduces her; in chapter 14, she develops a fever and spits blood; in chapter 15, she dies.

12. See M. de Charlus's delight in this Balzac story: IV, 526–30.

13. 'Est-ce un dénouement? Oui, pour les gens d'esprit; non, pour ceux qui veulent tout savoir.'

14. Jaloux, about to leave on holiday, had promised to arrange that all three should dine together beforehand.

15. In chapter 11, Darcy, complaining of the tedium of travel, says that he prefers 'a Parisian fog to the eternally blue skies of the Orient'. Proust makes a comparison with certain landscapes in Flaubert's *La Tentation de Saint Antoine*.

219 To Sir Philip Sassoon[1]

[June or July 1922]

Sir,

Our dear Madame Sert[2] (whom I love still but never see, so stupidly is my life arranged) has sent me three dilapidated copies of my books on your behalf, which I can easily have replaced with undilapidated ones.[3] (Alas, the contents will remain second-rate, they being the three worst books I've written.) If I don't return them with a simple signature, and if I'm making a colossal effort to write a letter when I'm hundreds of letters behind, it's for the following reason: I wish to reply to your courteous request as courteously as possible. But I don't yet know the identity of the female 'admirer' in question. Naturally, should this person be unknown to me but enjoy the privilege of being your friend, instead of a dedication, I would copy out a page over my signature, thus adding value to the book. On the other hand, should she turn out to be an enemy of mine who has used your name in order to obtain something for which she couldn't ask me herself, then even a simple signature would seem too much, and I would return the books to you unsigned. There is also a third possibility: that the lady thinks the book is by Marcel Prévost. In which case, I willingly undertake to ask the author of *Les Don Juanes*[4] to sign his latest novel.

After all that, forgive me for making such a fuss over a simple signature.

If I should ever see you (for my hand is beginning to tire) I'll tell you about the charming pastiche I did of you a year or so ago, and my noble motives for tearing it up.[5] All I have heard from you for a very long time is a watery murmur. I was dining in the Ritz (where I often take a room for a few hours in order to avoid the guests in the dining-room) and, unaware that I had a neighbour, was explaining to a waiter[6] who had been learning the part of Sosie for the Conservatoire (the Conservatoire having sent him back to his old job at the Ritz), what Molière's play was all about.[7] Suddenly, a menacing rumble from next door, followed by a veritable deluge, left me in no doubt that Jupiter had loosed his thunderbolt as a punishment for my irreverent explanations. But no, I was told that it was only Sir Philip Sassoon taking his bath.

With these explanations, dear Sir, you have a far worse deluge, and to little purpose other than to ask you to accept my sincere respects.

Marcel Proust

1. Sir Philip Sassoon (1888–1939), scion of the banking family.
2. See letter 70.
3. The three volumes of *Sodom and Gomorrah* Part Two.
4. See letter 205.
5. Proust alludes to the abandoned sequel to his Saint-Simon pastiche.
6. Camille Wixler, a Swiss, later the source of many anecdotes about Proust who, as promised, put his name in a book: see II, 96.
7. Allusion to Molière's comedy *Amphytrion*. Jupiter and Mercury disguise themselves as the Theban general Amphytrion and his servant Sosie, in order that Jupiter may make love to Amphytrion's wife – with farcical results when the general and his servant return from the wars. The play contains lines that have become famous sayings in French: 'Le véritable Amphytrion / Est l'Amphytrion où l'on dine' (Amphytrion having taken on the meaning of one's host), and 'Le Seigneur Jupiter sait dorer la pillule' ('Jupiter knows how to gild the pill').

220 To Madame Soutzo

[Early July 1922]

Dear Princesse,

A note to explain a card which must have seemed inexplicable to you. I was about to leave to dine at the Ritz (in *daylight*!) where, once again, I dine almost every night, when your pneumatique arrived. You wrote very illegibly, and the little I was able to decipher seemed to me rather offensive. But being a sensible man, I told myself that, whatever else, it was a favour to receive a note of that length from you, a favour that at one time (not so long ago I was still able to reanimate 'the tarnished mirrors and the lifeless flames')[1] I would have thought beyond price; and, still no doubt in thrall to that flame ('She half-alive and I half-dead',[2] to quote Hugo rather than Baudelaire this time), having said 'To the Ritz', I made the taxi turn around and go via the avenue Charles Floquet where some well-intentioned person who is, I suppose, your female concierge, told me that, alas, you were out. I wasn't too disappointed, for if you had guests I wouldn't have come in. I took a chance on finding you alone. I lost my bet. If I didn't 'give you a call' when dining at the Ritz (where I was alone, so I must ask you not to mention it, too many people having expected me to dinner on those nights), it's because I assumed, from all the invitations which even I receive daily, reclusive, entombed as I am, that you who are, thank God, so very alive, so much in demand, could have scarcely a moment to yourself. Besides, I never go to the Ritz anymore. For after several months of sending round for ice-cream,[3] cold beer and beef salad, whenever I arrive total strangers emerge from kitchens and cellars to assure me that it was they who had frozen the raspberries or sliced the meat, all of which costs me a fortune (don't imagine that I'm ga-ga because I put *œufs* instead of *eux*;[4] veronal has made me do that sort of thing for fifteen years, and I'm still here). Tell Morand (has his Ireland taken up residence beneath the Invalides dome to punish England, I wonder[5]) that Marcel Boulenger has written a highly eulogistic and agreeable piece about him in the *Renaissance*.[6] What's more, the same issue has a note by Jacques Boulenger, equally agreeable but shorter and more elliptical, as my dear, my increasingly dear Léon Daudet would say (he is leaving for Brittany, alas). Which re-Boulengizes me somewhat. But he should certainly read Marcel Boulenger. In sending you my admiring respects and sensing, in spite of everything, an overlong separation (and also, perhaps, too glacial an approach[7] the other evening) effacing features so dear, so special to me that I had thought them fixed in my mind for ever, I bid you, with, perhaps, a more melancholy inflection, a more synthesized meaning than formerly, Adieu Princesse.[8]

Marcel Proust

1. See letter 79, n.5.
2. See letter 60, n.1.
3. See Albertine's rhapsodies over the Ritz ice-cream: V, 140–1.
4. In the previous sentence, for *eux* (they), Proust had first written, then crossed out, the assonant *œufs*.
5. The parenthesis is very unclear, but Proust may allude to conversations (or correspondence) about the recent ratification of the Irish Free State by Parliament, preceded by the withdrawal of the notorious British 'Black and Tans'.
6. *La Renaissance* had conducted a survey on modern literary style; Jacques and Marcel Boulenger had both cited Morand's latest novel, *Ouvert la nuit*.
7. *approche*: conceivably, Proust had meant to write *reproche* ('reproach').
8. Proust implies a combination of the finality and spiritual meaning of *Adieu*.

221 To Gaston Gallimard

[2 or 3 July 1922]

Dear Gaston,

1. A totally insignificant point before I answer your question, to be read in the spirit in which it is written, that is, solely in order to spare you a problem that is highly unlikely to arise. I received no cheques at all at the end of June. It goes without saying that there's no question of its being overdue, and I would be ashamed to mention it but for the fact that I have a very careless concierge and wanted to put you on your guard lest it has gone to somebody else (again, highly unlikely), in which case it's essential that your bank stops it at once. Note that no other possibility has entered my mind. But it always arrives so punctually on the 30th that I had doubts which aren't really doubts at all. In all likelihood, you are adding on royalties, and that's delaying things.

2. Announce my books for 1923 *by all means* if you wish, dear friend. But if to announce them means committing yourself to a publication date, I can make no promises. For neither party is 'ready', whatever 'ready' may mean. And as you know, even when one party is, there are always delays. I don't want to deliver you botched work but the best I can manage within my feeble capabilities. Let's face it, there's a lot to be done on both sides. Being slightly less ill at the moment, I can get down to work. But who knows what tomorrow has in store. Therefore, if to announce my books means committing me, then, no, don't announce them. In any case, you have everything to gain. People are rather put off by my three volumes. The reported number of characters is a little daunting.[1] It would be better to give my readers a chance to catch their breath and regain their appetite. Yet there mustn't be too long an interval, for not everybody will remember that, at the end of *Sodome et Gomorrhe II*, I leave to make my life with Albertine, and since this life constitutes the whole of *Sodome III* (which will have a different title), it would be better (within the limits of my strength) not to give people time to forget. Another reason for not announcing them is that I had thought of calling the first part *La Prisonnière* and the second *La Fugitive*. Now, Mme de Brimont[2] has just translated a book by Tagore,[3] calling it *La*

Fugitive. So, no *Fugitive*, as it would cause confusion. And no *Fugitive*, no *Prisonnière*, which is its exact antithesis.[4] Knowing her slightly, I could of course write to Mme de Brimont, but that would be the act of a cad, and my letter would arrive too late. It would therefore be better not to give too many details in advance. Moreover, Chaumeix,[5] in his very nice article in the *Gaulois*, points out that I don't always publish what has been announced in advance.

Dear friend, I'm too tired to say all I wanted to say. I'm in none of your current crop of catalogues, advertisements etc. Without expecting you to put, as for Morand, '5000 copies sold in 10 minutes'[6] (joke), it's not good enough, especially when my old enemy and calumniator of many years' standing, the *Crapouillot*, makes out that it publishes all your best authors.[7] I must stop.

Do you think it would please Jacques if I wrote a 'Reply to M. Thibaudet' for the August issue: a 'My dear Thibaudet' on Flaubert?[8]

Ever yours,
Marcel Proust

1. See letter 216, n. 5.
2. Renée de La Bonninière de Brimont (1886–1943), poet, Lamartine's grandniece.
3. Indian devotional lyrics by the Bengali poet and novelist Rabindranath Tagore (1861–1941).
4. The symmetry was to be restored in October: see Tadié, *op. cit.*, 886.
5. André Chaumeix: see letter 223.
6. The *NRF* had advertised *Ouvert la nuit* as 'Book of the Week: 5000 copies sold in 14 days'.
7. Apparently, *Le Crapouillot* was re-issuing leading writers for lending libraries: see *MP-GG*, 552. (Proust seemed unlikely to be among them, the paper having called him 'a snobbish, misanthropic windbag'.)
8. Albert Thibaudet having published his literary criticism on Flaubert in book form, Proust was contemplating another of his epistolary articles.

222 To Madame Soutzo

[Shortly after 2 July 1922]

Dear Princesse,

Adorable friend, I sent Odilon round to you last night, but as there were no cars outside he was afraid of waking you up if he rang the bell. He was to tell you that I was up and dressed but not well enough to go downstairs. Also, a dinner I had had sent round from the Ritz had disagreed with me.

You talk so brilliantly about Charlus that I would love to write something just for you, on anything you like, as a reminder of the old days. I'm very ill, you know, to the point, this morning, of jumping out of the window. Léon Daudet is so good to me.

Adieu Princesse, your admiring and respectful friend
Marcel Proust

223 To André Chaumeix[1]

44 rue Hamelin
[4 or 5 July 1922]

Dear Sir (Dear friend would be more appropriate, but you might think me familiar),

Barely twenty-four hours ago I was writing to M. Rageot[2] (to whom my thanks were long overdue) when the press-cutting agency (usually so inefficient) delivered your charming and profound review in the *Gaulois*[3] and an extract from the same article in *L'Action française*.[4] My pleasure was all the greater for being unexpected. You had told me that, after Rageot, you could write no further essays on my book; admiring and liking you for disinterested reasons, I easily reconciled myself to that. But I'm delighted. Your *Gaulois* essay, like the one you wrote on *Swann* for the *Débats*,[5] ends with a description of nature, a miniature landscape. This resemblance probably escaped you. It merely emphasizes the spontaneity of your line of thought. And so often this line follows the crest. One regrets that, with this eagle's eye view, this breadth of horizon, you should give the best of your ideas, quasi-anonymously, to this or that newspaper or review, when one would like to see them collected so that one would have them to hand, condensed in your effortlessly pure, perfect style, and could turn to them at will. You're on a level with cathedral stone-masons whose masterpieces were never signed. One dislikes anonymity for one's friends (decidedly, I am becoming familiar

> 'It's a fault, I confess it,
> And I'll find a way to correct it.')[6]

In any case, your first drafts being definitive, could you not put them together as they are, without any need for re-setting?

A word or two more about your article. You quote France's dictum: 'Clarity etc.' He must have said that, since you say so.[7] But then, a great mind encompasses many contradictions. One day, in my presence (for I saw a great deal of him), somebody complained to him that a certain author (very probably Mallarmé) was obscure. Slightly irked, Monsieur France replied that everything had once seemed obscure, and he cited texts proving that Racine was thought obscure by his contemporaries.[8]

This idea being very close to me (though I had never confided it to my Master), I was moved to hear him unsuspectingly give it his authority. I was later to apply it to Painting and Music, in essays which attracted much attention abroad, notably in Germany.[9] I cannot, alas, apply this theory to myself, aware that some writings possess neither novelty nor merit, and seem lacking in clarity. And I very much fear that À la Recherche du temps perdu must be classed among them. If I weren't beginning to tire, I would admit to you that I, too, was sickened at having to give such prominence to the analysis of unhealthy passions.[10] Thank God it's almost over. I say almost. For in the rather healthier part to come, Charlus reappears – as little as I can manage – and his behaviour grows worse and worse. He's a madman.

Unable to go on, I abridge the usual formula and remain your grateful and devoted

Marcel Proust

1. André Chaumeix (1874–1955), critic.

2. Gaston Rageot (1873–1942), critic. His review of *Sodom and Gomorrah* Part Two in *Le Gaulois* of 10 June had compared Proust to Saint-Simon.

3. 'Marcel Proust and the study of sensibility', *Le Gaulois*, 1 July, a long, eulogistic article that praises Proust's portrayal of the human condition.

4. Perhaps at the instigation of Léon Daudet: see previous letter.

5. Chaumeix had reviewed *Swann's Way* in the *Journal des Débats* in January 1914.

6. Proust freely adapts lines from Musset's prefatory verse to *Poésies*: 'Ce livre est toute ma jeunesse / Je l'ai fait sans presque y songer / Il y paraît, je le confesse, / Et j'aurais pu le corriger.'

7. 'Anatole France once said that three things are essential to good writing, the first being clarity, the second clarity, the third again clarity.' Chaumeix, *loc. cit.*

8. See Proust, in 1896, in his essay 'Against Obscurity': 'Our obscurity [young poets may say] is the same obscurity as was held against Hugo, as was held against Racine. In language, whatever is new is obscure.' *AS-B*, 136.

9. Presumably an allusion to his essay for *L'Opinion* (see letter 57) and to 'On Flaubert's Style' and 'Concerning Baudelaire' for the *NRF*. Also to the essay by Curtius (see letter 164).

10. '[. . .] one may see a legitimate originality in the author's analyses of Sodom and Gomorrah. In any case, it could be said that his writing apes the actual emotional state that it analyses, and if it occasionally shocks or exasperates us with its picture of society, and its descriptions, it has the singular merit, when dealing with the impulses of susceptibility, of an uncompromising frankness that is not only stimulating but has a new and strange kind of beauty.' Chaumeix, *op. cit.*

224 To Sydney Schiff

[5 July 1922]

My dear Sydney,

You write me a shocking letter,[1] purely and simply to shock me, and in order that I, horrified, should be obliged to write to you in reply. Which I do, while asking myself if I'm not wrong to give in to such blackmail. You know perfectly well that I see nobody, and that, apart from the soirée I told you about,[2] I haven't seen a living soul but you and Madame Schiff for many months. You know that I can't write letters (this is the exception, and as I can't find my letter-paper and Céleste is asleep, I'm writing on the papers I use for lighting my fumigation powders). You know that I don't lead the life with which you reproach me, whereas you yourself do. You have only to read my book to see the stupid likes and dislikes of this social life which I put behind me at the age of twenty. Not that that prevented the N.R.F. twenty years later from dismissing *Swann* as the work of a social butterfly.[3] But you don't read my book because, in common with all the other society people who dislike it, you are too restless in Paris, too busy in London and hold too many house-parties in the country. Moreover, as the first thing a really good book does is to make the shattered spirit whole and calm the troubled breast, the fault lies not with me but with my book. Yet from the day it came out, people were reading it in the metro, in their carriages, in trains, oblivious of their neighbours, forgetting their stops. I have no time for the purely social theory that one can like the man but not his work. I would refute this sophism in two minutes, if I were less tired. Besides, I'm not sure that you like the author. I remember once asking you to subscribe to a volume of *Jeunes filles en fleurs*, and you replied that it annoyed you to think that one could have bought the entire print-run at the price. On that basis, one would never buy a single book, and not only would authors die for lack of the means to buy the bread of life, one would perish oneself, through one's refusal to buy the bread of the spirit. And I think of the story that Whistler used to tell about a luncheon at which his belongings were seized by the bailiffs despite the presence of every imaginable lord and millionaire. 'It would have been nothing to them,' he said, 'to have bought a painting or two to satisfy the bailiffs. But not one of them lifted a finger. Not, I think, out of meanness. Nor out of spite, for they were all perfectly happy to be in my house, in my company. No,' concluded the painter of the *Nocturnes*, 'I think the truth is that that it never occurred to them, it was *lack of imagination*.'[4]

Dear Sydney, Whistler is a far cry from the unfinished indictment I am drawing up against you. But I'm too tired. I confine myself to citing but one example of my fidelity: as evidence of the fact that I see nobody except the Schiffs, I keep at your disposal the fifty or so telegrams I have received from Antoine Bibesco since his return saying: 'Won't you dine with us tonight anywhere you like with anybody you choose?' And never once have I accepted.

With my humble respects to Madame Violet, yours
affectionately,
Marcel Proust

Another thing, more shocking than all the rest put together. Fancy saying that I claimed to have felt better once you had left. Your departure could only have reduced me to tears. It's as stupid as your thinking that I felt better for your presence. The relationship between one's state of mind and one's body is not as simple as that. I'll pursue this with you one of these days, when I'm not so tired and overworked, for my ideas on the subject are absolutely clear and, I believe, rather profound.

My dizzy spells, and the weakness in my arms and legs, have almost completely disappeared.

'Don't drink!' (Alas, I've rather taken after you in that respect.)[5] Don't take adrenalin if you suffer from hypertension, it could be very dangerous. Otherwise, it will do you a great deal of good. Be sure to ask me beforehand how to use it. And, to avoid any possible risk, make sure a *reliable* doctor takes your blood-pressure and examines your heart. Boissy's pills, taken as a laxative every two weeks, can only do good. But don't take them without eating afterwards (or after having eaten).

1. Missing letter.
2. Mme Hennessy's party: see letter 205.
3. Proust may have had in mind this cutting (doubtless supplied by Antoine Bibesco) from an article entitled 'A History of the NRF' in the *New York Evening Post* of 10 July: 'When Marcel Proust offered them his first long novel it was rejected because the author [...] happened to be a rich man, and the taboo against society amateurs in the world of letters is such that, at first, the publishers couldn't believe in the quality of the work they were being offered.'
4. Proust has already said most of the foregoing in letter 71 to Sydney Schiff.
5. See letter 141 to Walter Berry.

225 To Percy Wyndham Lewis[1]

44 rue Hamelin
(for your address was incorrect)
[Friday evening 7 July 1922]

Dear Sir,

The letter you did me the honour of writing, and which will always remain for me a most precious autograph, arrived only this evening, Friday. To save time, as soon as I had opened it I sent my maid to fetch you in her husband's taxi (he is a taxi-driver). They may have told you at your hotel that, at about eight o'clock, just after you had gone out, a very tall woman wearing a black hat had come to fetch you. Unfortunately, I have a cold this evening and am very much afraid that, if you are leaving on Monday, I shall be too unwell to receive you on Saturday and Sunday. So don't count on our meeting, think no more about it, and if I happen to be well enough I will send somebody round for you. But don't wait in on my account, it being most unlikely that I shall be able to receive you. And yet to be drawn by you would have been my one chance to be remembered by posterity! That being so, and because of the great pleasure I would have had in meeting you, kindly thank my great friend Monsieur Sydney Schiff, when you see him, for his exquisitely thoughtful idea which has at least afforded me the opportunity of expressing to you, dear Sir, together with my keen regrets, my warmest regards.

Marcel Proust

1. Percy Wyndham Lewis (1882–1957), artist, novelist and critic, a leading figure in the Vorticist movement.

226 To Edmond Jaloux

[Saturday evening 15 July 1922]

Dear friend,

I thank you again with all my heart – on paper unworthy of you[1] (but Céleste is asleep and has forgotten to leave out my letter-paper) – for the great pleasure it gave me to see you this evening,[2] a pleasure tinged with trepidation, I having scarcely dared hope to see you (I'm wrong to say 'see') and thus failed to notice that you were wearing a white tie, nor, till afterwards, that you were there one minute and gone the next.[3] And you were much missed for the rest of the evening. And you can't imagine how it ended, in that apparently quiet place. Maleissye[4] and the others (I don't think I'm being indiscreet in telling you this, but better not mention it, just in case) got into a fight with some unspeakable pimps. Everybody was drunk (I wasn't), it was appalling. As far as I could see, the owner[5] and his staff took the side of the pimps and fancy-boys. I'll tell you all about it when I see you, meanwhile, say nothing, especially not in front of the owner, who is a pretty dubious character. I was glad that you had left before these scenes began, not that you would have understood what was happening any more than I did because, although the bar is small, it all took place at the other end, where the drunken adversaries appeared to be joking. I thought my delightful duelling days were back again, but it seems that our assailants were not the sort of people with whom one fights. One can take such principles too far, in my opinion, for if one consented to cross swords only with the likes of Monsieur Baudrillart[6] or Monsieur de Luynes,[7] one would obviously never fight anybody! But my friends adhering to this code, and my having no personal quarrel with anybody, I couldn't 'go it alone'.[8] At any rate, this Moses,[9] whom I had taken for Brach's friend, evidently keeps tables which are outside the Law. I prattle about these stupid goings-on in a letter to you out of sorrow that we should have parted so soon, under the illusion of finding you again, and in the hope that, once the dialogue between two men who think of one another constantly (for you kindly told me that you too think of me) has given way to a cheerful, carefree familiarity, we shall be able to enjoy, in the Real, a friendship that, till now, has existed mainly in Spirit and in Truth.[10]

Marcel Proust

1. Probably the paper he used to light his powders: see letter 224.

2. Jaloux had been invited to join Proust, Paul Brach (see letter 211, n. 1) and Brach's friends at Le Bœuf sur le Toit. This bar, which Cocteau had made his headquarters (it was named for his burlesque), remained one of most fashionable rendezvous in Paris for the rest of the 1920s.

3. Jaloux had arrived dressed for a party he was to attend later in the evening.

4. Charles, Comte de Maleissye-Melun.

5. Louis Moyse, formerly proprietor of Cocteau's anti-Dada bar, Le Gaya.

6. Alfred Baudrillart (1859–1942), scholar and wit, principal of the Catholic Institute.

7. The Duc de Luynes.

8. Proust nevertheless exchanged addresses with one of the brawlers: see following letter.

9. See note 5.

10. See letter 90, n. 2. This letter was never sent, for reasons which Proust explains in letter 251.

227   To Jacques Delgado[1]

44 rue Hamelin
[Sunday 16 July 1922]

Sir,
    You owe me no apology whatsoever; that you should offer me one testifies to your sensitivity and 'good manners'.
    For a moment, in the unaccustomed confusion and hubbub of the bar, I almost hoped to become involved in some way in this quarrel which I had at first taken for horse-play. Hoped, not because I contemplated joining in a café brawl that would have been incompatible with my tastes, age and health, but because I had glimpsed an opportunity for something I used to enjoy very much and for which my health is absolutely no bar to my enjoying again: a duel. But my friends swore that it was out of the question, that the quarrel had nothing to do with me, and that to send my seconds to call on you would be absurd and a waste of time. Were they lying to me out of misplaced tact, and being over-protective? Only you can tell me the answer to that. Yet it's virtually certain that I shall never see you again. I shall thus remain in a state of perpetual doubt, albeit one that will very soon be cured by oblivion. However, your noble sentiments give me precisely the pleasure I would have enjoyed after a duel, and without the necessity of having first crossed swords with you, namely, Sir, the pleasure of shaking you very cordially by the hand.

                                                  Marcel Proust

1. One of the drunken brawlers of the night before: see previous letter. Proust had dispatched Odilon to Delgado's address at dawn, prompting his apology.

228   To Jean Schlumberger[1]

[Sunday evening 16 July 1922]

Dear friend,
    I have such cramp in my hand today, due to poisoning for which I have only myself to blame, having been tolerably well till then,

that I doubt if you can read my handwriting. But feelings of gratitude prevail, and my heartfelt thanks cannot wait. I was rather indiscreet about this review,[2] Flers having suggested various famous authors and I having felt that you (in addition to being famous) were much more talented. So I dismissed all these names and – herein lies the indiscretion – asked him if he couldn't get Jean Schlumberger. I wouldn't have done the same in the case of the *NRF*, for there would have been no point to my indiscretion. But remembering how I was once obliged to return a categorical no to a request from Gide[3] (*I implore you to keep this strictly between ourselves*), I felt that the chore of doing this review, which you could always refuse, would at least have the advantage of giving you 'top-billing', as we used to call it, in a publication not your own, and it's no bad thing to have different milieux in which to expand one's ideas. I meant it when I told Flers that your review was excellent. What I didn't tell him, but won't hide from you, being too fond of you to conceal it, is that I found the transpositions of gender you attribute to me[4] – without premeditation, I'm sure – particularly hurtful after everything that has been said.[5] Your paragraph is perfectly logical, and contains no hint of spite. But coming on top of so many absurd remarks about my young girls being young men in disguise, it looks as if you are giving the blessing of your infallible mind and great talent to an absurd hypothesis. Anyhow, it's a mere bagatelle in what is a superb article.

I fear I may have hurt Flers' feelings by insisting on the real Schlumberger, Jean, as opposed to the fake, Gustave,[6] who has always retained a false prestige in his eyes, being a former colleague of his grandfather, M. de Rozière.[7] With any luck, I may have discredited him once and for all by telling Flers the story – which I won't repeat here, being unable to write as you see; indeed, my letter must be full of spelling mistakes – of a soirée I attended recently. I gave Flers a full description of the arrival of Gustave-Vercingétorix,[8] and of his sudden transformation, thanks to Comtesse de Murat having spat at him, which was her way of convincing him that he should vote for Maurras, into a hippopotamus.[9] I left out the best part, alas. When the music stopped, your uncle, thinking the evening was over, got to his feet, grumbling about 'social life' and declaring musical soirées to be his 'greatest torture', thereby exciting the admiration of Mme de Ganay,[10] herself a witness to the daily abnegation suffered for years by a man of the world by way of mortification. Unfortunately, Gustave

Schlumberger, having chatted to every X-*de-la*-X in sight all through the music without looking at his programme, didn't realize that the second part of the soirée was still to come. When it began, he was already half-way downstairs, mad with rage, soaking wet, and raving about the joys of solitude. At once, with a nimbleness commendable in this wild cave-man, he turned on his heel and ran back upstairs to snuggle up to a pair of duchesses. That's what I forgot to tell Robert de Flers; I'll make up for my omission another time.

Dear friend, despite being so paralysed by drugs that I can hardly hold my pen, I want to ask you if you are leaving Paris, and if so, when. For while love at a distance is sweet, real friendship requires rather less mystery.[11] In other words, when I'm better I would love to see you, here, at your house, at the N.R.F., wherever you say. I only wish that extracts from your review could appear in the papers (preferably not the transpositions of gender), especially in *L'Action française*, which does an excellent Review of the Press. Unfortunately, Léon Daudet is away, and I'm afraid it may have escaped his notice. I don't really get on with Maurras, although we're on good terms (at a distance, that is, for though I'm anything but idle, I lead the life of a recluse, and am 'walled up', to quote M. de Luynes).[12] In fact, I believe that the soirée where I had the fun of seeing the fake Schlumberger but not the joy of meeting the real one, was my first such outing for years. I'm not an anchorite from choice, like the admirable Gustave, but I go out less than he does.

I'm astonished that people should take *Sodome et Gomorrhe* for a moral tale. The *Gaulois*, where I know nobody, has already had five articles about it. The *Écho de Paris* says that I deserve the Nobel Prize.[13] The *Revue de Paris* talks about me as if I were a superior Madame de Ségur.[14]

Dear friend, my hand is giving out. Adieu. Thank you.

Marcel Proust

1. See letter 184, n. 4.

2. The *Figaro* review Proust had been angling for: see letter 216, n. 8. Entitled 'Une nouvelle *Comédie Humaine*', it had appeared that morning.

3. In 1914, Gide, having had several letters from Proust about *Les Caves du Vatican*, had asked him to review it for *Le Figaro*. See *Selected Letters Volume Three*.

4. 'True, here and here one recognizes a person, a character, an anecdote; but, as ever, this artist makes free use of everything he observes, lending one the experi-

ences of another, placing a head on shoulders where it doesn't belong, turning an adolescent boy into a young girl, a dowager into an old gentleman.' Schlumberger, *loc. cit.*

5. By Souday, for example: see letter 77.

6. See letter 205, n. 8. Gustave Schlumberger was Jean Schlumberger's uncle.

7. Eugène de Rozière, the death of whose wife in 1907 had prompted Proust's *Figaro* article 'Une Grand-mère', an essay prefiguring his narrator's anguish over the death of his grandmother: see *CS-B*, 545–8.

8. See Proust to Flers, 12 June: 'I saw this imbecile [. . .] snorting in the hall and twirling his Vercingétorix moustaches.' See Proust's description of Schlumberger as a 'buffalo' in letter 205.

9. See Proust to Flers, *op. cit.*: 'The Comtesse Murat, while explaining to him why it was essential he vote for Maurras, spat in his face to such an extent that he emerged streaming with water like a hippopotamus.' Allusion to Maurras's candidacy for the French Academy. See also letter 205.

10. See letter 205, n. 5. Apparently, her sick brother-in-law was on a strict diet.

11. Proust alludes to the dialogue between Oronte and Alceste in Act I, scene 2 of *Le Misanthrope*.

12. See letter 176.

13. These statements were all true.

14. Allusion to the style of the moral tales for children by the Comtesse de Ségur (1799–1874). Vandérem wrote in the *Revue de Paris*: 'Here, for example, we have a newcomer, a young musician called Morel who is discovered by poor M. de Charlus and loved by him in a fashion even more explicit than Vautrin's for young Rubempré.' (Vandérem alludes to recurring characters in Balzac.)

229   To Paul Brach[1]

[Shortly after 16 July 1922]

As I told you, I wrote to M. Delgado.[2] I forgot to add that he may not have had my letter, for he wasn't at the rue Greuze address he gave. The concierge didn't know him, but took my money and letter anyway, presumably out a mixture of curiosity and cupidity. I also forgot, when thanking you, to tell you that the chicken was delicious. What a pity, when it had been so beautifully roasted, that somebody thought fit to throw it at your head. I haven't been able to identify the horrible waiter I was so certain I knew.

Your
Marcel

Please turn over.

The chicken I meant was at the Bœuf sur le Toit, and it being under that roof reminded me of the night I took Sem[3] from Trouville to Cabourg in a taxi. It was pitch dark, with bullocks charging us at every corner, and Sem was less than pleased, saying to me: 'You suggested that we went for a drive, not to a corrida in the wilds of the pampas.' Thanks to your gallantry and good sense, the sizzling chicken wasn't followed by an ice-bucket, that being precisely what happened some years ago in a lunatic asylum which you may know, for it has a sublime sculptured gate called – as a preventive measure, it being mediaeval – the 'Well of Moses'.[4]

P.S. Do you think, in case Montesquiou attacks me in his Memoirs, that I would be entitled to sue M. Louis Couchoud?[5] I ask because I had a very long and very nice letter from him about a week ago.

1. See letter 211, n. 1. This note carries no salutation.
2. See letter 227.
3. Alias the famous cartoonist Georges Goursat (1863–1934); the occasion was the summer of 1907.
4. Proust is reminded by the name of the proprietor of Le Bœuf sur le Toit, Louis Moyse, of the fourteenth-century monument at the Chartreuse de Champmol, in Dijon, with its magnificent figure of Moses by Claus Sluter. The monastery later became the city asylum. Proust visited Dijon in 1903.
5. Dr Paul-Louis Couchoud, Montesquiou's executor. In fact, Montesquiou's memoirs were to prove innocuous where Proust was concerned.

230 To Sydney Schiff

[Saturday evening 18 July 1922]

My dear Sydney,

Our letters crossed. Not having yours beside me as I write, I'm sure to forget everything I wanted to say. It was full of inaccuracies (unintentional, of course). There is no question of my being cured.

I cited Antoine Bibesco not as an example of a man-about-town but as your proof that I've broken the rules only with you and Madame Violet.[1] You should know that he and his brother read part of the manuscript of *Swann* around 1911 and were so enthusiastic (forgive my talking about myself like this) that they begged Copeau, whom they knew at the *NRF*,[2] to print some fragments, which were rejected, and more importantly, to publish the book, which was also rejected. As a result, I went from publisher to publisher, ending up with Grasset. The book having had some success with Grasset, whose firm then closed down for the duration, the N.R.F. confessed their error in having turned it down and approached me, which is how I came to join them. All this to show you that the Bibescos (one died a horrific death, alas)[3] were the first to admire *Swann*, and that it's a travesty to call my ultra-intellectual relations with Antoine worldly. What's more, not a day passes but he sends me cuttings from America. It's entirely thanks to him that I keep in touch with the foreign press.

Thirdly, to say that reading a book by a person one knows is as pointless as listening to the voice of a living person on the gramophone, is absurd. There is a world of difference between what a person *says* and what he dredges up, through meditation, from the veiled depths of the Mind. True, there are people who are better than their books, but that's because their books aren't *Books*. I believe that old fool Ruskin, who occasionally said a sensible thing, expressed at least some of that rather well.[4] I no longer remember where, but I can find it for you if you like.

If it would amuse you, I'll send you some of the rather remarkable (and at bottom, idiotic) articles about me which have appeared in various newspapers and magazines. But they're very uninteresting.

You talk as if I go about in society. I've been out once, as I told you, and that was the first time for a year.

I'm too tired to go on. I still haven't written to M. Eliot,[5] not having seen anybody from the N.R.F. they all being on holiday. 'Deus nobis haec otia fecit',[6] as they're probably saying about what they earn from my books, and I earn less than they do.

Fondest love, my dear Sydney, I kiss Madame Violet's hand.
Marcel Proust

Pay attention to the pagination, I've muddled up the pages.

1. See letter 224.
2. Jacques Copeau was editor at the time.
3. Emmanuel Bibesco: see letter 14.
4. See Proust's profound essay 'On Reading', the preface to his translation of *Sesame and Lilies*: *AS-B*, 195–226.

5. T.S. Eliot had asked for an extract for *The Criterion*. But Proust feared complications: Eliot acted as London correspondent for Rivière and also published Schiff, a story of whose Proust had urged on Rivière in vain.

6. 'A God has brought us this leisure time'. Virgil, *Eclogues*, I, vi.

231   To Gaston Gallimard

[Thursday 20 July 1922]

To be read to the end

My dear Gaston,

Your letter touches me without convincing me. The publicity given to *Sodome et Gomorrhe II* is entirely due to the friendship which some writers have for me.[1] In the case of M. Havard de La Montagne[2] I cannot talk of friendship, but I had a letter from him only yesterday, Wednesday. And precisely because his letter, forwarded either from rue Laurent-Pichat or boulevard Haussmann, the envelope isn't here (but I haven't thrown it away and can show you that it bears me out in every particular) thanks me for a favour, I certainly hope that he will charge advertising rates for any extract he inserts,[3] if he inserts anything (very likely, he will do nothing, which could for all I know be more advantageous for me on account of hidden dealings in which you are not involved. In that case, we should be careful not to insist and, rather than ask again, fall back on *L'Œuvre*, which is excellent). That way, we avoid putting ourselves in the humiliating position of appearing to ask him to repay my trifling favour within twenty-four hours. Robert de Flers said that he wouldn't charge me a sou,[4] but what's the point of going into all that again. The fake Morand advertisement 'Unsuitable for young girls' never appeared in *Ève*,[5] nor did 'Wanted on voyage', which is plastered all over the newspapers, though not for me. Lastly, and you're going to find me insufferable, I'm not happy about the extracts you propose using in the August number of the *NRF*. 1. I would have preferred to choose them for myself *from the the moment we decided to use them*. 2. But why use them at all? *NRF* readers are my readers. You even kindly suggested sending the extracts to the Librairie Gallimard. But don't you see that that is simply to hold up a mirror to ourselves? Isn't to tell readers of Gallimard books that 'M. Bidou has eulogized M. Proust in the *Revue de Paris*'[6] rather like that trick one played as a child when one wrote love-letters and posted them to oneself? On one point I owe you an apology, for you seem to think I was implying that Tronche used to manage these things better (I haven't seen him for months, by the way. I hope he is well. And his wife?).[7] Now, that's the last thing I meant, for it never occurred to me that you would be so kind as to trouble yourself about them. What I meant was: 'Rather than some awkward secretary, send somebody with Tronche's authority and tact.'[8] You didn't enter my mind, how could you have thought so! Any more than I would mean you to think that Tronche was involved in what I'm about to tell you, which I learnt from an entirely different source. I find it only natural that writers of the stature of Gide and his equals should be paid as much or more than me. But I confess that it hurt me (the material backlash being especially painful) to learn that one particular author of yours, a very intelligent man, competent in working-class matters, but whom you yourself consider a third-rate writer[9] (there I take his side, for in my opinion you attach too much importance to his French and his style) is paid far better than I am.[10] The other day, I didn't pursue the matter of reprints for which I haven't been paid. You were certainly in the right. I had understood that my monthly cheques were in payment for past books, and that new works would be paid per reprint, according to our contract (without which we should never be of one mind!). I obviously misunderstood, and even to think of my mistake makes me blush. But I find it hard that M. P.H. and others should take precedence over me.

Dear Gaston, this eternal money-talk is like spewing up mud, and I would like to cleanse myself by giving you a brotherly handshake (the comic aspect of this incoherent metaphor consoles me a little for having said anything so vulgar). And I'm sure that you would do me more good by giving me sound practical advice than by paying me better. One gains as much from cutting down on one's expenses as from increasing one's income. Those may not be the words of a good businessman, but they come from the heart of a friend who is very truly yours.

Marcel Proust

You distress me greatly when you say that your life is stupid. It is superb. Your name is associated with the most important literary movements of our time. Abroad (as I well know, for reasons I won't go into for fear of reviving our differences), the N.R.F. is regarded as being on a par with the Parnassians, or the Symbolists. I understand why there can be no pleasure in putting one's name to a work when, as in my case, that pleasure is marred by constant physical pain which precludes its slightest sensation. In that case, cut off from happiness by constant ill-health, one can feel nothing. But that's not so in your case, thank God: you have your health, and you are a sensible man who drinks Vittel. Furthermore, your name isn't just associated with one individual book, but with a cycle of books: the N.R.F. Only see your life from this angle and you can be proud and happy. Happiness, provided that it's not one's aim, is indeed a noble cause. I've known people be unhappy because they find that they're a year older, or something. Taken as a goal, happiness is unobtainable. It can be attained only by those who don't seek satisfaction but live outside themselves, for an idea. I repeat, one can't go by me, I'm a pure exception. Somebody like me, who lives in constant pain, is almost a monster (I don't mean of meanness, for I'm anything but mean). But I can only argue from such exceptions, fortunately very rare. Otherwise one could object to everything on the basis of an absurd example. Poverty, indigence, may favour intellectual life. But it doesn't follow that dire penury, days without bread, nights without a roof, are productive in themselves.

Dear Gaston, I must stop, having tired myself a little too much in my desire to persuade you that your life is a very good one (of which I'm convinced). A final word, I need to know as soon as possible if *La Revue rhénane* has published part of Curtius's article in translation. Several books I sent off have been returned 'address unknown'. It's distressing. Your list is atrocious. Do you have De Quincey's *Confessions of an English Opium-eater*? As for *The Possessed*, I think Morand will lend me a copy.[11] I can't go on.

Ever yours,
Marcel Proust

1. See the correspondence between Proust and Gallimard on the subject of the N.R.F.'s promotion of *Sodom and Gomorrah* Part Two: *MP–GG*, 550–73.

2. Robert Havard de La Montagne, editor in charge of the 'Review of the Press' at *L'Action française*.

3. See n. 8.

4. See letter 178, n. 5.

5. See letter 184, n. 2.

6. See Henri Bidou, *Revue de Paris*, 1 June '... his sense of reality is so strong that it communicates itself to us. Less a reading than a presence [. . .] This Vanity

Fair not only grips us, it persuades us that its characters are real people.'

7. Mme Tronche was expecting a baby.

8. See Proust to Gallimard, 17 July: 'We should immediately arrange to pay for an extract from Schlumberger's article to appear in *L'Action française*'s "Review of the Press" without its looking as if it came from me. It may well happen automatically, since I have friends there. But one can't be sure and I'm very anxious that steps be taken at once, on a commercial basis, by somebody with Tronche's authority. Should the *AF* refuse, it must be in writing, so that I can refer to it. Meanwhile, I want to keep myself out of it.' Cf. letter 228, n. 2.

9. Proust alludes to Pierre Hamp (real name Henri Bourrillon: 1876–1962), a novelist being hailed as the new Zola.

10. 'Who on earth could have told you such a thing? Invite me to meet your informant and I'll show him my contracts. André Gide receives 75 centimes a copy [...], Pierre Hamp [...] one franc a copy. [...] You are *far and away* our best-paid author.' Gallimard to Proust, *MP–GG*, 568.

11. Proust was making notes on Dostoevsky: see *AS-B*, 313–14. See also the conversation about Russian writers with Albertine: V, 430–34.

232 From Jacques Rivière

22 July 1922

My dear Marcel,

I finished re-reading *Sodome* three days ago. (I knew perfectly well that you hadn't believed me when I wrote that my state of mental turmoil was such that I couldn't immerse myself in it while still in Paris.)¹ Let what follows convince you that this wasn't just a vain excuse!

My dear Marcel, it's wonderful! It's life itself!

If, on the one hand, you set one thinking about a thousand different things in general (one thing apparent to me for the first time, for example, is your relationship to the Cubist movement, and, more importantly, the depth of your immersion in the world of modern aesthetics; one day, I'll explain what I mean), on the other, such a book, *being so close to what it portrays*, leaves one with nothing to say. No writer has ever equalled your close identification with the subject. At the moment, people are chiefly aware of what they are missing through this (a certain 'facility', a certain 'slickness' to which they are accustomed and equate with readability); for the most part, they have yet to perceive the tremendous gain this represents in terms of reality, of life.

Never have supposedly identical things been illuminated from so many different angles;[2] sometimes to the point where it seems that they must disintegrate, would disintegrate, if the impetus, the implacable drive of your story didn't ensure their reconstruction.

It's life itself! with its fundamental discontinuity and paradoxical unity. You are the first man to adapt yourself to its scale, bending and stretching, to follow it to its limits and give form to its multitudinous variety.

Listen, if anybody can recognize how remarkably innovative your book is, it's me, for I've written a book according to the rules, being incapable of doing otherwise.

I have a friend who has a habit of 'authenticating' his praise by supplementing it with the odd criticism. I shall follow his example. My one criticism, indeed the only one I can come up with, is this: perhaps, at times, your prodigious skill in reproducing the way people speak, and more especially in bringing out the contrast between what they say and what they mean, becomes a source of subjective pleasure (as every organic function is said to engender its own pleasure), which then tempts you to go too far and add touches that are simply amusing, picturesque, by which a character is neither enriched nor transformed but actually paralysed, and which tend slightly to create a stereotype. I'm thinking of certain phrases uttered by Brichot, by Cottard, in the invention of which, perhaps, *given the character*, you have over-indulged yourself. You see what I'm driving at: the natural effervescence, the constant creativity of your work matter so much to me that the minute the hint of anything mechanical creeps in, I seize on it.

But it's no more than a hint, and noticeable only (and perhaps erroneously, furthermore) to somebody as passionately engrossed as I was.

Charlus is a marvel! a character greater than any in Balzac because more self-aware, by which I mean more analytical. Never has the strangeness to which human nature is susceptible been more accurately pinpointed, rendered so understandable, so familiar. No being has ever lived in a book in quite that way before!

And then, the miracle, for after having been shown in a quasi-repulsive light, he becomes progressively more sympathetic. For he becomes so more and more, and as he takes shape, one recognizes his bond with common humankind. It's magnificent!

You know that, for reasons of personal taste (and perhaps – I hardly dare believe it – vocation), it's the analyses of love in your work which have always given me the greatest pleasure. Although

I tend to regret that their ratio to the whole diminishes with each volume, I find them quite astonishing in this latest volume. In particular, your study of the generation of love through jealousy seems to me extraordinarily novel and profound, as does everything you say about 'the binary rhythms of love';[3] and the inability of people 'whose self-analysis outweighs their self-esteem'[4] to believe that they are loved. I am far more grateful for these pages than for all the kindness you have ever shown me. From them, I derive even more precious nourishment than I do from the real thing. Thank you!

* * * *

I'm a little worried at not having received an answer to the letter I dictated in haste before I left, in which I told you how delighted I would be to have your latest thoughts on Flaubert.[5] Could it be that you have changed your mind? I hope not. I could keep the lead for you in the September issue. But I need to know at once if I can count on receiving your copy by early August. In case you are too tired to write, telephone your answer to Paulhan and he can tell me.

You know with what a full heart I hope that this letter finds you in better health.

I shake your hand in all friendship.
Jacques Rivière

You may have heard that, as of yesterday, Tronche is the father of a little girl. He is very happy, having always longed for children!

1. Rivière, demoralized by the effort of finishing his novel *Aimée*, had written to say that he was waiting for the summer holidays to read *Sodom and Gomorrah* Part Two.
2. Evidently, Rivière is thinking of Cubism.
3. See IV, 263.
4. See IV, 264.
5. See letter 221, n. 8. Nothing was to come of this project.

233   To Charles Du Bos[1]

[Sunday evening 23 July 1922]

My dear friend,
   How can your wonderful book[2] have taken a month to reach me (unless you ante-dated your dedication). I'm so dazzled by the 'Baudelaire' that – for the moment – I can hardly take in the pages on me. I can find nothing to criticize in this astonishing 'Baudelaire'. It's quite true that, generally speaking, I feel that preciosity (that's too strong a word) is to be eschewed in the abstract, like everything stemming from what you term Baudelaire's 'incompatibility' with life.[3] It reminds me of certain criticisms I ventured to make to Rivière, about his 'Rimbaud'. But (and you must know that this in no way affects my profound and loving admiration for Rivière's mind, heart and talent) perhaps because I don't know Rimbaud and do know Baudelaire, his Rimbaud seems to me nothing like as alive as your Baudelaire, who was truly a Michelangelo figure of our times. However much I might have preferred a more deductive critique, one calling more upon the simple impression gained from the close comparison of two readings, I have to say that, by the very perfection of its realization, your stupendous and poignant and inhuman and so human Baudelaire refutes any possible objections I might have. And yet, now and again, think of the divine Joubert's innocent simplicity when he wrote: 'We simple folk exchange the season's greetings' (or nearly that).[4] And would you not say that Baudelaire himself also participates in the lives of others:

> 'To your son I'll restore the glow of power
> And become, for that frail athlete of life,
> The oil that firms the limbs of wrestlers.'[5]

   Alas, I'm very much afraid that you are right after all, and that he is truly solitary, truly 'distinctive',[6] when he enjoys going to

> 'Those concerts, rich in brassy sounds,
> With which soldiers sometimes flood our parks
> And who, on golden evenings when one feels revived,
> Pour a drop of heroism into townsmen's hearts.'[7]

   I don't know the 'Baudelaire' by Rivière to which you refer, are you not confusing it with some simple notes which I, not Rivière, wrote for the *NRF*?[8] But that was only a sort of reading aloud (in the mind), and in the company of unknown friends; it is nothing compared to your magisterial constructions. But never lose touch with the honest impression,[9] which can't be forced into a mould.

Dear friend, I'll write to you again; today, I'm too ill. How I should profit from you advice, and how true is that which you give me about *Guermantes*,[10] even if indirectly, and which must be my guide. But all I can think of at the moment is that we should talk about your book (not that we should talk about me!). Has Rivière spoken to you about a review? Do you know Flers, Jaloux, or would you like me to speak to them (the former for the *Figaro*)? My relations with Jacques Boulenger are somewhat cool, but I know the proprietor of *L'Opinion*, Serge André,[11] whom I met only once but found charming. Would you like me to speak to him? Tiredness forces me to stop. I shall be writing to you, but in the meantime tell me your wishes.

Ever yours,
Marcel Proust

1. Charles Du Bos (1882–1939), man of letters.

2. *Approximations*, a collection of essays on art and religion, including 'Méditation sur la vie de Baudelaire', and 'Marcel Proust'.

3. 'Baudelaire's supreme tragedy is that whatever the blessings life wished to bestow upon him, it offered him nothing in tune with his nature; at its most terrible, his originality lies in his hatred of life, contingent upon nothing – simply a hatred stemming from this absolute *incompatibility*.' Du Bos, *op. cit.*

4. Allusion to a phrase not by the French moralist Jean Joubert but occurring in a letter to him from the Comtesse de Beaumont. (See *Les Correspondants de J. Joubert* [1884]).

5. From a stanza of 'L'âme du vin', *Les Fleurs du Mal*: 'À ton fils je rendrai sa force et ses couleurs / Et serai pour ce frêle athlète de la vie / L'huile qui raffermit les muscles des lutteurs.' (Proust writes 'membres' for 'muscles'.) The rendering 'glow of power' is Richard Howard's, in his translation of *Les Fleurs du Mal* (The Harvester Press, 1982). See also Proust in 'Concerning Baudelaire', *AS-B*, 290–1.

6. 'Give back to the word "distinguished" its original meaning of "that which is distinct"; free it from the vulgarities that beset it; there you will find the closest approximation to this innate, indomitable, anguished greatness. On the one hand, the impossibility of escaping life, on the other, the impossibility, even for a single instant, of becoming part of it.' Du Bos, *op. cit.*

7. From a stanza of 'Les Petites vieilles', *Les Fleurs du Mal*: '. . . ces concerts, riches de cuivre, / Dont les soldats parfois inondent nos jardins, / Et qui, dans ces soirs d'or où l'on se sent revivre, / Versent quelque héroïsme au cœur des citadins.' See *AS-B*, 291.

8. Du Bos was to reply that, although much impressed by 'Concerning Baudelaire', he was referring to an essay by Jacques Rivière published in December 1910.

9. See 'Concerning Baudelaire', *AS-B*, 287.

10. '[. . .] on a first reading, one finds *The Guermantes Way* a little disturbing: one feels that the author is equally interested in everything, so that even knowing this to be untrue (as is evident from the prefaces to his Ruskin translations, as well as in many passages in *Swann*), one finds it rather difficult to resist the impression that, for him, all of *Guermantes* is on the same scale and has equal importance.' Du Bos, 'Marcel Proust, *op. cit.*

11. Proust had met Serge André in June, at Le Bœuf sur le Toit.

234 To Paul Brach

[Thursday evening 27 July 1922]

Dear friend,

It's not worth your coming tomorrow, Friday. There's no hope of my seeing you before you leave. You weren't very nice the other evening, but your 'credit balance' of kind attentions to me is such that you can afford to be less and less nice for some time to come. It was this evening, Thursday, that you were expected. I had myself woken on purpose (something I should never do). This disruption so disrupted my timetable that Odilon, confused as if by summertime, left two hours early to fetch my beer etc.

I'm not well. I never am when I've been in bed too long, for I stream with sweat to such an extent that I need 'changing', as the 'smiling presence'[1] puts it, every quarter of an hour, and I then catch cold, which I never do out of doors. I've got a stiff neck again. From five to seven,[2] it was disagreeably caressed by a draught whenever somebody, never you, alas, opened my door. It horrifies me to think of my life. Since *Sodome II*, I haven't had the courage to correct *Sodome III*,[3] although it would be a great deal less tiring than giving Odilon lessons in French history.

You say you are out of paper; I must need a pen, for I can't manage to write these few lines legibly, dull and empty as they are. I don't know where you're going, nor when you return. Perhaps I shall go away, unless I decide to stay with the charming family to whom, disregarding the dawn Angelus,[4] I teach night-school; and once having left, I shan't be coming back, to the great relief of my friends.

Devotedly yours,
Marcel Proust

1. Brach's name for Céleste.
2. *cinq à sept:* the classic time for a lovers' rendezvous.
3. Cf. Proust to Gallimard, 22 July, *MP-GG*, 572: 'Shortly, I intend to send you the manuscript of *Sodome et Gomorrhe III* (*La Prisonnière*), so as to get the first proofs, which will need a lot of work.'
4. Allusion to the title of an early collection of poems by Francis Jammes, *De l'Angélus de l'aube à l'angélus du soir.*

235   To Jacques Porel

Thursday night [27 July 1922]

My dear Jacques,

I'll explain another time why I'm unable to come tomorrow, but I wanted to write and express my regret. (I nearly came to do so in person yesterday.) My disappointment is all the keener for a rather sudden recrudescence of affection for you, murmurs of the heart having brought back the old days. When I can, I'll tell you all about it. And my disappointment includes the new owner of Guermantes.[1] I'm not being polite, I really would have liked to meet her. I think it very kind, and very intelligent of her to have given a thought to the *name* of the château where she lives. I imagine that to be unique in the history of châtelaines. And also to have followed her train of thought to the author. The name of Guermantes (kindly tell her how much I would like to know its etymology) has always brought me luck. When *Swann* came out, an unknown 'admirer' asked to meet me in order to present me with a book stamped with the Guermantes arms. It was Walter Berry, who was to become one of my two or three closest friends.

Dear Jacques, between the effects of an accident and a bout of rheumatic fever, I've had a dreadful month, with *one* night's respite. Thank your dear and charming wife again for the pleasure of that evening so long ago at rue Laurent-Pichat, give her my regards, and believe me, my dear Jacques – my thoughts united with yours daily in sad memory of your wonderful Mother – to be your loving friend,

Marcel Proust

Two months ago, in the *Gaulois*, I wrote something about *Germinie*;[2] the phrasing was clumsy, but neither you nor anybody else could have mistaken the sentiment!

1. Mme Maurice Hottinger, whose daughter had written a monograph on the Château de Guermantes (which she seems to have bought from the Pâris family: see letter 89, n. 5).

2. Allusion to 'Les Goncourts', the essay Proust wrote for the Goncourt centenary, in which he describes Porel's mother, Réjane, in the role of the eponymous heroine of *Germinie Lacerteux*: see also *AS-B*, 311–12.

236 To Benjamin Crémieux

[5 or 6 August 1922]

Dear friend,

You've behaved monstrously, for by offering to single me out just when I had refused others you have caused me to be rude to the entire Italian press[1] (which writes about me daily to the utter despair of M. Barrère,[2] who thinks that simply because he dined once a week at home when I was a child, I meant to portray him in M. de Norpois. Now, M. de Norpois, though just as detestable, is exactly the opposite type of diplomat).

You wrote me a remarkable letter which I think you should publish (not as addressed to me, without my being involved), as if, for example, you were taking the opportunity to give a friend your (Paris) address.[3] Certain things would have to be cut, but there would be more than enough with such riches in almost every quarter of a line.

I don't think that the anachronisms on which you are quick to congratulate me are to be found in my book. I couldn't swear to it, and would find it too boring to open that tedious work in order to give you a positive answer. But to the best of my recollection, a long interval has elapsed between the Guermantes dinner and my second arrival at Balbec.[4] Let us Einstein-ize it, by all means, if it suits you. On the other hand, I think it's after 1900. In any case, it seems to me that I talk about the Ballets Russes only in the future.[5] And then, by the time Swann has his conversation with the Prince de Guermantes, the revision is over and done with.[6] Now, it seems to me that there will still be a small gap. But that was always happening in previous volumes, because of the flattened form which my people take on as they rotate in time. It would be terribly complicated to make that clear in a letter.

Regarding Caillaux's Germanophilia,[7] I probably anticipated it a little. I'll ask Léon Daudet when he first started to denounce him. Moreover, I imagine that it was a good thing to be pro-German at the time. I didn't follow it all well enough to have an opinion, but it seems to me that the Kiderlin-Waechter[8] Caillaux differed from the wartime one.

I don't know Nemours, apart from its name,[9] which is magnificent, but you make the countryside sound enchanting. What sad folly, in that case, to be leaving it on 11 August.

> 'But the true travellers are those who leave
> For leaving's sake . . .'[10]

Kindly give my respects to Madame Crémieux.

Ever yours,
Marcel Proust

P.S. I much regret not having chatted to you about the street-traders which, you tell me, are to be found near the Passage des Favorites.[11] For I've just finished a long passage for *Sodome et Gomorrhe III* on the street-cries of Paris (chiefly the cries of food-sellers, tinkers etc.).[12] Now, the originality of the shop-signs you describe may well complement the beguiling cries of the hawkers of vegetables, fruit etc. . . . and the variety of tools. In fact, my own harvest is fairly abundant, and sometimes felicitous, but you could probably have supplemented it.

A word about the following would be extremely useful (but I'm not sure I can wait for your answer): who is the Monsieur C., the multiple devices on whose superb writing-paper are variations on the letter C., and to whom I've owed letters and books for a time so long that I no longer dare to go in search of it?

1. The matter referred to is unclear.
2. Camille Barrère, French Ambassador to Italy. See letter 170, n. 4.
3. The address which had so intrigued Proust: see his p.s.
4. i.e. between the Duchesse de Guermantes's dinner towards the end of *The Guermantes Way*: III, 80 ff., and 'The Intermittencies of the Heart' in *Sodom and Gomorrah* Part Two: IV, 174 ff.
5. The narrator himself says: 'Certainly [. . .] I have no time left, before my departure for Balbec (where to my sorrow I am going to make a second stay which will also be my last), to start upon a series of pictures of society which will find their place in due course'; he immediately goes on to discuss salons, the Russian Ballet and the Princess Yourbeletieff, their 'youthful sponsor'. See IV, 163–5.

6. Allusion to the revision of the Dreyfus Case. See IV, 121-32.

7. See IV, 175. Allusion to Joseph Caillaux (1863-1944), progressive cabinet minister hounded by the *Figaro* (for which his wife assassinated its editor, Gaston Calmette in 1914: see letter 10, n. 6); after the war he was denounced as a collaborator, then pardoned.

8. Allusion to the German Secretary of State for Foreign Affairs at the time of the Franco-German diplomatic crisis over Agadir, Morocco, in 1911. See III, 469.

9. A town in the Seine-et-Marne. The Duc de Nemours is the romantic hero of Mme de La Fayette's novel *La Princesse de Clèves*.

10. 'Mais les vrais voyageurs sont ceux-là seuls qui partent / Pour partir [...]'. Lines from Baudelaire's 'Le Voyage', *Les Fleurs du Mal*.

11. Crémieux's Paris address: see letter 152.

12. See V, 136-8, 148-51.

237 To Paul Brach

[Wednesday 9 August 1922]

Dear friend (what a pen, not to mention my difficulty in writing this morning),

You said that you would come on Monday. I was so certain of it that when the bell went while Jacques Rivière was here, I knew at once that it was you. It was my friend Reynaldo Hahn.[1] As it's bad for me to stay in bed too long,[2] I decided to go out today, Tuesday (that is, yesterday, for on the days when I go out, I stay out all night and don't go back to bed in the morning). I was on the point of leaving when I had your card, which seemed a little distant. 'Are you sure you won't join us etc.' I interpreted this as 'Don't come'. In fact, I've never been to the grill-room at the Ritz, I don't know why. The manager there was poor old Vespis[3] (or lucky old Vespis, depending on your point of view, he being dead. I don't know if that's lucky or not), who was always asking me to come. Anyhow, I never did, I've been to the Ritz kitchens, and down to the cold-rooms where I frightened the cockroaches (in 1906, I even had M. Risler's[4] piano brought in, so that Mme de Haussonville's osprey feather could mark time knowledgeably), I can work the showers etc., only, stupidly, I've never been to the 'joint' you've chosen tonight. I'm really staying away out of sympathy for M. Serge André.[5] Had I seen him, I would have asked him to print an extract from Vettard's *NRF* article in *L'Opinion*.[6] I prefer to keep my friendships disinterested. I was enchanted by the cutting you sent me from *L'Illustration*.⁷ Of those portrayed, I knew only Haas, Edmond de Polignac and Saint-Maurice.⁸ But how delightful to see them again. I keep asking for this cutting, it gives me infinite pleasure. Now that I've been out (it's two o'clock in the afternoon on Wednesday, and I'm still in my hat and coat, in a dreadful state), I wonder when I'll be able to get up again. And the moment I can, you'll be off to Domfront. Anyhow, it doesn't matter, one thinks of people and one can so easily do without them. I had something to ask you, but I forget what. I don't say 'I'll drown you in an ocean of shit' quite so often these days.⁹

Adieu, dear friend.
Your
Marcel Proust

1. Hahn was beginning to call regularly for news of Proust's health.
2. Cf. letter 234.
3. Italian head-waiter of the Ritz grill-room.
4. Edouard Risler (1873–1929), concert pianist. Proust alludes to a sumptuous dinner he gave at the Ritz in 1907, which was followed by a recital by Risler. See *Selected Letters Volume Two 1904–1909*.
5. The proprietor of *L'Opinion*.
6. Proust feared that Jacques Boulenger would ignore Vettard's essay 'Proust et Einstein': see letter 217, n. 2.
7. A reproduction of James Tissot's painting *Le Balcon du Cercle de la Rue Royale en 1867*, a famous group portrait being shown in a current exhibition. Proust was to include a reference to it in the narrator's eulogy of Swann: see V, 223.
8. Respectively, Charles Haas, Proust's principal model for Swann, the Prince de Polignac and Gaston de Saint-Maurice, whom Proust had known in Dieppe.
9. See Tadié, *op. cit.*, 900: 'Proust's strange declaration [. . .] shows a reversion to the thoroughly infantile, anal state also characteristic of his sexuality.'

238 *From Jules Romains*¹

Hyères, 6 place Frédéric Mistral
16 August 1922

Dear Sir,

I was very touched and honoured to receive your kind letter about *Lucienne*.² There are few people whose opinion I value as much as I do yours, and I'm happy to know that it's not entirely unfavourable.

You're wrong to think that I haven't read you. Certainly, I admit to a very limited knowledge of your work, and to having waited too long before I knew anything of yours other than by repute. Thus I read *Le Côté de Guermantes* (and the beginning of *Sodome et Gomorrhe* in the same volume) for the first time when you kindly sent it to me; and Mademoiselle Monnier,[3] who oversees my reading, having since sent me *Du Côté de chez Swann*, I've begun its slow perusal (I'm halfway through).

Do your phrases of which you found the equivalent in *Lucienne* occur in this volume and a half?[4] I can't be positive, but I doubt it, for being very conscious of such things, I think I would have noticed, either in reading your sentences or in writing mine – I began *Lucienne* some time ago, and had written at least half of it when I came into contact with your mind. Indeed, it was a subject which interested me passionately. I would have felt no less admiration, no less pleasure, had I discovered you when composing *Comedeyre*, or *Donogoo*.[5] But my curiosity would have been more detached. However, my work on *Lucienne* was presenting me with many of the same technical and psychological problems as I was watching you solve, in your different fashion. It was very exciting, I assure you, and we had some very animated conversations and debates, without your being aware of it, you and I. Did they influence my work, I wonder? Possibly, but in the sense that I placed myself under an increasingly strict aesthetic discipline, something that has always mattered a great deal to to me, whereas I could see that it mattered less to you. Yes, on re-reading the 150 pages I had already written, I definitely think that where I had allowed myself to be carried away, I was more severe than ever on any extravagances of thought or expression, any moments of 'self-indulgence'.

When you say that you admire me, I feel I owe your admiration in part to your great courtesy and your natural inclination to be kind. Personally, I admire you enormously. The richness of your gifts never ceases to dazzle me. But I regard you as a magnificent heretic. I don't need to explain why. You are not one of those who 'falls' into heresy. You go out to meet it; you blithely espouse it (Mallarmé does the same).[6]

How I should like to meet you, to chat with you! I know that your state of health condemns you to a very reclusive life. Yet were I sure of not being a nuisance if I knocked on your door one morning – or one evening – during the coming autumn, I would do so with great pleasure.

Your sincere and devoted admirer,
Jules Romains

I hardly dare tell you that, once I've read *Swann*, a matter of a few days, I shall have an even heartier appetite for *Sodome et Gomorrhe* – and here, at Hyères, all the solitude and time I need in order to meditate on such a considerable work. I could perfectly well ask our friend Gaston Gallimard for the books, but it would give me much more pleasure to receive them from you. Forgive my asking, and thank you in any case.

1. Jules Romains (real name Louis Farigoule: 1885–1972), poet, playwright, essayist and novelist. His major work, the series of novels collectively entitled *Les Hommes de bonne volonté* (*Men of Goodwill*) was to be published between 1932 and 1947.
2. His latest novel, the first of the *Psyche* trilogy, an erotic study of marriage.
3. Adrienne Monnier, co-proprietor with Sylvia Beach of the famous Left-Bank bookshop Les Amis du livre.
4. See Proust to Romains, early August: 'One impression filled me with joy and a certain sadness. I found in *Lucienne* sentences of mine almost word for word, which proves that, naturally enough, you haven't read me. For you're one of those people who are self-sufficient, incapable of borrowing from others. But this purely subjective sadness was replaced by an even greater joy. If he too has thought and felt that (I told myself), a man whom I so much admire, then my books cannot be as bad as I thought. Every chance discovery that you think as I do (as also happens when I read the masters of the Past) I see as a certificate of authenticity, and imagine myself communing with the Sages.'
5. A verse-drama, *Comedeyre-le-vieil* and a film-script, *Donogoo-Tonka ou les miracles de la science*, both published in 1920.
6. Allusion to Mallarmé's 'Hérésies artistiques. L'Art pour tous', published in *L'Artiste* in 1862.

239 To Henri Ghéon

[Shortly after 17 August 1922]

Dear Sir,

I was very moved, the other day, to see my name cited by you – which was the greatest honour – in *L'Action française*, and in such illustrious company.[1] I'm under no illusions, and I know perfectly well that, in naming me alongside these great Masters, you hadn't the slightest intention of suggesting that I was their equal, but that, at a lesser altitude, you were struck by some resemblance, and kindness did the rest. You know what importance I have always attached to what you write, and the only response I ever made to a critic, in 1914, a reproachful letter for your review of *Du Côté de chez Swann* in the *NRF*,² was made precisely because your judgment, being more profound than anybody else's, went straight to my heart. Call it *Le Dépit amoureux*,³ if you like.

I wouldn't want your conversion, potent fertilizer of your plays, to stunt your critical style. I recall an article you once wrote on Francis Jammes, reproaching him for having applied to literary criticism, and to literature, strictures which, you said, were undreamt-of in all the centuries of rule by the Catholic Church.⁴ Being better aquainted than I am with the Way and the Life, you were more precise, citing Councils and Popes. Without wishing to set you against yourself, it certainly seems to a layman that as far as literature is concerned 'render unto Caesar' has been the Catholic Church's maxim since the days of those early monks who shaped our landscape and guided our still-stumbling efforts at language. I had hoped to write to you at greater length, but am far too ill. I'm incapable of writing, and a letter of these dimensions is an event in my life, if merely an intrusion in yours.

Your devoted admirer,
Marcel Proust

---

1. 'Some authors openly reveal their secrets, "unbutton" themselves, confess. Probably, without this need to confess, they wouldn't write at all. They are men like Montaigne, Rousseau, Stendhal, Proust. Others voluntarily hide behind their latest work.' Ghéon, *L'Action française*, 17 August.

2. See letter 34, n. 9.

3. Allusion to Molière's comedy of love-hate relationships.

4. Here, Proust may appear to repeat letter 34 to Ghéon – except that he had had second thoughts about sending it: see its note 11.

240 To Camille Vettard

44 rue Hamelin
[Around 20 August 1922]

Dear friend,

It's very annoying, not being able to write to you myself.[1] Your article in the *NRF*[2] has caused a considerable stir and been the subject of analysis in several newspapers. That in *L'Écho de Paris* being one of the simplest and the best, in my opinion.[3] Do you have it? Or would you like me to send it to you? Where should I have it sent? That in *L'Opinion* is less good, owing to a misunderstanding (but I'm too tired to go into all that), and in any case you should know that it wasn't me, but Serge André, who asked for this analysis, so whatever you do – I give you this advice because I think of you as a little impulsive – don't answer back[4] – I still haven't made it up with Jacques Boulenger, it would be the last straw. Allard wrote me a note full of praise for your article.

Dear friend, I take up my pen myself despite my fatigue because I can see that my maid can't cope. What I want to say to you is this: I'm still unable to write to you about *Pauper le Grand*[5] because I've broken my glasses and must somehow get out to buy new ones, and you can't imagine what a drama that is for me. But I want to make a trivial point: don't 'ruin' your book by ending it with your comments on a quotation. In my preface for Morand (whom I admire a hundred thousand times less than I do Giraudoux while remaining a hundred thousand times closer to him, which closeness explains the preface), I talked in similar terms about the wonderful *Nuit à Châteauroux*.[6] But that was in a Preface, a critical study. Within a novel, it would be bad enough; as an ending, it's impossible. If you want to express your admiration for Giraudoux, do so in your dedication to me. There, a sentence or two of literary criticism wouldn't come amiss. But seeing it at the end of a novel, everybody will think that, instead of making the effort to find the 'right' ending, you have borrowed one from Giraudoux. Mind you, at a pinch you could use the same sentence without citing Giraudoux, it not being so out of the ordinary that you couldn't both have hit on it (as is probably the case). If you really wanted to end like that, while being scrupulous about crediting Giraudoux, you could put a little 1 to indicate a note ('Giraudoux says, at the end of the marvellous ... etc.'). But let your text finish with something of yours.

    I feel badly about the delay I shall be causing you over *Pauper le Grand*. However, since both Gallimard and Rivière are on holiday, it doesn't really matter (Rivière comes back soon). Even if I haven't finished *Pauper le Grand* (but I shall have) by the time Gallimard gets back (Rivière being solely concerned with the Review), you can rely on me to send him your manuscript. But he is sure to turn it down, especially after all that trouble with Copeau,[7] unless I warn him beforehand that he would be making a great mistake in not publishing it. I don't think that you're sufficiently self-critical. In your excellent article on me (Einstein), you cite Léon Daudet word for word but without, inadvertently I'm sure, putting quotation marks. You are so remarkable (and, unlike me, you have the strength) that you must never stop digging, probing, until you reach those depths where one finds oneself.

               In all loving and grateful admiration, your devoted
                                         Marcel Proust

I have a feeling that an article by Jacques Boulenger will soon settle our differences. But nobody has told me a thing, so for heavens' sake don't mention it.

1. The beginning of this letter was dictated to Céleste.
2. Vettard's epistolary essay 'Proust and Einstein': see letter 162, n. 1.
3. An anonymous column in *L'Écho de Paris*, 17 August: 'M. Camille Vettard has written a letter to the *NRF* [...] which throws much light on the comparison some critics have made between [...] the great psychological novelist and the great mathematician–physicist. Henri Poincaré says that "astronomy is the soul which enables us to understand nature". This soul, M. Vettard says, is as apparent in a Proust as it is in an Einstein. In both we find the same sense, intuition and understanding of the laws of nature. One might add that the Proustian world, where time plays so large a part, is four-dimensional, like the Einsteinian world of relativity [...].'
4. See letter 188 to Jacques Boulenger.
5. The novel for which Vettard had written a long dedication to Proust: see letter 162, n. 1.
6. See 'Preface to Morand', *AS-B*, 284.
7. See Gallimard to Proust, 27 April, *MP–GG*, 511: 'Copeau brought me Camille Vettard's manuscript, which I've read. [It] is rather incoherent and very badly

constructed. His influences are all too apparent. [...] He may succeed in writing a novel, but this doesn't seem to be it.'

241 To Henri Duvernois

44 rue Hamelin
[Shortly after 21 August 1922]

My dear friend,

I apologize for writing to you about anything so mundane, and for asking you to reply, by hand, if possible and with the utmost frankness (I mean without being polite or sparing my feelings). And, to cap it all, to keep this ignominious note ultra-confidential. So – I have just written a novel called *La Prisonnière* (more Sodom and Gomorrah, but greatly toned down) and, to please Rivière, refused it to all the magazines. But such are the complications of my life at present, I would let *Les Œuvres libres* have it[1] simply because they pay far better than the others. But first I need to know if it would be a pleasure or a burden to *Les Œuvres libres* (I quite see that it might not suit you at the moment). I want to do it only if it's a pleasure, for while I make no attempt to disguise the purely financial motives behind my request, the 'complications of life' to which I refer are not so serious that I need burden your magazine with unwanted prose. I only need to be a little less insanely extravagant,[2] and to stop refusing offers from American reviews. Secondly, I need to know that the 'advance' will be substantial. Gallimard, by virtue of some grotesque logic, is determined to get his hands on half of whatever *Les Œuvres libres* would pay me.

As for *La Prisonnière*, it's more of a novel than 'Jalousie',[3] also longer, too, I think, and, I fear, less good (by less good, I mean worse, for 'Jalousie' was nothing special). Answer me as a friend, turning me down if you don't like the idea, and, if the opposite is the case (what style!), leaving me the option of sending you nothing, lest Rivière, who is in the Gironde and whose despair at the thought of not getting his 'extracts'[4] has already caused him to weep rivers of tears,[5] should succeed in extracting from me in a weak moment, once he is back in Paris and no longer breaking my heart, at least by letter, a renunciation in his favour.

Very sincerely yours,
Marcel Proust

You're a dreadful wrecker of sleep. Normally, my life is spent awake. Yesterday, I was dozing; in my dream, I kept hearing the words 'I myself am not without sin. Swine! Blonde? Blonde.' Eventually, the whole apartment was blue.[6] I woke up.

1. But see Proust's undertaking to Gallimard in letter 125.
2. Proust had lent 5000 francs to some friends in need: see Proust to Schiff, *c.* 14 September.
3. See letter 125.
4. From his next book, *The Captive*, Proust had offered Rivière a choice of 'Albertine's Sleep' (V, 71–7) or 'The Street-Cries of Paris': see letter 236, n. 12.
5. Word-play on the River Gironde and Rivière.
6. Proust seems to be dreaming of an orgy: see n. 4 to letter 88 to Mme de Clermont-Tonnerre.

242 To Daniel Halévy

[Shortly before 26 August 1922]

My dear friend,

I'm very uneasy about this letter. I was first going to write to congratulate you on your decoration.[1] It gave me the *greatest pleasure*. Now, the request I'm about to add to my congratulations will – quite wrongly – give the impression that it was the primary motive for my letter. And the fact that I'm unable to write myself[2] simply adds to my embarrassment. Anyhow, here goes:

I know that you're one of the judges for the Prix Balzac,[3] and, naturally, a very influential one. Now, I wish to draw your attention to my friend Jacques Rivière's fine novel *Aimée*.[4] I won't say more, because I know that you're not the sort of person one can influence, and I'm sure that Rivière's sense of honour would revolt at the idea of being beholden to anybody's recommendation, even yours. But I thought that, with so many manuscripts, his might not come to your attention. You'll find that it has none of the gloom and tedium of those valleys of sulphur and brimstone ringing with curses where, for the present, my novel is taking place – only a wholesome love of women, analysed in the best classical manner.

I suppose I ought not to add that Rivière's health has never recovered from a terrible war, during which he was imprisoned and condemned to death by the Germans, and that he and his wife and children are terribly poor . . .

His wife is Alain-Fournier's[5] sister.

Believe me, my dear Daniel, as well as my affection, you have my warmest congratulations on a decoration which makes me very happy.

Marcel Proust

1. Halévy had just been made Chevalier of the Legion of Honour.
2. Letter dictated to Céleste.
3. A new literary prize for unpublished work, worth 20,000 francs.
4. See letter 232, n. 1.
5. Alias Henri-Alban Fournier (1886–1914), author of *Le Grand Meaulnes* (1913).

243 *To Suzy Proust*

[25 or 26 August 1922]

My dearest little Suzy,

If I had sent you all the letters I write you nightly in my thoughts, you would have received a huge tome by now. The result so far having been Silence, I don't know whether the impression it has given you is one of plenitude, of affection, or of emptiness, of blank forgetfulness. You know that nothing is easy for me, least of all writing. And not having been out of Paris since 1914, whereas I always used to spend my summers by the sea, with every year that passes, besides growing weaker, I have this feeling of soaring while tethered to the spot, what Mallarmé called '. . . flights that never flew',[1] and it gives me slight nausea, like those lifts which fail to get off the ground while still making just as much noise.[2]

I very much hope that you are all well. You've probably seen the articles about your uncle that appear daily in the *Figaro*, the *Gaulois*, *L'Action française* etc., and the thought of the thoroughly frivolous idea they must have given you of me never ceases to make me tremble. It only needs a newspaper to talk about new frocks for Deauville à propos of my young girls[3] for me to tear it up in a rage, imagining your picture of me as a mere dabbler in fashion. But now that a mathematician, who is also, I believe, a sous-préfet, has written an article called 'Proust et Einstein', I feel much more worthy to be your uncle. You may have read an extract from it in *L'Écho de Paris*. If you would like to read it 'in extenso', as our great-uncle Louis[4], whom you never met, would say, I'll send it to you.

If you go to Venice, let me know; it may be that a very knowledgeable friend of mine will be there.[5] I kiss you all, in particular my dear little brother, with the deepest affection.

Marcel

1. Proust quotes from the sonnet beginning 'Le vierge, le vivace et le bel aujourd'hui / Va-t-il nous déchirer avec un coup d'aile ivre / Ce lac dur oublié qui hante sous le givre / Le transparent glacier des vols qui n'ont pas fui!' ('The primeval, the perennial and perfect dawn / Won't it break for us with one frantic beating wing / This forgotten lake of ice, this hard frozen / Transparent glacier, haunt of flights that never flew.')

2. See the narrator's sensation, just before helping his grandmother into Professor E.'s lift, of 'the abyss of sickness and death', the 'shudder that pierces us to the marrow': III, 361–3.

3. Allusion to 'Fashion notes', *Le Figaro*, 16 August: 'If one can admire the best of Parisian chic in the streets around the Bois de Boulogne this summer, the beaches and tennis-courts under softer, more changeable skies evoke certain parts of *À l'Ombre des jeunes filles en fleurs*. There they all are, M. Marcel Proust's Albertines, Andrées and Gilbertes, brightening their surroundings with the sparkle of jerseys in wool or silk, their deliciously fresh complexions flushed with exertion [...].'

4. Proust's maternal great-uncle, Louis Weil (1816–96), by all accounts a lovable if irascible man; the model for Oncle Adolphe.

5. Possibly Jean-Louis Vaudoyer.

244 To Charles Maurras

[Monday 28 August 1922]

Dear Sir and friend,

I'm extremely behindhand in thanking you for your books.[1] And yet I live in them. But for me, alas, living is being unable to see properly, or to turn over in bed so as to reach a pen, still less leave for the country, for that 'stony, golden land where the eternal wind blows'.[2] That's where I would go, could I leave Paris, something I haven't done for an hour since 1914. That's where I would go, for great poets clothe in desire and mystery sites that would, perhaps, be lacking in charm if not embellished through their eyes, like those in the lines from *Bérénice* which you so rightly admire.[3] I esteem you too much not to tell you that while *Le Chemin de Paradis* charms me, it doesn't always completely satisfy me (though more so than anything else I read these days). There, unfortunately, I don't think we'll ever agree, for what you have deliberately set out to achieve is precisely what gives me pause. Oh! It's not that I blame you for your personal disbelief in the divinity of Jupiter whom you would have us worship (rather, I have often wanted to ask you, in your post-war articles, not to give the Muses too lowly a rank). But this affectation in the use of words (found also in Moréas[4] and, to a lesser extent, in M. France, whom I haven't seen for twenty-two years, alas!) designed to flatter and to denote their origin, distracts me, just as it distracted that same poet, from following his line of thought. That so many charms should be wilfully tarnished by a touch of negligence here and there, an occasional repetition or ambiguity, also too obviously deliberate, doesn't make up for it. All that vanishes with *L'Avenir de l'intelligence*, a book worthy of its name,[5] admirable in every way. And it would be a simple matter to show that, beside your 'Invocation à Minerve',[6] 'La Prière sur l'Acropole'[7] is merely a lame exercise in rhetoric (with the exception of the ravishing phrase about the eyes of the young Breton girls).[8] I keep finding myself in the grip of the indescribable charm, the nostalgia, of *Le Chemin de Paradis*, where what Mallarmé called 'a flight that never flew'[9] cannot come to frolic. One detail makes me envy you (not that I don't envy you your entire life and work, but I'm talking here about something specific), and that is to hear you refer so nonchalantly to Phidias's lover and mistress.[10] In those days, such tastes, so often explained by fashion, the wish to emulate others, were natural. Centuries of opprobrium later, they survive only in those who are sick and cannot help themselves. And that's why, in my books, as I walk without pleasure through valleys that reek of sulphur and pitch, I appear to blame what I myself don't blame.[11] Which has earned me the curses of those who would have preferred me to paint an acceptable portrait of this or that young friend of Pantarces;[12] while M. Francis Jammes, for the opposite reason, has started to offer Masses, and to implore the Seraphim and all the heavenly powers to make me quit caverns where my companion is the Prince of Darkness.

Believe me, dear Sir, Master and friend, when I say that if I were less ill, I would write you a letter more worthy of the two books you were good enough to send me.

Your grateful admirer,
Marcel Proust

1. Two books of early essays, recently republished as *Le Chemin de Paradis* and *L'Avenir de l'intelligence*.

2. Evocation of Provence in the preface to *Le Chemin de Paradis*, a book of essays on paganism.

3. In 'Le Romantisme feminin', an essay in *L'Avenir de l'intelligence*, Maurras had quoted Racine's lines: 'Dans l'Orient quel devint mon ennui! / Je demeurais longtemps errant dans Césarée, / Lieux charmants où mon cœur vous avez adorée.' ('How dreary was my sojourn in the East! / Too long did I wander through Cesarae / By charmed sites detained, my heart worshipped thee.' See Antiochus to Bérénice, *Bérénice*, Act I, scene 4.

4. Maurras, like Moréas, was a founder of the movement for a return to the classical style in poetry. See letter 63, n. 8.

5. A deliberate echo of Renan's *L'Avenir de la science*.

6. Appendix to *L'Avenir de l'intelligence*.

7. Renan's 'La Prière sur l'Acropole', an invocation to Athena, comes into *Souvenirs d'enfance et de jeunesse*.

8. See Renan, *Souvenirs d'enfance et de jeunesse*, II, 1, 63: 'The clouds seemed colourless, and even our joy a little sad, but ice-cold springs gushed from the rock, and these same green fountains in which the sky was reflected over a bed of waving grasses were like the eyes of the young girls.' Cf. letter 189 to Francis Jammes.

9. See previous letter, n. 1.

10. Maurras alludes to the Athenian sculptor who loved both Pantarces, a young man, and Polydamia, a young woman.

11. This passage reiterates Brichot's musings about M. de Charlus in *The Captive*, V, 229–31.

12. See n. 10.

245 From Jacques Rivière

3 September 1922

My dear Marcel,

Despite my regret at starting my tenth year at the *NRF* without a piece by you, I will wait till November for the fragment which you are (I speak hypothetically, you understand) kindly reserving for me, no matter what.

Even should you decide against *Les Œuvres libres*, it would be too late, given my distance from Paris, for me to have any hope of getting it into the October issue.

I imagine that you will shortly have Gaston's reply.

You forget, when talking to me about these fragments, that, not knowing your book, I have no idea, though I'm terribly curious, what you mean by *La Prisonnière* and *La Fugitive*, nor whether the fragments correspond, in whole or in part, with 'Le Sommeil d'Albertine' and 'Les Cris de Paris'.[1] Do tell me, if you have a moment.

My dear Marcel, it's so good of you to have campaigned for me yet again, and to have written to Halévy[2] and Pierrefeu. I know the weight your letters carry; can it be a sign of their effect that I've been told, confidentially, that I'm rather well-placed, my manuscript being on the short list.

I had a very nice talk with Jaloux at Pontigny.[3] But, I beg you, Daudet must be left out of it. My political passions are too fierce for me to bear the idea of his being solicited on my behalf, even indirectly.[4]

I've just put the finishing touches to my dedication to *Aimée*. I trust you're not too displeased at receiving the homage of my little book.[5]

I'll ask somebody at the magazine to send you Curtius's home address. We met at Pontigny, but he greeted me very coldly because of my *L'Allemand*.[6] We were reconciled only towards the end.

In the next issue (October), there'll be a note on Lacretelle's book[7] by Faure-Biguet of *L'Écho de Paris*. This in response to your anxiety about our coolness to that newspaper.

To meet the November deadline, you need to let me have your copy by the last week in September at the latest. I'll be back in Paris by then in any case.

My dear Marcel, my gratitude to you is boundless, as is my wish to see you in better health.

Jacques Rivière

---

1. See letter 241, n. 4.

2. See letter 242.

3. Allusion to the first post-war sesssion of the philosopher Paul Desjardins's 'Décades', the famous literary seminar held annually at Pontigny Abbey in Burgundy. Proust's work was one of the main topics discussed.

4. Léon Daudet was a judge for the Prix Balzac, and Rivière's scruples were probably to cost him the prize.

5. Rivière dedicated his novel to Proust as 'the great painter of love'.
6. The title of Rivière's memoirs as a prisoner-of-war: see letter 242.
7. *La Fiancée morte*, which Proust had asked Rivière to review.

246 To Gaston Gallimard

[Sunday 3 September 1922]

Post-script or rather second letter[1]

My dear Gaston,

Remembering what happened a year or two ago saves me the fatigue of having to explain to you why, since yesterday, I lean more and more towards *Les Œuvres libres*. When I gave them 'Jalousie', you were kind enough to say that, in the event of their making me another such lucrative offer, while you would prefer me to refuse, you would give me (not that I would ever accept) the sum they would have advanced me.[2] Robert de Flers once asked to make exactly the same proposal to Réjane, when she wanted to play *Madame Sans Gène*[3] under conditions which, he felt, would have harmed both her and the play. I was to offer her so much for each performance in which she agreed not to act. But having nothing in common with Réjane except illness (and not wishing to criticize a woman who I believed had great moral qualities), I never accepted the commission. Only the difference, the contradiction, between being paid not to write in *Les Œuvres libres* – and handing over half of what they would they pay to the N.R.F. – is too great.

I see that the *NRF* has announced 'Le Sommeil d'Albertine' without my consent. I'm sorry for Jacques, but if I give *La Prisonnière* to *Les Œuvres libres*, it won't be to denude it of its least bad part.

Anyhow, advance announcements mean nothing. Years ago, the *Figaro* announced a long instalment of 'Odette mariée' (accompanied by a whole rigmarole about me, unlike the *NRF*).[4] When I thought better of it a month later, they made not the slightest objection.

My dear Gaston, you'll be receiving this postscript at the same time as my letter, but it being a weekend, when you're away, I didn't hurry, having had the most dreadful asthma. Moreover, I have a colossal amount of work, for you can't imagine the pains

I take to ensure that the books I give you are not wholly bad. And, dissatisfied with the opening of my *Prisonnière*, I'm re-writing it for the third time, and having endless trouble in deciphering all the corrections and insertions I made on my typist's once pristine pages.

I trust you'll find the arguments in both letter and postscript *irrefutable*. Above all, I hope you believe in my loyal and affectionate friendship.

Marcel Proust

I'm killing myself writing volumes on Jacques's behalf for the Prix Balzac. Unfortunately, it's Grasset's prize to such an extent that I dare not hold out too much hope.

1. The previous day, Proust had replied to a cold letter from Gallimard that formally objected to his giving The Captive to Les Œuvres libres. See MP–GG, 590–2.
2. See letter 125.
3. Comedy by Victorien Sardou, Flers's father-in-law. The lead had been one of Réjane's favourite roles.
4. In fact, this extract, the chapter entitled 'Madame Swann at home', had been cancelled owing to the outbreak of war.

247 To Armand de Guiche

[Shortly after 4 September 1922]

Dear friend,

You've written me a letter that is a remarkable piece of literary criticism. I didn't have it published, being polite and not knowing whether it would please you. But it deserves more than one reader. I smiled to learn that, this year, Madame Hennessy had invited me with the unfashionable 'crowd'.[1] Smiled, because I was shrewd enough to have guessed as much on arrival, and because nothing amuses me less than parties which, twenty years ago, were known as 'select'. What amuses me are large, mixed parties that produce fireworks. The Ritz gives me a sense of that, but it's always the same. What amuses me above all is to dine tête-à-tête with you. But I've given up all hope of that.

You've banned 'Marcel' for good, and the photograph of Madame Greffulhe.[2] I mention the two things I desired so much only because, having too often asked for them, I desire them no longer. In the end, what can be obtained only through nagging ceases to give pleasure. At least, to me. For I know what it is to wear oneself out inviting people who start by refusing and end up by accepting.

You would do me a favour by giving my warmest regards to M. Pierre Lafitte.[3] But it has become an annual ritual for me to ask you that, and it never works, alas. Why don't I do it myself, I hear you ask. I'm very unwell once again. My attacks are so violent that I'm beginning to wonder if my chimney, which is full of cracks, isn't to blame.[4] What makes me think so is the fact that on the very rare days when I dine out, having found a way of dining (alone) at four o'clock in the morning,[5] my symptoms disappear. But another possibility is the imminence of death. It's a nuisance, my book being unfinished. As I don't see well any more, I never read the papers. I don't know how I chanced upon this uninteresting item of news: 'Mme Georges Stoïcesco[6] held a tea-party in honour of the King of Spain, and gave an afternoon tea in honour of the Shah of Persia.' The difference between a tea-party and afternoon tea escapes me.[7] Immediately underneath, it says: 'Refugees starve to death on the roads of Austria', which makes the previous item rather painful reading. I don't feel the slightest ill-will towards the lady who makes this distinction between a tea-party and afternoon tea, and whom I don't know, especially since her mother (as a girl) was the second great love of my life (the first was Mademoiselle Benardaky).[8] But it seems to me that when people are dying of hunger, it might be better, not to starve oneself to death, but at least not to be seen eating 'in the Press'.

I say I never reply to anybody (let alone to 'coronets', dear friend), yet when I write to you I can't tear myself away! I send you my warmest regards and my humble respects to Madame the Duchesse de Guiche.

Your
Marcel Proust

1. Allusion to Mme Hennessy's musical soirée in June: see letter 205.
2. See letter 52, n.4.
3. A newspaper proprietor.
4. See Albaret, *op. cit.*, 340–1.
5. i.e. at the Ritz.

6. *Née* Simone de Caillavet (see letter 177, n. 3), Jeanne Pouquet's daughter, whom Proust had known as a child. She had married a Romanian diplomat he detested. Her mother was a model for Gilberte in *Swann's Way*, and in *Time Regained* Simone makes a brief but significant appearance as Gilberte's daughter, Mlle de Saint-Loup: VI, 425–40.

7. Reported in the *Figaro* of 21 August.

8. See letter 17, n. 5; letter 18, n. 26.

248 To Henri Duvernois

44 rue Hamelin
[Shortly after 6 September 1922]

My dear friend,

You're quite right. I've re-read your letter, it is indeed a 5 and not a 3 (five thousand lines). Moreover, M. Fayard's letter (dictated to somebody whose signature is illegible, but I shall reply to M. Fayard) confirms it.[1] That already seems like luxury to me, and if, without paying me a centime more, he could allow me six thousand instead of five, it would save my having to compress quite so much. (Naturally, it would add nothing to the ten thousand francs, I would simply be providing him with some extra copy.) I've already had I don't know how many typescripts done in an effort to abridge it. For it can't be said of everybody as it can of you:

'Two words from Horace would say more than you.'[2]

That I was determined to answer you at once is to my credit, for I'm in a dreadful and peculiar state, which I beg you not to mention to anybody. The minute I put a foot out of bed, I spin round and go sprawling. Of course I know there are doctors; and as Léon Daudet (who doesn't know about my fits of giddiness) wrote to me: 'Probably some little thing, easily curable, lies between you and health – which lies in your ink.'[3] But I feel too ill even to see a doctor.

Thank you again for *Les Œuvres libres*. It gives me enormous pleasure. Gallimard is so disappointed that he has suddenly left Paris for I don't know where to lick his wounds. Anybody would think, from all the arguments he put up, that the Nouvelle Revue française, more powerful than any parliament, governed my right to marry, eat, live and die. He even slipped in a 'Duvernois himself said', which I ignored. I paid no attention to any of it; he has been extremely nice. You know that he likes you, that I like him, that we all like one another. I would therefore be very grateful if you kept this letter quiet, it being quite without animosity towards him and in any case could only have made you laugh if I weren't so ill and had been able to include all the precedents he invoked. The fact that I negotiated with M. Gallimard, *editorial* director of the Nouvelle Revue française, and was refused the dispensation I sought by M. Gallimard, *managing* director of the Nouvelle Revue française, the two being embodied in the same person, our dear Gaston Gallimard whom we love, enchants me.

With all my love, deserter of Paris for La Baule. Personally, I haven't left Paris since 1914. Not that I'm proud of it!

Your
Marcel Proust

1. Proust had now signed a contract with Arthème Fayard, proprietor of *Les Œuvres libres*, for his abridgement of *The Captive*. See letter 241 ff.

2. 'Horace avec deux mots en eût dit plus que vous.' Proust adapts Agnès's reply to Arnolphe in Molière's *École des Femmes* (Act V, scene 4): 'Tenez, tous vos discours ne me touchent pas l'âme;/Horace en deux mots en feroit plus que vous.'

3. *Sic*. Proust has misread *encre* for *œuvre* in Daudet's letter. See letter 169.

249 *From Sydney Schiff*

9 September 1922

My dear Marcel,

A few words only. I have just seen the announcement of which I enclose a cutting.¹ I hope the translation at least will be good enough to give an idea of the original. The art of translation is difficult and little understood, and no author demands more from his translator than you do, nor has a better right to be admired. I don't like the titles. 'Memories of the past' and 'In the manner of Swann' or 'Swann's method'.² I would have thought it possible to find titles closer to yours,³ which are so wonderfully well-chosen. There is a melancholy nuance to *À la Recherche du temps perdu*, a suggestion of poignancy, of impropriety, even – a double meaning to the word *perdu* – has the time been wasted? is the past regretted? So many things come to mind. And *Du Côté de chez Swann*, containing as it does the double meaning of Swann's point of view and the locality – a double meaning miraculously hit upon and which in turn suggests a third, expressing the psychology of the adorable youth across the way, living out his dreams and desires, his hopes and regrets.

I shall get hold of the book as soon as it comes out, and having read it, tell you what I think of it.

We leave for London on Wednesday. Could you not send me a few lines? I've been very depressed lately, and need to have news of you. Above all, to know how you are.

With much love from us both,
Your
Sydney

---

1. Announcement in *The Athenaeum*, 9 September. 'Messrs Chatto & Windus, as publishers, and Mr Scott-Moncrieff, as author, have almost ready the first instalment of M. Marcel Proust's *Remembrance of Things Past* in the English translation. The title of this initial volume is *Swann's Way*.'

2. Schiff translates literally, evidently unaware that Scott-Moncrieff's overall title is taken from Shakespeare's Sonnet XXX: 'When in the sessions of sweet silent thought / I summon up remembrance of things past [...].' (Most of Scott-Moncrieff's titles were taken from English literature.)

3. For the new six-volume edition in 1991, Chatto & Windus and their translator, Terence Kilmartin, chose to return to Proust's own overall title: *In Search of Lost Time*. Already, for the first revised edition of 1981, they had replaced Scott-Moncrieff's *Cities of the Plain* with Proust's *Sodom and Gomorrah*, and, instead of *The Sweet Cheat Gone*, had restored the symmetry of *The Captive* and *The Fugitive* (as, it turns out, Proust would have wished: see letter 221).

250 To Gaston Gallimard

[Thursday 14 September 1922]

My dear Gaston,

(I don't know if I've written to you since I started to fall down at every step and to be unable to articulate. It's frightful. But a moment's respite this morning gives me a chance to write to you.) Not, alas, to say what I would like to say, and it horrifies me that a loving friendship like ours should constantly be overtaken by events that make no fundamental difference but vitiate its joys. I want to tell you two things. The second is unimportant. But you are too cultured a man not to realize that somebody who no longer lives except for his book cannot ignore the first. My English friends the Schiffs – who are above all friends of my books – have written me an appalled letter (I can't lay my hands on it, it must be tangled up in my sheets). They've seen an announcement of my book with a title that means (I repeat it roughly) *Souvenirs des choses passées* instead of *À la Recherche du temps perdu*. This ruins my title. What is more serious still (and to confirm this, I must find the letter), *Du Côté de chez Swann* is to be translated in English as *À la manière de Swann*. I can hardly believe it, let alone sanction it. You know the significance of the title *Du Côté de chez Swann*, the principal meaning of which is that there are two walks from Combray, one path leading to the Château de Guermantes and the other to the property owned by Swann. The title as told to me (but there has to be some mistake, you must find out)[1] would be meaningless, while the first might be from H. Bordeaux.[2] Yet my friends tell me that my titles (which they admire, but that's only their opinion) can be accurately translated in a number of different ways. In any case, when a publisher sells the translation rights, he doesn't sell the right to distort the work. And titles like these make my friends the Schiffs anxious for the translation itself.

The unimportant thing is this. I have a brother, a surgeon, who is very fond of me. Having been away, he came round to tell me: 'Everywhere I went, I saw Morand's book[3] (which pleased him as much as it does me). At every station, and I travelled all over the place, I asked for *Sodome*. I didn't find a single copy. You may pride yourself on having a publisher who doesn't spend a sou on promoting your books. And considering how much your sad life costs you, I wonder that you don't complain.'[4]

But, as I say, all this is very minor. What really matters to me is my book, which I refuse to let the English destroy, and your affection. For I am, with much love, your

Marcel

It's such an effort to write after attacks like these that my letter is incomplete. Forgive me.

1. Gallimard, back in Paris, was to reply that Chatto & Windus hadn't kept him informed, and that he would protest. See *MP-GG*, 616.
2. See letter 63, n. 3.
3. *Ouvert la nuit*: see letter 184, n. 2.

4. In his reply, Gallimard gives Proust precise details of publicity campaigns and the distribution of his books to station kiosks. See *MP-GG*, 612–16.

251 To Edmond Jaloux

[Around mid-September 1922]

My dear friend,

I still haven't thanked you for the wonderful article,[1] I couldn't, having been in a state of living death for the past month, deprived in turn of speech, sight and movement. And, medicine being comical, it's now thought to be due to a chimney which is leaking in several places and letting carbon-dioxide seep into a room with permanently closed windows. I prefer this explanation, for it gives me hope of an improvement, even a rapid one. But it's too ingenious and reassuring to be true. I doubt whether carbon-dioxide would send one sprawling every time one tries to get out of bed. I would rather you didn't mention any of this. 'To weep, to moan, are equally craven.'[2] I just wanted you to know why I hadn't yet thanked you. Today, I can, at last! thanks to adrenalin and caffeine. What you don't know is that on the night of Le Bœuf sur le Toit, I wrote you what amounted to a love letter. The letter is still here, because the next day I discovered that I had told you an untruth.[3] But even its rectification will amuse you, if only I can come back to life a little. I don't want to abuse my strength (!) by prolonging this first letter. Otherwise, I feel like going on and giving you both story and rectification. But I must be careful. Not that it will do much good.

Your grateful admirer,
Marcel Proust

1. Jaloux, writing in *L'Éclair* of 7 September, said that he wished he could identify what it was about Proust's work that made it 'new and essential, to the point where it seems likely to overturn all our conceptions of the French novel.'
2. Alfred de Vigny, 'La Mort du loup'. Proust quotes the verse fully in letter 174.
3. An allusion to Proust's description of 'pimps and fancy-boys' in letter 226, he having concluded that Jacques Delgado, at least, was neither: see letter 227.

252 To Ernst Robert Curtius

[17 or 18 September 1922]

Dear Sir,

    This note which accompanies a copy of *Sodome et Gomorrhe II* is merely to apologize to you, you, whom I admire so much and, dare I say, like so much, for its being so long overdue. I can't bear to talk about myself or my woes, but I would find it even more unbearable to have you think me indifferent. I've been deprived, successively, of speech, sight and movement (I fall down with every step I take). I prefer not to dwell on this torment. But I've said enough to make you forgive me. Medicine as a science (?) being extremely comical, the latest theory is that as my chimney is cracked, and as I never open a window, I inhale – O precious breath! – large amounts of cardon-dioxide daily. I don't want to speak disrespectfully of doctors, my father having been a professor at the Faculty of Medicine, and my brother, than whom nobody could be braver, wiser or more intelligent, also being a professor at the Faculty of Medicine. But my father is dead, alas, and as for my brother, I'm too ill to receive him. It's true that there are days when I could go to him in a taxi. But it's always at four o'clock in the morning. And I don't like to wake him as he has to be at the hospital by eight. It really is odious to go on and on about oneself and one's family like this. But it's no less than an overflowing of this admiring friendship for you.

    I read a very fine article by you, in which you talk in profound and magnificent terms about what post-war Germany should be.[1] Note that despite the greatly exaggerated, but also greatly moving praises lavished on me daily by Léon Daudet in *L'Action française*, and despite my brother's affection for General Mangin, a mutual affection, sealed on the battlefield, I am not (and neither is my brother) a 'nationalist'. It's rather vulgar of me to tell you all this, but it helps to get things straight. Not that we need to talk politics. Literature is our field, a very fertile one. Renan talked of people suffering from 'morbo litterario',[2] which is absurd. Bad literature shrinks things. But the real thing reveals unknown parts of the soul.[3] It's rather like Pascal's dictum, which I misquote, not having my books here: 'A little science turns one away from God, a lot brings one back.'⁴ One should never be afraid of going too far, for the truth lies beyond. But you know that much better than your friend

Marcel Proust

1. 'Intellectual relations between France and Germany' (*Neue Merkur*, June 1921), cited at length by André Gide in the *NFR* after its appearance, translated into French, in *La Revue rhénane* in October 1921.
2. '"Morbus litterarius"! The characteristic of this trait is to be more interested in its literary effect than in the thing itself.' Remark by Renan in his speech to the French Academy in 1889.
3. Cf. letter 19 to Lionel Hauser.
4. Not Pascal, but Francis Bacon. Proust seems to have remembered two of Bacon's sayings: 'A little philosophy inclines one to atheism, but depth in philosophy brings men's minds back to religion' ('Of Atheism', *Apothogems*). And: 'Books must follow science, and not science books' ('Proposition touching amendment of laws'.)

253 To Jacques Rivière

[Wednesday evening 20 September 1922]

Monsieur Marcel Proust[1] informs Monsieur Jacques Rivière in confidence that he has been suffering the worst asthma of his life for the past three days, during which he has found it impossible to work, either on the book, which he has re-started for the fourth time, or on the extracts,[2] and that, since these attacks, dreadful as they are, don't seem to have affected his health in general, he hopes to see Monsieur Rivière in a few days' time. At first glance, he feels that 'Le Sommeil d'Albertine' is a little short and needs to be reinforced by adjoining passages.[3] In any case, as he will explain to Monsieur Rivière, and only to Monsieur Rivière, he, Monsieur Proust, having thus far been content with any position, no matter what, would like in this instance to have the leading one. Should Monsieur Rivière find this impossible, which Monsieur Proust would well understand, it is unlikely that Monsieur Rivière will have any extracts at all, December and January being a little too close to New Year's Day.

Monsieur Proust is happy to hear that Monsieur Rivière had a good holiday, which affords him some consolation in his pain.

Marcel Proust

1. Letter dictated to Céleste.
2. The late September deadline for Proust's 'copy' was fast approaching.
3. Evidently Proust had not after all included 'Albertine's Sleep' (see letter 241) in his abridgement for *Les Oeuvres libres*: see letter 246. Rivière was to reply that he would lengthen it and make it the leading article in the *NRF* of 1 January.

254 To Jacques Rivière

[Saturday 23 September 1922]

My dear Jacques,

A mixture of evatmine and Kola[1] makes it just possible for me to write (legibly, by hand, that is) for an hour. I regret sending you what I'm about to send you. The reader would find my 'Cris de Paris'[2] more amusing than the results of my plumbing the depths of sleep. But that would already take up almost fifteen pages of the *NRF*, and one mustn't exaggerate. The piece I'm sending you is called:

I. 'La regarder dormir'. II. 'Mes réveils'.[3]

The cutting I did, with creditable energy considering the state I'm in, made putting the book back together again sentence by sentence a torture. Don't have qualms when you see Gisèle's name instead of Albertine's.[4] I'm too honest in my dealings with you, and in my dealings with Fayard, come to that, to allow a single line of what I am sending you to appear in *Les Œuvres libres*. He will have that much less for his extracts. Not to mention many other things. But I think I'll leave him the 'Cris de Paris' (it isn't the 'Cris de Paris', I'm wrong), otherwise the task of extraction will be impossible. We'll discuss it when I'm better. In fact, I'm much better already (thanks to the evatmine). My doctor, seeing me kill myself over your extracts, thinks I'm mad to work in such a state.

I would ask you to come and see me (now that I could perhaps receive you) but I know that going out at night doesn't suit you. I'm still too weak to write to Gaston, so give him my warmest regards. Write at once and tell me what you think of the pieces, and whether they have stood up to cutting. Gaston wanted to know if I had recommended you to Léon Daudet. But you forbade me to do so.[5]

Yours affectionately,
Marcel Proust

I would be very grateful for proofs, even before you read it. Kindly don't tell anybody which cuts I have made. Ignore the numbers in pencil.

1. The first is an anti-asthmatic drug, the second a heart stimulant.
2. See letter 241, n.4.
3. 'Watching her sleep' and 'My awakenings': V, 74–6; 131–3. Proust had thus lengthened 'Albertine's Sleep' himself.
4. Unless he means Andrée, Proust seems to have brought in Gisèle, Albertine's treacherous friend, from later in the story.
5. See letter 245.

255 To René Gillouin[1]

[End of September 1922]

Dear Sir and colleague,

Unfortunately for me, your diagnosis of my condition in your splendid article is incorrect.[2] But whatever illness I suffer from, it has been aggravated these past few days by such violent attacks of asthma that I was unable to thank you immediately, and find it very difficult to do so now, otherwise I would have taken great pleasure in dwelling on the exceptional beauties, the profound insights, of your article.

You may be surprised to learn that this isn't the first letter I have written to you. Indeed, though very ill even then (but still hoping to leave my bed to see beautiful things from time to time), I had thought of seeking advice about aesthetic excursions from the one man who I felt was qualified to give it. But my letter written, I lost my nerve. I have often thought about it since. But the time had come to make my retreat.

There are several factual errors in your article. But not having slept, eaten or drawn breath for six days, I'm in no condition to point them out. And then, an error of fact is unimportant. In the end, the friendly spirit in which I write to you (and yet I've virtually given up letter-writing) is your proof that, in an article of yours, I attach more importance to the spirit than to the letter.

Very gratefully yours,
Marcel Proust

1. René Gillouin (1881–1971), critic and civil servant.

2. In *La Semaine littéraire*, Geneva, 1 July. Having described Proust's 'severely neuro-pathological condition', Gillouin goes on: 'we never cease to be surprised at what M. Proust reveals to us about ourselves simply through talking aloud in our presence. On the other hand, his illness introduces a strongly morbid element [by] tackling certain aspects of reality which, till now, have been the subject of treatises by doctors and psychiatrists, or else of obscene books carried under a raincoat. *Sodom and Gomorrah* [. . .] is the literary equivalent of Freud's psychoanalysis. [. . .]. The most scabrous of subjects may be treated in a salubrious way [. . .] and the author of *Sodom and Gomorrah* is also the author of some of the noblest, highest and purest pages ever to honour French literature.'

256 To Gaston Gallimard

[Tuesday 3 October 1922]

My dear Gaston,

I've just sent you, instead of the long letter I've owed you for ages and couldn't write because, though you weren't to know it, I was dying and finding the process terribly slow, a request for information which I've been asked to supply.

1. The tax people want to know what I received in the way of royalties in 1921.[1] I would never have passed their request to you, being fed up with such bureaucratic nonsense, had a chance combination of physiological factors not revived me sufficiently to allow me to write these frivolous things to you. But once I write to you, I oblige you to write to me by return, in order that we keep in step and avoid the regrettable possibility – I'm assuming that you, too, would regard it as regrettable – of our contradicting one another.

2. Some friends write to say that they can't get hold of *Guermantes I* anywhere, nor, which is really extraordinary, the second volume of *Sodome* (to be precise, the second volume of the three-volume *Sodome II*).[2] Does this mean that both, the last so recent, are out of print? Please take action, this dearth is extremely bad for me. Others, I'm glad to say, have the freedom of the universe. I no longer enjoy movement, or speech, or thought, or even the simple pleasure of being free from pain. Therefore, as it were expelled from myself, I take refuge in palpating books I'm unable to read, adopting for their sake the stratagems of the burrowing wasp about which Fabre wrote the marvellous passages quoted by Metchnikoff that you must know.[3] Doubled-up like her and totally

bereft, I devote myself to providing them through the world of the mind with the future denied to me.

Thus, dear Gaston (and this is quite apart from the promised letter), I urgently need firstly, my royalties for 1921, and secondly, a note to the printer so that he reprints (instead of so many things he would do better to 'repress', modest pun)[4] *Guermantes I* (there are still some *Guermantes II*s and *Sodome I*s) and *Sodome II* (the book in three volumes).

Very affectionately yours,
Marcel Proust

(I stupidly said, writing badly, that I wanted the royalties for 1921. Now, it's not the royalties I need, but a note from you giving me the figures.) One evening this week, if I'm a little stronger, could I ask you to come round for a minute so that we can discuss all this. But kindly reply in the meantime.

1. Proust's royalties for 1921 totalled 30,000 francs. See *MP–GG*, 624.
2. This report was much exaggerated.
3. See Françoise's stratagems 'for establishing the greatness of her house', which the narrator compares to those of the solitary wasp burrowing to lay her eggs: I, 145–7. Allusion to a passage by the great entomologist Jean-Henri Fabre (1823–1915), quoted in an essay on the prolongation of life by his contemporary, the zoologist Élie Metchnikoff.
4. Play on the words *tirer* and *retirer*.

257 To Charles Scott-Moncrieff[1]

[9 or 10 October 1922]

Sir,

I'm very flattered and touched by the pains you have taken over the translation of *Swann*. It's a miracle that I can thank you. Indeed, I am so gravely ill (my illness is not contagious) that I write to almost nobody; in any case, of all my translators in different languages, you are the only one to whom I have written. Perhaps it was on seeing the fine gifts you have brought to this translation (I haven't finished reading it yet, but you should know that I'm bedridden, take no nourishment etc.). There are one or two points I would like to raise with you. For example, À la Recherche du temps perdu doesn't mean that at all. The lines you add, the dedication to your friends, are no substitute for the ambiguity of *temps perdu*, also present at the end of the work, in *Le Temps retrouvé*.[2]

As for *Swann's Way*, it can mean *Du Côté de chez Swann*, but also *à la manière de Swann*. You could have solved everything by adding 'to'.[3]

Forgive my writing to you in French, but my English is so pitiful that nobody would understand it. In saying this, I provide you with a good argument against me. 'What,' you say, 'you have scarcely a word of English' – at least nowadays – 'and yet you feel you have the right to raise objections' – tempered with much praise – 'about my translation.'

Kindly give your publishers my compliments on a most noteworthy translation of *Swann*.

Yours faithfully,
Marcel Proust

1. Charles Kenneth Scott-Moncrieff (1889–1930). His previous translations included Stendhal's *Red and Black* and *The Charterhouse of Parma*.
2. The 'dedication to friends' being, of course, the first two lines, quoted on the title-page of the English translation, of the Shakespeare sonnet from which Scott-Moncrieff took his overall title: see letter 249.
3. Proust writes 'to' in English.

258 *From Charles Scott-Moncrieff*

Savile Club
12 October 1922

My dear Sir,

I beg that you will allow me to thank you for your very gratifying letter in English[1] as my knowledge of French – as you have shown me, with regard to the titles – is too imperfect, too stunted a growth for me to weave from it the chaplet that I would fain offer you. As you are still suffering – which I am very sorry to hear, and wish that my real sympathy could bring you some physical relief – I am making my reply to your critiques on another sheet,[2] and by the aid of a machine which I hope you do not abominate: it is the machine on which *Swann* and one third of the *Jeunes filles* have been translated. Thus you can throw away this sheet unread, or keep it, or inflict it upon M. Gallimard.

Charles Scott-Moncrieff

1. Scott-Moncrieff means, of course, that his letter, not Proust's, is in English.
2. This sheet is missing.

259   To Céleste Albaret

[Shortly after 10 October 1922]

I've just coughed more than 3000 times and have no back or stomach left, nothing. It's madness. I need very well-warmed underclothes, ditto woollies. *But please think of this.* It's the smell of your laundry that brings on these needless coughing fits. I trust that my *orders* are understood. Otherwise I shall be *extremely cross*.[1]

1. A word always accompanied by a smile, according to Céleste: see Albaret, *op. cit.*, 349.

260   To Céleste Albaret

[Shortly after 12 October 1922]

Use rhino-gomerol,[1] so that if you pick up germs out of doors we won't have a repeat performance. Your arrangements for this afternoon are beyond my understanding.

Nobody should suffer such terrible cramp. But whatever happens, you are to come and stand at the foot of my bed for a nice long time.[2]

Is there still no letter from Mme Schiff?

1. A nasal antiseptic. See *The Captive*, where the narrator is struck by the unpleasant smell of rhino-gomerol emanating from Mme Verdurin, who has used it to counteract the 'appalling sniffles' brought on by Vinteuil's music: V, 271–2.
2. See the photograph of Céleste in Albaret, *op. cit.*

261 To Céleste Albaret

[October 1922]

'Tall, lissom, comely, spare,
Now carefree, now full of care,
Charming alike princes and cooks,
Flinging Marcel caustic looks,
Rendering him acid for hydromel,
Moral, sharp-tongued, original,
Such is the niece of Nègre, Albert.'[1]

1. 'Grande, fine, belle et maigre, / Tantôt lasse, tantôt allègre, / Charmant les princes comme la pègre, / Lançant à Marcel un mot aigre, / Lui rendant pour le miel le vinaigre, / Spirituelle, agile, intègre, / Telle est la nièce de Nègre.' Allusion to Albert Nègre, Archbishop of Tours, Céleste's sister-in-law's uncle.

262 From Reynaldo Hahn

[Shortly after 21 October 1922]

My dearest little Marcel,

I'm writing to you on the machine because holding a pen tires me and because my handwriting is so illegible.

I ran into Robert yesterday evening, after he had left you, and he asked me if we could have a chat about you. Naturally, I didn't say that I had seen you, and he has no idea that you talked to me about him. Here, word for word, is what he had to say: 'Marcel's illness isn't serious, it's pneumococcal, that is, something treatable and easily cured.[1] Yet it needs looking after, and Marcel won't let himself be looked after. The other day, I talked to him too much *like a doctor*, which I know was wrong of me, and that it agitated him. I mentioned the word clinic, thinking only of its advantages in terms of treatment, but I shouldn't have done so, any more than I should have suggested a nurse; but what is one to do, the good Céleste may be very dutiful, but she isn't capable of looking after an invalid. Anyhow, there'll be no more talk of clinics or nurses, or of anything else that might upset him, and I shan't go back unless he sends for me; but, you know, it's very hard for me to stand by and see him refuse treatment, when nothing could be simpler. After all, if he broke a leg, he would have to put up with having it in plaster and agree to it, whatever the cost to his nervous sensibilities. The only difference in this case is that it involves no operation or unpleasant treatment. I would be very grateful if you could persuade him to think it over, making him see that what isn't dangerous at present could become so. If I came across a patient in Marcel's condition on my hospital rounds, I would say: "Here we have a patient *whose care is being neglected*." That is the exact expression. There will be no more question of his having a nurse, nor of anything else that might vex him; I would gladly nurse him myself, and would make sure that nothing was done to upset him, or we could work out some other solution together, but it's unreasonable to expect me to leave him ill, without proper care, and even he himself, having gained confidence in me thanks to my successful treatment of Marie Laurencin,[2] seems to think that I may be able to do him good.'

I replied: 'Robert, you know how difficult it is to persuade Marcel of anything, especially anything to do with his health, and for my part, I never like to bring up the subject, being very ignorant about medicine and, above all, convinced that I would be wasting my breath. I'm sure that he won't see me tonight, but I'll write and tell him what you say. I quite agree that one should avoid vexing or tiring or agitating him, and when I call, it won't be in the hope of seeing him, but to get more detailed news than is possible over the telephone.' He told me that Céleste hadn't wanted to let him in, no doubt for fear of displeasing you, but that, not having seen you for some time, it was essential for him to see your condition for himself.[3] He was very sorry to find you no better. And that, my little Buncht,[4] was our conversation.

You know without my telling you how much I wish I had the smallest degree of influence over you. It makes me very unhappy that you refused to eat even a little purée, as you promised me you would, and that you persist in fasting, which cannot be good for you just now. I know that you won't allow anybody to tell you what to do, and that I'm powerless when it comes to doing anything I consider reasonable or desirable for my dearest friend, one of the people whom I have loved most in my life. But the last thing I want is for you to accuse me of making your illness worse with my nagging and boring advice. I'll do whatever you say and, since I have no choice, resign myself to getting nowhere.

With all my love,
Your
Reynaldo

1. Robert Proust had diagnosed bacterial pneumonia, Dr Bize having shown him the analysis of Proust's sputum.
2. Marie Laurencin (1885–1956), painter and theatre designer, notably for Stravinsky's ballet with Diaghilev, *Les Noces*.
3. This account agrees with Céleste's own: see Albaret, *op. cit.*, 345–8.
4. Term of endearment used between Proust and Hahn during their long correspondence. See *Selected Letters Volumes Two* and *Three*.

263 To Céleste Albaret

[October 1922]

You see, my coughing fits have come back through talking to you.

Cross out everything (except what we left in *Albertine disparue*)[1] – up to my arrival in Venice with my mother.

1. Proust's only reference to an alternative, truncated, version of *Sodome et Gomorrhe IV* (see letter 103, n. 3), the completed typescript of which was discovered among the papers of Proust's niece Suzy Mante-Proust after her death in 1986 by her son-in-law Claude Mauriac. In it, Proust ends the Albertine story at the conclusion of 'Sojourn in Venice' (the narrator having learned details of her death from which he deduces the brutal truth of her liaison with Mlle Vinteuil). Edited by Nathalie Mauriac and Étienne Wolff, this version was published as *Marcel Proust. À la recherche du temps perdu. Albertine disparue* (Grasset, 1987). It has been translated by Terence Kilmartin as *Albertine Gone* (Chatto & Windus, 1988).

264 From Jacques Rivière

[23 or 24 October 1922]

My dear Marcel,

I'm so sorry! but I'm afraid that the proof-copy you want *doesn't yet exist*. I haven't even passed the magazine for press. I won't have it before the 30th at the earliest.

Meanwhile, in the vague hope that it might be of some use, I enclose page-proofs of your extracts.[1]

Believe me, I would love to help and save you trouble, but it's a *physical* impossibility to give you what you want.

With affectionate regards and best wishes for a speedy improvement.

Your friend,
Jacques Rivière

1. See letter 254, n. 3. The extracts were to appear in the *NRF* of 1 November.

265 To Jacques Rivière

[Tuesday 24 October 1922]

My dear Jacques,

Forget about the proof of the magazine. But what appals me is that the article (I trust it precedes the corrections I asked you to make) ends exactly as before. It can't end like that, it's dreadful. Wire Bruges,[1] anything. I'll reimburse your expenses, but it cannot end like that.

Much love,
Marcel

Just in case, I've left you a set of galleys at the office.

1. The *NRF* printers were in Bruges.

266 From Jacques Rivière

11 o'clock Wednesday [25 October 1922]

My dear Marcel,

I've just held up printing, which was just about to begin. But for goodness sake tell me *as soon as possible* how the extract is to end. When you wrote to say that the ending was awful, you didn't give me the slightest indication of how I should change it. So I took it for a purely platonic regret.

True, your copy included a page that I didn't send to be set. But as you see, for I enclose it, it consists purely and simply of one sentence that had already occurred, word for word, higher up in the text I had sent to the printers. I couldn't believe that you wanted to repeat it a second time, so I left it out.

Tell me quickly (tonight, if at all possible) what I should do about the ending. And please bear in mind that it's now too late for me to change the layout. Anything you add has to fit into the blank space at the foot of the page, and anything you cut shouldn't cause the text to finish on the previous page; in short, you can't cut more than seven or eight lines.

I await your instructions, and only hope they arrive in time for me to telephone them to Paulhan in the morning.

Warmest regards,
Jacques Rivière

267 To Jacques Rivière

[Wednesday afternoon, 25 October 1922]

Dear Jacques,

I take advantage of a lull in my coughing fits (which have been going on for days) to say that the part of 'Mes Reveils' you sent me means nothing to me. All I can usefully do is to return your page-proof, and tell you not to include *anything from the last few lines*. But, if you can, insert the man who is running as he jumps off the train get back on it[1] before 'O miracle, Françoise, could have no suspicion of the sea of unreality'.[2] (Above all, don't forget the goddess of Mnemotechnia)³ and end with 'I had re-integrated myself with reality'.⁴ Don't worry too much about all this chopping and changing. But don't leave in a single line about Eliot⁵ and suchlike idiocies, nor about the life of the night before⁶ etc. The ending needs to be dramatic. We've jumped at least 12 pages.

And then, Jacques, leave a poor wretch in peace, for he is exhausted, and, yesterday, feeling better, corrected an entire book for Gaston as well as writing letters on your behalf about the Prix Balzac. You confused me by making me believe in corrections not one of which has been done. Leave me to my suffering, which today has reached the point of agony. I've lost faith in you.

[Unsigned]

Dear Jacques, forgive me, but one really detests you when one sees that the lives of others, their souls, are as nothing to you compared to ten lines, so miserably bad, furthermore, that they will ruin all the rest.

Remember to tell me what I owe for expenses incurred on my behalf.⁷ I'll settle them at once.

1. See V, 131.
2. See V, 133.
3. From Mnemotechnics, the art of assisting memory.
4. See V, 132–3.
5. Allusion to George Eliot. Her name occurs in the narrator's dream: V, 132.
6. See V, 134.
7. See letter 265.

268 To Henri Duvernois

[28 or 29 October 1922]

My dear friend,

If you knew the state I was in you would be astonished to learn that, by some wonderful stroke of luck, I opened your letter, and that, by an even more wonderful stroke of luck, I have the strength to answer it. To be brief, don't worry about cheques for the moment,¹ there will be plenty of time for that if I recover from this tiresome breakdown in health. As for the 'novel', there being nothing left of it, arrange the rest as you please, or throw it on the fire. I'm not surprised that nobody has understood my insane corrections.

In fact, once I thought I had cut all there was to cut, we worked it out at nine thousand lines. Therefore (my breakdown in health having begun), I had the lines taken from the typescript of the exercise-books without counting. So I don't mind if you cut a little more or a little less. I make the exhausting effort to tell you all this in case the book (Gallimard) should come out immediately afterwards.[2] There is nobody whom I would have liked to meet more than your friend. But visitors are forbidden, out of the question. If I survive, we'll meet. 'Précautions inutiles' is absurd as a title,[3] but the only one which doesn't present problems of one kind or another. If I have another hour of strength later, I'll write to Robert de Flers and ask him to spare me 'after a long illness, bravely borne',[4] which would in any case be false, the one having nothing to do with the other. Besides, I still hope to pull out of it. But, if so, I face a convalescence the thought of which makes me shudder.

Dear friend, don't write back. Don't ask to be told how I am (nobody knows). I've been too ill to write to you on behalf of Rivière (Prix Bourget),[5] but you know my affection and admiration for him.

And it must be all over by now.

If there is anything left about my dreams, my sleep, it must be cut; if I left any of that in, which would cause duplication, it was an oversight.

You will hear nothing but silence from me now, and I expect the same from you.

Ever yours,
Marcel Proust

---

1. Allusion to the 10,000 francs he was to be paid for his abridgement of *The Captive* for *Les Œuvres libres*. See letter 248.

2. After Proust's death, the extracts from *The Captive* appeared in *Les Œuvres libres* in February 1923. Publication of *The Captive* by Gallimard was delayed until January 1924.

3. The title used in *Les Œuvres libres*.

4. Allusion to his obituary.

5. Allusion to the Prix Balzac: Paul Bourget was chairman of the judges, one of whom was Duvernois. They had voted on 28 October: see following letter.

269 To Jacques Rivière

[30 October or 1 November 1922]

My dear Jacques,

I use the same miraculous force granted me in the same quarter hour that I write to Gaston to tell you, briefly, for the moment, of my sorrow about the Prix Balzac.[1] The strange thing is that I heard of it without taking it in, being in a state of near delirium. And that tonight, I took it in, instead of going for days without knowing. Make my apologies to your brother for my delay in thanking him for his charming 'Georgics' from the Bordelais,[2] in which each bacterium is a sign of good health. In the interests of the happy medical relations which I trust they will enjoy, I think it best if my brother doesn't know that I'm corresponding with your brother. Moreover, my brother (who is very fond of you) doesn't like anybody asking him about my health. If I wasn't so exhausted this evening, I would talk to you about Giraudoux. Another time.

Affectionately yours,
Marcel Proust

It's impossible for me to send something to M. Zavie.[3] I've been through too many dark days.

---

1. Giraudoux had been awarded the Prix Balzac for *Siegfried et le Limousin*; Rivière had been a close runner-up.

2. Dr Marc Rivière, head of a gynaecological clinic in Bordeaux, had written Proust a long letter about the functions of various bacteria, notably the pneumococcus (see letter 262).

3. Émile Zavie, editor in charge of the review of the Press for *L'Intransigeant*. In its next issue, he was to quote at length from Proust's extract from *The Captive* in the *NRF*.

270 *Céleste Albaret to Jacques Rivière*

[Early November 1922]

Monsieur Rivière,

Monsieur Marcel Proust, not being fully conscious, doesn't yet know that you have sent him his book.

But if he recovers, you may be sure that nothing would captivate him more than to read your book *Aimée*, it having given him so much pleasure previously.

Yours faithfully,
Céleste

271 *Reynaldo Hahn to Jacques Rivière*

[Saturday evening 18 November 1922]

Sir,

It is my sad duty to inform you that our beloved Marcel Proust died at five thirty this evening.

His brother and I wished you to be one of the first to know. Marcel had a very special liking and esteem for you, and we know that you will be deeply distressed by his death.

Yours sincerely,
Reynaldo Hahn

AFTERWORD: PHILIP KOLB AND PROUST

Jocelyne Kolb

The subject of Proust, specifically of his correspondence, is one that I know intimately if not expertly. It has been with me, literally, since the cradle. My father spent some sixty years of his life – longer than Proust lived – finding, deciphering, dating, annotating and publishing Proust's correspondence; and he took his family with him. He spent each of his sabbaticals in Paris, taking a year's leave at half pay every seventh year rather than a semester at full pay, partly for Proust but also so that his three children could spend an entire year in French schools. I escaped the schooling on my first voyage in 1951, when I was six months old, but profited from it twice later on, as I did from trips to France every summer after I turned 11. In Paris my father looked for letters, saw his publisher, worked in the Bibliothèque Nationale, visited autograph dealers, and sought out his friends, almost all of whom had a connection to Proust. His visits to Paris were to him what touching the soil was for Antaeus: they revived him and provided him with the inspiration as well as the material he needed to work on his edition when he returned to Urbana, Illinois. For my part, I took in what I know about Proust by osmosis at first and consciously later on; as a student I often read proofs or combed newspapers to find details that might help date or annotate a letter.

Proust was always with us when I was growing up, but in a comfortable way, like an elder member of the family who was sometimes quiet, sometimes noisy, and who always gave us focus. That he was treated more with irony than deference shows, I believe, that we knew him well; but it was the irony of affection and respect. Some would say that Philip Kolb knew Proust's whereabouts better than Proust himself, but there was no fetishism in his attachment to his Proust; he did not identify with his subject – except perhaps in later years, when he claimed to have inherited Proust's insomnia. He was as sensible as he was scrupulous in his scholarship, a man of determination who was wary of fanaticism and wanted to get things right by honest means, even when it slowed him down, as it did. He transferred to Proust one of the things that attached him to *In Search of Lost Time*: Proust's ability to catch human nature in its complexity, to be surprised by it and to rethink assumptions about people and things. In short, he granted to Proust the tolerance that Proust teaches in the novel and that can be found from reading his letters carefully, without prejudice. My father knew Proust's faults and quirks, but he cherished his greatness and was able – again not unlike Proust in the novel – to transfigure the ordinary, to complicate it with humour, and to keep sight of Proust's mind or of his capacity for hard work. Familiarity did not breed contempt. My father was not guilty of the modern complaint with which A.S. Byatt endows Mortimer Cropper, the wealthy, stereotypical, and sinister American scholar in *Possession* who has 'a peculiarly vicious version of reverse hagiography: the desire to cut his subject down to size'. If one wants to know what Philip Kolb was *not* like, in his person and in his scholarly methods, then one need only think of Mortimer Cropper.

This sense of perspective, this respect tinged with irony that is itself so Proustian, was one of his anchors. The other, which is connected but supersedes it, was *In Search of Lost Time*. My father told me once that whenever he was discouraged (and his work gave him many reasons to be discouraged), he would open Proust's novel at random and begin reading to regain his sense of purpose. He loved the novel. It was his fixed point, and this focus on the novel was the most persuasive argument I encountered at the height of my own venomous anti-positivist phase, when as a student I contemptuously discounted the facts of an author's life. I was dimly beginning to realize that scholarly methods are only as weak or as strong as the people who use them, that what counts is not the approach or ideology or nationality, but the intelligence and dedication one brings to a task.

When I realized that the search for letters was not an end itself but a way of getting closer to the novel, my father and I could meet on common ground; we could agree that much of the value of Proust's correspondence lies in what it reveals about his poetics. The letters help us read *In Search of Lost Time* not because of biographical details or because they introduce us to fragments of the figures we meet in the novel, but because they make clear the *difference* between the two, or between the historical Proust and the first-person narrator of his novel, to saying nothing of the difference in style. When we find echoes or anticipations of something from the novel, sometimes phrases that Proust uses later (in writing to Agostinelli, for instance), sometimes a character (for instance Montesquiou as a model for Charlus), it is the consciousness of their aesthetic transformation and stylistic refinement in the novel that thrills and arrests. My father always said that his ultimate task was not to edit the correspondence, but to write a biography of Proust; for selfish reasons I am not entirely sorry that he finished the correspondence but not his life of Proust, since the biography might have given the impression that the facts of Proust's life mattered to him in and of themselves, which was not the case. Knowing the facts of Proust's life was an essential tool for him, but here too he showed a sense of perspective. His aim was to reconstruct as well as he could the period in which Proust lived and to become familiar with the things Proust read and saw. His emphasis was on intellectual and cultural forces, which he considered more knowable than the psychological complications of Proust's existence; paradoxically but pragmatically (and I believe legitimately) he gave pride of place to psychology in the novel rather than in the letters. What we would have, if my father had written his biography, is truly a 'life and times'. And in a sense we do have that, both in the edition and in the material he collected and that is now available to other scholars in the Kolb-Proust Archive for Research at the University of Illinois Library.

Philip Kolb went about his work with precision and imagination, with drive, and (to the astonishment of his family) with a remarkable store of patience. At home his impatience was well-known to us all; in his study at the library, on the other hand, he was imperturbable. He once took me aback, when I was working for him, by reacting with serenity to my admission that I could not find what he needed in a newspaper from Proust's period. 'A negative result is a result nevertheless,' he said simply before giving me something else to look for. His way of working, his 'method' is a good place to start the story of Philip Kolb's quest for letters, since it was over the source of his 'method' that he suffered his first great setback. His edition began as a dissertation at the University of Chicago in the 1930s under the critic Robert Vigneron, known more for his victims than his work (my father's distinction, he said, was to be the first of many). Vigneron had mentioned in class that Proust's correspondence required editing – a suggestion that sounds in retrospect more like a taunt than an invitation – and when my father took up the challenge, Vigneron's anger and jealousy seem to have grown with every sign of his pupil's progress: the publication in 1935 of an article in the leading 'trade journal', *PMLA*; a grant from the French government to study in Paris in 1935–36; and finally, in Paris, the ultimate affront – an invitation from Proust's niece to collaborate on an edition of letters.

From Paris my father wrote to Vigneron to report on his work; he sent sections of his thesis (without making a copy); and he sent two copies of a book that Vigneron had mentioned, one for the University of Chicago Library and one as a gift. He received no reply and no acknowledgment. Understandably nervous, my father cut short his stay in Paris - without having used the generous sum his father had given him to start his own library – and returned to Chicago, where Vigneron would not see him, would not return his thesis, and where the chair of the Romance Languages Department told him that he would have to abandon his topic and start on another if he wanted to receive his Ph.D. from the University of Chicago. Vigneron felt 'betrayed', it seems, because my father had used 'his' method. So my father left Chicago and went to Harvard, where they were unafraid of and unimpressed by Vigneron. But first he had to retrieve what was written of his thesis, which was not easy, and he had to face the prospect of doing another year of course work and of taking another set of qualifying exams (he had already taken twenty hours of doctoral exams at the University of Chicago). That was in the autumn of 1936, and in the spring of 1938 he received his doctorate from Harvard with a dissertation entitled *La Correspondence de Marcel Proust, chronologie et commentaire critique*.

With the clearness of hindsight, Vigneron's responses sound more like traps and obstacles than scholarly wisdom, a kind of hazing ritual that the French call *bizutage*. Was Vigneron rigorous or cynical, for example, when he told my father to reread the entire novel before sending off his article on textual repetitions in the posthumous part of *À la Recherche*, 'just in case he missed something'? Did he suggest that my father visit his own thesis advisor in Paris, Paul Hazard, because he suspected that Hazard would respond discouragingly when my father told him what he was working on, as indeed Hazard did? It didn't help that Vigneron was an anti-Semite (he is supposed to have said of Erich Auerbach's candidacy at the University of Chicago that 'we don't want people like that here'), but whatever his motive, he misjudged his pupil's tenacity and powers of concentration. Reading the novel a second time so soon after the first was the best foundation my father could have for his work, and contributed to his sense that the novel mattered most. Hazard's comment that it was 'futile' to base a dissertation on a published correspondence so poorly edited, delivered with what my father called 'chilling candour', had anything but a chilling effect. Instead it forced my father to realize that he would have to establish the text from which to work, a realization that transformed an academic exercise into a work of scholarship lasting a lifetime. Finally, the move to Harvard made my father familiar with one of the world's great university libraries and probably opened doors to him in Europe, where Harvard meant more to people than the University of Chicago, especially in those days. Even taking a second set of doctoral exams, though painful, was useful preparation for dealing with Proust's encyclopedic range. My father often spoke of himself as a naïve graduate student, which doubtless was true. But his naïveté was his armour. and I think of him as a latter-day if agnostic Parzival: he was fearless and foolish; he had luck, or knew the secret of turning bad luck into good; he had charm to offset flashes of temper; and for every foe he acquired several friends of equal or greater strength.

Finding a job was another hurdle, but here too my father was the architect of his fortune, having realized that the University of Illinois library, though in the middle of cornfields, was ideally suited for his work. Jobs were scarce in the late 1930s, even with a Ph.D. from Harvard, and it did not help to be from a Jewish family. My father held a replacement position of one year at Williams College in Massachusetts, where he said that the countryside was so enticing that he could never have finished his edition if he had stayed. He held a second position of one year at Cumberland College, a small college near Nashville, Tennessee, where he had what he freely acknowledged to be his greatest stroke of luck: to meet my mother (whose jesting comment, delivered with her usual emphasis, that my father would be on Volume II if it weren't for her was not the exaggeration she thought, and prompted in him one of his endearing fits of the giggles). In the autumn of 1941, he was newly married and unemployed; in December the US Navy became his employer, and his work in military intelligence began in Florida before taking him to London and Brussels. Even the war had its connections to Proust. He found time to visit Marie Nordlinger Riefstahl in

Manchester, the cousin of Reynaldo Hahn, with whom he worked on his edition of Proust's correspondence with Hahn, and in London he shared a flat with one of his oldest and closest friends, the fellow-Proustian Douglas Alden. After World War II, he found a job at the University of Illinois teaching Spanish; the job was for only one year and was not in his specialty, so he assumed that he would have to move again soon. But the University of Illinois had a library in the league of Harvard's (the third-ranked university library in the United States) and a generous budget for acquisitions. When he was offered a position in the French Department, he readily accepted, and one year stretched into forty-seven. It was not the library alone that secured the success of his endeavour, but something else that he could not foresee at the time: the fact that the University of Illinois's productive scholars retain their privileges even after they retire. This combination of largesse and good sense has continued even after my father's death, notably so in the person of the University Librarian, Robert Wedgeworth, who from the very beginning saw the merit of establishing the Kolb–Proust Archive for Research and gave it his enthusiastic support.

There was more of the quotidien to my father's quest for letters than meets the eye or feeds the spirit. Dating the letters was a central task that took ingenuity and a good memory, since Proust rarely dated them himself (partly, my father surmised, because they did not hold much importance for him). When I read through French newspapers from Proust's lifetime, of which my father had acquired complete sets on microfilm for the University of Illinois (1737 reels in all, the only complete set outside France, I'm told), I was looking for news of local or passing interest and details about the weather, the stock market (which greatly interested Proust), society gossip, concerts or exhibitions. Looking for weather reports made me suspect my father of inventing a task to make me feel useful. Like the narrator's affected literary friend Bloch in *Swann's Way*, who arrives at the narrator's house late and soaking wet because he despises those 'pernicious and besides frankly bourgeois instruments, the watch and the umbrella', I had learned neither the value of precision nor the fact that precision is not an enemy of the imagination.

That my father did not resist or resent the routine doubtless accounts in large part for his success, and in trying to describe how he worked, I am reminded of the renowned chef Fernand Point, who said that his secret was 'du buerre, du beurre, et beaucoup de temps' – 'butter, butter, and a lot of time.' The library was for my father what butter was for Fernand Point, and it was there that he spent most of his time. It is hard to imagine what Vigneron had in mind when he felt that my father had betrayed him by using what he called his method, because my father's manner of proceeding could not have been more straightforward. He did not think of it as particularly original, and if there was anything specifically American about him (or perhaps Anglo-American), it was his pragmatism, the desire to be accurate, and a tendency to understate. His approach had the elegance of simplicity: he wanted to collect as many letters as he could; to date them and publish them in chronological order so that it was possible to retrace Proust's life as he lived it; to be fastidious in his transcription of the text and to work only from originals or photocopies (he mistrusted transcriptions, even his own, and had photocopies of all the letters in his study, even when the originals were at the University of Illinois); and to explain as completely as he could Proust's allusions to literature and art, to current events, and to personal matters. He had chosen to work on Proust because he realized very early that Proust was extraordinary (Proust had been dead only ten years when my father first read the novel), but he wanted to show Proust as a part of his world rather than cut off from it, and to demonstrate how eagerly and generously Proust reacted to things that happened not just to him but around him. The novel was my father's compass, but he considered its significance historical as well as aesthetic, and in presenting the letters of the man who wrote À la Recherche, my father was able to dispel the myth of Proust as aloof from his time, living in a cork-lined room and by extension with cork-lined thoughts. When the first volume of selected letters appeared in English in 1982, reviewers commented as one and with astonishment on Proust's forceful and active response to the Dreyfus Affair. Yet my father would have said that such a response is typical, and his edition supports the claim.

The attempt to be complete and not to isolate Proust was the motive behind one characteristic of his edition that he did consider original, which was to publish both sides of the correspondence whenever he could. He held that the letters to Proust were in some ways more precious than those from Proust, because they are more rare and because they reveal much about Proust's ability to shape his style according to his recipient. As a collector (which by temperament he was not, since he loved fine things but did not care much about acquiring them for himself), my father sought out those letters, and the Rare Book Room of the University of Illinois library therefore contains the largest number of letters to Proust to be found anywhere, among them Gide's apology for having misjudged *Du Côté de chez Swann*. The value of having letters to Proust in the edition is obvious: some letters, even those that sound obsequious or affected, leave a different impression when read alongside the answers to them, and in most exchanges the bantering tone and allusiveness resemble witty conversation. This is the case for the correspondence with Anna de Noailles or Robert de Montesquiou, for example. When Montesquiou returns one of Proust's letters with comments, corrections, and a failing mark, we are amused but likewise conscious that the pot is calling the kettle black. In the letters between Proust and his cousin the banker Lionel Hauser, Proust's naïveté about finances is balanced by Hauser's naïveté about literature; Proust may sound silly when he asks about stocks, but so does Hauser when he talks about his own literary aspirations. Some critics are revolted by Proust's tone and call him insincere, which is at least debatable; but in any case, doesn't the ability to manipulate style and tone also permit him to imagine and capture the psychology and the style of his characters in the novel? Proust's letters show him to resemble the characters from *In Search of Lost Time* whom he complicates by setting them up to appear one way before showing them in a different light, particularly – and logically – the artists whose transfiguration is invariably positive. There are letters that confirm and those that dispel the myth of Proust as a snob, as a dandy. But to wish away the less flattering ones, those that contain so much of their own flattery, is to miss the point and to show, I believe, a lack of imagination. Among other things, these letters are a kind of stylistic warm-up exercise for Proust, and even when his compliments are excessively flowery, especially for readers now, the flowers are exotic ones that befit the turn of the century and the milieux Proust frequented, settings he later reproduced in his novel.

The beauty of my father's approach was its flexibility, its flaw that it was not easily transferable. Not because it was so complicated, since as I have said it was straightforward, but because he carried most of it with him in his head. This I know at first hand, having at one point decided that I was the logical person to finish the edition if he could not. My father was diagnosed with leukemia when he was 70, not long after he had retired from teaching and could work without distractions; it was a blow, and his usual way of turning his luck seemed to have left him. I had just completed by own doctorate in German literature (an expression of rebellion remarkable only for its feebleness), and I decided to spend a month in Urbana learning what to do if he could not finish. My sister is a scholar of French literature and could have performed the task better, but she was not free (though now she is Director of the Archive), and my brother had stated his rebellion more effectively than I, having become a musician (albeit a musician who performs and publishes music of the Renaissance that he has found in archives, and a musician with a very literary mind). I arrived in Urbana armed with a little notebook in which to record what I learned. But my notebook was neither as handsome nor as useful as the leather notebooks Proust used when he was composing his novel, one of which, the *Carnet de 1908*, my father deciphered and published to give scholars a glimpse of Proust's creative process. Notebook in hand, I watched my father work and asked him where to look things up. Two times out of three he would point to his head and answer with an impish smile, 'It's in there.' So I quickly put away my notebook and took my customary seat at the microfilm reader or in the reference room or across the hall in what then was called the Modern Language Library and performed the same tasks I had performed since I was a teenager. What I could not know was that my father would will himself the fifteen years he needed to complete the edition, nor that two especially remarkable French assistants would receive the training I did not: Françoise Leriche and Virginie Eschenbrenner Greene. They began as assistants and became his successors.

It was in the library, then, that my father spent his most productive time, in the long, narrow study under the eves that was his workshop. He was in awe of Proust's capacity to work, and he worked hard himself, but he had no desire to imitate Proust's eccentric rhythm and hours. Except when he was in Paris from May to late August, my father could be found in his study between 7.30 in the morning and 5 in the afternoon, closing shop only on Saturday afternoon and Sunday and for lunch from 12 to 1, when he would take a brisk walk home to have lunch with my mother or across the campus to join a group of like-minded scholars from different disciplines. He was granted a key to the library after he found it closed on a day when he thought it shouldn't be; he made a legendary call to the University Librarian, who got out of bed, came to open the door, and had a key made for him. The library was a haven to him from academic politics; there he had a space to work, the competent and friendly staff to help him find what he needed, and library administrators who allowed him to act as the library's agent when he acquired manuscripts. That he was granted such a privilege is proof, I now realize, that he must never have abused it. His background as the son and brother of businessmen must have stood him in good stead when he dealt with autograph dealers, and in that sense at least he was not the black sheep he and his family thought him to be.

The library was so important because of the holdings there and because the powers that be were willing to acquire more; but my father always insisted that a library is only as useful as the librarians in it are good. He felt secure about the quality of his work, but he was modest; he willingly acknowledged the help he received and always said that he would have made little progress without the help of librarians, especially those in Urbana and at the Bibliothèque Nationale. Likewise he appreciated the work of his French research assistants, a series of supremely intelligent and well-trained young women from the École Normale, who in the last twenty years of his life came to Urbana for a year or sometimes more and whose work was funded by the National Endowment for the Humanities. One of their tasks was to find and identify quotations in Proust's letters. Proust read and remembered everything and quoted with or without warning; sometimes he manipulated what he quoted, and sometimes he misremembered just enough to make his source elusive. The young women who came to work in Urbana brought with them not only intelligence and a willingness to work, but also the benefits of a French education; they were better suited than anyone to work as literary detectives, and my father spoke increasingly of their collaboration rather than of their assistance.

It is one of the ironies of the edition – or perhaps one of its most heartening characteristics – that an important contribution to the national heritage of France should have been subsidized by the United States government, a government not exactly famous for its awareness of literary traditions. In that sense the edition itself, like the letters in it, undermines rather than confirms stereotypes, and the regular presence in Urbana of young French scholars offers another example of how practical needs were fused with philosophy. Philosophy in this case is that of the eighteenth-century French *philosophes*, and my father always underscored the common intellectual heritage of France and the United States. He admired the wit, style and religious scepticism of Voltaire in particular, and he thought of national distinctions as interesting rather than divisive; when he was asked, as he often was, whether it was odd for an American to have chosen to work on Proust, he spoke without apology or embarrassment of the universality of genius, yet with an appreciation for what made Proust distinctively French. My father's own easy ability to move in two cultures generally met with respect, though naturally people in France knew his work better than people in the United States. Anti-American sentiment was rare, but I can think of one example replete with ironies of a Proustian sort that is connected to the debt he owed to the young French scholars who worked with him.

As the edition progressed and my father's speed increased, one could mark the seasons by his arrival in Paris and the appearance of a new volume in the windows of the bookshops there. He and his edition increasingly acquired the status of an institution, and the reviews in the French press were almost always favourable, to the special delight of his publisher Plon and of my mother. Some wrote about the letters as if they grew on trees, which either amused or annoyed him, depending on how the work itself was going; but most of the reviewers, like most of the people my father met in France, admired the skill and integrity with which he produced his edition and the erudition of his notes (some concrete demonstrations of French admiration were a prize from the Académie française at the beginning of his career, in 1951; the awarding of the *légion d'honneur* at the end, in 1984 – 'Better late than never', was my father's remark; and since his death two volumes about the correspondence and about his work on it by the scholar Luc Fraisse). The reviews in *Libération* by Mathieu Lindon therefore stood out for their condescending tone and their sharp attack on the notes of the edition, which were said to belabour the obvious or to provide picky and idiotic details for pedants (Lindon uses the argot term '*thésards*'). Lindon further objects to the inclusion of both sides of the correspondence and to the accurate transcription, including mistakes, of Proust's letters and of those he dictated to his secretaries and to Céleste. Someone at Plon should have explained to 'this American' the standards of French scholarship, he writes, and familiarized him with French cultural history. Why, he asks, would one need to identify for a French reader quotations familiar to every French school child? This zeal to explain the obvious, Lindon says, is one of the edition's 'cardinal sins', making it ungainly for any but an American audience. Yet clearly not every French school child knows the quotations whose source he says is obvious, since some of France's brightest and best-trained school children worked long and hard to help identify Proust's literary allusions; and in the example he himself cites as a gross error, Lindon admits that his own identification is not definitive, thereby undermining his claim.

There is some merit to the charge that the notes are too detailed, that too much information can be more of a distraction than a help; but readers of this or any scholarly edition quickly learn to sift out what they need from the notes, a process that may change from one reading to the next. My father held to the principle that it is better to be inclusive, that what one person knows, another may not, in France as elsewhere. Different generations are familiar with different literary fashions; they will read and memorize different things. My father was the last to consider himself infallible, and was actually grateful (to my own thin-skinned amazement) when people pointed out mistakes in his edition. He always noted corrections or suggestions like Lindon's and went on with his work. But as the Germans say, the tone is what makes the music, and Lindon's tone and criticism are disproportionate to the offence. Lindon is clearly delighted by the letters themselves, but seems to resent the fact that an American would have been the one to find and to publish them. The politics of his newspaper may have shaped his own views.

In good Proustian fashion, the reviewer for *Libération* demonstrates the risks and traps of jumping to conclusions based on prejudices and insufficient knowledge. My father tried to avoid that kind of mistake in working on his edition, and his attempt to find all the facts and his insistence on laying all his cards on the table (for example in explaining his reasons for dating a letter) slowed him down and added details to his notes that are not equally interesting to everyone. His editorial decisions, however, aside from the fact that they are consistent, were made not in the name of pedantry but often as a corrective, out of a need to set the record straight. Being systematic in editing the letters did not mean that there was only plodding and no guessing; it meant that clues needed to be examined anew every time, and that nothing could be taken for granted. My father's work made of him a detective, often an inspired detective. He frequently needed to identify the recipients of the letters, for example, something that seems clear once the letters are printed (as does the handwriting) but is not. He relied principally on internal evidence and knew to be cautious about external evidence like writing paper and envelopes. If Proust used the same writing paper, for instance, it did not necessarily mean that all letters written on that paper were of the same period; there could have been (and often was) a stray piece that Proust used at a different period. Even a letter in an envelope with a postmark was not to be trusted, since the two could be mismatched.

Why would such things matter? One example that my father liked to cite can serve as an illustration of the kind of surprises that come from collecting and ordering and annotating the letters, and that force a re-evaluation of received ideas about Proust and his work. In what has become a famous letter of December 1902, Proust writes to Antoine Bibesco of his frustrated creative urge 'for the first time since my long torpor', and says that 'a thousand characters for novels, a thousand ideas urge me to give them body, like the shades in *The Odyssey* who plead with Ulysses to give them a little blood to drink to bring them back to life and whom the hero brushes aside with his sword.' This letter was first published in fragmentary form and given the date of 1906; Bibesco, who was known for his pranks, kept that date when he published the same fragment, but published another part of the same letter with the date of 1903. When my father saw the originals – which was possible only because he acquired them for the University of Illinois – he found that what Bibesco had published separately and with different dates came from one letter written on 20 December 1902. Without the manuscript and the real date, it was assumed that by 'torpor' Proust meant his response to the death of his parents, who died in 1903 and 1905, and that Proust conceived of *À la Recherche* in 1906. The letter to Bibesco proves that the gestation of the novel is longer and Proust's dissipation less than had been assumed before, that Proust was frustrated at not yet being able to begin his novel, and considered his translation of Ruskin to be 'wasted time' – 'temps perdu' – while his parents were alive and he was living at home. Once he does begin to write *À la Recherche*, the early references to its structure show that in beginning his novel, he knew where he was heading. He writes in 1909 that he has 'written the beginning – and the end – of a long work'; the first part of the novel, *Swann's Way*, appeared only in 1913. The letters refute the charges of Proust's idleness and of the novel's formlessness.

Doubtless the review in *Libération* rankles because it differs so from the open welcome my father received on his first visit to Paris in 1935 and that extended throughout his life and to his family. My father never considered it limiting to work on Proust, because he was led through Proust to so many different subjects; personally, too, his circle off friends and acquaintances widened immensely thanks to Proust and became more varied rather than more uniform. Through Proust he met people from different professions and social classes to whom most academics would not normally have access. Not that the sailing was always smooth when my father went in search of letters, usually with my mother as fellow diplomat; but on balance the rewards were greater than the frustrations. Occasionally I joined my parents or took my mother's place on an outing that eventually might lead to a letter, and even though the benefit was more often culinary than epistolary (which suited me fine), I was astonished to witness the complications and the delicacy and the time that were involved in each search. I met some fascinating people, among them Proust's devoted housekeeper Céleste Albaret, whose comment that I was 'the portrait of my father' gave me the licence, shamelessly abused, to resist paternal criticism or turn it back against its source. We often saw Proust's niece, Suzy Mante-Proust, who was generous to us children but quarrelsome with my father. We met people whose names sound familiar to those who know Proust: Helleu, Baignères, Gramont, Lauris, Lacretelle, Rothschild, the sons of Jacques Rivière and Anna de Noailles, and my particular favourite, Mary Springer Fould Wooster, who received us at the Ritz but otherwise reminded me of my grandmother. Often on Sunday afternoons we met artists and intellectuals at the country home of the Cains at Louveciennes. Julien Cain was the director of the Bibliothèque Nationale and later of the Musée Jacquemart André, and it was at the house in Louveciennes that as a child I met Marc Chagall, whom my brother photographed, and that as a student I was introduced to Jean-Louis Barrault, dashing in his leather jacket, and to Madeleine Renaud, elegant and gentle, whom my father and I instantly cast as the narrator's grandmother in the novel (this was just at the time when Harold Pinter had done his screenplay of *À la Recherche*, and casting the figures was a favourite pastime). Twice we attended a Proust décade at Cerisy-la-Salle, where Anne Heurgon-Desjardins had revived the 'Entretiens de Pontigny' begun by her father, Paul Desjardins, and where my sister vividly recalls meeting Ionesco.

Afterword: Philip Kolb and Proust

These were only some of the more famous or glamorous people; many others left strong impressions and became lasting friends.

Clearly the entire family gained from my father's work. But what gains are there for those besides us? If Proust had used e-mail and there were little record of his correspondence, what would be lost? (He would surely have used e-mail the way he used pneumatiques and his chauffeur to get his letters from one end of Paris to the other quickly; and he surely would have found a way to include e-mail in the novel, just as he did the telegram, the telephone, the automobile, the aeroplane.) Proust himself wrote loudly to correspondents that they should burn his letters and wrote eloquently about the fallacy of reading authors' works to learn about their biography. His own fascination with the lives and letters of great figures served to underscore for him the distance between their biography and their works. No one seriously argues, I don't believe, that Proust's letters should be left unpublished, any more than they think that Max Brod should have followed Kafka's wishes and destroyed Kafka's works, acting not as his literary executor but rather as his literary executioner. It is hard to imagine anyone wishing that Proust's letters would suffer the fate of the documents in Henry James's *The Aspern Papers* (though life imitated art when Proust's sister-in-law reputedly burned many of his papers before she learned what they were worth). In her introduction to the present volume, Joanna Kilmartin makes the case for the value of the correspondence as a whole when she draws attention to letters at the end of his life in which Proust responds to historical and cultural events, reflects on the composition of his novel, and reveals how distinct the novel is from his life.

My father used the image of a tapestry seen from the front or the back to describe the relationship between the novel and the correspondence: the threads are the same but look completely different, and less beautiful, from the back, yet they tell us how the front was made. Just the glimpse we get of Proust's reading is enough to make us glad for the letters, since he absorbed his reading completely and remembered it; likewise one appreciates what he says of art and music, of philosophy and science. Over and over the range of his knowledge astounds and his humour enchants. The letters prove that Proust never chose a metaphor haphazardly (which led my father to seek the genesis and meaning of the seemingly strange metaphor in *Swann's Way* that Gide gave as a reason for turning down the novel for the *Nouvelle revue française*); we see

Proust seeking information for his metaphors just as we see him studying people or works of literature, music, painting, architecture, or the gowns of Fortuny that are indeed woven into the novel. And it is through the letters (and his dating of them) that my father discovered the existence of an early story of Proust's, 'L'Indifférent', probably of 1893, which he published in 1978 and in which we find Proust testing his themes and his style.

The letters give us a terminology for discussing traits of his novel's composition, the psychology of his characters, some of his themes, and the novel's form. In a letter of 1919, for example – the year he received the Prix Goncourt – Proust compares the structure of the novel to a cathedral, saying that he had planned to give each part of the novel a name taken from the architecture of cathedrals but rejected the idea as pretentious (letter of 1 August 1919 to Jean de Gaigneron). Proust also speaks of how he has constructed, or 'prepared' (he puts the term in quotation marks) his characters, and it is now customary in Proust criticism to use the term for his method of introducing a figure's personality and dismantling it in another setting, at another time, with different people. This is how he describes the technique, and indeed the novel, in a letter of 23 February 1913 to René Blum: 'There is a gentleman who tells the story and says "I"; there are lots of characters; they are "prepared" as early as this first volume, which is to say that in the second they will do exactly the opposite from what one expects after reading the first.'* The Swann as perceived by the narrator from his childhood in Combray is not the Swann he knows and learns about later; the painter Biche is not the same as Elstir later; Vinteuil the pathetic piano teacher reappears as the composer of genius; Françoise when she tortures the asthmatic kitchen maid is not the same as the woman who cries when she reads about the very asthmatic symptoms she causes.

In many letters Proust shows himself to be an acute and sympathetic critic and an astute theorist of literature. He read everything that was sent to him and commented on it at length and with generosity. At the end of his life, when he was racing to finish his novel before he died, he even took the time to answer questionnaires that were fashionable at the time, one of them about the difference between classicism and romanticism. He questions literary labels

---

* Translations are those of Terence Kilmartin from volumes Two and Three of *Marcel Proust, Selected Letters*.

and argues that every work of art is *sui generis*, and he redefines what it means to be classical: 'I believe that all art is classical but that the laws of the mind often prevent it from being recognized as such at its first appearance' (letter to Émile Henriot of 2 December 1920).

In an earlier letter, dated 6 November 1908, he makes a related argument when he discusses French literary style and defends the prerogatives of great writers. The letter is to Madame Straus, the widow of Georges Bizet and mother of his school friend Jacques Bizet, a brilliant woman whose salon was legendary. He writes after reading in the *Figaro* the preface by Louis Ganderax – a founder of the conservative *Revue de Paris* and a self-proclaimed oracle of French style – to a forthcoming book of Georges Bizet's letters. True to his name, Ganderax takes an axe to the style of others, especially those more talented than he, and he evokes the great language debate of the Renaissance when he claims to write 'in illustration and defence of the French language'. Proust echoes the phrase 'illustration and defence' to mock Ganderax in a response that combines indignation with wit and makes an analogy to the Dreyfus case:

> Illustration, no; defence neither. The only people who defend the French language are those who 'attack' it (as [they attacked] the Army during the Dreyfus Case). The idea that there is a French language which exists independently of the writers who use it, and which must be protected, is preposterous. Every writer is obliged to create his own language, as every violinist is obliged to create his own 'tone'. And between the tone of a run-of-the-mill violinist and that of Thibaud (playing the same note) there is an infinitesimal difference that represents a whole world!

Proust envisages the exclusion of Racine's verses from the *Revue de Paris* under Ganderax, and he concludes with a vigorous defence of subtlety and differentiation:

> Alas, Madame Straus, there are no certainties, even grammatical ones. And isn't it happier that way? Because in that way a grammatical form can itself be beautiful, since only that which bears the imprint of our choice, our taste, our uncertainty, our desire and our weakness can be beautiful.

It is because Proust does not believe in certainties that he is such a good observer of his period and that his letters, as my father always emphasized, are a valuable document of French cultural history, not merely of French literary history. The task my father undertook as a graduate student was sometimes a thankless one, and he often remarked that for some critics the letters seemed to have been edited by the Holy Ghost. It strikes me that the work of translators is similarly invisible and often unappreciated, the sort of work where flaws more than felicities are brought into view. In making texts accessible – just as my father made the letters accessible – the best translators are faithful to the original without abandoning their own linguistic creativity, which they need in order to remake the text; they are secure about their task without putting themselves forward. These are qualities that Terence Kilmartin demonstrated in his translation of *In Search of Lost Time* and that made him the ideal collaborator for the English edition of selected letters, all the more so because both he and my father drew their inspiration from the novel (and, like Proust, inspiration from music). When both of them died within a little over a year of each other, their families were determined that Volume Four should be completed. Yet this would have been unrealistic if Joanna Kilmartin had not been a skilled translator in her own right who shared her husband's philosophy of translation.

The letters in English translation represent only a fraction of those Proust wrote. The French edition contains about five thousand letters, or perhaps one in twenty of those my father estimated Proust to have written, and its long history is intertwined with the history and technological changes of the twentieth century. In 1935 my father naturally made his first trip to Paris by boat, and when he began writing his dissertation that same year, although he used the typewriter and was therefore technologically more advanced than some, he found it tedious to make a duplicate, which is why he sent his thesis advisor the only copy of his work. By contrast, he wrote the last prefaces to his edition on the Macintosh computer, which he started using just before his eightieth birthday, and he sent his last letters by fax (his very last having been to the publishers about Volume Four of the *Selected Letters*). He never had a telephone in his study at the University of Illinois library, however, which may be one reason why he was able to finish the edition.

There were other than technological obstacles that my father faced while working on the letters. When he first began, he had to overcome the doubts of his family, who were convinced that it was impossible to make a living as a professor. Some of them did not really believe that he was working at all until 1982, when the first volume of the *Selected Letters* appeared and was reviewed in newspapers like the *Chicago Tribune*, the *New York Times* and the *Washington Post* (the fact that the French volumes had been reviewed for the *TLS* by another distinguished Proustian, John Cocking, went unnoticed). He also had to cope repeatedly with the capriciousness of Proust's niece, who sometimes granted, sometimes refused permission to publish the same documents, and who published a volume of Proust's correspondence in 1936, using my father's datings but nowhere his name. My father worked on the edition long enough for his work to have gone out of fashion and come back in again; or rather, his work on the correspondence is the necessary tool for a fashionable topic among literary critics today, the study of letters as a genre. He worked on the edition for so long, in fact, that one reviewer began his review by praising 'the late and irreplaceable Philip Kolb', which prompted my father to say that when *he* was a graduate student, they taught him to check his facts; he corrected the error in print, quoting Corneille and saying that 'Les morts que vous tuez se portent assez bien' ('The dead you kill off are enjoying rather good health'). Until he retired in 1975, when his pace accelerated, he had classes to teach, and after that he had to outwit his illness. When he completed the edition, it was in keeping with Byron's lines from *Don Juan* that truth is stranger than fiction: he was reading proofs of the final volume when he went to the hospital a few days before he died in November 1992, in the same month and exactly seventy years later than Proust. To the end he kept his strength of will intact, having waited to die until he saw the proofs of the last volume arrive from Paris and his three children arrive from places equally far.

My father's last assistant, Virginie Greene, took the proofs of Volume XXI to the hospital and worked with him there almost as if they were in his study. Having received his ready answers to her questions, she expected to return the next day, but instead she found herself responsible for the proofs and for a biographical dictionary of Proust's correspondents that she completed in a manner that my father would greatly have admired. As my father's last assistant, she also helped transform his study into the Kolb-Proust Archive for Research, where one can consult what he collected besides letters: the newspapers and reference works from Proust's period; all the published material by and about Proust;

and his *fichier*, the immense catalogue of facts he assembled and ordered throughout his life.

I recently returned to Urbana to visit my mother and the Archive (one follows from the other), and realized that Proust's influence on my family has its counterpart in the sense of family – I can think of no other term for it – that unites the people who brought the Archive into being and who now run it, people who combine the professional and personal commitment that my father appreciated in the library's staff. Principal among them are Caroline Szylowicz, the young French librarian who never met my father but has come to know and to speak of him as if she had, and Thomas Kilton, the Modern Languages and Linguistics Librarian whose contributions to my father's work did not stop in November 1992 and who is now the Coordinator of the Archive. My father's spirit seems to hover over the Archive just as Proust's spirit hovered over my family.

The present volume is meant to capture Proust's spirit through his letters, but it is likewise meant as a tribute to the spirit and to the work of Terence Kilmartin and Philip Kolb.

INDEX

Page references in **bold** refer to the first page of a letter from or to Proust. Identifying footnotes, both for Proust's correspondents and other persons mentioned in the letters, are indicated with an italic *n* wherever more than one footnote reference occurs.

Writings by Proust appear directly under title, followed by the symbol '(P)'; works by others appear under author's name.

A l'Ombre des jeunes filles en fleurs, see *Within a Budding Grove*
'A propos de Baudelaire', *see* 'Concerning Baudelaire'
Abrami, Dr, 262
Abrantes, Duchesse d': *Histoire des salons de Paris*, 137n
Académie Française, 139, 140n, 142, 157, 170, 172n, 352, 377, 406n
Action française, L' (journal), 177, 314; Maurras and, 87n, 169n; Léon Daudet founds, 88n; praises and defends P, 124, 190n, 261, 263, 264n, 358n, 430, 443; Léon Daudet writes in, 159, 160n, 214, 215n, 241, 242n, 261, 263, 264n, 275n, 315n, 358n, 443; Vandérem reviews Benoit in, 238; Vandérem's review of P banned in, 239n; on P's duel, 242n; attacks Briand, 275n; prints Chaumeix's article on P, 296; Review of Press, 405, 411n
Action Française (organization), 8n
Adam, Paul, 333, 334n
Agadir crisis (1911), 421n
'Against Obscurity' (P), 398n
Against Sainte-Beuve and Other Essays (P; *AS-B*), 15n, 16n, 24n, 70n, 84n, 92n, 99n, 116n, 127n, 130n, 140n, 142n, 167n, 169n, 171n, 173n, 176n, 196n, 208n, 215n, 242n, 325n, 360n, 398n
Agapit, Baron Albert (Jacques Doäzan), 211, 212n, 222, 354
Agostinelli, Alfred, 40n, 152n, 463
Alain-Fournier (Henri-Alban Fournier), 142n, 430 & n
Albaret, Odilon, 18n, 36, 38n, 357, 396, 400, 403n, 417

Albaret, Mme Odilon, *née* Céleste Gineste: marriage, 18n, 36, 400; as P's housekeeper and protector, 18, 21n, 29, 48, 61, 114, 131, 206, 218, 229, 235–6, 252, 262, 263n, 264, 265n, 276, 277n, 285, 322, 378, 398, 400, 401, 474; qualities, 18n, 27; in Paris during war, 33, 35, 37–8, 49; acts as P's amanuensis, 71, 257n, 427n, 430n, 445n, 453, 471; and P's move to new apartment, 84; mentioned in Morand's 'Ode', 95, 96n; feathered hat, 134; and publication of P's letters, 183n; and P's visit to Jeu de Paume, 217n; and Beaumont's device, 282; P provides reference for, 349n; Brach names 'smiling presence', 417, 418n; and P's illness, **450** & n, 451–3, **453**; P's poem to, **451**; protects P, 452, 453n; letter to Rivière, **459**
Albaret, Yvonne, 291n, 305n, 322, 327
Albertine Gone (P), 453n
Albufera, Marquis Louis d', 12n, 35, 36n, 72n, 211, 286–7 & n
Alexander, King of Greece, 159, 160n
Allard, Mme Jules, 26n
Allard, Roger, 126n, 240, 241n, **248** & *n*, 250, **337** & *n*, 338*n*, 373, 374*n*, 384 & n
Alton, Charles, Vicomte d', **34**
Alton, Charles, Vicomtesse d', *née* La Roque Ordan, 34
Alton, Colette d', 34, 36n
Alton, Hélène d', 34, 36n
Alton, William d', 34 & n
André, Serge, 416, 417n, 421, 426
Angennes, Julie d', 178n
Annales politiques et littéraires, Les, 167n, 259n, 309n, 327n

482　Index

Annunzio, Gabriele d', 343n; *The Martyrdom of St Sebastian* (with Debussy), 248n; *Forse che si, forse que non*, 282n
Antoinette (Mme Soutzo's personal maid), 5, 6n
Antraigues, Comte Urbain (*earlier* Chevreau), 222, 223n
Apollinaire, Guillaume, 83n
art galleries: Louvre, 129, 130n, 217n, 398n; Jeu de Paume, 216, 217n, 381n
Asche, Comtesse d' (Vicomtesse de Saint-Mars), 146, 147n
Asquith, Elizabeth, *see* Bibesco, Princesse Antoine
Astier de la Vigerie, Baron Maurice, 131, 132n
Astruc, Gabriel, 20n
Athenaeum, The (journal), 440n
Aubernon, Mme Georges, née Lydia de Nerville, 52, 53n
Auric, Georges, 283n
auto-suggestion, 239
Aux Écoutes (journal), 187
Avenir, L' (journal), 170
Averescu, General Alexander, 300, 301n

Babinski, Professor Joseph, 211n, 243n
Bach, Johann Sebastian, 217n
Bacon, Francis, 240n, 444n
Baignères, Arthur, 69, 70n
Baignères, Mme Arthur, née Charlotte de Formeville, 52, 53n, 68–9, 70n
Baignères, Mme Henri, née Laure Boilay, 68, 70n
Baignères, Mlle Louise, **67**, 70n
Baignères, Paul, 216, 217n
Bailby, Léon, 236, 237n
Bainville, Jacques, 87n, 316n
Ballets Russes, 365n, 419, 420n
Balzac, Honoré de, 141, 162n, 389, 413; P parodies, 23n; preface to Stendhal's *Chartreuse de Parme*, 146, 147n; names for fictional characters, 172, 183; character of Vautrin, 222, 223n, 406n; praises own books, 255; Souday compares P with, 343n; *Histoire des Treize*, 147n; *Lys dans la vallée*, 178 & n
Banque Varin-Bernier, 79n
Banquet, Le (magazine), 24n, 87n, 133n
Banville, Théodore de, 53n
Bargone, Frédéric, *see* Farrère, Claude
Barrère, Camille, 317n, 419, 420n
Barrès, Maurice: P's relations with, 51, 52n, 90, 92, 103, 138; promotes anti-Dreyfusism, 88n; and P's *Sodom and Gomorrah*, 156–7; sponsors P at Academy, 170; writes on Empress Elisabeth, 177; praises Vézelay, 225; attends Montesquiou's funeral, 302n;

and P's illness, 314; apologizes to Binet-Valmer, 334n
Barrie, Sir James Matthew: *Margaret Ogilvy*, 91, 92n
Barthou, Louis, 330, 331n
Baudelaire, Charles: delayed reputation, xxvii, 259; and new language, 44; Sainte-Beuve on, 97; Rivière and, 141; and Racine, 168, 169n; P quotes, 191 & n, 212, 323n, 367, 368n, 392, 420, 421n; Gide writes preface to, 214, 215n; homosexuality, 218n; on numbers and music, 329n; Du Bos on, 415, 416n; *Les Fleurs du mal*, 169n, 214n, 258n, 259n; 'La Mort des amants', 165n; 'La Mort des pauvres', 200n; 'Spleen et Idéal', 56n
Baudrillart, Alfred, 402 & n
Bauër, Gérard, 387n
Beach, Sylvia, 424n
Béarn, Comtesse René de, née Martine de Béhague, 22, 23n, 35
Beaulaincourt, Comtesse de, née Contades, 153, 158, 211, 222
Beaumont, Comtesse de, née Henriette de Boisgelin (Étienne's mother), 283n, 416n
Beaumont, Comtesse de, née Jeanne de Castries, 281, 283n, 300–1 & n, 304
Beaumont, Étienne, Comte de, 33, 34n, 35, 37, 38n, 132n, 147, **281**, 282n, **283**, 294, 300–1 & n, 303–4
Beaunier, André, 87n
Beauvau-Craon, Louis, Prince de, 114, 115n
Beethoven, Ludwig van, 57n, 205n, 308 & n
Bellmand, Louis, 76n
Bénac, Jean, 51, 52n
Benardaky, Dimitri, 37, 38n
Benardaky, Marie (*formerly* Princesse Michael Radziwill), 37, 38n, 40, 41n, 437
Benda, Julien, 266, 268n, 342, 343n
Benoist-Méchin, Baronne (Jacques' mother), 351
Benoist-Méchin, Jacques, **349**, 350n, 351, 352n, **365**
Benoit, Pierre, 238–9 & *n*
Béraud, Jean, 9n
Bergerat, Émile, 110, 111n
Bergson, Henri, 44, 46n, 170, 171n, 190n, 219, 221n, 227, 229n, 264, 306, **334**, 351
Bergson, Mme Henri, née Louise Neuburger, 334 & n
Berl, Emmanuel, 96, 97n
Bernstein, Henri, 78, 79n
Berry, Walter Van Rensselaer: P's friendship with, xix, xxiv, **3**, 4n, **235**, 243, **273**, **276**, **277**, 280, **285**, **357**, 368; P teases over women, xxx, 274–5, 278; and P's investments, **64**, 67n, 274; Blanche's dedication to, 66n; exchanges books with P,

67n, 275n, 285, 286n, 418; P dedicates *Pastiches et mélanges* to, 67n; looks after P's furniture, 71; in Venice, 150n; gives Guermantes arms to P, 183, 418; and Henry James's reading of P, 183; and Blanche's portraits, 194; befriends Hauser, 204n, 243; and Beaumont, 281; P asks about article for US magazine, 285, 302n; and P's drinking, 315n; speeches, 357–8; and Jaloux, 360; on Prix Blumenthal jury, **367**, 371n, 372
Berthelot, Philippe, 314, 315n, **316**, 317n, 318n
Berthelot, Mme Philippe, 317
Best of Marcel Proust, The (P), 188n
Bethmann, Baron Hugo von, 39, 41n
Bhageu, de (Montesquiou's contemporary), 221
Biarritz, 48–9
Bibesco, Prince Antoine, 31, 32n, 41n, 152n, 169, **174**, 276, 285, 286n, 296 & n, 299, 399, 400n, 407–8, 473
Bibesco, Princesse Antoine, *née* Elizabeth Asquith, 152 & n
Bibesco, Prince Emmanuel, 31–2 & n, 47, 53n, 408n
Bibesco, Princess Marthe, *née* Marthe Lahovary, **31**, 285
Bidou, Henri, 144 & n, 166, 167n, 409, 411n
Binet-Valmer, Gustave (Jean Binet de Valmer), 124, 126n, 255 & n, 261, 261n, 267, **332**, 333n, 334n, **356**
Bisaccia, Duc de, 181n, 276, 277n, 305n
Bize, Dr Maurice, 157 & n, 262
Bizet, Georges, 62n
Blanche, Dr Antoine-Émile, 190n
Blanche, Jacques-Émile: on P, xviii; portrait of P, xxvi, 8n, 19, 358n; dispute with P over preface, **6**, **8***n*, **13**, 14n, 15n, **19**, **20** & n, 21n, 52n, 63, 68, 99n, **188**, 190n, **194**; dedication to Berry, 66, 67n; and Degas portrait, 95; article on P, 126n; and Berry, 194; Vaudoyer deplores comments on P, 217n; *Cahiers d'un artiste*, 50; *Propos de peintre: Dates*, 180, 190n, 196n, 216, 320, 321n; *Propos de peintre: De David à Degas*, 8n, 67n, 21n, 188, 190n; *War Journals*, 52n
Blériot, Louis, 270, 271n
Blocqueville, Marquise de, 211, 212n, 222
Blum, René, 476
Blumenthal, Mme Cécilia (*earlier* Duchesse de Montmorency), 60 & n, 71, 93
Blumenthal, Mme Georges, 351, 352n, 367, 370–1, 373, 385; *see also* Prix Blumenthal
Boëx-Borel, Joseph, *see* Rosny aîné
Boileau-Despréaux, Nicolas, 168, 259
Bois Boudran, 182, 183n

Boisgelin, Comtesse Bruno de, *née* Harcourt, 283n
Boisgelin, Henri de, 283n, 300–1
Boissard, Maurice (Paul Léautaud), 272n
Bonaparte, Marie, *see* Marie Bonaparte, Princess of Greece
Bonnard, André, **375**, 376*n*, 377n
Bonnard, Pierre, 149n
Borda, Gustave ('Sword-thrust'), 9n
Bordeaux, Henry, 138, 140n, 441
Borel, Petrus, 125, 127n
Borodin, Alexander, 16
Bouffe de Saint-Blaise, Dr, 296 & n
Boulenger, Jacques: P cultivates as champion, xxv, **103**, 104n, **113**, 113n, 115*n*, 116n, **169**, 171*n*, **241**, **260**, **266**, **312**; and dispute with Martin-Chauffier, **232**, 235*n*, 250n, 254, 257n, 261n, 310, 311n, 312; and P's Prix Goncourt, 104*n*; and Mauriac's article on P, **199**, 200n; P praises Montesquiou to, 212n, 233–4, 235n; Martin-Chauffier reviews, 232, 242n, 261n, 312; criticizes P's 'On Flaubert's Style', 242n, 249; and P's caffeine overdose, 257; on Chardonne's *L'Épithalame*, 267, 269n; and Léon Daudet, 312 & n, 313–14, 316; and Vettard's 'Proust and Einstein', **344**, 345n, **373**, 422n; and reviews of P's *Swann*, 352; breach with P, **384**, 416, 426–7 & n, *Mais l'Art est difficile*, 171n, 235n, 310, 311n
Boulenger, Marcel, 104, 105n, 113n, **122**, 124, 313, 316, 336, 352, 393
Bourges, Émile, 104, 105n, 171
Bourget, J.M., 313
Bourget, Paul, 87n, 169, 171n, 313, 457n
Bourrillon, Henri, *see* Hamp, Pierre
Boutroux, Émile, 44, 46n
Boylesve, René (René Tardiveau), 6, 8n, 100, 102, 138, 187
Brach, Paul, 377 & n, 402 & n, **406**, **417**, 418n, **421**
Brancovan family, 79n, 175n
Brantes, Mme Roger Sauvage de, *née* Louise de Cessac, 222, 223n
Briand, Aristide, 275*n*, 331n, 362
Briey, Comtesse Théodore de, 40, 41n
Brimont, Renée de La Bonninière de, 394–5 & n
Brissaud, Dr Edouard, 153, 154n, 346, 347n
Broglie family, 44, 46n
Bruneau, Alfred, 82
Bugnet, Captain Charles, 264, 265n
Bussé, Rita de, *see* Maugny, Comtesse de
By Way of Sainte-Beuve (P), 109n

Cabourg, 33, 34n, 35, 40n, 49, 407
Cabrières, Cardinal de, 291n
Caillaux, Joseph, 419–20, 421n

Caillaux, Mme Joseph, 23n, 421n
Caillavet, Mme Armand de, *née* Léontine Lippmann, 328, 329n
Caillavet, Gaston de, 133n, 328–9 & n
Caillavet, Simone de, *see* Stoïcesco, Mme Georges
Calmann-Lévy (publishers), 24n, 64
Calmette, Gaston, 22, 23n, 421n
Cambacérès family, 71
Cambon, Jules, 54, 56n
Canard enchaîné (magazine), 263
Cannan, Gilbert, 103n
Capet, Louis, 41n, 56, 57n
Captive The (*La Prisonnière*; P): and Vermeer's *View of Delft*, xxvii; posthumous publication and title, 188n, 327n, 386, 394; violin playing in, 41n; Morel's engagement in, 238n; typing of, 291n; La Bruyère cited in, 339n; writing, 428; extracts published, 429n, 434, 435–6, 458n; Brichot's musings on Charlus in, 433n; P's contract with Fayard for, 439n; English translation, 440n; antiseptic smell in, 450n; payments for, 457n; Zavie quotes from, 458n
Capus, Alfred, 330, 331n
Caraman-Chimay, Princesse Alexandre de, *née* Hélène Bassaraba de Brancovan, 52, 53n
Casella, Georges, 113n, 356–7 & n
Castellane, Boniface, Marquis de ('Boni'), 112, 113n, 114, 154n, 369, 370n
Castex, Dr André, 157, 158n
Castiglione, Comtesse de, 304, 305n
Catholic Church, 87, 88*n*, 106, 108n
Catusse, Mme Anatole, **33**, 34n, 37, 209n
Catusse, Charles, 33, 34n
Cendrars, Blaise, 153, 154n
Cézanne, Paul, 83, 84n
Chabert (Montesquiou's contemporary), 221
Chabrillan, Comtesse Aynard de, 46n, 300
Chambord, Comte de (Henry V of France), 229n
Chamisso, Adelbert von, 203, 204n
Chaponay-Courval, Marquise de, 211, 212n
Charasson, Henriette, 124, 126n
Chardin, Jean-Simeon, 83, 84n, 130, 142, 143n, 216, 217n
'Chardin and Rembrandt' (P), 130n
Chardonne, Jacques: *L'Épithalame*, 267, 269n
Charles V, Holy Roman Emperor, 280, 281n, 302
Charpentier, Gustave, 82
Chassaigne, Anne de (Liane de Pougy), 315n
Chateaubriand, Vicomte François-René de, 15n, 109, 230, 232n, 259; *Mémoires d'outre-tombe*, 121n, 166, 167n
Chatto & Windus (publishers), 291n, 386, 440*n*, 441n, 453n
Chauffard, Dr Anatole, 154 & n
Chaulnes, Duc de, 223n

Chaumeix, André, 395 & n, **396**, 397n, 398*n*
Chauvelot, Mme, *née* Esmée Daudet, 154, 155n
Chénier, André, 184, 185n
Chevigné, Comte de, 229n
Chevigné, Comtesse Adhéaume de, *née* Laure de Sade, 35, 36n, 73, 74n, **158** & n, **179** & n, **256**, 257n; as model for Duchesse de Guermantes, xxix, 229n
Chevreuse, Duc de, *see* Luynes et de Chevreuse, Duc de
Chimay, Hélène de, 174, 175n
Chimay, Princesse de, *see* Caraman-Chimay, Princesse de
Cholet, Comte de, 153, 154n
Chrissoveloni, Jean, 37, 38n
Cicero, 282n
Clary, Comte Joachim, 47, 48n
Claudel, Paul, 14, 63, 272
Clemenceau, Georges, 157
Clermont-Tonnerre, Marquise Philibert de, *née* Elisabeth de Gramont, xxx, **180**, 181n, **182**, 183n, 229, **302**, 429n; *Almanach of the good things of France*, 182n
Clomesnil, Léonie de, 40, 41n, 354, 355n
Cocteau, Jean, xxv, **82**, 83*n*, 84*n*, 125, 131, 153, 154n, 257n, 285, 402*n*; *Le Coq et l'Arlequin*, 82, 83n
Communist Party Manifesto, 86, 87n, 91
Comœdia (journal), 126n, 205, 261n, 309n, 314, 333n
Comptoir d'Escompte, 65, 71–2, 203
'Concerning Baudelaire' ('A propos de Baudelaire'; P), xxvi, 46n, 127n, 169n, 208n, 215n, 398n, 416n, 417n
Connolly, Cyril, 272n
Constant, Benjamin: *Adolphe*, 339n
Constitutionnel, Le (newspaper), 99n
Contre Sainte-Beuve (*CS-B*), xvi, 24n, 56n, 74n, 79n, 87n, 96n, 135n, 288n, 363n; *see also Against Sainte-Beuve and Other Essays*
Copeau, Jacques, 75, 77n, 100–1, 133n, 385n, 407, 408n, 427 & n
cork-lined room, 27, 28n, 78, 79n, 83, 96n
Corneille, Pierre, 60n, 95n; *Horace*, 96n
Corot, Jean-Baptiste Camille, 129
Côté de Guermantes, Le, see *Guermantes Way, The*
Cottet, Dr Jules, 262, 263n
Cottin, Mme Nicolas (Céline; P's cook), 37, 38n
Cottin, Nicolas (P's manservant), 107, 108n, 113n
Couchoud, Dr Paul-Louis, 407 & n
Coué, Émile, 239n
Cox & Co. (bankers), 243 & n
Crapouillot, Le (review), 121n, 395 & n
Crédit Industriel, Paris, 46n, 135
Crémieux, Benjamin: reviews in *NRF*, 266–7,

268n, **291**, 292n, 311n; P supports for Blumenthal bursary, 366, 367n, 370–2 & n, **372**; and P's anachronism, **419**; *Du Côté de Marcel Proust*, 292n; *Premier de la Classe*, 291
Criterion, The (magazine), 409n
Croisset, Francis de (Franz Wiener), 228, 229n, 235n
Cruppi, Mme Jean, *née* Louise Crémieux, 52, 53n
Cubism, 83n, 84n, 412, 414n
Curtius, Ernst Robert: essay on P, 303, 305n, **307**, 308n, 312 & n, 319, 321, 325, 326, 398n; recommends Benoist-Méchin, 352n; meets P at Pontigny, 434; P compliments on Franco-German article, **443**

Dabescat, Olivier, 273, 275n, 303, 321, 323, 350
d'Annunzio, Gabriele, *see* Annunzio, Gabriele d'
'Dans les mémoires de Saint-Simon' (P), 72n, 74n, 93n
Daudet, Alphonse, xxv, 8n, 26n, 105, 108n, 185n; and Rivière, 335; *Les Contes du lundi*, 184, 185n
Daudet, Mme Alphonse, *née* Julia Allard, 154, 155n, 316–17
Daudet, Léon: extreme views, xxv, 8n; P's relations with, xxv, 7, 8n, 106, **315**, 360, 393, 411n; Blanche cites, 19–20; co-founds *L'Action Française*, 88n; supports P for Prix Goncourt, 104, 108n, 110, 124, 139; champions *Within a Budding Grove*, 109n, 170, 172n; P dedicates *The Guermantes Way* Pt.I to, 154n, 157; article on *The Guermantes Way*, 159; on Hervieu, 160n; writes on Baudelaire, 214; and Vandérem's review of Benoit, **238**, 239n; on auto-suggestion, 239 & n; medical training, 240n; on P as lion, 241, 242n, 250; P's article on, 260–1, 268n, 269n, 312 & n, 313, 316n, 344; praises P, 263, 264n, 443; attacks Briand, 275n; P forwards J. Boulenger letter to, **313**; and Meunier's arrest, 315n; in Brittany, 316, 393, 405; and Berthelot, 317, 318n; and nationalism, 358; article on Goncourt, 361, 363*n*; in NRF, 374; and Chaumeix, 396, 398n; and Caillaux, 420; Vettard cites, 427; acts as judge for Prix Balzac, 434 & n; on P's health, 438, 439n; 'Les cent portraits', 358n; *L'Entremetteuse*, 261n, 267; *Salons et journaux*, 8n; *Vers le Roi*, 314, 315n
Daudet, Mme Léon, *née* Marthe Allard (LD's second wife), 154, **177**, 178n, **183**, 314, 316
Daudet, Lucien, xxii, xxv, xxix, xxx, 9n, **24**, 26*n*, 27*n*, 36–7, **47**, **153**; *La Dimension nouvelle*, 26n

'Days of Reading' (P), 24n
Deacon, Gladys Marie, *see* Marlborough, Duchess of
'Death-bed, A' (P), 178n
Débats, le Journal des, 3, 4n, 99n, 112, 113n, 120–1, 144n, 169, 313, 396, 398n
Debussy, Claude, 83n, 248n, 329n; *Pelléas et Mélisande*, 95
Degas, Edgar, 19, 20n, 95
Delacroix, Eugène: *Dante et Virgil*, 129, 130n
Delaunay, Guy, 35
Delavigne, Casimir, 296 & n
Delessert, Mme, 161, 162n
Delgado, Jacques, **403** & n, 406, 442n
De Quincey, Thomas: *Confessions of an English Opium-eater*, 411
Desbordes-Valmore, Marcelline, 175, 176n
Descartes, René, xxvi; *Discours de la méthode*, 23, 24n
Descaves, Lucien, 110, 111n
Deschanel, Paul, 331 & n
Desjardins, Abel, **88**, 89n
Desjardins, Paul, 434n
Diaghilev, Serge, 20n, 83n, 149n, 364, 365n, 453n
Dieulafoy, Professor Georges, 295, 296n
Dimier, Louis, 120, 121n
Dimitri Pavlovitch, Grand Duke of Russia, 305 & n
Disque vert, Le (Belgian magazine), 121n, 351, 352n
Doäzan, Jacques, *see* Agapit, Baron Albert
Don (illustrator), 327n
Donnay, Maurice: *Amants*, 272 & n
Dorgelès, Roland (Lacavelé), xxv, 104, 105n, 106, 110, 115, 124, 126n, 268n; *Les Croix de bois*, 104, 105n, 106, 108n, 110, 248, 249n, 266; *Saint Magloire*, 299 & n
Dostoevsky, Fedor, 16; *The Possessed*, 411, 412n
Doucet, Jacques, 386, 387n
Doudeauville, Duchesse de, 181 & n
Doudeauville, Sosthènes de La Rochefoucauld, Duc de, 305 & n
Doumic, René, 313, 314n, 316, 374
Dreyfus, Captain Alfred, xxv, 8n, 62n, 87, 88n, 106, 108n, 110–11, 248n, 362
Dreyfus case, 135n, 260, 370n, 421n, 467, 477
Dreyfus, Robert, 126n
Du Bos, Charles, **415**, 416*n*, 417*n*
Duccio di Buoninsegna, 29
Du Côté de chez Swann, see *Swann's Way*
Dufy, Raoul, 132n
Duhamel, Georges, 166, 167n
Dumarchey, Pierre, *see* Mac Orlan, Pierre
Duplay, Marcel, xviii
Dupuy, Jean, 76, 77n

Durfot, Comtesse Jacques du, *née* Sybille de Chateaubriand, 369, 370n
Duvernois, Henri (Simon Schabacher), 242 & n, 244, 245n, **246**, 247n, 249, 254, 333, **428**, **438**, **456**

Écho de Paris, 362, 405, 426, 427n, 431, 434
Éclair, L' (journal), 442n
Écrits nouveaux, Les (magazine), 297n, 337n
Edward VII, King of England (*earlier* Prince of Wales), 73, 74n, 153
Eglise du Village, L', 23n
Einstein, Albert, xxv, 190n, 219, 221n, 264, 277 & n, 306n, 326, 419, 427
Eliot, George, 190n, 456 & n
Eliot, T.S., 408, 409n
Ellès, Henry, 321–3 & n
Émile-Paul (publisher), 6, 8n, 19, 21, 188
Enesco, Georges, 39, 41n
Ephrussi, Charles, 51, 52n
Ève (magazine), 337n, 409
Évian-les-Bains, 64n, 262, 263n, 287n, 288n
Excelsior, L' (journal), 163, 164n

Fabre, Jean-Henri, xxx, 447, 448n
Faguet, Emile: P parodies, 23n
Fargue, Léon-Paul, 264, 265n, 294, 295, 296
Farigoule, Louis, *see* Romains, Jules
Farrère, Claude (Frédéric Bargone), 245 & n
Fasquelle (publisher), 109n
Faucompré, Mlle de, 222
Faure, Félix, 140n, 153, 154n
Fauré, Gabriel, 39, 41n
Faure, Jean-Louis, 334n
Faure-Biguet (of *L'Écho de Paris*), 434
Faÿ, Bernard, 281, 283n, 286n
Fayard, Arthème, 244, 245n, 438, 439n, 445
Fels family, 71
Fels, Edmond Frisch, Comte de, 93–4, 95n, 96n
Fénelon, *see* Salignac-Fénelon
Fernandez, Ramon, 300, 301n
Ferval, Claude, *see* Pierrebourg, Baronne Aiméry Harty de
'Fête chez Montesquiou à Neuilly' (P), 93n
Féterne (villa), near Évian-les-bains, 175n
Feuillet, Octave, 369, 370n
Feuillets d'Art, 96n
Figaro, Le: P writes for, xxvi, 18n, 22, 24n, 40n, 56n, 70n, 92; editor (Calmette) assassinated, 22, 23n, 421n; and death of d'Alton's nephew, 34; manifesto 'In Favour of a Party of Intelligence', 86, 87n, 91n, 98, 113n; Hermant praises P in, 103n; reports Seine floods (1919), 111n; P meets Vandérem at, 117; praises P, 124; Flers edits, 133n, 330, 416; Régnier praises P in, 165; P reviews Mme de Noailles in, 175, 176n; Benda writes in on P as romantic, 266; prints extracts from *Sodom and Gomorrah*, 330, 331n; P recommends Schlumberger for, 336, 353n, 387n, 405n; article on P, 430; fashion notes, 431n; promises extract on 'Madame Swann at Home', 435, 436n; on Mme Stoïcesco's tea-party, 438n
Finaly, Mme Hugo, 68, 70n
Firdausi, 382
Fitau, Félicité, 36n
Fitz-James, Duc de, 228, 229n
Fitzgerald, Ellen, 351, 353n
Flaubert, Gustave: P writes on style, xxvi, 24n, 116n, 129, 130n, 141, 142n, 167n, 242n, 343n, 398n; in P's *NRF* correspondence, xxvi, 242, 251n; P parodies, 23n, 115; epilepsy, 44; P praises, 97; despises Stendhal, 98; letters, 115; on grammar, 342, 343n; P proposes article on to Rivière, 395n, 414; Thibaudet writes on, 395 & n; *L'Éducation sentimentale*, 162n, 343n; *Madame Bovary*, 87, 88n; *La Tentation de Saint Antoine*, 390n
Fleming, Irène von, 92n
Flers, Marquise de, *née* Geneviève Sardou, 133n
Flers, Robert, Marquis de: praises P, **132**, 133n; edits *Le Figaro*, 133n; and Gaston de Caillavet, 329; prints extract of *Sodom and Gomorrah*, **330**, 331n; and reviews of *Sodom and Gomorrah*, 352, 386, 409; and Vettard's 'Proust and Einstein', 384 & n; and Schlumberger, 404–5, 406n; and Maurras's candidacy for Academy, 406n; and Du Bos's *Approximations*, 416; and Réjane, 435; and P's illness, 457
'Foggy Evening, A' (P), 200n, 212n
Forain, Jean-Louis, 7, 8n, 14, 19–21, 189, 190n
Forssgren, Ernest, 181n
Fosca, F., *see* Traz, Georges de
Foucart (of Cabourg), 35
Fouquet, Nicolas, 111n
Fournier, Henri-Alban, *see* Alain-Fournier
Fragonard, Jean-Honoré, 250
France, Anatole, 23, 55, 90, 92, 328, 329n, 397, 398n, 432
Francfort, General, 30
Franck, César, 39, 41n, 82
Frederick von Hohenzollern, Crown Prince of Germany, 61, 62n
Freud, Sigmund, xxv, 248n, 249n, 447n
Frisch, Edmond, *see* Fels, Edmond
Frisch, Comte de Fromentin, Eugène: *Dominique*, 339n
Froments, Les (villa), 68, 70n
Fugitive, The (P): title and posthumous

publication, 188n, 208n, 386, 394; on Venice, 18n; adoption and names in, 128n, 173n; 'Grieving and Forgotten' chapter, 145n; typing of, 291n; on Louis XV's secret correspondence, 315n; extracts published, 434; English translation, 440n; typescript notes, 453n

Gabory, Georges, 294, 295n, 297, 298n, 299, 370-3, 371n, 385, 386n
Gabriac, Alexandre, Comte de, 119 & n
Gagey, Dr Émile, 157, 158n
Gahier, Joseph, 240 & n, 251n, 351 & n
Gaigneron, Jean, Comte de, 89, 90n, 112, 114, 476
Galliffet, General Gaston, Marquis de, 62 & n
Galliffet, Marquise Gaston de, 68
Gallimard, Claude (Gaston's son), 293-4, 295n, 297, 299
Gallimard, Gaston, 75, 76n, 100, 185, 192, 201, 206, 243, 253, 269, 271, 288, 293, 297, 298, 336, 351, 385, 394, 409, 435, 440, 447; publishes P, xxiii, 12n, 56n, 75, 77n, 100, 188n, 201, 387, 457; P corresponds with, xxiii; and success of *Within a Budding Grove*, xxviii; and Montesquiou as model for Charlus, xxix; P complains to, xxix, 253-5, 269, 270n, 394, 447; and P's decline, xxx; and translations and foreign rights of P's works, 101, 199, 270n, 291n, 350-1, 386n, 440-1 & n; and publication of *Sodom and Gomorrah*, 109n, 201-2, 207, 269, 271, 289-90, 295n, 297, 298-9, 321n, 386n, 418n; attempts to visit P, 169; owns bookshop (Librairie Gallimard), 187, 188n, 409; escapes mobilization, 188n; payments to P, 192, 288, 297; modifies Gide's article, 193n; as subject of gossip, 193n; Rivière's infatuation with wife, 199n; and Gide's preface to Baudelaire, 214; and Duvernois's offer to P, 242 & n, 245n, 246-7, 249, 435, 438; criticizes *Les Œuvres libres*, 245n; and P's approach for publication by Boulenger, 260; and Morand's *Tendres Stocks*, 267; and *Le Merle blanc*, 270, 271n; and printing style for P's works, 270n, 297, 362; Berry and, 285; and P's health, 291n, 336; and publicity for P's works, 291n, 337 & *n*, 394, 409, 411n, 441, 442n, 447; denies NRF bankruptcy rumours, 295n; son's illness, 295n, 297; P requests Morand's discretion with, 296; payment to Gabory, 298n; and Curtius's essay on P, 305n; places extract of *Sodom and Gomorrah* in *Le Figaro*, 330-1 & n; delays despatch of complimentary copies of *Sodom and Gomorrah*, 334n; and Schiff's stories, 364; distributes books to E. Europe at cost, 386n; and P's book titles, 386, 441; and Doucet's purchase of P material, 387n; and Schlumberger's review of *Sodom and Gomorrah*, 387n, 412n; and reputation of NRF, 410-11, 439; Romains and, 424; difficulties with Copeau, 427 & n; holiday, 427; and P's extracts in other magazines, 428, 435, 436n, 438-9; and P's royalties, 447, 448n; P corrects for, 456
Gallimard, Mme Gaston, *née* Yvonne Redelsperger, 199n, 241, 297
Gallimard, Raymond (Gaston's brother), 288, 290n, 297
Gambetta, Léon, 300
Ganay, Marquise Jean de, *née* Berthe de Béhague, 369, 370n, 404
Ganderax, Louis, 477
Gans, Henri, 176, 177n, 203
Garrett, Mrs John W., 4 & n, 274, 275n, 278
Gaulois, Le (newspaper), 124, 229n, 333n, 352n, 359 & n, 361, 363*n*, 395, 396, 397n, 398*n*, 418, 430
Gautier, Théophile, 33, 125, 127n, 168
Gautier-Vignal, Comte Albert, 152n
Gautier-Vignal, Comtesse Albert, *née* Edith Schiff, 152n
Gautier-Vignal, Louis, Comte, 150, 152n, 237, 300
Genevois, Maurice, 370-2 & *n*
Genoa: European Economic Conference (1922), 321n, 330, 331n, 379
Geoffrin, Mme Pierre François, *née* Marie Thérèse Rodet, 69, 70n
Germany: and 1918 peace, 61-2; reconciliation with, 275n; reparations, 315n, 331n; post-war prospects, 443, 444n
Ghéon, Henri (Dr Henri Vangeon), 40n, 79, 81n, 87n, 127n, 171n, 424, 425n; *The Man Born of War*, 81n
Gide, André: P's friendship with, xxiv, 9, 101, 324; and P's homosexuality, xxx, 218 & n; founds NRF publishing house and journal, 12n; published by NRF, 63; intimacy with Ghéon, 81n; lectures, 132, 133n; and Rivière, 153, 154n, 193; writes on P, 213, 214n, 215n, 217; preface to *Fleurs du mal*, 215n; reads *Sodom and Gomorrah*, 217; and Montesquiou's *Les Délices de Capharnaüm*, 222; and Allard's review of *Sodom and Gomorrah*, 241 & n; on Freud, 249n; Curtius writes to, 319, 322, 325; sends P extracts from Curtius letter, 319, 325; and Wilde, 324, 325n; Gahier praises, 351; and Jaloux, 360; and Prix Blumenthal, 370, 371; on NRF, 384; praises Gallimard, 385; P declines to review, 404 & n; payments to,

Gide, André – *cont.*
  410; cites Curtius's article, 444n; turns down *Swann's Way*, 468, 475; 'Billets à Angèle', 192, 193n, 214 & n, 218n, 221n; *Les Caves du Vatican*, 405n; *In Memoriam: Oscar Wilde*, 325n; *Journals*, 12n, 215n, 218n; *Les Nourritures terrestres*, 6n; *La Porte Étroite* (*Strait is the Gate*), 133n; *Saul* (play), 386
Gillouin, René, **145**, 146n
Gineste, Marie (Céleste's sister), 305n, 318, 319n
Giotto, 29
Giraudoux, Jean, xxvi, 94, 96n, 104n, 147–8, 268n, 297n, 426–7, 458 & n
Goncourt Academy, 108n, 111n, 140, 171, 264; *see also* Prix Goncourt
Goncourt brothers: P parodies, 23n, 100, 363n; will, 151; centenary, 419n; *Journal*, 108n, 315n
Goncourt, Edmond de, 359 & n, 361; *La Fille Elisa*, 102n; *Germinie Lacerteux*, 28 & n, 342, 343n, 418, 419n
'Goncourts, The' (P), 28n, 360n
Gonse, General Charles-Arthur, 91 & n
Gorki, Maxim, 16n
Gounod, Charles François, 82, 370n
Gourgaud, Baron Napoléon, 276, 277n
Goursat, Georges ('Sem'), 407 & n
grammar, 341–2, 343*n*, 352
Gramont, Agénor, Duc de, 326
Gramont, Duchesse de, 41n
Gramont, Ferdinand de (Balzac's secretary), 183n
Grasset, Bernard (publisher): publishes *Swann's Way*, xxiii, 12n, 77n, 101, 103n, 270n, 289, 408; P leaves for NRF, 75–6, 77n, 192; proposed extracts from P, 187, 188n, 270; publishes *Albertine disparue*, 453n
Greffulhe, Comtesse Henri, *née* Elisabeth de Caraman-Chimay, **118**, 119*n*, 437; as supposed model for Princesse de Guermantes, xxix, 227–8, 354
Greffulhe, Henri, Comte de, 119 & n, 180, 183n, 295
Gregh, Fernand, xviii, xix
Grunebaum (friend of Gaston de Caillavet), 328
Grunebaum, Paul, 328
Guermantes Way, The (*Le Côté de Guermantes*; P): proofs, 77n, 102, 145n, 201; reviewed, xxvi, 162n, 198n, 219, 220n, 248n, 337n, 353n; references to asparagus, 182n; acclaimed, xxviii; P writes to Daudet on, xxix; monocles in, 40–1; dedication, 66, 154n, 178; on music, 83n; on military life, 84n; extracts published, 107, 178; abbess portrait in, 122n; on high society, 128n;

Mme Straus's witticisms in, 134; dress conventions in, 135n; Rivière praises, 145n, 163, 164n; publication, 148n, 157, 162n, 185–6, 198n, 201; anti-Dreyfusism in, 151; P sends to Daudets, 154n; and false titles, 157n; complimentary copies, 160n, 179n, 193n, 206n, 224; P sends to Mme de Chevigné, 179n; payment for, 193n; Montesquiou complains of condition of copy, 206n; Montesquiou praises, 234; reprise of opening of *Swann's Way* in, 259n; length, 290; English translation, 353n; Du Bos on, 417n; P complains of unavailability, 447–8
Guiche, Armand, Duc de: as model for Saint-Loup and Duc de Guermantes, xxiv, 36n; P's friendship with, xxiv, 35, 112, 138, **226**, 273, 277n, **436**; P describes Mme de Chevigné to, xxix, 229n, 256; visits USA, 35, 36n, and P's finances, 71, 78; P asks to help obtain Mme Greffulhe's photograph, 119n, 436; and P's candidacy for Academy, 138–9; daughter's baptism, 181n; and Mme de Clermont-Tonnerre, 181n; P denies Mme Greffulhe to be Duchesse de Guermantes, 227, 355n; in P's Saint-Simon pastiche, 229n; home at Vallières, 276, 277n; on Ritz, 326; and P's gossip, 368–9
Guiche, Duchesse de, *née* Élaine Greffulhe, 78, 181n, 279, 280n, 281n
Guitry, Sacha, 245n

Haas, Charles, xxix, 172, 173n, 422 & n
Hahn, Carlos and Elena, 155n
Hahn, Reynaldo: P loses touch with, xxiv, 154, 158n; P holidays with at Bénacs, 52n; and Mme de Polignac, 53; intimacy with P, 55n, 349n, 453n; and P's move to new apartment, 84; Wicard and, 157; and Prince Constantin's liaison with Lady Pirbright, 182n; and Mme de Chevigné, 256; calls on P, 263, 421, 422n; musical activities, 263n, 288, 375n; and P's ill health, **451**; informs Rivière of P's death, **459**; correspondence with P, 466
Halévy, Daniel: war commentaries, 3, 4n; P criticizes *Figaro* manifesto, **86**, 87n, 90, 91n; co-founds *Le Banquet*, 87n; praises Sainte-Beuve, 98, 99n; translates Nietzsche's term as *egotisme sacré*, 126n; on P and Sainte-Beuve, 129, 130n; made Chevalier of Légion d'Honneur, 429, 430n; P recommends Rivière to for Prix Balzac, **429**, 434; *Charles Péguy et les Cahiers de la Quinzaine*, 87n
Halévy, Mme Daniel, *née* Marianne Vaudoyer, 57 & n
Halévy, Fromental, 61, 62n, 341n

Index

Halévy, Ludovic, 87n
Hallays, André, 120, 121n
Halphen family, 29
Hamp, Pierre (Henri Bourrillon), 410, 412n
Hanotaux, Gabriel, 138, 140n, 362
Hauser, Lionel, xxiv, xxix, xxx, **29**, 30n, **42**, **57**, 65, 67, **135**, 136n, **202**, 204n, **210**, **243**, 468; *The Three Levers of the Modern World*, 45n, 46*n*
Hauser, Mme Lionel, 29
Hauser, Philippe (Lionel's father), 204 & n
Haussonville, Comtesse Othenin d', *née* Pauline d'Harcourt, 421
Havard de La Montagne, Robert, 409, 411n
Hayman, Laure, xxix, **353**, 354n, 355n
Hébrard, Adrien, 18n
Hecht, Alfred, 51, 52n
Hecht, Mme Alfred, *née* Mathilde Oulman, **50**, 52n
Hellens, Franz, 351, 352n
Helleu, Paul, 13, 14n, 119, 302n, **307** & n, 330, 331n
Helvétius, Claude-Adrien, 237n
Hendaye, near Biarritz, 48, 49 & n
Hennessy, Mme Jean, *née* Marguerite, Comtesse de Mun: claims Mme Greffulhe to be model for Mme de Guermantes, 227; gives dinner for Gladys Deacon, 229n, 232n, 237n; and P's ill health, 236; P praises arms, 237n, 274, 278; Laszlo paints portrait, 275n, 278; P attends soirée, 367–8, **368**, 371n, 400n, 436, 437n
Henriot, Émile (*born* Maigrot), **167**, 168n, **325**, 327*n*, 477
Heraclitus, 301n
Heredia, José-Maria de, 125, 127n, 138, 140n, 362
Heredia, Marie de (Mme Henri de Régnier; *alias* Gérard d'Houville), 125, 140, 141n, 166, 268, 346 & n, 361, 363
Hermant, Abel, 51, 101, 103n, 126n, 313, 340, 341n, 377 & n; *Affranchis*, 38 & n
Hérold, Louis Joseph Ferdinand: *La Pré aux clercs*, 266, 268n
Herrick, Myron T., 370n
Hervieu, Paul, 159, 160n
Hinnisdael, Jeanne d', 35, 36n
Hinnisdael, Thérèse d', 35, 36n, 300, 301n
'Historic Salon, A' (P), 70n, 90n
Hommes du jour, Les (weekly journal), 312n
homosexuality, xxx, 56n, 218 & n, 234, 255n, 277n, 338, 339n
Horace, 438, 439n
Houville, Gérard d', *see* Heredia, Maria de
Howard, Richard, 416n
Hudson, Stephen, *see* Schiff, Sydney
Hugo, Victor: on maternal love, 10, 12n; suppresses name in book, 95; P quotes, 135, 279, 281n, 379, 392; reputation, 175, 176n, 217n; romanticism, 259; 'Booz endormi', 135n, 380n; *Les Quatre vents de l'esprit*, 29, 30n; *Ruy Blas*, 181n
Huysmans, Joris-Karl, xxvi; *Des Esseintes*, 93n

Ibsen, Henrik, 343n
Illiers, 23n
'Illimitable Wit and a Genius, An' (P), 269n
Illustration, L' (magazine), 422
Indépendance belge, L' (newspaper), 351
Industrial Bank of China, 317n, 362
Ingres, Jean Auguste Dominique, 83, 84n, 259; *La Grande Odalisque*, 169n
In Search of Lost Time (P): declined by NRF, xxiii; P refers to as *Swann*, 4 & n, 22–3, 117; monocles in, 39–40; music in, 39; proposed dedications, 53–5, 56n, 66; printing, 75–6 & *n*; printing and design, 75–6 & n, 270n, 297, 362; construction, 98; translations and foreign rights, 101, 141, 290, 291n
Characters, models for: Berma, 28n; Bloch, 466; Borodino, Prince of, 153, 154n; du Boulbon, Dr, 153, 154n, 346; Breauté, M. de, 40; Brichot, xxvii; Charlus, Baron de, xxix, 56n, 93n, 211, 212n, 222, 234, 291, 355n, 463; Elstir, 14n, 217n, 476; Forestelle, M. de, 39; Froberville, General de, 39; Gilberte (Swann), 15, 223n, 329n, 438n; Guermantes, Duc de, 36n, 122n; Guermantes, Duchesse de, xxix, 62n, 119n, 134, 158n, 169n, 180n, 256, 354; Guermantes, Prince de, 56n; Guermantes, Princesse de, xxix, 119n; Guermantes, Sosthènes de, 305n; Leroi, Blanche, 70n, 331n; Luxembourg, Princesse de, 70n, 380n; Morel, 41n; Norpois, M. de, 54, 317n, 419; Odette de Crécy, xxix, 352, 353, 355; Palancy, M. de, 39; Rachel, 36n, 287n; Saint-Candé, M. de, 39; Saint-Loup, Marquis de, xxiv, 36n, 47n, 56n, 211, 355; Saint-Loup, Mlle de, 438n; Swann, 52n, 172, 476; Swann, Mme, 40, 355; Verdurin, Mme, 40, 53n, 64n, 329n; Villeparisis, Mme de, 64n, 153, 158n, 211, 222; Vinteuil, 476; Yourbeletieff, Princesse, 149n
Places: Balbec, 52n, 89, 179, 247n, 252, 357n, 419, 420n; Combray, 16n, 23n, 39, 56n, 222; La Raspalière (house), 70n
see also constituent parts: *Albertine Gone*; *Captive, The*; *Fugitive, The*; *Guermantes Way, The*; *Sodom and Gomorrah*; *Swann's Way*; *Time Regained*; *Within a Budding Grove*
Intentions (magazine), 319n

'Intermittencies of the Heart, The' (P), 241n, 250n, 255, 268, 390n, 420n
Intransigeant, L' (journal), 143n, **146** & n, 458n

'Jalousie, Une', *see* 'Jealousy'
Jaloux, Edmond: P discusses work with, xxvi, **382**, **388**; contributes to *Figaro* manifesto, 87n; P sends book to, 351, 352n; P entertains, **358**, 359n, **360**, **401**, 402n; entertains P, 364, 365n; preface to Merimée's *La Double méprise*, 388–9, 390*n*; and Charles du Bos, 416; P meets at Pontigny, 434; praises P's writing, 442n; and P's ill health, **442**; *Escalier d'Or*, 382, 383n
James, Henry, 135, 136n, 137n, 475
Jammes, Francis: P discusses work with, **345**, 346n, 347*n*, 433n; storytelling, 10, 12n; and immunity to criticism, 80, 81n; praises *Swann's Way*, 81, 85 & n; neo-Catholicism, 91; requests P cut scene in *Swann's Way*, 98, 99n, 347n; stands for Academy, 231; dinner in honour of, 315n; on *NRF*, 384; Ghéon writes on, 425; religious invocations, 432; *De l'angélus de l'aube à l'angélus du soir*, 418n; *Le Livre de Saint-Joseph*, 231, 232, 346, 347n; *Mémoires*, 345
Jansen (Paris antique dealer), 66, 67n
Janzé, Vicomtesse Frédéric de, *née* Alix de Choiseul-Gouffier, 211, 212n, 222
Jarry, Alfred, 272 & *n*; *Ubu Roi*, 272n
Jaucourt, Marquise de, 35, 36n
'Jealousy' ('Une Jalousie'; P), 244, 245n, 246, 247n, 267, 270n, 271n, 428, 435
Jean Santeuil (P), 24n
Jews: and Catholic Church, 29–30; *see also* anti-semitism
Joubert, Jean, 415, 416n

Kant, Immanuel, 42, 45n
Kemp, Robert, 337 & *n*
Kiderlin-Waechter, Alfred von, 420, 421n
Kilmartin, Terence, 343n, 440n, 453n, 476n, 478, 480
'Kiss, The' (P), 200n
Koenigswarter, Louis de, 328
Kolb, Philip, xvi, xxiii, 461–80

La Béraudière, Mme de, 182, 276, 277n
Labiche, Eugène: *La Clé*, 22, 23n
La Bruyère, Jean de, 9, 12n, 339n
La Calprenède, Gauthier de Costes, Seigneur de, 343n
Lacretelle, Jacques de, **39**, 40n, **377**; *La Fiancée morte*, 434, 435n
La Fayette, Marie Madeleine Motier, Comtesse de: *La Princesse de Clèves*, 421n

Lafitte, Dr, 58–9, 262
Lafitte, Pierre, 437 & n
La Fontaine, Jean de: *Fables*, 31n, 111n, 208n, 273, 275n, 342
Lahovary, Marguerite, 31, 32n
Lamartine, Alphonse de, 158, 159n, 175, 176n, 177n, 200 & n, 202, 205 & n
La Moussay, Comtesse Eugène de, 221, 223n
Landowska, Wanda, 300, 301n
Landowski, Dr, 262
Landru, Henri, 275 & n
Lang, André, **258**, 309n, 325, 327n
'La regarder dormir', *see* 'Watching her sleep'
Lariboissière, Mme de, 277n
La Rochefoucauld, François, Duc de: *Maxims*, 126n
La Rochefoucauld, Gabriel, Comte de, xx, **355** & n, 360
La Rochefoucauld, Gabriel, Comtesse de, *née* Odile de Monaco, 380 & n
La Rochefoucauld, Stanislas de, 305 & n
Lasserre, Pierre, 145 & *n*, 154 & n, 268n
Laszlo, Philip, 119 & n, 275n, 278
La Tour, Quentin de, 195, 196n
Lau, Marquis de, 355
Laurencin, Marie, 452, 453n
Lauris, Georges de, xix, 88n
Lavoisier, Antoine Laurent, 44
Léautaud, Paul, *see* Boissard, Maurice
Le Bargy, Simone, 78, 79n
Le Cuziat, Albert, 96n, 181n
Legrand, Mme Gaston, *née* Clotilde de Fournès, 330, 331n
Leibnitz, Gottfried Wilhelm, 334
Lemaire, Madeleine, *née* Jeanne Magdeleine Coll, 24n, 63, 64n, 348–9 & n
Lemaire, Suzette, 348, 349n
Lemaître, Jules, 22, 23n, 184, 185n
Lemarié, Berthe, 11, 12n
lending libraries, 146, 147n
Lenin, Vladimir Ilich, 16
Leonardo da Vinci, 142, 143n, 258; *St John the Baptist*, 29
Leuchars (Paris stationers), 222
Lévi-Alvarès (friend of Gaston de Caillavet), 328
Lévy, Raphaël-Georges, 59, 60n, 65, 71–2
Lewis, Percy Wyndham, **400**, 401n
Liane de Pougy *see* Chassaigne, Anne de
Liberté, La (journal), 337n
'Little Train to La Raspelière, The' (P), 261n, 265n
Lloyd George, David, 3, 330, 331*n*
London & County Westminster Bank, 31n, 64, 203
London Mercury (journal), 142n
Longnon, Auguste, 120, 121n

Lorrain, Jean, 7, 9n, 106, 108n, 242n, 333, 363n
Loti, Pierre, 139, 140n
Louis XV, King of France, 315n
Louis-Napoléon, Prince, 89, 90n
Louis-Philippe, King of France, 99n
Louise, Princess Royal (of England), 172, 173n
Ludwig III, King of Bavaria, 61, 62n
Luynes et de Chevreuse, Honoré, Duc de, 47 & n, 312, 327, 349, 402 & n, 405

Mac Orlan, Pierre (Pierre Dumarchey), 289, 291n
MacSwiney, Terence, Mayor of Cork, 159, 160n, 311
'Madame Swann at Home' ('Odette mariée'; P), 435, 436n
Madelin, Louis, 377, 378n
Madrazo, Frédéric de ('Coco'), 47 & n, 154n, 155n
Madrazo, Raymond de, 154 & n, 155n
Madrazo, Mme Raymond de, *née* Maria Hahn, 154, **155** & n
Maes, Nicolas, 217n
Maeterlinck, Maurice, 95
Mâle, Émile, **125**, 226*n*
Maleissye-Melun, Charles, Comte de, 401, 402n
Malexis, Charles, 336, 337n
Malherbe, François de, 80, 143, 213, 281, 282n
Mallarmé, Stéphane: Valéry and, 80, 143; Mme Sert befriends, 149n; Montesquiou on Gide and, 222; and Duchesse d'Uzès, 223 & n; P quotes, 236, 275, 430, 431n, 432; introduces Hahn concert, 374, 375n; Anatole France denies obscurity of, 397; espouses heresy, 423; 'Hérésies artistiques', 424n; 'Le Tombeau d'Edgar Poe', 196n
Manet, Edouard, 51, 52n, 83; *Olympia*, xxvii, 129, 139, 140n, 168 & n, 259
Mangin, General Charles, 140 & n, 156, 157n, 313, 314n, 443
Manoury, Dr Gabriel, 157n
Manoury, General Michel-Joseph, 156, 157n
Mansfield, Katherine, 358, 359n
Mante-Proust, Suzy (P's niece), 157, 263, 294, 295, **430**, 453n, 474
Marguerite d'Autriche, 159n
Margueritte, Victor, 267, 269n
Marie, Queen of Romania, 131, 132n, 247n
Marie Bonaparte, Princess of Greece, xxv, 305 & n
Marlborough, Duchess of, *née* Gladys Marie Deacon, 229n
Martel, Aymar de, 333
Martel de Janville, Thierry, Comte de, 333 & n, 334n
Martel de Janville, Vicomtesse de ('Gyp'), 332, 333n

Martin, Dr, 239
Martin du Gard, Maurice, 296, 297n, 301, 336, 337n
Martin-Chauffier, Louis: dispute with J. Boulenger, 232, 235n, 242n, 250n, 257n, 261n, 310, 311n, 312; P thanks for review of *Guermantes Way*, xxvi, **196**, 198n; helps P with etymologies, **120**, 121n; and P's pastiches, 120, 121n; P congratulates on engagement, **309**
Marx, M. (Madeleine Paz), 115, 116n
Massis, Henri, 87n
Mathilde, Princesse, 68, 70n, 89, 375
Matin, Le (newspaper), 158
Maugny, Clément, Comte de, 35, 36n, **63**, 64n, **287**, **292**, 378–9
Maugny, Comtesse de, *née* Rita de Bussé, 64 & n, 288 & n, 378–9
Mauriac, Claude, 453n
Mauriac, François, xxvi, xxx, **209**, 210*n*, **230**, 272n, **332**, **335**, 339n, 346n, 347n; 'L'Art de Marcel Proust', 199, 200n; *Préséances*, 230, 232n; *Le Baiser aux lépreux*, 336
Mauriac, Nathalie, 453n
Maurras, Charles: collaborates with Léon Daudet, xxv, 8n, 88n; anti-Dreyfusism, 87, 88n; and *Figaro* manifesto, 87n; writes as 'Criton', 168, 169n; objects to Vandérem review, 239n; hostility to Briand, 362; candidacy for Academy, 404, 406n; relations with P, 405; P thanks for books, **431**, 433n; *L'Avenir de l'intelligence*, 433n; *Le Chemin de Paradis*, 433n
May, Pierre-André, **318**, 319n
Mendelssohn family, 30
Mendès, Catulle, 215n
Mercure de France (magazine), 296, 297n
Mercure de France (publishing house), 109n
Mérimée, Prosper, 43, 225, 226n, 375; *La Double Méprise*, 388, 389, 390*n*
Merle blanc, Le (weekly), 264n
Mérode, Cléo de, 348, 349n
'Mes reveils', *see* 'My awakenings'
Metchnikoff, Élie, 447, 448n
'Method of Sainte-Beuve, The' (P), xvi–xvii, 99n
Meunier, Paul, 314, 315n
Meyer, Arthur, 40, 41n, 228, 229n, 231
Meyer, Mme Arthur, *née* Marguerite de Turenne d'Aynac, 41n
Michel, Albin (publishers), 299n
Michelet, Jules: P parodies, 23n; *La Mer*, 85 & n
Milhaud, Darius, 130
Mill, John Stuart, 308, 309*n*
Millet, Jean François, 129
Minerve française, La (journal), 129, 130n
Miomandre, Francis de, 124, 126n, 360, 361n

Mogador, Céleste (Comtesse Lionel Mobreton de Chabrillan), 146, 147n
Molé, Louis-Mathieu, Comte de, 97, 99n
Molière, Jean-Baptiste Poquelin, 13–14, 164n, 389, 425 & n; *L'Amour Médecin*, 79n; *Amphytrion*, 391, 392n; *Le Bourgeois gentilhomme*, 272n; *École des femmes*, 439n; *Les Femmes savantes*, 341, 343n; *Le Misanthrope*, 339n, 406n
Monaco, Prince Albert de, 128n
Monaco, Princesse Albert de (Alice), 380n
Monaco, Prince Louis de, 128n
Monet, Claude, 129
Moniteur Universel, Le (newspaper), 99n
Monnier, Adrienne, 423, 424n
Montabré, Maurice, 142, 143n
Montaud, Louise, *see* Mornand, Louisa de
Monte Carlo, 151, 152n
Montesquieu, Charles Louis de Secondat, Baron, *Lettres persanes*, 226, 229n, 342
Montesquiou-Fezensac, Comte Robert de: as supposed model for Charlus, xxix, 56n, 212n, 463; sends violets to P, 35, 36n; Mme de Polignac quarrels with, 53; entertains P, 67n; P portrays in *Pastiches et mélanges*, 72n, **92**, 93n; P sends books to, 92, 159, **205**, **208**, **221**; correspondence with P, 93n, 135n, 151, 160n, 468; and Mme Greffulhe's photograph, 93n; P's relations with, 93n, 233–5, 235n; qualities, 93n; sells Whistler portrait, 95; Heredia entertains, 140n; nickname for Forssgren, 180, 182; stands godfather to Guiches' daughter, 181n; on writer's scope, 197, 198n; and keys to P's books, **211**, 230n; ill health, 213n; literary allusions, 223n; P praises, 228; death and funeral, 279–80, 281*n*, 291n, 302 & n; P proposes article on for US magazine, 285, 302; medical treatment, 295; rejection, 361, 363n; memoirs, 407 & n; *Brelan de Dames*, 222, 223n; *Les Délices de Capharnaüm*, 223n; *La Divine Comtesse*, 283n; *Élus et appelés*, 302 & n; *Paul Helleu*, 119n
Montholon, Tristan, Comte de, 153, 154n
Montmorency, Comte Othenin de, 122n
Montmorency, Henri II, Duchesse de (*later* Mother Superior), 120, 121n, 122n
Montmorency, Louis de Talleyrand-Périgord, Duc de, 60n
Morand, Paul, xix, **93**, 95n, **147**, **295**, **296**, **378**; P confesses admiration for Giraudoux to, 94, 147; engagement to Princess Soutzo, 5n, 38n, 49n, 95n, 131, 305; letter to Truelle, 38; friendship with P, 49, 131–2, 188n, 302–3, 389; published by NRF, 63; P satirizes, 74 & n; on Dorgelès's *Les Croix de bois*, 124; P writes preface for, 142n, 148n, 426, 427n; on Allard's review, 250; Robert Proust recommends doctors to, 262, 263n; and P's foreign rights, 270n; and Maugnys' money difficulties, 288n, 378; translates for P, 290; and rumours of NRF bankruptcy, 294, 295n; payments for medical treatment, 295–6; and Martin du Gard, 297n, 301; physical charms, 303–4; reviewed by Clauzel, 336; fake advertisement, 337n, 409; and Prix Blumenthal, 351; and Jaloux, 360; Boulenger reviews, 390; P borrows Dostoevsky's *The Possessed* from, 411; *Adorable Clio*, 147; 'L'hôtel contre la nuit', 96n; *Nuit à Charlottenberg*, 297n; 'Ode à Marcel Proust', xxvi, xxviii, 93–5 &*n*, 96n, 132n, 196n; *Ouvert la nuit*, 336, 337n, 393n, 395 & n, 409, 441 & n; *Tendres Stocks*, 148n, 267, 303
'Morceaux choisis' (P), 188n
Moréas, Jean, 139, 140*n*, 432, 433n
Mornand, Louisa de (Louise Montaud), 36n, 212n, **286**, 287*n*
Moyse, Louis, 402 & n, 407n
Mozart, Wolfgang Amadeus, 217n, 263n
Mugnier, Abbé Arthur, xxvi, 17, 18n, **22**, 23n, 43, **109**, 156
Muhlfeld, Mme Lucien, 139, 140n, 351, 371
Murat family, 71
Murat, Comtesse Joachim de (Thérèse), 369, 370n, 404, 406n
Murat, Princesse Joachim, 93, 94n
Murat, Princesse Lucien, *née* Marie de Rohan-Chabot, 93, 94n, 161, 162n, 169, 194
Murry, John Middleton, 322, 323n, **335** & n, 358, 359n, 360
Musset, Alfred de: output, 13–14; P quotes, 31, 32n, 125, 127n, 199, 200*n*, 202, 204n, 342, 343n, 397, 398n; drunkenness, 44; Vaudoyer on, 217n; 'La Mi-Carême', 389
Mussorgsky, Modeste: *Boris Godunov*, 20n
'My awakenings' ('Mes reveils'; P), 445, 446n, 455

Nahmias, Albert, 12n
Napoleon III, Emperor of the French, 305n
Nègre, Albert, Archbishop of Tours, 451 & n
Nerval, Gérard de, 259
Neuburger, Léon, 30, 31n, 203
Neue Merkur, Die, 308n, 322, 444n
Neufmoustiers, Mme Singer, 29
New York Evening Post, 400n
Nice, 33
Nicolas II, Tsar, 305n
Nietzsche, Friedrich, 126n, 382
Nijinsky, Vaslav, 82
Nivelle, General Robert, 124, 126n
Noailles, Anna de (Comtesse Mathieu de), *née* Princesse Anne-Élisabeth Bassaraba de Brancovan, xx, **77**, 78n, **175**, 468; and Mme Soutzo, 5 & n; P praises poetry, 79n, 176n; P

fails to send books to, 90, 92, 103; admires Musset, 125; P sends letter to A. Bibesco, 174 & n; A. Bibesco entertains, 175n; on dying to improve, 176n; P entertains, 190; relations with Viviani, 293; at Montesquiou's funeral, 302n; at Prix Blumenthal, 372; *Le Cœur innombrable*, 29, 30n, 176n; *Les Éblouissements*, 176n; *Les Forces éternelles*, 174n, 176n; *Premières Méditations*, 176; *Recueillements*, 176
Noailles, Comtesse Hélie de, *née* Corisande de Gramont, 230n
Noailles, Mathieu, Comte (*later* Marquis) de, 78, 79n, 176, 292–3, 379
Noailles, Comtesse Mathieu de, *see* Noailles, Anna de
Nordlinger, Marie, xviii
Nouvelle revue française éditions (publishing house; N.R.F.): publishes P, xxiii, 63, 101–2, 103n, 107, 133n, 185–7, 244–5, 249, 290, 387, 408, 438–9, 457n; turns down *Swann's Way*, xxiii, 109n, 398, 407–8; printing and proofs, 10–11, 102, 255, 298; founded by Gide, 12n; book club ('Original Editions'), 102, 103n; P visits, 131; Morand and, 132; and de luxe edition of *Within a Budding Grove*, 151; P gives as accommodation address, 225–6, 405; owes payments to P, 244; P's dissatisfaction with, 253–4, 264, 384; P's non-exclusive contract with, 260; and Benda, 266; negotiates translations of P's works, 270n; bankruptcy rumours, 294, 295n; and publicity, 337, 409, 411n; Rivière and, 352; advertises Morand's *Ouvert la nuit*, 395n; reputation, 410–11; *see also* Gallimard, Gaston
Nouvelle revue française, La (journal; *NRF*): founded by Gide, 12n; publishes extracts from P's works, 54, 56n, 75, 107, 123, 125–6, 159, 178, 200n, 243, 245n, 249, 253, 255 & n, 291n, 294, 318, 409, 445n, 454n, 457n, 458n; Vandérem reviews *Swann* in, 85 & n; Giraudoux contributes to, 94; on press hostile to P, 124; Rivière writes in, 124, 126n, 141, 145n, 164n; Vaudoyer on, 128; printed in Bruges, 130n; P admires, 133; Review of Reviews, 145; P writes and reviews for, 153, 242 & n; advertises P's works, 164n, 289, 435; Rivière edits, 190, 264; Gide contributes to, 193n, 214n, 215n, 444; and rival reviews, 193, 249, 333; P answers Valéry in, 208n; and Martin-Chauffier/Boulenger dispute, 235n, 242n; and Benda, 266; Crémieux reviews in, 267, 292n; Gabory contributes to, 295n; Vettard contributes to, 306n, 384; and Doumic, 313; article on Léon Daudet, 314; and Schiff, 322, 364; and Curtius's article on P, 384; P claims not read in summer, 388n; and P's letter to Jaloux, 389; and Schlumberger, 404; Ghéon reviews *Swann's Way* in, 425
Nouvelles de la Bourse de Berlin (newspaper), 270

'Odette mariée', *see* 'Madame Swann at Home'
Œuvre, L' (newspaper), 108n, 409
Œuvres libres, Les (journal): payments to P, 242n, 428, 435, 457n; publishes extracts from P's works, 242n, 244, 245n, 246, 249, 252, 253–5, 260, 267, 318, 428, 433, 435, 436n, 445n; Fayard publishes, 245n; Gallimard objects to, 245n, 253, 436; prints story by Marguerithe, 269n; P's articles in, 330, 354, 355; P's contract with, 438, 439n
Offenbach, Jacques: *Belle Hélène*, 228, 229n, 232
Olibrius the Gaul, 315, 316n
Ollendorf (publisher), 109n
Ollone, Max d', 39, 41n
'On Flaubert's Style' (P), xxvi, 24n, 116n, 130n, 142n, 167n, 242n, 343n, 398n
'On Reading'(P), 408n
On Reading Ruskin (P), 24n, 408n
Opinion, L' (journal): J. Boulenger edits, 104n; J. Boulenger's articles on P in, 113 & n, 115n, 169, 171n, 250n, 313; Vaudoyer's articles on art in, 128, 130n, 217n, 380, 381n; and Mauriac's defence of P, 199, 200n; P offers article to, 260; supports P, 267; and Vettard's article on P, 312n, 421, 426; on 'shameful vices' of P's characters, 373; reviews Gide's play *Saul*, 386; and P's essay on Louvre masterpieces, 398n; Serge André owns, 416, 422n
Owen, Peter (publisher), 24n

Paderewski, Ignacy Jan, 148, 149n
Paillart, Frédéric, 76n
Painlevé, Paul, 313, 314n
Palms, Jules, 67n, 73
Parent, Pierre, 35
Pâris, François, Vicomte de, 182, 183n, 311
Paris-Midi (newspaper), 115, 116n
Pascal, Blaise, 44–5, 443, 444n; *Pensées*, 46n, 60n
Pasquier, Étienne, 97, 99n
Pastiches et mélanges (P), xxv, 24n, 56n, 60, 66, 67n, 72n, 73, 77, 77n, 92, 93n, 95, 97, 109, 142, 159, 273
Patin, Henri, 220n, 221n
Paulhan, Jean: and printing of extracts from P's works, 243, 249, 251–3, 255, 455; edits *NRF* in Gallimard's absence, 245n; as candidate for Prix Blumenthal, 351, 352n, 366–7 & n, 370; on editorial board of *Le Disque vert*, 352n; letter to P unread, 388; and P's proposed article on Flaubert, 414

Paz, Madeleine, *see* Marx, M.
Pechkoff, Zinovii Alekseevich (Gorki's adopted son; 'Zina'), 15, 16n
Péguy, Charles Pierre, 63
Péret, Benjamin, 379, 380n
Pérochon, Ernest, 268n
Petit Parisien, Le (journal), 77n, 106, 124
Petrarch, 158, 159n, 256
Philibert le Beau, 159n
Picasso, Pablo, 149n
Picquart, Georges-Maris, 106, 108n
Pierrebourg, Baronne Aiméry Harty de (Claude Ferval), 140, 141n
Pierrefeu, Jean de, **111**, 113*n*, 116n, 313, 434
Pilon, Germain, 281, 283n
Pirbright, Sarah, Lady, 181
Plaisirs et les jours, Les (P), 23, 24n, 56n, 64n, 107, 170, 191 & n, 233
Plantevignes, Marcel, xx, 35, 48
Plato, 43, 324, 325n, 338, 339n
Pleasures and Regrets, see *Plaisirs et les jours, Les*
Pléiade, Bibliothèque de la, 24n, 208n
Poe, Edgar Allan, 275
Poincaré, Henri, 427n
Poincaré, Raymond, 330, 331n
Poland, 149, 150n
Polignac, Edmond, Prince de, 53-5, 56*n*, 422 & n
Polignac, Princesse Edmond de, *née* Winaretta Singer, 35, 36n, **53**, 55n, 56n, 364, 369
Polignac, Pierre, Comte de (*later* Duc de Valentinois), 112, 113n, 114, **127**, 128*n*, 134, 142n, 152n, 369, 370n
Politiken (Danish newspaper), 179, 180n
Pontigny Abbey, Burgundy, 434, 435n
Populaire, Le (newspaper), 171
Porel, Jacques, **27**, 28n, 84, **144**, 264, 288, **418**
Porel, Réjane, *see* Réjane
Porgès, Jules, 130n
Porgès, Mme Jules, 29, 223 & n
Porto-Riche, Georges de, 272 & n, 377 & n
Poulet Quartet, 217n
Pouquet, Mme Eugène, *née* Marie Rousseau, 329 & n
Pouquet, Maurice, 329 & n
Pouquet, Mme Maurice, *née* Jeanne Pouquet, 41n, **327**, 329n, 438n
'Preface to Blanche' (P), 70n, 190n, 196n
'Preface to Morand' (P), xxvi, 148n, 176n, 191n, 205n, 292, 306, 426, 427n
Prévost, Fernand, 328
Prévost, Marcel, 369, 370n, 374, 386, 387, 388n, 391
Prisonnière, La, see *Captive, The*
Prix Balzac, 429, 430n, 434n, 436, 456, 457n, 458 & n

Prix Blumenthal, 351, 352n, 367n, 368n, 370-2 & *n*, 378
Prix de la Vie Heureuse (Prix Femina), 106, 108n, 116n
Prix Goncourt: P wins, xxiv, 103-4, 106-8, 110, 111, 113n, 115, 118n, 126n, 133n, 135, 192, 245, 257n, 267, 476; Duhamel wins, 167n; awarded to Genevoix, 371n
Proust, Dr Adrien (P's father), 58, 60n, 108n, 263n, 379, 443
Proust, Mme Adrien, *née* Jeanne Weil (P's mother), 51, 52n, 67n, 108n, 214n, 262, 263n; death, 6n
Proust, Marcel: duelling, 7, 9n, 106, 242n, 333, 363n; lives in cork-lined room, 27, 28n, 78, 79n, 83, 96n; financial investments, 30, 31, 42, 45, 46n, 65-6, 67n, 71-2, 202-3, 204n; sells furniture, 30, 65-7, 71; moves to new apartment, 63, 65, 67n, 71, 84; military service, 84n; caffeine overdose, 257 & n; death, 459
WORKS: *Books: see Against Sainte-Beuve and Other Essays; Best of Marcel Proust, The; By Way of Sainte-Beuve; In Search of Lost Time* (and constituent parts); *Jean Santeuil; On Reading Ruskin; Pastiches et mélanges; Plaisirs et les jours, Les; Essays, extracts and shorter articles: see* 'Against Obscurity'; 'Albertine's Sleep'; 'Chardin and Rembrandt'; 'Concerning Baudelaire'; 'Dans les mémoires de Saint-Simon'; 'Days of Reading'; 'Death-bed, A'; 'Fête chez Montesquiou à Neuilly'; 'Foggy Evening, A'; 'Goncourts, The'; 'Historic Salon, A'; 'Illimitable Wit and a Genius, A'; 'Intermittencies of the Heart'; 'Jealousy'; 'Kiss, The'; 'Little Train to La Raspelière, The'; 'Madame Swann at Home'; 'Method of Sainte-Beuve, The'; 'Morceaux choisis'; 'My Awakenings'; 'On Flaubert's Style'; 'On Reading'; 'Preface to Blanche'; 'Preface to Morand'; 'Quarrel with Gilberte, The'; 'Sainte-Beuve and Balzac'; 'Sentiments filiaux d'un parricide'; 'Sojourn in Venice'; 'Street-Cries of Paris'; 'Swann explained by Proust'; 'Watching her sleep'
Proust, Dr Robert (P's brother): wartime service in Italy, 30, 31n, 33, 35; marriage and financial status, 58; waives interest in Boulevard Haussmann property, 67n; friendship with Mangin, 140, 141n, 156; and honour for P, **156**, 157n; and P's posthumous manuscripts, 208n; and bedside manner, 212; and P's ill health, **262**, 263n, 443, 451-2, 453n, 458; and sales of *Sodom* II, 352; and Morand's *Ouvert la nuit*, 441; professorship, 443; and P's death, 459

Proust, Mme Robert, *née* Marthe Dubois-Amiot (P's sister-in-law), 30, 31n, 157, 263
Proust, Suzy (P's niece), *see* Mante-Proust, Suzy

'Quarrel with Gilberte, The' (P), 76n, 127n
Quarterly Review, The, 335n
Quintilian, 380n

Racine, Jean, xxvi, 98, 124–5, 126n, 137, 143 & n, 168, 259, 318n, 397; *Bérénice*, 432, 433n; *Cantiques*, 80, 376n; *Esther*, 343n; *Phèdre*, 83, 127n, 168, 242n, 272, 337 & n
Radziwill, Prince Constantin, 180–1 & n
Radziwill, Princesse Constantin, 181
Radziwill, Prince Michael, 41n
Radziwill, Princesse Michael, *see* Benardaky, Marie
Rageot, Gaston, 126n, 396, 397n
Regnard, Jean-François, 259, 260n
Régnier, Henri de: P discusses literary work with, xxvi, **138**, **165**, 167n; campaigns for honours for P, 102, 103n, 138, 140n, 157; admires Musset, 125; P's pastiche of, 167n; P fails to send book to, 170; praises Mme de Noailles, 175; friendship with Boulenger, 313, 316; Léon Daudet mocks, 316; P offends, 351, 352n; praises P's piece on E. de Goncourt banquet, **359**, 360n; tribute to E. de Goncourt, 360n, 361; *Le Bon plaisir*, 166, 176; *La Double Maîtresse*, 166, 176, 361
Régnier, Mme Henri de, *see* Heredia, Marie de
Rehbinder, Comtesse Wladimir de, 22, 23n
Reims cathedral, 348, 349n
Réjane, *née* Gabrielle Réju, 28n, 85n, 418n, 435, 436n; death, 144n
Rembrandt van Rijn: *Portrait of Jan Six*, 189, 190n
Renaissance politique, littéraire, artistique, La (journal), 168n, 393n
Renan, Ernest, 77, 78n, 191 & *n*, 433*n*, 443, 444n; P parodies, 23n, 176n
Renoir, Auguste, 129
Revue Blanche, La, 140n
Revue de France, La, 238
Revue de Genève, La, 249n
Revue de la semaine, La, 260, 344
Revue de Paris, La, 104n, 118n, 148n, 191n, 208n, 225, 292n, 375, 388n, 405, 406n, 409, 411n
Revue des jeunes, La, 138n
Revue hebdomadaire, La, 199, 200n, 211
Revue mondiale, La, 116n
Revue parisienne, La, 147n
Revue rhénane, La, 411, 444n
Revue universelle, La, 145, 193, 250, 315, 345, 346n, 363n, 374

Rimbaud, Arthur, 44, 125, 198, 415
Rimestad, Charles, 180n
Risler, Edouard, 421, 422n
Rivière, Jacques, **123**, 126n, **141**, **144**, **163**, **198**, **240**, **249**, **251**, **252**, **264**, **366**, **387**, **412**, **433**, **444**, **445**, **454**, **455**, **458**, **459**; edits *NRF*, xxiv, 100–1, 102n; and psychological aspects of P's writings, xxv, 125, 144, 145n; P behaves badly to, xxix; and P's attitude to Halévy, 91n; publishes P extracts in *NRF*, 125–6, 127n, 241n, 247, 249, 250n, 251n, 252, 253–4, 264–5, 387, 433–4, 444–5 & n, 454 & n, 455; articles on P, 126n, 163, 164*n*; ill health, 126n, 129, 142n, 241n; P and Gide seek prize for, 153, 155n; defends P against Lasserre, 154 & n; calls on P, 169–70; and gossip over Gallimard, 187; fondness for Gallimard, 192; and NRF, 193, 196; praises Martin-Chauffier, 197; love for Yvonne Gallimard, 199n; and P's manuscript of *Albertine disparue*, 207, 208 & n; sends Gide's articles to P, 213–14; and Martin-Chauffier's review of Boulenger, 232, 235n, 242n, 261n, 310–11; P sends cuttings to, 240, 241n; absence from *NRF*, 245n, 427; and *NRF* drama critics, 272; and Crémieux, 291; and copy-editing of *Sodom and Gomorrah*, 299; and Sydney Schiff, 322, 364, 365n, 409n; and Allard, 338; life at NRF office, 352; wins Prix Blumenthal, 352n, 373; and P's support for Paulhan's candidacy for Prix Blumenthal, 366; and Vettard's 'Proust and Einstein', 384; and Gallimard's whereabouts, 386; denies *NRF* unread in summer, 388n; and T.S. Eliot, 409n; praises *Sodom and Gomorrah*, 412–14; on Baudelaire, 415–16 & n, 417n; and Rimbaud, 415; friendship with P, 421; and P's *La Prisonnière*, 428; and Prix Balzac, 434n, 457–8 & n; as prisoner of war, 435n; and publishing of P's extracts in other journals, 435; informed of P's illness and death, **459**; *Aimée*, 198, 199n, 250, 414n, 430, 434, 435n, 459; *L'Allemand*, 434, 435n
Rivière, Mme Jacques, *née* Isabelle Fournier, 142 & n, 250
Rivière, Dr Marc, 458 & n
Robert, Louis de, **224** & n
Robin, Albert, 314, 315n
Rochat, Henri (P's secretary), xxx, 26n, 60n, 114, 116n, 130n, 142n, 150, 230, 232n, 238n
Rochefort-Luçay, Henri, 146n, 261 & n
Rodenbach, Georges, 346, 347n, 361, 363n
Rodier (Montesquiou's contemporary), 221
Roget, General Gaudérique, 62 & n
Rohan-Chabot, Mme Gerard, 228
Rolland, Romain, 343n; *Jean Christophe*, 101, 103n

Romains, Jules (Louis Farigoule), **422**, 424*n*
Rosny *aîné* (Joseph Boëx-Borel), 104, **105**, 105n, 108n, 124, 126n, 171, **204**, 295*n*, **308**, 309n; *L'Imperieuse bonté*, 309n
Rostand, Maurice, 245n
Rothschild, Baronne Henri de, 29
Rothschilds' bank, 203–4
Roussy, Dr Gustave, 207, 208n
Rozière, Eugène de, 404, 406n
Rudolf, Crown Prince of Austria, 177, 178n
Ruhe, Algot, 264, 265*n*, 380n
Ruskin, John: P's prefaces and annotations to, 23, 24n, 408n; and Hauser, 43–4; P translates, 107, 473; on philistinism in readers, 150, 152n, 408; P writes on, 334n

Sade, Donatien Alphonse François, Marquis de, 343n
Sade, Hugues de, 159n
Sagan, Prince Hélie de, 118n
Sagan, Princesse de, *née* Jeanne Seillière (*later* Duchesse de Talleyrand), 68, 70*n*, **172**
Saint-Marceaux, Charles-René de Paul de, 347–8, 349n
Saint-Marceaux, Mme Charles-René de Paul de, *née* Marguerite Fred-Jourdain, **347**, 349n
Saint-Maurice, Gaston de, 422 & n
Saint-Saëns, Camille, 39, 41n, 82
Saint-Simon, Louis de Rouvroy, Duc de, 5 & n, 161, 162n, 220, 398n; P's pastiche of, xxvi, 6n, 72n, 73–4 & n, 77, 79n, 92, 93n, 96n, 135n, 160n, 212n, 229n, 275n, 392n
Saint-Victor, Paul de, 279, 281n
Sainte-Beuve, Charles-Augustin, xvi, 13, 14n, 61, 97–8, 99n, 109n, 130n, 141
'Sainte-Beuve and Balzac' (P), 84n, 173n
Sala, Comte Antoine de, 276, 277n
Salignac-Fénelon, Bertrand, Vicomte de, 47 & n, 211
Salmon, André, 289, 291n
Salomé, Lou, 126n
Sardou, Victorien, 133n; *Madame Sans Gène*, 435, 436n
Sassoon, Sir Philip, **391**, 392n
Satie, Erik, 83n
Schabacher, Simon, *see* Duvernois, Henri
Scheikévitch, Marie, **15**, 16n, **17**, 37, 67n, 273, 300, 301n
Schiff, Mortimer, 321
Schiff, Sydney (Stephen Hudson), xvi, xxiv, **150**, 152n, **364**, **398**, **407**; misunderstands Scott-Moncrieff's translated titles, **439**, 440n, 441; P sends books to, **237**; P attempts to meet in Paris, **321**; introduces P to Middleton Murry, 323n, 335 & n; gives party for Diaghilev, 365n; and Wyndham Lewis, 401; and T.S. Eliot, 408n; *Elinor Culhouse*, 323n
Schiff, Mme Sydney, *née* Violet Beddington,

151, 152n, 237, 365 & n, 398–9, 408, 441
Schlumberger, Gustave, 369, 370n, 404–5, 406n
Schlumberger, Jean, 87n, 336, 337n, 352, 353n, 387n, **403**, 412n
Schopenhauer, Arthur, 382
Schubert, Franz, 39
Scott-Moncrieff, Charles Kenneth, 386n, 440*n*, **448**, **449** & *n*, 450n
Scudéry, Madeleine de, 343n
Ségur, Comtesse Eugène de, *née* Sofia Rostopchin, 405, 406n
Sem, *see* Goursat, Georges
Semaine Littéraire, La (Geneva weekly), 367, 447n
'Sentiments filiaux d'un parricide' (P), 87n
Sert, José-Maria, 149 & n
Sert, Mme José-Maria, *née* Maria Godebska (*then* Mme Thadée Natanson; *then* Mme Alfred Edwards), **149** & n, 391
Sévigné, Marie de Rabutin-Chantal, Marquise de, 168
Shakespeare, William, 61
Shelley, Percy Bysshe, 386, 387n
Sibilat, René, 61, 62n
'Six, Les' (musical group), 83n
Sluter, Claus, 407n
Socrates, 339
Sodom and Gomorrah (P): proofs and printing, xxiii, 207, 297; P's apprehension over reception, xxv, 224; cries of Paris in, xxvii, 420; acclaimed, xxviii; inverts and homosexuality in, xxx, 56n, 84n, 161, 255n; Céleste Albaret depicted in, 18n; undedicated, 66; Gallimard returns typescript to P, 102; writing of, 107, 109n, 271; Dreyfusism in, 135n, 151; character of Albertine in, 145, 326, 394; publication, 156, 161, 178n, 185–6, 188n, 199, 201, 251n, 255n, 271, 289–90, 294, 321n, 326, 331n; doctors in, 206; reviews and reception, 220n, 234, 241 & n, 248n, 338 & n, 343n, 374n, 387n, 405, 409, 411n, 412n; extracts published, 241 & n, 244, 254–5, 319n, 330, 331n, 420 & n; manuscript, 270 & n; success in USA, 273; advertised and promoted, 290, 291n, 386n, 409, 411n, 442n; Gabory proof-reads, 294, 297, 298n, 299, 371n, 385, 386n; title, 326, 345, 386; complimentary copies, 334n, 335n, 340, 391, 392n; and Halévy's opera, 341n; special paper edition, 345n, 362–3; sales, availability and price, 352, 353n, 441, 448; Mme de Régnier reads, 363; and 'sequels', 386; Doucet offers to buy corrected proofs, 387n; psychological content, 447n; P requests reprint, 448
Soissons, Eugène, Chevalier de, 5n
'Sojourn in Venice' (P), 214n, 453n
Soria, Franck de, 328, 329n

Souday, Paul, **97**, 99n, **160**, **191**, **219**, **320**, **341**; criticizes P's style and grammar, 341, 352; mother's death, 97, 99n; articles and reviews on P, 115, 116n, 124, 162*n*, 191n, 219, 220*n*, 221*n*, 343*n*; P sends *Within a Budding Grove* to, 191; on Binet-Valmer, 255 & n; entertains P, 320; P's pastiche of, 341
Soutzo, Princesse, *née* Hélène Chrissovelno, **5** & n, **36**, **48**, **73**, **130**, **164**, **299**, **303**, **392**, **396**; engagement and marriage to Morand, 5n, 49n, 95n; operation, 10, 12n; Mme Scheikévitch confides in, 16n; entertains, 23n, 131, 247n, 282, 300n, 305n, 365n; and P's illness, 35, 36n; and transposition of sexes, 37, 350n; in P's Saint-Simon pastiche, 73, 74n; offends P, 74n; photographed as Minerva, 74n, 304, 305n; and P's change of apartments, 84; buys *Within a Budding Grove*, 165n; as model for Odette, 165n
Spinoza, Benedictus de, 331n
St-Germain-en-Laye, treaty of (1919), 116n
St-Jean-de-Luz, 48
Staël, Anne Louise Germaine, Baronne de, 122n
Stendhal (Marie-Henri Beyle), 98, 125; *La Chartreuse de Parme*, 146, 147n, 449n; *Le Rouge et le noir*, 449n
Stevenson, Robert Louis, 258, 259n, 374
Stoïcesco, Georges, 131, 132n
Stoïcesco, Mme Georges, *née* Simone de Caillavet, 329n, 437, 438n
Straus, Émile, 62 & n, 71, 134, 160, 302n, 340 & n, 356n
Straus, Mme Émile, *née* Geneviève Halévy, **61**, 62n, **71**, **133**, **159**, **339**, 477; ill health, xxiv, 62n, 133; as model for Duchesse de Guermantes, xxix, 62n, 161, 202n, 353, 355 & n, 356n; salon, 68; in P's Saint-Simon pastiche, 72n, 135n, 159; and P's delayed correspondence with Montesquiou, 93n, 135n, 160n; quotes Hugo, 135n; at Montesquiou's funeral, 302n; outlives P, 340n
Strauss, Richard, 83, 84n
Stravinsky, Igor, 82, 149n, 453n
'Street-Cries of Paris, The' (P), 429n, 434, 445
Sue, Eugène: *Les mystères de Paris*, 177, 178n
Sully Prudhomme, René François Armand, 114, 115n, 275
surrealism, 83n
'Swann explained by Proust' (P), 127n
Swann, Harry, xxix, **172**
Swann's Way (*Du Côté de chez Swann*; P): first published by Grasset, xxiii, 12n, 77n, 107, 172, 408; go-between in, 12n; NRF publishes edition of, 12n, 77n; P presents to Mme Scheikévitch, 16n; Léon Daudet reviews, 27n; Ghéon reviews, 81n, 425; Souday criticizes, 99n, 219; Régnier and, 166; Combray church in, 222; sado-masochistic scene in, 224 & n;

opening, 259n; printing type, 270n; Léonie de Clomesnil portrayed in, 354; Chaumeix reviews, 398n; Bibescos read in manuscript, 407–8; English translation, 440n

Tägliche Rundschau, 350n, 351
Tagore, Rabindranath, 394, 395n
Talleyrand, Duchesse de, *see* Sagan, Princesse de
Tardiveau, René, *see* Boylesve, René
Temps, Le (newspaper), 4n, 18, 103n, 127n, 162n, 220n, 221n, 327n, 343*n*
Temps retrouvé, Le, see Time Regained
theatres: Théâtre Astruc, 20n, 195; Théâtre des Champs-Élysées, 132n; Théâtre des Mathurins, 287 & n; Théâtre du Vieux Colombier, 12n, 76n, 77n, 133n, 291n, 387n
Theocritus, 266, 268n
Thérive, André, 374, 375n
Thibaud, Jacques, 39, 41n
Thibaudet, Albert, 141, 142n, 250, 251n, 395 & n
Time Regained (*Le Temps retrouvé*; P): completed, xxiii, 107, 292; air raid in, 31n; and cooking, 77n; on telescope/microscope view, 121n; Schiff translates, 152n; on memory, 167n; on dinner parties, 237n; on French classics, 259n; publication, 282; on Deschanel's death, 331n
Times, The, 141
Times Literary Supplement, The, 101, 102n
Tinseau, Léon, Comte de, 39, 41n
Tissot, James: *Le Balcon du Cercle de la Rue Royale en 1867* (painting), 422n
Tolstoy, Count Leo, 7, 16, 269n
translations, 101, 141, 290, 291n, 305n, 350 & n, 385, 386n, 439–41, 448–50
Traz, Georges de (F. Fosca), 381, 382n
Treilhard, Comtesse, 296
Tronche, Gustave: at NRF, 100–1, 102n, 192, 201, 410, 412n; P delivers *Guermantes Way* Pt.I to, 141; makes payment to P, 186, 188n; P acknowledges gifts from, **284**; retires, 284n; and P's book titles, 386; wife expects child, 412n
Tronche, Mme Gustave, 410, 412n
Truelle, Jacques, 38 & n, 58, 60n
Truelle (Jacques' father), 58
Turenne d'Aynac, Louis, Comte de, 39–40, 41n

Uzès, Duchesse de, 223 & n

Vacaresco, Hélène, 300, 301n
Valentinois, Charlotte Grimaldi, Duchesse de, 128n, 134
Valéry, Paul, 80, 81n, 143, 207, 208n
Vallery-Radot, Robert, **137**, 138*n*
Vandérem, Fernand, 85 & n, **116**, 118*n*, 238–9 & n, 406n

Vangeon, Dr Henri, *see* Ghéon, Henri
Vanzype, Gustave: *Jan Vermeer of Delft*, 382n
Vaquez, Dr Henri, 262, 295, 296
Varèse, Louise, 24n
Vaudoyer, Mme Alfred (Jean-Louis' mother), 56, 57n
Vaudoyer, Jean-Louis, **56**, 57n, **128**, **216**, **380**; and P's admiration for Vermeer, xxvii, 216, 217n, 380–1; bereavements, 56, 57n; collaborates on Diaghilev's *Spectre de la rose*, 83n; subscribes to *Figaro* manifesto, 87n; writings on art, 130n, 216n, 217*n*, 381*n*; friendship with Henriot, 327; in Venice, 431 & n
Vaudoyer, Michel, 57n
Vercingétorix, 404, 406n
Verlaine, Paul, 44, 82, 84n, 175, 176n, 180, 181n, 251n, 375, 376n; 'Sagesse', 81n
Vermeer, Jan: P admires, xxvii, 129, 216, 381; Vaudoyer writes on, 216, 217n, 380, 381n; and P's *The Captive*, 382n; *The Lacemaker* (*La Dentellière*), 129, 130n, 285, 286n; *View of Delft*, xxvii, 216, 381n
Versailles, Treaty of (1919), 261n, 331n
Vespis (Ritz head waiter), 421, 422n
Vettard, Camille, **306** & n, **383**, **426**; dedicatory essay on P, 306n, 312n, 344, 345n, 374, 375n, 427n; on P's view of time, 326, 427n; official post, 344, 345n; *Pauper le Grand*, 426–7 & n; 'Proust and Einstein', 306n, 373, 374n, 384n, 388n, 421, 422n, 426, 427 & n, 430–1
Vézelay, 225, 226n
Victor-Napoléon, Prince, 89, 90n
Vigier, René, Vicomte, 93, 94n
Vigny, Alfred de, xxix, 7, 9n, 62, 81n, 175, 176n, 185n, 261, 323n, 345, 442n; 'La Colère de Samson', 202n, 326
Virgil, 46n, 98, 192n, 409n
Viviani, René, 193 & n, 379
Voltaire, François Marie Arouet de, 58, 60n, 471
Vuillard, Jean Édouard, 149n, 216, 217n

Wagner, Richard, 31n, 39, 41n, 44, 82, 129, 130n, 164, 165n, 238n
Wagram, Princesse Alexandre Berthier de, 39, 41n, 68
Wales, Prince of, *see* Edward VII, King of England
Walewski, Comte, 153, 154n
Warburg's Bank, Hamburg, 46n, 65, 72, 135, 202, 243
Warner, Sylvia Townsend, 109n
Waru, Mme Jacques de, 330, 331n
'Watching her sleep' ('La regarder dormir'; P), 445, 446n

Watteau, Antoine, 129, 180, 216, 217n, 380
Weil, Adèle, 52 & n
Weil, Georges (P's uncle), 67n
Weil, Mme Georges, *née* Amélie Oulman (P's aunt and landlady), 31n, 52n, 63, 64n, 67n, 71–2
Weil, Louis (P's uncle), 67n, 129, 354n, 431 & n
Weil, Nathé (P's maternal grandfather), 379, 380n
Wells, H.G., 306n
Wessbecher, 35
Wharton, Edith, 137n
Whistler, James McNeill, 7, 8n, 95, 150, 399
Whitman, Walt, 94
Wicard, Dr Alexis, 157, 158n
Widal, Dr Fernand, 239, 240n, 262
Wiener, Franz, *see* Croisset, Francis de
Wilde, Oscar, 83, 84n, 219, 221n, 324, 325n; *The Picture of Dorian Gray*, 248 & n
William II, Kaiser, 61
Williams, Dr Charles, 72 & n
Wilson, Mme Philip Duncan, *née* Germaine Porel, 28n
Wilson, Woodrow, 61–2 & n
Within a Budding Grove (*A l'Ombre des jeunes filles en fleurs*; P): proofs, xxiii, 12n, 24n, 26n; P awarded Prix Goncourt for, xxiv, 104n, 113n, 171; success and sales, xxviii, 100–1, 103n, 104, 109, 270n; complimentary copies and dedicatory inscriptions, 4n, 89n, 93n, 170, 191; P copies passages for Mme Scheikévitch, 16n; P sends proofs to Léon Daudet, 26n; Balbec circle in, 36n, 89; P describes to Mme de Polignac, 54; lacks dedication, 55, 56n, 66; P complains to Gallimard of production faults, 75, 76n; extracts published, 76n, 109n; publication, 77n; and new art, 82; reviews and reception, 98, 99n, 109n, 112, 117, 118n, 137, 138n, 172, 198n; writing of, 107; Cambremer's vulgarity in, 122; Schiff orders, 151, 399; limited edition, 152n, 170, 191, 271; Montesquiou reads, 160n, 211; character of Charlus in, 222, 335; jealousy scene, 326; Reims cathedral in, 349n; sexual transposition in, 350; character of Odette in, 353; title, 376
Wixler, Camille, 149n, 392n
Wolff, Étienne, 453n
Wright brothers (Orville and Wilbur), 191

Yturri, Gabriel de, 93n

Zavie, Émile, 458 & n
Zola, Emile: *J'accuse*, 88n